Lecture Notes in Computer Science 9283

Commenced Publication in 1973
Founding and Former Series Editors:
Gerhard Goos, Juris Hartmanis, and Jan van Leeuwen

More information about this series at http://www.springer.com/series/7409

Josiane Mothe · Jacques Savoy
Jaap Kamps · Karen Pinel-Sauvagnat
Gareth J.F. Jones · Eric SanJuan
Linda Cappellato · Nicola Ferro (Eds.)

Experimental IR Meets Multilinguality, Multimodality, and Interaction

6th International Conference
of the CLEF Association, CLEF'15
Toulouse, France, September 8–11, 2015
Proceedings

 Springer

Editors

Josiane Mothe
Institut de Recherche en Informatique
  de Toulouse
Toulouse
France

Jacques Savoy
University of Neuchâtel
Neuchâtel
Switzerland

Jaap Kamps
University of Amsterdam
Amsterdam
The Netherlands

Karen Pinel-Sauvagnat
Institut de Recherche en Informatique
  de Toulouse
Toulouse
France

Gareth J.F. Jones
Dublin City University
Dublin
Ireland

Eric SanJuan
Université d'Avignon et des Pays
  de Vaucluse
Avignon
France

Linda Cappellato
University of Padua
Padua
Italy

Nicola Ferro
University of Padua
Padua
Italy

ISSN 0302-9743   ISSN 1611-3349 (electronic)
Lecture Notes in Computer Science
ISBN 978-3-319-24026-8   ISBN 978-3-319-24027-5 (eBook)
DOI 10.1007/978-3-319-24027-5

Library of Congress Control Number: 2015947945

LNCS Sublibrary: SL3 – Information Systems and Applications, incl. Internet/Web, and HCI

Springer Cham Heidelberg New York Dordrecht London
© Springer International Publishing Switzerland 2015

Printed on acid-free paper

Springer International Publishing AG Switzerland is part of Springer Science+Business Media
(www.springer.com)

Preface

Since 2000, the Conference and Labs of the Evaluation Forum (CLEF) has played a leading role in stimulating research and innovation in the domain of multimodal and multilingual information access. Initially founded as the Cross-Language Evaluation Forum and running in conjunction with the European Conference on Digital Libraries (ECDL/TPDL), CLEF became a standalone event in 2010 combining a peer-reviewed conference with a multi-track evaluation forum. CLEF 2015[1] was hosted by the *Institut de Recherche en Informatique de Toulouse* UMR 5505 CNRS, *Université de Toulouse*, France, SIG team.

The CLEF conference addresses all aspects of information access in any modality and language. The conference has a clear focus on experimental IR as done at evaluation forums (CLEF Labs, TREC, NTCIR, FIRE, MediaEval, RomIP, SemEval, TAC, ...), paying special attention to the challenges of multimodality, multilinguality, and interactive search. We invited submissions on significant new insights demonstrated on the resulting IR test collections, on analysis of IR test collections and evaluation measures, as well as on concrete proposals to push the boundaries of the Cranfield/TREC/CLEF paradigm. The conference format consisted of keynotes, contributed papers, lab sessions, and poster sessions, including reports from other benchmarking initiatives from around the world. It was an honor and a privilege to have Gregory Grefenstette (INRIA Saclay, France), Mounia Lalmas (Yahoo Labs, London, UK), and Douglas W. Oard (University of Maryland, USA) as keynote speakers. Greg talked about personal information systems and personal semantics, Mounia addressed the topic of user engagement evaluation, and Doug examined issues in privacy and ethics when searching among secrets.

CLEF 2015 received a total of 68 submissions, a dramatic increase over previous years. Each submission was reviewed by at least three PC members, and the two program chairs oversaw the reviewing and often extensive follow-up discussion. Where the discussion was not sufficient to make a decision, the paper, went through an extra review by the PC. A novel feature of the CLEF 2015 conference was to invite CLEF 2014 lab organizers to nominate a "best of the labs" paper, which was reviewed as a full paper submission to the CLEF 2015 conference according to the same review criteria and PC. This resulted in 8 full papers accepted corresponding to each to the CLEF 2014 labs. We received 24 regular full paper submissions, of which 8 (33 %) full papers were accepted for regular oral presentation, 7 further full paper submissions (29 %, making a total of 63 %) accepted with short oral presentation and a poster. We received 36 short paper submissions, and accepted 20 (55 %).

---

[1] http://clef2015.clef-initiative.eu/

In addition to these talks, the eight benchmarking labs reported results of their year long activities in overview talks and lab sessions[2]. The eight labs running as part of CLEF 2015 were as follows:

CLEFeHealth provided scenarios aiming to ease patients' and nurses' understanding and accessing of eHealth information. The goals of the lab were to develop processing methods and resources in a multilingual setting, to enrich difficult-to-understand eHealth texts, and provide valuable documentation. The tasks were: information extraction from clinical data, and user-centered health information retrieval.

ImageCLEF provided four main tasks with a global objective of benchmarking automatic annotation and indexing of images. The tasks tackled different aspects of the annotation problem and aimed at supporting and promoting cutting-edge research addressing the key challenges in the field: image annotation, medical classification, medical clustering, and liver CT annotation.

LifeCLEF provided image-based plant, bird, and fish identification tasks addressing multimodal data by (i) considering birds and fish in addition to plants, (ii) considering audio and video content in addition to images, (iii) scaling-up the evaluation data to hundreds of thousands of life media records and thousands of living species. The tasks were: an audio record-based bird identification task (BirdCLEF), an image-based plant identification task (PlantCLEF), and a fish video surveillance task (FishCLEF).

Living Labs for IR (LL4IR) provided a benchmarking platform for researchers to evaluate their ranking systems in a live setting with real users in their natural task environments. The lab acted as a proxy between commercial organizations (live environments) and lab participants (experimental systems), facilitated data exchange, and made comparisons between the participating systems. The task was: product search and web search.

News Recommendation Evaluation Lab (NEWSREEL) provided two tasks designed to address the challenge of real-time news recommendation. Participants could: a) develop news recommendation algorithms and b) have them tested by millions of users over the period of a few weeks in a living lab. The tasks were: benchmark news recommendations in a living lab, benchmarking news recommendations in a simulated environment.

Uncovering Plagiarism, Authorship, and Social Software Misuse (PAN) provided evaluation of uncovering plagiarism, authorship, and social software misuse. PAN offered three tasks at CLEF 2015 with new evaluation resources consisting of large-scale corpora, performance measures, and web services that allowed for meaningful evaluations. The main goal was to provide for sustainable and reproducible evaluations, to get a clear view of the capabilities of state-of-the-art algorithms. The tasks were: plagiarism detection, author identification, and author profiling.

Question Answering (QA) provided QA from the starting point of a natural language question. However, answering some questions may need to query linked data

---

[2] The full details for each lab are contained in a separate publication, the Working Notes, which are available online at http://ceur-ws.org/Vol-1391/.

(especially if aggregations or logical inferences are required); whereas some questions may need textual inferences and querying free-text. Answering some queries may need both. The tasks were: QALD: Question Answering over Linked Data, entrance exams: questions from reading tests, BioASQ: large-scale biomedical semantic indexing, and BioASQ: biomedical question answering.

Social Book Search (SBS) provided evaluation of real-world information needs which are generally complex, yet almost all research focuses instead on either relatively simple search based on queries or recommendation based on profiles. The goal of the Social Book Search Lab was to investigate techniques to support users in complex book search tasks that involve more than just a query and results list. The tasks were: suggestion track, and interactive track.

A rich social program was organized in conjunction with the conference, starting with a welcome reception with local food and wine specialities, continuing with a city hall reception, which included the local band "*La mal Coiffée*". The social dinner was enjoyed in a famous organic restaurant named "*Saveur Bio*", and master classes in (1) traditional polyphonic singing with Bastien Zaoui from the famous Vox Bigerri band and (2) wine and food pairing with Yves Cinotti, were also offered.

The success of CLEF 2015 would not have been possible without the huge effort of several people and organizations, including the CLEF Association[3], the Program Committee, the Lab Organizing Committee, the Local Organization Committee in Toulouse, the reviewers, and the many students and volunteers who contributed along the way. We would like to acknowledge the *Institut de Recherche en Informatique de Toulouse* UMR 5505 CNRS and its director, Prof. Michel Daydé, for the support we got, first for bidding to host the conference, then for organizing it. We also received the support from the following universities and schools: Ecole supérieure du professorat et de l'éducation, Université Toulouse-Jean Jaurès, Université Paul Sabatier, and Université du Capitole. We also gratefully acknowledge the support we received from our sponsors. The ESF Research Networking Program ELIAS, the ACM SIG-IR, the *Université Toulouse-Jean Jaurès*, and the *Région Midi-Pyrénées* for their strong financial support; but also: Springer, the *Université Paul Sabatier*, *Institut de Recherche en Informatique de Toulouse* UMR 5505 CNRS, INFORSID, *Université Toulouse Capitole*, EGC, ARIA, and ACL. The level of sponsorship allowed us to offer 20 grants for students in addition to a free registration for the 25 volunteers including 11 further students.

July 2015

Josiane Mothe
Jacques Savoy
Jaap Kamps
Karen Pinel-Sauvagnat
Gareth J.F. Jones
Eric SanJuan
Linda Cappellato
Nicola Ferro

---

[3] http://www.clef-initiative.eu/association

Organization

CLEF 2015 Conference and Labs of the Evaluation Forum, Experimental IR Meets Multilinguality, Multimodality, and Interaction, was organized by the University of Toulouse, France.

General Chair

Josiane Mothe	IRIT, Université de Toulouse, France
Jacques Savoy	University of Neuchâtel, Switzerland

Program Chair

Jaap Kamps	University of Amsterdam, The Netherlands
Karen Pinel-Sauvagnat	IRIT, Université de Toulouse, France

Lab Chair

Gareth J.F. Jones	Dublin City University, Ireland
Eric SanJuan	Université d'Avignon et des Pays du Vaucluse, France

Program Committee

Maristella Agosti	University of Padua, Italy
Krisztian Balog	University of Stavanger, Norway
Patrice Bellot	LSIS - Université de Marseille, France
Toine Bogers	Aalborg University Copenhagen, Denmark
Mohand Boughanem	IRIT - Université Paul Sabatier Toulouse 3, France
Guillaume Cabanac	IRIT - Université Paul Sabatier Toulouse 3, France
Tiziana Catarci	Università di Roma "La Sapienza", Italy
Paul Clough	University of Sheffield, UK
Nicola Ferro	University of Padua, Italy
Norbert Fuhr	University of Duisburg-Essen, Germany
Eric Gaussier	Université Joseph Fourier (Grenoble I), France
Lorraine Goeuriot	Université Joseph Fourier (Grenoble I), France
Julio Gonzalo	UNED, Madrid, Spain
Allan Hanbury	Vienna University of Technology, Austria
Donna Harman	NIST, USA
Djoerd Hiemstra	University of Twente, The Netherlands
Frank Hopfgartner	University of Glasgow, UK
Gilles Hubert	IRIT - Université Paul Sabatier Toulouse 3, France
Peter Ingwersen	University of Copenhagen, Denmark
Alexis Joly	INRIA Sophia-Antipolis, France
Gareth J.F. Jones	Dublin City University, Ireland

Evangelos Kanoulas	University of Amsterdam, The Netherlands
Gabriella Kazai	Lumi, UK
Jaana Kekäläinen	University of Tampere, Finland
Liadh Kelly	Trinity College Dublin, Ireland
Benjamin Kille	DAI Lab, Berlin Institute of Technology, Germany
Marijn Koolen	University of Amsterdam, The Netherlands
Birger Larsen	Aalborg University, Denmark
Mihai Lupu	Vienna University of Technology, Austria
Thomas Mandl	University of Hildesheim, Germany
Henning Müller	HES-SO, University of Applied Sciences Western Switzerland, Switzerland
Jian-Yun Ni	Université de Montréal, Canada
Iadh Ounis	University of Glasgow, UK
Gabriella Pasi	Università degli Studi di Milano Bicocca, Italy
Anselmo Peñas	NLP and IR Group, UNED, Spain
Benjamin Piwowarski	CNRS/Université Pierre et Marie Curie, France
Martin Potthast	Bauhaus University Weimar, Germany
Paolo Rosso	Technical University of Valencia, Spain
Eric SanJuan	Université d'Avignon, France
Ralf Schenkel	Universität Passau, Germany
Anne Schuth	University of Amsterdam, The Netherlands
Efstathios Stamatatos	University of the Aegean, Greece
Benno Stein	Bauhaus-Universität Weimar, Germany
Lynda Tamine	IRIT - Université Paul Sabatier Toulouse 3, France
Xavier Tannier	LIMSI-CNRS, Université Paris-Sud, France
Theodora Tsikrika	Information Technologies Institute, CERTH, Greece
Christina Unger	CITEC, Universität Bielefeld, Germany
Mauricio Villegas	Universitat Politècnica de València, Spain

Local Organization

Adrian Chifu	IRIT, Université de Toulouse, France (Sponsoring)
Véronique Debats	IRIT, France (Communication)
Marlène Giamporcaro	SAIC, INP Toulouse, France (Administration and Registration)
Laure Soulier	IRIT, Université de Toulouse, France (Advertising)
Nathalie Valles-Parlengeau	IRIT, Université de Toulouse, France (Co-resp. for UT1-Capitole University)

Platinum Sponsors

Silver Sponsors

Bronze Sponsors

Keynotes

Personal Information Systems and Personal Semantics

Gregory Grefenstette

INRIA Saclay, France

People generally think of Big Data as something generated by machines or large communities of people interacting with the digital world. But technological progress means that each individual is currently, or soon will be, generating masses of digital data in their everyday lives. In every interaction with an application, every web page visited, every time your telephone is turned on, you generate information about yourself, Personal Big Data. With the rising adoption of quantified self gadgets, and the foreseeable adoption of intelligent glasses capturing daily life, the quantity of personal Big Data will only grow. In this Personal Big Data, as in other Big Data, a key problem is aligning concepts in the same semantic space. While concept alignment in the public sphere is an understood, though unresolved, problem, what does ontological organization of a personal space look like? Is it idiosyncratic, or something that can be shared between people? We will describe our current approach to this problem of organizing personal data and creating and exploiting a personal semantics.

Evaluating the Search Experience:
From Retrieval Effectiveness to User Engagement

Mounia Lalmas

Yahoo Labs, London, UK

Building retrieval systems that return results to users that satisfy their information need is one thing; Information Retrieval has a long history in evaluating how effective retrieval systems are. Many evaluation initiatives such as TREC and CLEF have allowed organizations worldwide to evaluate and compare retrieval approaches. Building a retrieval system that not only returns good results to users, but does so in a way that users will want to use that system again is something more challenging; a positive search experience has been shown to lead to users engaging long-term with the retrieval system. In this talk, I will review state-of-the-art approaches concerned with evaluating retrieval effectiveness. I will then focus on those approaches aiming at evaluating user engagement, and describe current works in this area. The talk will end with the proposal of a framework incorporating effectiveness evaluation into user engagement. An important component of this framework is to consider both within- and across-search session measurement.

Beyond Information Retrieval:
When and How Not to Find Things

Douglas W. Oard

University of Maryland, USA

The traditional role of a search engine is much like the traditional role of a library: generally the objective is to help people find things. As we get better at this, however, we have been encountering an increasing number of cases in which some things that we know exist simply should not be found. Some well known examples include removal of improperly posted copyrighted material from search engine indexes, and the evolving legal doctrine that is now commonly referred to as the "right to be forgotten." Some such cases are simple, relying on users to detect specific content that should be flushed from a specific index. Other cases, however, are more complex. For example, in the aspect of the civil litigation process known as e-discovery, one side may be entitled to withhold entire classes of material that may not have been labeled in advance (because of attorney-client privilege). An even more complex example is government transparency, in which for public policy reasons we may want to make some information public, despite that information being intermixed with other information that must be protected. Professional archivists have long dealt with such challenges, so perhaps we should start thinking about how to build search engines that act less like a library and more like an archive. In this talk, I will use these and other examples to introduce the idea of "search among secrets" in which the goal is to help some users find some content while protecting some content from some users (or some uses). We'll dive down to look at how this actually works today in a few specific cases, with particular attention to how queries are formulated and which parts of the process are, or might be, automated. With that as background, I will then offer a few initial thoughts on how we might evaluate such systems. I'll conclude with an invitation to think together about how information retrieval researchers might, together with others, begin to tackle these challenges.

Contents

Short Papers

Best of the Labs

Labs Overviews

Experimental IR

Experimental Study on Semi-structured Peer-to-Peer Information Retrieval Network

Rami S. Alkhawaldeh$^{(\boxtimes)}$ and Joemon M. Jose

School of Computing Science, The University of Glasgow, University Avenue,
Glasgow G12 8QQ, UK
r.alkhawaldeh.1@research.gla.ac.uk, Joemon.Jose@glasgow.ac.uk

Abstract. In the recent decades, retrieval systems deployed over peer-to-peer (P2P) overlay networks have been investigated as an alternative to centralised search engines. Although modern search engines provide efficient document retrieval, they possess several drawbacks. In order to alleviate their problems, P2P Information Retrieval (P2PIR) systems provide an alternative architecture to the traditional centralised search engine. Users and creators of web content in such networks have full control over what information they wish to share as well as how they share it. The semi-structured P2P architecture has been proposed where the underlying approach organises similar document in a peer, often using clustering techniques, and promotes willing peers as super peers (or hubs) to traffic queries to appropriate peers with relevant content. However, no systematic evaluation study has been performed on such architectures. In this paper, we study the performance of three cluster-based semi-structured P2PIR models and explain the effectiveness of several important design considerations and parameters on retrieval performance, as well as the robustness of these types of network.

Keywords: Semi-structured Peer-to-Peer · Clustering peers · Query routing · Resource selection · Evaluation

1 Introduction

Over the last decade, the Internet has emerged as a wide pervasive network over the world handling a rich source of information. It contains an immense amount of content such as text, image, video and audio that are scattered over many distributed machines. People use search engines to access information on these networks. Although search engines have advantages of simplicity in document management and high efficiency in comprehensive search to retrieve relevant information, they are susceptible to various deficiencies [1]. The drawbacks include: (i) the monopolisation of the search engine where few companies have control of the entire domain [2,3]; (ii) search engines leave users prone to privacy risk by pursuing their behaviours [4]; (iii) search engines have to be updated regularly to keep track of the modified information on the Internet [5]; (iv) centralised search engine can easily become a bottleneck during periods of

© Springer International Publishing Switzerland 2015
J. Mothe et al. (Eds.): CLEF 2015, LNCS 9283, pp. 3–14, 2015.
DOI: 10.1007/978-3-319-24027-5_1

high demand and may have a single point of failure; and (v) crawlers in search engines are incapable of locating web pages in the hidden web (or deep web) that are invisible from indexation [1, 6]. It would be better if users and creators of web content could collectively provide a search service and have a full control over what information they wish to share as well as how they share it. P2P overlay networks could be used as a promising surrogate network to alleviate the ethical and technical drawbacks of centralised search engines, to handle dynamic content, and provide scalability.

Retrieval approaches on P2P networks have been proposed in the past [7–9]. However, retrieval effectiveness over P2P networks was very poor and hence the initial enthusiasms receded. Semi-structured P2P network is proposed as a promising network to build retrieval approaches, which contains two types of peers; super (or hub) and regular peers [10]. Super peers have a high level of willingness to store the meta-data of their associated regular peers and communicate between each other to cast queries on behalf of their own regular peers. Semi-structured P2P network combines the advantages of the two centralised and decentralised P2P overlay networks in load balancing between super and regular peers and through providing heterogeneity across peers to improve the performance [11]. In this paper, we study the performance boundaries of semi-structured P2PIR systems. We study a set of semi-structured topologies built with different settings to study the effectiveness of information retrieval.

The reminder of the paper is organised as follows: Section 2 discusses the problem and some related works along with research questions. Section 3 explains the experiments settings and the retrieval process along with the evaluation framework. Section 4 creates the semi-structured P2PIR topologies and compares them with the centralised system. Section 5 studies the effectiveness of some retrieval models in the suggested semi-structured P2PIR system. Section 6 studies a set of resource selection methods on semi-structured P2PIR system, followed by our conclusion in section 7.

2   Related Work

The efficient and effective P2P retrieval systems combine peers with similar content semantically into the same cluster [9]. Consequently, the peers can reach each other via a shortest path as small-world networks [12,13]. However, such approaches are hindered by the effectiveness of the clustering technique used.

Lu and Callan [7] study the performance of a set of resource selection algorithms and retrieval effectiveness of the hybrid P2P network. This study uses a large scale test-bed and a set of queries. Precision, recall, and F-score metrics are calculated as retrieval effectiveness where the efficiency of the system is evaluated as the number of queries routed. They shows the accuracy and the effectiveness of content-based resource selection and text retrieval algorithms in comparison with name-based and flooding methods.

In [8] the retrieval effectiveness is evaluated on different P2PIR architectures using a large test-bed. The architectures use the Decision-theoretic Framework

(DTF) [14] and COllection Retrieval Inference network (CORI net) [15] as query routing that depends on global hub statistics for centralised and decentralised information selection. The comparison study depends on three main topologies of P2P networks for evaluation. Their results show that there is no preferred architecture and the solid theoretical framework, DTF, can be used on P2P networks in an efficient and effective manner.

Klampanos and Jose [9] proposed a single pass cluster-based P2P architecture; However, the effectiveness of the network is not satisfactory and it is not clear what alternate forms of clustering can be used. Applying single-pass clustering to a large collection of documents is computationally expensive and it is also dependent on the threshold used. Hence, alternative computationally feasible models need to be explored. They further proposed two features used for improving the performance, which are replications of relevant documents through the network and using relevance feedback by increasing the values of past queries' terms at the super peer level.

A recent method called PCAP [16] exploits co-clustering for improved resource selection. It uses a query log to build a matrix where each document-query combination is assigned a relevance scores. This matrix is then co-clustered to identify clusters that have two parts, a set of documents and a set of queries for which the documents are relevant. These separate co-clusters are then managed by separated peers, and a subset of co-clusters are chosen to route each query too. Though the usage of clustering overlaps conceptually with our method, it may be noted that the clustering is done on query logs, and thus, PCAP cannot work in the absence of accumulated historical query log information. This is different from the conventional co-operative resource selection setting that we target in this paper; in such a setting, the resource selection algorithm is expected to work before query log is available.

One of the difficulty in P2P architectures is that it is almost impossible to collect global statistics which are needed to be estimated [17] to route queries to those relevant peers. These challenges along with the lack of systematic evaluation framework dampens the research in this area. In this paper, we investigate the behaviour of number of factors in a semi-structured co-operative P2P architecture.

- We propose to use three different clustering approaches for content organization and compare their performance.
  RQ1: How do different clustering approaches compare in terms of performance for the purposes of semi-structured P2P information retrieval?
- In centralised IR systems, we have clear understanding on how the state of the art retrieval models behave. However, we conjecture that due to the variations in the number of documents within peer's collection, the retrieval effectiveness will vary with centralised systems.
  RQ2: How does the retrieval effectiveness vary with respect to various retrieval models in P2P testing?
- Resource selection (or query routing) is considered one of the important challenges in Distributed Information Retrieval (DIR) systems especially in P2PIR systems.

RQ3: What are the retrieval effectiveness and message routing efficiency in using a well-known resource selection methods on Semi-structured P2PIR systems?

3 Experimental Methodology

3.1 Testbeds and Queries

Our study uses large-scale test-beds as a real baseline to evaluate the retrieval effectiveness in P2PIR systems [18]. These test-beds are developed based on the TREC WT10g collection (11680 web domains) for information retrieval. Three properties of P2P Information Retrieval test-beds are: (i) a peer shares a limited number of topics, (ii) documents are distributed in a power-law pattern, (iii) and content replication. Some statistics are given in Table 1. The individual test-

Table 1. Testbeds general properties

Characteristics	ASISWOR	ASISWR	DLWOR	DLWR	UWOR	UWR
No.of Peers	11680	11680	1500	1500	11680	11680
No.of Docs	1692096	1788248	1692806	1740385	1692096	1788896
Average.Peers Docs	144.87	153.1	1128.54	1160.26	144.87	153.16
Max.Peer of Docs	26505	33874	26505	33874	145	7514
Min.Peer of Docs	5	5	171	174	140	8

beds are designed to simulate a number of P2PIR applications through different document distributions and concentrations of relevant documents. The test-beds are categorised into three different environments with two collections for each; **W**ith **R**eplication (WR) and **W**ith**O**ut **R**eplication (WOR). These environments are as follows: (i) Information sharing environment ($ASIS^*$ family), (ii) Digital library environment (DL^* family), (iii) and uniformly distributed environments (U^* family).

The standard query set for the TREC WT10g corpus, which is TREC topics 451-550[1], is used along with standard judgement assessments provided by the US National Institute for Standards and Technology (NIST) and generated by a group of experts from different areas.

3.2 Retrieval Process and Evaluation

In semi-structured P2P retrieval systems two layers of clustering are used for organising the content. Firstly, each peer's documents are clustered to find semantic groupings. Then, at the super peer level, peers' cluster centroids are clustered again to discover semantic groupings at network level which are distributed over super peers of the network. This super peer level grouping is used

---

[1] TREC English Test Questions (Topics). http://trec.nist.gov/data/webmain.html

to route queries to appropriate super peers and their peers [9]. We used TER-RIER (Terabyte Retriever) [19] as an indexer and searcher for each peer. The user (i.e. the owner of the peer) initiates and sends a query to the connected super peer. The super peer routes the query to its local peers and other selected super peers. The requested peers execute the information retrieval process on their indices and return a list of result, which is fixed to 1000 documents, using the BM25 retrieval model [20]. Then, the computed result lists of requested peers are merged by the super peer of the requesting peer to produce the final result. We used a well known merging algorithm, called COMBMNZ [21]. The COMBMNZ is an unsupervised merging algorithm which is simple, effective and well-studied [22]. We compute the retrieval accuracy using the following popular metrics: (i) precision, (ii) recall, (iii) P@10, (iv) P@30, (v) P@100, (vi) average precision, (vii) and Mean Average precision (MAP) metrics.

4 Retrieval Effectiveness of Semi-structured P2PIR Systems

4.1 Centralised System

Although P2PIR effectiveness is not comparable with centralised systems [23], we compare our results to a centralised system as a point of reference to determine which topology is closer to such a system. Table 2 shows seven metrics discussing the IR effectiveness of a centralised system averaged over all TREC topics of the WT10g collection.

Table 2. Retrieval performance using our centralised system

Topics	Recall	Precision	P@10	P@30	P@100	MAP
100	0.7008	0.0406	0.299	0.2293	0.1418	0.1903

As shown, the average number of relevant documents retrieved is 38.53 which is 4% of the retrieved documents; approximately 3, 7, 14, and 38.53 documents at positions 10, 30, 100, and 203 respectively with 970.5 retrieved documents on average.

4.2 Semi-structured P2PIR Architecture

In the P2P networks, the peer holds a limited set of semantic topics which motivated [9] to group the peers' documents that have the same semantics, using a hierarchical clustering algorithm as briefly described in Subsection 3.2. Our three topologies follow this methodology and clusters each peer's documents using the Bisect K-means clustering algorithm. It may be noted that any clustering algorithm can be used to identify peer clusters; our choice of bisecting K-Means is driven by efficiency considerations [24]. However, the cluster-based architecture, unlike other architectures, has an elaborate set-up phase that involves clustering

Table 3. The Bisecting K-means Clustering analysis

Meta-Info	No.of.Clusters per Peer			Av.Docs.per Peers' Clusters			Av.Terms.per Peers' Clusters			Clustering Time (in secs)		
Test-beds	Min	Max	Mean	Min	Max	Mean	Min	Max	Mean	Min	Max	Mean
DLWOR	1	119	12.3	304.2	601.1	371.3	4090.4	9172.5	5360	2.26	349.87	14.90
DLWR	1	137	12	15.2	268.7	628.7	359.3	163.4	4120.4	9403.5	5497.8	2213.99
ASISWOR	1	166	3.9	39.2	68.5	46.8	853	1713.5	1129.3	0.09	469.14	2.56
ASISWR	1	154	4	6.7	40.5	71.4	48.05	13.43	915.6	1840.3	1202.2	405.44
UWOR	1	23	6.2	4.6	26.5	54.8	35.5	13.92	1293.2	3126	1891.6	827.22
UWR	1	29	6.2	4.7	30	61.3	40.1	15.8	1400.2	3332.05	2037.3	883.91

of documents. Thus, an understanding of the computational and memory costs of the clustering phase is important in analysing the applicability of routing algorithms that work upon it. The statistics of the Bisect K-means clustering algorithm appear in Table 3. The table details the number of clusters, documents per cluster, the number of terms per cluster, and the time taken for clustering on average. The clustering is seen to just take a few seconds to complete on the average, and a few minutes at worst; we presume that these would be regarded as very low overheads for the setup phase. The Bisect K-means clustering algorithm was seen to be even faster, since the clustering is done on the peer clusters that were seen to be fewer than the number of documents per peer, on the average.

In this work, we propose to use three other alternative clustering approaches to construct the super peer level of the network which are: (i) K-means, (ii) Half K-means, (iii) and Approximation single pass topologies. In k-means topology, the peers' centroids are used as input to the K-means clustering algorithm (where $k = 50$), resulting in 50 super peer centroids. This is similar to gather all peers' centroids in one file and perform a K-means clustering. In the HalfK-means Single pass topology, the clustering starts with the half of the peers and builds a K-means topology as attractor of other peers. Then, the topology uses single pass clustering to connect the other half peers' centroids with already built super peers' centroids. The half K-means single pass algorithm assumes that the half of the resources in the network are available and they can be used from the other arrived peers to discover the related semantic groupings for joining the system. Finally, as single pass clustering is computationally intensive, we use an approximation single pass approach, which is executed on a distributed Hadoop cluster of 8 nodes. In the approximation single pass method, we divided the peers into eight packets and then used the single pass algorithm on each packet to create super peers for each packet. The super peers in all packets were used as a topology from the assumption that the super peers might be created separately as independent components from each other.

Our results are shown in Table 4, which is much lower than the centralised retrieval result in Table 2. The results can be more fairly compared with other works which use the same evaluation framework. The authors in [9] use the same test-beds and build the network in the same way with single pass clustering algorithm. In their work, they uses the P@10 metric at different thresholds of clustering on four test-beds (i.e non-replication test-beds). The best P@10 values are 0.0196, 0.0063, and 0.060 for ASISWOR, DLWOR, and UWOR respectively. In the three test-beds (ASISWOR, DLWOR, and UWOR) our clustering formu-

Table 4. The Retrieval Effectiveness of three semi-structured P2PIR topologies

Testbed	Topology	Recall	Precision	P@10	P@30	P@100	MAP
ASISWOR	K-means	0.2984	0.0161	**0.078**	**0.0527**	**0.0317**	**0.024**
	Half K-means Single Pass	0.1354	0.0113	0.0602	0.0405	0.0219	0.0216
	Approximation Single Pass	**0.3627**	**0.0202**	0.0293	0.0195	0.0236	0.0197
ASISWR	K-means	**0.253**	**0.014**	0.028	0.025	**0.0208**	**0.0138**
	Half K-means Single Pass	0.1248	0.0108	**0.0296**	**0.0282**	0.0173	0.0115
	Approximation Single Pass	0.2397	0.0131	0.009	0.0097	0.0142	0.0107
DLWOR	K-means	**0.3655**	**0.0194**	**0.0717**	**0.0502**	**0.0336**	**0.0354**
	Half K-means Single Pass	0.0466	0.0045	0.0598	0.0292	0.0126	0.0145
	Approximation Single Pass	0.2892	0.0151	0.064	0.0437	0.0243	0.022
DLWR	K-means	0.2564	0.0134	0.0173	0.0238	**0.0198**	**0.0132**
	Half K-means Single Pass	0.0512	0.0077	**0.0463**	**0.027**	0.0128	0.0053
	Approximation Single Pass	**0.3294**	**0.0165**	0.012	0.0127	0.0161	0.0131
UWOR	K-means	0.3428	0.0202	**0.058**	**0.051**	0.0381	0.0243
	Half K-means Single Pass	0.0597	0.0082	0.0286	0.0235	0.0132	0.0044
	Approximation Single Pass	**0.4513**	**0.0255**	0.0172	0.0259	**0.042**	**0.0302**
UWR	K-means	0.2027	**0.0120**	0.0150	**0.0197**	**0.0177**	0.0104
	Half K-means Single Pass	0.0498	0.0086	**0.0184**	0.0153	0.0096	0.0031
	Approximation Single Pass	**0.2699**	0.014	0.009	0.0123	0.0157	**0.0133**

lations outperform their approach. But, the approximation single pass topology in our semi-structured P2PIR system on UWOR has a lower value than the 0.060 which means that their approach outperforms ours in such scenarios. We can conclude that the retrieval effectiveness of P2PIR depends on the clustering algorithm used to build the network which confirms our research question (i.e. **RQ1**). Finally, on average the best topology of three scenarios is the K-means topology, with 0.0201 over all test-beds. The approximation single pass approach has value of 0.0182 and the worst topology is half-kmeans single pass with 0.0102 MAP value. This clearly shows the need for developing a robust content organization methodology.

5   Retrieval Models in Semi-structured System

In this section, a set of retrieval models are used to compare the retrieval effectiveness on the semi-structured P2PIR networks. Retrieval models have characteristics and assumptions which differ from one to another in retrieving relevant documents. However, the comparison between retrieval models on the centralised system were conducted and studied in the literature. It is assumed that same level of performance is expected in P2PIR systems. Given that the content characteristics of peers change, it is important to study the relative performance differences of P2PIR systems with respect to the retrieval models.

The retrieval models that we studied come from different families implemented in TERRIER framework [19]. The Figure 1 shows the effectiveness of retrieval models on centralised test-bed and the other P2P test-beds. We used the F-score values as the average value combining the precision and recall values. The retrieval models behaves in different manner between test-beds and the centralised test-bed, because of the terms and documents distribution in P2PIR systems. The retrieval models behave based on the terms statistics in the collection and each of them has a specific intuition and parameters.

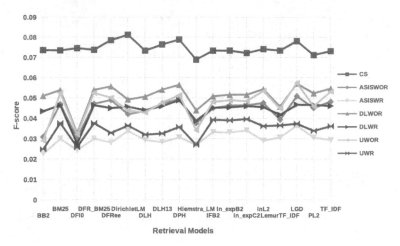

Fig. 1. Effectiveness of Retrieval models over Semi-structured P2PIR system

As shown in Figure 1, the Language models retrieval models which are DirichletLM and Hiemstra_LM occupies the best and worst retrieval models in CS systems with F-score 0.081 and 0.0689 respectively. In contrary, the retrieval models in semi-structured P2PIR models is performs differently where the best retrieval model for test-beds without replication is LGD retrieval model with F-score 0.051, 0.0571, and 0.0574 for ASISWOR, DLWOR, and UWOR respectively. The worst retrieval models on the same test-beds is DFI0 model with F-score 0.030, 0.032, and 0.032 for ASISWOR, DLWOR, and UWOR respectively. The test-beds with replication perform in different way in comparing with the test-bed without replication, because the replicating models replicate relevant documents on different peers which change the term distribution for retrieval selection. The best retrieval models in test-beds with replication are LGD for ASISWR, DPH for DLWR, and In_expC2 for UWR with F-score 0.036, 0.049, and 0.04 respectively, while the worst ones are BB2 for ASISWR, DFI0 for DLWR, and BB2 for UWR with F-score 0.022, 0.03, 0.045 respectively. Ultimately, on average the best retrieval model on all test-beds is LGD model with approximate F-score 0.05 where the worst one is DFI0 model with approximate F-score 0.029. We conclude that there are differences in the retrieval effectiveness of retrieval models in the centralised and distributed systems, especially given the heterogeneity distribution of collections in P2P networks, which means that the retrieval models' parameters have to be studied carefully in the designing phase (**RQ2**).

6   The Resource Selection Methods on Semi-structured P2PIR Systems

The experiment settings we used are the number of messages and retrieval effectiveness. The number of messages setting is the number of hops that the system uses to send the given query to those relevant peers. The small number of messages can achieve high performance in reducing the cost of bandwidth limit in the system. Retrieval effectiveness focuses on information user need by calculating the number of relevant documents retrieved for each query (or topic). The high performance model of retrieval effectiveness and routing efficiency are achieved at small number of messages with more relevant retrieved documents. In this section, we will study the performance of the Semi-structured P2P network in routing efficiency and retrieval effectiveness and compared it the flooding method (**RQ3**).

6.1   Message Complexity

The Semi-structured P2PIR system is studied under four test-beds. The number of messages are averaged over 100 topics and the baseline for comparison is flooding method that cast query to whole peers under specific super peer level.

As shown in Figure 2, The CVV method has a small number of messages in $ASIS^*$ family and vGIOSS method performs better in small number of messages

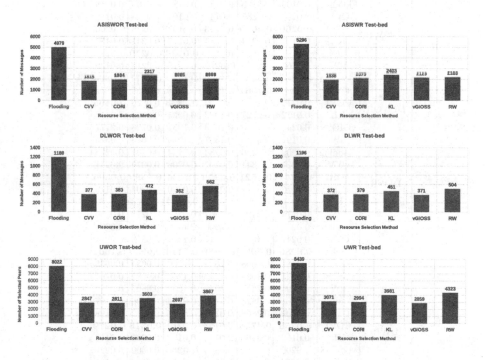

Fig. 2. Message Complexity on Semi-structured P2PIR system

in other test-beds. The worst method in number of messages are KL method and Random walk (RW) method. The message routing is related with retrieval effectiveness. The system design is acceptable with more retrieval effectiveness and little bit high in message routing efficiency.

6.2 Retrieval Effectiveness

The information retrieval systems whatever if it is centralized or distributed retrieval model can be evaluated through the number of relevant documents retrieved for a specific query and the ranks of that documents in search result list. The proposed model was tested under four test-beds which are DLWOR and ASISWOR as test-beds without replication and DLWR and ASISWR as test-beds with replication. The table 5 shows the result of retrieval of such

Table 5. The performance of Resource Selection Methods

Test-bed	Methods	Precision	Recall	P@10	P@30	P@100	MAP
ASISWOR	Flooding	0.025	0.463	0.164	0.1200	0.076	0.071
	CVV	0.0252	0.4594	**0.1635**	0.1205	0.0765	0.0714
	CORI	**0.0260**	**0.4658**	0.1633	**0.1224**	**0.0782**	**0.0744**
	KL	0.0188	0.3368	0.1347	0.0988	0.0619	0.0530
	vGIOSS	0.0226	0.4089	0.1593	0.1149	0.0724	0.0705
	RW	0.0174	0.2583	0.1223	0.0877	0.0528	0.0389
ASISWR	Flooding	0.0163	0.3385	0.0141	0.0182	0.0190	0.0173
	CVV	0.0193	0.3885	0.0148	0.0191	0.0208	0.0189
	CORI	**0.0209**	**0.4070**	0.0143	0.0195	0.0226	0.0206
	KL	0.0171	0.3254	0.0157	0.0217	0.0241	0.0177
	vGIOSS	0.0199	0.3859	0.0153	**0.0236**	**0.0270**	**0.0217**
	RW	0.0163	0.2430	**0.0205**	0.0215	0.0218	0.0136
DLWOR	Flooding	**0.0287**	**0.5479**	0.1690	0.1323	**0.0877**	**0.0866**
	CVV	0.0266	**0.4961**	0.1757	0.1308	0.0855	0.0842
	CORI	0.0274	0.4913	0.1732	**0.1333**	0.0876	**0.0865**
	KL	0.0172	0.2727	0.1323	0.0924	0.0577	0.0453
	vGIOSS	0.0245	0.4510	0.1643	0.1251	0.0796	0.0777
	RW	0.0192	0.3035	0.1337	0.1019	0.0613	0.0524
DLWR	Flooding	0.0209	0.4256	0.0184	0.0184	0.0231	0.0223
	CVV	0.0221	0.4341	0.0202	0.0208	0.0279	0.0241
	CORI	**0.0244**	**0.4521**	**0.0296**	0.0336	**0.0399**	**0.0300**
	KL	0.0158	0.2511	0.0281	0.0290	0.0304	0.0179
	vGIOSS	0.0216	0.4051	0.0294	**0.0337**	0.0378	0.0280
	RW	0.0174	0.2423	0.0267	0.0285	0.0273	0.0153
UWOR	Flooding	0.0277	0.4900	0.1900	0.1337	0.0906	0.0974
	CVV	0.0247	0.4341	0.1917	0.1364	0.0858	0.0915
	CORI	**0.0286**	**0.4951**	**0.1930**	**0.1414**	**0.0950**	**0.1002**
	KL	0.0181	0.3008	0.1522	0.1060	0.0634	0.0633
	vGIOSS	0.0225	0.4055	0.1733	0.1243	0.0781	0.0791
	RW	0.0195	0.2622	0.1535	0.1036	0.0607	0.0482
UWR	Flooding	0.0188	0.3818	0.0120	0.0153	0.0196	0.0197
	CVV	0.0201	0.3868	0.0125	0.0177	0.0212	0.0198
	CORI	**0.0256**	**0.4755**	0.0153	0.0219	**0.0313**	**0.0279**
	KL	0.0169	0.3168	0.0142	0.0189	0.0225	0.0174
	vGIOSS	0.0209	0.3959	0.0145	**0.0234**	0.0300	0.0229
	RW	0.0172	0.2528	**0.0182**	0.0213	0.0197	0.0127

test-beds using the resource selection techniques. In order to reflect the selection parameter setting, the results are averaged over six percent of selection peers from 5% to 50% that are performed at super peer for the requested query. The methods column clarifies the selection techniques for comparison.

The results shows that the CORI resource selection method obtains the high values in all test-beds in each measurement score in comparison with other resource selection approach. The CORI method has acceptable number of messages in number routed query which could be selected as an effective and efficient selection method in semi-structured P2PIR systems.

7 Conclusion

Semi-structured P2PIR has an important role as a promising retrieval system to alleviate drawbacks of centralised systems. Despite this, a systematic study on the behaviours of P2PIR systems are not done yet. In this paper, we executed the first comparative evaluation of its kind in the P2PIR domain, considering the effect of architectural decisions have on the retrieval effectiveness of such systems. In a nutshell, three cluster based P2PIR topologies were studied which confirms the need for better clustering or semantic organisation techniques. The study evaluates the effectiveness of different retrieval models in a semi-structured P2PIR system and results show surprisingly different behaviours for the considered retrieval models. Finally, the effectiveness and efficiency of resource selection methods in distributed information retrieval systems is studied, where the CORI selection method is the best approach experimentally. Overall, this is the first systematic study on P2P retrieval which highlights and opens up need for new researches.

References

1. Shokouhi, M., Si, L.: Federated search. Foundations and Trends in Information Retrieval 5(1), 1–102 (2011)
2. Kulathuramaiyer, N., Balke, W.T.: Restricting the view and connecting the dots - dangers of a web search engine monopoly. J. UCS 12(12), 1731–1740 (2006)
3. Mowshowitz, A., Kawaguchi, A.: Assessing bias in search engines. Inf. Process. Manage. 38(1), 141–156 (2002)
4. Tene, O.: What google knows: Privacy and internet search engines. Utah Law Review 2008(4), 1434–1490 (2009)
5. Lewandowski, D., Wahlig, H., Meyer-Bautor, G.: The freshness of web search engine databases. J. Inf. Sci. 32(2), 131–148 (2006)
6. Bergman, M.K.: The deep web: Surfacing hidden value. Journal of Electronic Publishing 7(1) (2001)
7. Lu, J., Callan, J.: Content-based retrieval in hybrid peer-to-peer networks. In: CIKM, pp. 199–206 (2003)
8. Nottelmann, H., Fuhr, N.: Comparing different architectures for query routing in peer-to-peer networks. In: Lalmas, M., MacFarlane, A., Rüger, S.M., Tombros, A., Tsikrika, T., Yavlinsky, A. (eds.) ECIR 2006. LNCS, vol. 3936, pp. 253–264. Springer, Heidelberg (2006)

9. Klampanos, I.A., Jose, J.M.: An evaluation of a cluster-based architecture for peer-to-peer information retrieval. In: Wagner, R., Revell, N., Pernul, G. (eds.) DEXA 2007. LNCS, vol. 4653, pp. 380–391. Springer, Heidelberg (2007)
10. Androutsellis-Theotokis, S., Spinellis, D.: A survey of peer-to-peer content distribution technologies. ACM Comput. Surv. **36**(4), 335–371 (2004)
11. Yang, B., Garcia-Molina, H.: Designing a super-peer network. In: ICDE, pp. 49–60 (2003)
12. Watts, D., Strogatz, S.: Collective dynamics of 'small-world' networks. Nature **393**(6684), 440–442 (1998)
13. Kleinberg, J.: The small-world phenomenon: An algorithmic perspective. In: Proceedings of the Thirty-Second Annual ACM Symposium on Theory of Computing, STOC '00, pp. 163–170. ACM, New York (2000)
14. Fuhr, N.: A decision-theoretic approach to database selection in networked IR. ACM Trans. Inf. Syst. **17**(3), 229–249 (1999)
15. Callan, J.P., Lu, Z., Croft, W.B.: Searching distributed collections with inference networks. In: Proceedings of the 18th Annual International ACM SIGIR Conference on Research and Development in Information Retrieval, SIGIR '95, pp. 21–28. ACM, New York (1995)
16. Puppin, D., Silvestri, F., Perego, R., Baeza-Yates, R.: Tuning the capacity of search engines: Load-driven routing and incremental caching to reduce and balance the load. ACM Trans. Info. Syst. (TOIS) **28**(2), 5 (2010)
17. Richardson, S., Cox, I.J.: Estimating global statistics for unstructured P2P search in the presence of adversarial peers. In: Proceedings of the 37th International ACM SIGIR Conference on Research and Development in Information Retrieval, SIGIR '14, pp. 203–212. ACM, New York (2014)
18. Klampanos, I.A., Poznański, V., Jose, J.M., Fischer, F.: A suite of testbeds for the realistic evaluation of peer-to-peer information retrieval systems. In: Losada, D.E., Fernández-Luna, J.M. (eds.) ECIR 2005. LNCS, vol. 3408, pp. 38–51. Springer, Heidelberg (2005)
19. Ounis, I., Lioma, C., Macdonald, C., Plachouras, V.: Research directions in terrier: a search engine for advanced retrieval on the web. CEPIS Upgrade Journal **8**(1) (2007)
20. Jones, K.S., Walker, S., Robertson, S.E.: A probabilistic model of information retrieval: Development and comparative experiments. Inf. Process. Manage. **36**(6), 779–808 (2000)
21. Shaw, J.A., Fox, E.A.: Combination of multiple searches. In: Text REtrieval Conference, pp. 243–252 (1994)
22. Lee, J.H.: Analyses of multiple evidence combination. SIGIR Forum **31**(SI), 267–276 (1997)
23. Xu, J., Callan, J.P.: Effective retrieval with distributed collections. In: SIGIR, pp. 112–120 (1998)
24. Steinbach, M., Karypis, G., Kumar, V.: A comparison of document clustering techniques. Technical Report 00–034, University of Minnesota (2000)

Evaluating Stacked Marginalised Denoising Autoencoders Within Domain Adaptation Methods

Boris Chidlovskii[✉], Gabriela Csurka, and Stephane Clinchant

Xerox Research Centre Europe, 6 Chemin Maupertuis, Meylan, France
chidlovskii@xrce.xerox.com

Abstract. In this paper we address the problem of domain adaptation using multiple source domains. We extend the XRCE contribution to Clef'14 Domain Adaptation challenge [6] with the new methods and new datasets. We describe a new class of domain adaptation technique based on *stacked marginalized denoising autoencoders* (sMDA). It aims at extracting and denoising features common to both source and target domains in the unsupervised mode. Noise marginalization allows to obtain a closed form solution and to considerably reduce the training time. We build a classification system which compares sMDA combined with SVM or with Domain Specific Class Mean classifiers to the state-of-the art in both unsupervised and semi-supervised settings. We report the evaluation results for a number of image and text datasets.

1 Introduction

Domain adaptation problem rises each time when we need to leverage labeled data in one or more related domains, hereafter referred to as *source* domains, to learn a classifier for unseen data in a *target* domain. Such a situation occurs in multiple real world applications with embedded machine learning components. Examples include named entity recognition across different text corpora, object recognition in images acquired in different conditions, and some others (see [18] for a survey on domain adaptation methods).

Domain adaptation has received a particular attention in computer vision applications [19, 22, 23] where domain shift is a consequence of taking images in different conditions (background scene, object location and pose, view angle changes) [24]. A large number of very different approaches have been proposed in the last few years to address the visual domain adaptation [3, 14–17, 21]. Due to this high interest, ImageCLEF 2014 organized the Domain Adaptation Challenge on multi-source domain adaptation for the image classification. XRCE team participated and won the challenge [6], by combining techniques of the instance reuse and metric learning.

In this paper, we extend our last year contribution in three ways. First, we lean on new methods for domain adaptation, in particular, ones based on *stacked marginalized denoising autoencoders* (sMDAs) [5, 26] developed in the

© Springer International Publishing Switzerland 2015
J. Mothe et al. (Eds.): CLEF 2015, LNCS 9283, pp. 15–27, 2015.
DOI: 10.1007/978-3-319-24027-5_2

deep learning community. These methods aim at extracting features common to both source and target domains, by corrupting feature values and then marginalizing the noise out. Second, we extend the semi-supervised classification task to a more challenging unsupervised mode, where no target labeled instances are available. Finally, we include in the evaluation new, both image and text datasets.

The remainder of the paper is organized as follows. In Section 2 we introduce the problem of domain adaptation from multiple sources to a target domain. We recall the previous methods and describe in details sMDA. Section 3 describes datasets used in evaluation. Section 4 is a core part of the paper, it reports results of multiple comparative evaluations. Section 5 concludes the paper.

2   Domain Adaptation Problem and Methods

We define a domain $\mathcal{D}$ as composed of a feature space $\mathcal{X} \subset R^d$ and a label space $\mathcal{Y}$. Any given task in domain $\mathcal{D}$ (classification, regression, ranking, etc.) is defined by function $h : \mathcal{X} \to \mathcal{Y}$. In traditional machine learning, learning the task is to estimate a classifier function $\tilde{h} : \mathcal{X} \to \mathcal{Y}$ from the sample data $D = \{(\mathbf{x}_1; y_1), \dots, (\mathbf{x}_n; y_n)\}$, $\mathbf{x}_i \in \mathcal{X}$; $y_i \in \mathcal{Y}$, that best approximates h, according to certain criteria.

In the domain adaptation setting, we assume working with $N + 1$ domains, including N *source* domains S_j and a *target* domain T. From the source domain $S_j, j = 1 \dots, N$, we can sample data with labels, $D_{S_j} = \{(\mathbf{x}_{j1}, y_{j1}), \dots, (\mathbf{x}_{jn_j}, y_{jn_j})\}$, $\mathbf{x}_{ji} \in \mathcal{X}$, $y_{ji} \in \mathcal{Y}$. From the target domain, we are able to sample data $D_T = \{\mathbf{x}_1, \dots, \mathbf{x}_{n_T}\}$, $\mathbf{x}_i \in \mathcal{X}$. In the unsupervised case, data is sampled without labels; in the semi-supervised setting, initial $r_T \ll n_T$ items in D_T have labels $\{y_1, \dots, y_{r_T}\}$. The domain adaptation goal is then to learn a classifier $h_T : \mathcal{X} \to \mathcal{Y}$ with the help of the labeled sets D_{S_j} and the (mostly) unlabeled set D_T, to accurately predict the labels of data from the target domain T.

In [6] we addressed the domain adaptation problem by techniques which either selectively reuse source domain instances for target domains, or transform both target and source domains in one common space. Here we extend our previous results with a new class of methods based on stacked marginalized denoising autoencoders (sMDAs) [5,26], described in the following section.

2.1   Stacked Marginalized Denoising Autoencoders

A denoising autoencoder (DA) is one-layer neural network trained to reconstruct input data from partial random corruption [25]. The denoisers can be stacked into multi-layered architectures (sDAs) where the weights are fine-tuned with back-propagation. Alternatively, the outputs of intermediate layers can be used as input features to other learning algorithms. These learned feature representations are known to improve classification accuracy in many cases. For example, Glorot et. al.[13] applied sDAs to domain adaptation and demonstrated that these learned features, when used with a simple linear SVM classifier, yield record performance in benchmark sentiment analysis tasks.

The main downside of sDAs is a long training time, which often entails specialized computing supports such as GPUs, especially for large-scale tasks. To address this problem, a variation of sDA was proposed [5], in which the random corruption is marginalized out. This crucial step yields the optimal reconstruction weights computed in closed-form and eliminates the use of back-propagation for tuning. Features learned with this approach lead to classification accuracy comparable with sDAs [5, 26], with a remarkable reduction of the training time.

The basic building block is a one-layer linear denoising autoencoder. From a given set of inputs D, we sample inputs $\mathbf{x}_1, \ldots, \mathbf{x}_m$. These inputs are corrupted by random feature removal, when each feature is set to 0 with probability p; the corrupted version of $\mathbf{x}_i$ is denoted as $\tilde{\mathbf{x}}_i$. Then, the corrupted inputs are reconstructed with a linear mapping $\mathbf{W} : R^d \to R^d$, that minimizes the squared reconstruction loss

$$\mathcal{L}(\mathbf{W}) = \frac{1}{m} \sum_{i=1}^{m} ||\mathbf{x}_i - \mathbf{W}\tilde{\mathbf{x}}_i||^2. \tag{1}$$

The constant feature can be added to the input, $\mathbf{x}_i = [\mathbf{x}_i; 1]$, and an appropriate bias is incorporated within the mapping $\mathbf{W} = [\mathbf{W}; b]$. Note that the constant feature is never corrupted. Inputs design the matrix $\mathbf{X} = [\mathbf{x}_1, \ldots, \mathbf{x}_m]$ and its corrupted version is denoted by $\tilde{\mathbf{X}} = [\tilde{\mathbf{x}}_1, \ldots, \tilde{\mathbf{x}}_m]$. Then, the solution of (1) can be expressed as the closed-form solution for ordinary least squares

$$\mathbf{W} = \mathbf{P}\mathbf{Q}^{-1}, \quad \text{where} \quad \mathbf{Q} = \tilde{\mathbf{X}}\tilde{\mathbf{X}}^T \quad \text{and} \quad P = \mathbf{X}\tilde{\mathbf{X}}^T. \tag{2}$$

The solution to (2) depends on the sample inputs $\mathbf{x}_1, \ldots, \mathbf{x}_m$ and which features are randomly corrupted. Ideally, it is preferable to consider all possible corruptions of all possible inputs when the denoising transformation $\mathbf{W}$ is computed, i.e. letting $m \to \infty$. By the weak law of large numbers, the matrices $\mathbf{P}$ and $\mathbf{Q}$ converge to their expected values $\mathbb{E}[\mathbf{Q}], \mathbb{E}[\mathbf{P}]^{-1}$ as more copies of the corrupted data are created. In the limit, one can derive their expectations and express the corresponding mapping for $\mathbf{W}$ in closed form as $\mathbf{W} = \mathbb{E}[\mathbf{P}] \cdot \mathbb{E}[\mathbf{Q}]$, where

$$\mathbb{E}[\mathbf{Q}]_{ij} = \begin{bmatrix} \mathbf{S}_{ij}q_iq_j, & \text{if} & i \neq j, \\ \mathbf{S}_{ij}q_i, & \text{if} & i = j, \end{bmatrix} \quad \text{and} \quad \mathbb{E}[\mathbf{P}]_{ij} = \mathbf{S}_{ij}q_j, \tag{3}$$

with $q = [1 - p, \ldots, 1 - p, 1] \in R^{d+1}$ for the noise level p, and $\mathbf{S} = \mathbf{X}\mathbf{X}^T$ being the covariance matrix of the uncorrupted data $\mathbf{X}$. This closed-form denoising layer is denoted as *Marginalized Denoising Autoencoder* (MDA).

In the case of sDAs, the key component of their success consists in multiple stacked layers of denoising autoencoders, which create a *deep learning* architecture. Several MDA layers can also be stacked together by feeding the representations of the t-th denoising layer as the input to the $(t + 1)$-th layer. Each transformation $\mathbf{W}^t$ is learned to reconstruct the previous MDA output $\mathbf{h}_t$ from

its corrupted equivalent. In order to extend our mapping beyond a linear transformation, a non-linear function between layers is applied. Each layer's representation is obtained from its preceeding layer through a non-linear transformation
$\mathbf{h}_t = \tanh(\mathbf{W}^t \mathbf{h}_{t-1})$, with $\mathbf{h}_0 = \mathbf{x}$ denoting the input.

Beyond the stacking and noise level, the performance of sMDA may depend
on the data normalization and pre-processing. In Section 4, we test different
options and parameters of sMDA.

3   Datasets and Evaluation Framework

We tested sMDA on a large set of domain adaptation tasks, using three image
and one text datasets.

ICDA. We denote by ICDA the dataset that was used in the ImageClef 2014
Domain Adaptation challenge. It consists of a set of SIFT BOV[1] features provided for 12 common classes of five different image collections: Caltech-256 (C),
ImageNet (I), PascalVOC (I), Bing (B) and SUN (S). The first four collections
are treated as *source* domains; for each of them 600 image features and the corresponding labels were provided. The SUN dataset served as the *target* domain,
with 60 annotated and 600 non-annotated instances. The domain adaptation
task is to provide predictions for the non-annotated target data. Neither the
images nor their low-level features used to generate the BOV are available. The
Challenge run in two phases where the participants were provided with a similar configuration but different features. We distinguish them by denoting the
corresponding feature sets as ICDA1 or 3 (phase 1) and ICDA2 (phase 2). The
ICDA1 and ICDA3 share the same feature sets but different in the evaluation
setting; the former applies the cross validation on the full train and test set with
11 folds [8], while ICDA3 corresponds to results obtained with the provided
train-test split at phase 1.

OC10. Office+Caltech10 is a dataset frequently used for testing domain adaptation techniques [1,11,14,15]. In our experiments we use the SURF BOV[2] available from http://www-scf.usc.edu/~boqinggo/domain_adaptation/GFK_v1.zip.
The dataset consists of four domains: Amazon (A), Caltech (C), dslr (D) and
Webcam (W) , with 10 common classes. Each domain is considered in its turn
as a *target*, with the other domains considered as *sources*. First, we followed the
experimental setting of [11,14,15], to build the training set with 8 images from
each class (for D or W as source domains) or 20 images (for A or C) randomly
selected, to which 3 target instances per class were added in the case of semi-
supervised (SS) setting. All experiments were repeated 10 times and averaged.
We denote this case by OC10s referring to the small source set. The case when
all source data is used is denoting OC10a.

---

[1] Bag-of-visual (BOV) words [9] built using SIFT features [20] extracted on interest points.
[2] Bag-of-visual (BOV) words [9] built on SURF features [2] on interest points.

OFF31. Another popular dataset used to compare domain adaptation methods is the Office31 dataset [22] containing images of 31 product classes downloaded from amazon.com (Amazon) or taken in an office environment using a webcam or digital SLR camera (dslr), respectively. Note that the 3 corresponding domains in OffCal10 are subsets of this dataset. We consider the provided SURF BOV features available on http://www.cs.uml.edu/~saenko/projects.html#data, and the corresponding experimental framework, which is similar to the OC10 setting. We also consider the case where all available source data is used and denote it OFF31a, while the small set is denoted OFF31s.

AMT. The Amazon text dataset consists of products reviews in different domains. If a book review can be quite different from a kitchen item review, there are nevertheless some common features to assess whether the customers were satisfied with their purchase. Blitzer et al. [4] preprocessed a sub-part of this collection which has been used subsequently in several studies for domain adaptation. The task is to predict whether a customer review is positive or negative where a review with more than 3 stars is considered as positive and (strictly) less than 3 as negative. After preprocessing, documents are represented by a bag of unigrams and bigrams. For our experiments, we only considered the top 10,000 features according to document frequency and the four domains used in most studies: *kitchen* (K), *dvd* (D), *books* (B) and *electronics* (E). Furthermore, we varied the training set size as we considering first 'all' source data with roughly 5,000 document for each class, (denoted with AMTa), then considering a 'medium' size experiment (denoted by AMTm) with 2000 source documents for training and 2000 targets document for tests (this is the classical setting on most other domain adaptation studies). Finally, we also built random 'small' collections (denoted by AMTs) where 200 documents were selected randomly from each source (100 per class) and from the target as labeled set in the semi-supervised setting, and tested on the remained unlabeled target documents. This latter selection process was repeated 10 times and the results were averaged over the 10 runs.

4 Evaluation Results

We run two series of evaluations. In the first one, we test different aspects of the sMDA method, in particular, the number of stacking layers, the amount of noise, the data normalization and data pre-processing. In the second one, we compare these methods with the state-of-the art methods, both in unsupervised and semi-supervised settings.

Varying the Noise Level. First, we study the sensitivity of the sMDA methods to the noise by varying the probability p between 0.1 to 0.9, with all other parameters being fixed. In the experiments with the ICDA image dataset we used the linear SVM with 5 stacking layers on z-score normalized features concatenated to the original features (as in [5]). In the case of the AMT text set we used only a single layer on L2 normalized TFIDF+L2 features.

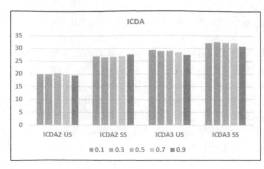 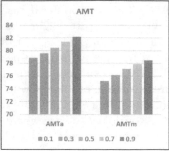

Fig. 1. ICDA2 and ICDA3 (left) and AMT (right) average accuracy for different noise levels.

Figure 1.left) shows the results for ICDA sets averaged over 15 configurations: (C)→S, (I)→S, ..., (C,I,P,B)→S, both in unsupervised (US) and semi-supervised (SS) modes. It is easy to see that for the image data, the sMDA methods seem to be fairly robust to the noise level, the globally most convenient value is close to 0.5. On contrary, Figure 1.right) shows results on AMT set where increasing the noise level increases the accuracy. In the followings, we systematically use $p=0.5$ for the image sets, and $p=0.9$ for the text set.

Feature Normalization for Images. Like in any deep learning architecture, we pay a particular attention to the data preprocessing when using sMDAs, as these methods appear to be highly sensitive to the spread and variance of feature values. We mainly focus on the features themselves, therefore instead of combining the results with SVM, in this section we use them with domain specific class mean classifier[3] (DSCM)[6,8], because the DSCM does not require any meta parameter tuning and is extremely fast. Furthermore, we consider only a single stacking layer, and we concatenate the MDA output (denoted by L1) with the original (NO) or previously normalized features; we then train the DSCM in this concatenated space.

We experimented with two feature normalizations on the image datasets. The first denoted as **P05** is the power normalization ($x_{ij} = x_{ij}^{0.5}$), previously used in [6,8]. The second is the z-score function $\mathcal{Z}(\mathbf{X})$. For the input data $\mathbf{X} = [\mathbf{x}_1, \ldots, \mathbf{x}_n]$, we set $x_{ij} = (x_{ij} - \mathbb{E}(\mathbf{X}_j))/std(\mathbf{X}_j)$, where $\mathbb{E}(\mathbf{X}_j)$ and $std(\mathbf{X}_j)$ are the mean and standard deviation of feature j. It can be applied in three following ways:

- **ZA**: *jointly* on all sources S_j and the target data, $\mathcal{Z}([S_1, \ldots, S_N, T])$;
- **ZS**: *independently* on each source and target data, $\mathcal{Z}(S_1), \ldots, \mathcal{Z}(S_N), \mathcal{Z}(T)$;

---

[3] The domain specific class mean classifier assign a test data to a class based on a weighted softmax distance to domain-specific class means: $p(c|\mathbf{x}_i) = \frac{1}{Z_i} \sum_{d=1}^{D} w_d \exp\left(-\frac{1}{2}\|\mathbf{x}_i - \boldsymbol{\mu}_d^c\|_2\right)$, where μ_d^c is the average of the class c in domain d, w_d re domain specific weights and Z_i is a normalizer. We used $w_s = 1$ for all sources and in the semi-supervised setting $w_t = 2$ for the target.

Table 1. Different normalization and pre-processing strategies for image datasets. Strategy-best cases are underlined, overall best ones are shown in red.

Dataset	S_i	Semi supervised					Unsupervised				
		NO	P05	ZA	ZS	ZSZT	NO	P05	ZA	ZS	ZSZT
ICDA2	S_0	19.82	24.83	25.91	25.74	25.69	11.83	13.4	13.81	15.67	15.69
	S_1	17.92	25.08	25.27	24.51	24.46	13.33	13.44	13.74	15.5	15.58
	S_2	14.84	17.58	25.89	25.51	25.29	10.51	10.82	13.74	15.41	15.6
	S_3	17.92	25.08	25.94	25.91	25.77	13.33	13.44	13.69	15.57	15.63
ICDA3	S_0	22.49	32.16	35.2	33.99	32.98	18.09	23.83	24.96	26.79	26.7
	S_1	21.73	32.21	35.01	34.27	34.27	17.3	23.72	25.36	26.84	26.84
	S_2	22.96	26.63	34.68	34.84	33.81	18.83	20.96	24.74	26.29	26.16
	S_3	21.73	32.21	34.82	33.96	34	17.3	23.72	24.78	26.71	26.53
OC10s	S_0	52.05	56.42	55.35	56.15	56.15	43.63	45.94	48.52	49.84	49.4
	S_1	54.97	57.16	56.71	57.27	57.3	46.15	46.82	49.59	49.92	50.07
	S_2	54.48	55.12	56.26	56.74	56.76	45.88	46.43	49.17	49.91	49.81
	S_3	54.97	57.16	56.76	57.09	57.11	46.15	46.82	49.73	49.93	50.11
OFF31s	S_0	33.33	43.03	42.64	45.33	44.77	15.06	20.71	20.74	25.75	23.76
	S_1	34.47	41.11	43.48	45.52	45.03	14.78	20.24	21.55	26.44	24.66
	S_2	34.14	30.94	44.95	47.08	46.75	14.85	16.22	21.54	26.7	25.1
	S_3	34.47	41.11	43.48	45.88	45.42	14.78	20.24	21.04	26.19	24.33

- **ZSZT**: *separately* on the source combination and the target data, $\mathcal{Z}([S_1, \ldots, S_N])$, $\mathcal{Z}(T)$.

In addition we compare the normalization effects to the *no normalization* (**NO**) case.

The feature normalization can be further coupled with the following pre-processing options, applied after normalization but before using the sMDA:

- S_0, *baseline*: features are used directly to learn a classifier, without any MDA layer;
- S_1: features are used as such by the MDA;
- S_2: features are binarized; this can help MDA to capture the feature co-occurrences;
- S_3: all negative feature values are set to zero.

Note that these pre-processing options are applied on the input of the MDA, but not on the original (normalized) features that are concatenated with the MDA output.

We test all image normalization and pre-processing combinations on all image datasets, both in unsupervised and semi-supervised modes. In Table 1) we report average results over all possible DA tasks (target and source combinations). For example, for Office 31, the USL scores are averaged over 9 possible tasks: D→A, W→A, (D,W)→A, A→D, W→D, (A,W)→D, A→W, D→W and (A,D)→W.

We analyze Table 1 and draw the following conclusions:

- Feature normalization is an important factor for the MDA+DSCM classification. With no normalization (S_i,NO) the results are always low. Z-score normalization performs better than with P05. Among normalization strategies,

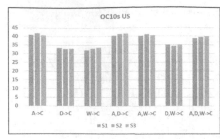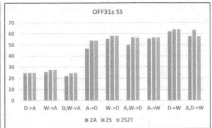

Fig. 2. Further examples comparing different feature correlation strategies results.

independent source normalization (**ZS**) is either the best or close to the best. Note that **ZS** and **ZSZT** differ when we have more than one sources.

- Combining normalized features with the output of the MDA (O+L1) does not seem to always help in the case of ICDA dataset, but we have a consistent gain in the case of OC10 and OFF31. The tree feature preprocessing strategies seem to give relatively similar results except for OC10s, where binarizing the z-scored feature vectors performs better.
- Amongst the three preprocessing strategies we do not have a clear winner, but strategy S_2 seems to be a good compromise in most cases.

When we analyze the results for every individual domain adaptation task for each dataset (see also Figure 2) and tracked the correlation between the best normalization and pre-processing strategies again we find the strategy S_2 with **ZS** normalization as a good choice in most cases.

Feature Normalization for Text. Feature normalization for text is more known as term weighting. It often differs from the normalization of image features, due to a higher sparsity of textual representation. Here we experiment with the AMTa (all) and AMTm (small) cases using the following six strategies:

- raw term frequency, without normalization (**TF**) and with L2 normalization (**TF+L2**),
- term frequency binarization (**BIN**),
- TF-IDF with L2 normalization (**TFIDF+L2**),
- Q-Learning term weighting function [7] without (**QLN**) and with L2 normalization (**QLN+L2**).

Previous experiments showed that a stronger noise level is needed for the text reconstruction, so we set the noise level p to 0.9. We use linear SVM and a single layer MDA without feature concatenation (L1). We only test the unsupervised domain adaptation case, where the SVM classifiers are cross-validated on the source data, and then evaluated on the target documents. Table 2 shows the results averaged over all domain adaptation tasks. While the gain and the accuracy varies a lot from one configuration to another, MDA always helps, independently of the initial normalization.

Different Number of Stacking Layers. In the previous experiments, we used DSCM for the sake of simplicity and speed. However, DSCM did not benefit from

Table 2. Different term weighting strategies for text.

Dataset	S_i	TF	TF +L2	BIN	TFIDF +L2	QLN	QLN+L2
AMTa	S_0	79.75	79.62	80	80.4	81.24	80.72
	S_1	84.34	84	84.04	83.88	84.16	83.97
AMTm	S_0	76.38	75.72	76.26	77.02	78	77.69
	S_1	79.98	79.13	79.87	79.3	79.69	79.76

using multiple layers. For DSCM, neither increasing the number of dimensions nor using feature redundancy is necessarily helpful. This is why, in this section, we turned to SVM classifiers as they can cope with both.

To analyze the stacking effect, when two or more layers are used we use the linear multi-class SVM from the LIBSVM package[4] with the fixed cost $c = 0.1$ in all experiments. In Table 3 we report only results for the normalization and preprocessing strategy (**ZS**,S_2) as one performing well with DSCM; for other strategies we observe a similar behavior.

We tested configurations including 1 to 5 layers and the feature concatenation options including:
- (**Li**) uses the last layer as features in the SVM,
- (**O+Li**) concatenates the original features with last layer output (O+Li),
- (**O+L1→Li**) concatenates the original features with all the layers up to Li.

As in the case of DSCM, Table 3 shows results averaged over all different domain adaptation tasks and configurations. From the results we can conclude that in general (except for ICDA2 US) best results are obtained when we concatenate the output of all the layers (**O+L1→Li**). However it is rare that we need to stack more than 3 layers to get significantly better results. In Figure 3 we show some configuration results for **O+L1→Li**. While the best stacking option varies from configuration to configuration, considering 3 layers seems a good compromise in general.

On the AMT text set, we limited the stacking to 3 layers due to the high feature dimensionality. In these experiments, we tested both the semi-supervised and the unsupervised settings for the small collection (200 document per domain) with the (TFIDF+L2) normalization and a noise level of 0.9. In the case of semi supervised settings, we added randomly 100 documents per class (satisfied and unsatisfied) from the target. We show the average results over all possible target sets and all possible source configurations in Table 4 where we varied the number of stacking layers. From the table we can see that adding extra stacks helps but the gain is relatively small except for the unsupervised case where using a more than a single stacking layers really helps.

4.1   Comparing sMDAs to Other Domain Adaptation Approaches

In this section we compare our domain adaptation results to the ones published recently in [10,12] using the same experimental settings (see Section 3).

---
[4] http://ww.csie.ntu.edu.tw/cjlin/libsvm/

Table 3. Different normalization and pre-processing strategies for image datasets.

Dataset	Layer	Semi supervised					Unsupervised				
		L1	**L2**	**L3**	**L4**	**L5**	**L1**	**L2**	**L3**	**L4**	**L5**
ICDA2	Li	25.83	24.70	22.88	21.89	22.24	20.46	19.39	18.78	16.31	17.08
	O+Li	26.14	25.73	25.00	25.15	25.45	18.36	18.10	17.99	18.37	18.65
	O+L1→Li	26.14	25.96	25.86	25.86	25.96	18.36	18.50	18.39	18.39	18.84
ICDA3	Li	30.25	28.76	27.00	25.79	22.95	26.96	25.47	24.27	22.82	20.60
	O+Li	31.09	31.20	30.84	30.70	30.30	28.10	28.11	27.99	27.80	27.59
	O+L1→Li	31.09	31.75	31.75	31.78	31.45	28.10	28.36	28.53	28.33	28.02
OC10s	Li	54.58	55.11	55.42	53.88	51.92	52.13	52.60	52.23	49.59	47.52
	O+Li	52.97	53.41	53.72	53.75	53.44	50.73	51.44	51.94	51.71	51.26
	O+L1→Li	52.97	54.27	54.82	55.32	55.51	50.73	51.99	52.69	52.99	53.03
OFF31s	Li	43.78	43.3	42.29	40.75	39.31	22.89	22.15	18.31	15.23	13.20
	O+Li	42.61	43.82	43.86	43.86	43.16	26.97	26.91	26.46	26.07	25.50
	O+L1→Li	42.61	44.52	45.32	45.17	45.23	26.97	27.31	26.73	25.91	25.31

Table 4. Different number of stacking layers for the text dataset.

Dataset	Layer	Semi supervised			Unsupervised		
		L1	**L2**	**L3**	**L1**	**L2**	**L3**
AMTs	Li	79.97	80.08	80.63	74.89	76.23	76.93
	O+Li	80.14	80.16	80.64	74.98	76.3	76.94
	O+L1→Li	80.14	80.55	80.81	74.98	76.54	77

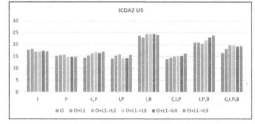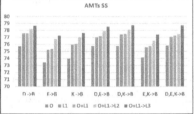

Fig. 3. Different stacking evaluations for ICDA2 and AMTs cases.

In the case of ICDA datasets, Table 5 compares our results to the Self-adaptive Metric Learning for Domain Adaptation (SaMLDa) as it also exploits the unlabeled target instances to iteratively adjust the metric learned for the DSCM [8]. From these results, we can see that using DSCM with independent (**ZS**) feature normalization performs the best on both ICDA datasets. This is an interesting finding, as the DSCM method is very fast and requires no parameter tuning. In addition, as Table 1 shows this method performs extremely well also in the case of the unsupervised learning.

Table 5. Classification accuracy on ICDA1.

	SVM P05	SVM ZS	SVM+sMDA + ZS,S2,(O+L1→L3)	DSCM P05	DSCM ZS	DSCM+MDA ZS,S_2(O+L1)	SaMLDa [8] P05
ICDA1 SS	30.31	35	32	31.37	**35.21**	34.97	33.67
ICDA2 SS	25.92	24.61	25.65	26.13	**27.37**	26.95	27

Table 6. Results on OC10. We show our best results in underlined and the overall best results in red.

	SVM P05	SVM ZS	SVM+sMDA + ZS,S2,(O+L1→L3)	DSCM P05	DSCM ZS	DSCM+MDA ZS,S2(O+L1)	[11] SA
OC10a (US)	42.69	41.54	44.22	43.13	45.49	45.84	**45.9**
OC10a (SS)	53.83	51.03	53.68	55.83	53.7	54.37	53.67
OC10s US	44.8	45.66	47.99	41.2	43.07	43.56	51.4
OC10s SS	51.7	49.65	52.62	54.72	54.13	54.81	-
A→W (US)	14.8	16.87	17.86	17.95	22.36	20.8	15.3
A→W (SS)	47.59	40.91	44.07	54.13	53.99	56.55	45
D→W (US)	49.97	48.18	55.13	42.88	42.59	48.29	50.1
D→W (SS)	68.73	63.7	67.22	56.98	58.97	63.96	63.8
W→D (US)	39.65	45.83	47.19	37.53	48.89	51.85	56.9
W→D (SS)	58.42	64.44	66.05	52.12	56.79	58.02	69.9

Table 6 compares our results to the results of [11,12], for the OC10a and OC10s cases[5], and the 3 available source target configuration available in the literature from OFF31 datasets always using the same experimental protocol (described in Section 3). From the table we can conclude the following. Again DSCM with z-normalization and even without sMDA performs extremely well in the case of semi-supervised setting in spite of its simplicity, but SVM performs better when we do not have any labeled target sample. sMDA in general helps to increase the accuracy in average with 2-3% both in the case of DSCM and SVM.

5 Conclusion

In this paper we address the problem of domain adaptation using multiple source domains. In particular we intensively evaluated the deep learning technique of the *stacked marginalized denoising autoencoders* (sMDA). A detailed analysis of evaluations of sMDA parameters and comparison to other state of art methods allow us to make the following conclusions:

– sMDA gives a consistent classification improvement in different domain adaptation scenarios;

---

[5] We average the results for only the 12 "one source versus one target" for OC10 and only 9 "one source versus one target" cases, as in [11,12].

- It is complementary to any other components, like learning from multiple sources, available target labels instances, image or text classification, etc.
- Due to the noise marginalization in the closed form, sMDA is a fast and low-cost alternative to the energy-expensive deep learning solutions [13];
- Optimal values of two main parameters, the stacking size and the noise level, can be detected by cross validation, but the default setting $p = 0.5$ and $m = 3$ works well in most cases;
- Data normalization plays an important role; independent or joint domain data normalization are top preferences;
- Due to unsupervised feature extraction, sMDA yields a larger gain over the baselines in unsupervised learning, when no target label information is available.

References

1. Baktashmotlagh, M., Harandi, M.T., Lovell, B.C., Salzmann, M.: Unsupervised domain adaptation by domain invariant projection. In: ICCV (2013)
2. Bay, H., Tuytelaars, T., Van Gool, L.: SURF: speeded up robust features. In: Leonardis, A., Bischof, H., Pinz, A. (eds.) ECCV 2006, Part I. LNCS, vol. 3951, pp. 404–417. Springer, Heidelberg (2006)
3. Beijbom, O.: Domain adaptations for computer vision applications (2012). arXiv (1211.4860)
4. Blitzer, J., Foster, D., Kakade, S.: Domain adaptation with coupled subspaces. In: ICAIS (2011)
5. Chen, M., Xu, Z., Weinberger, K.Q., Sha, F.: Marginalized denoising autoencoders for domain adaptation (2012). arXiv (1206.4683)
6. Chidlovskii, B., Csurka, G., Gangwar, S.: Assembling heterogeneous domain adaptation methods for image classification. In: Working Notes for CLEF 2014 (2014)
7. Clinchant, S.: Concavity in IR models. In: CIKM (2012)
8. Csurka, G., Chidlovskii, B., Perronnin, F.: Domain adaptation with a domain specific class means classifier. In: Agapito, L., Bronstein, M.M., Rother, C. (eds.) ECCV 2014 Workshops. LNCS, vol. 8927, pp. 32–46. Springer, Heidelberg (2015)
9. Csurka, G., Dance, C., Fan, L., Willamowski, J., Bray, C.: Visual categorization with bags of keypoints. In: SLCV, ECCV Workshop (2004)
10. Donahue, J., Jia, Y., Vinyals, O., Hoffman, J., Zhang, N., Tzeng, E., Darrell, T.: Decaf: A deep convolutional activation feature for generic visual recognition. In: ICML (1999)
11. Fernando, B., Habrard, A., Sebban, M., Tuytelaars, T.: Unsupervised visual domain adaptation using subspace alignment. In: ICCV (2013)
12. Fernando, B., Habrard, A., Sebban, M., Tuytelaars, T.: Subspace alignment for domain adaptation (2014). arXiv (1409.5241)
13. Glorot, X., Bordes, A., Bengio, Y.: Domain adaptation for large-scale sentiment classification: a deep learning approach. In: ICML (2011)
14. Gong, B., Grauman, K., Sha, F.: Reshaping visual datasets for domain adaptation. In: NIPS (2013)
15. Gopalan, R., Li, R., Chellappa, R.: Domain adaptation for object recognition: an unsupervised approach. In: ICCV (2011)

16. Hoffman, J., Kulis, B., Darrell, T., Saenko, K.: Discovering latent domains for multisource domain adaptation. In: Fitzgibbon, A., Lazebnik, S., Perona, P., Sato, Y., Schmid, C. (eds.) ECCV 2012, Part II. LNCS, vol. 7573, pp. 702–715. Springer, Heidelberg (2012)
17. Jhuo, I.-H., Liu, D., Lee, D.T., Chang, S.-F.: Robust visual domain adaptation with low-rank reconstruction. In: CVPR, pp. 2168–2175 (2012)
18. Jiang, J.: A literature survey on domain adaptation of statistical classifiers (2008). https://scholar.google.com.sg/citations?user=hVTK2YwAAAAJ
19. Kulis, B., Saenko, K., Darrell, T.: What you saw is not what you get: domain adaptation using asymmetric kernel transforms. In: CVPR (2011)
20. Lowe, D.G.: Object recognition from local scale-invariant features. In: ICCV (1999)
21. Patel, V.M., Gopalan, R., Li, R., Chellappa, R.: Visual domain adaptation: An overview of recent advances. IEEE Transactions on Geoscience and Remote Sensing **52**(2) (2007)
22. Saenko, K., Kulis, B., Fritz, M., Darrell, T.: Adapting visual category models to new domains. In: Daniilidis, K., Maragos, P., Paragios, N. (eds.) ECCV 2010, Part IV. LNCS, vol. 6314, pp. 213–226. Springer, Heidelberg (2010)
23. Tommasi, T., Caputo, B.: Frustratingly easy NBNN domain adaptation. In: ICCV (2013)
24. Torralba, A., Efros, A.: Unbiased look at dataset bias. In: CVPR (2011)
25. Vincent, P., Larochelle, H., Bengio, Y., Manzagol, P.-A.: Extracting and composing robust features with denoising autoencoders. In: ICML (2008)
26. Xu, Z., Chen, M., Weinberger, K.Q., Sha, F.: From sBoW to dCoT marginalized encoders for text representation. In: CIKM (2012)

Language Variety Identification Using Distributed Representations of Words and Documents

Marc Franco-Salvador[1]([✉]), Francisco Rangel[1,2], Paolo Rosso[1], Mariona Taulé[3], and M. Antònia Martít[3]

[1] Universitat Politècnica de València, Valencia, Spain
mfranco@prhlt.upv.es, prosso@dsic.upv.es
[2] Autoritas Consulting S.A., Madrid, Spain
francisco.rangel@autoritas.es
[3] Universitat de Barcelona, Barcelona, Spain
{mtaule,amarti}@ub.edu

Abstract. Language variety identification is an author profiling sub-task which aims to detect lexical and semantic variations in order to classify different varieties of the same language. In this work we focus on the use of distributed representations of words and documents using the continuous Skip-gram model. We compare this model with three recent approaches: Information Gain Word-Patterns, TF-IDF graphs and Emotion-labeled Graphs, in addition to several baselines. We evaluate the models introducing the Hispablogs dataset, a new collection of Spanish blogs from five different countries: Argentina, Chile, Mexico, Peru and Spain. Experimental results show state-of-the-art performance in language variety identification. In addition, our empirical analysis provides interesting insights on the use of the evaluated approaches.

Keywords: Author profiling · Language variety identification · Distributed representations · Information Gain Word-Patterns · TF-IDF graphs · Emotion-labeled Graphs

1   Introduction

Author profiling aims to identify the linguistic profile of an author on the basis of his writing style. It is used to determine an author's gender, age, personality type and native language, among other traits. In this work we focus on language variety identification. Native language identification aims at identifying

This research has been carried out within the framework of the European Commission WIQ-EI IRSES (no. 269180) and DIANA - Finding Hidden Knowledge in Texts (TIN2012-38603-C02) projects. The work of the second author was partially funded by Autoritas Consulting SA and by Spanish the Ministry of Economics by means of a ECOPORTUNITY IPT-2012-1220-430000 grant. We would like to thank Tomas Mikolov for his support and comments about distributed representations.

© Springer International Publishing Switzerland 2015
J. Mothe et al. (Eds.): CLEF 2015, LNCS 9283, pp. 28–40, 2015.
DOI: 10.1007/978-3-319-24027-5_3

the native language of an author on the basis of a text he has written in another language. In contrast, the aim of language variety identification sub-task is to label the texts with its corresponding variant. For example, with a text written in Spanish, the Argentinean, Chilean, Mexican, Peruvian or European Spanish variant. This task has special relevance in text mining in social media. Given that there are millions of user blogs and posts in any given language, it is important to identify the concrete variety of the language in order to attribute and exploit correctly the information they contain, e.g. opinions about political elections in Mexico do not have the same relevance in Spain, which is at 9,000 kilometers away.

In this work, we are interested in comparing the performance of three recent approaches that we previously applied to other author profiling tasks: Information Gain Word-Patterns, TF-IDF Graphs and Emotion-labeled Graphs. Furthermore, due to the increasing popularity of distributed representations [5], we use the continuous Skip-gram model to generate distributed representations of words, i.e., n-dimensional vectors, applying further refinements in order to be able to use them on documents. In addition, we use the Sentence Vector variation to directly generate representations of documents. We also compare the aforementioned approaches with several baselines: bag-of-words, character 4-grams and TF-IDF 2-grams. In order to evaluate these models, we are presenting the Hispablogs dataset, a new collection of Spanish blogs from five different countries: Argentina, Chile, Mexico, Peru and Spain.

The rest of the paper is structured as follows. Section 2 studies related work in the field of language variety identification. In Section 3 we overview the continuous Skip-gram model, its Sentence Vectors variation, and explain how we generated distributed vectors of documents. Section 4 details the three compared approaches. Finally, in Section 5 we introduce the Hispablogs dataset and evaluate the different approaches to the task of language variety identification.

2   Related Work

Author profiling is a field of growing interest for the research community. In the last years several tasks have been hold on different demographic aspects: i) native language identification at the BEA-8 workshop at NAACL-HT 2013[1]; ii) personality recognition at ICWSM 2013[2] and at ACMMM 2014[3]; and iii) age and gender identification (both in English and Spanish) at PAN 2013[4] and PAN 2014[5] tracks at the CLEF initiative. In PAN 2015[6] the task is concerned with

---

[1] https://sites.google.com/site/nlisharedtask2013/

[2] http://mypersonality.org/wiki/doku.php?id=wcpr13

[3] https://sites.google.com/site/wcprst/home/wcpr14

[4] http://www.uni-weimar.de/medien/webis/research/events/pan-13/pan13-web/author-profiling.html

[5] http://www.uni-weimar.de/medien/webis/research/events/pan-14/pan14-web/author-profiling.html

[6] http://www.uni-weimar.de/medien/webis/events/pan-15/pan15-web/author-profiling.html

predicting the author's age, gender, and personality. Interest in author profiling was also expressed by industry representatives in the Kaggle platform[7], where companies and research centers share their needs and independent researchers can join the challenge of solving them. A small number of tasks related to author profiling have been organised: i) psychopathy prediction based on Twitter usage[8]; ii) personality prediction based on Twitter stream[9]; iii) and gender prediction from handwriting[10].

With respect to previous works on author profiling, in [17] the author divides writing style features in two types: content and style-based features. In [19,20] participants in the PAN shared task at CLEF approached the task of age and gender identification using combinations of style-based features such as frequency of punctuation marks, capital letters, quotations, etc., together with part-of-speech (PoS) tags and content-based features such as bag-of-words, the TF-IDF of words, dictionary-based words, topic-based words, entropy-based words, and content-based features obtained with Latent Semantic Analysis [3]. Affectivity is explored in [15], showing the relationship between gender and the expression of emotions.

Despite the growing interest in author profiling problems, little attention has been given to language variety identification. In [24] the authors investigated varieties of Portuguese. They collected 1,000 news articles and applied different features such as word and character n-grams to them. Similarly, in [21] the authors differentiate between six different varieties of Arabic in blogs and forums using character n-gram features. Concerning Spanish language varieties, in [9] the authors collected a dataset from Twitter, focusing on varieties from Argentina, Chile, Colombia, Mexico and Spain. They applied four types of features: character n-gram frequency profiles, character n-gram language models, LZW compression and syllable-based language models, all combined with a meta-classifier and evaluated with cross-validation.

In this work we focus on Spanish language variety identification with some differences with regard to the previous works: i) we focus on larger social media texts because we are interested in investigating more complex features which may also model discourse structure; ii) we evaluate the proposed methods both with cross-validation and with an independent test set generated from different authors in order to reduce possible overfitting; iii) the Twitter dataset compiled in the previous work is not publicly available; in contrast, in line with the CLEF initiative we are making our datset available to the research community.

3 Continuous Skip-Gram Model

The use of log-linear models has been proposed [11] as an efficient way to generate distributed representations of words, since they reduce the complexity of the

---

[7] http://www.kaggle.com/

[8] http://www.kaggle.com/c/twitter-psychopathy-prediction

[9] http://www.kaggle.com/c/twitter-personality-prediction

[10] http://www.kaggle.com/c/icdar2013-gender-prediction-from-handwriting

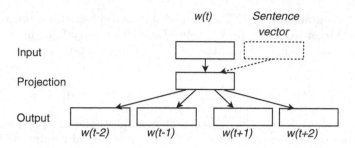

Fig. 1. Skip-gram model architecture. The objective is to predict words within a certain range before and after the current word. Dashed part is used only in place of $w(t)$ when learning sentence vectors.

hidden layer thereby improving efficiency. The continuous Bag-of-Words model attempts to maximize the classification of a word by using the surrounding words without taking into account the order of the sequence. In contrast, the continuous Skip-gram model uses word ordering to sample distant word that appear less frequently during training time. Compared to traditional approaches such as the Feedforward Neural Net Language model [2] and the Recurrent Neural Net Language model [12], these approaches obtained better performance with a considerably lower training time in semantic and syntactic word relationship tasks. Experimental results also demonstrated that the Skip-gram model offers better performance on average, excelling especially at the semantic level. Therefore, in this work we selected that approach to generate our distributed representations.

The continuous Skip-gram model [11,13] is an iterative algorithm which attempts to maximize the classification of the context surrounding a word (see Figure 1). Formally, given a word $w(t)$, and its surrounding words $w(t-c)$, $w(t-c+1)$, ..., $w(t+c)$ inside a window of size $2c+1$, the training objective is to maximize the average of the log probability:

$$\frac{1}{T} \sum_{t=1}^{T} \sum_{-c \leq j \leq c, j \neq 0} \log p(w_{t+j}|w_t) \tag{1}$$

$$p(w_O|w_I) = \frac{\exp(v'_{w_O}{}^T v_{w_I})}{\sum_{w=1}^{W} \exp(v'_w{}^T v_{w_I})} \tag{2}$$

Although $p(w_{t+j}|w_t)$ can be estimated using the softmax function (Eq. 2) [1], its normalization depends on vocabulary size W which makes its usage impractical for high values of W. For this reason, more computationally efficient alternatives are used instead. Hierarchical softmax has been proposed [16] to approximate the results of the softmax function. This function is based on a binary tree with all $w \in W$ as leaves, each node being the relative probabilities of its child nodes. The algorithm makes it necessary only to process $\log_2(W)$ words for each probability estimation. An alternative introduced in [13] is negative sampling. This function is a simplified version of the Noise Contrastive Estimation (NCE) [4,14], which is only concerned with preserving vector quality in the context of Skip-gram learning. The basic idea is to use logistic regression to distinguish the target word W_O from a noise distribution $P_n(w)$, having k negative samples for each word. Formally, the negative sampling estimates $p(w_O|w_I)$ as follows:

$$\log \sigma(v'_{w_O}{}^T v_{w_I}) + \sum_{i=1}^{k} \mathbb{E}_{w_i} \sim P_n(w) \left[\log \sigma(-v'_{w_i}{}^T v_{w_I}) \right] \tag{3}$$

where $\sigma(x) = 1/(1 + \exp(-x))$. Note that computational complexity is linear with the number of negative samples k. The experimental results in [13] show that this function obtains better results at the semantic level than hierarchical softmax and NCE. Therefore, in this work we will use negative sampling in all our experiments.

3.1   Learning Sentence Vectors

The continuous Skip-gram model can be easily adapted to generate representative vectors of sentences (or documents). Sentence vectors (SenVec) [7] follows Skip-gram architecture to train a special vector sv representing the sentence. Basically, before each context window movement, SenVec uses sv in place of $w(t)$ with the objective of maximizing the classification of the surrounding words (see Figure 1).

3.2   Classification Using Distributed Representations

Although SenVec is directly applicable as input to a classifier, we need to combine the word vectors generated with the Skip-gram model to use them when classifying documents. The use of Convolutional Neural Networks with Skip-gram word vectors as input has been proposed [6] with excellent results for sentence classification tasks. However, due to the computational complexity of these networks, we will explore that option in the future and we now employ a simpler solution. Having a list of word vectors[11] $(w_1, w_2, ..., w_n)$ belonging to a document, we generate a vector representation v of its content by estimating the average of their dimensions: $v = n^{-1} \sum_{i=1}^{n} w_i$. This combination is directly named Skip-gram in the evaluation.

4   Alternative Methods for Language Variety Identification

We are interested in comparing the performance of distributed representation against three alternative representations successfully used in other author profiling tasks: TF-IDF graphs[12], Information Gain Word-Patterns and Emotion-labeled Graphs. We describe the latter two below. We also compare them

---

[11] We allow the use of word repetitions.

[12] We represent each word as a node and each edge defines a sequence between words.

against different baselines in author profiling such as Bag-of-Words (BOW), Char. 4-grams and TF-IDF 2-grams[13].

4.1   Information Gain Word-Patterns

Information Gain Word-Patterns (IG-WP) [10] is a bottom-up method for obtaining lexico-syntactic patterns aiming to represent the content of documents. This method is based on the pattern-construction hypothesis, which states that those contexts that are relevant to the definition of a cluster of semantically related words tend to be (part of) lexico-syntactic constructions[14]. This method consists of a pipe-line of the following processes. First, the source corpus is morphologically annotated with lemma and PoS tagging using Freeling library[15], and syntactically annotated with dependencies using Treeler[16]. Secondly, a Vector Space Model (VSM) [22] matrix is built, in which contexts are modeled as dependency relations between two lemmas. For each lemma in the rows (source lemma) of the matrix, a context is defined by a tuple of three elements: the direction of the dependency, the dependency label and the target lemma:

$$matrix\_context = (dep\text{-}dir,\ dep\text{-}lab,\ lemma\text{-}context),$$

followed by the examples of matrix-context:

$$context_1 = (<,\ subj,\ \textbf{robar}\ (to\ steal)),$$
$$context_2 = (<,\ dobj,\ \textbf{peinar}\ (to\ comb)),$$

where, 'subj' and 'dobj' stand for subject and direct object respectively, $<$ indicates the dependency direction, that is, that the lemma in the context is the parent node of the source lemma (in these cases, 'robar' ('to steal') and 'peinar' ('to comb')).

Then, we used the CLUTO toolkit[17] to obtain the clusters of semantically related words that share the same contexts. Next, the relationships between clusters are established using the most descriptive and discriminative contexts of each cluster. Each context consists of a dependency direction, a dependency label, a lemma and a score:

$$cluster\_context = (dep\text{-}dir,\ dep\text{-}lab,\ lemma\text{-}context,\ score)$$

---

[13] We tested the value of n iterating for each representation from 1 to 10. The best results were achieved with n equal to 1, 4 and 2 respectively. In all of them the 10,000 most frequent grams were selected.

[14] A construction is a recurrent pattern in language.

[15] http://nlp.lsi.upc.edu/freeling/

[16] Treeler is an open-source C++ library of structure prediction methods focussing on tagging and parsing. To get Treeler: http://devel.cpl.upc.edu/treeler/svn/trunk

[17] http://glaros.dtc.umn.edu/gkhome/cluto/cluto/overview

Table 1. Cluster 25 with theirs corresponding lemmas

Cluster: 25	
Lemmas	barba, bigote, cabellera, cabello, cana, ceja, hebra, mecha, mechón, melena, pelo, peluca, pestaña, rizo, trenza (*beard, moustache, head of hair, hair, grey hair, eyebrow, thread, wick, lock of hair, fur, wig, eyelash, curl, braid*)

Table 2. Cluster 643 related to cluster 25

Related_cluster	Context_set	Lemmas
643	<:* (2.2) <:subj (2.2) <:cd (1.3)	afeitar, ahuecar, alisar, cepillar, encrespar, enmarañar, erizar, mesar, ondear, peinar, rapar, rizar, sombrear, trenzar, tupir (*to shave, to hollow out, to straighten, to brush, to frizz, to tangle, to make stand on end, to pull on, to wave, to comb, to crop, to curl, to tint, to braid, to thicken*)

We obtain as a result a graph of related clusters, exemplified in Table 1 and 2, where cluster 25 is related to cluster 643 by means of the subject and direct object relationships. Table 1 describes the lemmas in cluster 25 (translated lemmas in English appear in italics). Table 2 shows one of the related clusters (i.e., 643) (first column) as a result of the linking cluster process for cluster 25. The second column shows the context_set that relates cluster 25 to cluster 643, and the third column describes the lemmas in the related cluster.

All members (nouns) in cluster 25 are good candidates to be subjects and direct objects of all members (verbs) of cluster 643.

Finally, a set of lexico-syntactic patterns are derived after applying different filters to avoid spurious relationships. The lexico-syntactic patterns are tuples involving two lemmas, related by both a dependency direction and a dependency label:

$$pattern = (lemma_u, \text{ } dep\text{-}dir, \text{ } dep\text{-}lab, \text{ } lemma_v)$$

Considering the examples of cluster 25 and 643, we generated all possible combinations of every lemma from cluster 25 with every lemma in cluster 643. Examples of lexico-syntactic patterns derived from the related clusters 25 and 643 are:

$$(\textbf{bigote}_{c25} \text{ (}moustache), <, dobj, \textbf{afeitar}_{c643} \text{ (}to \text{ } shave)),$$
$$(\textbf{peluca}_{c25} \text{ (}wig), <, dobj, \textbf{peinar}_{c643} \text{ (}to \text{ } comb)),$$
$$(\textbf{pelo}_{c25} \text{ (}hair), <, subj, \textbf{encrespar}_{c643} \text{ (}to \text{ } curl))$$

In the experiments carried out we selected as features the set of 1,000 words from the obtained patterns with the highest information gain. We used the Araknion dataset [10] as input to IG-WP to generate our Spanish patterns.

4.2 Emotion-labeled Graphs

The Emotion-labeled Graphs (EmoGraphs) model [18] obtains morphosyntactic categories from the Freeling library for each word in the text. Each PoS is modeled as a node in the graph and each edge defines a PoS sequence in the text. The graph obtained is enriched with semantic and affective information. Adjectives are annotated with their polarity and the Spanish Emotion Lexicon [23] is used to identify their associated emotions. WordNet Domains[18] is used to obtain the topics of nouns. On the basis of what was investigated in [8], verbs are annotated with one of the following semantic categories: i) perception (see, listen, smell...); ii) understanding (know, understand, think...); iii) doubt (doubt, ignore...); iv) language (tell, say, declare, speak...); v) emotion (feel, want, love...); vi) and will (must, forbid, allow...). We can see an example in Figure 2.

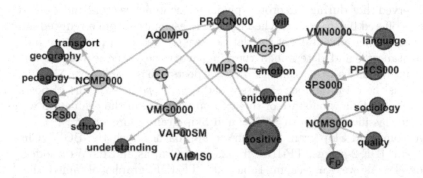

Fig. 2. EmoGraph of "He estado tomando cursos en línea sobre temas valiosos que disfruto estudiando y que podrían ayudarme a hablar en público" (*"I have been taking online courses about valuable subjects that I enjoy studying and might help me to speak in public"*). Node sizes are proportional to its eigenvector and node colors depend on its betweenness.

Once the graph is built, the objective is to use a machine learning approach to classify texts into its corresponding language variety. We obtain two kind of features on the basis of graph analysis: i) general properties of the graph describing the overall style of the modelled texts, such as nodes-edges ratio, average degree, weighted average degree, diameter, density, modularity, cluster

---

[18] http://wndomains.fbk.eu/

coefficient or average path length; ii) and specific properties of its nodes and how they are related to each other, such us eigenvector and betweenness values.

EmoGraphs aims at modelling the way the authors express their emotions in the discourse structure and offers a competent representation in age and gender author profiling tasks [18].

5 Evaluation

In this section we evaluate the performance of the aforementioned models for the language variety identification task. Given a document d and a corpus D_{tr} with documents in C different language varieties, a system has to classify d into one of the categories of C using the labeled collection D_{tr}.

Dataset and Methodology To perform this task we created and used the Hispablogs dataset,[19] a new collection of Spanish blogs from five different countries: Argentina, Chile, Mexico, Peru and Spain. There are 450 training and 200 testing blogs respectively for each language variety, with a total of 2,250 and 1,000 blogs. Each user blog is represented by a set of user posts, with 10 posts per user/blog. We measured the quality of the models by evaluating the accuracy of the classification of the test set using a model trained with the training set. We observed that during the prototyping step, sentence vectors and word vector averages offered better results when they were estimated from a reduced number of words. Taking advantage of the dataset, we treated each post as an independent instance[20], and determined the language variety of the blog in function of the probabilities of classification of its posts: $class = \text{argmax}_{c \in C} \sum_{i=1}^{n} P(c|po_i)$, where C is the total number of classes and $(po_1, ..., po_n)$ is the list of posts in a concrete blog. Following state-of-the-art approach [7], in the evaluation we used a logistic classifier[21] for both SenVec and Skip-gram approaches[22].

We compared Skip-gram and SenVec approaches with the BOW, Char. 4-grams, TF-IDF 2-grams, TF-IDF graphs, EmoGraphs and IG-WP models (cfr. Section 4). As we can see in Table 3,[23] TF-IDF graphs obtained the lowest results, even lower than the random baseline (0.2 accuracy), followed by EmoGraphs. Looking at the results of TF-IDF 2-grams, we think that in this concrete task TF-IDF-based models are not able to capture differences between

---

[19] The Hispablogs dataset can be dowloaded at: https://github.com/autoritas/RD-Lab/tree/master/data/HispaBlogs

[20] Although our method ensures that all contexts are kept together, a sliding window could be used as an alternative.

[21] Similar results with higher training time were obtained with other classifiers such as Support Vector Machines.

[22] We used 300-dimensional vectors, context windows of size 10, and 20 negative words for each sample. We preprocessed the text with word lowercase, tokenization, removing the words of length one, and with phrase detection using word2vec tools: https://code.google.com/p/word2vec/

[23] In this work, statistically significant results according to a χ^2 test are highlighted in bold.

Table 3. Accuracy results in language variety identification.

Method	Accuracy
Skip-gram	**0.722**
SenVec	**0.708**
BOW	0.527
IG-WP	0.520
Char. 4-grams	0.515
EmoGraphs	0.393
TF-IDF 2-grams	0.322
Random baseline	0.200
TF-IDF graphs	0.181

language varieties. However, EmoGraphs took advantage of additional information (topics, verbs, sentiments, emotions) to achieve a better performance. The
two baselines, BOW and Char. 4-grams, were competitive despite their simplicity. Character n-gram models proved able to extract syntactic variations
(differences in vocabulary, verbal inflections) between speakers of different language varieties. The IG-WP approach does not seem to outperform BOW, but
demonstrated the potentiality of word-patterns and has the advantage of reducing considerably dimensionality by taking into account linguistic information.
We note that in this task of language variety identification, content-based features such as BOW or IG-WP obtained better results than style-based ones such
as EmoGraphs or TF-IDF graphs. This may be due to the fact that language
variety relies more on the use of words than on discourse structure. Finally, both
Skip-gram and SenVec models based on distributed representations significantly
outperformed the others. Using the average of the word vectors, the Skip-gram
model performs slightly better than SenVec, which infers a unique representation
of documents, and proves to be a good alternative to more complex approaches.
We think that the use of user blog posts as representations, instead of complete
blogs, may have helped to reduce the noise in the vectors in both approaches.

In Figure 3, we highlight the capability of distributed representations to
model the semantic properties of language. Comparing how all the models learn
their features over the complete training partition, and evaluating their classifiers
with cross-validation on the same dataset, we appreciate a very low improvement
compared to training features on a different dataset (test set setting). Other
models seem to experience some kind of over-fitting, obtaining much higher
results in the cross-validation setting.

We can observe in Table 4 the difference in difficulty in the classification
of Spanish language varieties using the Skip-gram model. The Spain-Spanish
variety is the easiest one to detect compared to the Argentinian variety, which
has the lowest results. In general, Latin American varieties are closer to each
other and it is more difficult to differentiate between them.

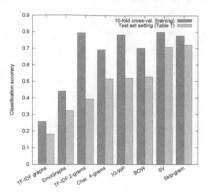

Fig. 3. Models over-fitting analysis.

Table 4. Test set confusion matrix (in %) of Skip-gram model in language variety identification.

Lang.	Classified as...				
	AR	CL	ES	MX	PE
AR	58.5	8	8.5	11	14
CL	5	73.5	5	6	10.5
ES	3	3.5	85.5	4	4
MX	8	4.5	5	70	12.5
PE	6.5	6	4	10	73.5

6 Conclusions

In the task of Spanish language variety identification, we introduced Hispablogs -a new collection of Spanish blogs from five different countries-, and evaluated two continuous Skip-gram-based approaches: vectors of words and documents. Compared to the alternative approaches that we previously used in other author profiling tasks (e.g. EmoGraphs), the results obtained using Skip-gram are significantly superior, especially when evaluated with an independent dataset. This may be due to their ability to model semantics. In this particular task, features that model contents perform better than features which model the discourse structure. This suggest that language varieties differ more in the use of words at the lexical level than in the discourse structure, that is, what is said is more important than the way it is said. Future work will investigate further how to apply distributed representations to other author profiling tasks. We are also interested in comparing our approaches to [9] when they release their dataset.

References

1. Barto, A.G.: Reinforcement learning: An introduction. MIT press (1998)
2. Bengio, Y., Ducharme, R., Vincent, P., Janvin, C.: A neural probabilistic language model. The Journal of Machine Learning Research **3**, 1137–1155 (2003)
3. Dumais, S.T.: Latent semantic analysis. Annual Review of Information Science and Technology **38**(1), 188–230 (2004)
4. Gutmann, M.U., Hyvärinen, A.: Noise-contrastive estimation of unnormalized statistical models, with applications to natural image statistics. The Journal of Machine Learning Research **13**(1), 307–361 (2012)
5. Hinton, G.E., McClelland, J.L., Rumelhart, D.E.: Distributed representations. In: Rumelhart, D.E., McClelland, J.L., (eds.) Parallel Distributed Processing: Explorations in the Microstructure of Cognition. MIT Press (1986)
6. Kim, Y.: Convolutional neural networks for sentence classification. In: Proceedings of the International Conference on Empirical Methods in Natural Language Processing (2014)
7. Le, Q.V., Mikolov, T.: Distributed representations of sentences and documents. In: Proceedings of the 31st International Conference on Machine Learning (2014)
8. Levin, B.: English verb classes and alternations. University of Chicago Press, Chicago (1993)
9. Maier, W., Gómez-Rodríguez, C.: Language variety identification in Spanish tweets. In: Proceedings of the EMNLP'2014 Workshop on Language Technology for Closely Related Languages and Language Variants, pp. 25–35. Association for Computational Linguistics, Doha, Qatar, October 2014. http://emnlp2014.org/workshops/LT4CloseLang/call.html
10. Martí, M.A., Bertran, M., Taulé, M., Salamó, M.: Distributional approach based on syntactic dependencies for discovering constructions. Computational Linguistics (2015, under review)
11. Mikolov, T., Chen, K., Corrado, G., Dean, J.: Efficient estimation of word representations in vector space. In: Proceedings of Workshop at International Conference on Learning Representations (2013)
12. Mikolov, T., Karafiát, M., Burget, L., Cernockỳ, J., Khudanpur, S.: Recurrent neural network based language model. In: INTERSPEECH 2010, 11th Annual Conference of the International Speech Communication Association, Makuhari, Chiba, Japan, pp. 1045–1048, September 26–30, 2010
13. Mikolov, T., Sutskever, I., Chen, K., Corrado, G.S., Dean, J.: Distributed representations of words and phrases and their compositionality. In: Advances in Neural Information Processing Systems, vol. 26, pp. 3111–3119 (2013)
14. Mnih, A., Teh, Y.W.: A fast and simple algorithm for training neural probabilistic language models. arXiv preprint arXiv:1206.6426 (2012)
15. Mohammad, S.M., Yang, T.: Tracking sentiment in mail: how gender differ on emotional axes. In: Proceedings of the 2nd Workshop on Computational Approaches to Subjectivity and Sentiment Analysis (2011)
16. Morin, F., Bengio, Y.: Hierarchical probabilistic neural network language model. In: Proceedings of the International Workshop on Artificial Intelligence and Statistics, pp. 246–252. Citeseer (2005)
17. Pennebaker, J.W.: The secret life of pronouns: What our words say about us. Bloomsbury Press (2011)
18. Rangel, F., Rosso, P.: On the impact of emotions on author profiling. Information Processing & Management, Special Issue on Emotion and Sentiment in Social and Expressive Media (2015, in press)

19. Rangel, F., Rosso, P., Chugur, I., Potthast, M., Trenkmann, M., Stein, B., Verhoeven, B., Daelemans, W.: Overview of the 2nd author profiling task at pan 2014. In: Cappellato, L., Ferro, N., Halvey, M., Kraaij, W. (eds.) CLEF 2014 Labs and Workshops, Notebook Papers. CEUR-WS.org, vol. 1180 (2014)
20. Rangel, F., Rosso, P., Koppel, M., Stamatatos, E., Inches, G.: Overview of the author profiling task at pan 2013. In: Forner P., Navigli R., Tufis, D. (eds.) Notebook Papers of CLEF 2013 LABs and Workshops. CEUR-WS.org, vol. 1179 (2013)
21. Sadat, F., Kazemi, F., Farzindar, A.: Automatic identification of arabic language varieties and dialects in social media. In: Proceeding of the 1st International Workshop on Social Media Retrieval and Analysis SoMeRa (2014)
22. Salton, G., Wong, A., Yang, C.S.: A vector space model for automatic indexing. Communications of the ACM **18**(11), 613–620 (1975)
23. Sidorov, G., Miranda-Jimnez, S., Viveros-Jimnez, F., Gelbukh, F., Castro-Snchez, N., Velsquez, F., Daz-Rangel, I., Surez-Guerra, S., Trevio, A., Gordon-Miranda, J.: Empirical study of opinion mining in spanish tweets. In: 11th Mexican International Conference on Artificial Intelligence, MICAI, pp. 1–4 (2012)
24. Zampieri, M., Gebrekidan-Gebre, B.: Automatic identification of language varieties: the case of portuguese. In: Proceedings of the Conference on Natural Language Processing (2012)

Evaluating User Image Tagging Credibility

Alexandru Lucian Ginsca[1,4]([✉]), Adrian Popescu[1], Mihai Lupu[2],
Adrian Iftene[3], and Ioannis Kanellos[4]

[1] CEA, LIST, Vision and Content Engineering Laboratory,
91191 Gif-sur-yvette, France
{alexandru.ginsca,adrian.popescu}@cea.fr
[2] Vienna University of Technology, Vienna, Austria
lupu@ifs.tuwien.ac.at
[3] "Al.I.Cuza" University of Iasi, Iasi, Romania
adiftene@info.uaic.ro
[4] TELECOM Bretagne, Brest, France
ioannis.kanellos@telecom-bretagne.eu

Abstract. When looking for information on the Web, the credibility of
the source plays an important role in the information seeking experience.
While data source credibility has been thoroughly studied for Web pages
or blogs, the investigation of source credibility in image retrieval tasks
is an emerging topic. In this paper, we first propose a novel dataset for
evaluating the tagging credibility of Flickr users built with the aim of
covering a large variety of topics. We present the motivation behind the
need for such a dataset, the methodology used for its creation and detail
important statistics on the number of users, images and rater agreement scores. Next, we define both a supervised learning task in which
we group the users in 5 credibility classes and a credible user retrieval
problem. Besides a couple of credibility features described in previous
work, we propose a novel set of credibility estimators, with an emphasis
on text based descriptors. Finally, we prove the usefulness of our evaluation dataset and justify the performances of the proposed credibility
descriptors by showing promising results for both of the proposed tasks.

1 Introduction

When searching for information, offline or online, one of the main questions that
arises refers to the information's degree of credibility. While there are many studies covering credibility for offline sources of information, for Web 1.0 sites [14],
for Twitter [20] or blogs [19], where credibility has been successful integrated
in information retrieval algorithms, there is little work dealing with credibility
in image sharing websites. Depending on the choice of platform, the notion of
credibility can be covered by different definitions. In this paper, we look at the
credibility of users in image sharing platforms. This setting imposes a view on
credibility that regards simultaneously the user and his contributions. In this
way, we find ourselves in the lines of work that portray the common assumption

© Springer International Publishing Switzerland 2015
J. Mothe et al. (Eds.): CLEF 2015, LNCS 9283, pp. 41–52, 2015.
DOI: 10.1007/978-3-319-24027-5_4

that a credible source produces credible content and vice-versa. This relation can be found in studies on credibility where user profile information is analyzed together with content features [12,18].

Having an indication on the credibility of the source can also be beneficial for the performance of an image retrieval system. This has been recently proven by the introduction of user credibility in the 2014 MediaEval Retrieving Diverse Social Images Benchmarking Initiative [9], where some of the participating teams [3,5] have improved the relevance and diversity of an image retrieval system using user credibility estimators. This Benchmarking Initiative also offers the only available dataset that provides manual credibility estimations for Flickr users, the Div150Cred dataset [10]. This dataset provides, among others, ground truth credibility scores for 685 users and gives a small set of credibility descriptors. Beside these, using a single user credibility estimator derived from visual information has been proven useful in diversifying a set of results for landmark image retrieval [7]. Although the aforementioned works are groundbreaking in their use of user credibility estimates for image retrieval, this process is however performed in a confined setting(i.e. diverse image search).

In this paper, we go beyond the direct usage of user credibility estimators in an image retrieval system and propose a medium for a complex analysis of user tagging credibility that can serve multiple purposes, including credibility class prediction, user ranking or the study of topic specific credibility. We first describe a novel dataset that serves the goal of evaluating the credibility of Flickr users. We provide ground truth credibility estimations for 1009 users whose evaluated images cover a large set of visually coherent topics. Our proposal diverges from recent image retrieval datasets that are either domain specific [11] or built for ad-hoc retrieval of complex topics [17]. It is closer in terms of topic coverage to the original MIR Flickr collection [8]. Our target is obtaining a reliable collection of ground truth scores for user credibility and not proposing another image retrieval dataset. A second part of the paper is dedicated to the introduction of a new set of credibility features. We are particularly interested in features that can be derived from the textual metadata that accompany Flickr images. We then propose two different tasks that use the new collection and the credibility descriptors. For each of them, we study the best choice of models and evaluation metrics that can serve as guidelines for future work involving this dataset. The first one is a user credibility classification problem that is more closely related to the previous work on credibility and provides a proof on concept on how the newly introduced dataset and features can be successfully used to predict the credibility of a Flickr user. The second one is inspired by expert retrieval tasks [1] and deals with ranking users according to predicted credibility scores. We conclude by providing future directions and use cases for the proposed dataset.

2   A Multi-Topic Tagging Credibility Dataset (MTTCred)

We propose in this section a novel dataset, designed with the goal of analyzing user credibility for a diversified set of topics.

2.1   User Credibility Dataset Design

We describe here the desiderata in creating a dataset tailored for the investigation of features that are potentially useful in assessing a user's tagging credibility. We identify the following requirements for a dataset of this nature:

- It should contain contributions from a substantial number of different users. This allows the exploitation of the dataset both as a relevant collection on which correlations between synthetic features and manual credibility scores can be estimated, but also leaves room for a learning scenario in which the credibility score can be predicted by a trained model. It should offer enough training instances so that commonly used machine learning models are able to learn a pattern, if one would exist.
- Each user should have a significant number of contributions evaluated so that we could derive a reliable manual credibility score. This score is obtained by averaging the relevance scores of individual contributions.
- Contributions sampled for each user should be images depicting a diverse set of topics. On the first hand, this choice is imposed by the nature of how we define the credibility score in an image tagging context. Our goal is to study a user's global credibility score. Having more than one topic represented for each user also promotes the re-usability of this dataset and enables studies on domain specific user credibility.

In practice, all of the desired features mentioned above are subject to limitations coming from the availability of data but mostly from the cost of annotation. As a result, when setting the targeted values for each of the three features, a trade-off between any of them has to be made. After a series of internal studies, we settled for the following approximate values: Around 1000 users, 50 images for each user and at least 5 topics represented in the contributions of each user. Next, we present the dataset annotation protocol and the dataset statistics.

2.2   Dataset Creation

For the annotation effort, we follow a methodology similar to that proposed for the construction of the datasets used in the ImageCLEF Wikipedia retrieval evaluation campaigns [17]. For each topic, we present the annotator with a couple of relevant images and a narrative which has the purpose of clarifying what is relevant and what is not for each topic. For example, in the case of the *sunset* topic, we provide the following narrative: *Assume that you want to illustrate different aspects of sunset with images. Please select all images which are relevant for sunset from the list below. Diversified views or aspects of sunset are relevant.* Then, for each topic we present a maximum of 300 images per page. The annotator's task is to select only the images he/she finds relevant for the given topic. The relevance assessments of the images in the dataset were provided by a total of 6 trusted annotators (faculty members), with 3 annotations per image. An image is considered to be relevant if at least two raters agree.

Before starting the annotation process, the users were first involved in a feedback loop. This entailed them expressing the ambiguities they identified in some topics and, from our side, modifying the narratives, where necessary. We first fix a number of diverse but simple topics that have a clear visual representation. This means having confident assessments of images depicting easily recognizable topics.

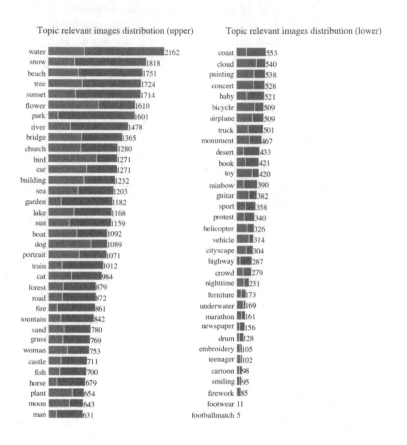

Fig. 1. Distribution of relevant and non relevant images for each topic

We use the Flickr API[1], to download both user and image metadata. We start with the *flickr.photos.search* function to download photo metadata for more than 90 topics. These topics were chosen from those used in the ImageCLEF Wikipedia Retrieval 2010 evaluation campaign. Then, we collect statistics on the users that have contributions to the retrieved set of images for all the topics. We retain the users with most images across topics. We keep the top 3000 users as candidates for the credibility dataset. For each of these users, we call the *flickr.people.getPhotos* function to gather metadata for the users' photos.

---

[1] http://www.flickr.com/services/api/

We download metadata for a maximum 10 000 images per user. Finally, we keep only the users that have at least 50 images covering at least 10 topics.

2.3   Dataset Statistics

Using the protocol described above, we obtain a dataset containing a total of 1 009 users and 50 450 images evaluated for relevance covering 69 topics. There is no overlap between the users from our dataset and those present in the Div150Cred dataset. Each user has exactly 50 images in the dataset. In Figure 1 we present the names of the topics we retained in the dataset and the number of images that were evaluated for each topic. We also show the distribution of positive and negative images for each topic. The blue bar represents the percentage of images found relevant by the annotators and the red bar gives the percentage of non-relevant images. We observe that some topics are very well represented (e.g. *water, snow, beach*), while others have fewer than 100 images (e.g. *firework, footwear, footballmatch*). We can also see from this figure that most of the images are rated as being non-relevant to the queries. A few notable exceptions, where the relevant images are predominant are the *dog, plant, vehicle or firework* topics.

We observe the agreement between raters by measuring Randolph's free marginal multirater kappa score [16]. We use this method to evaluate agreement, as opposed to Fleiss multirater kappa, because we do not know a priori the quantities of cases that should be distributed into each category (relevant vs. non relevant images). We observe an agreement score of 0.581 when combining annotation for all the topics, which can be interpreted as moderate to high agreement. This score shows that although we took precautions to ensure a simple and clear annotation process, providing relevance ratings for a diverse set of topics remains a difficult task.

When computing Randolph's free marginal multirater kappa for each individual topic, we notice high scores for some of the least ambiguous topics (e.g. *fire, man, cat*). Among the topics with low agreement scores, we find those that may present with some level of incertitude, such as *teenager* or *smiling* but also, surprisingly, topics that seem to have a clear visual representation, such as *boat or truck*.

2.4   Deriving a Ground Truth Credibility Score

As for the Div150Cred dataset [10], we build the manual user credibility scores by taking the percentage of images found relevant among the 50 images that were evaluated for each user. In Figure 2 we show the distribution of the manual credibility scores. We observe that the scores follow an approximate normal distribution. The fact that the majority of images are labeled as non-relevant can also be observed in this figure, from which we see that the mean of the credibility scores is 0.41.

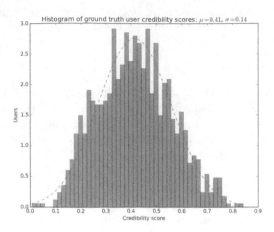

Fig. 2. Histogram of manual credibility scores

3   User Credibility Features

We provide in this section a list of features that can be used as indicators for credibility. Our goal here is not to extract a large set of features but to show the variety of useful features that can be derived from a user's Flickr metadata, textual content (e.g. image tags, title) or the visual content. These features are used in the next section for the classification experiments in which we predict a user's credibility class. We first start with the credibility descriptors proposed for the Div150Cred dataset, eliminating those that are specific to the landmark image retrieval task (e.g. the percentage of face proportion in images or the location similarity descriptor). In order to cover the multimodal aspect of user credibility, we introduce a couple of new credibility descriptors, with a focus on textual ones. We note here that the set of features used in these experiments is not exhaustive and its main purpose is to serve as a proof of concept for the importance of the proposed task and the usefulness of the newly introduced dataset. Other features extracted from Flickr metadata may be proposed with a possible increase in classification scores but this is beyond the scope of this paper.

In order to extract the credibility descriptors, for each user in our datasets, we downloaded metadata for up to 10.000 images. From the credibility descriptors proposed in [10], we use the following:

- *visualScore*: A credibility descriptor that estimates the relevance of a user's tags to the visual content of the image for a set of predefined ImageNet[2] concepts.
- *photoCount*: The total number of photos a user has uploaded to Flickr.

---

[2] http://www.image-net.org

- *uploadFrequency*: The average time (in hours) between two consecutive uploads in Flickr.
- *tagBulkProportion*: The percentage of tag sets which appear identical for at least two distinct photos.

A more detailed description of the aforementioned features is provided in [10]. Besides these features, we also extract descriptors derived from the photo metadata, with an emphasis on textual descriptors. For some of the tag based features, we require tag frequency and co-occurrence statistics from a large sample of Flickr images. To obtain a representative set of tag lists, we first gather a collection of Flickr images metadata by download information for 50 000 Flickr groups. We eliminate bulk tagging and obtain a set of 20 737 794 unique tag lists out of which we extract our tag statistics. We rank the tags in regards to their frequency and keep a list containing the top 10 000 most frequent tags and then extract a matrix with co-occurence counts for these tags. We propose the following set of new features:

- *tagVocabularySize*: The number of unique tags with which a user has labeled his photos.
- *titleVocabularySize*: The number of unique words that appear in the titles of a user's photos.
- *titleBulkPercentage*: The percentage of photo titles which appear identical for at least two distinct photos.
- *meanPhotoViews*: The average number of views for the user's photos.
- *meanTagsPerPhoto*: The average number of tags that a user puts for his photos.
- *tagsWithNumbersPercentage*: The percentage of tags that contain numbers. In most cases, these tags are not relevant to the visual content of the image.
- *meanTagRank*: The average rank in the tag list sorted by frequency for a user's tags. This feature represents an indicator to whether a user prefers to use more specific or generic tags.
- *meanPMI*: We first compute the mean pointwise mutual information (PMI) for any pair of tags from a tag list, according to Equation 1. The final feature is obtained by averaging the $mean\_pmi(T)$ values for all tag lists T of a user. This feature serves as an indicator to whether a user's tagging behavior is similar or diverges to that of a large sample of the Flickr community.

$$mean\_pmi(T) = \frac{\sum_{t_i \in T} \sum_{t_j \in T \setminus t_i} \frac{p(t_i,t_j)}{p(t_i)p(t_j)}}{|T|}, \tag{1}$$

where T is a list of tags associated with an image, $p(t_i)$ is the probability that the tag t_i appears in our tag list collection and $p(t_i,t_j)$ is the probability that t_i and t_j appear together.

4   Problem Definition

We showcase the use of the *MTTCred* dataset and the relevance of the credibility features introduced in the previous section both on a classical multi-class supervised learning problem and a retrieval task inspired by expert retrieval work, in which we rank users based on predicted credibility scores. Like most of the work that deals with predicting credibility in social media, such as the credibility of tweets [4], the problem is viewed as a classification problem. In those scenarios, two (credible / not credible) or several credibility classes are considered. Here, we first define a classification problem in which we have 5 credibility classes as follows:

- *C5:* highly credible users. Users that have a ground truth credibility score $\in [0.8, 1]$.
- *C4:* credible users. Users that have a ground truth credibility score $\in [0.6, 0.8)$.
- *C3:* uncertain credibility. Users that have a ground truth credibility score $\in [0.4, 6)$.
- *C2:* not credible users. Users that have a ground truth credibility score $\in [2, 0.4)$.
- *C1:* highly not credible users. Users that have a ground truth credibility score $\in [0, 0.2)$.

For the credible user retrieval task, we have different unions of the credibility classes, dictated by the different evaluation measures that we use. We provide more details in Section 4.3.

4.1   Data Exploration

Each user from the *MTTCred* dataset is described by 12 features. In Figure 3, we provide a visualization of a projection of those features in the two dimensional space for the 1009 users using the t-SNE algorithm [13]. We first observe in the upper left corner a small cluster including 4 out of the 7 highly credible users.

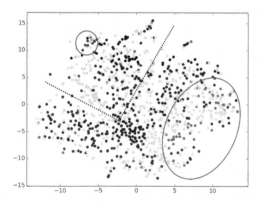

Fig. 3. Visualization of the 1009 users from the *MTTCred* dataset using the t-SNE algorithm. The values from both axes are automatically determined by t-SNE. The strong blue points represent users from the *C5* class, pale blue the ones from the *C4* class, while strong red and pale red represent users from the *C1* and *C2* classes, respectively. Black points correspond to *C3* users.

On the contrary, towards the right side of the plot we can see the users belonging to the *C1* class. Although most of the users fall under the *uncertain credibility* category and are scattered all over the plot, the dotted black lines mark a separation between most of the credible users and the others. Just by looking at this plot, we can assume that a non linear classifier can potentially be able to discern between credible and non credible users. We show in the next section that this hypothesis is partially confirmed.

4.2   User Classification Experiments

Given the fact that we have few instances in our dataset (1009 users) we afford to perform tests using a Leave-One-Out Cross Validation (LOOCV) method. On each iteration, we train a model on 1008 users and predict for the one left aside. Before the classification, all the features are L2 normalized. We tested several classifiers(e.g. support vector machines with different kernels, random forests etc.) and the best accuracy, reported in Table 1 is obtained with and Extra Trees Classifier model. For all the experiments in this section and in the following subsection, we perform parameter tuning and compare models from the scikit-learn toolkit [15].

Table 1. Confusion matrix of user credibility class prediction.

		Predicted Class					*Accuracy*
		C1	C2	C3	C4	C5	
True Class	C1	47	18	2	0	0	0.701
	C2	4	272	116	2	0	0.693
	C3	0	107	305	12	0	0.719
	C4	0	10	33	73	1	0.692
	C5	0	0	1	4	2	0.285
Overall Accuracy							**0.692**

Considering that the main goal of this experiment is to analyze the potential of multi-class classification on our proposed dataset and not to maximize the accuracy score, we still obtain a good overall accuracy (0.692) using only 12 credibility features. While proposing a fine-grained user classification task renders the classification problem more difficult, it allows us to perform a deeper analysis of Flickr user credibility. Although the accuracy scores for individual classes are not very high, the confusion matrix presented in Table 1 gives us an insight on where the classifier makes mistakes. As it can be also observed in Figure 3, most of the misclassifications fall in the *C3* class. We also consider a possible real world scenario, similar to tweet credibility classification, where we are interested to differentiate between credible and non credible users and disregard the degree of credibility and the users of *uncertain credibility*. This entails that we will have a *Cred* class composed by the union of *C4* and *C5* and a *NotCred* class, containing users from *C1* and *C2*. In this case, we obtain a 0.888 accuracy for the *Cred* class and 0.994 for the *NotCred* one.

4.3   Credible Users Retrieval Experiments

In this section, we describe how the *MTTCred* dataset can be used for a credible user retrieval task. In order to obtain a user ranking, we employ a LOOCV method but unlike the models used in the previous section, we test regression models that predict a credibility score instead of the credibility class. The users are ranked in descending order of the predicted credibility scores.

Table 2. Comparison of regression models for credible user retrieval.

	P@10	P@100	AP	NDCG@10	NDCG@100	NDCG
Linear Regression	0.2	0.42	0.349	0.193	0.515	0.851
SVR	0.2	0.43	0.348	0.224	0.527	0.855
Extra Trees Regressor	**0.8**	0.56	**0.532**	**0.593**	**0.72**	**0.917**
RF Regressor	0.6	0.57	0.505	0.423	0.673	0.892
GBR	0.6	**0.58**	**0.532**	0.529	0.709	0.912

In Table 2, we compare a set of regression models with several standard metrics used to test the relevance of ranked lists in regards to ground truth labelings. We test both linear models, such as Linear Regression and Support Vector Regression (SVR) and ensemble models, such as Extra Trees, Random Forests (RF) and Gradient Boosting (GB) Regressors. Similar to the evaluation protocol for expert retrieval in social networks described in [2], we consider the following metrics: Precision at two cut-off points (10 and 100), Average Precision over the complete list (AP), Normalized Discounted Cumulative Gain (NDCG) at 10, 100 and for the full list. While AP provides a compact measure of the precision of the retrieval capability, NDGC measures the ability of a model to retrieve different levels of credible users at high positions in the result set. P@10 and NDCG@10 are well suited for understanding the perceived quality of the first 10 retrieved users. For the precision metrics, we consider each user with a ground truth score higher than 0.6 as credible (relevant in terms of information retrieval) and the rest as not credible (not relevant). For the NDCG metrics, we consider the users from the *C1* and *C2* classes as non relevant and are given a relevance score of 0, *C3* users are given a relevance score of 1 (i.e. slightly relevant), *C4* users a score of 2 and *C5* users a score of 3. Using this approach, we can use the property of the NDCG metric of evaluation different levels of relevance in a retrieved list.

Confirming the observation drawn from Figure 3, linear models perform poorly over all metrics. With the exception of P@100, the Extra Trees Regressor model performs the best over all other metrics. This confirms the classification results from the previous section, where the best performing model was the Extra Trees Classifier and comes in lines with the recent findings presented in [6], in which the authors found that ensemble methods provide the best global results over a large number of diverse datasets.

5   Conclusions and Future Work

After motivating the importance of estimating the credibility of users in image sharing platforms in respect to image retrieval, we described the process behind building an evaluation dataset for the credibility of Flickr users. We provided detailed information about the annotation process, rater agreement scores and how we construct a user ground truth credibility score. We also introduced a user classification task and a credible user retrieval one. We found that ensemble models perform best on both of the proposed tasks. This observation may serve as a guideline for future experiments carried on *MTTCred* dataset.

The dataset described in this paper and the credibility descriptors that we used both for predicting user credibility classes or for credible user retrieval pave the road for future research towards user credibility estimation in image sharing platforms.

Although the dataset that we introduced in this paper is also designed to allow a fine-grained topic specific credibility analysis of Flickr users, this is left for future work. When doing retrieval, one possible way of taking into consideration the topical expertise of a user is by deriving his visual credibility estimator by guarding only the predictions from the binary visual classifiers that are semantically close to the query. Besides the credibility features presented in this paper, other credibility descriptors may be extracted from the image metadata but also from other data sources (e.g. user contacts, image comments, groups). Also, mainly due to space constraints, an in-depth analysis of feature importance and feature selection for both proposed tasks is left for future work.

Acknowledgments. This work is supported by the MUCKE FP7 CHIST-ERA project, partly funded by ANR, France, and by the USEMP FP7 project, partly funded by the EC under contract number 611596.

References

1. Balog, K., Fang, Y., de Rijke, M., Serdyukov, P., Si, L.: Expertise retrieval. Foundations and Trends in Information Retrieval **6**(2–3), 127–256 (2012)
2. Bozzon, A., Brambilla, M., Ceri, S., Silvestri, M., Vesci, G.: Choosing the right crowd: expert finding in social networks. In: Proceedings of the 16th International Conference on Extending Database Technology, pp. 637–648. ACM (2013)
3. Calumby, R.T., Santana, V.P., Cordeiro, F.S., Penatti, O.A., Li, L.T., Chiachia, G., da Silva Torres, R.: Recod@ mediaeval 2014: Diverse social images retrieval
4. Castillo, C., Mendoza, M., Poblete, B.: Information credibility on twitter. In: Proceedings of the 20th International Conference on World Wide Web, pp. 675–684. ACM (2011)
5. Dang-Nguyen, D.T., Piras, L., Giacinto, G., Boato, G., De Natale, F.: Retrieval of diverse images by pre-filtering and hierarchical clustering. Working Notes of MediaEval (2014)
6. Fernández-Delgado, M., Cernadas, E., Barro, S., Amorim, D.: Do we need hundreds of classifiers to solve real world classification problems? The Journal of Machine Learning Research **15**(1), 3133–3181 (2014)

7. Ginsca, A.L., Popescu, A., Ionescu, B., Armagan, A., Kanellos, I.: Toward an estimation of user tagging credibility for social image retrieval. In: Proceedings of the ACM International Conference on Multimedia, pp. 1021–1024. ACM (2014)
8. Huiskes, M.J., Lew, M.S.: The mir flickr retrieval evaluation. In: Proceedings of the 2008 ACM International Conference on Multimedia Information Retrieval, MIR 2008. ACM, New York (2008)
9. Ionescu, B., Popescu, A., Lupu, M., Ginsca, A.L., Müller, H.: Retrieving diverse social images at mediaeval 2014: challenge, dataset and evaluation. In: MediaEval 2014 Workshop, Barcelona, Spain (2014)
10. Ionescu, B., Popescu, A., Lupu, M., Gînscă, A.L., Boteanu, B., Müller, H.: Div150cred: a social image retrieval result diversification with user tagging credibility dataset. In: Proceedings of the 6th ACM Multimedia Systems Conference, MMSys 2015, pp. 207–212. ACM, New York (2015). http://doi.acm.org/10.1145/2713168.2713192
11. Ionescu, B., Radu, A.L., Menéndez, M., Müller, H., Popescu, A., Loni, B.: Div400: a social image retrieval result diversification dataset. In: Proceedings of the 5th ACM Multimedia Systems Conference, pp. 29–34. ACM (2014)
12. Juffinger, A., Granitzer, M., Lex, E.: Blog credibility ranking by exploiting verified content. In: Proceedings of the 3rd Workshop on Information Credibility on the Web, pp. 51–58. ACM (2009)
13. Van der Maaten, L., Hinton, G.: Visualizing data using t-sne. Journal of Machine Learning Research **9**(2579–2605), 85 (2008)
14. Metzger, M.J.: Making sense of credibility on the web: Models for evaluating online information and recommendations for future research. Journal of the American Society for Information Science and Technology **58**(13), 2078–2091 (2007)
15. Pedregosa, F., Varoquaux, G., Gramfort, A., Michel, V., Thirion, B., Grisel, O., Blondel, M., Prettenhofer, P., Weiss, R., Dubourg, V., Vanderplas, J., Passos, A., Cournapeau, D., Brucher, M., Perrot, M., Duchesnay, E.: Scikit-learn: Machine learning in Python. Journal of Machine Learning Research **12**
16. Randolph, J.J.: Free-marginal multirater kappa (multirater k [free]): An alternative to fleiss' fixed-marginal multirater kappa (2005) (online submission)
17. Tsikrika, T., Kludas, J., Popescu, A.: Building reliable and reusable test collections for image retrieval: The wikipedia task at imageclef. IEEE MultiMedia **19**(3), 0024 (2012)
18. Weerkamp, W., De Rijke, M.: Credibility improves topical blog post retrieval. Association for Computational Linguistics (ACL) (2008)
19. Weerkamp, W., de Rijke, M.: Credibility-inspired ranking for blog post retrieval. Information Retrieval, 1–35 (2012)
20. Westerman, D., Spence, P.R., Van Der Heide, B.: A social network as information: The effect of system generated reports of connectedness on credibility on twitter. Computers in Human Behavior **28**(1), 199–206 (2012)

Web and Social Media

Tweet Expansion Method for Filtering Task in Twitter

Payam Karisani[1(✉)], Farhad Oroumchian[2], and Maseud Rahgozar[1]

[1] Database Research Group, Control and Intelligent Processing Center of Excellence,
School of Electrical and Computer Engineering, University of Tehran, Tehran, Iran
p.karisani@gmail.com, rahgozar@ut.ac.ir
[2] University of Wollongong in Dubai, Dubai, United Arab Emirates
oroumchian@acm.org

Abstract. In this article we propose a supervised method for expanding tweet contents to improve the recall of tweet filtering task in online reputation management systems. Our method does not use any external resources. It consists of creating a K-NN classifier in three steps. In these steps the tweets labeled related and unrelated in the training set are expanded by extracting and adding the most discriminative terms, calculating and adding the most frequent terms, and re-weighting the original tweet terms from training set. Our experiments in RepLab 2013 data set show that our method improves the performance of filtering task, in terms of F criterion, up to 13% over state-of-the-art classifiers such as SVM. This data set consists of 61 entities from different domains of automotive, banking, universities, and music.

Keywords: Twitter · Classification · Filtering · Content expansion

1 Introduction

Twitter is one of the widely used social networks in the world. According to reports[1] as of February 2015, Twitter had 288 million users. This large number of users, has made this website to be one of the most studied social networks in computer science [1-3]. On Twitter website users can post their messages in less than 140 characters; then their followers can read and re-tweet these messages. The huge source of information is spread in Twitter and other social networks every day; this has caused the emergence of Online Reputation Management systems (ORM.) ORM is about monitoring the Internet users' opinions regarding organizations, products, or celebrities [4]. The main tasks of ORM systems are retrieving the messages posted by users, analyzing the messages, and visualizing the results [3].

An important step in ORM is detecting the messages that are related to a specific entity; in other words, classifying messages based on their context. This step is known as the filtering task. If this step is carried out properly, it will result in reduction of noise and one could expect a higher quality of results. This task is quite challenging due to the ambiguity in the name of entities and the short length of messages. For

---

[1] http://www.statista.com/statistics/282087/number-of-monthly-active-twitter-users/

© Springer International Publishing Switzerland 2015
J. Mothe et al. (Eds.): CLEF 2015, LNCS 9283, pp. 55–64, 2015.
DOI: 10.1007/978-3-319-24027-5_5

instance, if an ORM system wants to analyze users' impression of BMW Company, it must be able to recognize the tweets that contain this name (or other related names.) However, this is not an easy task because users may also abbreviate other phrases to BMW. For example, 90s TV series "Boy Meet World" is also abbreviated to BMW in tweets due to the constraints on the message length. Therefore, more sophisticated methods than simple keyword matching are required to carry out this step correctly.

The short length of messages is the main challenge of applying regular classification and disambiguation techniques for tweet filtering [3]. In this research, we propose a supervised method to address this problem through tweet expansion. We expand the content of each tweet with more related words in order to increase the accuracy of matching tweets with keywords. Although we only use the data extracted from the tweet contents in the collection for tweet expansion, the results show that our expansion method improves the performance of tweet filtering by up to 13% on F measure, over state-of-the-art classification techniques. In recent years, much researches have been conducted in this area; Meij et al. [5] have tried to retrieve a ranked list of Wikipedia pages for a given tweet; they used the Wikipedia link structure and the matching score between tweet contents and Wikipedia articles to find the most related articles. Spina et al. [3] have tried to classify tweet contents through detecting positive and negative keywords; their experiments show that using only the top 5 keywords, the related tweets of a company can be classified with 28% accuracy in average. They also investigated the role of keywords extracted from the data set, the web, and both. Saleiro et al. [6] (the best run in RepLab 2013 exercise) have investigated a variety of internal and external features and classification techniques to find the best setting. Their best result is achieved with a Random Forest classifier and a number of external features extracted from Wikipedia, Freebase, and entity homepages.

The rest of this paper is organized as follows, section 2 explains our expansion method for tweet filtering problem; section 3 reports our experimental results, and section 4 concludes the paper.

2   Filtering Method

Our filtering method is a two-step approach. The first step is training in which we try to expand the training tweets for each entity; then we use these expanded tweets to filter new tweets using cosine similarity.

2.1   Overview

The short length of tweets is the main reason that we believe content expansion can be helpful. The users on Twitter website must enter their messages in less than 140 characters. This restriction constrains users to use as few as possible words by abbreviating as much as they can in order to fit their messages into a single tweet. This constraint results in creation of a large set of creative and context sensitive abbreviations. As mentioned earlier, these context sensitive abbreviations hinder accuracy of the classification and retrieval methods. We try to address this issue by adding more content to each tweet; expansion methods have shown their effectiveness in text retrieval [7]. In this research, we use a tweet expansion method in order to increase the chance of matching new tweets with the previously labeled and expanded tweets.

Note that we expand both sets of the related and unrelated tweets in the training set of each entity separately. Although the set of unrelated tweets of an entity can be considered as all the tweets in the training set that are not labeled as related, we only use the tweets that are explicitly labeled as unrelated for this purpose. The reason is that we are only interested in the tweets that contain the name of the entity and are unrelated. Moreover, note that we use the same process for expanding both sets of related and unrelated data.

We only expand the tweets in the training set since the labels in this set are known, and this reduces the probability of content drift [8]. We do not use tweet expansion on the tweets from the test set due to the lack of information which makes it difficult to decide which terms must be added.

Let's assume R to be the set of related tweets of a specific entity, and U denotes the set of unrelated tweets of the same entity. Our expansion method consists of three steps. First, for each entity, we select the words that highly discriminate R and U from the whole collection, and add those terms to all the tweets in the related and unrelated tweets respectively. Second, we select the terms which are the most frequent terms in R and U, and add those terms to all related and unrelated tweets respectively. Finally, we re-weight the original terms of the expanded tweets based on their discrimination scores. A term is a good discriminator for R (or U) if its frequency in R (or U) is higher than its frequency in the whole collection.

2.2   Expansion Steps

Initially, for each tweet in our training set, we create an expanded tweet which only consists of the original terms of the tweets with equal weights (we assume this weight is 1.) Then, we use the following steps to enrich and reformulate these tweets. Note that we only describe the steps for the related tweets (set R) of an entity; however, the same steps are followed for the unrelated tweets (set U) of that entity.

Step One. In this step, we extract the top k terms which discriminate the set of related tweets of an entity from the rest of training collection; then, we add those terms to all related tweets. In other words, we try to emphasize the role of discriminative terms. The weight of the new terms are set to w. The value of w is experimentally defined as described in section 3.1; if a new term already exists in a tweet, the value of w is added to its current weight in that tweet. To find the most discriminative terms we use equation (1) as follows:

$$d(t) = P_R(t) \times \log(\frac{P_R(t)}{P_{col}(t)})$$ (1)

In which, $d(t)$ is the discrimination score of word t, $P_R(t)$ is the probability of observing word t in the set of related tweets, and $P_{col}(t)$ is the probability of observing word t in the training collection. We estimate $P_R(t)$ and $P_{col}(t)$ by creating two meta documents from all tweets of R and the collection; thus, probabilities are calculated using term frequencies.

Equation (1) is derived from the conditional entropy [9] of any two distributions A and B; the conditional entropy of two distributions, for instance A and B, estimates the difference between these distributions by measuring the amount of information which is needed to estimate A using B, conditional entropy is evaluated as follows:

$$D(A|| B) = \sum_{w \in V} P_A(w) \times \log(\frac{P_A(w)}{P_B(w)})$$ (2)

Where, V is the sample space. In other words, we select the terms which have the highest positive contribution to the conditional entropy of the related tweets.

Step Two. In the second step, we extract the terms with the highest tweet frequency in the related tweets, and add these terms to all the related tweets again. The rationale behind this step is that, if users were permitted to post their messages in any length, they would use these terms more frequent than they are using now. Therefore, we try to simulate this fact, by extracting the top k_2 high tweet frequency terms and adding these terms to all related tweets again to increase their weight. Similar to pervious step, the weights of the new terms are set to w_2; the value of w_2 is also defined experimentally as described in section 3.1 below. If a new term already exists in a tweet, the value of w_2 is added to its current weight in that tweet.

Step Three. In this step we try to re-weigh the original terms of the tweets. The rationale behind this step is that, there might be some words in each tweet that describe the subject of the tweet more accurately than the others. We increase the weight of these words by 1. We hypothesize that these words most of the time have a high discriminative score; therefore, we use equation (1) to find these terms in each tweet. The weights of the top k_3 terms which have the highest discriminative value are increased by 1 in each related tweet. Note that k_3 is different from k; since we add the top k terms to tweets, but we only increase the weight of the top k_3 terms which are already present in tweets.

Using these three steps, we expand all the tweets in R and U sets. To label new tweets, we use the expanded tweets and cosine similarity measure to find the expanded tweet which has the highest similarity to the new tweet—the obtained weights in the expanded tweets and term frequencies in the test tweets are used as the feature vectors. The label of the expanded tweet is assigned to the new tweet (if there is more than one tweet, we randomly choose one.) This is similar to nearest neighbor method that looks at only one neighbor (1-NN).

3   Experimental Results

In this section, we report our results. First, the data set, the baselines, and the training process are described; then, the results are reported, and finally the method is discussed in more detail.

3.1   Experimental Setup

We used RepLab 2013 data set to test our method [1]; the data set consists of 61 entities from 4 different domains of automotive, banking, universities, and music. The
name of the entities are used to retrieve the tweets of that entity; the tweets are in two
languages of English and Spanish. Each entity at least has 2200 tweets; the first 700
tweets are used in the training set, and the rest of the tweets are used in the test set.
RepLab team crawled the training tweets and the test tweets in different time periods,
in order to separate these two sets temporally. For each tweet in the set, the tweet id,
author screen name, tweet URL, language, timestamp, entity, and label are provided.
The labels determine whether the tweets are related or unrelated to the entities. Because of Twitter terms of service, they did not provide the tweet contents; therefore,
we developed a tool for this purpose and downloaded the contents of the tweets directly. Table 1 summarizes the number of tweets which were available at the time of
our crawl.

Table 1. The statistics of the tweets which were available at the time of our crawl. (Rel=the
number of related tweets, Unrel=the number of unrelated tweets)

	Automotive		Banking		Universities		Music	
	Rel	*Unrel*	*Rel*	*Unrel*	*Rel*	*Unrel*	*Rel*	*Unrel*
Training	10460	3374	5431	1904	3238	3320	12835	1299
Test	22428	6386	11286	4168	7029	6455	27497	1934

In order to improve the quality of the tweet texts, we took the following pre-
processing steps:

1. URLs and HTML tags. We removed all URLs and HTML tags.
2. Hashtags and mentions. We removed all hash signs (#) and mention signs (@).
3. '-' and '_' signs. We did not remove signs '-' and '_'. Terms which contain one of
   these two signs remained intact; moreover, we added to their tweets the components of those terms. For instance, if a tweet contained term "BMW-Siri", we added to that tweet words "BMW" and "Siri".
4. Uppercase characters. We converted all uppercase characters to lowercase characters.
5. Stopword removal. We used the standard INQUERY stop word list [10] to remove
   common English words from tweet texts. Besides, we used a list of 351 common
   Spanish words to remove Spanish stop words[2].
6. Entity names. We did not tokenize the entity names which contain the characters
   other than alphabet. For instance, we did not tokenize entity names "AC/DC" or
   "Wells Fargo".

To measure the performance of our method we used the standard Accuracy criterion
[8] and F measure which is the combination of Reliability and Sensitivity proposed by
Amigo et al. [11]. As a baseline, we chose SVM with polynomial kernel classifier
[12] which is one of the best classifiers; the polynomial kernel usually has a good

---

[2] http://members.unine.ch/jacques.savoy/clef/index.html

performance when data is not linearly separable. Our method selects the nearest neighbor after the expansion process; therefore, we also chose K-Nearest Neighbor classifier as the second baseline. Weka [13] is used for implementing the baselines, and R^3 tool is used for significance testing.

In the training process, we optimized the parameters of SVM classifier, KNN classifier, and our method based on Accuracy criterion. For SVM classifier, we have experimented with different values of the complexity parameter $C=\{10^{-5}, 10^{-3}, 10^{-1}, 10, 10^3, \ldots 10^{15}\}$ and kernel degree $Exp=\{1, 2, 3, 4, 5\}$ and their combinations. For the KNN classifier, we have experimented with $K=\{1, 3, \ldots 9\}$ to find the best performance.

In step one of our method, there are two parameters w and k; w is the weight of the new terms and k is the number of the new terms. Because this step selects the terms that best discriminate sets R and U from the rest of the tweets in the training collection, therefore, we have experimented with the weights close to 1 in order to maximize the differences. The values we tried are $w=\{0.7, 1, 1.3\}$, and for the number of the new terms we tried $k=\{10, 20, 30\}$. In step two of our method, there are parameters w_2 and k_2 which must be also optimized; as before, w_2 is the weight of the new terms and k_2 is the number of the new terms. The criterion in this step is tweet frequency; we believe tweet frequency does not fully represent the importance of terms in a subject; therefore, we assigned the weights that are less than the weights of the original terms and the weights of the terms in the first step. In this step, we tried $w_2=\{0.2, 0.3, 0.4, 0.5\}$ and $k_2=\{10, 20, 30\}$. In step three, k_3 is the number of the discriminative terms which we use to re-weigh the original tweet terms. Although a number of highly discriminative terms are already added to the tweets in the first step, we use this step to detect and increase the weight and number of the terms which carry more information than other terms. We selected a wider range for k_3 than what we used for k in the first step; thus, we tried $k_3=\{10, 30, 50, 70, 90\}$. To find the best parameter setting, we also experimented with the combination of these parameters.

Note that for each entity the classifiers are trained separately. We also used standard 10 fold cross validation in order to insure the generalization of our training procedure; that is, we randomly divided each training set into 10 folds—the ratio of the related tweets to the unrelated tweets are kept the same in each fold—and in each step we used one fold as the test set and the rest of the folds as the training set to optimize the parameters. The final parameters are averaged over these optimal values for each entity and used to label the main test set of that entity.

3.2   Results

Table 2 reports the performance of our expansion method (EPM) in comparison to the performance of SVM and KNN classifiers[4]. We can observe that our method improves the performance of tweet filtering, in terms of F measure, up to 13.51% over

---

[3] http://www.r-project.org/
[4] We also tested Naïve-Bayes classifier; because the performance of this classifier was highly similar to SVM, we did not report the results here.

SVM classifier which is statistically significant—using paired t-test at $p<0.05$. Although our method EPM decreases Accuracy less than 2.36% over SVM, statistical analysis shows that this effect is not significant. As stated in [1], 77% percent of the tweets in the data set are related to the profiles; therefore, achieving high accuracy results per se is not a challenging task if we do not take recall into account—one might achieve high accuracy results by considering all the tweets to be positive. Normally an increase in recall results in a decrease in precision. An analysis of our results also shows the improvement exhibited by F measure for our method also has come in the expense of lower precision (or reliability) [8] rate.

Table 2. The performance of our method in comparison to SVM and KNN classifiers. α, β, and γ indicate statistically significant improvements over KNN, SVM, and our method respectively.

	Reliability	Sensitivity	F	Accuracy
KNN	0.70^{γ}	0.30	0.36	0.84
SVM	$\mathbf{0.86}^{\alpha\gamma}$	0.31	0.37	**0.85**
EPM	0.59	$\mathbf{0.40}^{\alpha\beta}$	$\mathbf{0.42}^{\alpha\beta}$	0.83

Table 3 reports the performance of all the methods, in terms of F measure, in each domain separately. We can observe that the most improvement is made in universities domain, and the least improvement is in banking domain. These results indicate that the tweets which are written about universities are more sensitive toward expansion and enriching their contents.

Table 3. The performance of our method, in terms of F, in comparison to SVM and KNN classifiers in the four domains of RepLab 2013 data set.

	Automotive	Banking	Universities	Music
KNN	0.36	0.50	0.38	0.26
SVM	0.38	0.49	0.40	0.28
EPM	**0.42**	**0.53**	**0.48**	**0.31**

In order to measure the expansion process directly, we also did the following experiment. We extracted the features from steps one and two, and built two feature vectors for sets R and U separately; using cosine similarity measure and these two feature vectors we labeled the test sets according to the most similar feature vector (the same as 1-NN). Table 4 presents the result of this experiment; the improvements signify that the re-weighting procedure and using original terms have a high impact on the final results. Because the only difference between the methods are these two steps. In fact, enriching tweet contents, although with the same content for all tweets, helps to improve the probability of matching keywords, and in turn improves the sensitivity (or recall) of the filtering task.

Table 4. The performance of our method (EPM) in comparison to filtering using only feature vectors of steps one and two.

	Reliability	Sensitivity	F	Accuracy
Feature Vectors	**0.70**	0.30	0.34	0.82
EPM	0.59	**0.40**	**0.42**	**0.83**

3.3   Discussion

Our expansion process consists of three independent steps; in order to measure the effectiveness of each step, we ran our method four times with different settings. First, without taking any step we only used the most similar tweet in the training set to label the test sets; then we took step one and measured the performance again, and so on. Fig. 1 plots the result of these experiments in terms of F measure. The results show that as we expected, adding the most discriminative terms to all tweets, has the highest impact. The results also suggest that the second step has the minimal impact on F measure because the tweet frequency is constrained by the length of the tweets and does not fully reflects the importance of terms.

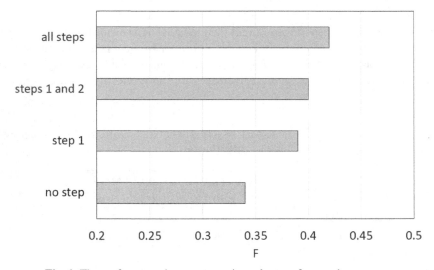

Fig. 1. The performance improvement in each step of expansion process

Table 5 reports the performance of our method EPM in comparison to the performance of the top 5 runs in RepLab 2013; the runs are sorted by F criterion. Users in Twitter may delete a post or make it private; due to these changes, the data which was available for us was less than what was available for the teams in RepLab 2013. At our crawling time, 91% of the training data and 90% of the test data were available. In this experiment, for measuring the performance criteria, we only used the tweets that were present in the available data and their content was downloadable. If we assume that the difficulty of the collection does not change over time, our method is comparable to the top runs in Replab 2013. Note that some runs use external data like Wikipedia articles, or Twitter profile contents, and some others use resource consuming techniques like N-gram indexing. Our method does not use any external data and only uses training set for classification.

Table 5. The performance of our method (EPM) in comparison to the best runs of RepLab 2013

Method	Reliability	Sensitivity	F	Accuracy	Notable tasks and used resources
POPSTAR 2	0.73	0.45	0.49	0.91	Wikipedia, Freebase
SZTE NLP 7	0.60	0.44	0.44	0.93	N-gram, LDA
EPM	**0.59**	**0.40**	**0.42**	**0.90**	-
LIA 1	0.66	0.36	0.38	0.87	Authors and Entities Meta Data
UAMCLYR 04	0.56	0.4	0.38	0.91	-
UNED ORM 2	0.43	0.38	0.34	0.86	Wikipedia, ODP

Methods shown in Table 5 are the best runs of RepLab 2013 [1]. POPSTAR experimented with a large set of internal and external features; such as the similarity scores between tweet texts and Wikipedia articles and entity homepages. They also created two bi-grams, containing the query terms and the previous/subsequent word in the tweet texts; these bigrams were used to retrieve a list of entities from Freebase to calculate a score which shows the importance of that bigram in the context of the entity. SZTE NLP used a series of normalization steps; then they used bigram indexing, LDA topic modeling, and the presence and absence of the entity names as feature vector. LIA experimented with TF-IDF combined with Gini purity criteria; they also used a set of tokens extracted from the authors and entities metadata in the Twitter website as feature vector. UAMCLYR investigated the role of Distributional Term Representation [14] to represent terms by means of contextual information given by the term co-occurrence statistics. They used SVM classifier, and their best result was achieved with bag-of-word representation and Boolean weighting. Finally, UNED ORM proposed a method to automatically detect positive and negative keywords that reliably predict the relatedness and non-relatedness of tweets to a specific entity. They extracted these keywords from the collection, Wikipedia articles, entity homepages, search results in Wikipedia site, and search results in Open Directory Project.

4   Conclusion and Future Work

In this article we proposed a supervised method for expanding tweet contents. Our method does not use external resources; it consists of three steps: extracting and adding the most discriminative terms, adding the most frequent terms, and re-weighting of the original tweet terms. To carry out these steps, we used the manually tagged tweets in the training set. Expansion methods are often used to improve recall; these methods potentially can harm precision. Our method is more a recall tool than precision tool. Although as expected the overall accuracy of our method decreases, this drop in accuracy is not statistically significant. On the other hand, the improvements in sensitivity (or recall) amount to 13% in terms of F criterion over SVM classifier. Our method is easily adaptable to real life situations as many companies which use Twitter for their reputation management, tend to categorize the tweets to related or unrelated manually or semi-automatically. Therefore, creating a sizable training data set is not difficult for these companies. In the next step, we have planned to investigate the role of external resources in the expansion procedure. Besides, we believe a more sophisticated re-weighting method can improve the performance even further.

References

1. Amigó, E., Carrillo de Albornoz, J., Chugur, I., Corujo, A., Gonzalo, J., Martín, T., Meij, E., de Rijke, M., et al.: Overview of RepLab 2013: evaluating online reputation monitoring systems. In: Forner, P., Müller, H., Paredes, R., Rosso, P., Stein, B. (eds.) CLEF 2013. LNCS, vol. 8138, pp. 333–352. Springer, Heidelberg (2013)
2. Amigó, E., Carrillo-de-Albornoz, J., Chugur, I., Corujo, A., Gonzalo, J., Meij, E., de Rijke, M., Spina, D.: Overview of RepLab 2014: author profiling and reputation dimensions for online reputation management. In: Kanoulas, E., Lupu, M., Clough, P., Sanderson, M., Hall, M., Hanbury, A., Toms, E. (eds.) CLEF 2014. LNCS, vol. 8685, pp. 307–322. Springer, Heidelberg (2014)
3. Spina, D., Gonzalo, J., Amigó, E.: Discovering filter keywords for company name disambiguation in twitter. Expert Systems with Applications **40**(12), 4986–5003 (2013)
4. Hoffman, T.: Online reputation management is hot—but is it ethical. Computerworld, p. 2, February 2008
5. Meij, E., Weerkamp, W., de Rijke, M.: Adding semantics to microblog posts. In: Proceedings of the Fifth ACM International Conference on Web Search and Data Mining. ACM (2012)
6. Saleiro, P., Rei, L., Pasquali, A., Soares, C., Teixeira, J., Pinto, F., Nozari, M., Félix, C., Strecht, P.: POPSTAR at RepLab 2013: name ambiguity resolution on twitter. In: CLEF 2013 Eval. Labs and Workshop Online Working Notes (2013)
7. Lavrenko, V., Bruce Croft, W.: Relevance based language models. In: Proceedings of the 24th Annual International ACM SIGIR Conference on Research and Development in Information Retrieval. ACM (2001)
8. Baeza-Yates, R., Ribeiro-Neto, B.: Modern information retrieval, vol. 463. ACM Press, New York (1999)
9. Kullback, S., Leibler, R.A.: On information and sufficiency. The Annals of Mathematical Statistics, 79–86 (1951)
10. Allan, J., Connell, M.E., Bruce Croft, W., Fang-Fang F., Fisher, D., Li, X.: Inquery and trec-9, DTIC Document (2000)
11. Amigó, E., Gonzalo, J., Verdejo, F.: A general evaluation measure for document organization tasks. In: Proceedings of the 36th International ACM SIGIR Conference on Research and Development in Information Retrieval. ACM (2013)
12. Keerthi, S.S., Shevade, S.K., Bhattacharyya, C., Murthy, K.R.K.: Improvements to Platt's SMO algorithm for SVM classifier design. Neural Computation **13**(3), 637–649 (2001)
13. Hall, M., Frank, E., Holmes, G., Pfahringer, B., Reutemann, P., Witten, I.H.: The WEKA data mining software: an update. SIGKDD Explor. Newsl. **11**(1), 10–18 (2009)
14. Lavelli, A., Sebastiani, F., Zanoli, R.: Distributional term representations: an experimental comparison. In: Proceedings of the Thirteenth ACM International Conference on Information and Knowledge Management. ACM (2004)

Real-Time Entity-Based Event Detection
for Twitter

Andrew J. McMinn$^{(\boxtimes)}$ and Joemon M. Jose

School of Computing Science, University of Glasgow,
Glasgow G12 8QQ, Scotland, UK
a.mcminn.1@research.gla.ac.uk, joemon.jose@glasgow.ac.uk

Abstract. In recent years there has been a surge of interest in using
Twitter to detect real-world events. However, many state-of-the-art event
detection approaches are either too slow for real-time application, or can
detect only specific types of events effectively. We examine the role of
named entities and use them to enhance event detection. Specifically, we
use a clustering technique which partitions documents based upon the
entities they contain, and burst detection and cluster selection techniques
to extract clusters related to on-going real-world events. We evaluate our
approach on a large-scale corpus of 120 million tweets covering more than
500 events, and show that it is able to detect significantly more events
than current state-of-the-art approaches whilst also improving precision
and retaining low computational complexity. We find that nouns and
verbs play different roles in event detection and that the use of hashtags
and retweets lead to a decreases in effectiveness when using our entity-
base approach.

Keywords: Event detection · Social media · Reproducibility · Twitter

1 Introduction

Today, if a major event occurs, many people turn to social media services for
up-to-the-second information about what is happening. Twitter is one of the
most popular social media services, with over 200 million active users who make
more than 500 million posts every day. Twitter makes it possible for users to
post first-hand information about ongoing events in real-time, allowing Twitter
to be used as a coordination tool for protests and demonstrations, with examples
including the Arab Spring, and anti-government protests in Turkey.

Given this, it is not surprising that many of the most popular accounts are
those which report breaking news and events. For example, the Twitter account
@breakingnews, which aims to report breaking news in real-time, has over 6 million followers and a team of over a dozen journalists who work around the clock
to monitor Twitter, but still rely on tips from over 300 other news organizations.
A tool which could automatically detect, track and organize these events would
be valuable to journalists and other fields, such as finance or security. However,

© Springer International Publishing Switzerland 2015
J. Mothe et al. (Eds.): CLEF 2015, LNCS 9283, pp. 65–77, 2015.
DOI: 10.1007/978-3-319-24027-5_6

Twitter poses a number of significant challenges which make this a hard task. The vast majority of social media content is trivial and unrelated to on-going real-world events. It is not uncommon to find a user who only posts about the food they eat or music they listen to. The low quality of social media content poses further issues; spelling and grammar errors very common, as is the use of abbreviations and acronyms. Additionally, the massive volume of data produced by social media services makes it incredibly difficult to process in real-time, and many traditional event detection approaches, such as those proposed as part of the Topic Detection and Tracking Project, fail to scale to Twitter-sized corpora. These challenges, combined with the fact that event detection and tracking is hard (even on newswire documents [3]), make it a worthy challenge.

We propose the use of named entities for the efficient and effective detection and tracking of events on Twitter. We conjecture that named entities are the building blocks of events; the people, places and organizations involved are crucial in describing an event. For example, given the event *"Hilary Mantel wins the 2012 Man Booker Prize for her novel Bring Up the Bodies"*, it is clear that named entities (highlighted in bold) play a crucial role in describing an event, and are often enough to decipher what happened. Our real-time approach identifies bursty named entities and uses an efficient clustering approach to detect and break events into individual topics, each of which describes a different aspect of an event. We evaluate our event detection approach on a large-scale Twitter dataset of 120 million Tweets and over 500 events, showing that our approach gives significant increases in precision and recall over current state-of-the-art approaches whilst maintaining real-time performance.

2   Background

The Topic Detection and Tracking (TDT) project aimed to produce a system that was capable of monitoring broadcast news and could produce an alert when a new event occurred. A simple nearest neighbor clustering approach was used by most TDT systems, and produced some reasonably effective systems [2–4,22]. However, TDT datasets used long newswire documents, and had several orders of magnitude fewer documents than Twitter datasets. This mean that systems were designed without regard for real-time performance or noise and spam, making them inefficient and ineffective when applied to Twitter. Despite these issues, TDT-inspired clustering models are still commonly used in event detection approaches for Twitter, although often with efficiency optimizations to cope with the increased volume of data [1,18] and additional filtering steps to remove spam and non-event clusters [6]. However, these efficiency optimizations and filtering steps often come at the cost of reduced effectiveness [1,18] or mean that significant delays must be introduced at the cost of real-time performance [6].

In recent years, interest in events (significant things that happen at some specific time and place [15]) on social media, and in particular Twitter [5], has exploded as real-time social media streams have become available for research. Hu et al. [9] demonstrated the effectiveness of Twitter as a medium for breaking news by examining how the news of Osama bin Laden's death broke on Twitter. They found that Twitter had broken the news, and as a result, millions knew of his death before the official announcement. Kwak et al. [12] analyzed the top trending topics to show that the majority of topics (over 85%) are related to headline news or persistent news. Osborne et al. [16] measured the delay between a new event appearing on Twitter and the time taken for the same event to be updated on Wikipedia, finding that Twitter appears to be around 2 hours ahead of Wikipedia. These findings show that Twitter is a valuable resource and viable platform for the real-time detection and tracking of events and breaking news.

Although there have been many event detection approaches proposed for Twitter [1,5,6,17,18,20,21], Petrović et al. [18] were perhaps the first to propose a scalable, real-time, event detection system for Twitter. They use Locality Sensitive Hashing (LSH) to perform approximate nearest neighbor clustering in a fixed time. Recent evaluations [15] show that although the approach performs reasonably, it is susceptible to insignificant and mundane events, and has relatively low precision. Other approaches have been proposed which have high precision [6,21], however generally these approaches require significant amounts of training or curated data. Our approach achieves extremely high precision (a 100% improvement over [18]) without the need for training or curated data.

2.1 Named Entities in Events and Twitter

We believe that named entities play a key role in describing events, such as the people involved, or the location where the event took place. Without this information, or some other contextual clue, it is unreasonable to expect a person or machine to determine the specifics of an event. For cxample, given the document "*A bomb exploded.*", it is impossible to determine who was involved or where the event took place – we are only able to say that a bomb exploded somewhere. Only by introducing entities or other contextual information can we begin to determine the specifics of an event: "***Boko Haram*** *claims responsibility for a bomb which exploded in the northeast* ***Nigerian*** *town of* ***Potiskum***.". Given this information, we are now able to say who was involved (Boko Haram), where the event took place (Potiskum, Nigeria), and due to Twitter's real-time nature, infer with some confidence that the event took place recently.

Previous work has examined the use of named entities for event detection as part of the TDT project, with some success at improving detection performance [10,11,23]. However, these approaches were mainly adjustments to similarity measures so that named entities were given increased weight compared to other terms, and do not address the efficiency and effectiveness issues outlined in Section 2. In the context of Twitter, Choudhury and Breslin [7] examined how linguistic features and background knowledge could be used to detect specific types of sports events with high precision, however requires significant domain knowledge and large amounts of manual labeling to prepare a classifier. More similar to our work, Ritter et al. [20] used named entities, "event phrases" and temporal expressions to extract a calendar of significant events from Twitter. However, their approach requires that tweets contain temporal resolution phrases, such as "tomorrow" or "Wednesday" to resolve between an entity and a time. This means that smaller and unexpected events, which are often the events which are of most interest, are unlikely to be detected. Our approach requires no domain knowledge or temporal phrases to perform event detection, instead relying on statistical information about common named entities, which is automatically extracted from the corpus in real-time.

Natural Language Processing (NLP) software struggles when faced with the short length and noise found in Tweets [8,13,14,20]. Several attempts have been made to address this, particularly in the tasks of Part Of Speech (POS) Tagging [8] and Named Entity Recognition (NER) [8,13,14,20]. A number of new methods have been proposed which provide significant improvements to effectiveness [13,14,20], and a number of improved models designed specifically for Twitter [8] have been released for commonly used NLP software such as the Stanford NLP Toolkit, including the GATE Twitter POS model [8].

3   Entity-Based Event Detection

In this section we describe our entity-based event detection approach. The approach comprises of 6 key stages, as shown in Figure 1. Tweets are processed in order using a pipelines architecture which allows for simple parallel processing, and with each component relying only on the output of the previous component to complete its task.

3.1   Pre-processing

Parsing and Tagging. We perform Part of Speech (POS) tagging and Named Entity Recognition (NER) on the text of each Tweet using the GATE Twitter POS model [8] which was trained using English language tweets. We extract lemmatized nouns and verbs, and named entities (persons, locations, and organizations) from each tweet.

Filtering. Event detection on Twitter relies heavily on filtering as many non-event related tweets as possible. We apply a set of filters which remove over 95% of tweets, resulting in considerably less noise, and unlike other approaches which filter after clustering [6,18], it significantly reduces the amount of data which

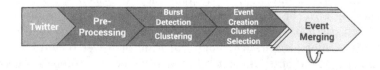

Fig. 1. The pipeline architecture and components of our approach.

needs to be processed. Our first and most aggressive filter (removing around 90% of tweets), removes Tweets which contain no named entities. As discussed in Section 2.1, we believe that named entities play a crucial role in describing events, thus do not believe that this filter significantly harms detection performance, and analyze this in Section 5.1. Furthermore, in order to efficiently cluster tweets, our clustering approach (described in Section 3.2) requires each tweet to contain at least one named entity, making this filter necessary. The second filter removes retweets, which make up approximately 30% of tweets. We examine the effect of removing retweets in Section 5.2. We also have a number of term-level filters that remove terms that are unlikely to be related to an event or that are known to be associated with spam and noise (e.g. "watch", "follow", "listen", etc.).

3.2 Clustering

Clustering is commonly used in event detection, however it is also inherently slow for large numbers of documents. We address this using the premise that tweets discussing an event must describe at least one of the named entities involved in the event, and partition tweets based upon the entities they contain, as shown in Figure 2, which reduces the computational complexity significantly. For the purpose of clustering, this can be thought of as having a unique Inverted Index for each named entity. For each named entity e in tweet d, a list of tweets D is retrieved from the inverted index for e and the maximum TF-IDF weight cosine similarity score is calculated between d and each tweet in D. If the maximum score is above a set threshold (usually in the range $0.45 - 0.55$ [18]), then d is added to the same cluster as its nearest neighbor. If the nearest neighbor does not already belong to a cluster, then a new cluster is created containing both tweets and assigned to entity e. The new tweet is then added to the inverted index for entity e. To ensure real-time performance, we limit the number of tweets that can be retrieved from an entity's inverted index to N (in our experiments, N=200 resulted in no significant differences from an unlimited number of tweets), and use only the top 10 TF-IDF weighed terms per tweet, ensuring an upper bound of $10N$ comparisons (less than 1% of tweets contain more than 10 terms).

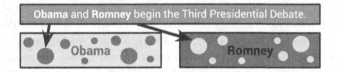

Fig. 2. Our clustering approach which partitions tweets based upon the entities they contain. The example shows how a Tweet containing both 'Obama' and 'Romney' would be put into two clusters, one for 'Obama' and one for 'Romney'.

3.3   Burst Detection

For an effective event detection approach, it is important to have a method of detecting significant events and filtering the mundane. We do this by looking for temporal bursts in the frequency of an entity, which can occur over periods ranging from a few minutes to several hours. To model this, we use a set of windows for each entity to capture their frequency over time, starting at a 5 minutes, and doubling in length up to 360 minutes (i.e. 5, 10, 20, ..., 360). We use the Three Sigma Rule as the basis for a light-weight burst detection approach, which states that a value is considered to be practically impossible if it is further than 3 standard deviations from the expected value [19]. For the windows, we maintain mean and standard deviation values, updating them periodically with the current entity frequency. It is possible to efficiently compute moving mean (μ) and standard deviation (σ) values using a set of three power sums s_0, s_1 and s_2, where s_j, μ and σ at time period $n + 1$ for data series x is shown below:

$$s_{jn+1} = s_{jn} + x_{n+1}^{j} \qquad \mu = \frac{s_1}{s_0} \qquad \sigma = \sqrt{\frac{s_2 - s_1^2}{s_0}}$$

The μ and σ values for each window are updated periodically based upon the length of the window (i.e., a 5 minute window is updated every 5 minutes). When a tweet is no longer covered by the largest window it is removed from all inverted indexes. Once a tweet has been clustered and added to an entity's inverted index (as described in Section 3.2), each window is checked, and if the number of tweets in a given window is greater than $\mu + 3 \cdot \sigma$ then we say that the given window is bursty. In order to smooth and reduce noise, statistics are not updated while a window is bursting, and windows are kept in a bursting state for $1.5 \times window\_length$ after the window's statistics suggest that it has stopped bursting. This prevents large events from saturating an entity's statistics, which would make it difficult for future events to cause a burst.

3.4   Cluster Identification

Once a burst has been detected, an event is created and associated with the bursting entity for the duration of the burst (we address how an event could be associated with multiple entities in Section 3.5). However, the event does not yet have any tweets associated with it since many of the tweets posted during the burst will discuss background topics and noise. To solve this, we associate entity clusters with the event, and require that the centroid time of a cluster (i.e. the average timestamp of tweets in the cluster) is after the initial burst. This helps to ensure that clusters which discuss background topics are not included as they are likely to have existed for some time before the burst took place. A cluster's centroid time is updated as new tweets are added, ensuring that clusters which initially had a centroid time prior to the burst can still be added to an event, allowing clusters containing early reports of the event (which often occur before any burst takes places) to be included. We also require that a cluster meets a

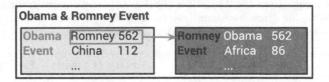

Fig. 3. An example of event merging, where two events which are happening at the same time can be merged if more than half of the tweets mention another entity.

minimum size threshold (we use 10 in our experiments) to prevent small but noisy clusters from being included. An event is kept alive as long as it has at least one bursting entity associated with it. Once all entities associated with an event have stopped bursting, the event is finalized, and no more clusters can be added to it.

3.5 Event Merging

It is common for more than a single entity to be involved in an event, such as football matches or political debates. Rather than have a single event for each entity involved in a real-world event, we attempt to automatically detect links and merge events where a link is found. If an entity is mentioned in at least 50% of tweets in an event and the mentioned entity is currently part of an another event, we merge the two events, as shown in Figure 3. This merging process can happen any number of times to produce events with many entities, and from each entity, many topics/clusters.

Entities are kept in their longest form rather than being split into individual components (e.g. 'Barack Obama', rather than 'Barack' and 'Obama'). It is unlikely that single tweet will mention both 'Barack Obama' and 'Obama', meaning that our event merging approach is unlikely to ever create a link between the two. To solve this, we perform a normalization step which splits Person names into their individual components when computing entity frequencies within events, allowing 'Barack Obama' events to be easily linked to both 'Barack' and 'Obama.'

4   Experimentation

To perform repeatable evaluations, we used the Events2012 Twitter Dataset created previously [15]. The collection provides a sample of the Twitter garden hose: 120 million tweets, covering a 28 day period, starting 10th October 2012 and ending 7th November 2012. The collection contains over 150,000 relevance judgments for over 500 events, and was created using the Wikipedia Current Events Portal[1] and 2 state-of-the-art event detection approaches, namely the

---

[1] http://en.wikipedia.org/wiki/Portal:Current_events

Table 1. The results from the 2 baselines (LSH & CS) and our entity-based approach when measured using Crowdsourcing (events with 30+ tweets) and automatic using the 500 events from the Events2012 collection (best run, events with 75+ tweets).

	CS	LSH	Entity (Crowd)	Entity (Auto)
Precision	53/1097 (0.048)	382/1340 (0.285)	**769/1210 (0.636)**	181/586 (0.302)
Recall	32/506 (0.063)	156/506 (0.308)	**194/506 (0.383)**	159/506 (0.310)
F1	0.054	0.296	**0.478**	**0.306**

Locality Sensitive Hashing (LSH) approach proposed by Petrović et al. [18] and the Cluster Summarization (CS) approach proposed by Aggarwal et al. [1].

Given that no event detection technique for Twitter has been robustly evaluated against a publicly available Twitter collection, the only available baselines are the LSH and CS approaches used to generate the collection. The results of the baseline approaches are taken from those given in [15]. We ran our entity based approach on the collection, treating it as a stream ordered by the creation time of each tweet. Evaluations were performed on all events with more than 30 tweets. We say that a candidate event has detected an event from the relevance judgments if at least 5% or more than 15 of the candidate's tweets match those in the relevance judgments for an event. The rationale for these choices is described in Section 5.

Although the collection contains a very large number of events and relevance judgments, we note that it does not guarantee full coverage of events, or full coverage of relevance judgments for each event. Whilst this is an issue in many IR collections, we note that the effect is more pronounced when dealing with event detection, as it is very likely that we will detect events which are not in the judgments. We verify this hypothesis and show that we detect a large number of events which are not in the relevance judgments through crowdsourcing. In order to keep the comparison between the baselines approaches and our approach as fair as possible, we used the same methodology used to gather relevance judgments for the collection. We will also make our events and judgments available as a baseline and to enhance the judgments available in the collection. We replicate the methodology described in our previous work [15], using 5 crowdsourced annotators to judge each event, and gather descriptions and category information. We perform a number of spam and quality controls, and use majority judgment for each event. Full details can be found in [15].

5   Results and Discussion

As shown in Table 1, our approach is able to significantly outperform the two baseline approaches when evaluated using Crowdsourcing and, to a lesser extent, using the test collection. Note that the crowdsourced results were only obtained for events with at least 30 tweets in order to match the evaluation carried out in [15], however the collection based evaluation was carried out on events with

Table 2. The types of event broken down by category [15] which our entity-based approach was able to detect in events with at least 30 tweets.

Category	Events	Recall
Armed Conflicts & Attacks	51	0.520
Arts, Culture & Entertainment	12	0.226
Business & Economy	9	0.391
Disasters & Accidents	13	0.448
Law, Politics & Scandals	54	0.386
Miscellaneous	4	0.190
Science & Technology	4	0.250
Sports	47	0.373

at least 75 tweets as this gave the highest F1 measure. For a direct comparison to the crowdsourced evaluation, an automatic evaluation on events with at least 30 tweets results in a precision of 0.200 and recall of 0.383, substantially below the precision of 0.636 found using crowdsourcing. We discuss possible reasons for this in Section 5.3.

Table 2 shows the breakdown of the events detected by our baseline run for events with at least 30 tweets. Our approach seems to be most effective at detecting events categorized as "Disasters & Accidents" ($R = 0.448$) and "Armed Conflicts & Attacks" ($R = 0.520$). This is extremely promising as these are the types of event that are most likely to benefit from citizen journalism and the use of social media. The ability to find and post information about these types of event can be crucial, and is one of main motivations for event detection on Twitter. Our approach also seems to be effective at detecting events categories as "Sports" ($R = 0.373$), "Business & Economy" ($R = 0.391$), and "Law, Politics & Scandals" ($R = 0.386$). Law, Politics & Scandals, as well as the Sports events make up over 50% of the total events in the collection, so given our approaches high recall, it is not surprising to find that it performs well on events in these categories. This is most likely due to a number of factors. Firstly, these types of event tend to focus on a small number of easily identified entities, such as sports teams or politicians. Secondly, these types of event are of interest to a large number of people, making them more likely to burst and be detectable, with sports events in particular being well suited to discussion on social media.

Our approach performs worst on "Miscellaneous" ($R = 0.190$), "Arts, Culture & Entertainment" ($R = 0.226$), and "Science & Technology" ($R = 0.250$) events. The low recall for science and technology events can be somewhat explained by a lack of easily detectable named entities, particularity for science events, such as "Astronomers detect what appears to be light from the first stars in the universe". Certainly, of the 21 Miscellaneous events, 10 of them have fewer than 15 tweets in the relevance judgments which contain named entities. This lack of named entities makes miscellaneous very difficult to detect for our approach, and the effect is examined in detail in Section 5.1.

5.1   Effect of Named Entities

One of the concerns using our entity-based approach is tweet recall. Since we discard any tweets without named entities we must examine the impact this has on both our tweet and event recall. Running the Stanford POS Tagger and NER over tweets from the relevance judgments from [15] shows that 47.4% of event-related tweets contain at least one named entity. This is promising, and considerably higher than the 11% of tweets that contain name entities across the collection as a whole, confirming our hypothesis that there is a relationship between entities and events. Our approach achieves a tweet recall of 0.242 across the events it detects (0.511 if we measure only against tweets which contain named entities). However, even if we were to detect every event in the collection, we could never achieve a tweet recall above 47.6%. Some of this is likely down to the difficulty of NER on Twitter, as noted by Li et al. [13], and could be improved with better NER models for Twitter. However, it is likely that the majority of tweets do not contain named entities, meaning that we must consider the effect this has on detection effectiveness – if an event has very few or no tweets with named entities then our approach will be unable to detect them.

Of the 506 events[15], 14 have fewer than 5 relevance judgments, 42 have fewer than 15, and 72 have fewer than 30. In addition, 41 events in the relevance judgments have fewer than 5 tweets with entities, 109 events have fewer than 15, and 163 have fewer than 30. For those 41 events with fewer than 5 tweets containing entities, even if our system was to perform perfectly, we would be unable to detect them – that accounts for just over 8% of all the events in the collection. However, given than these events on average contain just 32 tweets, it seems unlikely that they are of any real-world significance.

5.2   Nouns, Verbs, Hashtags and Retweets

Table 3 shows the effect of using different terms combinations for clustering. Note that for verb only clustering, named entities were still used, despite being classified as proper nouns. This is because our clustering and event merging approaches require them to work, however we feel that conclusions drawn from the result of this run are still valid and can be used to provide insight. The use of only nouns gives the highest recall but the lowest precision ($F1 = 0.249$), whereas using verbs only results in the lowest recall but the highest precision.

Table 3. The effect of using different combinations of nouns (NN), verbs (VB) and hashtags (HT) as terms for clustering on events with at least 30 tweets.

POS	Precision	Recall	F1
NN Only	242/1324 (0.183)	198/506 (0.391)	0.249
VB Only	196/912 (0.215)	165/506 (0.326)	0.259
NN, VB	242/1210 (0.200)	194/506 (0.383)	0.263
NN, VB, HT	232/1174 (0.198)	192/506 (0.379)	0.260

Using both nouns and verbs seems to take best the characteristic of both, giving the highest F1 measure. The high recall associated with nouns fits with our hypothesis that events are about entities, as named entities are proper nouns, and entity classes (i.e. city, person, plant) are common nouns. If nouns had not been used to describe these events then we would not have been able to detect them. This is again reflected in the low recall when using only verbs, and we suspect that had named entities (i.e. proper nouns) not been used, then the recall would be even lower.

The use of Hashtags seems to cause a small but insignificant reduction in both precision and recall, a somewhat unexpected result, as Hashtags are commonly thought to be very good indicators for the topic of a tweet. We hypothesis that this is due to the specificity of named entity, and by requiring every tweet to contain a named entity, we are removing the topical uncertainty and rendering Hashtags redundant as an indicator of topic. The use of retweets has a significant impact, reducing precision from 0.200 to 0.063. The use of retweets does provide a small, but insignificant increase in recall (0.390), and can likely be attributed to a 60% increase in the average number of tweets per event from 125 to 198, creating many events with more than 30 tweets. These findings are somewhat unsurprising as retweets have previously been associated with the spread of spam and require little effort to produce.

5.3 Evaluation Measures

Event detection on Twitter is a relatively new task, with very little work looking at how to perform reproducible and reliable evaluations. The work in this paper presents, to the best of our knowledge, the first evaluation of an event detection approach on a large-scale, publicly available dataset, and as such it is important to examine our choice of evaluation measures and thresholds. In this work, we required that at least 5% or at least 15 tweets in a candidate event must be relevant to a single event from the relevance judgments for it to be considered detected. The rational for this is two-fold. Firstly, it is impossible that the collection has judgments for every event which occurred over the 28 days it covers. Even for events which are in the collection, it is unlikely to have complete coverage of all relevant tweets. Secondly, because automated methods were used to generate the events, each with differing levels of granularity, there are a number of events in the judgments where only part of an event has been detected (for example, a single goal in a football matcher, rather than the football match itself). This means that a high threshold will make it difficult for an event to be relevant if the system has detected a "full" event rather than the specific sub-event which the collection has judgments for. While this may seem like a somewhat low threshold, we feel that it is reasonable, and by comparing the precision of our approach using the collection (0.200) and using crowdsourcing (0.636), it is clear that it does not result in an overestimate of precision.

6 Conclusion

In this paper, we proposed a novel, efficient, real-time, event detection approach for Twitter using the role that named entities play in events. We used a clustering technique which partitions tweets based upon the entities they contain, burst detection and cluster selection techniques to extract clusters related to ongoing real-world events. We demonstrated that our approach is able to outperform state-of-the-art approaches, whilst retaining a very low computational complexity and guaranteeing real-time performance. We found that nouns and verbs have significant roles in determining recall and precision respectively, and that Twitter-specific features seem to have either no effect or a detrimental effect on detection performance when using our entity-based approach.

References

1. Aggarwal, C.C., Subbian, K.: Event detection in social streams. In: Proc. of SDM Conference (2012)
2. Allan, J., Harding, S., Fisher, D., Bolivar, A., Guzman-Lara, S., Amstutz, P.: Taking topic detection from evaluation to practice. In: HICSS 2005. IEEECS, Washington, D.C. (2005)
3. Allan, J., Lavrenko, V., Jin, H.: First story detection in TDT is hard. In: CIKM 2000, pp. 374–381. ACM, New York (2000)
4. Allan, J., Lavrenko, V., Malin, D., Swan, R.: Detections, bounds, and timelines: UMass and TDT-3. In: TDT-3 Workshop (2000)
5. Atefeh, F., Khreich, W.: A survey of techniques for event detection in twitter. Computational Intelligence (2013)
6. Becker, H., Naaman, M., Gravano, L.: Beyond trending topics: real-world event identification on twitter. In: ICWSM 2011 (2011)
7. Choudhury, S., Breslin, J.G.: Extracting semantic entities and events from sports tweets. In: Proceedings of #MSM2011 at ESWC (2011)
8. Derczynski, L., Ritter, A., Clark, S., Bontcheva, K.: Twitter part-of-speech tagging for all: overcoming sparse and noisy data. In: ICRA-NLP (2013)
9. Hu, M., Liu, S., Wei, F., Wu, Y., Stasko, J., Ma, K.-L.: Breaking news on twitter. In: CHI 2012. ACM, New York (2012)
10. Kumaran, G., Allan, J.: Text classification and named entities for new event detection. In: SIGIR 2004, pp. 297–304. ACM, New York (2004)
11. Kumaran, G., Allan, J.: Using names and topics for new event detection. In: HLT 2005, pp. 121–128. ACL, Stroudsburg (2005)
12. Kwak, H., Lee, C., Park, H., Moon, S.: What is twitter, a social network or a news media? In: WWW 2010. ACM, New York (2010)
13. Li, C., Weng, J., He, Q., Yao, Y., Datta, A., Sun, A., Lee, B.-S.: Twiner: named entity recognition in targeted twitter stream. In: SIGIR (2012)
14. Liu, X., Zhang, S., Wei, F., Zhou, M.: Recognizing named entities in tweets. In: HLT 2011. ACL, Stroudsburg (2011)
15. McMinn, A.J., Moshfeghi, Y., Jose, J.M.: Building a large-scale corpus for evaluating event detection on twitter. In: CIKM 2013. ACM (2013)
16. Osborne, M., Petrovic, S., McCreadie, R., Macdonald, C., Ounis, I.: Bieber no more: first story detection using twitter and wikipedia. In: SIGIR 2012 Workshop TAIA (2012)

17. Ozdikis, O., Senkul, P., Oguztzn, H.: Semantic expansion of tweet contents for enhanced event detection in twitter. In: ASONAM. IEEE CS (2012)
18. Petrović, S., Osborne, M., Lavrenko, V.: Streaming first story detection with application to twitter. In HLT 2010. ACL (2010)
19. Pukelsheim, F.: The three sigma rule. The American Statistician **48**(2), 88–91 (1994)
20. Ritter, A., Mausam, Etzioni, O., Clark, S.: Open domain event extraction from twitter. In: Proceedings of ACM SIGKDD 2012. ACM (2012)
21. Sankaranarayanan, J., Samet, H., Teitler, B., Lieberman, M., Sperling, J.: Twitterstand: news in tweets. In: ACM SIGSPATIAL 2009 (2009)
22. Yang, Y., Pierce, T., Carbonell, J.: A study of retrospective and on-line event detection. In: SIGIR 1998, pp. 28–36. ACM, New York (1998)
23. Yang, Y., Zhang, J., Carbonell, J., Jin, C.: Topic-conditioned novelty detection. In: ACM CIKM 2002, pp. 688–693 (2002)

A Comparative Study of Click Models
for Web Search

Artem Grotov, Aleksandr Chuklin, Ilya Markov[(✉)], Luka Stout,
Finde Xumara, and Maarten de Rijke

University of Amsterdam, Amsterdam, The Netherlands
{a.groto,a.chuklin,i.markov,derijke}@uva.nl, lukastout@gmail.com,
finde.findexumara@student.uva.nl

Abstract. Click models have become an essential tool for understanding user behavior on a search engine result page, running simulated experiments and predicting relevance. Dozens of click models have been proposed, all aiming to tackle problems stemming from the complexity of user behavior or of contemporary result pages. Many models have been evaluated using proprietary data, hence the results are hard to reproduce. The choice of baseline models is not always motivated and the fairness of such comparisons may be questioned. In this study, we perform a detailed analysis of all major click models for web search ranging from very simplistic to very complex. We employ a publicly available dataset, open-source software and a range of evaluation techniques, which makes our results both representative and reproducible. We also analyze the query space to show what type of queries each model can handle best.

1 Introduction

Modeling user behavior on a search engine result page (SERP) is important for understanding users, supporting simulation experiments [12,11], evaluating web search results [1,4] and improving document ranking [2,7]. In recent years, many models of user clicks in web search have been proposed [3]. However, no comprehensive evaluation of these click models has been performed using publicly available datasets and a common set of metrics with a focus on an analysis of the query space. As a result, it is not clear what the practical advantages and drawbacks are of each proposed model, how different models compare to each other, which model should be used in which settings, etc.

In this paper we aim to compare the performance of different click models using a common dataset, a unified implementation and a common set of evaluation metrics. We consider all major click models for web search ranging from simple the Click-Through Rate model (CTR), Position-Based Model (PBM) and Cascade Model (CM) [5] through the more advanced Dependent Click Model (DCM) [10] to more complex User Browsing Model (UBM) [8], Dynamic Bayesian Network model (DBN) [2], and Click Chain Model (CCM) [9].

A. Chuklin—Currently at Google Switzerland.

© Springer International Publishing Switzerland 2015
J. Mothe et al. (Eds.): CLEF 2015, LNCS 9283, pp. 78–90, 2015.
DOI: 10.1007/978-3-319-24027-5_7

Table 1. Notation used in the paper.

Symbol	Description	Symbol	Description
u	A document	E	A random variable for document examination
q	A query	R	A random variable for document relevance
s	A search query session	C	A random variable for a click on a document
j	A document rank	ϵ	The examination parameter
c	A click on a document	r	The relevance parameter
$\mathcal{S}$	A set of sessions		

These models are evaluated using log-likelihood, perplexity, click-through rate prediction, relevance prediction, ranking performance and computation time.

We also analyze two different factors that influence performance of click models, namely, query frequency and click entropy. Intuitively, it is easier to predict clicks for frequent queries than for less frequent ones because of the larger size of the training data and the relatively more uniform click patterns associated with frequent queries. Click entropy can be used to distinguish between navigational and informational queries. Navigational queries tend to have low click entropy (usually only the top result is clicked), while informational queries tend to have high click entropy (several results may be clicked before a user's information need is satisfied).

Our main finding is that no single model excels on each of the considered metrics and that sometimes simple models outperform complex ones and that the relative performance of models can be influenced by the data set characteristics such as query frequency and click entropy. These results can guide the application of existing click models and inform the development of new click models.

2 Click Models

In this section, we give an overview of all major click models for web search, which we will then use in our comparative study

Click-Through Rate Models. Three simple click models, all based on click-through rates, predict click probabilities by counting the ratio of clicks to the total number of impressions. In the simplest case of Global CTR (GCTR) this ratio is computed globally for all documents, while in Rank CTR (RCTR) it is computed separately for each rank j and in Document CTR (DCTR) for each document-query pair uq:

$$P_{GCTR}(C_u = 1) = r = \frac{1}{\sum_{s \in \mathcal{S}} |s|} \sum_{s \in \mathcal{S}} \sum_{u \in s} c_{uq} \tag{1}$$

$$P_{RCTR}(C_{u_j} = 1) = r_j = \frac{1}{|\mathcal{S}|} \sum_{s \in \mathcal{S}} c_j \tag{2}$$

$$P_{DCTR}(C_u = 1) = r_{uq} = \frac{1}{|\mathcal{S}_{uq}|} \sum_{s \in \mathcal{S}_{uq}} c_{uq}, \text{ where, } \mathcal{S}_{uq} = \{s_q : u \in s_q\} \tag{3}$$

Position-Based Model. This model builds upon the CTR models and unites DCTR with RCTR. It adds a separate notion of examination probability (E)

which is subject to *position bias* where documents with smaller rank are examined more often; the document can only be clicked if it was examined and is relevant:

$$C_{uq} = 1 \Leftrightarrow (E_{j_u} = 1 \text{ and } R_{uq} = 1) \tag{4}$$

The examination probability $\epsilon_j = P(E_{j_u} = 1)$ depends on the rank j, while the relevance $r_{uq} = P(R_{uq} = 1)$ depends on the document-query pair. Inference of this model is done using the Expectation Maximization algorithm (EM).

Cascade Model. The Cascade Model [5, CM] is another extension to the CTR models. The model introduces the *cascade hypothesis*, whereby a user examines a search result page (SERP) from top to bottom, deciding whether to click each result before moving to the next one; users stop examining a SERP after first click. Inference of the parameters of CM is done using Maximum Likelihood Estimation (MLE). The click probability is defined using the examination (4) and the cascade assumptions:

$$P(E_1 = 1) = 1 \tag{5}$$
$$P(E_j = 1 \mid E_{j-1} = e, C_{j-1} = c) = e \cdot (1 - c), \tag{6}$$

where e and c are 0 or 1, and the only parameters of the models are $r_{uq} = P(R_{uq} = 1)$. The fact that users abandon a search session after the first click implies that the model does not provide a complete picture of how multiple clicks arise in a query session and how to estimate document relevance from such data.

User Browsing Model. [8] propose a click model called the User Browsing Model (UBM). The main difference between UBM and other models is that UBM takes into account the distance from the current document u_j to the last clicked document $u_{j'}$ for determining the probability that the user continues browsing:

$$P(E_{j_u} = 1 \mid C_{u_{j'}} = 1, C_{u_{j'+1}} = 0, \ldots, C_{u_{j-1}q} = 0) = \gamma_{jj'}. \tag{7}$$

Dependent Click Model. The Dependent Click Model (DCM) by [10] is an extension of the cascade model that is meant to handle sessions with multiple clicks. This model assumes that after a user clicked a document, they may still continue to examine other documents. In other words, (6) is replaced by

$$P(E_j = 1 \mid E_{j-1} = e, C_{j-1} = c) = e \cdot (1 - c + \lambda_j c), \tag{8}$$

where λ_j is the continuation parameter, which depends on the rank j of a document.

Click Chain Model. [9] further extend the idea of DCM into the Click Chain Model (CCM). The intuition behind CCM is that the chance that a user continues after a click depends on the relevance of the previous document and that a user might abandon the search after a while. This model can be formalized with (4) and the following conditional probabilities:

$$P(E_{j_u+1} = 1 \mid E_{j_u} = 1, C_{uq} = 0) = \tau_1 \tag{9}$$
$$P(E_{j_u+1} = 1 \mid E_{j_u} = 1, C_{uq} = 1) = \tau_2(1 - r_{uq}) + \tau_3 r_{uq}. \tag{10}$$

Dynamic Bayesian Network Model. The Dynamic Bayesian Network model [2] takes a different approach in extending the cascade model. Unlike CCM, DBN assumes that the user's perseverance after a click depends not on the relevance r_{uq}, but on a different parameter s_{uq} called satisfaction parameter. While r is mostly defined by the snippet on the SERP, the satisfaction parameter s depends on the actual document content available after a click. The DBN model is defined by (4) and the following formulas:

$$P(E_{j_u+1} = 1 \mid E_{j_u} = 1, C_{uq} = 0) = \gamma \tag{11}$$

$$P(E_{j_u+1} = 1 \mid E_{j_u} = 1, C_{uq} = 1) = \gamma(1 - s_{uq}), \tag{12}$$

where γ is a continuation probability after a non-satisfactory document (either no click, or click, but no satisfaction).

In general, the inference should be done using the EM algorithm. However, if γ is set to 1, the model allows easy MLE inference. We refer to this special case as the Simplified DBN model (SDBN).

3   Evaluation Measures

Different studies use different metrics to evaluate click models [3]. In this section we give an overview of these metrics. We will then use all of them in our comparative study.

Log-likelihood. Log-likelihood evaluates how well a model approximates observed data. In our case, it shows how well a click model approximates clicks of actual users. Given a model M and a set of observed query sessions $\mathcal{S}$, log-likelihood is defined as follows:

$$\mathcal{LL}(M) = \sum_{s \in \mathcal{S}} \log P_M(C_1, \ldots, C_n), \tag{13}$$

where P_M is the probability of observing a particular sequence of clicks $C_1, \ldots, C_n$ according to the model M.

Perplexity. Perplexity measures how surprised a model is to see a click at rank r in a session s [8]. It is calculated for every rank individually:

$$p_r(M) = 2^{-\frac{1}{|\mathcal{S}|} \sum_{s \in \mathcal{S}} \left(c_r^{(s)} \log_2 q_r^{(s)} + \left(1 - c_r^{(s)}\right) \log_2 \left(1 - q_r^{(s)}\right) \right)}, \tag{14}$$

where $c_r^{(s)}$ is the actual click on the document at rank r in the session s, while $q_r^{(s)}$ is the probability of a user clicking the document at rank r in the session s as predicted by the model M, i.e., $q_r^{(s)} = P_M(C_r = 1)$.

The total perplexity of a model is defined as the average of perplexities over all positions. Lower values of perplexity correspond to higher quality of a click model.

Click-trough Rate Prediction. Click-through rate (CTR) is a ratio of the cases when a particular document was clicked to the cases when it was shown. In [2], the following procedure was proposed to measure the quality of click models using CTRs:

- Consider a document u that appears both on the first position and on some other positions (in different query sessions).
- Hold out as a test set all the sessions in which u appears on the first position.
- Train a click model M on the remaining sessions.
- Use the model M to predict clicks on the document u on the held-out test set (predicted CTR).
- Compute the actual CTR of u on the held-out test set.
- Compute the Root-Mean-Square-Error (RMSE) between the predicted and actual CTRs.

Relevance Prediction. It was noticed in [2] that click models can approximate document relevance. A straightforward way to evaluate this aspect is to compare document relevance as predicted by a model to document relevance labels provided by human annotators. We measure the agreement between the two using the Area Under the ROC Curve (AUC) and Pearson correlation.

Predicted Relevance as a Ranking Feature. The predicted relevance can also be used to rank documents [2]. The performance of such a ranker can be evaluated using any standard IR measure, such as MAP, DCG, etc. In this study, we use NDCG@5 [13]. To calculate NDCG@5 we only consider documents for which we have relevance labels. The evaluation is performed as follows:
- Retrieve all sessions that have complete editorial judgments.
- Sort sessions by session id
- The first 75% are training sessions, the remainder are test sessions.
- Train the model on the training sessions and predict relevance for the test sessions.
- Sort the documents w.r.t the predicted relevance given by the model.
- Compute the NDCG@5.
- Average over all sessions.

Computation Time. Historically, in machine learning a big problem in creating accurate models was the amount of data that was available. However, this is no longer the case, and now we are mostly restricted by the time it takes to learn a model based on a large amount of available data. This makes the ability to efficiently compute parameters an important feature of a successful model. Therefore, we also look at the time it takes to train a click model.

4   Experimental Setup

Our goal is to evaluate and compare the click models presented in Section 2 using the evaluation metrics described in Section 3. To this end we use the first 32 million query sessions from the 2011 Yandex Relevance Prediction contest.[1] In this contest participants were asked to predict document relevance based on click log data. We split the session set into 32 batches of one million sessions each and measured, for every click model, the log-likelihood, perplexity, RMSE of

---

[1] http://imat-relpred.yandex.ru/en/datasets

CTR prediction and computation time for each of the batches. Then we average the measurements across the batches.

The sessions in each batch are sorted based on their session id and divided into a set of training sessions used to train the click models and a set of test sessions used in the evaluation of the models; the number of sessions in these sets have a 3 to 1 ratio.

To measure the quality of relevance prediction and ranking performance we use sessions for which all the documents have relevance labels. For each query all except the last session is used for training and the last session is used for testing. There are 860861 search sessions and 178 unique queries in the training set and 112 queries in the test set.

To determine whether observed differences are statistically significant we use the two-tailed student-t test with p values below 0.05 indicating significant differences. The error bars in the plots below are standard errors of the means.

Performance Impacting Factors. To evaluate the effect of *query frequency* on click model performance, we split the data into four parts (see Table 2).

Another factor that may influence click model performance is *click entropy*. Click entropy has been used to analyze queries in [6]. The formal definition of the entropy of query q is:

$$ClickEntropy(q) = -\sum_{d \in \mathcal{P}(q)} P(d \mid q) \log_2 P(d \mid q) \tag{15}$$

where $\mathcal{P}(q)$ are documents clicked on for query q and $P(d \mid q)$ is the fraction of clicks on document d among all clicks on q, $P(d \mid q) = \sum_p c_{r_d}^{(q)} \cdot (\sum_{u \in \mathcal{P}(q)} c_{r_u}^{(q)})^{-1}$. Click entropy can be used to distinguish navigational and informational queries. In navigational queries users know what they are looking for so the click entropy will be low because almost all clicks within that query will be on the same document. In an informational query the users explore different results to find the optimal one because they do not know what document they are looking for yet. This gives these queries a high click entropy. We divide our search sessions into three bins with respect to click entropy and report on evaluation measures per bin; statistics of these bins are listed in Table 3.

Table 2. The distribution of session with respect to query frequency.

Query frequency	Number of sessions
2	6944438
3–5	12750938
6–19	16592812
20+	108132750

Table 3. The distribution of session with respect to click entropy.

Click entropy	Number of sessions
0–1	53380500
1–2	48844812
2+	42195625

5   Results

In this section we present the results of our experiments. For every evaluation measure we report the influence of the query frequency and click entropy. Table 4

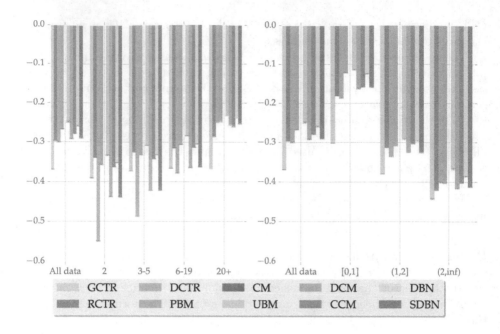

Fig. 1. Log-likelihood of click models, grouped by query frequency (left) and click entropy (right).

contains the evaluation outcomes for every model when trained on the entire dataset.

Log-likelihood. Figure 1 shows the results of the log-likelihood experiments; shorter bars indicate better results. The cascade model (CM) cannot handle multiple clicks in one session and gives zero probability to all clicks below the first one. For such sessions its log-likelihood is $\log 0 = -\infty$ and so the total log-likelihood of CM is $-\infty$.

When evaluated on the whole test set, UBM shows the best log-likelihood, followed by DBN, PBM and CCM. Note that the simplified DBN model (SDBN) has lower log-likelihood values compared to its standard counterpart (DBN). The simple CTR-based models show the lowest log-likelihood. This confirms that complex click models explain and approximate user behavior better than simply counting clicks.

Figure 1 (left) shows the log-likelihood of click models for different query frequencies. In general, the higher the query frequency (more training data available) the better the performance of click models. When comparing complex click models, there is variation in their relative performance based on the query frequency, but UBM consistently has the highest log-likelihood. SDBN and DCM have considerably lower log-likelihood than the similar models DBN and CCM (apart from the "20+" bin). In contrast, the log-likelihood of the CTR-based models varies considerably across query frequencies. On the "2" and "3–5" bins, GCTR outperforms SDBN and DCM, while RCTR is the second best model overall (after UBM). The DCTR model has the lowest log-likelihood for all query frequencies, but "20+". There, it outperforms SDBN, DCM and CCM and comes close to PBM. These results show two interesting facts. On the one hand, the log-likelihood of complex click models is more stable across different query frequencies than that of the CTR-based models. On the other hand, for each query frequency bin there is a CTR-based model that has log-likelihood scores comparable to complex models (RCTR for "2–19" and DCTR for "20+").

Figure 1 (right) shows the log-likelihood of click models for queries with different click entropy. In general, the lower the click entropy the easier it is to approximate clicks and, hence, the better the performance of click models. The relative log-likelihood of different click models for different values of click entropy is similar to that for different query frequencies: UBM is followed in different orders by DBN, PBM and CCM; SDBN and DCM have lower log-likelihood than the above; the log-likelihood of the CTR-based models varies across bins (RCTR is better than SDBN and DCM on $(1, 2]$, DCTR is comparable to PBM and CCM on $(2, \infty)$). As a future work, we plan to investigate the relation between query frequency and click entropy.

Perplexity. Figure 2 shows the perplexity of the click models; the lower the better. When evaluated on all test sessions, most of the complex click models (apart from CM and CCM) have comparable perplexity, with DBN and SDBN having the lowest one, but not significantly so. The CTR-based models have higher perplexity than the complex models, which again confirms the usefulness of existing click models for web search.

The trends for different query frequencies (Figure 2, left) are similar to those for log-likelihood (Figure 1, left): the variation of perplexity of complex click models is not large (but there are different winners on different bins), while the perplexity of the CTR-based models varies considerably (RCTR has the lowest perplexity overall on "2" and "3–5", DCTR is comparable to other models on "20+"). The trends for different values of click entropy are similar (see Figure 2, right). CM performs poorly in all query classes apart from the $[0, 1]$ entropy bin, which is related to the fact that CM is tuned to explain sessions with one click.

CTR Prediction. Figure 3 shows the impact of query frequency and click entropy on the CTR prediction task. Here, the simple models, RCTR and CM, outperform some of the more complex ones. This is because the intuition of these models is exactly what this task has set out to measure. The average rank of the documents in the training data set is 2.43, i.e., they were usually in some of the top positions. As the RCTR and CM models both perform well on documents that are ranked high, this high average rank influences the observed performance. The top performers on this task are sDBN and DCM. It is not clear why there is such a notable gap in performance between DBN and sDBN on this task; it could be speculated that DBN relies more on the satisfactoriness parameters that are not used in this task. Both UBM and PBM have poor performance on this task, we hypothesize that they rely even more on the position dependent

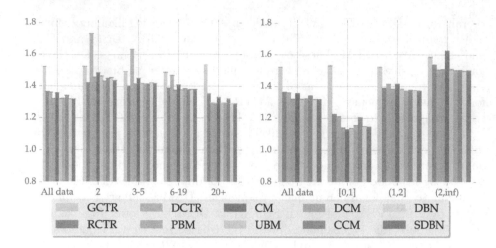

Fig. 2. Perplexity of click models, grouped by query frequency (left) and click entropy (right).

parameters and in this task the document under question was presented at a different position.

Relevance Prediction. The results of the relevance prediction task can be seen in Figure 4. The plot for different query frequencies could not be generated, because the queries with judged results do not occur often in the dataset, while the relevance prediction protocol only considers queries that occur at least ten times.

Table 4. Performance of click models according to various measures: log-likelihood ($\mathcal{LL}$), perplexity, RMSE of the CTR prediction task, AUC of the relevance prediction task, Pearson correlation between annotated relevances and predicted relevances, ranking performance (NDCG@5), and computation time. The symbol ▲ denotes a significant difference at $p = 0.01$ as measured by a two tailed t-test.

Model	$\mathcal{LL}$	Perplexity	RMSE	AUC	Pearson Correlation	NDCG@5	Time (sec.)
GCTR	-0.369	1.522	0.372	0.500	0.000	0.676	0.597
RCTR	-0.296	1.365	0.268	0.500	0.000	0.676	**0.589**▲
DCTR	-0.300	1.359	0.261	0.535	0.054	0.743	3.255
PBM	-0.267	1.320	0.354	**0.581**▲	0.128	0.727	34.299
CM	∞	1.355	0.239	0.515	0.024	0.728	4.872
UBM	**-0.249**▲	1.320	0.343	**0.581**▲	**0.130**▲	0.735	82.778
DCM	-0.292	1.322	**0.212**▲	0.516	0.035	0.733	5.965
CCM	-0.279	1.341	0.283	0.541	0.106	**0.748**	521.103
DBN	-0.259	**1.318**▲	0.286	0.517	0.089	0.719	457.694
SDBN	-0.290	**1.318**▲	**0.212**▲	0.529	0.076	0.721	3.916

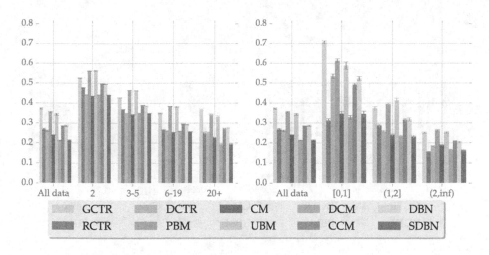

Fig. 3. Click-through rate prediction RMSE of click models, grouped by query frequency (left) and click entropy (right).

The relevance prediction performance of all click models is relatively low (between 0.500 and 0.581). The GCTR and RCTR models do not have a document-specific parameter and, thus, cannot predict relevance. So their AUC is equal to that of random prediction, i.e., 0.5. UBM and PBM have the highest AUC (0.581), while other models are closer to random prediction (from 0.515 for CM to 0.541 for CCM). These results show that existing click models still

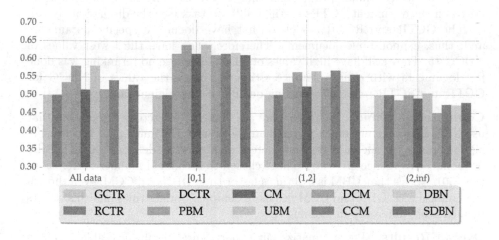

Fig. 4. Relevance prediction of click models on click entropy

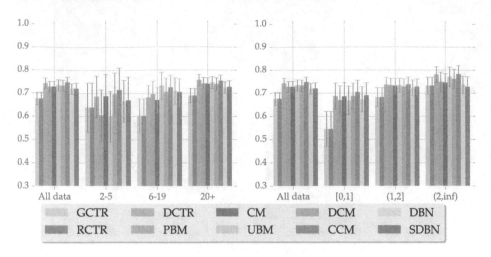

Fig. 5. Ranking performance (NDCG@5) of click models, grouped by query frequency (left) and click entropy (right).

have a long way to go before they can be used for approximating relevance labels produced by human annotators.

Predicted Relevance as a Ranking Feature. Figure 5 shows the results of using the predicted relevance as a ranking feature. The best model here is CCM, followed by the simple DCTR model. This is not surprising as relevant documents attract more clicks and usually have higher CTRs. Thus, ranking documents based on their CTR values only (as done by DCTR) results in high NDCG@5. Notice, though, that predicting actual relevance labels of documents based on the documents' CTRs is still a difficult task (see the discussion above).

The GCTR and RCTR models do not have document-specific parameters and, thus, cannot rank documents. Therefore, they have the lowest values of NDCG@5. They still have high values of NDCG because no reranking was done for documents with equal relevance estimates, hence the values of NDCG for GCTR and RCTR reflect the ranking quality of the original ranker.

Computation Time. In Table 4 we see that, as expected, the models that use MLE inference are much faster than those with EM inference. When using EM inference to calculate the parameters of a click model, one would ideally use some convergence criteria; we have chosen to do a fixed number of iterations (i.e., 50). Notice that UBM is 5–6 times faster than DBN and CCM, even though they all use EM. DBN and CCM use more complex update rules and this results in such a big difference in training time.

Overall Results. We summarize our experimental results in Table 4. There is no perfect click model that outperforms all other models on every evaluation metric. For example, UBM is the best in term of log-likelihood and relevance prediction, while DBN is the best in terms of perplexity and CTR prediction.

Even simple CTR-based models have relatively high performance according to some metrics (e.g., DCTR according to NDCG@5).

6 Conclusion

We have shown that a universal benchmark is necessary for developing and testing click models. The unified evaluation we performed gave important insights into how click models work. In particular, we found that complex click models dominate most of the evaluation metrics, however, in some cases simple click models outperform state-of-the-art models. We also found that none of the tested click models outperforms all others on all measures, e.g., DBN and sDBN are best when judged by perplexity, UBM is best when judged by likelihood, GCTR and RCTR are the fastest and CCM is best for ranking documents.

Our results suggest that different click models can excel at some tasks while having inferior performance at others. Hence, when introducing a new click model or improving an existing one it is important to keep in mind how it is going to be used. If a click model is going to be used for reranking, then the log-likelihood or the perplexity do not matter as much as the ability of the model to rerank documents, and if a click model is going to be used to understand user behavior, then the reranking performance is less important than its ability to explain observations as measured by log-likelihood and perplexity. It is not clear if a single click model can be designed to cater for all needs. Potentially optimizing the design of a click model to a particular use case may improve performance.

We also showed that considering query frequency and click entropy increases the amount of information that can be gained from click model evaluation. In some of the cases our findings were counter intuitive, e.g., higher query frequency did not always make log-likelihood higher. Also, when ranking models by performance, different rankings are observed depending on query frequency or click entropy. This again suggests that no single model can beat all other and that one may benefit from either designing different models for different settings or using an ensemble of models.

The CTR prediction task seems to mimic the behavior of perplexity at the first rank and as such does not give any additional insights into model performance. Relevance prediction also does not give any new insights, albeit for a different reason, the presence of a large set of unseen document-query pairs when evaluating the models.

Our evaluation only covers some of the many click models that have been proposed. The potential for future work is great in the sense that the same evaluation approach can be applied to other click models.

Acknowledgements. This research was supported by grant P2T1P2_152269 of the Swiss National Science Foundation, Amsterdam Data Science, the Dutch national program COMMIT, Elsevier, the European Community's Seventh Framework Programme (FP7/2007-2013) under grant agreement nr 312827 (VOX-Pol), the ESF Research Network Program ELIAS, the HPC Fund, the Royal Dutch Academy of Sciences (KNAW) under the Elite Network Shifts project, the Microsoft Research PhD program, the Netherlands eScience Center under project number 027.012.105, the Netherlands Institute for Sound and Vision, the Netherlands Organisation for Scientific Research (NWO) under project nrs 727.011.005, 612.001.116, HOR-11-10, 640.006.013, 612.066.930, CI-14-25, SH-322-15, and the Yahoo! Faculty Research and Engagement Program.

All content represents the opinion of the authors which is not necessarily shared or endorsed by their respective employers and/or sponsors.

References

1. Chapelle, O., Metzler, D., Zhang, Y., Grinspan, P.: Expected reciprocal rank for graded relevance. In: CIKM 2009, pp. 621–630 (2009)
2. Chapelle, O., Zhang, Y.: A dynamic bayesian network click model for web search ranking. In: WWW 2009, pp. 1–10 (2009)
3. Chuklin, A., Markov, I., de Rijke, M.: Click Models for Web Search. Morgan & Claypool (2015)
4. Chuklin, A., Serdyukov, P., de Rijke, M.: Click model-based information retrieval metrics. In: SIGIR 2013, pp. 493–502 (2013)
5. Craswell, N., Zoeter, O., Taylor, M., Ramsey, B.: An experimental comparison of click position-bias models. In: WSDM 2008, pp. 87–94 (2008)
6. Dou, Z., Song, R., Wen, J.R., Yuan, X.: Evaluating the effectiveness of personalized web search. IEEE TKDE 21(8), 1178–1190 (2009)
7. Dupret, G., Liao, C.: A model to estimate intrinsic document relevance from the clickthrough logs of a web search engine. In: WSDM 2010, pp. 181–190 (2010)
8. Dupret, G.E., Piwowarski, B.: A user browsing model to predict search engine click data from past observations. In: SIGIR 2008, pp. 331–338 (2008)
9. Guo, F., Liu, C., Kannan, A., Minka, T., Taylor, M., Wang, Y.M., Faloutsos, C.: Click chain model in web search. In: WWW 2009, pp. 11–20 (2009)
10. Guo, F., Liu, C., Wang, Y.M.: Efficient multiple-click models in web search. In: WSDM 2009, pp. 124–131 (2009)
11. Hofmann, K., Schuth, A., Whiteson, S., de Rijke, M.: Reusing historical interaction data for faster online learning to rank for IR. In: WSDM 2013, pp. 183–192 (2013)
12. Hofmann, K., Whiteson, S., de Rijke, M.: A probabilistic method for inferring preferences from clicks. In: CIKM 2011, pp. 249–258 (2011)
13. Järvelin, K., Kekäläinen, J.: Cumulated gain-based evaluation of IR techniques. ACM Transactions on Information Systems (TOIS) 20(4), 422–446 (2002)

Evaluation of Pseudo Relevance Feedback Techniques for Cross Vertical Aggregated Search

Hermann Ziak[(✉)] and Roman Kern

Know-Center GmbH, Inffeldgasse 13, 8010 Graz, Austria
{hziak,rkern}@know-center.at

Abstract. Cross vertical aggregated search is a special form of meta search, were multiple search engines from different domains and vary-ing behaviour are combined to produce a single search result for each query. Such a setting poses a number of challenges, among them the question of how to best evaluate the quality of the aggregated search results. We devised an evaluation strategy together with an evaluation platform in order to conduct a series of experiments. In particular, we are interested whether pseudo relevance feedback helps in such a sce-nario. Therefore we implemented a number of pseudo relevance feedback techniques based on knowledge bases, where the knowledge base is either Wikipedia or a combination of the underlying search engines themselves. While conducting the evaluations we gathered a number of qualitative and quantitative results and gained insights on how different users com-pare the quality of search result lists. In regard to the pseudo relevance feedback we found that using Wikipedia as knowledge base generally provides a benefit, unless for entity centric queries, which are targeting single persons or organisations. Our results will enable to help steering the development of cross vertical aggregated search engines and will also help to guide large scale evaluation strategies, for example using crowd sourcing techniques.

1 Introduction

Todays web users tend to always revert to the same sources of information[6] despite other potentially valuable sources of information exists. These sources are highly specialized in certain topics, but often left out since they are not familiar to the user. One key aspect to tackle this issue is to devise search methods that keep the users efforts minimal, where meta search serves as a starting point. This is motivated to improve the public awareness of systems in domains, which are considered to be niche areas by the general public, like cultural heritage or science. Meta search is the task of distributing a query to multiple search engines and combining their results into a single result list. In meta search there is usually no strict separation of domains, thus the results are expected to be homogeneous or even redundant, for example results from different web search engines. On the other hand vertical search engines try to combine results from sources of different domains. In our case these verticals or sources are highly specialized

© Springer International Publishing Switzerland 2015
J. Mothe et al. (Eds.): CLEF 2015, LNCS 9283, pp. 91–102, 2015.
DOI: 10.1007/978-3-319-24027-5_8

collections, for example medicine, business, history, art or science. These verticals might also differ in the type of items which are retrieved [3] (e.g. images, web pages, textual documents). An example of vertical search is the combination of results from an underlying images search with results from a traditional textual search. In our work we focus on cross vertical aggregated search engines [11], also known as multi domain meta search engines [14], where we do not make any assumptions about the domain of the individual sources. Hence, in such a scenario the challenges [11] of both types of aggregated search engines are inherited. In particular we are dealing with so called uncooperative sources, thus the individual search engines are treated as black boxes. The overall goal of our work is to gain a profound understanding on how to provide aggregated search results, which prove to be useful for the user. This directly addresses the question on how to assess this usefulness, i.e. how to evaluate such a system? The traditional approach for information retrieval evaluation follows the Cranfield paradigm [22]. Here the retrieval performance is assessed by a fixed set of relevant documents for each query and typically evaluated offline using mean average precision (MAP), normalized discounted cumulative gain (NDCG) or related measures. This type of evaluation does not appear to be appropriate, as it does not capture aspects like diversity, serendipity and usefulness of long-tail content which we consider to play an important role in our setting. Furthermore, these indicators are hard to measure since ground truth data is hard to create for cross vertical search systems where sources might be uncooperative. In order to fill this gap, we conducted user centred evaluations to get a better understanding of how users perceive search result lists and how to design evaluations in such a setting. In particular we are interested in how users evaluate longer result sets against each other, not only judging the top documents alone. Therefore we developed a dedicated evaluation tool allowing users to interactively vote for results which best match their expectations. The evaluation platform also allows us to evaluate the impact of different retrieval techniques: more specifically, the integration of pseudo relevance feedback. In pseudo relevance feedback the search is conducted two times. First the original query is issued and the top search hits are analysed. From those search hits a number of query term candidates are selected and added to the query. The expanded query is then used to generate the final search result list. As an extension to the basic procedure, the search engine for the first query might be different from the one of the second round. Thus different knowledge bases can be studied when used for the first search and how they impact the final results. Before conducting the actual evaluation, we did a preliminary test with few friendly users to fine tune the evaluation system. In our main evaluation we gathered qualitative insights and quantitative results, of the integration of pseudo relevance feedback into the retrieval process and whether it proves beneficial and helps to diversify results of specialized sources. Another outcome of our work is a guideline on how human intelligence tasks have to be designed for large scale evaluations on crowd-sourcing platforms like Amazon Mechanical Turk.

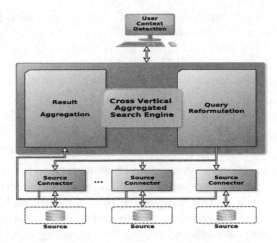

Fig. 1. Overview of the basic architecture of the whole system. In the *user context detection* component the query is extracted from the current user's context. The *cross vertical aggregated search engine* is the core of the system where queries are expanded and distributed to the sources. The *source connector* is responsible to invoke the source specific API and return the individual search results, which are finally merged by the *result aggregation* component

2 System Overview

Our cross vertical search algorithms are at the core of a bigger system, which is development within the EEXCESS[1] ("Enhancing Europes eXchange in Cultural Educational and Scientific reSources") project. The code is available under an open-source license[2]. An overview of the architecture is given in Figure 1. The vision of the project is to recommend high quality content of many sources to platforms and devices which are used on a daily basis for example in form of a browser add-on. In a traditional information retrieval setting the user is requested to explicitly state her information need, typically as a query consisting of a few keywords. We consider the case, where additionally to the explicit search capabilities, the information need is not explicitly given. In this case the query is automatically inferred from the current context, by the user context detection component [20]. Such a setting is also known as just-in-time information retrieval [18] and has a close connection to the field of recommender systems research. The search result list is continuously updated according to the users' interactions, for example when navigating from one web site to another. Next, the query is processed by the query reformulation step, where the query expansion takes place. Optionally one of the pseudo relevance feedback algorithms is applied to add related query terms to the original query. The query is then fed to

---

[1] http://eexcess.eu
[2] http://github.com/EEXCESS/recommender

all known sources, i.e. all search engines that are registered with the system, via source specific connectors. These source specific connectors then adapt the query to the source specific format and invoke the respective API calls, for example by the use of the Open Search API[3]. Finally, the results from all sources are collected and aggregated into a single search result list that is presented to the users.

3   System Details

The automatic query generation poses a set of challenges, as the true information need might be only partially present in these automatically inferred queries and might not cover the user's intent well. One approach to deal with such problems is to diversify results as suggested in the literature [19]. Diversification can be achieved by a number of methods, ranging from mining query logs to query reformulation strategies [17]. Other diversification techniques like IA-Select [1] rely on categorization of the query and the retrieved documents to greedily rearrange the given result lists. In the end, the final presented result should cover all topics of the query in proportion to its categories. Although we considered such approaches, we found that in our meta search environment some of the verticals returned insufficient information to do a categorization of the results. For example, digital libraries of images only supply short titles and no additional metadata. Farming query logs do also not apply to our scenario, as our system should also work with uncooperative sources. Another source of information are language models, which could provide benefit in the query expansion stage. One way to obtain a language model of an uncooperative source is probing. Here a number of search requests are issued to the individual sources to collect a sample set of the source's documents. Pass et al. [16] showed that an amount of about 30,000 to 60,000 documents are required for every source to get a decent representation of the source's language model. Again, such sampling methods will not work for our system for a number of reasons (e.g. the sources might restrict the number of API calls per day). Therefore we opted for an solution that does not rely on such datasets, namely pseudo relevance feedback with the help of knowledge bases.

3.1   Query Reformulation

We expect the user context detection component to produce short queries, which is an additional motivation to use query expansion as reformulation strategy. For the query expansion we followed the advise found in the literature. We limited the retrieved documents to the ten top-ranked documents as suggested by Montgomery et al. [15] to extract query expansion term candidates. Out of these documents we extracted the top terms and removed duplicate query terms. There are several suggestions on the number of query terms to be used for query

---

[3] http://www.opensearch.org/

expansion [4]. Harman [7] showed that after a certain amount of added expansion terms there is a drop in precision. Most recommendations vary from ten to twenty. We decided to use the twenty most frequent terms for our evaluation. Next, one needs to define which meta data fields to use when selecting the query expansion candidate terms. Most of our sources provide a description together with the title for each of their search results, while others just return the title. Existing work shows that using the title only might already result in a satisfying performance [4]. Therefore we opted to use just the title, even if a description is present for some of the search results. Another problem in pseudo relevance feedback is the so called query drift [12], where the additional terms introduced by the query expansion also cause a semantic drift away from the original user's information need. Shokouhi et al. [21] tackled this problem by running the query expansion separately for each source and using just the respective source to produce the candidate terms. They also pointed out one disadvantage of such a procedure: not all sources might be equally suited to produce expansion terms. In our case some of the sources return very sparse textual information (e.g. sources specialized on visual content with short similar titles). Here the query expansion algorithm will also pick semantically unrelated terms simply due to the data sparseness. Shokouhi, Azzopardi and Thomas [21] demonstrated that results could benefit from taking only selected sources for query expansion instead of following a global approach, where all sources are treated equally. Lynam et al. [13] showed that the extent to which a source is suited to serve as query expansion for other sources can be estimated by the performance benefit when used on itself. This implies that picking the source, which demonstrated the best result in a single search setting could also be a viable option to produce query expansion terms for other sources. This can be extended further, when an external knowledge base is used for query expansion, which is not actually used for the aggregated search. Finally, our system features three different strategies for query expansion together with a baseline.

No Query Expansion. In this setting, the query is not expanded and sent as it is to the sources - the baseline.

Multiple Sources. The multiple sources approach takes all sources into account by first retrieving a combined search result list of all sources using no query expansion. This initial aggregated result list is taken as input to compute and rank candidates for the query expansion step. Next, all sources are queried using these query terms.

Single Source. This approach is similar to the multiple sources approach but takes only a single, selected source into consideration. This source has been selected based on the observed behaviour when used to expand queries applied only on itself.

External Knowledge Base. For this query expansion strategy we used Wikipedia, which has already been used by existing research [8]. Motivated by the assumption raised by Cai et al. [4] regarding diverse content of web pages, we segmented Wikipedia pages into their main sections and indexed these sections as separate documents. For pseudo relevance feedback we ranked the terms contained in the top hits using the Divergence from Randomness approach [2]. Here, Wikipedia is not part of the sources which contribute to the final search result list.

3.2 Source Specific Query Reformulation

Every source may require a different, dedicated query language. Therefore the query has to be adopted specifically to the sources' capabilities. As a general strategy, we formulated the expanded query consisting of the original query terms as conjunction followed by the new terms as a disjunction query. We expect that this approach will generally produce satisfying results, although tweaking the query reformulation for every source would most likely provide benefit.

3.3 Result Aggregation

The final stage of our cross vertical aggregated search is the merging of the individual search results. Many different approaches have been proposed in the literature on how to combine search results from different sources [11,3]. For the evaluation we tried to keep the result aggregation as simple as possible to prevent any interference with the query expansion. Therefore we followed a simple round robin based approach. This is additionally motivated by our intention to keep the results deterministic and reproducible. Here results of all sources are combined, by picking the top ranked results of each list in a fixed sequence, i.e. first result of the first source followed by the first result of the second source.

4   Evaluation

The main goal of our evaluation was to arrive at a deeper understanding on how users judge the usefulness of the search results as produced by our system. Furthermore, we wanted to assess the impact of our pseudo relevance feedback configurations. Additionally, the evaluation should contribute to the understanding on how to design an evaluation for crowd-sourcing platform complementary to existing work in this area [9,10].

Evaluation Platform. We opted to build our own tool to conduct the user based evaluation, as this would allow us to control all parameters of the algorithms. See Figure 2 for a screenshot of the tool. The user is presented a fixed query together with an optional short description of the query and some background information. A number of different search result lists are presented next to each other. Now the user has to compare these search results and decide on a ranking

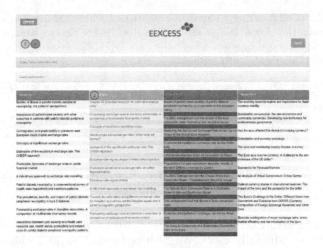

Fig. 2. Screenshot of the evaluation user interface, for the query "euro conversion rate". A total of four different search results are presented next to each other. The user already picked result list #3 (green) as the best and result list #2 (yellow) as the second best result. Third and fourth place are not decided yet.

of the lists. By clicking on the respective search result list, the user expresses her preference on the ranking of the results. Once the sequence is defined, the user is routed to the next query. All decisions of the user are recorded together with the consumed time for each task. In the design of the tool great attention has been dedicated to keep the results and behaviour of the tool deterministic and consistent. For example, the search result lists are identical for each user within one evaluation run. At the same time our tool is flexible enough to allow the search results to be configured on how they should look like. For example, they may contain an optional preview image, or may be composed of the title alone or a combination of the title plus a description. The individual search result lists are generated by different configurations of the pseudo relevance feedback techniques. The sequence, which technique comes first and so forth, has been randomly chosen to prevent any bias. The actual algorithm has been recorded by the tool, but not presented to the user. Thus no hints on the way the search result lists were generated are available to the user.

Query Selection. As input our evaluation tool requires a list of queries to be presented to the user. The query list was preselected by us. The decision to predefine queries was to create result lists with a balanced amount of results of each source which could not have been guaranteed otherwise. Thus we also did not follow the proposal of Diaz et al. [5], to give users the opportunity to commit own queries. Furthermore, in our system the user is typically not expected to manually define the query terms, as they should be automatically inferred from the current context. The final query terms were chosen from the AOL query

Table 1. Results of all four query expansion strategies, where the number indicates the accumulated rank, thus lower values are better. Results are also separated into entity-centric queries and topical queries, where the first type of query refers to individuals, organisation, and other types of entities.

Expansion Method	Overall Score	Entity-Centric Queries	Topical Queries
No QE	431	**103**	328
Multiple Sources	466	129	337
Selected Source	427	143	284
Wikipedia	**426**	155	**271**

log [16] and further individually selected to match the sources to prevent the search result to be dominated by specific sources.

Pre-test. Before starting the actual evaluation with our framework we conducted a small pre-test with friendly users. We gathered some insights, which allowed us to fine tune the evaluation tool and the procedure. In short the three main findings were: The results themselves should be uniformly presented. Thus, even if some results may provide an additional preview image or a rich textual description, it is preferable to stick with the smallest common denominator. Therefore in the evaluation just the title is displayed for all search results. A second result of the pre-test concerns the number of queries to be evaluated. Initially we have foreseen to have our users assess a total of 30 queries. Apparently, the introspection of the search results takes much time, therefore we reduced the number of queries to just 10 for the main evaluation. Finally, it has been observed that some of the sources also returned non-English results. Thus the feedback has been to filtered out these results and only keep English results.

Main Evaluation. The main evaluation took place during a computer science conference where we tried to motivate conference visitors to take part in the evaluation. From the visitors that were motivated enough to start the evaluation, a total of 20 managed to state their preference for all search result lists for all queries. Curious users were given a short background of the system and a brief introduction on the user interface. Apart from that, no hints were made by which means the search result lists should be measured. This has been done in order to prevent users to exert any bias. Comments and feedback from the users were collected in addition to the interactions recorded by the evaluation tool. Generally, none of the participants signalled having problems using the evaluation tool.

5   Results

Given the recordings of our tool and the feedback of the participants we can summarise the result in two ways, qualitatively and quantitatively. Finally, this allows us to provide a guideline on how our evaluation could be improved and how future evaluation should be designed.

5.1   Qualitative Evaluation

Users reported that deciding between results was often hard, since results appeared to be quite similar in many cases. The Krippendorff's Alpha as measure of disagreement lies between 0.66-0.78 for the different configurations. This agreement can only be considered as "fair", corroborating the subjective impression of the participants. This is also caused by the variety on how users conducted the process of comparing search result lists. Some users just focused on the top results, others picked the best overall result set studying each document in the lists. There does not appear to be a single, uniform strategy of users to assess search result lists. This could be also seen as an indicator why we observed a big variation of evaluation time, between 1 to 5 minutes per query. Further, since query terms where not randomized in our evaluation, studying each document might lead to a higher fatigue of the user and therefore might bias results. Generally, these results also hint that applying a form of personalisation on the search result to cater for the different assessment types. Some users showed a clear preference to result lists with more general top items, e.g. overview articles. One outcome of the qualitative evaluation suggests to design a system to have the first few search results to be of more general nature. This should maximise the chances that users perceive a search result as an appropriate response to the given query or information need. For our scenario of aggregating multiple sources, it appears to be advisable to reserve the first few spots of the aggregated search result to items from more generic sources, but allowing more specific sources to populate the remaining result list.

5.2   Quantitative Evaluation

Table 1 summarises the result from the recording of the evaluation tool and compares the four different pseudo relevance feedback strategies. The numbers represent the accumulated rank of the users' rating, hence a lower number indicates a preference for the respective configuration. Two of the three pseudo relevance feedback strategies yielded better results than the baseline without any query reformulation. The knowledge base setting using *Wikipedia* for query expansion appears to give the best overall results, followed closely by the *selected source* strategy although the distinctions are minimal. Though, when inspecting the result in more detail, we made an interesting observation. We discovered that there is a pronounced discrepancy between queries which can be described as entity-centric queries and topical queries. For entity-centric queries one would expect that there is a single, defining Wikipedia page, for example "Michelle Obama". For this kind of query, the query expansion using Wikipedia did not provide any benefit, in contrary it had a negative impact. This might be due to the way how the query expansion terms are constructed and that the terms used for expansion allow a too large query drift. From the result from the quantitative evaluation, one can conclude that pseudo relevance feedback might help, but not for all configurations and queries. Using Wikipedia as knowledge base demonstrated the best overall performance. For entity centric queries it is suggested to introduce a query pre-preprocessing where the type of a query is inferred and enable pseudo relevance feedback just for topical queries.

5.3 Evaluation Guideline

Taken from the feedback we got during the evaluation sessions we collected a number of criteria, which could guide future user based evaluations, that complement our findings:

- A clear rating strategy for comparing result lists should be defined prior to the task to prevent different rating schemes.
- Participants reported that it was often hard to decide between four lists. In particular if there were multiple similar sets for different configurations. Therefore only base line plus one of the configurations should be compared against.
- If one wants to research diversity or serendipity in result lists, the participants should be instructed to compare the entire result set, not just the first few items.
- The amount of queries judged by one user should be selected carefully. The judgement process may take longer than expected and workers tend to get indifferent later in the process, which might lead to randomly chosen results.
- To keep the task short one may consider using only the title of the search result. This requires the title to be informative enough, which might not always be the case.
- Introduce questions where participants have to give insights into their decision making process, similar to Kittur et al. [10]. This should also give the participants the impression that their decisions and answers will be examined closely and thus should help to improve the quality of their answers.

6 Conclusions and Future Work

In our evaluation we found that there is a large variety on how users assess the usefulness of search results, when they are not primed with a predefined scheme. Furthermore, users also showed a preference to more general search hits in the top results. Both findings can be exploited to improve future search systems, in particular for aggregated search scenarios. In our evaluation we found that different techniques for pseudo relevance feedback provide varying benefit. In particular, the use of Wikipedia as knowledge base and carefully selected single source approaches seem to be a sensible choice. In analysing the results, we found that queries should be pre-processed, whether they fall into the category of entity-centric queries or topical queries. In this case of entity-centric queries they should be processed differently to other types of queries. More research is needed to gain a deeper understanding why this kind of query does not respond well to be expanded and how an optimal strategy for query processing looks like. As future work we plan to follow our proposed guidelines in upcoming evaluations, in particular using crowd sourcing techniques. In particular we plan to extend the evaluation to study the impact of different aggregation methods and research on how to increase the diversity of search result, without negatively affecting the precision of the results.

Acknowledgments. The presented work was developed within the EEXCESS project funded by the European Union Seventh Framework Programme FP7/2007-2013 under grant agreement number 600601. The Know-Center is funded within the Austrian COMET Program - Competence Centers for Excellent Technologies - under the auspices of the Austrian Federal Ministry of Transport, Innovation and Technology, the Austrian Federal Ministry of Economy, Family and Youth and by the State of Styria. COMET is managed by the Austrian Research Promotion Agency FFG. We would also like to thank all our test users, who underwent the tedious job of scrutinising vast amounts of search results.

References

1. Agrawal, R., Gollapudi, S., Halverson, A., Ieong, S.: Diversifying search results. In: Proceedings of the Second ACM International Conference on Web Search and Data Mining, WSDM 2009, pp. 5–14. ACM, New York (2009)
2. Amati, G., Van Rijsbergen, C.J.: Probabilistic models of information retrieval based on measuring the divergence from randomness. ACM Transactions on Information Systems **20**(4), 357–389 (2002). http://doi.acm.org/10.1145/582415.582416
3. Arguello, J., Diaz, F., Callan, J., Carterette, B.: A methodology for evaluating aggregated search results. In: Clough, P., Foley, C., Gurrin, C., Jones, G.J.F., Kraaij, W., Lee, H., Mudoch, V. (eds.) ECIR 2011. LNCS, vol. 6611, pp. 141–152. Springer, Heidelberg (2011)
4. Cai, D., Yu, S., Wen, J.R., Ma, W.Y.: Block-based web search. In: Proceedings of the 27th Annual International ACM SIGIR Conference on Research and Development in Information Retrieval, pp. 456–463. ACM (2004)
5. Diaz, F., Allan, J.: When less is more: Relevance feedback falls short and term expansion succeeds at hard 2005. Tech. rep., DTIC Document (2006)
6. Gehlen, V., Finamore, A., Mellia, M., Munafò, M.M.: Uncovering the big players of the web. In: Pescapè, A., Salgarelli, L., Dimitropoulos, X. (eds.) TMA 2012. LNCS, vol. 7189, pp. 15–28. Springer, Heidelberg (2012)
7. Harman, D.: Relevance feedback and other query modification techniques (1992)
8. He, B., Ounis, I.: Combining fields for query expansion and adaptive query expansion. Information Processing & Management **43**(5), 1294–1307 (2007). http://linkinghub.elsevier.com/retrieve/pii/S0306457306001956
9. Kazai, G., Kamps, J., Koolen, M., Milic-Frayling, N.: Crowdsourcing for book search evaluation: impact of hit design on comparative system ranking. In: Proceedings of the 34th International ACM SIGIR Conference on Research and Development in Information Retrieval, SIGIR 2011, pp. 205–214. ACM, New York (2011). http://doi.acm.org/10.1145/2009916.2009947
10. Kittur, A., Chi, E.H., Suh, B.: Crowdsourcing user studies with mechanical turk. In: Proceedings of the SIGCHI Conference on Human Factors in Computing Systems, CHI 2008, pp. 453–456. ACM, New York (2008). http://doi.acm.org/10.1145/1357054.1357127

11. Kopliku, A., Pinel-Sauvagnat, K., Boughanem, M.: Aggregated search: A new information retrieval paradigm. ACM Computing Surveys (CSUR) **46**(3), 41 (2014)
12. Lam-Adesina, A.M., Jones, G.J.: Applying summarization techniques for term selection in relevance feedback. In: Proceedings of the 24th Annual International ACM SIGIR Conference on Research and Development in Information Retrieval, pp. 1–9. ACM (2001)
13. Lynam, T.R., Buckley, C., Clarke, C.L., Cormack, G.V.: A multi-system analysis of document and term selection for blind feedback. In: Proceedings of the 13th ACM International Conference on Information and Knowledge Management, pp. 261–269. ACM (2004)
14. Minnie, D., Srinivasan, S.: Meta search engines for information retrieval on multiple domains. In: Proceedings of the International Joint Journal Conference on Engineering and Technology (IJJCET 2011), pp. 115–118 (2011)
15. Montgomery, J., Si, L., Callan, J., Evans, D.: Effect of varying number of documents in blind feedback: analysis of the 2003 NRRC RIA workshop bfnumdocs experiment suite. In: Proceedings of the 27th Annual International ACM SIGIR Conference on Research and Development in Information Retrieval, SIGIR 2004 (2004)
16. Pass, G., Chowdhury, A., Torgeson, C.: A picture of search. In: Proceedings of the 1st International Conference on Scalable Information Systems, InfoScale 2006. ACM, New York (2006). http://doi.acm.org/10.1145/1146847.1146848
17. Radlinski, F., Dumais, S.: Improving personalized web search using result diversification. In: Proceedings of the 29th Annual International ACM SIGIR Conference on Research and Development in Information Retrieval, pp. 691–692. ACM (2006)
18. Rhodes, B.J.: Just-in-time information retrieval. Ph.D. thesis, Massachusetts Institute of Technology (2000)
19. Santos, R.L., Macdonald, C., Ounis, I.: Exploiting query reformulations for web search result diversification. In: Proceedings of the 19th International Conference on World Wide Web, pp. 881–890. ACM (2010)
20. Schlötterer, J., Seifert, C., Granitzer, M.: Web-based just-in-time retrieval for cultural content. In: PATCH14: Proceedings of the 7th International ACM Workshop on Personalized Access to Cultural Heritage (2014)
21. Shokouhi, M., Azzopardi, L., Thomas, P.: Effective query expansion for federated search. In: Proceedings of the 32th International ACM SIGIR Conference on Research and Development in Information Retrieval, SIGIR 2009, pp. 427–434. ACM, New York (2009). http://doi.acm.org/10.1145/1571941.1572015
22. Voorhees, E.M.: The philosophy of information retrieval evaluation. In: Peters, C., Braschler, M., Gonzalo, J., Kluck, M. (eds.) CLEF 2001. LNCS, vol. 2406, pp. 355–370. Springer, Heidelberg (2002)

Long Papers with Short Presentation

Analysing the Role of Representation Choices in Portuguese Relation Extraction

Sandra Collovini$^{(\boxtimes)}$, Marcelo de Bairros P. Filho, and Renata Vieira

Faculdade de Informática, Pontifícia Universidade Católica do Rio Grande do Sul -
PUCRS, Av. Ipiranga, Porto Alegre, RS 6681, Brazil
{sandra.abreu,marcelo.bairros}@acad.pucrs.br, renata.vieira@pucrs.br

Abstract. Relation Extraction is the task of identifying and classifying the semantic relations between entities in text. This task is one of the main challenges in Natural Language Processing. In this work, the relation extraction task is treated as sequence labelling problem. We analysed the impact of different representation schemes for the relation descriptors. In particular, we analysed the BIO and IO schemes performance considering a Conditional Random Fields classifier for the extraction of any relation descriptor occurring between named entities in the Organisation domain (Person, Organisation, Place). Overall, the classifier proposed here presents the best results using the IO notation.

Keywords: Natural Language Processing · Information Extraction · Relation extraction · Organisation domain · Portuguese language

1 Introduction

Relation Extraction (RE) is the task of identifying and classifying semantic relations that occur between entities recognized in a given text [13]. The ability to identify semantic relations in text can be useful in many Natural Language Processing tasks, such as Information Extraction, Information Retrieval, Text Summarization, Machine Translation, Question Answering, Thesaurus Construction, Semantic Network Construction, Word-Sense Disambiguation, Language Modelling, among others. Specifically, relation extraction from text is one of the main challenges in Information Extraction, given the required language knowledge and the sophistication of the employed language processing techniques.

The problem of relation extraction has been studied extensively from natural language texts, including news articles, science publications, blogs, e-mails, and resources like Wikipedia, Twitter, and the Web. There is an increasing interest in relation extraction, mostly motivated by the exponential growth of information made available through the Web, which makes the tasks of researching and using this massive amount of data impossible through manual means. That context makes relation extraction an even more complex and relevant research area.

Several approaches have been proposed to relation extraction from unstructured data. A very robust and generally applicable approach to the task of

© Springer International Publishing Switzerland 2015
J. Mothe et al. (Eds.): CLEF 2015, LNCS 9283, pp. 105–116, 2015.
DOI: 10.1007/978-3-319-24027-5_9

semantic relation classification is to use supervised classifiers. Among them stand out the sequential models, such as Hidden Markov Model (HMM), Maximum Entropy Markov Model (MEMM) or Conditional Random Fields (CRFs) model, which are very powerful for segmenting and labeling sequence data [14]. CRFs, the most sophisticated of the three families of models, have now become almost a standard for the task of Named Entity Recognition [16], and has more recently been applied to the task of relation extraction from text [11,2,15].

Another important question is the representation of the text segments that express the relations for the sequential models. In the literature there are works that study the performance on Named Entity Recognition task considering different encoding schemes [18,12]. The choice of the encoding scheme can have an impact on the system's performance. Ratinov and Roth in [18] compared the system performance with BILOU and BIO schemes, and show that the BILOU scheme significantly outperforms the widely adopted BIO scheme. Stanford NER [12] uses IO scheme to represent entities types, therefore it does not use the usually seen BIO scheme. The IO scheme is faster than the BIO scheme because it uses less labels, thus simplifying the classification. For the relation extraction task most of the works use BIO notation for sequence labeling [2,15,19].

In this paper, we analysed the impact of different representation schemes for the relation descriptors. Specifically, we evaluated the BIO and IO schemes performance considering a Conditional Random Fields classifier for the extraction of any relation descriptor occurring between named entities in the Organisation domain (Person, Organisation, Place) from Portuguese texts. We define relation descriptor as the text chunks that describe the explicit relation occurring between a pair of named entities in the sentence. For example, in the following sentence: *"Steve Jobs was a co-founder of Apple Inc."*, we can extract the relation descriptor *"co-founder"* that occurs between the named entities *"Steve Jobs"* and *"Apple Inc."* in this sentence.

This work is organized as follows. In Section 2, we review related work. The data annotation is described in Section 3. The proposed method is detailed in Section 4. In Section 5, we show the evaluation of our CRF classifier with the IO and BIO schemes, and discuss our results. We conclude in Section 6.

2   Related Work

Conditional Random Fields have been applied to a large variety of areas, including text processing, computer vision, and bioinformatics. Specifically, CRF model have been applied to many problems in NLP, including extraction of relations from text [11,2,15].

Among relation extraction applications stands out the O-CRF system based in CRF model [2]. The authors show that many relations can be categorized using a compact set of lexicon-syntactic patterns. Bellare and McCallum [4] extract 12 biographic relations by applying a CRF extractor trained from BibTeX records and research in articles citations. In [9] the CRF is applied to extract relations between knowledge elements, involving the relation types: *"preorder"*, *"illustration"*, and *"analogy"*. Culotta et al. [11] propose a CRF-based model for the extraction of familiar relations (mother, cousin, friend, education etc.) from biographical texts. Li et al. [15] also deal with familiar relations, they apply the CRF model for extraction of specific relations between two entities based on general relations.

Most of the relation extraction systems for Portuguese are based on rules and few external resources, such as Wikipedia and domain ontology, they usually do not make use of machine learning techniques, contrary to the situation for English [1]. The relevant systems for Portuguese that took part in the Recognition of Relation between Named Entities (ReRelEM) track of Second HAREM[1] are presented following.

The REMBRANDT (Recognition of Named Entities Based on Relations and Detailed Text Analysis) system [7] was developed to recognize all types of named entities and relations between them, using Portuguese Wikipedia and some grammar rules. The SeRELeP (System for Recognition of Relations for the Portuguese language) system [6] aimed at recognizing the relation types: *"identity"*, *"inclusion"* and *"placement"*, using the informations provided by PALAVRAS parser [5]. SEI-Geo [8], in contrast with the other systems, is focused on ontology enrichment. SEI-Geo is an extraction system that deals with NER concerning only the *Place* category and its relations, using Geo-ontologies. Also stands out the work of Batista et al. [3], which proposes an approach of distantly supervised relation extraction between two entities. The authors selected 10 relation types in articles written in Portuguese from Wikipedia, such as *"located-in"*, *"influenced-by"*, *"successor-of"*, and others.

In this work, we used a set of features for Portuguese language described in [10], which were based on previous works for the English language presented here to induce the CRF model for Portuguese. We defined the task of extracting relation descriptors from texts in Portuguese according to Li et al. [15]. The main challenge of our work is to extract relation descriptors that express any type of relation between the named entities in Portuguese (Organisation, Person and Place categories), differently from Li et al.'s work, in which the relation descriptors are extracted considering pre-defined types of relations (*"employment"* and *"personal/social"* relations). The following sentence fragment shows an example of relation descriptor : *"A Legião da Boa Vontade, instituição educacional, foi fundada em o Brasil"* (*"The Legião da Boa Vontade, educational institution, was founded in Brazil"*), where the relation descriptor *"fundada em o"* (*founded-in*) relates the named entities *"Legião da Boa Vontade"* and *"Brasil"*.

3   Data Annotation

In this work, we used a subset of the HAREMs Golden Collections[2] for Named Entity Recognition (NER). We only analysed texts that deal with the Organisation domain, such as opinion, journalistic, and political texts, among others. These texts already had the annotations of the named entities, and we opted

---

[1] http://www.linguateca.pt/LivroSegundoHAREM/
[2] http://www.linguateca.pt/harem/

for the categories Person, Organisation and Place; they were found to be the most relevant to the Organisation domain. A sum of 516 relation instances was selected to compound the reference corpus.

We added to these texts the annotation of the relation descriptors occurring between pairs of named entities (ORG-ORG, ORG-PERS, ORG-PLACE), considering only one pair of named entities by sentence of the texts. The manual annotation of the relation descriptors was performed by two linguists. The total number of relations and the number of positive and negative instances according to the categories of the pairs of named entities are summarized in Table 1. Positive instances are those that present an explicit relation descriptor between the two named entities. The small amount of instances is due to the difficulty in the manual annotation of the data. We can highlight the difficulty to determine which elements between the named entities are in fact part of the descriptor.

Table 1. Reference corpus.

NE categories	Relations	Positive instances	Negative instances
ORG-ORG	175	90	85
ORG-PERS	171	105	66
ORG-PLACE	170	109	61
TOTAL	**516**	**304**	**212**

In Table 2 are presented examples of positive instances expressing some relation types in the Organisation domain (i.e., expressing the type of activity realized by the Organisation, expressing an affiliation relation, and expressing an institutional bond relation). According to examples of relation instances, we can notice that the articles and prepositions were included in the descriptors.

The reference corpus has been automatically annotated on Part-Of-Speech (POS), syntactic and semantic information, with the PALAVRAS parser [5]. The example of output of the PALAVRAS is presented below, following the order: the word, the canonic form, semantic tag, POS tag, and syntactic information.

A [o] DET @>N
Legião=da=Boa=Vontade [Legião=da=Boa=Vontade] <inst> PROP @SUBJ>
,
instituição [instituição] N @N<PRED
educacional [educacional] ADJ @N<
,
foi [ser] V @FS-STA
fundada [fundar] V @ICL-AUX<
em [em] PRP @<PIV
o [o] DET @>N
Brasil [Brasil] <inst> PROP @P<

Table 2. Examples of the positive relation instances.

Relation instance	Relation descriptor
Goa Tourism Development Corporation Office **organiza excursões a** *Goa*	**organiza excursões a**
(*Goa Tourism Development Corporation Office* **organizes excursions to** *Goa*)	(**organizes excursions to**)
Confederação Brasileira de Cinofilia, **órgão filiado ao** *FCI*	**órgão filiado ao**
(*Confederação Brasileira de Cinofilia*, **agency affiliated to** *FCI*)	(**agency affiliated to**)
Steve Jobs, o **director-geral** da empresa, foi o ponto alto para os fãs da *Apple*	**director-geral**
(*Steve Jobs*, the **CEO** of the company, was the highest point for *Apple* fans)	(**CEO**)

4 Method

In this section we present the Conditional Random Fields model and data representation, as well as the used features.

4.1 Conditional Random Field Model

In this work, the relation extraction task was treated as a structured sequence labeling problem, thus, we chose to apply Conditional Random Fields (CRFs). CRFs have been applied in various sequential text processing tasks efficiently, including relation extraction [11,2,15,10].

According to [14], CRFs are undirected graphical models used to calculate the conditional probability of values on designated output nodes given values assigned to other designated input nodes. A conditional model specifies the probabilities of possible label sequences given an observation sequence. The conditional probability of the label sequence can depend on arbitrary, non-independent features of the observation sequence.

Initially, linear-chain CRFs were used to label and segment sequential data [14]. This type of CRF occurs when output nodes of the graphical model are linked by edges in a linear chain. Linear-chain CRFs can be understood as conditionally-trained Finite State Machines (FSMs). In order to define linear-chain CRF, let $\mathbf{o} = (o_1, o_2, ..., o_T)$ be the sequence of observed input data (values on T input nodes, such as the sequence of words in a text. Let S be a set of FSM states, in which each state is associated a with a label (L label $\in$ a set of ζ labels), for example, the categories of named entities in a text: Place, Person, etc. Finally, $\mathbf{s} = (s_1, s_2, ..., s_T)$ is the sequence of states corresponding to the T on output nodes. Linear-chain CRFs define the conditional probability of state sequence given an input sequence as $p(\mathbf{s}|\mathbf{o})$, described in (1):

$$p(\mathbf{s}|\mathbf{o}) = \frac{1}{Z_o} \exp(\sum_{t=1}^{T} \sum_{k=1}^{K} \lambda_k f_k(s_{t-1}, s_t, \mathbf{o}, t)) \tag{1}$$

- Z_o is the normalization factor over all state sequences;
- $f_k(s_{t-1}, s_t, \mathbf{o}, t)$ is an arbitrary feature function over its arguments;
- $\lambda_k \in (-\infty; +\infty)$ is a learned weight for each feature function.

Considering that the normalization factor Z_o corresponds to the sum of the scores of all possible state sequences, and that the number of state sequences is exponential in the input sequence length T, illustrated in (2):

$$Z_o = \sum_{s} \exp(\sum_{t=1}^{T} \sum_{k=1}^{K} \lambda_k f_k(s_{t-1}, s_t, \mathbf{o}, t)), \mathbf{s} \in S^T \tag{2}$$

Overall, the features functions f_k can ask arbitrary questions about the input sequence, including queries about previous words, next words, and combinations of all these. Thus, we can verify words in a window of two positions to the left/right of the actual position t. However, the feature functions do not depend on the value of t, because such value is used only as an index for observations $\mathbf{o}$. The features used in this work are presented in Section 4.3.

4.2   Representation

For the sequence labeling task in the relation extraction context, we consider each word of a sentence as an observation $\mathbf{o}$, which receives a L label according to a notation. Traditionally, in the literature the BIO notation [17] is used to indicate the words that form a relation [2,15,19]. We define the set of BIO labels {B-REL, I-REL, O}, being B-REL the Beginning of the relation descriptor, I-REL other words Inside the relation descriptor and O any word Outside of the relation descriptor.

In additional, we apply an IO scheme [12] where two labels are created, namely, I-REL and O. A word labelled with I-REL is Inside of a relation descriptor, while a word labelled with O is Outside of the relation descriptor. In this work, we applied IO and BIO schemes aiming at finding the most appropriate notation for the task of relation extraction. The BIO and IO notations here defined were applied based on the manual annotation of the relation descriptors presented in Section 3. Table 3 illustrates a distribution of BIO and IO labels following proposed representation.

To exemplify both proposed representation scheme, in Table 4 we present the sentence fragment "A Legião da Boa Vontade, instituição educacional, foi fundada em o Brasil" ("The Legião da Boa Vontade, educational institutuion, was founded in Brazil"), in which the bold part of the first column corresponds to the sequence of words indicating the relation descriptor "fundada em o" (founded-in), that relates the named entities "Legião da Boa Vontade" and "Brasil". This word sequence represents inputs for CRF model. The second column illustrates the output labels according to the BIO notation, and the last one illustrates output from IO notation. These labels (BIO or IO) represent the output nodes of the CRF model. The Person and Organisation named entities involved in the relation (*"Legião da Boa Vontade"* and *"Brasil"*, respectively) represent the arguments and receive the label O, because they are not part of the relation. As a result, considering the triple (*argumento1, REL, argumento2*), we have (*Legião da Boa Vontade, fundada em o, Brasil*).

Table 3. A distribution of BIO and IO schemes from reference corpus.

Labels	BIO	IO
B-REL	304	—
I-REL	885	1189
O	5012	5012

Table 4. Example with BIO and IO notations for sequence labeling

Words	BIO notation	IO notation
A	O	O
Legião da Boa Vontade	O	O
,	O	O
instituição	O	O
educacional	O	O
,	O	O
foi	O	O
fundada	B-REL	I-REL
em	I-REL	I-REL
o	I-REL	I-REL
Brasil	O	O

4.3 Features

The analysis of the features to represent relation instances is an essential element of the task of learning semantic relations between named entities.

In this work, we used relation-specific features for Portuguese analysed in [10], which are based on the related work [11,2,9,15]. Below we show a list of features and its brief description:

1. POS features: POS tags in a window of +-2 words; 2 consecutive POS tags in a window of +-2 words.
2. POS features: POS tags in a window of +-2 words; 2 consecutive POS tags in a window of +-2 words.

3. Lexical features: canonic form in a window of +-2 words; 2 consecutive canonic forms in a window of +-2 words; number of words in the segment.
4. Syntactic features: syntactic tags (appositive; direct object; head of segment; head of the appositive); syntactic tags in a window of +-2 words; 2 consecutive syntactic tags in a window of +-2 words.
5. Patterns features: patterns such as: a verb followed by a preposition or an article; an adverb followed by a preposition or an article; a noun followed by a preposition; a verb in a window of +-2 words.
6. Phrasal Sequence features: POS tags of the word sequence between two named entities.
7. Semantic features: semantic tags provided by parser Palavras in a window of +-2 words; named entity category.
8. Dictionary features: list of the words representing typical Person titles and jobs, and Place words.

5   Evaluation

We perform 10-fold cross validation in the reference corpus considering the two proposed representations described in Section 4.2 (IO and BIO schemes) and all features presented in Section 4.3. We evaluated the performance of the classification using the following measures: number of correct labels (#C), Recall (R), Precision (P), and F-measure (F).

Table 5 presents the results of the CRF model using the BIO scheme. In a total of 304 words labeled with B-REL (see Table 1) 133 words were correctly classified; for I-REL label we achieved 287 words correctly annotated of the total 885 words; and we also achieved a great number of words annotated with O label (4831 words of the total of 5012). We present high rates of Precision for all labels, and F-measure of 55% and 43% for B-REL and I-REL labels, respectively.

The results for the IO sheme, shown in Table 6, increased the number of words correctly annotated with I-REL label to 447 words (of 1189), and thus decrease the number of words annotated with O label. We achieved high rates of Precision and F-measure, 67% and 48%, respectively.

We also evaluated the classified instances using two different criteria: exact matching, when the extracted relation descriptor is exactly the same as the one manually annotated (i.e., having all words in common); and partial matching, when the extracted relation descriptor has at least one word common with the manual annotation. Table 7 presents the results of the classification with BIO and IO schemes. Overall, the best results in the classification of correct relation descriptors were obtained with IO scheme. We classified a greater number of correct instances with IO scheme compared to the BIO scheme, 118 correct instances for exact matching and 208 cases for partial matching, and thus increased the rates of recall for both exact and partial matching relation descriptors (39% and 68%, respectively). The best F-measure was 67% for partial matching and 46% for exact matching using IO and BIO schemes, respectively.

Table 5. Results of the CRF model with BIO representation scheme.

	#C	R	P	F
B-REL	133	0.43	0.74	0.55
I-REL	287	0.32	0.66	0.43
O	4831	0.96	0.86	0.91

Table 6. Results of the CRF model with IO representation scheme.

	#C	R	P	F
I-REL	447	0.37	0.67	0.48
O	4797	0.95	0.86	0.90

Table 7. Results of the classification with BIO and IO schemes.

	Exact matching				Partial matching			
	#C	R	P	F	#C	R	P	F
BIO	113	0.37	**0.63**	**0.46**	133	0.43	**0.74**	0.55
IO	**118**	**0.39**	0.38	0.38	**208**	**0.68**	0.66	**0.67**

5.1 Analysis and Discussion

From the results presented in Table 5 and Table 6, one can see that IO scheme is more adequate to be used on relation extraction task.

We can notice that a greater number of words that form a relation descriptor have been identified using only the I-REL label, compared to the application of both B-REL and I-REL labels. This is due to the fact that the IO scheme suggests to learn classifiers that identify only the Inside and the Outside of the text segments, and thus this scheme is more simple than the BIO scheme, that suggests to learn classifiers that identify the Beginning, the Inside and the Outside of the text segments.

Considering all correctly extracted relation instances (see Table 7) for each pair of named entities, we have the following distribution for BIO scheme: 30 cases of ORG-ORG, 52 of ORG-PERS, 51 of ORG-PLACE (total of 133 cases from 304 positive instances); and for IO scheme: 52 cases of ORG-ORG, 69 of ORG-PERS, 87 of ORG-PLACE (total of 208 cases from 304 positive instances). We can notice that a greater number of classified relation descriptors occur between Organisation and Place named entities, when applying the IO scheme. In the reference corpus there are 109 positive instances involving Organisation and Place named entities, among these, 51 cases were classified as exact matching and 36 as partial matching. The BIO scheme classified more relation instances occurring between Organisation and Person named entities, however the IO scheme classified more cases involving such entities (from 52 to 69 cases, respectively).

In Table 8, we show in (a) a relation instance expressing a "location" relation between Organisation and Place named entities in the following order: input relation instance, in which the bold part corresponds to the relation descriptor; IO output classification; and BIO output classification. In this example, there were elements interposed between the named entity *"Estância de Cinco Estrelas Martino"* and the relation descriptor *"em o"* (*"in"*), yet the IO scheme managed to correctly classify the instance, even though the BIO scheme did not classify the instance. The example of relation instance involving Organisation and Person named entities is presented in (b), in which all elements of describing the relation are classified using IO scheme, but the BIO scheme did not manage to classify this instance relation.

Table 8. Examples of extracted relation descriptor with IO and BIO schemes.

Relation instance	Output IO	Output BIO
a. *Estância de Cinco Estrelas Martino* é o lugar mais conveniente para se ficar **em a** *Costa Rica* (*Estância de Cinco Estrelas Martino* is the most convenient place to stay **in** *Costa Rica*)	**em**<I-REL> **o**<I-REL>	em<O> o<O>
b. *António Ribeiro* **em declarações ao** *Público* disse no saber o ocorrido. (*António Ribeiro* **in declarations to** *Público* said he does not know what happened.)	**em**<I-REL> **declaração**<I-REL> **a**<I-REL> **o**<I-REL>	em<O> declaração<O> a<O> o<O>
c. O *CEC* **foi reconhecido há dois anos como** *Câmara do Comércio e Indústria.* (The *CEC* **two years ago was recognized as** *Câmara do Comércio e Indústria.*)	**ser**<I-REL> **reconhecer**<I-REL> **há**<I-REL> **dois**<I-REL> **anos**<I-REL> como<O>	ser<B-REL> reconhecer<O> há<O> dois<O> anos<O> como<O>
d. Os *Estados Membros* estão a ignorar **as leis de a** *UE* em matéria de segurança marítma. (The *Estados Membros* are ignoring **the laws of the** *UE* concerning maritime safety.)	o<O> **lei**<I-REL> **de**<I-REL> **o**<I-REL>	o<O> lei<O> de<O> o<O>

In the analysis of results, we noticed that in most of the partial matching cases with IO scheme the elements of the relation descriptors are classified almost in totality, generally missing only an article or preposition. In the reference corpus there are many relation descriptors formed by several words, hence making difficult the exact tagging of the descriptors. Most of these relation descriptors occur between a pair of Organisations, which are more extensive compared to others.

We present examples of partial matching descriptors between the pair of Organisations in Table 8. We can see in (c) that IO scheme identified more elements of the relation instance compared to BIO scheme, missing only the preposition "como" ("as"), and in (d) the IO scheme identified almost all elements of the relation instance, missing the article "o" ("the"). In this case, the BIO scheme did not classify the relation instance.

6 Conclusions

In this work, we analysed the impact of representation choices in Portuguese relation extraction. We present a CRF classifier that uses specific features for Portuguese for the extraction of any relation descriptor occurring between named entities in the Organisation domain. Since there are very few proposals for relation extraction for Portuguese, contrary to the situation for other languages [1], the difficulty of the task is enhanced.

We explored the BIO and IO schemes and evaluated the performance of the CRF classifier with each scheme. We are now able to conclude that the choice of scheme has impact on the results, and we showed that the IO scheme outperforms the widely adopted BIO scheme for the relation extraction task. This is due to fact that the IO scheme simplifies the classification problem because it uses less labels, impacting positively on performance of the CRF classifier.

In future works, we intend to increase the size of the annotated data and to extract specific relations from Portuguese texts, such as relations of ReRelEM track; as well as to realize an extension of the work for other languages.

Acknowledgments. We thank the CNPQ and PNPD/CAPES for their financial support.

References

1. Abreu, S.C., Bonamigo, T.L., Vieira, R.: A review on relation extraction with an eye on portuguese. Journal of the Brazilian Computer Society, 1–19 (2013)
2. Banko, M., Etzioni, O.: The tradeoffs between open and traditional relation extraction. In: McKeown, K., Moore, J.D., Teufel, S., Allan, J., Furui, S. (eds.) ACL, pp. 28–36. The Association for Computer Linguistics (2008)
3. Batista, D.S., Forte, D., Silva, R., Martins, B., Silva, M.: Extracção de relações semânticas de textos em português explorando a DBpédia e a Wikipédia. Linguamatica 5(1), 41–57 (2013)
4. Bellare, K., Mccallum, A.: Learning extractors from unlabeled text using relevant databases. In: Sixth International Workshop on Information Integration on the Web (IIWeb) (2007)
5. Bick, E.: The Parsing System Palavras. Automatic Grammatical Analysis of Portuguese in a Constraint Grammar Framework. University of Arhus (2000)

6. Brucksen, M., Souza, J.G.C., Vieira, R., Rigo, S.: Sistema serelep para o reconhecimento de relações entre entidades mencionadas. In: Mota, C., Santos, D. (eds.) Segundo HAREM, chap. 14, pp. 247–260. Linguateca (2008)
7. Cardoso, N.: Rembrandt - reconhecimento de entidades mencionadas baseado em relações e análise detalhada do texto. In: Mota, C., Santos, D. (eds.) Segundo HAREM, chap. 11, pp. 195–211. Linguateca (2008)
8. Chaves, M.S.: Geo-ontologias e padrões para reconhecimento de locais e de suas relações em textos: o sei-geo no segundo harem. In: Mota, C., Santos, D. (eds.) Segundo HAREM, chap. 13, pp. 231–245. Linguateca (2008)
9. Chen, Y., Zheng, Q., Wang, W., Chen, Y.: Knowledge element relation extraction using conditional random fields. In: CSCWD, pp. 245–250 (2010)
10. Collovini, S., Pugens, L., Vanin, A.A., Vieira, R.: Extraction of relation descriptors for Portuguese using conditional random fields. In: Bazzan, A.L.C., Pichara, K. (eds.) IBERAMIA 2014. LNCS, vol. 8864, pp. 108–119. Springer, Heidelberg (2014)
11. Culotta, A., McCallum, A., Betz, J.: Integrating probabilistic extraction models and data mining to discover relations and patterns in text. In: Proceedings of the Main Conference on HLT-NAACL, HLT-NAACL '06, pp. 296–303. Association for Computational Linguistics, Stroudsburg (2006)
12. Finkel, J.R., Grenager, T., Manning, C.: Incorporating non-local information into information extraction systems by gibbs sampling. In: Proceedings of the 43rd Annual Meeting on Association for Computational Linguistics, ACL '05, pp. 363–370. Association for Computational Linguistics, Stroudsburg (2005)
13. Jurafsky, D., Martin, J.H.: Speech and Language Processing: An Introduction to Natural Language Processing, Computational Linguistics and Speech Recognition. Prentice Hall Series in Artificial Intelligence, 2nd edn. Pearson Education Ltd., London (2009)
14. Lafferty, J.D., McCallum, A., Pereira, F.C.N.: Conditional random fields: probabilistic models for segmenting and labeling sequence data. In: Proceedings of the Eighteenth International Conference on Machine Learning, ICML '01, pp. 282–289. Morgan Kaufmann Publishers Inc., San Francisco (2001)
15. Li, Y., Jiang, J., Chieu, H.L., Chai, K.M.A.: Extracting relation descriptors with conditional random fields. In: Proceedings of 5th International Joint Conference on Natural Language Processing, pp. 392–400. Asian Federation of Natural Language Processing, Chiang Mai (2011)
16. McCallum, A., Li, W.: Early results for named entity recognition with conditional random fields, feature induction and web-enhanced lexicons. In: Proceedings of the Seventh Conference on Natural Language Learning at HLT-NAACL 2003, CONLL '03, vol. 4, pp. 188–191. Association for Computational Linguistics, Stroudsburg (2003)
17. Ramshaw, L.A., Marcus, M.P.: Text chunking using transformation-based learning. In: Proceedings of the 3rd ACL Workshop on Very Large Corpora, pp. 82–94, Cambridge MA, USA (1995)
18. Ratinov, L., Roth, D.: Design challenges and misconceptions in named entity recognition. In: Proceedings of the Thirteenth Conference on Computational Natural Language Learning, CoNLL '09, pp. 147–155. Association for Computational Linguistics, Stroudsburg (2009)
19. Žitnik, S., Šubelj, L., Lavbič, D., Zrnec, A., Bajec, M.: Collective information extraction using first-order probabilistic models. In: Proceedings of the Fifth Balkan Conference in Informatics, BCI '12, pp. 279–282. ACM, New York (2012)

An Investigation of Cross-Language Information Retrieval for User-Generated Internet Video

Ahmad Khwileh[(✉)], Debasis Ganguly, and Gareth J.F. Jones

ADAPT Centre, School of Computing, Dublin City University, Dublin 9, Ireland
ahmad.khwileh2@mail.dcu.ie, {dganguly,gjones}@computing.dcu.ie

Abstract. Increasing amounts of user-generated video content are being uploaded to online repositories. This content is often very uneven in quality and topical coverage in different languages. The lack of material in individual languages means that cross-language information retrieval (CLIR) within these collections is required to satisfy the user's information need. Search over this content is dependent on available metadata, which includes user-generated annotations and often noisy transcripts of spoken audio. The effectiveness of CLIR depends on translation quality between query and content languages. We investigate CLIR effectiveness for the blip10000 archive of user-generated Internet video content. We examine the retrieval effectiveness using the title and free-text metadata provided by the uploader and automatic speech recognition (ASR) generated transcripts. Retrieval is carried out using the *Divergence From Randomness* models, and automatic translation using *Google translate*. Our experimental investigation indicates that different sources of evidence have different retrieval effectiveness and in particular differing levels of performance in CLIR. Specifically, we find that the retrieval effectiveness of the ASR source is significantly degraded in CLIR. Our investigation also indicates that for this task the Title source provides the most robust source of evidence for CLIR, and performs best when used in combination with other sources of evidence. We suggest areas for investigation to give most effective and robust CLIR performance for user-generated content.

Keywords: Cross-Language Video Retrieval · User generated content · User generated internet video search

1 Introduction

Recent years have seen a huge rise in the amount and diversity of content stored in online video repositories. In 2015, YouTube[1] the predominant online video sharing site, reported that 300 hours of video content are being uploaded every minute encompassing material in 61 languages [20]. This content comes from a wide variety of sources, with significant amounts created and uploaded privately

---

[1] www.youtube.com

© Springer International Publishing Switzerland 2015
J. Mothe et al. (Eds.): CLEF 2015, LNCS 9283, pp. 117–129, 2015.
DOI: 10.1007/978-3-319-24027-5_10

with little or no formal editorial control, meaning that the amount and quality of associated metadata is of widely varying quantity and reliability. Further, the amount of content and topical coverage of the content across different languages is very uneven, meaning that satisfying an information need for a user of one language can only be achieved by providing relevant content in another language. One of the challenges for the effective exploitation of this content in this setting is effective multilingual search.

Recent years have seen significant efforts in the area of Cross Language Information Retrieval (CLIR) for text retrieval initially focusing on formally published content and more recently beginning to look at informal social media content. However, while some limited work has been carried out on Cross-Language Video Retrieval (CLVR) for professional videos such as documentaries or TV news broadcasts, there has to date, been no significant evaluation of CLVR for user-generated Internet-based content. A key difference between user-generated Internet content and professionally produced content is the nature and structure of the textual data associated with it. In this setting, retrieval effectiveness may not only suffer from issues arising from translation errors common to all CLIR tasks, but also recognition errors associated with the automatic speech recognition (ASR) systems used to transcribe the spoken content of the video, and with inconsistencies, and frequently the sparseness of the associated user uploaded metadata for each video. There are many potential choices for how to design a robust CLIR framework for an Internet video search task, but the current lack of detailed investigation means that there is little or no guidance available for the choices that should be made.

In this paper we explore a known-item CLVR task based on a semi-professional Internet video archive constructed from the MediaEval 2012 Search and Hyperlinking [6]. To understand the complexities of the task better, we undertake a detailed performance analysis examining the impact of different source metadata information on CLIR behaviour. The video collection used for this investigation is the blip10000 dataset collected from the Internet video sharing platform Blip.tv [18]. We investigate the CLIR effectiveness of metadata based on ASR, Title and description fields for both short and long queries defined for the MediaEval 2012 task.

The remainder of this paper is structured as follows: Section 2 reviews related work, Section 3 describes the test set used in our experiments and the evaluation metric, Section 4 describes initial experiments examining CLIR robustness for each information source, Section 5 describes our approach to improving CLIR effectiveness, and Section 6 concludes and provides directions for further work.

2   Related Work

While we are not aware of a comparable study of CLIR for user-generated Internet video content, there is much related existing work. The most closely related work to that examined in this paper was carried out in tasks within the CLEF evaluation campaigns[2]. From 2002-2004 the Cross-Language Spoken Document Retrieval (CL-SDR) task investigated news story document retrieval using data from the NIST TREC 8-9 Spoken Document Retrieval (SDR) with manually translated queries [7,8]. Their tasks involved the retrieval of American English news broadcasts of both unsegmented and segmented transcripts taken from radio and TV news. A more ambitious Cross-Language Speech Retrieval (CL-SR) task ran within CLEF 2005-2007 [19,15,17]. This examined CLIR for a spontaneous conversational speech collection with content in English and Czech content consisting of oral history interviews. The task provided ASR transcripts, automatically and manually generated metadata for the interviews. The goal was to design systems to help searchers to identify sections of an interview that would be most relevant to their information need. The reported results of these tracks showed that the use of manual metadata yielded substantial improvement on the retrieval effectiveness, compared to using ASR transcripts and automatically created metadata.

The VideoCLEF track was then run at CLEF 2008 and CLEF 2009. This task provided Dutch TV content featuring English-speaking experts and studio guests. VideoCLEF piloted tasks involving performing classification, translation and keyword extraction on dual language video using either machine learning or information retrieval techniques. Participants were provided with Dutch archival metadata, Dutch speech transcripts, and English speech transcripts [10,11].

The multimedia CLIR tasks at CLEF focused on professionally curated content. Whether it was documentaries, TV shows or interviews, this had high quality metadata provided with it. For example, domain experts following a carefully prescribed format created the manual metadata for CLEF 2005-2007. The CLEF tasks were followed by the establishment of the MediaEval benchmarking campaign in 2010 [14]. Activities at MediaEval have focused on various multimedia search tasks, but have not included any CLIR elements.

Other recent work has explored searching video of user generated content, but this has not included an element of CLIR. The most relevant video search task is the known-item search task which was established by the TREC Video Retrieval Evaluation (TRECVID)[3] in it's known-item search task (KIS) [16]. This was included at TRECVid annually from 2010 to 2012. Results were rather inconsistent from year to year in terms of the retrieval effectiveness of different search approaches, one conclusion being the difficulty of setting up such a task on Internet collections.

While CLIR for published text has been ongoing with a wide variety of language pairs for many years, recent research has begun to explore CLIR for user-generated text. One example of this is the work described in [4], which explored the retrieval of questions posed in formal English across user-generated (informal) documents of Arabic collected from forum posts. Their results showed that the retrieval performance could be enhanced by applying an informal text classifier to help the translation of informal content. The work described in [12]

---

[2] www.clef-initiative.eu/
[3] http://trecvid.nist.gov

Table 1. Length statistics for indexed blip10000 fields

	Title	Desc	ASR
Stan.Dev	3.0	106.9	2399.5
Avg.Length	5.3	47.7	703.0
Median	5.0	24.0	1674.8
Max	22.0	3197.0	20451.0
Min	0.0	1.0	0.0

also reported a CLIR task for informal Chinese documents. They proposed to use pseudo relevance feedback (PRF) approaches to improve retrieval effectiveness, and showed they can be useful to reduce the impact of translation errors on retrieval effectiveness.

3 Experimental Test Set and Evaluation

To the best of our knowledge, our work is the first to explore the issues of CLIR on video that is collected from a user-contributed source on the Internet. Content creators from varied backgrounds with differing motivations and interests created this content without any central editor control of style, format or quality. This makes the uploaded videos very varied in terms of the amount and quality of manually added metadata descriptions, and thus challenging from multiple retrieval perspectives.

The blip10000 collection used in our experiments is described in detail in [18]. This collection is a crawl of the Internet video sharing platform Blip.tv[4]. It was originally used as the content dataset for the MediaEval 2012 Search and Hyperlinking task [6]. The blip10000 collection contains the crawled videos together with the associated metadata. This metadata is comprised of the Titles and short descriptions for each video that were manually provided by the video uploader. In addition, associated ASR transcripts were also provided. The collection consists of 14,838 videos having with a total running time of ca. 3,288 hours, and a total size of about 862 GB.

Table 1 shows the variations of individual fields between the videos. For example, while one video may have no ASR, another may contain over 20K terms. Of particular relevance to our investigation are the following aspects of the data:

- *The distribution of the document lengths*: since there is no restriction on document lengths and they are found to be highly variable. Such length variability poses a challenge for any retrieval task. A breakdown of the details of the various fields in our blip10000 test collection is shown in Table 1.
- *High variability in automatic speech recognition (ASR) quality of the transcripts of the video*: Even though the same ASR system is used, the variation in the audio quality, speaking styles and speakers leads to significant variability in the accuracy of the transcripts.

---

[4] http://blip.tv/

– *Inconsistencies and sparseness of the associated user uploaded metadata*: Titles may be very short having only one or two terms, while descriptions can be generic and incomplete, making their utility for retrieval very varied.

For our experiments we indexed the metadata fields separately and in combination, as described in the experiments in Sections 4 and 5.

3.1 Query Construction for the CLIR Task

The MediaEval 2012 Search and Hyperlinking task [6] was a known-item search task, a search for a single previously seen relevant video (the *known-item*). This task provided 60 English queries collected using the Amazon Mechanical Turk[5] (MTurk) crowd-sourcing platform. Each query contains a full query statement providing a detailed described of the required features of the single relevant target video (long query) and a terse web type search query for the same item (short query). To create our CLIR test set, we extended the original monolingual English by giving the queries to Arabic, Italian and French native speakers, and asking them to rewrite them into natural queries in their native language. Both short and long queries were expressed into Arabic. In addition, the short query set was also expressed in Italian, while the long query set was further expressed in French.

In order to explore CLVR for this task, we used the Google translate API[6] to translate these translated topics back into English. As would be expected, for some queries, machine translation (MT) produced a slightly different queries than the monolingual ones. In addition to the expected deletion/insertion edits, there were also some Named Entity Errors (NEEs) for Out-Of-Vocabulary (OOV) items that *Google MT translation* could not translate correctly. These edits and translation errors pose a challenge to the retrieval effectiveness of the CLIR over the monolingual one. For our investigation, we explored both the short and long queries to give a better understanding of the effect of query length on retrieval behaviour for both the monolingual and CLIR tasks. The query sets used in out investigation are labelled as follows:

– **Mn-Sh**: 60 EN short queries (monolingual)
– **Mn-Lg**: 60 EN long queries (monolingual)
– **CL-AR-Sh**: 60 AR short queries translated into EN
– **CL-AR-Lg**: 60 AR long queries translated into EN
– **CL-IT-Sh**: 60 IT long queries translated into EN
– **CL-FR-Lg**: 60 FR long queries translated into EN

Since the retrieval task is a known-item search for which we are seeking to retrieve the single known relevant item, we evaluate our investigations using the standard metric for this task, the mean reciprocal rank (MRR) metric computed as shown in Equation 1.

---

[5] http://www.mturk.com/
[6] https://developers.google.com/translate/

$$MRR = \frac{1}{n} \sum_{i=1}^{n} \frac{1}{rank_i} \tag{1}$$

where $rank_i$ indicates the rank of the ground truth known item that the ith query is intended to find.

4   CLIR Using Single Field Indexes

The first part of our investigation examines the behaviour of the separate information fields in the CLIR framework. We are particularly interested here in the impact of errors in automatic translation or inconsistencies on retrieval effectiveness, given the noise in ASR transcripts, the shortness of the title field, and the inconsistencies of the description field. We examine this question by evaluating the *CLIR robustness* of each field, to measure how the retrieval effectiveness behaves in the CLIR framework. We report this by observing the significance of change between the CLIR and monolingual performance using the same setting and across all query sets. For running our CLIR robustness evaluation experiment, we compare the CLIR effectiveness of each field against a monolingual baseline:

- **ASR_index** contains only the ASR transcript fields
- **Title_index** contains only the Title fields
- **Desc_index** contains only description fields

We report the results for both long and short query sets to examine the impact of query length and the natural language form of the long queries.

Our single field CLIR retrieval experiments were carried out using the Terrier retrieval engine[7]. Stop-words were removed based on the standard Terrier list, and stemming performed using the Terrier implementation of Porter stemming. We used the PL2 [2] model, a probabilistic retrieval model from *the Divergence From Randomness (DFR)* framework. The reason we selected this model over other retrieval models, is our data collection and experiments specifications; our Internet based data collection has very large variations in the lengths of the metadata and documents shown in Table 1. Previous studies such as [3] showed that the PL2 model has less sensitivity to length distribution compared to other retrieval models and works better for experiments that seek early precision, which aligns with our known-item experiment. The PL2 document scoring model is defined in Equation 2.

$$Score(d, Q) = \sum_{t \in Q} qt_w \cdot \frac{1}{1 + tf_n} (tf_n \log_2 \frac{tf_n}{\lambda} + (\lambda - tf_n) \cdot \log_2 e + 0.5 \log_2(2\pi.tf_n)) \tag{2}$$

where $Score(d, Q)$ is the score for a document d for each query term t of the query Q, λ is the Poisson distribution of F/N; F is the query term frequency

---

[7] http://www.terrier.org/

Table 2. Mono vs. CLIR performance per index

	Mn-Sh	CL-AR-Sh	CL-IT-Sh	Mn-Lg	CL-AR-Lg	CL-FR-Lg
Title_index	0.239	0.2288	0.2383	0.2827	0.2244	0.2239
ASR_index	0.4275	0.2748	0.3873	0.4513	0.3487	0.3833
Desc_index	0.2154	0.1943	0.2102	0.2432	0.2285	0.2316

Table 3. The t-values according to the % MRR reduction for each index

	CL-AR-Sh	CL-AR-Lg	CL-IT-Sh	CL-FR-Lg
Title_index	-1.69	-1.73	-0.05	-1.77
ASR_index	**-1.94***	**-2.50***	-1.58	**-2.04***
Desc_index	-0.829	-0.44	-0.32	-0.47

Statistically significant values with p-value < 0.05.

of t over the whole collection and N is the total number of documents at the collection. qt_w is the query term weight given by $qt_f/qt_f max$; qt_f is the query term frequency and $qt_f max$ is the maximum query term frequency among the query terms. tf_n is the normalized term frequency defined in Equation 3.

$$tf_n = \sum_d (tf.\log_2(1 + c.\frac{avg_l}{l})), (c > 0) \tag{3}$$

where l is the length of the document d. avg_l is the average length of documents, and c is a free parameter for the normalization. To set the parameter c, we followed the empirically standard settings used in [3,9], which are $c = 1$ for short queries and $c = 7$ for long queries.

Our results for each index are shown in Table 2, these show that MRR is *lower* in all cases for the CLIR task. Thus retrieval effectiveness of all fields is negatively impacted for CLIR. This confirms the expected additional retrieval challenge that arises from the imperfect query translation. MRR for the AR queries is reduced to a higher degree than for the French and Italian queries. This is likely to arise due to the relative difficulty of Arabic MT [1]. One significant challenge for Arabic to English MT relates to named entities. For instance, a query including the word 'dreamweaver' (the proprietary web development tool) was expressed as 'dreamweaver' for both FR and IT, while for AR, it was represented by "الدريموفر" which resulted in it being an OOV term for *Google Translate* and being transliterated into a completely different word 'Aldirimovr' which was not useful for retrieval using the English language metadata.

Also, looking at the MRR reduction rates for each index indicates they have different responses to the query translation; notable the impact is greatest on the ASR transcript indexes across all languages pairs using both short and long queries. To better understand the significance of these CLIR reductions in MRR, we computed the statistical significance of each drop. We calculated the t-value for the difference at the 95% confidence level after representing all monolingual and CLIR MRRs in pairs on every query level. The significance test results in terms of t-values for the indexes searched for all CLIR constructed queries are shown in Table 3. Looking at the t-values, we can observe that IT queries were less challenging than the others since the performance was not significantly different from monolingual. Table 3 indicates that when using the one-field per index, for both long and short queries, ASR_index has the least robustness, with a statistically significant negative drop in Arabic and in French with ($p < 0.05$). For the Italian queries, the MRR reduction rates of the ASR index (ASR_index) were not statistically significant, but still had the highest negative impact comparing to searching other fields (Title and description fields).

We conclude from this experiment that even if they are incomplete, informal, short and sometimes unreliable, the user-uploaded Titles and meta descriptions are yet more robust in the CLIR setting than the ASR fields. As noted earlier, the degree of ASR recognition errors may vary from video to another on Internet video due to the huge variation of the audio quality. The interaction between recognition error rate, document length and retrieval behaviour is highly complex, as observed in [5]. We plan to explore this effect in more detail in future work, with a view to improving the CLIR robustness of the ASR transcript field.

5   CLIR Using Combined Metadata Fields

Having examined the effectiveness of the three separate fields for monolingual retrieval and CLIR, in this section we explore the potential for combining them for improving retrieval effectiveness. For this investigation, we carried out another set of experiments that combined the evidence from the individual fields. We combined the three fields with varied field weighting. For these combined field experiments we use the DFR PL2F model [13] which is a modified version of the PL2 model [2] used in the previous section. The PL2F model is designed to adopt per-field weighting when combining multiple evidence fields into a single index for search. The term frequencies from document fields are normalised separately and then combined in a weighted sum. PL2F uses the same document scoring function as PL2, shown in Equation 2, but here tfn is the weighted sum of the normalised term frequencies in the normalised term frequencies tf_X for each field x. in our case $x \in (ASR, title, desc)$ as indicated by Equation 4.

$$tf_n = \sum_x (w_x.tf_x.\log_2(1 + c_x.\frac{avgl_x}{l_x})), (c_x > 0) \qquad (4)$$

where l_x is the length of the field x in document d. $avgl_x$ is the average length of the field x across all documents. and c_x, w_x are the per-field normalization parameters. This per-field normalization feature in PL2 modifies the standard PL2 document scoring function to include the weighted sum of the normalised term frequencies tf_x. tf_x also needs two parameters w_x, c_x to be set. Hence, for scoring every indexed document we needed to set these parameters: C_x which is the set of per-field length normalization parameters c_x that need to be set for every field as $C_x = \{ c\_asr, c\_title, c\_desc \}$. Also for W_x which is the set of

Table 4. Weighting scheme W_x for the single-weighted retrieval models

	ASR	Title	Desc
PL2ASR	w_x	1	1
PL2Title	1	w_x	1
PL2Desc	1	1	w_x

per-field boost factors w_x that need to be set for each field as $W_x = \{$ w_asr, w_title, $w\_desc\}$.

For our investigation of the retrieval effectiveness with combination of all three fields, we explore giving higher weight to a specific field over the others by creating a single-weighted retrieval model for each source of evidence (field). To set the parameter values for our proposed single-weighted retrieval models we followed these steps:

- Construct a model based on the PL2F that targets a single field x from each (ASR, title, desc) as PL2ASR, PL2Title, PL2Desc.
- Give an equal c_x value to all fields to allow full-length normalization for the term frequency of each field as in $C_x = \{1,1,1\}$ for short queries, $Cx = \{7,7,7\}$ for long queries. We also follow the empirically standard settings applied in [3,9].
- For W_x, we set the w_x value for the targeted field, and the rest to be fixed at 1, to give a priority for field x over the others as in $W_x = \{w_x,1,1\}$. The reason why we chose the fixed weights to be 1 was to allow for the presence of their term frequencies, but with normal (not boosted) weights.

The combination weighting schemes are shown in Table 4, in each case only one field has a weight boost of w_x. To examine retrieval behaviour, we varied the w_x boost parameters for each proposed model from 1 to 60 using increments of 1. The first weighting iteration at the weighting point 1 is the same for all models where they have $W_x = \{1,1,1\}$. Figure 1 shows the MRR performance at each weighting point for the long queries (the CL-AR-Lg and the CL-FR-Lg query sets), and the short queries (the CL-AR-Sh and the CL-IT-Sh query sets). As can be seen in Figure 1, fields behave *differently* with the weight boosting. The best CLIR precision performance is always achieved by giving a higher weight towards the Title field across the AR, IT and FR queries[8]. Across all the weighting points and all languages, the PL2Title model shows higher performance than other fields for both short and long query sets. It is also shown in these figures, that we even get lower performance when we give progressively higher weights to the ASR and Desc fields. The strong CLIR performance of the PL2Title indicates the stability and the robustness of Title fields for Internet videos over other fields. Also, the fact that these Titles may have been written by the video uploader with more attention than the descriptions could be attributed to the following reasons:

---

[8] Also worth mentioning that the MTurk task used to construct all query sets did not expose any associated video metadata to the query creators.

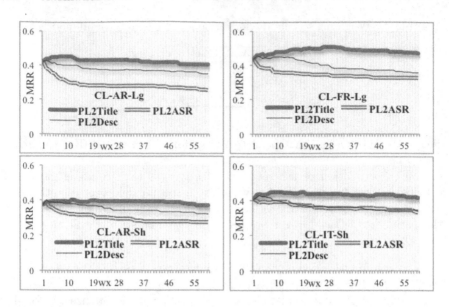

Fig. 1. CLIR peformance (MRR) of the single-weighted models across all weighting points (wx) using both short and long query sets

Table 5. Mono vs. CLIR Recall performance represented by the number of found documents on 100 results cut-off

	Mn-Sh	CL-AR-Sh	CL-IT-Sh	Mn-Lg	CL-AR-Lg	CL-FR-Lg
Title_index	25	23	24	32	29	29
ASR_index	46	41	45	47	40	43
Desc_index	34	27	31	34	32	32
TitleDesc_index	38	32	35	42	35	38
ASRDesc_index	50	47	49	50	43	47
ASRTitle_index	46	41	45	46	39	42
All_Index	50	45	50	52	43	49

- The uploader thought it is vital to have a meaningful Title for his video since it would help in promoting it on the video-sharing site.
- The uploader believed that it has more importance since it is shown at the header of his video, while the description is generally shown below the video and may not be examined at all by the video viewers.
- The quality of textual content of Title field, which is shown to have more CLIR robustness, can be attributed to its shortness; in which it was *only* helpful for limited amount of queries without introducing any noise that would negatively affect the overall retrieval performance.

Comparing the MRR for PL2Title with the values shown in Table 2, it can also be seen that performance for the PL2Title is almost double that of the result for the separate Title field run. While the MRR values for the ASR and

Desc fields are similar between the two experiments. As the w_x increases for the Title field, we can see that there is some further improvement, with the optimal weight depending on the query length and the language pair. In order to better understand how the field combination improves retrieval effectiveness, we examined the Recall of the individual fields and the combinations. Table 5 shows the total number of known-items retrieved in the top 100 results for each field set (including pairs-combined fields). It can be seen here that the Title field has low recall in isolation (due to its shortness issue), but it can boost the Recall of the other fields when used in combination. The results in Figure 1 suggest that the Title field brings additional evidence without bringing noise, unlike the Desc and ASR fields which degrade effectiveness when their weight is increased.

6   Conclusions and Further Research

This paper has examined CLVR based on text metadata fields for an Arabic-English, French-English and Italian-English known-item search task based on user-generated Internet video collection. We studied the retrieval effectiveness and challenges of three different sources of information: ASR transcripts, which are challenged by recognition errors, video Titles, which can be very short and lack content, and videos descriptions which can be informal, generic and incomplete. Our first set of experiments analysed the behaviour of these sources for CLIR by examining their CLIR robustness. We found that the ASR transcript field has the lowest robustness across other fields and its performance can significantly drop for CLIR. We then explored field combination and showed that giving higher weight to the Titles over other fields gives improved CLIR performance. In general, our experiments suggest that giving higher weight towards the fields which have a lower CLIR robustness degrades retrieval effectiveness.

Our analysis of these fields effectiveness gives us suggestions for further investigation. One potential direction for further work is to automatically assess the quality of ASR transcripts and the Description information and assign weights based on quality measures, and also to explore task dependent tuning of the machine translation process. Many CLVR search requests have the potential to exploit the use of visual features, we intend to explore the integration of visual features into our retrieval framework in further experiments.

References

1. Alqudsi, A., Omar, N., Shaker, K.: Arabic machine translation: a survey. Artificial Intelligence Review, 1–24 (2012)
2. Amati, G.: Probabilistic Models for Information Retrieval based on Divergence from Randomness. Ph.D. thesis, Department of Computing Science, University of Glasgow (2003)
3. Amati, G., Van Rijsbergen, C.J.: Probabilistic models of information retrieval based on measuring the divergence from randomness. ACM Transactions on Information Systems (TOIS) 20(4), 357–389 (2002)

4. Bagdouri, M., Oard, D.W., Castelli, V.: CLIR for informal content in Arabic forum posts. In: Proceedings of the 23rd ACM International Conference on Conference on Information and Knowledge Management, pp. 1811–1814. ACM (2014)
5. Eskevich, M., Jones, G.J.F.: Exploring speech retrieval from meetings using the AMI corpus. Computer Speech & Language (2014)
6. Eskevich, M., Jones, G.J.F., Chen, S., Aly, R., Ordelman, R., Larson, M.: Search and hyperlinking task at MediaEval 2012 (2012)
7. Federico, M., Bertoldi, N., Levow, G.-A., Jones, G.J.F.: CLEF 2004 cross-language spoken document retrieval track. In: Peters, C., Clough, P., Gonzalo, J., Jones, G.J.F., Kluck, M., Magnini, B. (eds.) CLEF 2004. LNCS, vol. 3491, pp. 816–820. Springer, Heidelberg (2005)
8. Federico, M., Jones, G.J.F.: The CLEF 2003 cross-language spoken document retrieval track. In: Peters, C., Gonzalo, J., Braschler, M., Kluck, M. (eds.) CLEF 2003. LNCS, vol. 3237, pp. 646–652. Springer, Heidelberg (2004)
9. He, B., Ounis, I.: On setting the hyper-parameters of term frequency normalization for information retrieval. ACM Transactions on Information Systems (TOIS) 25(3), 13 (2007)
10. Larson, M., Newman, E., Jones, G.J.F.: Overview of VideoCLEF 2008: automatic generation of topic-based feeds for dual language audio-visual content. In: Peters, C., Deselaers, T., Ferro, N., Gonzalo, J., Jones, G.J.F., Kurimo, M., Mandl, T., Peñas, A., Petras, V. (eds.) CLEF 2008. LNCS, vol. 5706, pp. 906–917. Springer, Heidelberg (2009)
11. Larson, M., Newman, E., Jones, G.J.F.: Overview of VideoCLEF 2009: new perspectives on speech-based multimedia content enrichment. In: Peters, C., Caputo, B., Gonzalo, J., Jones, G.J.F., Kalpathy-Cramer, J., Müller, H., Tsikrika, T. (eds.) CLEF 2009. LNCS, vol. 6242, pp. 354–368. Springer, Heidelberg (2010)
12. Lee, C.-J., Croft, W.B.: Cross-language pseudo-relevance feedback techniques for informal text. In: de Rijke, M., Kenter, T., de Vries, A.P., Zhai, C.X., de Jong, F., Radinsky, K., Hofmann, K. (eds.) ECIR 2014. LNCS, vol. 8416, pp. 260–272. Springer, Heidelberg (2014)
13. Macdonald, C., Plachouras, V., He, B., Lioma, C., Ounis, I.: University of Glasgow at WebCLEF 2005: experiments in per-field normalisation and language specific stemming. In: Peters, C., Gey, F.C., Gonzalo, J., Müller, H., Jones, G.J.F., Kluck, M., Magnini, B., de Rijke, M., Giampiccolo, D. (eds.) CLEF 2005. LNCS, vol. 4022, pp. 898–907. Springer, Heidelberg (2006)
14. MediaEval: MediaEval Benchmarking Initiative for Multimedia Evaluation (2014). http://www.multimediaeval.org/ (retrieved September 30, 2014)
15. Oard, D.W., Wang, J., Jones, G.J.F., White, R.W., Pecina, P., Soergel, D., Huang, X., Shafran, I.: Overview of the CLEF-2006 cross-language speech retrieval track. In: Peters, C., Clough, P., Gey, F.C., Karlgren, J., Magnini, B., Oard, D.W., de Rijke, M., Stempfhuber, M. (eds.) CLEF 2006. LNCS, vol. 4730, pp. 744–758. Springer, Heidelberg (2007)
16. Over, P., Awad, G., Fiscus, J., Antonishek, B., Michel, M., Smeaton, A.F., Kraaij, W., Quénot, G., et al.: TRECVID 2011-an overview of the goals, tasks, data, evaluation mechanisms and metrics. In: TRECVID 2011-TREC Video Retrieval Evaluation Online (2011)
17. Pecina, P., Hoffmannová, P., Jones, G.J.F., Zhang, Y., Oard, D.W.: Overview of the CLEF-2007 cross-language speech retrieval track. In: Peters, C., Jijkoun, V., Mandl, T., Müller, H., Oard, D.W., Peñas, A., Petras, V., Santos, D. (eds.) CLEF 2007. LNCS, vol. 5152, pp. 674–686. Springer, Heidelberg (2008)

18. Schmiedeke, S., Xu, P., Ferné, I., Eskevich, M., Kofler, C., Larson, M.A., Estève, Y., Lamel, L., Jones, G.J.F., Sikora, T.: Blip10000: a social video dataset containing SPUG content for tagging and retrieval. In: Proceedings of the 4th ACM Multimedia Systems Conference, pp. 96–101. ACM (2013)
19. White, R.W., Oard, D.W., Jones, G.J.F., Soergel, D., Huang, X.: Overview of the CLEF-2005 cross-language speech retrieval track. In: Peters, C., Gey, F.C., Gonzalo, J., Müller, H., Jones, G.J.F., Kluck, M., Magnini, B., de Rijke, M., Giampiccolo, D. (eds.) CLEF 2005. LNCS, vol. 4022, pp. 744–759. Springer, Heidelberg (2006)
20. YouTube Press: Statistics - YouTube (2015). http://www.youtube.com/yt/press/statistics.html (retrieved April 1, 2015)

Benchmark of Rule-Based Classifiers in the News Recommendation Task

Tomáš Kliegr[1,3] and Jaroslav Kuchař[2,3] (✉)

[1] Multimedia and Vision Research Group, Queen Mary University of London,
London, UK
t.kliegr@qmul.ac.uk
[2] Web Engineering Group, Faculty of Information Technology,
Czech Technical University in Prague, Prague, Czech Republic
jaroslav.kuchar@fit.cvut.cz
[3] Faculty of Informatics and Statistics, Department of Information and Knowledge
Engineering, University of Economics Prague, Prague, Czech Republic

Abstract. In this paper, we present experiments evaluating Association Rule Classification algorithms on on-line and off-line recommender tasks of the CLEF NewsReel 2014 Challenge. The second focus of the experimental evaluation is to investigate possible performance optimizations of the Classification Based on Associations algorithm. Our findings indicate that pruning steps in CBA reduce the number of association rules substantially while not affecting accuracy. Using only part of the data employed for the rule learning phase in the pruning phase may also reduce training time while not affecting accuracy significantly.

Keywords: Recommender · Association rules · Rule learning · Decision trees

1 Introduction

The large amount of content to choose from causes the *Information Overload* problem for visitors of news websites. Based on the analysis of past usage patterns, recommender systems can make a personalized list of preselected content, alleviating the users of the effort entailed in the process of choosing the content they should consume next and limiting the number of choices they need to make.

In this paper, we present experiments evaluating Association Rule Classification (ARC) algorithms on on-line and off-line recommender task of the CLEF NewsReel 2014 Challenge (further only Challenge). This research aims to investigate the execution time and accuracy of ARC algorithms on datasets with many target class values. For the on-line task with 100 millisecond response limitation, we received the best results with an association rule-based recommender, securing a 3rd place in the contest.

Obtaining promising results with a simple association rule learning approach deployed within our InBeat.eu open source recommender in the on-line task,

© Springer International Publishing Switzerland 2015
J. Mothe et al. (Eds.): CLEF 2015, LNCS 9283, pp. 130–141, 2015.
DOI: 10.1007/978-3-319-24027-5_11

we hypothesize that Association Rule Classification (ARC) algorithms can yield improved results over direct application of association rules. Our benchmark also involves related symbolic machine learning algorithms – standard rule induction (FOIL) and decision tree induction (ID3).

The second focus of the experimental evaluation is to investigate possible performance optimizations of the Classification Based on Associations (CBA) ARC algorithm – through removal of its individual pruning steps or through the use of lower amount of data for pruning. There are practical problems with real time processing that are not encountered when there is "unlimited time" to provide the recommendation.

This paper is organized as follows. Section 2 presents the InBeat.eu recommender system in the on-line task. Section 3 briefly introduces the CBA ARC algorithm and presents the results on the off-line task. Finally, Section 4 summarizes the results and outlines future work.

2 On-line Task: Setup and Results

This section gives a short introduction of the CLEF-NEWSREEL: News Recommendation Evaluation Lab[1], which aimed at evaluating recommender systems on the task of recommending news articles on real websites. A major constraint imposed by the Challenge was a limitation on response time. Recommendations had to be provided in real-time (within 100ms). The main evaluation metric was the total number of successful recommendations, rather than the prediction accuracy (clickthrough rate).

Inputs: The main inputs are the users' interactions and news item descriptions.

- $interaction(type, userId, itemId, context)$
  where $type = \{impression|click\}$ and $context$ describes the features of the user (e.g. browser version, geolocation, etc.) and special features related to items and their presentation (e.g. keywords, position).
- $item(itemId, domain, description)$
  where $domain$ is the identifier of items from the same group (e.g. news portal) and $description$ provides more detailed information about items (e.g. title, text, time of last update).

Outputs: Set of recommended items for the specific user who is reading the item within a given context.

- $(userId, itemId, context) \rightarrow \{item_x, item_y, ...\}$

2.1 Algorithms

As the baseline, we used two simple algorithms *top interacted* and *most recent*, which we found as very effective for the given domain in the News Recommender

---

[1] http://www.clef-newsreel.org/

Challenge'13 (our submission obtained a runner-up award).[2] The main focus of our evaluation were association rules.

Top Interacted. This algorithm is based on the daily popularity of news items. To avoid excessive effect of high short-time popularity of one item the interactions are aggregated on a daily basis. This approach addresses the evolution of popularity over time and decreases the influence of short-time peaks.

Most Recent. The recency of an article plays an important role in the news domain. Our baseline recency-based algorithm uses a simple heuristic based on the newest news item within the same group as the group of the item the user is reading at the time of the request. The results is ordered list of items sorted by creation time.

Association Rules. For each *interaction(type, userId, itemId, context)* stored in our database, we prepared one entry in the training dataset as described in Table 1. Interactions are described only by the contextual features that are provided by the platform (e.g. Location, Browser, ...) and by an identifier of the item the user interacted with.

Table 1. Two instances from the CLEF#26875 offline dataset.

browser	isp	os	context geo	weekday	lang	zip	class item
312613	281	431229	19051	26887	49021	62015	127563250
457399	45	952253	18851	26887	48985	65537	45360072

The training dataset was used to learn association rules. The contextual features could appear only in the rule body (antecedent) and the identifier of the item only on the right side of rule (consequent). We used the APRIORI algorithm [1] available within the *arules* package of R [6]. Example of a rule:

$$\text{isp} = \text{``281''} \wedge \text{os} = \text{``431229''} \rightarrow \text{item} = \text{``1124541''}$$

Additional mining setup is as follows. We used latest five thousand interactions as training dataset from our database. The APRIORI algorithm is run with minimum support of 0.1% (five interactions) and minimum confidence of 2%.

All discovered rules are imported into our simple rule engine. The engine finds all rules that match the contextual features of a recommendation request. The consequent of each matching rule represents a recommended item. The output is a list of unique item identifiers from the right side of the matching rules.

---

[2] https://sites.google.com/site/newsrec2013/challenge

2.2 Performance

In this section, we present the performance of our InBeat recommender in the Challenge. The metric used in the Challenge to select the winning recommender systems was the *cumulative number of clicks* (number of successful recommendations) over the three different evaluation periods. The additional metrics provided by the organizers include *number of impressions* and *click-through rate*.

Sum of the number of impressions with the number of clicks can be interpreted as the ability of the systems to process large number of interaction observing the response time limitation.

Table 2. Leaderboard with cumulative number of clicks and average click-through rate per team in the Challenge - last evaluation period (2014-05-25 – 2014-05-31). Source: http://orp.plista.com

team	requests	clicks ↓	CTR
labor	285533	5614	1.97%
abc	206330	3653	1.77%
inbeat	**268611**	**3451**	**1.28%**
insight	508851	2012	0.4%
ba214	158593	1828	1.15%
uned	370510	1215	0.33%
riemannzeta	99920	1156	1.16%
plista GmbH	9112	137	1.5%

Table 2 presents the results for the last evaluation period. The table is sorted by the cumulative number of clicks. InBeat team is on the third position (total clicks) and on the fourth position with respect to the click through rate (CTR).

The CTR reported in Table 2 is the average for all algorithms. We also report the numbers for the individual algorithms:

- *Top Interacted*: 1.4% CTR,
- *Most Recent*: 0.8% CTR,
- *Association Rules*: 1.5% CTR.

The best CTR was obtained with a margin of 0.1% by *Association Rules*, which we explain by the fact that this algorithm takes into account both popularity (as reflected in the support score) and contextual features (the condition expressed by the antecedent of the rule). *Most Recent* is influenced only by temporal aspects and *Top Interacted* takes into account only the popularity.

3   Off-line Task: Setup and Results

The objective of our experimental evaluation is to investigate the performance of Association Rule Classification (ARC) algorithms on the recommender problem cast as a standard classification task, and to compare the results with related mainstream classification algorithms.

3.1   Data and Task

We used the data published within the off-line task of CLEF-NEWSREEL'14. The entire dataset consisted of 84 million records collected across multiple news portals [8]. We selected the website with the smallest amount of data (26,875 records) denoting the resulting dataset as CLEF#26875.

The dataset consists of instances described by a fixed number of attributes. In our evaluation we process the data with standard machine learning algorithms that require data in tabular form.

The task is to predict the class label (item viewed). The CLEF#26875 off-line dataset has 1,704 distinct items (target class values). This is an unusually high number in comparison with other datasets typically used for evaluation of machine learning algorithms, such as the most frequently cited datasets from the UCI repository.[3] This distributional characteristic has an impact both on execution time and accuracy of the evaluated algorithms. The second notable feature of the dataset is that all its attributes are nominal. This is a favourable property for ARC algorithms in general, since they typically require that numerical attributes are discretized prior mining. The discretization algorithm and its parameters may have substantial impact on both accuracy and execution time.

The problem is cast as a standard machine learning classification task, where each row corresponds to a separate training instance. We also provide comparison with related mainstream machine learning algorithms that create rule or tree-based models (decision trees are convertible to rules).

3.2   Algorithms

The main focus of our evaluation is the Classification Based on Associations (CBA) ARC algorithm [10] and its two candidate successors – CMAR [9] and CPAR [16]. We compare the results with related symbolic machine learning algorithms, namely rule induction (FOIL, CPAR) and decision tree algorithms (ID3, CHAID).

The primary difference between ARC algorithms and rule induction is that the former class of algorithms first generates all association rules in the training data, and then performs pruning, while the rule learning algorithms add rules to the model one-by-one. The CPAR algorithm has some features of both ARC and rule induction algorithm, we list it under rule induction.

Association Rule Classifiers. In 1998, Liu et al. introduced CBA, the first association rule classifier according to [15]. The first step in CBA is association rule learning with a modified APRIORI algorithm. The learning is constrained to produce rules that have an item corresponding to a class label value in the consequent.

---

[3] https://archive.ics.uci.edu/ml/datasets.html

In the second step, the resulting rules are subject to several pruning algorithms:

1. Pessimistic pruning (optional). This pruning method attempts to simplify discovered rules by removing individual conditions from the rule antecedent. The rule is pruned if the pessimistic error rate [14] of the original rule is higher than that of the pruned rule.
2. Data coverage pruning[4]. This method removes rules preserving the following two conditions: i) each training case is covered by the rule with the highest precedence over other rules covering the case and ii) every rule in the classifier correctly classifies at least one training case.
3. Default rule pruning[5]. Rules pruned with data coverage pruning are ordered and all rules after the first rule with the lowest total error are replaced by a rule with empty antecedent predicting the majority class in the remaining data.

The gist of the CBA algorithm are the latter two pruning methods. The final ordered rule set is used as the classifier. Rules are sorted according to confidence, support and antecedent length. CBA performs single rule classification: for a given unlabeled instance, the first highest ranked rule whose antecedent matches the instance is selected, and its consequent is used to label the instance.

The CMAR algorithm is based on similar principles as CBA, but uses the newer FP-Growth [7] algorithm for association rule generation. In addition to data coverage pruning, CMAR performs also pruning based on chi-square test. The rule is pruned if the correlation between the rule's body and and the rule's head is not statistically significant. The data coverage pruning in CMAR is slightly different from CBA as it requires at least δ rules to cover an instance before the instance is removed from training data (in CBA, $\delta = 1$).

In our benchmarks, we used the LUCS-KDD implementations of the ARC algorithms available from http://cgi.csc.liv.ac.uk/~frans/KDD/Software/. According to the implementations' author the software matches the description in the original papers introducing the respective algorithms, apart from that in the first rule generation step, the Apriori-TFP algorithm [2] is used instead of the modified APRIORI algorithm (CBA) or FP-GROWTH (CMAR).

It should be also noted that the LUCS-KDD implementation of CBA does not include pessimistic pruning. In evaluations on 20 UCI datasets reported in [10] CBA with pessimistic pruning had exactly the same accuracy as CBA without pessimistic pruning, but order of magnitude smaller number of rules in the classifier.

For part of the experiments with CBA, we used our own implementation of CBA. While this is not as efficient as the LUCS-KDD implementation, this allows us to test the effect of the individual pruning stages in CBA on accuracy and rule count of the resulting classifier. For rule generation phase, our

---

[4] We adopt the name for this method from [15].
[5] This pruning type is omitted from the review [15], but we are of the opinion that "default rule pruning" could be perceived as a separate step from data coverage pruning.

implementation uses the APRIORI algorithm from the arules package followed by a filtering step which retains only rules that have one of the class labels in the consequent. For the rule generation phase we implemented the version M1 of CBA [10]. The most simplified form of the classifier has a learning phase roughly corresponding to the execution of the APRIORI algorithm.

Rule Learning (Baseline). As a second set of baseline algorithms, we selected the First-Order Induction Learner (FOIL) [13] and the Classification based on Predictive Association Rules (CPAR) algorithm. It was shown that FOIL is prone to overfitting the training data as the size of the theory learned by FOIL can grow with the number of training examples [4]. For this reason, we tried to include Repeated Incremental Pruning to Produce Error Reduction (RIPPER) [3] algorithm, which effectively addresses the overfitting problem [5]. We did not include RIPPER, because on the CLEF#26875 data the RapidMiner 5 implementation[6] of the algorithm did not finish within a 12 hour time limit.

Finally, CPAR was designed to combine advantages of rule learning algorithms with association rule classifiers. The algorithm tests more rules than traditional rule-based classifiers which is claimed to ensure it does not miss important rules.

We used again the LUCS-KDD implementation of FOIL and CPAR.

Decision Trees. Decision tree induction algorithms produce models that to an extent resemble those produced by ARC algorithms. Each path from the root of the tree to the leaf in a decision tree corresponds to a classification rule.

Out of the multiple proposed decision tree algorithms, we included those implemented in the RapidMiner 5 open source data mining suite: ID3, Rapid-Miner's "DECISION TREE" and CHAID.

ID3 [12] is a frequently used baseline decision tree algorithm. Since all input attributes in CLEF#26875 are nominal, the algorithm can be used directly on input data without any preprocessing.

The RapidMiner's DECISION TREE operator was found to be the most accurate decision tree classifier in [11], which evaluated decision tree learning algorithms in three common data mining suites: SPSS-Clementine, RapidMiner and Weka. This implementation supports prepruning and postpruning methods.

The RapidMiner's CHAID implementation uses the chi-square test as a goodness criterion, otherwise it is the same as DECISION TREE.

3.3   Experimental Evaluation

The algorithms described in the previous subsections were executed with parameters set according to Table 3.

The support and confidence parameters of CBA and CMAR had to be changed from the default values (of 20% and 80% respectively), since otherwise no rules were generated (no class item in the data had at least 20% support).

---

[6] http://sourceforge.net/projects/rapidminer/

Table 3. Algorithm parameters used in the off-line evaluation.

method	parameters
CBA	support = 2 records (0.008%), confidence = 2.0%, max size of antecedent = 6, max number of CARS = 80000, max number of frequent sets = 1,000,000
CMAR	support = 2 records (0.008%), confidence = 2.0%, max size of antecedent = 6, min cover (δ) = 1
CPAR	*default values*: K value = 5, min. best gain = 0.7, total weight factor = 0.05, decay factor = 1/3, gain similarity ratio = 0.99
DECISION TREE, CHAID	*default values*: criterion = gain ratio (Decision Tree), Chi-square test (CHAID), minimal size for split = 4, minimal leaf size = 2, minimal gain = 0.1, maximum depth = 20, confidence = 0.25, no prepruning, postpruning enabled
ID3	*default values*: criterion = gain ratio, minimal size for split = 4, minimal leaf size = 2, minimal gain = 0.1
FOIL	max number of attributes per rule = 6

The maximum number of frequent sets for CBA and CMAR was increased to 1,000,000 since for support threshold lower then approximately 0.01%, the default limit of 500,000 prevented further improvements of the classifier. For DECISIONTREE, we initially obtained very low accuracy of 2%. This was caused by the prepruning step, which is enabled in RapidMiner by default. The resulting tree was composed of only one leaf class, which is the most frequent class label in the training data. The (post)pruning feature had a small but positive impact on accuracy and model size, therefore we left it enabled. For CPAR the default parameters produced acceptable results. Additional parameter tuning could have improved the performance of the algorithm.

The data were preprocessed to the form shown at Table 1 and randomly split to a training dataset (90%) and test dataset (10%). The experiments were run on Intel core i5 3320M CPU@2.6 GHz with 16 GB of RAM.

Table 4. Model benchmark on CLEF#26875 dataset (single 90/10 split). Model size refers to the number of rules for rule models and number of leaves for decision trees. Time is measured in seconds.

	time			
algorithm	train	test	accuracy	model size
DECISIONTREE	273	4	23.0	13496
ID3	290	4	22.8	13579
CHAID	284	3	**25.4**	13224
FOIL	815	1.5	24.7	18047
CPAR	**87**	1.23	4.6	18907
CBA	279	**0.25**	21.2	**3681**
CMAR	205	1.781	16.9	22516

The results depicted in Table 4 indicate that the overall best accuracy was obtained by the CHAID decision tree algorithm. CBA obtained accuracy close to the decision tree classifiers, however, with smaller training times and - for the on-line setting most significantly - shorter testing times. There are several factors contributing to the fast testing: a) the fact that CBA performs single rule classification, b) small number of rules in the classifier (compared to models created by other algorithms). The difference in test times between decision trees and the rule learning algorithms might be to a large extent caused by implementation-specific issues. Our impression is that additional optimization for the evaluation of the decision tree models could lead to substantially shorter test times.

Trading Speed for Accuracy. Speed of training can be important in on-line recommender setting. Fast training also typically entails simpler models that are faster to apply. The accuracy/execution time balance can be controlled by the minimum leaf size and/or maximum depth parameters for decision trees and by the minimum support parameter for ARC classifiers.

Table 5. Effect of support threshold - CBA (ten-fold shuffled cross-validation). Time is measured in seconds.

metric	0.10%	0.09%	0.08%	0.07%	0.06%	0.05%	0.04%	0.03%	0.02%	0.01%
accuracy	6.68	6.88	7.07	7.64	8.1	8.65	9.48	10.4	13.47	17.55
train time	1.8	2.3	3	4.56	5.6	8.7	14.6	30.5	172	477
test time	0.02	0.03	0.03	0.04	0.03	0.04	0.05	0.05	0.1	0.19
rule count	148	178	193	228	270	317	452	576	1100	2303

Table 6. Effect of support threshold - CMAR (ten-fold shuffled cross-validation). Time is measured in seconds.

metric	0.10%	0.09%	0.08%	0.07%	0.06%	0.05%	0.04%	0.03%	0.02%	0.01%
accuracy	4.82	5.12	5.28	5.78	6.12	6.59	7.48	8	10.23	13.84
train time	0.744	0.89	1	1.39	1.75	2.13	3.83	6.5	36.34	178.92
test time	0.11	0.115	0.14	0.144	0.18	0.2042	0.32	0.46	1.05	2.26
rule count	834	999	1177	1557	1863	2251	3581	5116	11450	20561

Tables 5 and 6 show the impact of varying the support threshold on the accuracy and execution time of the CBA and CMAR classifiers. To obtain more reliable estimates especially at higher support thresholds, we performed ten-fold cross-validation. Table 7 shows the impact of minimum leaf size on the ID3 results.

The comparison between ID3 and CBA at 13% accuracy level shows that ID3 has much shorter training time (8.58s vs 172s), but it also produces more complex models (3278 leaf nodes vs 1100 rules for CBA). The more compact model size contributes to fast test times for CBA.

Table 7. Effect of minimum leaf size - ID3 (ten-fold shuffled cross-validation, *based on one 90/10 split). Time is measured in seconds.

metric	100	90	80	70	60	50	40	30	20	10
accuracy	13.67	13.89	14.1	14.4	14.7	14.9	15.3	16.2	17	18.7
train time	8.58	8.58	9.04	9.57	10.57	12.17	13.93	18.09	25.4	80.66
test time	2.36	1.41	1.36	1.35	1.34	1.43	1.29	1.3	1.28	3.9
number of leaves*	3278	3362	3427	3522	3708	3959	4167	4817	5596	7389

Optimizing CBA. In the field of decision tree induction, one of the mainstream pruning techniques is reduced error pruning, which uses different sets of data for learning the classifier and for pruning. Our experiments with CBA on CLEF#26875 showed that dividing available training data into a training set and a holdout set for pruning (validation data) does not have a positive effect on classifier accuracy. We tried multiple ratios of training set/holdout set size without obtaining a notable increase in accuracy.

An interesting finding follows from results presented in Table 8: if only part of the data used for the rule learning phase (i.e. APRIORI in CBA) is used for the pruning phase (i.e. data coverage and default pruning in CBA), the impact on accuracy is small. The training time can be reduced substantially as smaller amount of data is processed.

Table 8. Effect of pruning data set size. 100% of training data were used for rule generation, only x% used for pruning. For this experiment, we used our implementation of CBA M1.

metric	1%	2%	5%	10%	20%	30%	50%	75%
rule count	38	48	78	96	125	138	151	166
accuracy [%]	4.5	5.6	6.6	6.8	7.1	7	6.9	6.9

Table 9. Impact of pruning steps in CBA. Minimum support set to 0.1% and minimum confidence set to 2%.

algorithm	accuracy	rules
no pruning, direct use of association rules	6.4	1735
data coverage pruning	6.9	497
data coverage, default rule pruning	7	175

The results of the experiments with omission of individual pruning steps from CBA (Table 9) indicate that both data coverage pruning and default rule pruning not only reduce the size of the rule set, but also slightly improve the accuracy of the model. Interestingly, the absolute difference in accuracy between direct use of association rules (as in the on-line challenge) and CBA is very small. However, the order of magnitude decrease in the number of rules in the classifier justifies the use of CBA in on-line setting which puts emphasis on fast prediction times.

4   Conclusion and Future Work

This paper presented evaluation of multiple Association Rule Classification (ARC) algorithms in the CLEF NewsReel'14 challenge. The on-line track of the challenge required the competing systems to balance the architecture and technologies with the complexity of the involved algorithms. The practical experience that we obtained with our InBeat.eu recommender system underpin the choice of association rules as a fast on-line recommender algorithm. The experiments performed on the off-line dataset indicate that the CBA association rule classifier can further improve the results in terms of accuracy and especially speed, as it significantly reduces the size of the rule set. The best accuracy in our benchmark on the off-line dataset was obtained by the CHAID decision tree induction algorithm.

We further investigated the options for optimizing the pruning workflow in the CBA algorithm. The results indicate that the primary effect of the CBA pruning is the reduction of the number of rules in the model and that the impact on classifier accuracy is small. However, the potential saving in training time resulting from omission of these pruning steps might be offset by the increase of prediction time due to increased model size. Experiments showed that a viable direction of training time optimization might be using only part of the available training data for pruning. Further decrease in the number of rules could be attained by applying pessimistic pruning, an optional step in CBA, which was not covered in our evaluation.

Our benchmark on the off-line dataset was methodologically limited with respect to the typical setting for evaluation of recommender algorithms a) by ignoring the temporal dimension associated with the instances in the dataset and b) by providing results in terms of accuracy. Since recommender systems are frequently used as rankers other evaluation metric than accuracy could be more suitable. Future work could thus aim at addressing these limitations.

Acknowledgments. The authors would like to wish the anonymous reviewers for their helpful feedback. The participation in the CLEF recommender challenge was supported by the EC project FP7-287911 LinkedTV. The experimental evaluation of the CBA method was performed within grant IGA 20/2013. Tomáš Kliegr benefited in writing this paper from "long term institutional support for research activities" of the Faculty of Informatics and Statistics, UEP.

References

1. Agrawal, R., Imieliński, T., Swami, A.: Mining association rules between sets of items in large databases. SIGMOD Rec. **22**(2), 207–216 (1993)
2. Coenen, F., Leng, P., Ahmed, S.: Data structure for association rule mining: T-trees and p-trees. IEEE Transactions on Knowledge and Data Engineering **16**(6), 774–778 (2004)
3. Cohen, W.W.: Fast effective rule induction. In: Proceedings of the 12th International Conference on Machine Learning, ML'95, pp. 115–123. Morgan Kaufmann, Lake Tahoe (1995)

4. Fürnkranz, J.: FOSSIL: a robust relational learner. In: Bergadano, F., De Raedt, L. (eds.) ECML 1994. LNCS, vol. 784, pp. 122–137. Springer, Heidelberg (1994)
5. Fürnkranz, J., Gamberger, D., Lavrač, N.: Foundations of Rule Learning. Springer (2012)
6. Hahsler, M., Grün, B., Hornik, K.: Arules - a computational environment for mining association rules and frequent item sets. Journal of Statistical Software **14**(15), 1–25 (2005)
7. Han, J., Pei, J., Yin, Y.: Mining frequent patterns without candidate generation. SIGMOD Rec. **29**(2), 1–12 (2000)
8. Kille, B., Hopfgartner, F., Brodt, T., Heintz, T.: The plista dataset. In: Proceedings of the International Workshop and Challenge on News Recommender Systems, NRS'13, pp. 14–22. ACM, October 2013
9. Li, W., Han, J., Pei, J.: CMAR: accurate and efficient classification based on multiple class-association rules. In: Cercone, N., Lin, T.Y., Wu, X. (eds.) The 2001 IEEE International Conference on Data Mining (ICDM'01), pp. 369–376. IEEE Computer Society (2001)
10. Liu, B., Hsu, W., Ma, Y.: Integrating classification and association rule mining. In: Proceedings of the 4th International Conference on Knowledge Discovery and Data Mining (KDD'98), pp. 80–86. AAAI Press, August 1998
11. Moghimipour, I. Ebrahimpour, M.: Comparing decision tree method over three data mining software. International Journal of Statistics and Probability **3**(3) (2014)
12. Quinlan, J.: Induction of decision trees. Machine Learning **1**(1), 81–106 (1986)
13. Quinlan, J.R.: Learning logical definitions from relations. Machine Learning **5**(3), 239–266 (1990)
14. Quinlan, J.R.: C4.5: Programs for Machine Learning. Morgan Kaufmann (1993)
15. Vanhoof, K., Depaire, B.: Structure of association rule classifiers: a review. In: International Conference on Intelligent Systems and Knowledge Engineering (ISKE), pp. 9–12, November 2010
16. Yin, X., Han, J.: CPAR: classification based on predictive association rules. In: Proceedings of the SIAM International Conference on Data Mining, pp. 369–376. SIAM Press, San Franciso (2003)

Enhancing Medical Information Retrieval by Exploiting a Content-Based Recommender Method

Wei Li[✉] and Gareth J.F. Jones[✉]

ADAPT Centre, School of Computing, Dublin City University, Dublin 9, Ireland
{wli,gjones}@computing.dcu.ie

Abstract. Information Retrieval (IR) systems seek to find information which is relevant to a searcher's information needs. Improving IR effectiveness using personalization has been a significant focus of research attention in recent years. However, in some situations there may be no opportunity to learn about the interests of a specific user on a certain topic. This is a particular problem for medical IR where individuals find themselves needing information on topics for which they have never previously searched. However, in all likelihood other users will have searched with the same information need previously. This presents an opportunity to IR researchers attempting to improve search effectiveness by exploiting previous user search behaviour. We describe a method to enhance IR in the medical domain based on recommender systems (RSs) by using a content-based recommender model in combination with a standard IR model. We use search behaviour data from previous users with similar interests to aid the current user to discover better search results. We demonstrate the effectiveness of this method using a test dataset collected as part of the EU FP7 Khresmoi project.

Keywords: Information retrieval · Content-based filtering · Medical search

1   Introduction

The ever increasing volume of information available online is creating increasing challenges for information retrieval (IR) technologies. One significant area of growth of online content and user searching is information related to medical issues. Additionally, in recent years within IR research there has been growing interest in IR methods which personalize the search process by taking advantage of the user's previous search history, with the objective of enabling them to locate relevant information more efficiently. Where the user is searching in a topical area of ongoing interest such an approach can prove very effective. However, in practice, users may enter queries on new topics which they have not searched on previously. This is often likely to be the case when performing search for medical topics. For example, a relative of the searcher may have been diagnosed with a condition and the searcher wishes to learn about their prognosis, any treatments that are recommended or lifestyle implications of the condition. Or a patient may present to a medical practitioner with a

© Springer International Publishing Switzerland 2015
J. Mothe et al. (Eds.): CLEF 2015, LNCS 9283, pp. 142–153, 2015.
DOI: 10.1007/978-3-319-24027-5_12

combination of symptoms which they have not seen before, and they may wish to find information to support them in attempting to make an accurate diagnosis.

Developing search tools to support the medical information needs of the general public and medical professionals was the focus on the EU FP7 Khresmoi project[1]. As part of the Kreshmoi project, the Health on the Net (HON) Foundation carried out a questionnaire based user study to examine the behaviour of the general public health in search. In their study, 24% of the respondents looked for health information on the Internet at least once a day (some mentioned doing this from four to six times a day), while 25% did it several times a week. The 11% who answered "Other" specified that they look for health information "from time to time" or "when needed". From these numbers it is clear that health information search is a very popular topic. While these searchers may never have tried to use an IR system to address their current specific medical information need before, it is likely that multiple previous searchers will have had the same or similar information needs for which they will have entered the same or similar queries, and subsequently indicated documents relevant to their need by clicking on them.

Analysis of the medical IR task for ad hoc search of open online collections by both the general public and general practitioners within the Khresmoi project demonstrated two significant challenges. First, the online information sources are highly varied in content style, but also in accuracy and reliability of the medical information that they contain. Some of the material comes from official agencies, other material comes from reliable and useful sources, such as support groups for individuals living with a particular medical condition, but other material comes from highly unreliable and potentially dangerous sources, based on unproven or untested treatments, etc. While a professional is likely to be able to filter and select helpful material, this may not be the case for some members of the general public, who consequentially will follow useless or dangerous advice. Second, queries entered by the general public and, perhaps surprisingly, medical professionals are in general very short, one or two words, and thus often highly ambiguous in terms of the searcher's information need even if the overall topic is clear, e.g. "lung cancer", diabetes". These queries will often match with many documents of varying quality and relating to different facets relating to the contents of the query. A standard way of at least partially addressing these problems in web search is to incorporate link-based methods such as the Page-Rank algorithm to promote the rank of popular content which matches the query. In the context of medical IR, we could make the reasonable assumption that the link structure will give a reasonable indication of the reliability and general utility of the information. However, this assumes that a suitable link structure has actually been established by the users of the information and is available to the search engine. In this paper we describe part of the search technology developed within Khresmoi to improve the effectiveness of medical IR in the absence of rich link structures and details of information reliability. This method exploits logs of the queries and click behaviour of previous searchers. This work combines a traditional IR model with a

---

[1] http://www.khresmoi.eu/

recommender method, our positive experimental results using data collected in the Khresmoi project illustrate its potential effectiveness.

The remainder of this paper is structured as follows: Section 2 introduces the framework of the integrated retrieval model; Section 3 outlines the process for the collection of the medical search data used in our investigation; Section 4 describes the experimental set up itself and reports and analyzes the results obtained; and finally Section 5 concludes the paper.

2   Framework of the Integrated IR Model

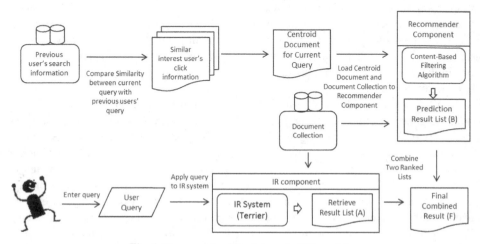

Fig. 1. Framework of the integrated IR model.

2.1   Background to Recommender Systems Applications

Recommender Systems (RSs) exploit the behaviour of multiple users to make predictions of items which future users may find useful if they are interested in the same topic. In recent years, RSs have started to appear in many applications where user feedback is available, for example in online applications such as *YouTube*[2], *Amazon*[3], and *EBay*[4]. These systems record the behaviour of users to build models of their interests, and use these to predict items which may be of interest to the current user based on feedback from previous ones.

By contrast, most existing personalized search engines require information from the specific current user in order to build a user profile [6]. This data can be collected by asking users to input their personal information preferences, including for example topics of interest or keywords, recording their search queries and click-through and viewing behaviour when browsing retrieved results, or by asking them to rate some

---

[2] http://www.youtube.com/
[3] http://www.amazon.com/
[4] http://www.ebay.com/

items or give other explicit feedback [6]. In other web search personalization technologies, data is collected without user involvement by exploiting the clustering of retrieved documents in order to create a complete personal user profile based on characterization of their search history. These approaches have been found to perform well in the modeled domains [4][5]. However, this approach will not work for new domains where the individual user has not provided personalized information, and it is not realistic to gather such information from the user before retrieval operations begin. In this situation we seek to make use of any information which is available from previous searchers with similar interests to improve retrieval effectiveness. To do this, we propose to exploit feedback from previous users' search behaviour. This information is used to suggest documents which may potentially be useful for a new searcher who is interested in the same topical area.

2.2   Combining Information Retrieval and Recommender Systems

IR and RSs have similar aims: they both attempt to provide users with items which meet their current information needs. For this reason, integrating IR with RSs has become a topic of research interest area in recent years. e.g. [2][3]. However most existing research in this area focuses only on applying collaborative data in IR models or developing a RS which makes use of the concepts and tools in an IR context [2][3]. This type of combination of IR and RSs is not integrating them in its true sense. By contrast, [10] introduces the I-SPY search system which performs personalized search by employing collaborative filtering methods. In [10], the collaborative filtering methods are used to represent user interests in terms of ratings over a set of items. Recommendations are then made to a target user by selecting items from a set of users with correlated rating histories. Finally collaborative filtering operates by exploiting a graded mapping between users and items. In this work, we utilize an approach to combining recommender technologies with standard IR models to produce an integrated IR model where user driven models are used to enhance the effectiveness of ranked IR systems. Similar to [10], we exploit the history information of similar users to perform search for the current user. However, since ratings are not available in our experiment, so use a content-based recommender method to aid the search results.

Most existing related work uses IR concepts to reformulate an RS model or the reverse of this using an RS scheme to reformulate an IR model. By contrast our integrated IR model combines recommendation results with IR results. We build IR and RS components separately, and carry out the combination in the final step before presentation of the search results. The aim of our integrated IR model is to better address the challenge of short, often ambiguous, queries where the user's intention is unclear. This problem typically arises for short queries where the terms match with many documents which may not be relevant or only focus on non-relevant facets of the topics represented by the query. In this situation here is no information available to help determine which facet is more likely to be relevant to the user. Personalized IR (PIR) is widely used to address this challenge, however in some conditions, including the medical environments which form the focus of our work, personal data for the user relating to their information need is not available. In this condition, we attempt to exploit the search behaviour of previous users to aid the current user to find better results to meet his/her information needs.

Figure 1 shows the framework of our integrated IR model. This method for integrating a recommender component into a standard IR system proceeds as follows:

- Capture user logs from previous searches. These include each query entered by each user to search the available document archive, and the sequence of documents that each user clicked in response to their query.
- When a new user enters a query into the system: i) pass the query to the standard IR component to retrieve a set of potentially relevant search results from the available document collection; ii) use the query to select a group of queries previously entered by users with similar interests by comparing it to the contents of the queries they entered.
- Use the search logs of the selected similar interest users to generate a centroid document for the current query.
- Use a content-based filtering method to process the centroid document and the data collection to generate a prediction ranked list.
- Integrate the results of the IR search and RS predictions using a linear combination of the scores for each retrieved document. This step effectively means that we use the prediction result list from the RS to re-rank the IR result list

The aim of this model is twofold. First, it addresses the short query problem for IR systems, when the user enters a short query to the system, and it is not clear which matching documents are most likely to be relevant. Second, it ameliorates the key cold start problem of RSs. If no similar interest previous user found, the output of recommender component may become unreliable. In this case, retrieval results can be used to aid the recommendations to provide users with useful information. Thus the integrated IR model aims to exploit IR and RSs to benefit each other.

3   Experimental Test Collection

The Kreshmoi project performed research using both existing search logs from the general public and medical professional, and logs from studies carried out within the project examining users' search behaviour, the effectiveness of search tools and user interaction with retrieved information. In order to gather query sets from specific groups, a user interface was constructed using the *ezDL*, open-source search system [1]. This was connected to public online health websites, including medical text and image information, across different languages, including English, Spanish and German. User queries and their search activities including click through behaviour were recorded. The dataset used for our experimental investigation was extracted from the English language user logs collected using the *ezDL* user interface for a
cohort of general practitioners searching publically accessible online medical information portals.

3.1   Query Set

For our investigation, a total of 10,713 queries were extracted from the query log archive. Since for this study we focus only on the textual content, we removed image-based queries and also filtered meaningless queries. Meaningless queries here were queries without particular meaning for the medical search, such as numbers, single letters or words like 'test', these filtered queries were defined manually. Finally a total of 7,161 queries were selected for our experimental query set. 6,000 of these were selected at random for use as the training set for our recommender model with the remaining 1,161 queries forming the test query set.

3.2   Click-Through Data

The click-through information for each selected query was extracted from the query log. Fig. 2 shows an example of a user's click-through information including the associated query, clicked urls and the click order of these urls. In Fig. 2, eventid indicates the query side information (eventid links to another table which includes both user information and the query associated with these clicked documents), the param-value column shows the list of urls that the user clicked, and sequence column shows the clicked sequence of each url.

eventid	paramname	paramvalue	sequence
12	item	mimir:knowyourabcs:2011:h.qes.subject.all	0
12	item	term:C0850356	1
12	item	clinicaltrial:http://data.linkedct.org/resource/trials/NCT00241956:The Royal Melbourne Hospital	2
12	item	clinicaltrial:http://data.linkedct.org/resource/trials/NCT00250731:State University of New York Upstate Medical University	3
12	item	term:C0085207	4
12	item	clinicaltrial:http://data.linkedct.org/resource/trials/NCT00201292:Department of Health-Yuli Hospital	5
12	item	clinicaltrial:http://data.linkedct.org/resource/trials/NCT00245882:VA Pittsburgh Healthcare System	6
12	item	term:C0011848	7
12	item	clinicaltrial:http://data.linkedct.org/resource/trials/NCT00091949:Center for Neurologic Research	8
12	item	clinicaltrial:http://data.linkedct.org/resource/trials/NCT00091949:University of New Mexico	9
12	item	clinicaltrial:http://data.linkedct.org/resource/trials/NCT00091949:Hartford	10
12	item	clinicaltrial:http://data.linkedct.org/resource/trials/NCT00091949:Denver Health and Hospital Authority	11
12	item	clinicaltrial:http://data.linkedct.org/resource/trials/NCT00091949:Beth Israel Deaconess	12
12	item	clinicaltrial:http://data.linkedct.org/resource/trials/NCT00091949:George Washington Univeristy	13
12	item	clinicaltrial:http://data.linkedct.org/resource/trials/NCT00091949:Via Christi Regional Medical Center	14
12	item	clinicaltrial:http://data.linkedct.org/resource/trials/NCT00091949:Yale University	15

Fig. 2. Example of a user's click-through information.

Again, we only consider the textual content, clicked image pages were removed from each user's search activities. From Fig. 2, we can see that, there some clicked data are not urls, e.g 'term:C08050356', these are the Mímir [5] index documents. Since we are unable to access these documents, they are also removed. This resulted in a total set of 3,374 distinct urls. The number of clicked pages is far less than the number of queries because many queries are the same or very similar. There are a large number of user queries on the same topic, e.g. 'diabetes' was queried 665 times and 'heart' 521 times. For these duplicate queries, their clicked-through search logs

---

[5] Mímir : Multiparadigm Indexing and Retrieval Tool. https://gate.ac.uk/mimir/

contain a large number of the same pages. This duplication is useful when recommendations for the current user with an interest in a similar topic are to be made based on the previous click-through behaviour.

3.3   Document Collection

Since the interface used to gather the user queries and click-through actions was connected to public information services, we did not have access to the underlying document sets used by these retrieval services. In order to explore the effectiveness of our integrated search model, and indeed to build our content-based recommender, we needed a document set. To construct an experimental document set we used Scrapy[6] to crawl the contents of all the pages clicked by the users and many of the other pages from the websites from which they were drawn, predominantly: http://www.biomedcentral.com, http://
data.linkedct.org/resource and http://wifo5-03.informatik.uni-mannheim.de The total number of documents crawled for use in our test collection was 102,600 documents. The textual content extracted for each page constitutes the data collection we used for this experiment.

3.4   Query Relevance Data

For each query, we assumed that its corresponding list of clicked pages corresponds to a reasonable relevance set for the query. While use of a more formal process for relevance assessment, for example using a pooling procedure with manual relevance assessment, might be expected to produce a richer set of relevance data, since we do not have access to the original creators of the queries to enquire about their information needs, and based on inspection of our dataset, we believe that the click-through information formed a reasonably representative relevance set.

4   Experimental Investigation

In this section, we first describe the components of the integrated retrieval system used in our investigation and their combination, we then report and analyse the experimental results for the test collection described in the previous section.

4.1   Information Retrieval Component

The IR component for our integrated model was constructed using the Terrier[7] platform. The Terrier implementation of the standard BM25 IR model [10] was used to generate ranked lists for the IR component, with the standard parameter settings of

---

[6] http://scrapy.org/
[7] terrier.org

b=0.75 and K1=1.2. The Terrier system stop-word list of 733 words was used with Porter stemming [8] applied to the documents and the queries.

Query expansion using relevance feedback is often found to be effective for ad hoc IR tasks. While relevance feedback using relevance data provided by users is generally found to be most effective, useful improvements are often found using pseudo relevance feedback where the top ranked documents are assumed to be relevant. We thus examined the potential for pseudo relevance feedback (PRF) to improve retrieval effectiveness for our task, we applied the standard Rocchio query expansion method.

4.2   Recommender Component

Most recommender systems can broadly be classified into content-based filtering (CBF) approaches and collaborative-filtering (CF) methods. In previous work we have demonstrated the potential for the use of CF methods in an integrated IR and RS model for news retrieval with a small query set gathered in a laboratory setting [12]. However, CF methods require ratings information to be available for previously accessed items, and since for our current task there is no rating information available, we apply a CBF recommender method for our current task.

CBF algorithms are based on the content of the document and a profile of the current user. In a CBF RS, keywords are used to represent the document, while a user profile needs to be built to indicate the type of document a user likes. In other words, these algorithms seek to provide users with documents which are similar to documents they liked in the past. Different retrieval models have been explored for use in CBF systems, including keyword matching and the Vector Space Model (VSM) with basic TF-IDF (Term Frequency-Inverse Document Frequency) weighting.

For this study, we chose the latter method. The standard TF-IDF function shown in Equation (1) is used to weight the terms.

$$TF - IDF(t, d) = TF(t, d) \cdot log \frac{N}{n_t} \tag{1}$$

where $TF(t,d)$ is the term frequency of term t in document . N denotes the number of documents in the corpus, and n_t denotes the number of documents in the dataset in which the term   occurs at least once.

In order for the term weights to fall in the [0,1] interval[8] and for the documents to be represented by vectors of equal length, weights obtained by Equation (1) are normalized using the cosine normalization shown in Equation (2).

$$T_{w_{t,d}} = \frac{TF - IDF(t,d)}{\sqrt{\sum_{s=1}^{|T|} TF - IDF(t_s,d)^2}} \tag{2}$$

where t_s indicates that a term occurs in document d, and $|T|$ is the total number of all terms in document vocabulary.

---

[8]   Here we do the normalizing for the term weight because we need to compare the document vector with the user profile vector for which term weight also fall into [0,1] interval.

The standard cosine similarity measure shown in Equation (3) is used to compare the similarity between two document vectors.

$$sim(d_i, d_j) = \frac{\sum_t w_{ti} \cdot w_{tj}}{\sqrt{\sum_t w_{ti}^2} \cdot \sqrt{\sum_k w_{tj}^2}} \tag{3}$$

where w_{ti} is the weight of term t in document d_i.

In CBF using the VSM, both user profiles and target documents are represented as weighted term vectors. Predictions of a user's interest in a particular document are calculated by computing the cosine similarity between them.

For the CBF recommender component of our integrated system, the first step is to find other users who share similar interests, and then to generate recommendations for a query based on the click-through information from these users. Since many searchers entered queries on the same topic, to identify similar search interests, we simply compare the current user's query with previous queries, if the query for comparison is the same or shares a term, we consider it to be similar.

Since the queries are typically very short, generally one or at most two words, they are too short to compute a reliable similarity measure between the current query and documents, we use a centroid representation [9] for the current query to perform the similarity computation.

Centroid Document

Since we presume that the current user only contributes the current query, and provides no other information, the entered query usually contains at most 2 to 3 terms, we need to generate a presentation of the query to operate the content-based filtering method. In order to generate a centroid representation for the current query q, we adopted the following procedure:

(i)   Find all similar previous users based on their entered queries. Since for most users, they query on the exactly same topic, like 'diabetes' ,'lung cancer' etc., in this work, we only consider the same query and queries which share the same terms to be similar queries.

(ii)   After selecting the similar queries, we go through their click data, and take the most frequently clicked 5 documents from these selected previous similar users' logs to generate its centroid document. This top 5 set is based on the results of an empirical training phase.

(iii)   For each of the selected most clicked documents d in the similar interest group, stopwords are first removed with subsequent application of Porter stemming

(iv)   The resulting document vector is then weighted using normalised TF-IDF to produce a weighted vector $d_{tf\text{-}idf}=(tf\text{-}idf_1, tf\text{-}idf_2,...)$.

(v)   For the set N of documents and their corresponding vector representations, we define the centroid vector C_q for the query using Equation (4).

$$C_q = \frac{1}{|N|} \cdot \sum_{i=1}^{N} d_i \tag{4}$$

Recommendations Generate

The procedure for application of the CBF method to the output recommendations for each test query is as follows:

- Generate the centroid document for the current query to be used as its representation.
- For each candidate document, compute its similarity with the representation of the query using cosine similarity, and rank all candidate documents in descending order based on their distance from the current query centroid document.

4.3   Combination of Results

The ranked lists produced by the IR and CBF components are combined using a standard *CombSUM* operation as shown below.

$$CombSUM_i = \sum_{i \in (IR\ scheme\ \cup RS\ scheme)} score_i = score\_IR_i + score\_RS_i$$

The *CombANZ* operator is then applied to the *CombSUM$_i$* result to create the ranked retrieval list. *CombANZ$_i$* is specified as the same sum of document scores as *CombSUM$_i$* but divided by the number of ranking schemes which contain document *i*.

$$CombANZ_i = \frac{CombSUM_i}{number\ of\ nonzero\ score_i} \tag{5}$$

4.4   Experimental Results

The results of our experimental results are shown in Table 1, where IR indicates the result for the standard search engine result without PRF query expansion (QE). IR+QE represents the IR results with QE, and IR+QE+CBF is the results obtained by combining the standard IR+QE results with the output obtained from the recommender component (CBF).

Results are shown for precision at rank cutoffs at 5, 10 and 20 documents, and standard MAP. For the IR+QE results, the top 5 ranked documents are assumed to be relevant and 5 additional terms are added to the original query. These parameters

Table 1. Results comparison for standard IR results with the output of the integrated model. †
indicates a statistically significant (where the Wilcoxon statistical significant evaluation method is used with 95% confidence or 5% error) increase compared to IR results.

	MAP	P@5	P@10	P@20

IR	0.4109	0.3726	0.3167	0.2730
IR+QE	0.4354	0.3973	0.3521	0.2789
IR+QE+CBF	0.5015†	0.4289†	0.3814†	0.2936

were varied in a series of runs with these values giving the best results. While assuming 5 relevant documents is a common value for PRF in other tasks, we might generally expect to obtain the best results by adding more than 5 additional terms to the query. However, for this dataset, the very short initial queries are generally somewhat ambiguous, leading to diverse focus in the retrieved documents, in this situation we found that adding more terms to the original query produced unfocused expanded queries with somewhat random retrieval behaviour.

From the results shown in Table 1, it can be seen that the addition of QE leads to a non-significant improvement in retrieved effectiveness according to all the evaluation metrics. Combining the IR+QE ranked list with the QBF ranked list produces further improvements in IR effectiveness for all evaluation metrics, which are significant according to the P@5, P@10 and MAP metrics. The results show that while using the only IR system obtains relatively good search results, the integrated model improves on these. The reason for this is that it promotes the rank of documents which have been clicked by previous users with similar search interests.

As mentioned previously, in this work, large numbers of users query on the same topic. This means that a large number of similar users' information can be found for these topics, and the final combined results improves significantly. However, for some rarer topics, only a few or non-similar users found, the overall results show that in this condition, the framework will also output reasonable retrieval results.

5   Conclusions and Further Investigations

This paper investigated the application of a retrieval method combining a standard IR algorithm and a CBF recommender model for an ad hoc medical IR task. Experimental results with a collection of queries and click-through data collected using a prototype search application from the Khresmoi project and a collection of crawled online medical information, showed that our integrated model is able to significantly improve high-end precision compared to a standard IR model. This demonstrates that we are able to make effective use of relatively small query log archives with user-click through data to improve retrieval effectiveness for related queries, even in the absence of formally collected relevance data.

While these results are encouraging, the document collection used here is relatively small and contains reliable medical information. In further work we intend to explore the application of this method in medical search settings where the searcher is accessing larger more diverse collections containing less reliable medical content. Also in this work, we only conduct one experimental run, a K-fold cross validation method will be investigated in the future work to examine the average performance of the proposed method, in order to further examine the effectiveness of the introduced framework and method.

In this paper, the methods employed are quite simple, in future work, we will apply more sophisticated methods to discover similar taste users for the current query, and attempt to use different recommender methods to compute recommendation and to investigate use of alternative fusion methods to do the final combination.

Acknowledgments. The research leading to these results received funding from the European Union Seventh Framework Program (FP7/2007-2013) under grant agreement no 257528 (KHRESMOI). This work was also partially supported by SFI (07/CE/I1142) as part of the Centre for Next Generation Localisation (CNGL) at Dublin City University.

References

1. Beckers, T., Dungs, S., Fuhr, N., Jordan, M., Kriewel, S.: ezDL: an interactive search and evaluation system. In: Proceedings of SIGIR 2012 Workshop on Open-Source Information Retrieval (OSIR 2012), August 2012
2. Bellogín, A., Wang, J., Castells, P.: Text retrieval methods for item ranking in collaborative filtering. In: Clough, P., Foley, C., Gurrin, C., Jones, G.J.F., Kraaij, W., Lee, H., Mudoch, V. (eds.) ECIR 2011. LNCS, vol. 6611, pp. 301–306. Springer, Heidelberg (2011)
3. Costa, A., Roda, F.: Recommender systems by means of information retrieval. In: Proceedings of the International Conference on Web Intelligence, Mining and Semantics (WIMS 2011), Sogndal, Norway, Article No. 57 (2011)
4. Jansen, B.J., Spink, A., Bateman, J., Saracevic, T.: Real Life Information Retrieval: A Study of User Queries on the Web. ACM SIGIR Forum **32**(1), 5–17 (1998)
5. Jeon, H., Kim, T., Choi, J.: Adaptive user profiling for personalized information retrieval. In: Proceedings of 3rd International Conference on Convergence and Hybrid Information Technology (ICCIT 2008), vol. 2, pp. 836–841. Busan (2008)
6. Li, W., Jones, G.J.F.: Utilizing recommender algorithms for enhanced information retrieval. In: Proceedings of OAIR 2013 - 10th International Conference in the RIAO series, Lisbon, Portugal (2013)
7. Mylonas, P., Vallet, D., Castells, P., FernÁndez, M., Avrithis, Y.: Personalized Information Retrieval Based on Context and Ontological Knowledge. Journal of The Knowledge Engineering Review **23**(1), 73–100 (2008)
8. Porter, M.F.: An algorithm for suffix stripping. Program **14**(3), 130–137 (1980)
9. Radev, D.R., Jing, H.Y., Styś, M., Tam, D.: Centroid-based summarization of multiple documents. In: Proceeding of Emerging Trends in Engineering and Technology, ICETET 2008 (2008)
10. Robertson, S.E., Walker, S., Jones, M.S.: Okapi at TREC-3. In: The Proceeding of Second Text Retrieval Conference (TREC-3) (1995)
11. Smyth, B., Freyne, J., Coyle, M., Briggs, P., Balfe, E.: I-SPY – anonymous, community-based personalization by collaborative meta-search. In: Proceedings of the 23rd SGAI International Conference on Innovative Techniques and Applications of Artificial Intelligence (2003)
12. Yu, J., Liu, F.F., Zhao, H.H.: Building user profile based on concept and relation for web personalized services. In: International Proceedings of Computer Science & Information Tech., vol. 36, pp. 172 (2012)

Summarizing Citation Contexts of Scientific Publications

Sandra Mitrović$^{(\boxtimes)}$ and Henning Müller

University of Applied Sciences Western Switzerland (HES–SO), Sierre, Switzerland
sandra.mitrovic1402@gmail.com

Abstract. As the number of publications is increasing rapidly, it becomes increasingly difficult for researchers to find existing scientific papers most relevant for their work, even when the domain is limited. To overcome this, it is common to use paper summarization techniques in specific domains. In difference to approaches that exploit the paper content itself, in this paper we perform summarization of the citation context of a paper. For this, we adjust and apply existing summarization techniques and we come up with a hybrid method, based on clustering and latent semantic analysis. We apply this on medical informatics publications and compare performance of methods that outscore other techniques on a standard database. Summarization of the citation context can be complementary to full text summarization, particularly to find candidate papers. The reached performance seems good for routine use even though it was only tested on a small database.

Keywords: Text summarization · Sentence similarity · Citation context

1 Introduction

The increasing volume of produced research papers makes their use difficult and time–consuming, even for a small scientific domain. One way to quickly grasp the main results of a set of existing papers is through paper summarization. However, since publications can be long, this approach is not always efficient to get the most important aspects of a paper. Instead, the context in which a paper is cited can be used as indicator for its main contributions [6]. This context (known as *citation context* or *citation summary*) refers to a set of sentences pointing to the paper [17] when cited. If the publication is frequently cited, its citation context is also long, so we propose summarizing citation contexts longer than two sentences (otherwise, we consider them concise). We opt for generic extractive summarization where the aim is to extract original sentences that preserve the substance of the original text, leaving out potentially irrelevant details. In order to complete our task, we combine several existing approaches into a novel workflow and apply it on 50 randomly selected publications from our research group. We first extract and segment references, detect citations and merge them into integrated citation contexts. Then, we summarize them using

© Springer International Publishing Switzerland 2015
J. Mothe et al. (Eds.): CLEF 2015, LNCS 9283, pp. 154–165, 2015.
DOI: 10.1007/978-3-319-24027-5_13

methods based on clustering and latent semantic analysis (LSA). We did not restrict summary length in advance, since previous work suggests that such an approach can affect summarization results [8]. Instead, we use an approach based on word distribution [1]. We compare algorithm performance using standard evaluation measures such as ROUGE [10] and the F1–measure on two data sets. We also explain challenges faced during different phases of our work including the small size of a citation context and relaxed grammatical structures, which increase the complexity of summarization.

2   Related Work

Reference Extraction and Segmentation. Reference formats are not standardized. Hence, despite much existing work, there are continuous efforts to improve reference extraction. ParsCit[1] (successfully used in [12]) is the current state–of–the–art reference extraction system that uses both heuristics and conditional random fields. Another freely available tool for extracting metadata from scientific publications is PDFmeat[2], based on Google Scholar[3]. On the other side, efficient results were obtained even with regular expressions and heuristics [2].

Citation Context Extraction. Identifying the full span of a citation context within a publication is a challenge. While previous work [4] suggests using a fixed character–length window around a citation, [19] concluded that sentence–based contexts are more effective than windows of equivalent length.

Text Summarization. During almost half a century, text summarization evolved into different branches. We constrain this overview to generic extractive single–document techniques. Generic means that summary refers to the main topic of the entire text. Extractive means that the parts of text conveying essential information are simply extracted without modification. A significant amount of work on extractive summaries uses statistical [24] and machine learning approaches [5,22]. One of the most recent approaches is based on prior sentence clustering [1,16], selecting for the summary the most representative sentences from each cluster. Another group of articles applies LSA [15,21]. Text summarization is a challenging task due to anaphors and cataphors. Moreover, extractive summaries usually require human intervention to smooth the transition from one topic to another.

Sentence Similarity. Text clustering relies on sentence similarity to distinguish the most relevant parts of the document. Since citation contexts are usually short, we aim at determining sentence semantic similarity which reduces to word semantic similarity. The latter can be ontology/thesaurus–based or information theory/corpus–based (also called distributional) [9]. Onthology–based measures

---

[1] http://aye.comp.nus.edu.sg/parsCit/
[2] http://dbs.uni-leipzig.de/pdfmeatdemo/demo.html
[3] http://scholar.google.com/

156   S. Mitrović and H. Müller

relate to the distance between concepts in onthology (known as path similarity) or to information content (e.g. [18]). Pointwise mutual information and LSA are two well–known techniques used in corpus–based similarity. The choice of the sentence similarity measure influences the summarization result [1,16].

Evaluation of Summaries. We focus on direct (*intrinsic*) evaluation of summaries, where a summary is compared with a gold standard. Although it is not easy to agree on a gold standard, if it is available, the standard F1–measure can be used, as well as ROUGE [10], a widely accepted measure introduced at DUC[4]. ROUGE is based on statistical overlapping of gold standard and automatically created summary. The pyramid method [13] is a semi–automatic content–based method based on construction of a pyramid containing so–called summarization content units. Methods without manual summaries appeared recently but the results obtained correlate well with ROUGE [23].

3   Materials and Methods

3.1   Data and Tools

We use 50 randomly selected publications belonging to researchers of the eHealth unit of HES–SO[5]. All publications are provided in PDF format (in English) and refer to medical information retrieval but differ in size and layout. We refer to this data set (and data extracted from it) as the HES–SO data set. Additionally, a benchmark called DUC2002 with 567 document–summary pairs was used for summarization evaluation (used as baseline in [1]).

Except for the Java library PDFBox[6], used to convert PDF to text, the code was entirely developed using Python NLTK [3] and the Scikit libraries. For storing all data we use MySQL. Summarization was implemented and run on a Hadoop[7] distributed computing platform. In our setting, map was performing summarization related calculations, while the reducer was responsible for storing summaries at the requested location in the database. In this manner, the reducer remains the same for different summarization methods.

3.2   Suggested Approach

Reference Extraction, Segmentation and Matching. To precipitate pre–processing, we tried applying ParsCit and PDFmeat on the HES–SO data but both provided unsatisfactory results (on a paper with 52 references, ParsCit correctly extracted only the first 19, while PDFmeat substituted all authors' names (except the first) with "et al."). Thus, we decided to implement this part

---

[4] Document Understanding Conference; http://duc.nist.gov/
[5] http://medgift.hevs.ch/
[6] http://pdfbox.apache.org/
[7] http://hadoop.apache.org

ourselves as a mixture of regular expressions and heuristics since we had no manually–annotated training set. Moreover, these fairly simple methods proved efficient [2].

Extracting References. For identifying the reference section, apart from common starting keywords (as in [2,12]), we had to include additional checks regarding section ends since 14% of the selected HES–SO papers had additional content behind references (e.g. correspondence addresses). Next, we constructed regular expressions capturing numbered references (e.g. *[1].* or *1.*) since only these appeared in the sample data and drastically outnumbered non–numbered references in the complete publication set. The HES–SO data contained 1055 references, thus on average each paper had 21,1 references (min 6, max 61).

Reference Segmentation. We extract from each reference: author names, title, year, journal/venue, volume, number and pages (where applicable). As mentioned, reference formats are not standardized, differing in content, order of mentioned elements, separators used. We used four pattern types to capture the most dominant patterns of author names (see Table 1). To avoid overlaps and

Table 1. Pattern types used for capturing author names

Pattern type description	Examples
initials followed by surname	A. García Seco de Herrera; D. M. Van De Ville; L.-T. Guo; M.-A. Keller-Rex; G. McLeman; C. E. Kahn Jr.
surname followed by name or name initials	Van De Ville Dimitri; van Ginneken BJ; McLennan Geoffrey; da Costa JC; Shyu Chi-Ren; Leh TM (also Leh T M); Similowski Thomas
surname, initials	Fillion-Robin, J.-C.; Mazzoncini de Azevedo-Marques, P.; van Ginneken, B.; Guo, L.-T.; McLeman, G.; Bakke, B., Jr.; Leh, T.M.;
name surname	Jayashree Kalpathy-Cramer; Dimitri Van De Ville; Bruno van Ginneken; Lao-Tze Guo; Yasin Ben Salem

incorrect matches (e.g. "John Doe" matches both pattern 2 and 4), we developed four pre–parsers (one per pattern). While this handled situations where among several different author formats in a paper one was predominant, we still encountered a few exceptions: different author formats appearing within the same reference (e.g. *Thomas M. Deserno, Sameer Antani, and L. Rodney Long*), missing authors, typos etc. For extracting titles, we used NLTK [3] sentence extraction, working well except when title contained a dot sign or consisted of more than one affirmative sentence. For years, we modified 4 digit patterns to cover different date formats (e.g. *May/Jun 2012*), usually scanning reference string backwards. For volume, number and pages, we combined their dedicated patterns (e.g.: *vol. 3* or *p. 12-16*) with those allowing their common retrieval (e.g. *20(May(3)):26-39* or *75(1-2): 11-9*). Finally, the remainder of the reference was taken as journal/venue.

Reference Matching. As the same publication can be cited in different papers and using various formats (see Figure 1), it was essential to identify all the re–occurrences of the same paper in order to properly define citation context. We implemented 4 matching scenarios ranging from exact matching to similarity estimation based on heuristically determining similarity thresholds and Damerau-Levenshtein distance, modified to tolerate reasonable differences between two strings. These allowed matching when a list of authors is replaced with "et al.", when one author is accidentally omitted or when differences stem from special character misspellings (e.g. "Müller" (correct) vs. "Muller"/"Mueller") etc.

Müller, H., Michoux, N., Bandon, D., Geissbuhler, A.: A review of content-based image retrieval systems in medicine-clinical benefits and future directions. Int. J. Med. Inf. 73(1) (2004) 1-23

H. Müller, N. Michoux, D. Bandon and A. Geissbuhler, "A review of content-based image retrieval systems in medicine-clinical benefits and future directions," *Internation Journal of Medical Informatics*, vol. 73, no. 1, pp. 1-23, 2004.

Fig. 1. Two formats of the same reference

3.3   Text Summarization

We perform text summarization using two approaches: clustering and LSA.

Similarity Measures for the Clustering-Based Approaches. We used two types of similarity measures for clustering: one based on a thesaurus referred to as **combined** and other, referred to as **distributional**.

1. Thesaurus–Based Similarity Measures. This similarity measure is an adaptation of the similarity measure used in [16] and represents a linear combination of three similarity measures. With all of them, for each particular citation context we dynamically create vocabularies eliminating stop words using the Python NLTK library. Then, each sentence is considered a bag of words.

For the first measure, the similarity between two sentences was calculated in the same way as in [16]: $sim_1(S_1, S_2) = \dfrac{2 * matched(S_1, S_2)}{num\_words(S_1) + num\_words(S_2)}$, where $matched(S_1, S_2)$ is the number of words that the two sentences S_1 and S_2 share and $num\_words(S)$ is the number of words that sentence S contains.

The second similarity measure in [16] was based on TF–IDF scores using uni–grams, bi–grams and tri–grams. We took into account only uni–grams, since cocitation formulations usually differ significantly [6]. The similarity between two sentences $sim_2(S_1, S_2)$ is calculated as cosine similarity of the corresponding sentences' TF–IDF vectors (more precisely, TF–ISF as in our setting, sentence corresponds to document, word to term and citation context to corpus).

It is worth noting that despite their similarities, first and second similarity measures express different concepts: while the first focuses exclusively on vocabulary overlap, the second emphasizes the overlapping word importance.

The third similarity measure focuses on semantic similarity. Since we did not deal with Chinese, instead of using HowNet[8] (as in [16]), we decided to use WordNet[9] [11], an enormous lexical database and online thesaurus in English. In WordNet, similarity is defined on the level of synsets (sets of near synonyms that share a common meaning (sense)). Thus, we define word–word similarity as maximal similarity between any two of their senses [9]:

$$ww\_sim(w_1, w_2) = max\{ss\_sim(s_1, s_2) : s_1 \in synset(w_1), s_2 \in synset(w_2)\},$$

where ss_sim is similarity between two senses s_1, s_2 (calculated using provided Python NLTK functions). Further, we define word–sentence similarity as in [16]: $ws\_sim(w, S) = max\{ww\_sim(w, v) : v \in S, v \ word\}$ and finally, sentence-sentence similarity as:

$$sim_3(S_1, S_2) = \frac{\sum_{w_i \in S_1} ws\_sim(w_i, S_2) + \sum_{w_j \in S_2} ws\_sim(w_j, S_1)}{num\_words(S_1) + num\_words(S_2)}$$

The final similarity measure is obtained as a linear combination of the three calculated measures: $sim(S_1, S_2) = \sum_{i=1}^{3} \lambda_i sim_i(S_1, S_2)$. We repeat the entire procedure twice: first, setting ss_sim in sim_3 to be a path similarity measure (obtaining thus similarity measure sim that we refer to as COMB_PATH), and second, using the Resnik similarity measure for ss_sim in sim_3 (denoting final similarity sim as COMB_RES). It is also worth mentioning that we use a general-purpose corpus $wordnet\_ic$ for generating an information content file applied to calculate the Resnik similarity.

Initially, we borrowed values of parameters λ from [16], since they also gave more importance to semantic similarity, but we also performed a small experiment varying the values (while retaining $\lambda_1 + \lambda_2 + \lambda_3 = 1$).

2. Distributional Similarity Measures. In distributional algorithms words are similar if they have similar distributional contexts [9]. They are used to overcome the problems of missing or incomplete thesauri. In this approach, we construct a word–context matrix which is based on positive pointwise mutual information (PPMI) [14], calculated as:

$$PPMI(w, c) = \begin{cases} PMI(w, c) = log_2 \frac{freq(w, c)}{freq(w) * freq(c)} : \ if \ PMI(w, c) > 0 \\ 0 : otherwise \end{cases}$$

where $freq(w, c)$ is the number of times that word w has context c, $freq(w)$ is the number of word w occurrences, $freq(c)$ is the number of context c occurrences. We build a PPMI matrix (with words as rows and contexts as columns) taking 20 words around the word as its context (to avoid computational complexity), apply add–one smoothing (to avoid bias toward infrequent occurrences) and define a word–word similarity measure, using Dice: $sim_{Dice}(v, w) = \frac{2 * \sum_i min(v_i, w_i)}{\sum_i (v_i + w_i)}$ and Jaccard similarity: $sim_{Jaccard}(v, w) = \frac{\sum_i min(v_i, w_i)}{\sum_i max(v_i, w_i)}$, where v_i is the PPMI value for word v in the context i and w_i is PPMI value for word w in the context i. These two measures are selected as they perform better than cosine [20]. We then calculate similarity between sentences

---

[8] http://www.keenage.com/
[9] http://wordnet.princeton.edu/

as: $sim(S_1, S_2) = \frac{\sum_{w_1 \in S_1} \sum_{w_2 \in S_2} word\_sim(w_1, w_2)}{\sqrt{num\_words(S_1) * num\_words(S_2)}}$, where $word\_sim$ is once Dice (denoted in further text as PPMI_DICE) and another time Jaccard similarity (denoted as PPMI_JACCARD).

Clustering–Based Approach. Since we did not have training data, we experimented with three clustering methods: K-means, hierarchical agglomerative clustering (HAC) and affinity propagation (AP). For each of these, the four similarity measures were used. Due to different syntactic and semantic features of citation contexts, the number of clusters was not defined in advance. Instead, we calculated it based on the distribution of words [1] in the sentences of particular citation contexts: $K = n * \frac{|C|}{\sum_{i=1}^{n} |S_i|}$, where $|C|$ and $|S_i|$ are the number of words in citation context C and i–th sentence of citation context C respectively, n is the number of sentences in citation context C. Details can be seen in [1].

With K–means, we randomly selected K sentences for the K initial cluster centroids (Forgy method). A convergence to a global optimum with K–means cannot be guaranteed. Thus, to avoid obtaining clusters not reflecting the real situation, we ran the algorithm 10 times with random initializations and selected as final clustering the one with minimal intercluster similarity and maximal intracluster similarity.

In HAC, we followed the "bottom–up" approach, starting from clusters containing only one sentence and progressively merging them into bigger clusters. Among the three most popular linkage criteria determining how the distance/similarity between clusters can be calculated, we decided to apply average linkage clustering which defines linkage between two sets A and B as: $\frac{1}{|A||B|} \sum_{a \in A} \sum_{b \in B} d(a, b)$, where d is dissimilarity or similarity measure.

AP is a clustering method based on message passing between data points in the initial data set [7]. Unlike other clustering methods, for AP we used a method from the Python Scikit library. We kept all default parameters, except for three. First, we determined the number of clusters in the same way as for previous clustering algorithms; second, we used the explained similarity measures instead of the default (negative Euclidean) and third, we increased the number of iterations until convergence from a default 15 to 20. Since we did not use the default affinity, the obtained result contained only cluster labels so additional coding was done to determine centroids.

LSA–Based Approach. LSA discovers latent semantic interrelationships among words, which allows identifying independent concepts hidden in the text. It applies singular value decomposition (SVD), factorizing a term–document matrix A (in our case word–sentence matrix) into a product of three matrices $U \Sigma V^T$. Σ is a diagonal matrix where non–zero entries are singular values, representing concepts. The magnitude of a singular value reflects the importance of the appropriate concept. The matrix V^T, with concepts as rows and sentences as columns, describes how important each concept for each sentence is, allowing capturing the most informative sentences.

Here, we implement two methods based on LSA.

CROSS Method. This method (introduced in [15]) is actually the modification of the Steinberger and Jezek [21] method and it often performs better than other LSA methods. In [21] sentence selection is based on sentence length, calculated as: $len(s_i) = \sqrt{\sum_{j=1}^{k} \sigma(j,j)^2 * v(j,i)^2}$, where s_i is i-th sentence, $v(j,i)$ is element of matrix V^T corresponding to the j–th concept and i–th sentence, and $\sigma(j,j)$ is singular value for j–th concept. The novelty in [15] (compared to [21]) is that the additional preprocessing step for matrix V^T is introduced in order to eliminate underrepresented sentences (where scores per concept are lower than the average sentence score per concept). Then, only the K longest sentences are taken for the summary, calculating K in the same way as with clustering methods.

HYBRID Method. As a second method we are proposing an approach where only a subset of singular values is taken into consideration based on the amount of information that we want to retain. After selecting the top X singular values to keep we calculate the strength of each sentence as: $strength(s_i) = \sum_{j \in sel\_concept} v(j,i)$, where $v(j,i)$ is corresponds to the j-th concept and i–th sentence in V^T. In the end, we select for the summary the top K strongest sentences, choosing K the same way as in previous methods.

We applied both methods on three types of word–sentence matrices:

1. *binary* matrix with $b_{ij} = 1$ if word i appears in sentence j and 0 otherwise
2. *root* matrix with values $r_{ij} = 1$ if word i appears in sentence j and word i is a noun, and 0 otherwise
3. *TF-ISF* matrix with values t_{ij} which represent TF-ISF score of word i with respect to the sentence j

4   Experimental Results

The accuracy of the reference extraction was 82% (of 1055 references to extract). It was evaluated by manually scanning original references and extracted information, considering that a reference is successfully processed only if all relevant data are correctly extracted.

For the citation extraction, we again manually checked the quality of the extracted citations. We obtained an accuracy of 83.5%. Actually, all extracted data contain valid citation sentences but we were not always able to exclude unnecessary (sub)titles, footers/headers, tables. Additionally, even though they were technically correctly extracted, citations obtained from table cells were considered as incorrect, due to their lack of context.

After matching, 885 unique papers remained, out of which 786 papers where cited only once, while 31 paper had more than 2 citations (1 paper had 16 citations, the maximum). We consider only these 31 papers for the summarization task. An example of the obtained summary compared with manually made one

Table 2. Citation context, corresponding manual and generated summaries

citation context	manual summary	automatic summary
ImageCLEFmed is part of ImageCLEF focusing on medical images. 1 Introduction A medical retrieval task has been part of ImageCLEF1 since 2004. 1 Introduction ImageCLEF1 started in 2003 as part of the Cross Language Evaluation Forum	A medical retrieval task has been part of ImageCLEF1 since 2004. ImageCLEF1 started in 2003 as part of the Cross Language Evaluation Forum	1 Introduction A medical retrieval task has been part of ImageCLEF1 since 2004.ImageCLEFmed is part of ImageCLEF focusing on medical images

and original citation context can be seen in Table 2. We evaluate summaries using the ROUGE–2 measure:

$$ROUGE\text{-}2 = \frac{\sum_{\Sigma \in \{ReferenceSummaries\}} \sum_{bi\text{-}gram \in \Sigma} count_{match}(bi\text{-}gram)}{sum_{\Sigma \in \{ReferenceSummaries\}} \sum_{bi\text{-}gram \in \Sigma} count(bi\text{-}gram)}$$

and the standard F1-measure. As both measures require manual summaries and having a single summary can be problematic [8], we used two sets of summaries (provided by domain experts, mimicking extractive summarization). For DUC2002, we selected [1] as a baseline since it obtained better results than SVM or CRF. [1] used a normalized Google distance (NGD) as similarity measure.

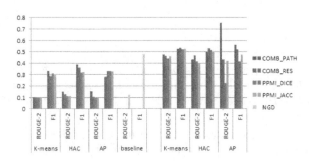

Fig. 2. Clustering results on the DUC2002 (violet) and HES–SO data sets (red)

Figure 2 shows the average results for three clustering techniques when both manual summaries are taken into account for the HES–SO and DUC2002 data sets. It can be seen that the same clustering methods perform differently on the two data sets, which is expected considering that they belong to different domains. Additionally, results vary both on similarity measures and clustering

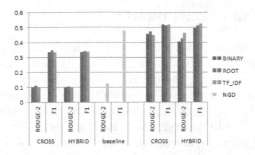

Fig. 3. LSA results on DUC2002 (violet) and HES–SO (red)

techniques. For DUC2002, better results were mainly obtained using a combined similarity measure with path similarity. For this similarity measure and two clustering methods: HAC and AP, we obtained better average ROUGE–2 results than the one provided by the baseline (0.15015 and 0.15155, versus 0.12368 respectively). At the same time, the F1 measure obtained (0.3893 for HAC and 0.2868 for AP) is worse than for the baseline (0.47947).

LSA results on both data sets (with both manual summaries) can be seen in Figure 3. The LSA CROSS method applied on the ROOT word–sentence matrix scored the best (average ROUGE–2 on DUC2002 was 0.11135). The best result on DUC2002 for the HYBRID method was also obtained for ROOT word–sentence matrix (0.10434). When two sets of manual summaries for the HES–SO data set are considered separately, results for the average ROUGE–2 vary (Figure 4). The smallest difference is achieved for LSA CROSS on the ROOT matrix, the highest for K–Means with a combined Resnik similarity. In general, results are better with the summary of the domain expert.

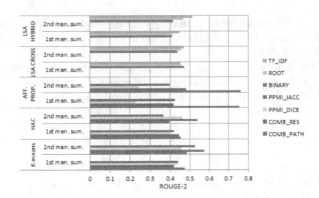

Fig. 4. Comparison of ROUGE–2 for different manual summaries (HES–SO data set)

5   Discussion and Conclusions

The reported reference extraction and parsing accuracy of 82%, better than 80% reported in [12], is suffient for further analysis but maybe not the maximum that is reachable. However, solving the mentioned exceptions was not the focus of this work. Using plain text resulted in difficulties to eliminate headers/footers, (sub)titles and even table/figure captions from the text, deteriorating citation extraction accuracy. Our ROUGE–2 results for HAC and AP with combined path similarity are higher than the compared baseline, which indicates that these methods generate summaries with correct bi–grams (as compared to manual summaries). On the other side, F1 (related to uni–gram matches and to ROUGE–1) is lower than the baseline, so we can not be certain that the number of uni–grams is higher than the baseline. This situation may seem inconsistent but it actually indicates that our algorithms have the ability of generating summaries with a high number of overlapping bi–grams compared to manual summaries.

This work aims to help researchers reviewing scientific publications in a more efficient way by providing summaries of articles based on citation contexts. For this, we implement a novel workflow and carry out experiments applying several unsupervised extractive summarization techniques, based on clustering and LSA. We extend the claims of [1] and [16], demonstrating that not only similarity measures have impact on the summarization result but that different clustering techniques lead to different summarization results even when the same similarity measure is used. We show an improvement of the average ROUGE–2 measure on DUC2002 for HAC and AP clustering with a combined similarity measure using the WordNet path similarity. As future work, we consider using a medical thesaurus (e.g. MeSH) instead of general purpose WordNet.

References

1. Aliguliyev, R.: A new sentence similarity measure and sentence based extractive technique for automatic text summarization. Expert Systems with Applications **36**(4), 7764–7772 (2009)
2. Bergmark, D.: Automatic extraction of reference linking information from online documents. Tech. rep., Cornell University, Ithaca, NY, USA (2000)
3. Bird, S.: NLTK: the natural language toolkit. In: Proceedings of the Coling/ACL on Interactive Presentation Sessions, pp. 69–72, Stroudsburg, PA, USA (2006)
4. Bradshaw, S.: Reference directed indexing: redeeming relevance for subject search in citation indexes. In: Koch, T., Sølvberg, I.T. (eds.) ECDL 2003. LNCS, vol. 2769, pp. 499–510. Springer, Heidelberg (2003)
5. Conroy, J., O'Leary, D.: Text summarization via Hidden Markov models. In: Proceedings of the 24th Annual International ACM SIGIR Conference, pp. 406–407, New York, NY, USA (2001)
6. Elkiss, A., Shen, S., Fader, A., Erkan, G., States, D., Radev, D.: Blind men and elephants: What do citation summaries tell us about a research article? Journal of the American Society Information Science and Technology **59**(1), 51–62 (2008)
7. Frey, B., Dueck, D.: Clustering by passing messages between data points. Science **315**(5814), 972–976 (2007)

8. Jing, H., Barzilay, R., McKeown, K., Elhadad, M.: Summarization evaluation methods: experiments and analysis. In: AAAI Symposium on Intelligent Summarization, pp. 51–59 (1998)
9. Jurafsky, D., Martin, J.: Speech & Language Processing. Pearson Education India (2000)
10. Lin, C.Y.: Rouge: a package for automatic evaluation of summaries. In: Text Summarization Branches Out: Proceedings of the ACL-04 Workshop, pp. 74–81 (2004)
11. Miller, G.: Wordnet: A lexical database for english. Communications of the ACM **38**(11), 39–41 (1995)
12. Haddou ou Moussa, K., Mayr, P.: Automatische referenzextraktion mit parscit. In: Social Media and Web Science - Das Web als Lebensraum, DGI, pp. 425–428 (2012)
13. Nenkova, A., Passonneau, R.: Evaluating content selection in summarization: the pyramid method. In: Proceedings of Conference of the North American Chapter of the Association for Computational Linguistics: Human Language Technologies, pp. 145–152 (2004)
14. Niwa, Y., Nitta, Y.: Co-occurrence vectors from corpora vs. distance vectors from dictionaries. In: Proceedings of the 15th Conference on Computational Linguistics, COLING '94, vol. 1, pp. 304–309 (1994)
15. Ozsoy, M.G., Cicekli, I., Alpaslan, F.N.: Text summarization of turkish texts using latent semantic analysis. In: Huang, C.R., Jurafsky, D. (eds.) Proceedings of the 23rd International Conference on Computational Linguistics, pp. 869–876. Tsinghua University Press (2010)
16. Pei-Ying, Z., Cun-He, L.: Automatic text summarization based on sentences clustering and extraction. In: Proceedings of 2nd IEEE International Conference on the Computer Science and Information Technology, pp. 167–170. IEEE (2009)
17. Qazvinian, V., Radev, D.: Scientific paper summarization using citation summarynetworks. In: Proceedings of the 22nd International Conference on Computational Linguistics, vol. 1, pp. 689–696 (2008)
18. Resnik, P.: Using information content to evaluate semantic similarity in a taxonomy. In: Proceedings of the 14th International Joint Conference on Artificial Intelligence, vol. 1, pp. 448–453 (1995)
19. Ritchie, A., Robertson, S., Teufel, S.: Comparing citation contexts for information retrieval. In: Proceedings of the 17th ACM Conference on Information and Knowledge Management. CIKM '08, pp. 213–222. ACM, New York (2008)
20. Saad, S.M., Kamarudin, S.S.: Comparative analysis of similarity measures for sentence level semantic measurement of text. In: IEEE International Conference on Control System, Computing and Engineering, pp. 90–94. IEEE (2013)
21. Steinberger, J., Ježek, K.: Using latent semantic analysis in text summarization and summary evaluation. In: Proceedings of Industrial Management, ISIM '04, pp. 93–100 (2004)
22. Svore, K.M., Vanderwende, L., Burges, C.: Enhancing single-document summarization by combining ranknet and third-party sources. In: Proceedings of Conference on Empirical Methods on Natural Language Processing and Computational Natural Language Learning, pp. 448–457 (2007)
23. Torres-Moreno, J.M., Saggion, H., da Cunha, I., SanJuan, E.: Summary Evaluation With and Without References. Polibits: Research Journal on Computer Science and Computer Engineering with Applications **42**, 13–19 (2010)
24. Zechner, K.: Fast generation of abstracts from general domain text corpora by extracting relevant sentences. In: Proceedings of the 16th Conference on Computational Linguistics, vol. 2, pp. 986–989 (1996)

A Multiple-Stage Approach to Re-ranking Medical Documents

Heung-Seon Oh$^{(\boxtimes)}$, Yuchul Jung, and Kwang-Young Kim

Korea Institute of Science and Technology Information, Daejeon, South Korea
{ohs,jyc77,glorykim}@kisti.re.kr

Abstract. The widespread use of the Web has radically changed the way people acquire medical information. Every day, patients, their caregivers, and doctors themselves search for medical information to resolve their medical information needs. However, search results provided by existing medical search engines often contain irrelevant or uninformative documents that are not appropriate for the purposes of the users. As a solution, this paper presents a method of re-ranking medical documents. The key concept of our method is to compute accurate similarity scores through multiple stages of re-ranking documents from the initial documents retrieved by a search engine. Specifically, our method combines query expansion with abbreviations, query expansion with discharge summary, clustering-based document scoring, centrality-based document scoring, and pseudo relevance feedback with relevance model. The experimental results from participating in Task 3a of the CLEF 2014 eHealth show the performance of our method.

Keywords: Medical information retrieval · Document re-ranking · Medical abbreviations

1   Introduction

Health-related content has become one of the most searched-for topics on the Web[1]. Nowadays, people are using Web search engines to acquire medical information. Even doctors themselves are frequently using Web search engines to facilitate diagnoses because of the difficulty in keeping up with the rapidly generated medical knowledge.

Recently, medical information retrieval (IR) has been actively researched to tackle diverse medical information sources including the general web, journal articles, social media, hospital records, etc. However, medical IR is still challenging because it should consider various information needs from a wide range of users including patients and their care givers, researchers, clinicians, practitioners, etc. Moreover, it is highly co-related with the background medical knowledge and language skills of those users.

---

[1] Health Fact Sheet, http://www.pewinternet.org/fact-sheets/health-fact-sheet/

© Springer International Publishing Switzerland 2015
J. Mothe et al. (Eds.): CLEF 2015, LNCS 9283, pp. 166–177, 2015.
DOI: 10.1007/978-3-319-24027-5_14

To mitigate the difficulties of laypeople (e.g., patients and their relatives) who have different information needs, Conference and Labs of the Evaluation Forum (CLEF) have launched the eHealth Evaluation Lab [5, 6]. Especially, Task 3 of CLEF 2014 eHealth extends the previous IR task by cleaning document collection and introducing new query generation methods and multilingual topics. Task 3 is divided into two sub-tracks: Task 3a and Task 3b. The former is a monolingual English retrieval track, and the latter includes cross-lingual retrieval challenges to the lab. The overall goal of task 3 is to develop more advanced techniques that can provide more valuable and relevant documents to laypeople.

Most of the previous research has focused on using external medical resources (e.g., MetaMap [2] and NegEx [19]) and natural language processing (NLP) [7] to understand the meanings of medical words at a semantic level. We, however, are interested in applying several retrieval techniques such as query expansion with different resources, document scoring methods, and the relevance feedback model.

In this paper, we designed five different components that can be merged for multi-stage re-ranking to elevate the ranked position of the most relevant documents. The first component expands queries with abbreviations. The abbreviations are obtained taking into consideration their frequencies and a simple rule-based extraction method [12] from the entire collection. The second component uses discharge summary for query expansion. To do that, we devised a random-walk based discharge summary model. In the third component, a hierarchical agglomerative clustering is applied to incorporate the cluster information of the documents [10]. In addition, the fourth component, centrality-based document scoring, considers the associations among the documents. The associations can be obtained through similarity matrix construction and random-walk [8]. The final component is pseudo relevance feedback (PRF) with a relevance model [1].

In our experiments, we recognized that the PRF provides a strong baseline, and it was used for every evaluation run. In terms of the precision measure, the best performance, 0.7400 (P@10) was obtained when the queries were expanded with abbreviations and discharge summary. In addition, the best performance in NDCG, 0.7333, was achieved by combining all five components together in the re-ranking method.

2   Related Work

Recently, much IR research has been performed with different types of medical collections. TREC 2011 and 2012 covered medical record tracks in which particular retrieval tasks were defined. Most approaches in TREC's medical track depend on external medical resources to enhance the retrieval performance. Cengage learning's approach [7] presented a two-stage method for the 2011 medical track. They first extracted useful attributes such as age and gender from a collection with NLP techniques and then applied hand-created regular expressions to identify the major attributes of a patient and the patient's visit. They used three kinds of techniques for query expansion which used UMLS related terms, terms from a network built from UMLS, and terms for their medical reference encyclopedias.

For the 2012 medical record track, [19] investigated three research problems – evidence aggregation, expansion sources, and retrieval models. In their study, several ranking functions were proposed to combine several evidences of different levels including various external medical resources. They found that the following was effective: factor-based query expansion with external resources, scoring models which incorporate term proximity information, and aggregated evidences from both the report and visit levels. Although other approaches have considered negation handling, interestingly, [4] presents two different algorithms based on syntactic analysis to deal with negations in the task of retrieving medical reports. One is to detect negations, and the other is to infer their scope. Their experiments have shown that negation handling improves retrieval performances even though the improvement is not significant.

Task 3 of the CLEF 2013 eHealth is designed to simulate web searches for health information by patients. In the task, [18] presents a two-step ranking system utilizing three different external resources (i.e., external medical collections, medical concept mapper, and discharge summaries). It first retrieves documents in the text-space by using the Markov random field, a mixture of relevance models, and the Medical Subject Headings-based query expansion, and then re-ranks them in the concept space where every concept is represented as UMLS concept unique identifiers (CUI). Assuming that the discharge summary (DS) may contain 'hidden' concepts that did not appear in the query, they convert text DS to CUI DS with a clinical NLP annotation tool.

The MedSearch system [9] proposed three techniques to deal with special requirements in medical IR. First, it provides query reformulation which transforms a long descriptive query to a moderate-length query. Second, it supports the diversification of web search results. Third, it provides medical phrases semantically related to a query from the MeSH ontology. These solutions are known to help ordinary users obtain satisfactory search results in medical IR.

3   Methods

The key concept of our proposed method is to re-rank top-k documents through multiple stages that are designed to compute more accurate similarity scores with respect to a query. For a given query Q, a set of documents, $D_{init} = \{D_1, D_2, \ldots, D_k\}$, are retrieved from a collection C using a search engine. In our implementation, the initial documents are retrieved by Lucene[2] using a query-likelihood method with Dirichlet smoothing [17]. Based on the initial documents, re-ranking is performed by combining multiple components. Fig. 1 shows the overview of our multiple-stage re-ranking method. For re-ranking, components 1~4 can be combined selectively or sequentially except for the pseudo relevance feedback with relevance model. The rest of this section explains the details of the re-ranking method.

---

[2] http://lucene.apache.org/

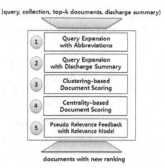

Fig. 1. Overview of our document re-ranking method: documents are re-ranked through multiple stages based on the initial retrieved documents

Basics: Throughout the re-ranking, we use the KL-divergence method to compute a similarity score between a query and a document [8, 11]:

$$score(Q,D) = \exp\left(-KL(\theta_Q||\theta_D)\right) = \exp\left(-\sum_w p(w|\theta_Q) \log \frac{p(w|\theta_Q)}{p(w|\theta_D)}\right), \quad (1)$$

where θ_Q and θ_D are the query and document language models, respectively.

In general, a query model is estimated by the maximum likelihood estimate (MLE) shown below:

$$p(w|\theta_Q) = \frac{c(w,Q)}{|Q|}, \quad (2)$$

where $c(w,Q)$ is the count of a word w in a query Q, and $|Q|$ is the number of words in Q.

To avoid zero probabilities and improve retrieval performance, a document model is estimated using Dirichlet smoothing [17]:

$$p(w|\theta_D) = \frac{c(w,D) + \mu \cdot p(w|C)}{\sum_t c(t,D) + \mu}, \quad (3)$$

where $c(w,D)$ is the count of a word w in a document D; $p(w|C)$ is the probability of a word w in a collection C, and μ is the Dirichlet prior parameter.

Component 1: The first component expands the abbreviations in a query. In a large number of medical documents, abbreviations are frequently used to represent important meanings and to save space. Unfortunately, the clear interpretation of abbreviations is quite difficult due to the existence of several different meanings for a same abbreviated expression. Similarly, medical queries generated by users may also contain abbreviations. If we submit a query that includes abbreviations, it may not match with relevant documents due to a term mismatch problem or may match documents with abbreviations having different meanings. Query expansion resolving abbreviations deals with this problem. To do that, we extract pairs of abbreviations and corresponding full representations with an occurrence count using a simple rule-based extraction method [12] from the entire collection. Then, a query model is estimated by incorporating words from the full representations of an associated abbreviation as follows:

$$p(w|\theta_Q') = (1 - \lambda_{abbr}) \cdot p(w|\theta_Q) + \lambda_{abbr} \cdot \sum_{t \in full(w)} p_{abbr}(t|w), \qquad (4)$$

where $p(w|\theta_q)$ is MLE; λ_{abbr} is a control parameter; $full(w)$ is a set of words consisting of a full representation for an abbreviation w, and $p_{abbr}(t|w)$ is estimated by $\frac{count(t)}{count(t,w)}$.

Component 2: The second component is built to reflect information from the discharge summary. A query used in the CLEF eHealth Task 3 is generated by a human expert after reading the discharge summary corresponding to the query. Therefore, it may contain hidden but useful information not captured by a query. The use of the discharge summary can improve the retrieval performance by using such hidden information. To do that, the query model can be expanded by combining a random-walk based discharge summary model. For the model, we should construct a word-to-word transition matrix in terms of measuring the associations among words in the discharge summary. A simple solution is to use a co-occurrence count between two words among all sentences [16]. However, words are strongly associated when they appear closely in a sentence. In addition, associations between topical words are more important than those between common words. To consider this situation, we use the hyperspace analogue to language (HAL) [14] function with the inverse document frequency (IDF):

$$HAL(w, u) = \sum_{n=1}^{N} wt(n) \cdot co(w, u, n) \cdot IDF(w) \cdot IDF(u), \qquad (5)$$

where n is the distance between words w and u; N is the window size; $wt(n) = N - n + 1$; $co(w, u, n)$ is the co-occurrence count of w and u within the k-distance, and $IDF(w) = \log\left(\frac{|C|}{doc\_freq(w)}\right)$

Then, a transition probability is computed:

$$p_{HAL}(w|u) = \frac{HAL(w, u)}{\sum_{t \in DS} HAL(t, u)}, \qquad (6)$$

where DS is the discharge summary document.

Based on the translation matrix $p_{HAL}(w|u)$, word centralities are computed using random-walk:

$$cent(w) = \frac{\lambda_{DP}}{|V_{DS}|} + (1 - \lambda_{DP}) \cdot \sum_{u \in DS} \frac{cent(u)}{p_{HAL}(w|u)}, \qquad (7)$$

where $|V_{DS}|$ is the number of unique words in the discharge summary DS, and λ_{DP} is a damping factor .

We approximate the resulting $cent(w)$ as the discharge summary model $p(w|\theta_{DS})$ and update the query model with it:

$$p\big(w\big|\theta_Q''\big) = (1 - \lambda_{DS}) \cdot p\big(w\big|\theta_Q'\big) + \lambda_{DS} \cdot p(w|\theta_{DS}), \qquad (8)$$

where λ_{DS} is the control parameter, and $p(w|\theta_{DS})$ is the discharge summary model.

Component 3: The third component incorporates the cluster information of documents. Namely, a score for a document is computed by incorporating the membership of the document to a cluster that we constructed.

To partition the top-k documents D_{init} into a set of disjoint clusters, we apply bottom-up hierarchical agglomerative clustering [10]. At first, k-clusters for every document in D_{init} are constructed. Then, two clusters, which have the highest similarity, are selected and merged into a single cluster if the similarity is above the threshold T. This procedure stops when there are no more clusters above the threshold. Similarity scores are computed using the KL divergence method between a query model and the Dirichlet-smoothed cluster model.

A new score is computed by combining the initial search score and the cluster score:

$$score_{sc}(Q, D) = score_{search}(Q, D) \cdot score_{cluster}(Q, CL_D), \qquad (9)$$

where CL_D is the cluster of a document D. $score_{sc}(Q,D)$ is used after normalization over all document scores.

Component 4: The fourth component, centrality-based document scoring, is to use the associations among documents in the search results. The centralities are computed through two steps - similarity matrix construction and random-walk [8]. Among the initial documents, implicit links are generated because there are no explicit links among them.

For each document $d \in D_{init}$, α documents in D_{init} are selected according to high generation probabilities:

$$score(D_1, D_2) = \exp\left(-KL\big(\theta_{D_1}||\theta_{D_2}\big)\right). \qquad (10)$$

Based on the generation probabilities, a similarity matrix with the initial documents and the corresponding α documents are constructed. Then, random-walk is executed on this matrix to produce centrality scores for the initial documents. This score is multiplied with the previous score:

$$score_{scs}(Q, D) = score_{sc}(Q, D) \cdot score_{centrality}(Q, D) \qquad (11)$$

Component 5: The fifth component is the pseudo relevance feedback (PRF) with relevance model. PRF is a very popular used query expansion method to update a query. Updating a query with PRF assumes that top-ranked documents $F = \{D_1, D_2, \ldots, D_{|F|}\}$ in the initial search results are relevant to a given query, and terms in F are useful to modify a query for a better representation. The relevance model (RM) is to estimate a multinomial distribution $p(w|q)$ that is the likelihood of a term w given a query q. The first version of the relevance model (RM1) is defined as follows:

$$
\begin{aligned}
p_{RM1}(w|Q) &= \sum_{D \in F} p(w|\theta_D)p(\theta_D|Q) \\
&= \sum_{D \in F} p(w|\theta_D)\frac{p(Q|\theta_D)p(\theta_D)}{p(Q)} \\
&\propto \sum_{D \in F} p(w|\theta_D)p(\theta_D)p(Q|\theta_D)
\end{aligned}
\tag{12}
$$

RM1 consists of three components: document prior $p(\theta_D)$, document weight $p(Q|\theta_D)$, and term weight in a document $p(w|\theta_D)$. In general, $p(\theta_D)$ is assumed to be a uniform distribution without the knowledge of a document D. $p(Q|\theta_D) = \prod_{w \in Q} p(w|\theta_D)^{c(w,Q)}$ indicates the query-likelihood score. $p(w|\theta_D)$ can be estimated using various smoothing methods such as the Dirichlet-smoothing. Various strategies are applicable to estimate these components.

To improve the retrieval performance, a new query model can be estimated by combing the relevance model and the original query model. RM3 [1] is a variant of a relevance model to estimate a new query model with RM1:

$$
p(w|\theta_Q''') = (1 - \beta) \cdot p(w|\theta_Q'') + \beta \cdot p_{RM1}(w|Q),
\tag{13}
$$

where β is the control parameter between the original query model and the feedback model.

Before estimating a new query model, RM1 is re-estimated by retaining M words which are topical words in the feedback model. Based on the query model, final scores for the documents are computed.

The above five components originate from different starting points, but can be merged for re-ranking purposes. In our approach, PRF is essentially used because it delivers a very strong baseline.

4   Experiments

4.1   Data

For the evaluation, the CLEF 2014 eHealth document collection was used. It consists of more than a million web documents related to health topics focusing on the general public and healthcare professionals [5] and 50 test queries. Relevance for each query is judged from 0 to 3 where 3 indicates a stronger relevance while 0 indicates non-relevance. Except for non-relevant documents, 3,756 query-document pairs were used to compute the evaluation measures. Table 1 summarizes the data statistics. The lengths of documents and queries[3] were computed after stop-word removal using the mallet stop-word list[4].

Table 1. Data statistics

#Docs	Voc. Size	Avg. Doc. Len
1,102,289	2,647,062	540.0

#Queries	Avg. Query Len.	#Query-Doc
50	7.2	3,756

Fig. 2 shows an example of a test query and its corresponding discharge summary. A query has a corresponding discharge summary that presents the complete context of the query. Generally, title and description are utilized as a query text. In addition, we can use the discharge summary as query text to investigate the usefulness of the complete context.

```
<topic>
    <id>qtest2014.2</id>
        <discharge_summary>01234-029456-DISCHARGE_SUMMARY.txt</discharge_summary>
        <title>Sepsis</title>
        <desc>Could sepsis be the cause of death?</desc>
        <narr>The document should contain information about sepsis in general and its possible consequences</narr>
        <profile>The patient was an 83 year-old lady who died after sepsis. Her daughter wants to know if sepsis    is the
possible cause of her death. She does not know what sepsis means.</profile>
    </topic>
```
```
<01234-029456-DISCHARGE_SUMMARY.txt >
...
Service: MEDICINE
Allergies:
No Drug Allergy Information on File
Attending:[**Attending Info 1071**]
Chief Complaint:
hypoxia
Major Surgical or Invasive Procedure:
n/a
...
Physical Exam:
t 99.8, bp 111/44, p 115, r 18, 98% 10L NRB
Minimally arousable, localized pain.
Pupils pinpoint.
OP- midline lesion of upper hard palate, generally yellow and discolored.
Dry MMM.
Regular s1,s2. no m/r/g
...
</01234-029456-DISCHARGE_SUMMARY.txt >
```

Fig. 2. An example of a test query and corresponding discharge summary

---

[3] Length of query was counted by including title and description.
[4] http://mallet.cs.umass.edu/

4.2   Evaluation Settings

Lucene was exploited for indexing and searching the initial documents D_{init}. A query-likelihood method with Dirichlet smoothing was chosen for a scoring function. $|D_{init}|$ was set to 1,000. Based on D_{init}, we did 7 runs by differentiating the components of our re-ranking method.

Table 2 shows the parameters and corresponding values for each component in the experiments. The parameters were set according to our empirical experiments.

Table 2. Parameter setup used in the re-ranking method

Component	Description	Parameters
1	Query expansion with abbreviations	$\lambda_{abbr} = 0.15$
2	Query expansion with discharge summary	$N=3$ $\lambda_{DP} = 0.85$
3	Clustering–based document scoring	$T = 0.9$
4	Centrality-based document scoring	$\lambda_{DP} = 0.85$ $\alpha = 10$
5	Pseudo relevance feedback with relevance model	$\|F\| = 10$ $M = 100$ $\beta = 0.1$ $\mu = 1500$

4.3   Results

Table 3 describes the components used at each run and the evaluation results from the corresponding runs. Basically, component 5, which indicates the use of PRF, was applied to all runs and thus, regarded as the baseline method of our experiments. All runs used component 1. The distinction between RUN2-4 and RUN5-7 is that the former uses the discharge summary while the latter does not. Precision and normalized discounted cumulative gain (NDCG) were used to measure the performance of the top-10 ranked documents from D_{init}. They are denoted as P@10 and NDCG@10, respectively. * indicates that the performance passed determined by paired t-test with $p = 0.05$.

Our baseline achieved 0.7300 and 0.7235 in P@10 and NDCG@10, respectively. It shows that PRF is an effective solution to find relevant medical documents. For precision, the best performance, 0.7400, was obtained from RUN2 which utilized abbreviations and the discharge summary. For NDCG, the best performance, 0.7333, was obtained from RUN4 which used all the components in the re-ranking method. This shows that sequentially combining the components contributed to achieving the best performance in the NDCG measure. However, clustering and centrality-based document scoring were not effective in enhancing the precision measure.

Table 3. Performances of our re-ranking method

RUN ID	Components					Evaluation Measures	
	1	2	3	4	5	P@10	NDCG@10
1					O	0.7300	0.7235
2	O	O			O	*0.7400	*0.7301
3	O	O	O		O	0.7160	0.7171
4	O	O	O	O	O	0.7380	**0.7333**
5	O				O	0.7280	0.7211
6	O		O		O	0.7240	0.7187
7	O		O	O	O	0.7260	0.7233

Due to quite a high baseline (i.e., RUN1) obtained by PRF with the relevance model and lack of in-depth study on the provided healthcare dataset, our experiments only obtained small success in showing drastic improvements in the evaluation measures. However, our best results are included in the top 10 runs in Task 3a of the CLEF 2014 eHealth [5]. Especially, component 2, which uses the discharge summary, made an improvement over the method used in CLEF 2013 eHealth. We assume that the best performances observed in our multi-stage approach to re-ranking documents (i.e., RUN4) could originate from the synergistic effects between the involved components.

Table 4. Performance comparison with other top-ranked methods in CLEF 2014 eHealth. (sorted by P@10 in desecding order)

Group-Run ID	P@10	NDCG@10
GRIUM-5 [13]	0.7560	0.7445
SNUMedinfo-2 [3]	0.7540	0.7406
KISTI-2 (Our run)	0.7400	0.7301
IRLabDAIICT-1 [15]	0.7060	0.6869

In [5], performances of all participants of CLEF 2014 are summarized. Table 4 shows the best performance of four different groups which produced high performance. Other top groups except us employed external biomedical resources for query expansion (e.g., GRIUM and SNUMedino: UMLS and MetaMap, and IRLabDAIICT: Mesh and MetaMap). Although the use of external resources is quite effective, it requires a huge amount of time to process medical documents. Our re-ranking method achieved a meaningful result without resorting to external resources.

5   Conclusion

This paper presents a multiple-stage approach to re-ranking medical documents. Our method focuses on combining different retrieval techniques rather than utilizing biomedical knowledge resources and advanced natural language processing to understand medical meanings. Through our experiments, we found that the use of abbreviations and discharge summary in query expansion play an important role in finding more relevant medical documents. Our future work includes further development of the two components and in-depth error analysis based on standard assessment dataset.

References

1. Abdul-Jaleel, N., et al.: UMass at TREC 2004: novelty and HARD. In: Proceedings of Text REtrieval Conference (TREC) (2004)
2. Aronson, A.R., Lang, F.-M.: An overview of MetaMap: historical perspective and recent advances. Journal of the American Medical Informatics Association: JAMIA 17(3), 229–236 (2010)
3. Choi, S., Choi, J.: Exploring effective information retrieval technique for the medical web documents: SNUMedinfo at. CLEFeHealth2014 Task 3. In: Proceedings of CLEF 2014, pp. 167–175 (2014)
4. Diaz, A. et al.: UCM at TREC-2012: does negation influence the retrieval of medical reports? In: Proceedings of Text REtrieval Conference (TREC) (2012)
5. Goeuriot, L. et al.: ShARe/CLEF eHealth Evaluation Lab 2014, Task 3: User-centred health information retrieval. In: Proceedings of CLEF 2014 (2014)
6. Kelly, L., et al.: Overview of the ShARe/CLEF eHealth evaluation lab 2014. In: Kanoulas, E., Lupu, M., Clough, P., Sanderson, M., Hall, M., Hanbury, A., Toms, E. (eds.) CLEF 2014. LNCS, vol. 8685, pp. 172–191. Springer, Heidelberg (2014)
7. King, B., et al.: Cengage Learning at TREC 2011 medical track. In: Proceedings of Text REtrieval Conference (TREC) (2011)
8. Kurland, O., Lee, L.: PageRank without hyperlinks: structural re-ranking using links induced by language models. In: Proceedings of the 28th Annual International ACM SIGIR Conference on Research and Development in Information Retrieval - SIGIR 2005, pp. 306–313. ACM Press, New York (2006)
9. Luo, G. et al.: MedSearch. In: Proceeding of the 17th ACM Conference on Information and Knowledge Mining - CIKM 2008, pp. 143–152. ACM Press, New York (2008)
10. Manning, C.D. et al.: Introduction to Information Retrieval. Cambridge University Press (2008)
11. Oh, H.-S., Myaeng, S.-H.: Utilizing global and path information with language modelling for hierarchical text classification. Journal of Information Science 40(2), 127–145 (2014)
12. Schwartz, A.S., Marti, A.: Hearst: a simple algorithm for identifying abbreviation definitions in biomedical text. In: Proceedings of Pacific Symposium on Biocomputing, pp. 451–462 (2003)
13. Shen, W., et al.: An investigation of the effectiveness of concept-based approach in medical information retrieval. In: Proceedings of CLEF 2014, pp. 236–247 (2014)

14. Song, D., Bruza, P.: Discovering information flow using high dimensional conceptual space. In: Proceedings of the 24th Annual International ACM SIGIR Conference on Research and Development in Information Retrieval - SIGIR 2001, pp. 327–333. ACM Press, New York (2001)
15. Thakkar, H., et al.: Team IRLabDAIICT at ShARe / CLEF eHealth 2014 Task 3: User-centered information retrieval system for clinical documents. In: Proceedings of CLEF 2014, pp. 248–259 (2014)
16. Weeds, J., Weir, D.: Co-occurrence retrieval: a general framework for lexical distributional similarity. Computational Linguistics **31**(4), 439–475 (2005)
17. Zhai, C., Lafferty, J.: A study of smoothing methods for language models applied to information retrieval. ACM Transactions on Information Systems **22**(2), 179–214 (2004)
18. Zhu, D. et al.: Using Discharge Summaries to Improve Information Retrieval in Clinical Domain. ShARe/CLEF eHealth Evaluation (2013)
19. Zhu, D., Carterette, B.: Exploring evidence aggregation methods and external expansion sources for medical record search. In: Proceedings of Text REtrieval Conference (TREC), pp. 1–9 (2012)

Exploring Behavioral Dimensions in Session Effectiveness

Teemu Pääkkönen[1], Kalervo Järvelin[2], Jaana Kekäläinen[2(✉)], Heikki Keskustalo[2],
Feza Baskaya[2], David Maxwell[3], and Leif Azzopardi[3]

[1] Flockler, Tampere, Finland
teemu@flockler.com
[2] School of Information Sciences, University of Tampere, Tampere, Finland
{kalervo.jarvelin,jaana.kekalainen,
heikki.keskustalo,feza.baskaya}@uta.fi
[3] School of Computing Science, University of Glasgow, Glasgow, UK
d.maxwell.1@research.gla.ac.uk, Leif.Azzopardi@Glasgow.ac.uk

Abstract. Studies in interactive information retrieval (IIR) indicate that expert searchers differ from novices in many ways. In the present paper, we identify a number of behavioral dimensions along which searchers differ (e.g. cost, gain and the accuracy of relevance assessment). We quantify these differences using simulated, multi-query search sessions. We then explore each dimension in turn to determine what differences are most effective in yielding superior retrieval performance. The more precise action probabilities in assessing snippets and documents contribute less to the overall cumulative gain during a session than gain and cost structures.

Keywords: Session-based evaluation · IR interaction · Behavioral dimensions · Simulation · Multi-query scanning models

1   Introduction

Studies in *Interactive Information Retrieval (IIR)* generally agree that novices and experts of a particular domain differ in their search performance [12,13,24]. First, experts may differ from novices in domain expertise. As such, experts may provide better queries and more informed relevance assessments. Secondly, experts and novices may differ in searching expertise, potentially resulting in better use of interface tools and better querying strategies employed. Many factors affect a searcher's performance, yet it is unknown how effective they are in bringing up a novice to the level of an expert. In the present paper, we look at this issue through simulation of an IIR search session using a test collection.

Simulation is an established approach to analyze and evaluate searcher interaction with retrieval systems (e.g., [2,4,21]). Traditional test collection-based *Information Retrieval (IR)* experimentation and evaluation exemplifies simulation with minimal interaction [10]. Session-based simulation of interactive IR offers evaluation with explicit modeling of behavioral dimensions in IR interaction. Its strengths include

© Springer International Publishing Switzerland 2015
J. Mothe et al. (Eds.): CLEF 2015, LNCS 9283, pp. 178–189, 2015.
DOI: 10.1007/978-3-319-24027-5_15

control over experimental factors, an unlimited supply of 'test subjects' with no fatigue, low costs, no (non-programmed) learning effects, and reproducibility of experiments. Limitations of a simulation-based approach include the lack of fully-fledged human subjects, which may lead to unrealistic or biased findings. [2]

In traditional IR evaluation - and often in IIR simulations - ideal behavior of the (simulated) searcher is assumed. Human behavior, however, is better modeled as stochastic across behavioral dimensions. For this work, we consequently employ an automaton-based, discrete-time stochastic simulator for IIR. With this simulation, we perform a comparative analysis in order to avoid assuming ideal behavior.

Based on past studies [12,13,24], we identify a number of search effectiveness related dimensions along which searchers are likely to behave differently. We then quantify the differences in multi-query session simulations. For each of these dimensions, we identify two sets of values based on earlier simulated session studies [5,15] and reasonable inference. In order to simplify terminology, we associate the term 'novice' to one set of values representing the behavior of an ordinary searcher, and the term 'expert' to another set of values representing the behavior of a more experienced searcher. We then test which of the behavioral dimensions contribute most to the performance difference between novices and experts. We run our experiments over the TREC7-8 test collection with graded relevance assessments.

The next section discusses some relevant prior studies. The simulator is described in Section 3, followed by the study design in Section 4. Section 5 describes the results, and Section 6 concludes the paper.

2   Prior Studies on IR Simulation

There is a large number of both IR simulation studies and empirical studies discussing behavioral dimensions related to searching. As far back as 1992, Harman [9] conducted a simulation study on the effectiveness of *Relevance Feedback (RF)* in IR. Keskustalo and colleagues [14] evaluated the effectiveness of simulated RF based on a searcher model defining various RF characteristics of a simulated searcher. Järvelin [11] conducted a simulation study on the effectiveness of pseudo-RF based on query-biased summaries. Carterette and colleagues [6] evaluated system performance in a simulation study, and considered the effects of variance in searcher behavior related to their scanning profiles. Baskaya and colleagues [3] simulated the effects of searchers providing partially incorrect RF. In their study, RF with realistic levels of searcher fallibility yielded results that were close to perfect RF. Keskustalo and colleagues [15] simulated searchers performing direct query reformulations as multi-query sessions in a test collection, and discovered that sequences of extremely short queries combined with shallow browsing were surprisingly effective. Smucker [20] explored the time and accuracy of searchers making decisions while searching ranked lists of documents. Among two strategies - *fast and liberal*, and *slow and neutral* - the former was more successful. Gwizdka [8] studied cognitive effort spent in text documents, presenting four degrees of relevance. He concluded that most effort was spent on partially relevant documents - relevant and irrelevant documents attracted less effort.

Kelly and Cool [13] studied the effect of topic familiarity in identifying specific information in documents. They observed that reading time decreased with topic familiarity; however, the difference was not statistically significant. Kharazmi and colleagues [12] found that experts made more queries with more query terms per session than non-experts in the medical domain. White and colleagues [24] studied the effect of in-domain vs. out of domain expertise to query vocabulary, and concluded that the domain experts issued longer queries and allocated longer sessions.

In summary, the dimensions of accuracy in making informed decisions and cognitive efforts are relevant to IIR studies focusing on novices vs. experts. In this paper, we focus on document utility (in gain units); average search subtask costs (in seconds); query formulation strategies; scanning and stopping behavior; session time allocation; and relevance-related behavior (clicking and judging probabilities). In particular, we study *(1)* the use of query formulation strategies; *(2)* snippet scanning behavior; *(3)* setting search goals (gain); *(4)* setting cost constraints (time); *(5)* snippet assessment; and *(6)* document assessment. We introduce a simulator for the interaction of these dimensions. The model that the simulator follows is depicted in Figure 1. Multiple arrows leaving a node in the figure represent different possible next steps in a session. Their probabilities add to one, each arrow having a probability $P \leq 1$.

It also seems plausible to conclude that there is, for each dimension, a range of justifiable values. For the purposes of the present study, we feel that a quantifiable difference is important but not so much the exact magnitudes. Section 4 provides the characteristics and their values used in the present simulations.

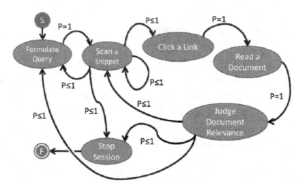

Fig. 1. A graphical illustration of the session simulation automaton, where P denotes the transition probabilities [5]

3   The Session Simulator

3.1   Simulator Definition

Due to the explorative nature of the study, we required a simulator framework that allows for multiple different kinds of searcher models, and easy swapping of behavioral parameter values. Furthermore, in anticipation of future studies, we required the framework to be as generic as possible, in order to be of maximal use in such studies.

To that end, we created a generic IIR simulator framework that allows us to model searcher interaction as a discrete-time stochastic process that forms a sequence of events over time. Each event represents the searcher completing some action or behavior (see Figure 1). Furthermore, each event affects how and when the next event should occur. The framework allows defining probabilities and conditions for behaviors to occur. Within the simulator, probabilistic behavior is approximated using pseudo-random numbers. Pseudo-randomness also brings forth the ability to repeat any simulation precisely, when the random number generator is given the same seed value every time.

With randomness, it becomes necessary to use Monte Carlo methods to produce sufficiently robust data. Therefore the simulator framework was built to run multiple iterations of each simulation, and then calculate average values for the metrics used.

Due to the generic nature of the framework, a similarly generic means to describe any simulation was required. Our approach was to define an input language ruleset for describing simulations, and the mechanism for processing it. The formal model of the ruleset is based on finite automata, as originally presented by Rabin and Scott [18]. We define our IIR simulator as an automaton-like construct, extended by adding elements from the IR domain. In order to make the definition usable for IIR simulation purposes, document collections and Markov-Chain-like probability-based decision-making need to be incorporated into the definition.

A finite automaton is formally defined as a tuple $(Q, \Sigma, \delta, q_0, F)$, where Q is a finite set of states, Σ a finite set of input symbols, δ a transition function $Q \times \Sigma \rightarrow Q$, $q_0 \in Q$ the initial state, and $F \subseteq Q$ a set of final states.

In terms of graph theory, our automaton is a directed graph. The nodes represent searcher actions, such as reading a document snippet or typing a query on the keyboard. Each action may cause side effects, such as changing the document that is currently being assessed. Actions may also have associated costs and gains. The actions can be as fine-grained as the research setting requires.

The edges of the automaton are directed. They represent decision-making, such as deciding whether to read a document. Each edge is associated with a conditional probability that represents the likelihood of making the decision based on a condition, such as the document relevance level being high enough.

For our simulator, we define a variant of the finite automaton, the *IR simulator automaton* as a tuple $(Q, X, \Delta_X, q_0, F, U)$, where $X \in [0,1]$ is the input of the system – a continuous random variable of standard uniform distribution, Δ_X a transition set that replaces the transition function δ, and $U = \{u_1, u_2, ..., u_n\}$ a set of result document sets. The transition set Δ_X resembles in many ways the definition of the transition function of a probabilistic automaton, as defined by Rabin [17], but instead of working with simple transition probabilities, it also considers run-time conditions, as defined below.

Each simulation iteration forms a sequence of transitions $T = (t_1, t_2, ..., t_n)$. Each transition t_i is a tuple (u, r, q), where $u = \{r_1, r_2, ..., r_n\}$, $u \in U$ is the result set of the last query made by the simulated searcher, $r \in u$ the current result document, and $q \in Q$ the source state. The result documents r_i possess inherent properties such as length and relevance which are used in the simulation process.

The set of states Q contains action tuples (f_c, f_g, E), where $f_c: R \rightarrow \mathfrak{R}$, $R = \cup_i u_i$, is a cost determining partial function, $f_g: R \rightarrow \mathfrak{R}$ a gain determining partial function, and E a set of events to trigger.

Within a simulation step, to make changes to the current transition tuple, each set of events E can change the result document set $u \in U$, and change the current result document $r \in u$.

Let C denote a set of run-time conditions, such as "current document is highly relevant" or "current cumulated cost exceeds 1000". The transition set Δ_X contains tuples (q_s, P), where $q_s \in Q$ is the source state, $P = \{(q_t, c, V) \mid q_t \in Q, c \in C\}$ a set of transition targets, with their conditions c and probabilities as defined by $V: C \rightarrow [0,1]$.

3.2   A Simulation Step

The simulation advances according to the algorithm defined below in a very similar fashion as a finite automaton. The random variable X is the input, and the output is a sequence of searcher actions and decisions, represented by the nodes and edges respectively. As a side effect, the accumulators for gain and cost are also updated.

Let q_i be the current state, x_i a random value for X, and T_i the sequence of transitions at this point. Let A_{gain} and A_{cost} be accumulators for gain and cost, respectively.

1. Trigger the set of events E associated with the current state q_i.
2. Let u_i be the current result set, and r_i the current result document, as set by events E.
3. Increment A_{gain} by $f_g(r_i)$. Increment A_{cost} by $f_c(r_i)$.
4. Stop if q_i is a final state ($q_i \in F$).
5. Establish accumulator $A_{prob} = x_i$.
6. Iterate over transition set Δ_X where $q_s = q_i$. For each transition, iterate over transition target set P.

    o Let (q_p, c_p, V_p) denote the current transition target $p \in P$.
    o If $V(c_p) + A_{prob} \geq 1$, choose q_p as target and end iteration.
    o Otherwise, increment A_{prob} by $V(c_p)$.

7. Insert transition element (u_i, r_i, q_i) into T.
8. Perform transition. Target state q_p becomes current state.

In the present study, we instantiate our simulator to IIR sessions of the type given in Figure 1.

4   Study Design

This section first presents the research questions (4.1), followed by the presentation of the test collection and search engine (4.2). We then provide the search goals, gains and cost constraints (4.3), query formulation strategies (4.4), snippet scanning and stopping behaviors (4.5), relevance related behavior (4.6), and conclude with session generation methods employed in simulation.

4.1   Research Questions

Observing a notable difference in the IIR performance between a novice and an expert, our overall research question is which behavioral dimensions contribute most to the difference. In the experiments, we measure the IIR performance of novices and experts through cumulated gain over cost (time).

Our baseline performances are: *(a)* the IIR performance of novices following likely novice behavioral parameters; and *(b)* the IIR performance of experts following likely expert behavioral parameters. There is a clear gap between them providing *(a)* the lower bound and *(b)* the upper bound performance (see experimental results). Our aim is to experiment what behavioral parameters or their combinations contribute most to closing the gap between the baselines. The behavioral dimensions are given as value dichotomies between more expert vs. more novice behavior. We utilize parameter values from prior studies when possible. In cases where this is not possible, we rely on plausible arguments. While empirically derived values are preferable, the effect of a behavioral dimension on session effectiveness can be assessed experimentally, using other plausible parameter values.

4.2   Test Collection and Search Engine

We used a subset of the TREC 7-8 test collection of about 500 K documents and 41 topics with graded relevance assessments (see [4]). For each topic, there are five candidate search terms generated by test subjects in a systematic way. The documents have graded relevance assessments on a four-point scale (n=non-relevant, m=marginal, f=fair, h=highly relevant). Among the relevant documents, the shares the relevance levels are m: 50%, f: 35% and h: 15%, respectively. The IR system *Indri* version 5.0 with language modeling and two-stage smoothing was used.

4.3   Search Goals, Gains and Cost Constraints

Search goals determine when the searcher is satisfied with what (s)he has found, and cost constraints determine how much effort (s)he is willing to invest in searching. We set the gain goal at cumulated gain $CG = 40$, and cost allowance up to 6 minutes of search time for both experts and novices.

Table 1. Gain of found and marked documents (in CG points), for both experts and novices

Underlying Document Relevance	Score/Expert	Score/Novice
Non-relevant	0	0
Marginal	0	2
Fair	5	4
Highly relevant	10	8

We employed a gain scoring scheme as shown in Table 1 for experts and novices with relation to relevance levels. The idea is that an expert earns no gain from low-value documents while a novice learns some from marginal ones, while benefitting less from the really good ones. These scoring alternatives clearly are artificial but make a difference in session effectiveness. It should be noted that the typical frequencies of documents of various relevance levels in search results are $F_{non-rel} \gg F_{marginal} > F_{fair} > F_{high}$, so this scoring favors novices.

Table 2. Average costs of subtask (in seconds)

Session subtask	Cost/Expert	Cost/Novice
Entering a query word character	0.6	0.6
Scanning one document snippet	4.5	6.0
Reading to assess one document		
- non-relevant	10.0	15.0
- marginally relevant	20.0	30.0
- fairly relevant	30.0	30.0
- highly relevant	20.0	25.0
Entering the relevance judgment	1.0	2.0

There is a cost involved with the subtasks of formulating the query, scanning, reading snippets and (full) documents, and judging their relevance. Table 2 gives the subtask costs used in the study. Baskaya and colleagues [4] used the following costs for subtasks: *(i)* 3.0 sec. to enter a query word; *(ii)* 4.5 sec. to scan one document snippet; *(iii)* 30.0 sec. to assess one document; and *(iv)* 1.0 to enter the relevance judgment. These values correspond to the values in the left column in Table 2, assuming an average query word length of 5 characters, and a fairly relevant document is assessed. The higher cost values in the right column describe a slower, novice searcher. Even though the time spent for reading and evaluating a document depends on document length, we have characterized the average costs by document relevance level and searcher type for reading a document, and evaluating its relevance.

The simulated sessions were not allowed to continue beyond the time allowance. However, subtasks (e.g. typing a query or browsing snippets) initiated before the time limit were carried out entirely. Our results therefore extend slightly beyond 6 minutes.

4.4   Query Formulation Strategies

We followed earlier studies [3, 4] in session generation. Both novices and experts applied same strategies and were bound to the same vocabulary. We limited the length of the sessions to at most four queries. Baskaya and colleagues [3] considered five query formulation strategies (*S1* to *S5*). Among them, *S2* (two word queries) and *S3* (three word queries) were most effective. The former represents here very short queries, and the latter longer queries. They are referred to here as strategies *2WV* and *3WV* respectively, and are illustrated as follows (see [3,10]):

   2WV: Two word variations: *w1w2 -> w1w3 -> w1w4 -> w1w5*
   3WV: Three word variations: *w1w2w3 -> w1w2w4 -> w1w2w5*

4.5   Snippet Scanning and Stopping Behavior

A searcher may scan in principle one or more *Search Engine Results Page (SERP)* items after each query before deciding to formulate the next query or end the session. In more detail, consider the handling of a *single* query Q_i result up to 10 document snippets: $Q_1->s_{1,1}->c_{1,1}->r_{1,1}->j_{1,1}->s_{1,2}->s_{1,3}->c_{1,3}->r_{1,3}->j_{1,3}->...$

Here, s_{ij} stands for scanning a snippet j, c_{ij} clicking on the snippet j, r_{ij} reading the linked document j, and j_{ij} judging its relevance for query i. We follow a fixed scan stopping strategy, where the searcher always scans n SERP items unless the search goal or the time limit is reached. We set the maximum scanning length to $n=10$ snippets for all SERPs. In another study [16], we found that actual searchers were well approximated by the fixed depth strategy.

4.6   Relevance Related Behavior

While scanning, the simulated searcher probabilistically clicks on snippets appearing to represent relevant documents, and reads and judges every clicked document. Snippets are not always informative, and/or the searcher may overlook their relevance [15]. Moreover, the searcher does not always understand (or notice) the relevance of the documents (s)he has read. Therefore, their relevance judgments may be incorrect; this depends on document relevance level [5, 15]. These can be modeled as probabilities over relevance levels given in the test collection. Table 3 shows clicking and assessment probabilities by the relevance degree of the underlying document.

For example, the simulated novice will click the snippet of a non-relevant document (of relevance degree n) with a probability of 27%. The probabilities increase toward highly relevant documents (cf. [15]), which are judged as relevant with a probability of 97%.

Table 3. Action probabilities by searcher type and snippet/document relevance degree

Feature of Behavior	Doc relevance degree			
	n	m	f	h
P(Click Snippet | Novice)	0.27	0.27	0.34	0.61
P(Click Snippet | Expert)	0.1	0.2	0.4	0.8
P(Relevant Doc | Novice)	0.2	0.88	0.95	0.97
P(Relevant Doc | Expert)	0.1	0.15	0.60	0.97

4.7   Session Generation

Because the execution of experiments entails probabilistic decisions, the outcome of every experiment varies accordingly. As we sought statistical stability in our findings, we applied the Monte Carlo method and iterated each experiment 50 times. Iterations were stopped when the search goal was reached, or the searcher ran out of time or queries. Altogether, we ran 41 topics * 2 session strategies * 8 searcher type variations * 50 stochastic iterations = 32800 sessions in the experiment.

5   Experimental Results

In the following experimental results, we encode behaviors as searcher types progressing from novices toward experts as follows (Table 4).

Table 4. Searcher type coding

Code	Searcher type description
Novice	Novices, see Tables 1-3
Novice2	Novices with expert costs
Novice3	Novices with expert action probabilities
Novice4	Novices with expert gains
Novice2+3	Novices with expert costs and action probabilities
Novice2+4	Novices with expert costs and gains
Novice3+4	Novices with expert action probabilities and gains
Expert	Experts, see Tables 1-3

Figure 2 shows the effectiveness of the sessions with short queries (*2WV*) as gain by session time. We note the following key points.

- There is a systematic and growing gap between novice and expert behaviors of about 3.4, 5.1, 5.5, and 5.0 gain units at 100, 200, 300, and 360 seconds, respectively.
- The effectiveness order of behavioral dimensions from worst to best is *Novice3*, *Novice2/Novice4*, *Novice2+3*, and *Novice2+4/Novice3+4*. This means that, among the individual dimensions, action probabilities affect less than gain and cost structures. Among the combined dimensions, action probabilities and costs are the least effective. This suggests that emphasis be given to exploring the action speed and document utility dimensions.

Figure 3 shows the effectiveness of the sessions with longer queries (*3WV*) as gain by session time. We note that:

- There is a smaller gap between novice and expert behaviors of about 1.8, 4.2, 4.6, and 3.8 gain units at 100, 200, 300, and 360 seconds, respectively, but an overall lower performance compared to the *2WV* case.
- The effectiveness order of behavioral dimensions is the same as in the *2WV* case. In the present simulation, the expectation that longer queries would be more effective was not supported. Both baseline behavioral combinations lost 1.8-3.2 gain units (14%-18%) respectively by using longer queries.

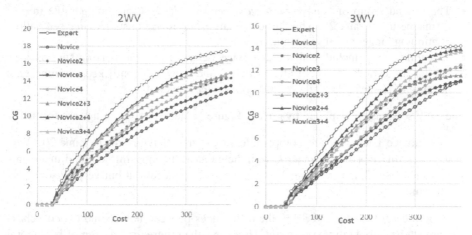

Fig. 2. Sessions with 2 word queries (2WV): gain by cost

Fig. 3. Sessions with 3 word queries (3WV): gain by cost

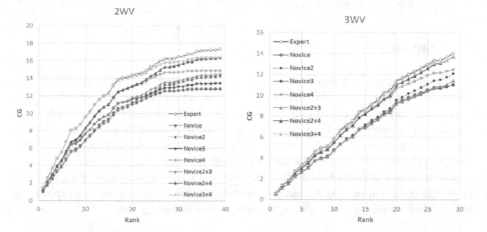

Fig. 4. Sessions with 2 word queries (2WV): gain by rank

Fig. 5. Sessions with 3 word queries (3WV): gain by rank

Traditional IIR evaluation uses gain by rank rather than by time. In Figures 4 and 5, and the associated text below, we therefore analyze session effectiveness by rank. Here the (seen) results from consecutive queries of a session are joined to a long list. All sessions are also extended up to rank 40 (*2WV*) or 30 (*3WV*) for visualization even if their time ran out earlier. However, the extended ranks add no gain.

- The sessions with short queries are depicted by rank in Figure 4. Looking at the results by ranks, the effects of costs are indirect and the gain dimension seems to give the strongest boost. Three groupings can be observed: The best novice behavior (*Novice3+4*) seems to be almost as effective as the expert behavior. Only from rank 20 onwards the *Novice3+4* curve starts to level off as the number of runs starts to decrease because time runs out.

- The second group of behaviors, *Novice4* and *Novice2+4*, are comparable in performance up to rank 25. The curves depart when lower costs (*Novice2+4*) allow continuing longer and thus gaining more.
- The third group includes all other novice behaviors whose performance is very similar up to rank 25 where after *Novice2* and *Novice2+3* still keep earning gain because of lower costs while *Novice* and *Novice3* level off.

The *3WV* sessions are depicted by rank in Figure 5. Here, two groupings are formed:

- Best novice behaviors are comparable to expert behaviors up to rank 20 (*Novice3+4*, *Novice2+4* and *Novice4*) with the gains as the most influential dimension.
- *Novice*, *Novice2*, *Novice3* and *Novice2+3* are less successful but very close in performance.

In both cases of *2WV* and *3WV*, the differences between novice and expert behaviors are statistically highly significant. However, the progressive design of behavioral combinations from the novice to the expert baseline fills the gap so that the set as a whole has no significant differences (ANOVA). Still, most of the pairwise differences are statistically significant (t-test).

6   Summary

The analysis shows that expert-like precise action probabilities contribute less than expert-like gain and cost structures to the overall search performance. However, we have made only a limited exploration of the IIR dimension space. For example, both experts and novices were bound to the same search vocabulary and session length, which is unlikely to occur in real life. Nonetheless, this work suggests that helping less experienced searchers to reduce their search costs would provide them with greater increases in performance. This may happen, for example, through search interfaces that make snippet and document assessment faster. Future work will explore the behavioral dimensions more thoroughly, using more empirical data.

References

1. Azzopardi, L.: The economics of interactive information retrieval. In: 34th Int. SIGIR Conf., pp. 15–24. ACM, New York (2011)
2. Azzopardi, L., Järvelin, K., Kamps, J., Smucker, M.: Report on the SIGIR 2010 workshop on the simulation of interaction. SIGIR Forum **44**, 35–47 (2010)
3. Baskaya, F., Keskustalo, H., Järvelin, K.: Simulating simple and fallible relevance feedback. In: Clough, P., Foley, C., Gurrin, C., Jones, G.J., Kraaij, W., Lee, H., Mudoch, V. (eds.) ECIR 2011. LNCS, vol. 6611, pp. 593–604. Springer, Heidelberg (2011)
4. Baskaya, F., Keskustalo, H., Järvelin, K.: Time drives interaction: simulating sessions in diverse searching environments. In: 35th Int. SIGIR Conf., pp. 97–106. ACM, New York (2012)
5. Baskaya, F., Keskustalo, H., Järvelin, K.: Modeling behavioral factors in interactive information retrieval. In: 22nd CIKM Conf., pp. 2297–2302. ACM, New York (2013)

6. Carterette, B., Kanoulas, E., Yilmaz, E.: Simulating simple user behavior for system effectiveness evaluation. In: 20th CIKM Conf., pp. 611–620. ACM, New York (2011)
7. Dupret, G., Piwowarski, B.: Model based comparison of discounted cumulative gain and average precision. J. of Discrete Algorithms **18**, 49–62 (2013)
8. Gwizdka, J.: Characterizing relevance with eye-tracking measures. In: 5th IIiX Symposium, pp. 58–67. ACM, New York (2014)
9. Harman, D.: Relevance feedback revisited. In: 15th Int. SIGIR Conf, pp. 1–10. ACM, New York (1992)
10. Harman, D.: Information retrieval evaluation. Morgan & Claypool (2011)
11. Järvelin, K.: Interactive relevance feedback with graded relevance and sentence extraction: simulated user experiments. In: 18th CIKM Conf, pp. 2053–2056. ACM, New York (2009)
12. Kharazmi, S., Karimi, S., Scholer, F., Clark, A.: A study of querying behaviour of expert and non-expert users of biomedical search systems. In: 19th Australasian Document Computing Symposium (2014). doi:10.1145/2682862.2682871
13. Kelly, D., Cool, C.: The effects of topic familiarity on information search behavior. In: 2nd JCDL, pp. 74–75. ACM, New York (2002)
14. Keskustalo, H., Järvelin, K., Pirkola, A.: Evaluating the effectiveness of relevance feedback based on a user simulation model: effects of a user scenario on cumulated gain value. Information Retrieval **11**, 209–228 (2008)
15. Keskustalo, H., Järvelin, K., Pirkola, A., Sharma, T., Lykke, M.: Test collection-based IR evaluation needs extension toward sessions – a case of extremely short queries. In: Lee, G.G., Song, D., Lin, C.-Y., Aizawa, A., Kuriyama, K., Yoshioka, M., Sakai, T. (eds.) AIRS 2009. LNCS, vol. 5839, pp. 63–74. Springer, Heidelberg (2009)
16. Maxwell, D., Azzopardi, L., Järvelin, K., Keskustalo, H.: An initial investigation into fixed and adaptive stopping strategies. In: 38th Int. SIGIR Conf., pp. 903–906. ACM, New York (2015)
17. Rabin, M.: Probabilistic automata. Information and Control **6**, 230–245 (1963)
18. Rabin, M., Scott, D.: Finite automata and their decision problems. IBM Journal of Research and Development **3**, 114–125 (1959)
19. Smucker, M.D.: Towards timed predictions of human performance for interactive information retrieval evaluation. In: 3rd Workshop on HCIR (2009). http://cuaslis.org/hcir2009/HCIR2009.pdf
20. Smucker, M.D.: An analysis of user strategies for examining and processing ranked lists of documents. In: 5th Workshop on HCIR (2011). https://sites.google.com/site/hcirworkshop/hcir-2011/papers
21. Smucker, M.D., Clarke, C.: Time-based calibration of effectiveness measures. In: 35th Int. SIGIR Conf., pp. 95–104. ACM, New York (2012)
22. Turpin, A., Scholer, F., Järvelin, K., Wu, M.F., Culpepper, S.: Including summaries in system evaluations. In: 32nd Int. SIGIR Conf., pp. 508–515. ACM, New York (2009)
23. Vakkari, P., Sormunen, E.: The influence of relevance levels on the effectiveness of interactive information retrieval. JASIST **55**, 963–969 (2004)
24. White, R., Dumais, S.T., Teevan, J.: Characterizing the influence of domain expertise on web search behavior. In: 2nd WSDM Conf., pp. 132–141. ACM, New York (2009)

Short Papers

Meta Text Aligner: Text Alignment Based on Predicted Plagiarism Relation

Samira Abnar[1]([✉]), Mostafa Dehghani[2], and Azadeh Shakery[1]

[1] School of ECE, College of Engineering, University of Tehran, Tehran, Iran
{s.abnar,shakery}@ut.ac.ir
[2] Institute for Logic, Language and Computation, University of Amsterdam,
Amsterdam, The Netherlands
dehghani@uva.nl

Abstract. Text alignment is one of the main steps of plagiarism detection in textual environments. Considering the pattern in distribution of the common semantic elements of the two given documents, different strategies may be suitable for this task. In this paper we assume that the obfuscation level, i.e the plagiarism type, is a function of the distribution of the common elements in the two documents. Based on this assumption, we propose META TEXT ALIGNER which predicts plagiarism relation of two given documents and employs the prediction results to select the best text alignment strategy. Thus, it will potentially perform better than the existing methods which use a same strategy for all cases. As indicated by the experiments, we have been able to classify document pairs based on plagiarism type with the precision of 89%. Furthermore exploiting the predictions of the classifier for choosing the proper method or the optimal configuration for each type we have been able to improve the Plagdet score of the existing methods.

Keywords: META TEXT ALIGNER · Plagiarism type · Text alignment · Plagiarism detection · Patterns of distribution of common elements

1 Introduction

The rapid growth of the facilities for accessing and publishing information has led to an increase in producing plagiarized content. Manual investigation of document collections for finding plagiarism cases is not realistic, and thus considering automatic techniques for this purpose is beneficial. The earliest efforts addressing this challenge have begun in 1980s [3,9]. Since then various methods have been proposed considering different problem formulations and evaluation settings. Stein et al. proposed a three step process for plagiarism detection in [10]. These steps are heuristic retrieval, detailed analysis, and knowledge-based post-processing. In order to make the efforts in this area more focused, PAN, an evaluation lab in CLEF, was initiated [7]. In PAN, plagiarism detection is formulated as two steps of source retrieval and text alignment. Source retrieval refers to identifying a small set of source documents that are likely sources for

© Springer International Publishing Switzerland 2015
J. Mothe et al. (Eds.): CLEF 2015, LNCS 9283, pp. 193–199, 2015.
DOI: 10.1007/978-3-319-24027-5_16

plagiarism for a given document. Text alignment is defined as comparing the source and the suspicious documents in details, in order to determine segments of plagiarized and source of plagiarism [7]. Based on the categorization in PAN's datasets, plagiarism cases reuse text employing four different strategies: 1) verbatim copies, 2) random obfuscation, 3) cyclic translation, and 4) summary.

Based on the type of plagiarism relation between two documents, different methods may be suitable for aligning plagiarized and source parts. So the main aim of this paper is to predict the type of plagiarism relation between two given documents and make use of this information to better align documents by employing different text aligners for different plagiarism types. We break this down into two concrete research questions:

RQ1 How can we determine the type of plagiarism relation between two documents before aligning their texts?

RQ2 How can we improve text alignment performance knowing the type of plagiarism?

Regarding the first research question, the main difficulty in determining the plagiarism type of a document pair is that we do not know which part of the two documents are related to the plagiarism cases, if there exist any. In this situation, a naive solution would be to use term frequencies to compare the documents, however, this method may fail to detect all types of plagiarism. We propose a supervised solution to detect plagiarism type, in which both the information about the frequency of common terms and concepts and the pattern of their distribution in the two documents are taken into account.

The second research question is inspired by the important challenge that has also been addressed in some of the working notes of PAN@CLEF. Based on PAN's reports of several years[7], there is no one for all optimized method performing well for all types of plagiarism. This means the performance of text alignment can be improved if we can choose the best method or customize a particular method based on the type and degree of obfuscation in the plagiarized text. In this paper we demonstrate that our proposed method, as a preprocessing step for the text alignment, improves the overall performance.

There are some related efforts addressing the same problem of predicting plagiarism type. One of the very first attempts goes back to 2001, when Paul Clough et al. have proposed to use Naive Bayes classifiers to classify newspaper articles in the three categories of wholly, partially or non-derived [4]. Later in [2], a scoring function based on Kullback-Leibler symmetric distance is applied on some distributional features of documents, such as $tfidf$ to select documents having a plagiarism relation other than *no-plagiarism*. Among participants in PAN, Yurii Palkovskii and Alexei Belov do some analysis to use different parameter presets proper for different obfuscation types [6]. Miguel A. Sanchez-Perez et al. apply two different strategies for text alignment and classify the results to detect if the plagiarism type is *summary* or not. Finally they select the result which corresponds to the detected type [8]. Demetrios Glinos has introduced a hybrid architecture that has a text alignment component to detect order-based

Table 1. Features reflecting pattern of intensity, frequency, and position of common elements

Features determining the pattern of intensity and the frequency of the common elements

Feature Name	Feature Description
Frequency of common bi-grams	*Total number of common bi-grams*
Frequency of common tri-grams	*Total number of common tri-grams*
Relative frequency of common bi-grams	*Ratio of the total number of common bi-grams to the whole number of bi-grams in both documents*
Relative frequency of common tri-grams	*Ratio of the total number of common tri-grams to the whole number of tri-grams in both documents*
Common bi-gram to tri-gram ratio	*Ratio of the total number of common bi-grams to the total number of common tri-grams*
Number of common stopwords	*Total number of common stopwords. For finding the common stopwords, we do the exact matching.*
Ratio of common stopwords	*Ratio of the total number of common stopwords to the whole number of stopwords in both documents*
Length of documents	*Length of both documents*
Length ratio of the documents	*Ratio of the length of the first document (suspicious) to the second document (source).*
Statistics of the similarity scores	*Average, min, max and standard deviation of the similarity scores of common elements separately for bi-grams and tri-grams*

Features determining the pattern of positions of the common elements that occur in the two documents

Feature Name	Feature Description
Statistics of the similarity scores	*Average, min, max and standard deviation of the distances between common elements in each document separately for bi-grams and tri-grams*

plagiarism and a separate and independent component for non-order based plagiarism [5].

The rest of the paper is organized as follows. Section 2 presents the proposed approach. In Section 3, experimental evaluations of the proposed approach are discussed. Finally, In Section 4 the paper is concluded and some future work is suggested.

2   META TEXT ALIGNER

In this section, we explain the proposed mechanism for the META TEXT ALIGNER. The process begins with predicting the type of plagiarism between a given document pair. The type of plagiarism is a function of the distribution of common elements. Depending on the the pattern of the distribution of common elements, different methods may be suitable for text alignment. So the META TEXT ALIGNER uses the predicted plagiarism type to select the best method or tune the parameters of a particular method for each document pair. We first discuss the classifier and the features it exploits. Then we discuss how the predictions of the classifier are used to do a better text alignment compared to the existing approaches.

2.1   Predicting the Plagiarism Type

In this section, we address our first research question: "How can we determine the type of plagiarism relation between two documents before aligning their texts?"

We solve this problem with a supervised method. Thus the problem is mapped to a classification task. Thus we should define a set of features to classify a given document pair based on the type of plagiarism between the documents. In this regard, the first type of features that comes to mind is the frequency of common n−grams in the two documents. In a more general context, we can use common elements instead of common n−grams. Thus similar concepts or synonym n−grams would also be considered as common elements. Considering these types of elements, we can estimate how two documents are lexically, semantically or conceptually similar. In predicting the type of plagiarism, degree of similarity between a document pair is not discriminative feature solely. Our hypothesis is that considering the pattern of the distribution of common elements in the two documents can help us predict the plagiarism relation more accurately. To this end, we define a set of features that reflects the pattern of intensity and positions of the common elements of a document pair. To compute the common elements between a document pair, each document is mapped to a set of elements. These elements are bi-grams and tri-grams of the documents along with their offsets. We denote an element by $e_d = < w, i >$, where w is the n−gram and i is the offset of the beginning of the n−gram in the document in terms of word index. A common element is a pair of elements that their degree of similarity is higher than a specified threshold using a specific method of computing the n−gram similarity. Formally, we denote a common element by $ce_{d,d'} = < e_d, e_{d'}, s >$, where e_d and $e_{d'}$ are two elements from the first and the second documents, and s determines the similarity of the two elements, which corresponds to the concept of "intensity" of element. To compute the similarity between two n−grams, we use the method described in [1].

Finally having a set of common elements for a document pair, we have defined a set of features to model the document pairs as feature vectors. These features are grouped into two categories: i) Features determining the distribution of "intensity" and "the frequency of the common elements". ii) Features determining the distribution of "positions of the common elements" in the two documents. Table 1 shows the whole list of employed features along with their descriptions. Using the defined features, a classifier is trained and used for determining the type of plagiarism between two documents.

2.2 Using Predicted Plagiarism Type to Improve Text Alignment's Performance

Now, we address our second research question: "How can we improve text alignment performance knowing the type of plagiarism?". According to the fact that there is no one for all optimized method of text alignment, an idea to improve the accuracy of text alignment is to choose the best aligning strategy based on plagiarism type. To this end, there are two possibilities:

1. Choosing the *appropriate text alignment method* for each type of plagiarism.
2. Optimizing the *parameters of a particular method* for each type of plagiarism.

Based on reports from PAN over several years, the best method for text alignment for one type is not necessarily the best for other types. So knowing the

Table 2. Accuracy of the classifier for detecting plagiarism relation between two documents

Feature Types	Precision	Recall	F1
distributions of frequency and intensity	0.866	0.865	0.865
distributions of frequency, intensity and positions	0.897	0.894	0.894

plagiarism type, it is possible to choose the best method for each type. On the other hand, usually text alignment strategies have some parameters whose optimal values are not identical for different plagiarism types, or in the supervised approaches, training on different plagiarism types results in different models. Hence, for a specific method, knowing the type of plagiarism, we can set the optimum configuration or choose the particular trained model. In the next section, we present experiments to indicate knowing the plagiarism type, the performance of text alignment can be improved by choosing either the best performing method or the best configuration for a particular method per plagiarism type.

3   Experiments and Analysis

In this section we discuss the performance of the proposed method for predicting the plagiarism type. Moreover, we show that using it as the core of META TEXT ALIGNER will improve the overall performance of the existing text alignment methods.

In our experiments, we have used PAN 2014 text alignment corpus. Moreover, for classifying document pairs, we have applied DTNB, a rule based classifier, on the computed features. Table 2 presents the accuracy of the classifier when it does not use features related to the positions of elements and when it uses this information. As shown in the results, by adding the features that reflect the pattern of distribution of common elements in the documents to the feature set, we can improve the precision.

Employing the proposed classifier, we have implemented META TEXT ALIGNER using the methods proposed in PAN 2014 which are the best methods for different types (two methods, each one outperforms text alignment on two types [8,5]). In META TEXT ALIGNER, if the predicted plagiarism type is No-Plagiarism, the document pair is reported as no-plagiarism. In any of the other cases, META TEXT ALIGNER chooses the text alignment method that has the best performance on the predicted type. Considering the Plagdet score evaluation table reported in the overview paper of PAN 2014, we have extracted the rows which correspond to at least the best result for one of the obfuscation types. The first two rows of Table 3 show the results. The last row in Table 3 presents the performance of META TEXT ALIGNER on different types as well as the entire corpus. As can be seen, using META TEXT ALIGNER, the Plagdet score on the entire corpus is improved. We expected META TEXT ALIGNER to improve the overall performance, while the performance for each type would slightly degraded compared to the best result for that type (since the classifier is not perfect). However, looking at the last row of Table 3, it is observed that

Table 3. Plagdet score of the methods that have the best performance at least for one plagiarism type in PAN 2014

Team	Year	no-obfus.	random-obfus.	circular-trans.	summary	Total
Sanchez-Perez	2014	0.9003	**0.8842**	**0.8866**	0.5607	0.8782
Glinos	2014	**0.9624**	0.8062	0.8472	**0.6236**	0.8593
META TEXT ALIGNER		0.9577	0.8698	0.8820	**0.6310**	**0.8900**

Table 4. Plagdet score of the general expanded n-grams based text aligner (GEN) vs the specialized expanded n-gram based text aligner (SEN)

Method	no-obfus.	random-obfus.	circular-trans.	summary	Total
GEN	0.8512	0.4906	0.6737	0.1715	0.6722
SEN	0.8917	0.6802	0.7008	0.5074	0.7521

META TEXT ALIGNER has an improved performance for the summary type. This indicates that the errors in classifying the document pairs can have positive impact on the text alignment results in some cases. In fact, it is the pattern of the frequency, intensity and positional distribution of the common elements which determines which method would perform better, and our assumption was that the plagiarism type can be a reflection of them. In some cases there might happen that these patterns in the distribution of common elements of a document pair with a plagiarism type are more similar to the ones that are labeled as another type, thus while the classifier may assign them to a wrong class, this can be a desired error. In other words, the wrong prediction of the classifier would lead to selecting the proper method of text alignment.

Table 4 shows how META TEXT ALIGNER improves the performance of a particular method by customizing its parameters per plagiarism type. To show this, the method introduced in [1] is employed. The original method is named as General Expanded N-gram (GEN). GEN is a one for all optimized method. It uses the same value of parameters and feature types for all cases. We have further implemented a Specialized Expanded N-gram (SEN), which makes use of the customized parameters (based on the suggestions in [1]) for the predicted plagiarism type. Comparing the rows in Table 4, it can be seen that SEN outperforms GEN generally and in individual plagiarism types.

4 Conclusion and Future Works

Text alignment is an important stage of plagiarism detection. Regarding the level of obfuscation, i.e. plagiarism type, aligning the text of two documents requires different considerations. Based on this fact, our main goal in this paper was to predict the type of plagiarism relation between two given documents and make use of this information to better align documents by employing different text aligners for different plagiarism types. We demonstrate that using distribution of frequencies, intensities, and positions of common elements of the two documents, we are able to effectively predict their plagiarism relation. We designed META TEXT ALIGNER which based on plagiarism type, improves overall performance of text alignment by either choosing the best performing method or the best configurations.

As an idea for extending this research, we are thinking about tuning parameters of text alignment methods dynamically and directly based on information about frequency, intensity and positions of common elements per instance instead of per type.

References

1. Abnar, S., Dehghani, M., Zamani, H., Shakery, A.: Expanded n-grams for semantic text alignment. In: Lab Report for PAN at CLEF (2014)
2. Barrón-Cedeño, A., Rosso, P., Benedí, J.-M.: Reducing the plagiarism detection search space on the basis of the kullback-leibler distance. In: Gelbukh, A. (ed.) CICLing 2009. LNCS, vol. 5449, pp. 523–534. Springer, Heidelberg (2009)
3. Brin, S., Davis, J., Garcia-Molina, H.: Copy detection mechanisms for digital documents. ACM SIGMOD Record **24**, 398–409 (1995)
4. Gaizauskas, R., Foster, J., Wilks, Y., Arundel, J., Clough, P., Piao, S.: The meter corpus: a corpus for analysing journalistic text reuse. In: Proceedings of the Corpus Linguistics 2001 Conference, pp. 214–223 (2001)
5. Glinos, D.: A hybrid architecture for plagiarism detection. In: Lab Report for PAN at CLEF (2014)
6. Palkovskii, Y., Belov, A.: Developing high-resolution universal multitype n-gram plagiarism detector. In: Lab Report for PAN at CLEF (2014)
7. Potthast, M., Hagen, M., Beyer, A., Busse, M., Tippmann, M., Rosso, P., Stein, B.: Overview of the 6th international competition on plagiarism detection. In: Cappellato, L., Ferro, N., Halvey, M., Kraaij, W. (eds.) Working Notes Papers of the CLEF 2014 Evaluation Labs (2014)
8. Sanchez-Perez, M., Sidorov, G., Gelbukh, A.: A winning approach to text alignment for text reuse detection at pan 2014. In: Lab Report for PAN at CLEF (2014)
9. Shivakumar, N., Garcia-Molina, H.: Scam: A copy detection mechanism for digital documents, pp. 1–13 (1995)
10. Stein, B., zu Eissen, S.M., Potthast, M.: Strategies for retrieving plagiarized documents. In: Proceedings of SIGIR 2007, pp. 825–826. ACM (2007)

Automatic Indexing of Journal Abstracts with Latent Semantic Analysis

Joel Robert Adams[✉] and Steven Bedrick

Center for Spoken Language Understanding, Oregon Health and Science University,
3181 SW Sam Jackson Park Road, Portland, OR, USA
{adamjo,bedricks}@ohsu.edu
http://www.ohsu.edu/cslu

Abstract. The BioASQ "Task on Large-Scale Online Biomedical Semantic Indexing" charges participants with assigning semantic tags to biomedical journal abstracts. We present a system that takes as input a biomedical abstract and uses latent semantic analysis to identify similar documents in the MEDLINE database. The system then uses a novel ranking scheme to select a list of MeSH tags from candidates drawn from the most similar documents. Our approach achieved better than baseline performance in both precision and recall. We suggest several possible strategies to improve the system's performance.

1 Introduction

When a new biomedical journal article is added to the MEDLINE database, professional indexers at the National Library of Medicine (NLM) manually annotate it with semantic descriptors from a controlled vocabulary of Medical Subject Headings (MeSH) in order to capture the primary concerns of the text. These descriptors, or "MeSH tags," are used as features in traditional document retrieval systems, such as PubMed, document classification, and recommendation systems [10] and even word sense disambiguation [15]. The manual indexing process is both time consuming and expensive [1].

BioASQ is an organization that sponsors challenges in biomedical question answering. One of their yearly challenges is an investigation into large-scale semantic indexing of journal abstracts. Participants are provided a set of MEDLINE abstracts in English, and are tasked with assigning MeSH tags to them. These tags are then evaluated against the MeSH tags manually applied by annotators. The work presented in this paper was initiated as part of the second iteration of the BioASQ track on biomedical semantic indexing.

Previous researchers have explored a variety of approaches to this problem, such as supervised learning approaches including Support Vector Machines [8], and tools based on more traditional natural language processing techniques [2]. We approach the problem from a document clustering perspective, based on the observation that similar documents often share MeSH terms. For example two articles about treatments prolonging the survival of patients with Glioblastoma — one annotated with 15 MeSH tags and the other with 17 — share 10 of these terms.

J. Mothe et al. (Eds.): CLEF 2015, LNCS 9283, pp. 200–208, 2015.
DOI: 10.1007/978-3-319-24027-5_17

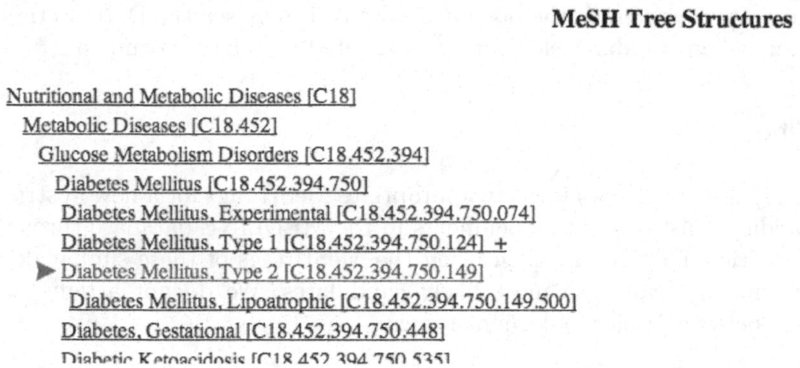

MeSH Tree Structures

Nutritional and Metabolic Diseases [C18]
  Metabolic Diseases [C18.452]
    Glucose Metabolism Disorders [C18.452.394]
      Diabetes Mellitus [C18.452.394.750]
        Diabetes Mellitus, Experimental [C18.452.394.750.074]
        Diabetes Mellitus, Type 1 [C18.452.394.750.124] +
▶ Diabetes Mellitus, Type 2 [C18.452.394.750.149]
         Diabetes Mellitus, Lipoatrophic [C18.452.394.750.149.500]
       Diabetes, Gestational [C18.452.394.750.448]
      Diabetic Ketoacidosis [C18.452.394.750.535]

Fig. 1. An example from the online MeSH Browser

This work presents a system that uses latent semantic analysis to identify semantically "similar" abstracts to an unlabeled "query" abstract. Given this set of similar abstracts, we use the human-assigned MeSH tags of the similar documents to build a set of candidate MeSH tags. We then use distributional features of these tags to attempt to rank the most likely candidate terms for our query abstract.

2 Background

2.1 MeSH Hierarchy

MeSH is a hierarchical thesaurus managed by the National Library of Medicine. As of the 2014 edition, there were 27,149 tags in MeSH. Objects in the MeSH hierarchy have two primary attributes. The first is a human readable name, such as "Diabetes, Mellitus, Type 2," and the second is a unique identifier, such as "D003924." As you can see from the small fragment of the MeSH hierarchy in Figure 1, the concepts range from general to extremely specific.

2.2 PubMed Annotation

The NLM gives its annotators clear guidelines for adding MeSH tags to a new document. They encourage their staff to select only subjects discussed at length in the paper, rather than those mentioned briefly. Once the annotator understands the subjects involved, she chooses the most specific heading possible. For example, if the focus of the article is "Type 2 Diabetes" then the annotator would use "Diabetes, Mellitus, Type 2." However, if the paper had a broader focus on Diabetes, a more general term such as "Diabetes Mellitus" is preferred [12]. The assigned MeSH tags for a given paper are divided into "major" topics, which represent the primary concerns of the article, and "non-major" topics, which are not the focus but are substantively discussed.

There are no rules about how many MeSH tags can or should be applied to a given document. However, in the documents we consider (see the Data section) there are an average of about eleven tags associated with each document.

3   Method

For this study, we attempt to identify appropriate MeSH tags for a new abstract by first building a list of similar documents in the MEDLINE database through Latent Semantic Analysis, and then using the MeSH tags of these similar documents to find and rank the most likely candidates. We do not attempt to differentiate between major and minor topics.

3.1   Data

Due to the immense size of the MEDLINE database, and the possibility of MeSH tags changing over time, we focus only on the documents after 2005 which are included in the list of 1,993 journals that BioASQ has identified as having "small average annotation periods" [16]. These journals are selected because they are updated only during short, discrete time periods, and should therefore have stable MeSH labelling for training and evaluation. In addition, we only include tags which appear in the 2014 edition of MeSH. We do not attempt to re-map tags that have changed between MeSH editions. Training documents which have no MeSH tags from the 2014 MeSH are ignored. These restrictions result in a training set of ≈ 1 million documents.

We evaluate our system on two BioASQ-provided batches of abstracts together with their manually-applied gold-standard MeSH tags. The first of these (Batch 3, Week 4) consists of 4,726 documents, and the second (Batch 3, Week 5) consists of 4,533 documents. We compare our performance against the BioASQ baseline system — an unspecified "unsupervised" approach [13] — evaluated on the same data.

3.2   Latent Semantic Analysis

Latent Semantic Analysis (LSA) is a technique for analyzing semantic relationships between documents. It is an extension of standard vector-space retrieval [14] but is more robust in the face of synonymy [5]. LSA has been applied to a wide variety of information retrieval tasks, ranging from standard ad-hoc retrieval [6] to cross-language information retrieval [11]. Using LSA, one may perform vector-space retrieval on a low-rank approximation of a term-document matrix, in which "related" words (i.e., words that frequently co-occur with one another in the corpus) end up grouped together — and are therefore retrieved together. The combination of dimensionality reduction and semantic grouping make LSA a natural fit for the problem of computing document similarity for automatic indexing.

LSA produces this matrix approximation using singular value decomposition (SVD). SVD effectively "splits" a term-document matrix X into three new matrices, T, S, and D, which may be multiplied together in order to approximate the original matrix ($X = TSD'$). The S matrix is said to contain the "singular values" of X and T and D map terms and documents (respectively) onto singular values [5].

Given the LSA-produced approximation of the term-document matrix, and a query document, one performs retrieval as follows: the query document is transformed into a term vector, and this vector is projected into the LSA space. Then, one may use standard vector-space techniques to score the similarity between low-rank approximations of corpus documents and the transformed query document.

Our implementation begins by pre-processing our training documents using the Python Natural Language Toolkit (NLTK) library.[1] We use NLTK's implementation of the Punkt sentence tokenizer [9] along with the standard NLTK word tokenizer to break the documents into their component sentences and then words. As part of pre-processing, we remove common words (such as 'or' and 'not') found in the standard NLTK English word list, and then apply the NLTK implementation of the Snowball stemmer.

We next use the Gensim library[2] to produce a term-document matrix, in which each "row" represents a term, and each "column" represents a document (i.e., a MEDLINE abstract), and the values in cells represent occurrence counts. We then weight the counts by their normalized term frequency-inverse document frequency scores, and perform LSA on the resulting matrix. Since the purpose of LSA is to produce a low-rank approximation of the complete term-document matrix, users of LSA must choose a dimensionality for their search space. We heuristically choose the first 200 features of our transformed matrix.

3.3 Choosing Closest Neighbors

We are now able to use cosine similarity (a measurement of the angle between two vectors) to determine the similarity between our query document and each of the training documents. We then select the n-closest neighbors from the training documents. We performed initial tuning experiments and settled on a provisional value for n of 20. However, we also set a minimum cosine similarity threshold of 0.1 to avoid considering documents with 0 or negative similarity.

3.4 MeSH Tag Scoring and Selection

Once the neighboring documents are selected, our system sorts and ranks the associated MeSH terms based on the following assumptions:

1. All else being equal, a MeSH tag from a *more* similar document should have a greater contribution to the final score than a tag from a *less* similar document.

---

[1] http://www.nltk.org/

[2] http://radimrehurek.com/gensim/

2. MeSH tags that appear more frequently in neighboring (i.e., more similar) documents are better candidates than those which only occur a single time.
3. Some MeSH tags — such as "Mutation" — appear far more frequently in the corpus than others, so the fact neighbors share one of these common tags should contribute less information than a more obscure tag.

Let our n neighboring documents $d_1, d_2, \ldots, d_n$ be represented as the ordered pairs $d_i = (s_i, M_i)$ where s_i represents the cosine similarity between document i and the new abstract, and M_i is the set of MeSH tags associated with document i.

Then for any MeSH tag m in our set of candidates, we can define a weighted frequency $f(m)$ as:

$$f(m) = \sum_{i=1}^{n} e(i) \cdot s_i \qquad (1)$$

Where:

$$e(i) = \begin{cases} 1 & \text{if } m \in M_i \\ 0 & \text{otherwise} \end{cases} \qquad (2)$$

And define an inverse document frequency $idf(m)$ over the training corpus:

$$idf(m) = \log(\frac{N}{1 + C_m}) \qquad (3)$$

where N is the number of documents in the training corpus and C_m is the number of documents in the training corpus that contain m.

Then our score for term m is:

$$score(m) = f(m) \cdot idf(m) \qquad (4)$$

We will refer to this formula as the "naive score" ranking.

3.5   Additional Ranking Experiments and Learning-to-Rank

During error analysis of the naive score results, it appeared that the weighted frequency factor, $f(m)$, seemed to be a better predictor of a good MeSH tag than our inverse document frequency formulation. Manual tuning of the score suggested that weighted frequency alone seemed to be more informative than the naive score.

We decided to attempt to apply a learning-to-rank algorithm to our ranking, both as a more principled way to evaluate our assumptions about features, and because similar approaches have lead to good results in automatic MeSH tag assignment [7].

We used the list-wise learning-to-rank algorithm ListNet [4] as implemented in the RankLib library.[3] In this implementation, a training document is associated with a list of mesh tags, each one of which is represented by its features (such as $f(m)$ and $idf(m)$). These <mesh tag, feature> pairs are assigned a

---

[3] http://people.cs.umass.edu/~vdang/ranklib.html

Table 1. Micro-precision and recall for our various ranking approaches over two epochs of BioASQ 2014 data.

Batch	System	Precision	Recall	F
Week 4	BioASQ Baseline	0.24	0.29	0.27
Week 4	Naive Score	0.28	0.24	0.26
Week 4	LtR Score	0.44	0.35	0.35
Week 4	TF	**0.45**	**0.36**	**0.40**
Week 4	LtR TF + Max Similarity	**0.45**	**0.36**	**0.40**
Week 5	BioASQ Baseline	0.23	0.31	0.26
Week 5	Score	0.27	0.24	0.25
Week 5	LtR Score	0.40	0.35	0.37
Week 5	TF	0.40	0.35	0.37
Week 5	LtR TF + Max Similarity	**0.41**	**0.35**	**0.38**

target value of '1' if the mesh tag was actually assigned to the query document, and '0' otherwise. ListNet then assigns scores so as to optimize a loss function based on the cross-entropy between the targets and assigned scores.

In addition to the naive score, we evaluated the following ranking models:

- **TF**: MeSH tags ranked using only weighted term frequency $f(m)$.
- **Learn to Rank Score**: ListNet trained on the features $f(m)$ and $idf(m)$ as defined in the naive score.
- **Learn to Rank TF + Max Similarity**: ListNet trained on unweighted MeSH tag frequency within neighboring documents, and 'maximum similarity' — the highest value similarity witnessed for a document containing the tag.

All ListNet models were trained on 2000 documents, with linear feature normalization.

4   Results and Discussion

The micro precision and recall results of our experiments are shown in Table 1.

Our inverse document frequency feature — $idf(m)$ — for MeSH terms did appear to be exceptionally helpful. While there do appear to be cases in the data where it would benefit our ranking to handle particularly obscure MeSH tags differently from very common terms, our current methods are not capturing this in a useful way.

Tables 2 and 3 demonstrate the difference between ranking by naive score and weighted term frequency on PMID 17400438: "Molecular characterization of the BvgA response regulator of Bordetella holmesii." The horizontal line in the tables (for example below the term 'Chromatography, Gel' in table 2) marks the 12 term threshold. Ellipses mark where tags were removed for clarity. MeSH tags in the actual — manually assigned — list are marked in bold.

Table 2. Example candidates and Naive Score values for a sample abstract. **Boldfaced** tags were present in the ground truth.

MeSH Tag	Score
Protein Binding	21.157
Amino Acid Sequence	20.93
Centromere Protein B	18.16
Protein Structure, Tertiary	16.97
Cytochromes b5	15.76
Molecular Sequence Data	15.10
Cytochrome P-450 CYP2E1	14.09
Arabidopsis	13.58
Mutagenesis, Site-Directed	13.17
Cloning, Molecular	12.75
Centromere	12.59
Chromatography, Gel	11.18
Recombinant Proteins	11.04
...	...
Bordetella pertussis	7.07
...	...
Phosphorylation	6.49
...	...
Gene Expression Regulation, Bacterial	4.28
...	...

In this particular example, a total of 201 candidate terms were considered. The candidate list includes *all* of the MeSH terms that were manually applied to the abstract. However, both systems fail to assign tags because they fall below the 12 tag cut-off.

The naive score does, indeed, give high scores to less frequently used MeSH tags witnessed in neighborhood documents — for example, "Centromere Protein B" appears in only 12 documents in the training set. However, this comes at a high cost in terms of noise. Essentially, this approach gives too much weight to tags from the "long tail" of MeSH tags, and often ranks spurious tags too highly.

The weighted term frequency system obviously does better in that fewer spurious and rare terms end up in the top 12. Under this ranking scheme, the cost is such that more infrequently used terms such as "Bordetella pertussis" — which is used in only 146 documents in the training set — are exceptionally unlikely to make it into the top 12 without somehow taking into consideration their relative rarity.

The learning-to-rank models perform well, but not significantly better than weighted term frequency on its own. This suggests that additional feature engineering is required, in order to provide ListNet with more information about our ranking criteria.

All methods other than the naive score consistently outperform baseline.

Table 3. Example candidates ranked by weighted term frequency, from the same article as shown in Table 2. **Boldfaced** tags were present in ground truth.

MeSH Tag	Weighted Term Frequency
Humans	9.98
Protein Binding	5.80
Amino Acid Sequence	5.76
Molecular Sequence Data	4.95
Protein Structure, Tertiary	4.18
Animals	4.09
Recombinant Proteins	2.52
Mutagenesis, Site-Directed	2.51
Models, Molecular	2.46
Base Sequence	2.45
Arabidopsis	2.43
Cloning, Molecular, 2.42	
...	...
Phosphorylation	1.63
...	...
Gene Expression Regulation, Bacterial	.84
...	...
Bordetella pertussis	.82
...	...

5   Conclusions

The comparison with the BioASQ baseline shows the LSA-based system is viable, however our system falls well short of being state of the art. The leading system in the most recent version of the BioASQ challenge has both precision and recall results above 0.6 [3]. However, there are a number of potential improvements to our system which are worth exploring.

Our experiments with learning-to-rank are suggestive, and it will be interesting to see how much improvement can be gained from further feature-engineering and training on larger data sets. Additional features could include additional MeSH-focused features (such as capturing whether the tag is included in the special set of extremely frequently used "checktags") or could focus on surface features of the query itself.

There is also still room for improvement in the LSA model. In our current work, we are exploring different methods of identifying stop words, so as to better reflect the word frequency distribution of biomedical literature. In addition, we are investigating a variety of domain-specific text normalization approaches. For example, we are currently working on automatic identification and normalization of acronyms, as well as automated identification of age ranges. We expect this to improve LSA's ability to "connect the dots" and recognize semantically similar documents.

References

1. Aronson, A.R., Bodenreider, O., Chang, H.F., Humphrey, S.M., Mork, J.G., Nelson, S.J., Rindflesch, T.C., Wilbur, W.J.: The NLM indexing initiative. In: AMIA Annual Symposium Proceedings, pp. 17–21 (2000)
2. Aronson, A.R., Lang, F.M.: An overview of MetaMap: historical perspective and recent advances. Journal of the American Medical Informatics Association : JAMIA **17**(3), 229–236 (2010)
3. BioASQ: Test results for task 3a (2015). http://participants-area.bioasq.org/results/3a/
4. Cao, Z., Qin, T., Liu, T.Y., Tsai, M.F., Li, H.: Learning to rank: from pairwise approach to listwise approach. In: Proceedings of the 24th International Conference on Machine Learning, pp. 129–136. ACM (2007)
5. Deerwester, S.C., Dumais, S.T., Landauer, T.K., Furnas, G.W., Harshman, R.A.: Indexing by latent semantic analysis. JASIS **41**(6), 391–407 (1990)
6. Furnas, G., Deerwester, S., Dumais, S., Landauer, T.K., Harshman, R., Streeter, L., Lochbaum, K.: Information retrieval using a singular value decomposition model of latent semantic structure. In: Proceedings of the 11th Annual International ACM SIGIR Conference on Research and Development in Information Retrieval, SIGIR 1988, May 1988
7. Huang, M., Névéol, A., Lu, Z.: Recommending mesh terms for annotating biomedical articles. Journal of the American Medical Informatics Association **18**(5), 660–667 (2011)
8. Jimeno Yepes, A., Mork, J.G., Wilkowski, B., Demner-Fushman, D., Aronson, A.R.: MEDLINE MeSH indexing: lessons learned from machine learning and future directions. In: Proceedings of the 2nd ACM SIGHIT International Health Informatics Symposium, pp. 737–742. ACM, New York (2012)
9. Kiss, T., Strunk, J.: Unsupervised Multilingual Sentence Boundary Detection. Computational Linguistics **32**(4), 485–525 (2006)
10. Lin, J., DiCuccio, M., Grigoryan, V., Wilbur, W.: Navigating information spaces: A case study of related article search in PubMed. Information Processing and Management **44**(5), 1771–1783 (2008)
11. Littman, M.L., Dumais, S.T., Landauer, T.K.: Automatic cross-language information retrieval using latent semantic indexing. In: Grefenstette, G. (ed.) Cross-Language Information Retrieval: The Spring International Series on Information Retrieval, pp. 51–62. Springer (1998)
12. National Library of Medicine: The medline indexing process: Determining subject content (2015). http://www.nlm.nih.gov/bsd/disted/meshtutorial/principlesofmedlinesubjectindexing/theindexingprocess/
13. Partalas, I., Gaussier, É., Ngomo, A.C.N.: Results of the first bioasq workshop. In: BioASQ@ CLEF, pp. 1–8 (2013)
14. Salton, G., Wong, A., Yang, C.S.: A vector space model for automatic indexing. Communications of the ACM **18**(11), November 1975
15. Stevenson, M., Guo, Y., Al Amri, A., Gaizauskas, R.: Disambiguation of biomedical abbreviations. In: Proc. Workshop Current Trends in Biomedical Natural Language Processing, pp. 71–79 (2009)
16. Tsatsaronis, G., Balikas, G., Malakasiotis, P., Partalas, I., Zschunke, M., Alvers, M.R., Weissenborn, D., Krithara, A., Petridis, S., Polychronopoulos, D., et al.: An overview of the bioasq large-scale biomedical semantic indexing and question answering competition. BMC bioinformatics **16**(1), 138 (2015)

Shadow Answers as an Intermediary
in Email Answer Retrieval

Alyaa Alfalahi, Gunnar Eriksson, and Eriks Sneiders[✉]

Department of Computer and Systems Sciences,
Stockholm University, 7003, 164 07 Kista, Sweden
{alyalfa,gerik,eriks}@dsv.su.se

Abstract. A set of standard answers facilitates answering emails at customer care centers. Matching the text of user emails to the standard answers may not be productive because they do not necessarily have the same wording. Therefore we examine archived email-answer pairs and establish query-answer term co-occurrences. When a new user email arrives, we replace query words with most co-occurring answer words and obtain a "shadow answer", which is a new query to retrieve standard answers. As a measure of term co-occurrence strength we test raw term co-occurrences and Pointwise Mutual Information.

Keywords: Email answering · Statistical word associations · Shadow answer

1 Introduction

Agents at customer care centers traditionally use standard answers (a.k.a. answer templates) to answer customer emails. Various methods for obtaining email answers may help with this task. Matching manually crafted text patterns yields the highest accuracy of answer retrieval [1], but it is a labor intensive approach. Machine learning is popular (e.g. [2-3]), but it works best with a few and broad text categories. Answer generation (e.g. [4]) is an interesting research problem, but not likely to reach commercial use in the nearest future.

Our contacts with customer care centers in Sweden show that they prefer technology support that requires minimum maintenance, and this minimum does not depend on rare professional competence. For email answering that means a focus on statistical text similarity calculation rather than building a knowledge base (e.g. [5]).

Our task at hand is retrieval of standard answers when a new customer email arrives. The difficulty of the task is different wordings: a standard answer is not a document similar to the query, it is a document that answers the query. We cannot rely on term similarity. There exist, however, statistical word associations: certain words in similar queries co-occur with certain words in their answers. This may be a machine learning task for Support Vector Machine (SVM). Alternatively, we can measure the strength of these associations and use them in order to replace words in a user email with the associated words from the answers. Thus, the user email is translated into a shadow answer, i.e., a user query made of anticipated answer words, which becomes a

© Springer International Publishing Switzerland 2015
J. Mothe et al. (Eds.): CLEF 2015, LNCS 9283, pp. 209–214, 2015.
DOI: 10.1007/978-3-319-24027-5_18

new search query in the database of standard answers. The question is – how can we measure the word associations between user emails and their answers? We compare two measures – raw term co-occurrence and Pointwise Mutual Information.

Further in this paper, Section 2 presents our answer retrieval method. Sections 3 and 4 introduce the experiment data and process. Section 5 shows the results, and Section 6 concludes the paper.

2   Shadow Answer

Because we cannot use the original user email as a search query among standard answers, we translate the user email into a shadow answer that contains terms expected in the answer, and use the shadow answer as a search query among standard answers. The idea of a shadow answer comes from Lamontagne et al. [6] who explored co-occurrences between words in archived problem descriptions and their solutions. Our messages and their answers are two parallel corpora; parallel corpora are traditionally used in machine translation to train the system to establish relationships between similar words in two languages. We have a similar task; our "two languages" are the wording of user emails and the wording of their answers.

The architecture of our answer retrieval process is shown in Fig. 1.

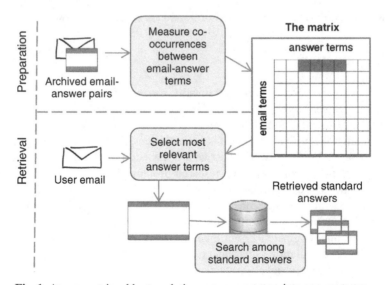

Fig. 1. Answer retrieval by translating user query terms into answer terms.

During the preparation phase, we measure term co-occurrences in archived emails and their answers, and fill the numeric co-occurrence values into the matrix. Every term in the email corpus has a corresponding row in the matrix; every term in the answer corpus has a corresponding column in the matrix. The numeric values in the matrix show the strength of co-occurrence of two terms in the email and its answer respectively.

During the answer retrieval phase:

1. The system takes each term in the user email and consults the matrix for one or several most co-occurring answer terms, and puts these answer terms into the shadow answer, which is a bag of words. If an email term has no corresponding answer term, it is ignored. The shadow answer is an equivalent of the user email re-written in answer terms.
2. We use the shadow answer as a search query for a standard text-retrieval system to get a ranked list of standard answers.
3. Because the shadow answer contains terms expected in the answer of the given user email, we hope that the retrieved answers are relevant.

Our research question is how we can fill and use the matrix in Fig. 1. In this paper, we explore two measures of term co-occurrence. First one is raw co-occurrence, i.e., the number of email-answer pairs where one term occurs in the email and the other term occurs in the answer. Second one is Pointwise Mutual Information (PMI).

PMI is a simple measure of co-occurrence strength between two items. It works by relating the probabilities of the individual occurrence of the items to the probability of both items occurring together. In this paper, the probabilities of query and answer term are based on their occurrence in all questions and answers, respectively. The joint probability of the co-occurrence of a pair of a question term and an answer term is based on their occurrence in the same question-answer pair. For more information on this measure, see e.g. Yang and Pedersen [7].

Our goal is to find out whether PMI is better than the raw term co-occurrence for generating shadow answers.

3   Experiment Data

Our data is 1431 email-answer pairs from the Swedish Pension Authority (Pensionsmyndigheten in Swedish). Because we had a text retrieval task, not a traditional machine learning task, we did not divide our email collection into training and test data. We used all 1431 email-answer pairs to fill the email-answer term co-occurrence matrix.

During the answer retrieval test, we used all 1431 emails as user emails, and all 1431 answers as simulated "standard answers". We increased the number of test answer texts by adding some FAQ answers from the Pension Authority's homepage.

4   Experiment Process

Measuring Co-occurrences between Email-Answer Terms. Two parallel sets of experiments were conducted. One set of experiments filled the email-answer term co-occurrence matrix with raw term co-occurrence values; the other set of experiments had the matrix filled with term PMI scores. The texts were not stemmed or lemmatized.

Separate sub-experiments were conducted with and without removal of stop-words from user emails and their answers.

Selecting Most Relevant Answer Terms and generating a shadow answer was conducted roughly the same way when using term PMI or raw term co-occurrences. The system took each email term, consulted the matrix, selected most co-occurring answer terms, and put those answer terms into the shadow answer.

Search among Standard Answers. The shadow answer becomes a query for Lucy, our text-retrieval system. Lucy (http://lucy.apache.org/) is an open source information retrieval system with a standard tf-idf-based ranking. In our experiments, document indexing was performed with Swedish stemming, but without any other modifications such as stop word filtering.

Retrieval Performance Measurements. At the moment of conducting the experiments, the only proof of email-answer relevance was the fact that both the email and the answer originally were in the same pair. We do not formally know whether the answer in a different email-answer pair is relevant to the given email or not, although in reality there are many similar answers. We measured the retrieval performance as follows:

- Lucy retrieved a ranked list of answers.
- In the list of answers, we looked for the original answer of the submitted user email; i.e., they both originally were in the same email-answer pair.
- We note the rank, i.e., the position in the list, of the original answer.
- The average rank of original answers across all 1431 submitted emails describes the potential of the retrieval method.

Baseline Method. Our baseline method was submitting the email message directly to the text retrieval system without the matrix and the shadow answer. The baseline method searched for answers similar to the text of the user email.

5   Experiment Results

Table 1 shows the answer retrieval results when we filled the email-answer term co-occurrence matrix with raw term co-occurrences. The last row shows the results of the baseline method – no matrix at all.

The first four rows in the table stand for sub-experiments: for each term in the submitted email we selected top n most often co-occurring answer terms to put into the shadow answer.

The second and third columns stand for another kind of sub-experiment: when the matrix was filled, stop-words were left in the text or removed from the text.

The cells of the table show the average rank of the original answer across all the submitted emails.

Table 1. Answer ranks, the matrix filled with raw term co-occurrence

Top *n* co-occurring	Avg. rank with stop-words	Avg. rank without stop-words
Top 1	431	202
Top 5	327	239
Top 20	256	304
Top 30	293	320
Baseline	463	184

The biggest surprise is the low rank of the original answers in the list of retrieved answers – the highest average is 184. Because we use a mixture of techniques, we cannot blame any single technique for that. The next biggest surprise is the baseline method, which is the best performing method if stop-words are removed from the texts. If we do use the shadow answer, it is better to remove stop-words and select fewer top co-occurring answer terms.

Table 2 shows the answer retrieval results when we filled the email-answer term co-occurrence matrix with term PMI scores. We extended our PMI experiments by using not only unigrams but also bigrams, terms made of two consecutive words. The email-answer term co-occurrence matrix was filled once by PMI scores between unigrams, bigrams, as well as between unigrams and bigrams.

During the retrieval, we selected only top 1 co-occurring answer terms to be placed into the shadow answer, which corresponds to the first row of Table 1. Furthermore, we experimented with selecting only unigrams, only bigrams, or both, in the user email, and putting only unigrams, only bigrams, or both, into the shadow answer. In Table 2, "$U_e \rightarrow U_{sa}$" stands for the experiment where unigrams were selected in the user email, and unigrams were placed into the shadow answer, as in the experiments in Table 1. "$U+B_e \rightarrow U+B_{sa}$" means that both unigrams and bigrams were selected in the user email, as well as both placed into the shadow answer; the co-occurrences between unigrams, bigrams, and between unigrams and bigrams were considered.

Not surprisingly, the best gain was from using longer sequences, i.e. bigrams: the best average rank of the original answer was obtained by selecting only bigrams from user emails and putting only bigrams into the shadow answers. On the other hand, mixing unigrams with bigrams performed worst, as the last row in Table 2 shows.

Table 2. Answer ranks, the matrix filled with term PMI scores

Selection of uni/bi-grams	Avg. rank	Selection of uni/bi-grams	Avg. rank
$U_e \rightarrow U_{sa}$	66	$B_e \rightarrow U+B_{sa}$	49
$B_e \rightarrow B_{sa}$	28	$U_e \rightarrow U+B_{sa}$	68
$U_e \rightarrow B_{sa}$	38	$U+B_e \rightarrow U_{sa}$	78
$U+B_e \rightarrow B_{sa}$	47	$U+B_e \rightarrow U+B_{sa}$	81
$B_e \rightarrow U_{sa}$	48		

6   Conclusions

The concept of a shadow answer is not new, yet barely used in answer retrieval. We believe this concept has a potential together with a good measurement of term co-occurrences. In our experiments, term PMI outperformed raw term co-occurrence. In experiment settings where only unigrams were used, PMI yielded 66 as the average rank of the original answer, while raw term co-occurrence yielded 202. Having the original user email as the search query (i.e., as the shadow answer) in the set of answers yielded the average rank 184. The best average rank – 28 – was achieved with PMI and bigrams.

We had an unusual method for measuring the performance of answer retrieval – the rank (i.e., position) of the original answer of the user email in the list of retrieved answers. We chose this method because we did not have expert-labeled documents as it is common in text retrieval evaluation. The average rank turned out to be much lower than we expected, although we saw relevant documents on the top of the answer list. For practical use, it appears that shadow answer alone may not be sufficient. Our ongoing research suggests that it can be used in a combination of retrieval methods that generates a merged result list.

We are in the process of labelling answers, which would allow us improving future relevance judgements.

References

1. Sneiders, E.: Automated email answering by text pattern matching. In: Loftsson, H., Rögnvaldsson, E., Helgadóttir, S. (eds.) IceTAL 2010. LNCS, vol. 6233, pp. 381–392. Springer, Heidelberg (2010)
2. Lapalme, G., Kosseim, L.: Mercure: Towards an automatic e-mail follow-up system. IEEE Computational Intelligence Bulletin 2(1), 14–18 (2003). IEEE
3. Itakura, K., Kenmotsu, M., Oka, H., Akiyoshi, M.: An identification method of inquiry e-mails to the matching FAQ for automatic question answering. In: Distributed Computing and Artificial Intelligence, pp. 213–219. Springer, Heidelberg (2010)
4. Marom, Y., Zukerman, I.: Towards a framework for collating help-desk responses from multiple documents. In: Proceedings of the IJCAI05 Workshop on Knowledge and Reasoning for Answering Questions, pp. 32–39 (2005)
5. Malik, R., Subramaniam, L.V., Kaushik, S.: Automatically selecting answer templates to respond to customer emails. In: IJCAI, vol. 7, pp. 1659–1664 (2007)
6. Lamontagne, L., Langlais, P., Lapalme, G.: Using statistical word associations for the retrieval of strongly-textual cases. In: FLAIRS Conference, pp. 124–128 (2003)
7. Yang, Y., Pedersen, J.O.: A comparative study on feature selection in text categorization. In: ICML, vol. 97, pp. 412–420 (1997)

Are Topically Diverse Documents Also Interesting?

Hosein Azarbonyad$^{(\boxtimes)}$, Ferron Saan, Mostafa Dehghani,
Maarten Marx, and Jaap Kamps

University of Amsterdam, Amsterdam, The Netherlands
{h.azarbonyad,dehghani,kamps,maartenmarx}@uva.nl, ferron.saan@gmail.com

Abstract. Text interestingness is a measure of assessing the quality of
documents from users' perspective which shows their willingness to read
a document. Different approaches are proposed for measuring the interestingness of texts. Most of these approaches suppose that interesting
texts are also topically diverse and estimate interestingness using topical
diversity. In this paper, we investigate the relation between interestingness and topical diversity. We do this on the Dutch and Canadian parliamentary proceedings. We apply an existing measure of interestingness,
which is based on structural properties of the proceedings (eg, how much
interaction there is between speakers in a debate). We then compute the
correlation between this measure of interestingness and topical diversity.

Our main findings are that in general there is a relatively low correlation between interestingness and topical diversity; that there are two
extreme categories of documents: highly interesting, but hardly diverse
(focused interesting documents) and highly diverse but not interesting
documents. When we remove these two extreme types of documents there
is a positive correlation between interestingness and diversity.

Keywords: Text interestingness · Text topical diversity · Parliamentary
proceedings

1 Introduction

The availability of user-generated text-based reviews stimulated research in automatically computing the interestingness of texts [3]. In [3] it is shown that
text interestingness is highly correlated with topical diversity on e-books and
e-commerce products description datasets. In this paper, we further investigate
the relation between interestingness and topical diversity of texts. Our main
research question is: *Are topically diverse documents also interesting?*

To answer this question, we independently measure interestingness and topical diversity of texts and compute their correlation. We carry out our research
on the parliamentary proceedings of The Netherlands and Canada and measure the interestingness of the debates in these proceedings using the method
proposed in [4] and their topical diversity using the method proposed in [1].
Parliamentary proceeding have structural measures of interestingness which are

© Springer International Publishing Switzerland 2015
J. Mothe et al. (Eds.): CLEF 2015, LNCS 9283, pp. 215–221, 2015.
DOI: 10.1007/978-3-319-24027-5_19

independent from the textual content. This makes them well suited to answer our research question. Our experiments show that interestingness and diversity reflect different characteristics of documents and in general there is a relatively low correlation between the two properties.

The rest of this paper is organized as follows. In Section 2, we describe the methods used for measuring text's diversity and interestingness. The results and analysis are presented in Section 3. Finally, Section 4 concludes the paper with a breif discussion on the possible future research directions.

2   Methods

In this section we describe how we measure interestingness and topical diversity of debates.

Measuring Debates' Topical Diversity. Different approaches are proposed for measuring the topical diversity of texts [1,3]. Most of these approaches first extract topics of documents using LDA [2] and then estimate the diversity of documents using the extracted topics. We use the method proposed in [1] for estimating the diversity of documents. This approach estimates the diversity of texts using Rao's coefficient [5]: for a document D,

$$div(D) = \sum_{i=1}^{T} \sum_{i=1}^{T} p_i^D p_j^D \delta(i,j),$$ (1)

where T is the set of topics; p_i^D and p_j^D are the probability of assigning topics i and j to document D, and $\delta(i,j)$ is the distance (dissimilarity) of topics i and j. This method first learns an LDA topic model and then uses that model to assign a probability distrobution over topics to documents. Different distance functions have been employed in [1]. However the used functions are not proper distance metrics. So, we use the normalized angular distance which is a distance metric and holds the properties of a metric for measuring the distance of topics [6]:

$$\delta(i,j) = \frac{ArcCos(CosineSim(i,j))}{\pi}$$ (2)

where $CosineSim$ is the cosine similarity of topics i and j. $ArcCos$ ($CosineSim(i,j)$) is the arc cosine of cosine similarity of topics i and j. To calculate the similarity of topics we identify a topic i with the vector consisting of all p_i^D for all documents D in our collection. The similarity of two topics is then the cosine similarity of their vectors.

Measuring Debate's Interestingness. Interestingness of a text could be defined in different ways [3,4]. Derzinski and Rohanimanesh [3] showed that texts' interestingness is highly correlated with its topical diversity. To measure the correlation of interestingness and diversity of documents we first need to estimate the interestingness of documents. To do so, we use the method proposed in [4] and estimate an interestingness value for each document. They define the interestingness of a document as "the probability that the public finds a document of great importance". They focused on measuring the interestingness of debates in parliamentary proceedings. Since the interestingness of texts in parliamentary proceedings is measurable using this method, we employ the approach proposed in [4] to measure the interestingness of debates in parliamentary proceedings. This method uses features extracted from debates for learning a supervised method to assign interestingness values to debates. The used features are categorized into three groups: features based on intensity of debates, features based on quantity and quality of key players in the debates, and features based on the length of debates. From the first category we use the number of switches between speakers in the debates. From the second category we use the most important features: the percentage of members present in the debate, whether the prime minister is present in the debate or not, whether the deputy prime minister is present in the debate or not, and the number of speakers who are floor (party) leaders as well. From the last category we use two most important features: word count of debates and closing time of debates. The importance of features are determined using weights of features in the model trained and reported in [4]. We use weighted linear combination of mentioned features to estimate the interestingness of a debate D:

$$I(D) = \sum_{i=1}^{7} w_i * f_i;$$ (3)

where f_i is a feature and w_i is the weight of f_i in the trained model reported in [4] for assigning interestingness values to debates and the sum is taken over the mentioned seven features.

Correlation of Debates' Topical Diversity and Interestingness. We express the correlation between our two variables of interest by Pearson's product-moment correlation coefficient.

3 Analysis

In this section we first describe the datasets and different setings and pre-processings we did, and then we analyze the text interestingness and topical diversity and their correlations on these datasets.

3.1 Datasets and Experimental Setup

We use two datasets to analyze the correlation of texts' diversity and interestingness: Dutch and Canadian parliamentary proceeding. These datasets are publicly available at http://search.politicalmashup.nl. From the Dutch parliamentary proceedings we use the debates from 1999 to 2011 to train an LDA model. This dataset contains 20,547 debates from parliament. For measuring

Table 1. Top three diverse debates in Dutch and Canadian parliaments

Canadian proceedings			Dutch proceedings		
Topic	#Speeches	Diversity	Topic	#Speeches	Diversity
competitiveness	140	0.224	kingdom relations	20	0.222
industry,science,technology	105	0.218	housing, integration	40	0.219
closed containment	72	0.217	transportation	24	0.216

the correlation of diversity and interestingness, we select a period of parliament from 2006 to 2010 and calculate the correlation on the debates of this period. This period contains 6,575 debates. We also remove the procedural debates which do not contain speeches of parliament members. From Canadian proceedings we choose the debates from 1994 to 2014 to train an LDA model. This subset of dataset contains 9,053 debates. We calculate the correlation of diversity and interestingness on a subset of this dataset from 2004 to 2014 which contains 7,823 debates.

We set the number of topics of LDA to 50. The LDA models are trained on the lemmatized nouns in the documents only. Words with less than five occurrences and 100 words with highest frequencies and 100 words with highest document frequencies in the corpus are considered as stop words and removed from documents. We also do the same feature normalization done in [4] before calculating text interestingness.

3.2   Results

Measuring Topical Diversity of Debates. Table 1 shows the information of top three most diverse debates in the Dutch and Canadian parliaments. The most diverse debate in the Canadian parliament is a debate on study of competitiveness. In this debate, members discussed different issues related to farming, agriculture, and petroleum which made this debate very diverse. The most diverse debate in the Dutch proceedings is a debate in which parliament members asked questions from minister of Interior and Kingdom Relations. Table 1 also shows that diverse debates have a high number of speeches in Canadian proceedings, but a low number of speeches in the Dutch proceedings.

Measuring Interestingness of Debates. Table 2 shows the top three most interesting debates in the Dutch and Canadian proceedings. Unlike diverse debates, interesting ones are mostly focused on a few topics. Also, since number

Table 2. Top three interesting debates in Dutch and Canadian parliaments

Canadian proceedings			Dutch proceedings		
Topic	#Speeches	Interestingness	Topic	#Speeches	Interestingness
government,budget	331	0.52	pension	823	0.86
government orders	325	0.51	economic crisis	681	0.74
crime	314	0.50	war in Iraq	454	0.74

Table 3. The correlation of debates' interestingness (all features) and diversity on Dutch and Canadian proceedings ($\blacktriangle$ indicates the significance using t-test, two-tailed, $p-value < 0.05$)

Interestingness	Canadian	Dutch
Interestingness(all features)	$0.13^{\blacktriangle}$	$0.11^{\blacktriangle}$
Interestingness(speaker switches)	$0.11^{\blacktriangle}$	0.03
Interestingness(prime minister)	$0.08^{\blacktriangle}$	$0.14^{\blacktriangle}$
Interestingness(deputy prime minister)	$0.06^{\blacktriangle}$	$0.1^{\blacktriangle}$
Interestingness(closing time)	$-0.12^{\blacktriangle}$	-0.01

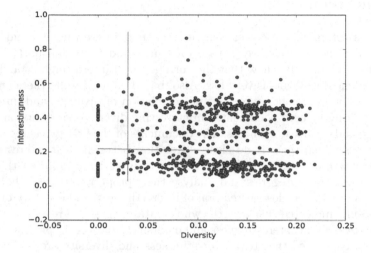

Fig. 1. Scatter plot of interestingness (y-axis) against diversity (x-axis) on debates from 2006 to 2010 on Dutch parliamentary proceedings. Each point in the plot corresponds to a debate.

of speaker switches is the most important feature in the interestingness prediction model, the number of speeches in interesting debates is high.

The Correlation Between Interestingness and Diversity. Table 3 shows the correlation of debates' diversity and interestingness. There is a relatively low correlation between diversity and interestingness in both Dutch and Canadian datasets. In fact, these two metrics are reflecting different characteristics of documents. The results also show that there is a negative correlation between closing time of debates and their diversity. In fact, the debates that take more time are very focused on a few topics. Figure 1 shows the scatter plot of interestingness against diversity on Dutch proceedings. From this figure it can be seen that most of diverse documents have low value of interestingness (the right bottom part of the plot). These are the debates which cover lots of topics but are not interesting from the users' perspective. Also there are a few debates with high value of interestingness and very low value of diversity (left part of the plot).

Besides these two types of debates, we can see from Figure 1 that there is a slight positive correlation between interestingness and diversity (top right part of the plot). If we remove the debates from the first and second category (indicated by red lines in the figure) and just consider the top right points in the Figure 1, the correlation of diversity and interestingness (using all features) increases to 0.35. This results indicates that other than extreme cases (interesting but not diverse documents and diverse but not interesting documents) interesting documents are also topically diverse.

4   Conclusion

We have investigated the correlation between text interestingness and topical diversity. For the analysis, we focused on Dutch and Canadian parliamentary proceedings. The results show that the correlation of interestingness and diversity over whole documents is very low. Also, based on our results there are three major types of documents based on the correlation of diversity and intersting-ness: interesting focused documents; uninteresting diverse documents, and both interesting and diverse documents. The documents of the first two categories are extreme ones which there is no clear correlation between their interestingness and diversity values. It would be interesting to investigate more on the documents of these two categories and analyse their properties to see what is the main reason behind the low correlation of interestingness and diversity on them.

Our results indicated that over the whole dataset there is a relatively low correlation between text interestingness and diversity. However, in previous studies it has been concluded that text interestingness and diversity are highly correlated [3]. There are some possible explanations: We used a method for measuring the interestingness of documents which is independent of the content of documents. However, text diversity is dependent to the content of the documents. Also, [4] used a manually selected debates to train the interestingness prediction model. The chosen debates are the debates which contain the information needed to estimate the interestingness. However we conducted our evaluations on whole debates. Therefore, the used interestingness measure may not be a proper measure to assess the interestingness of all kind of debates. Another reason for getting the low correlation value on debates is that based on our analysis, some of the topics of the LDA model trained on debates are not pure and contain words which should basically belong to different topics. Also, there are some general topics which contain procedural words and are not very informative. So, the impure and general topics make the diversity value estimated for debates very noisy.

Acknowledgments. This research was supported by the Netherlands Organization for Scientific Research (ExPoSe project, NWO CI # 314.99.108; DiLiPaD project, NWO Digging into Data # 600.006.014) and by the European Community's Seventh Framework Program (FP7/2007-2013) under grant agreement ENVRI, number 283465.

References

1. Bache, K., Newman, D., Smyth, P.: Text-based measures of document diversity. In: KDD 2013, pp. 23–31 (2013)
2. Blei, D.M., Ng, A.Y., Jordan, M.I.: Latent dirichlet allocation. Journal of Machine Learning Research **3**, 993–1022 (2003)
3. Derzinski, M., Rohanimanesh, K.: An information theoretic approach to quantifying text interestingness. In: NIPS MLNLP Workshop (2014)
4. Hogenboom, A., Jongmans, M., Frasincar, F.: Structuring political documents for importance ranking. In: Bouma, G., Ittoo, A., Métais, E., Wortmann, H. (eds.) NLDB 2012. LNCS, vol. 7337, pp. 345–350. Springer, Heidelberg (2012)
5. Rao, C.R.: Diversity and dissimilarity coefficients: a unified approach. Theoretical Population Biology **21**(1), 24–43 (1982)
6. Van Dongen, S., Enright, A.J.: Metric distances derived from cosine similarity and pearson and spearman correlations (2012). arXiv preprint http://arxiv.org/abs/1208.3145 arXiv:1208.3145

Modeling of the Question Answering Task in the YodaQA System

Petr Baudiš[(✉)] and Jan Šedivý

Department of Cybernetics, Czech Technical University, Technická 2,
Praha, Czech Republic
baudipet@fel.cvut.cz

Abstract. We briefly survey the current state of art in the field of Question Answering and present the YodaQA system, an open source framework for this task and a baseline pipeline with reasonable performance. We take a holistic approach, reviewing and aiming to integrate many different question answering task definitions and approaches concerning classes of knowledge bases, question representation and answer generation. To ease performance comparisons of general-purpose QA systems, we also propose an effort in building a new reference QA testing corpus which is a curated and extended version of the TREC corpus.

Keywords: Question answering · Information retrieval · Information extraction · Linked data · Natural language processing

1 Introduction

The Question Answering problem (converting an unstructured user query to a specific information snippet) is enjoying renewed research popularity, inspired in part by the high profile Jeopardy! matches of IBM Watson.

The problem is being applied both to open domain (general knowledge; e.g. the QALD challenge) and closed domain (specific knowledge; e.g. the BioASQ challenge). At the same time, the specific task can differ significantly based on the choice of a knowledge base — either a corpora of unstructured data (typically natural language text) or structured database (typically a linked data graph). Finally, when answering questions on top of unstructured data, some argue for yielding answer-bearing passages instead of specific answers.[1] These choices have repercussions on the very formulation of question answering problem, typically require vastly different systems, and lead in different research directions.

In Sec. 2, we review the competing approaches. In Sec. 3, we discuss a related issue of benchmarking question answering systems for comparison and propose a curated dataset initiative. In Sec. 4, we briefly present a system we have created for general question answering that aims to reconcile the competing paradigms. We conclude and outline future research in Sec. 5.

---

[1] See the **ACL Wiki** topic *Question Answering (State of the art)*.

© Springer International Publishing Switzerland 2015
J. Mothe et al. (Eds.): CLEF 2015, LNCS 9283, pp. 222–228, 2015.
DOI: 10.1007/978-3-319-24027-5_20

2   Question Answering Approaches

Likely the more popular area of research concerns structured databases, typically linked data, is often posed as a task of machine translation from naturally phrased question to a formal query based on processing the question parse tree [2] [8] or vector embeddings of the question and knowledge base subgraph [3].

Moving to querying an unstructured knowledge base, the problem becomes a mix of information retrieval, information and relation extraction, textual entailment and knowledge representation. In the era of the TREC QA track, systems with large amount of handcraft [10] or wrapping a web search engine [4] dominated (making results difficult to reproduce). The current high performance models for selection of answer-bearing passages relies on alignment of question and passage dependency trees [11] or vector embeddings [18]. The answer extraction can be regarded as a BIO sequence tagging problem alike named entity recognition. [17]

Another proposed task involves recognition of an entity described by a sentence using a TreeRNN-based vector embedding model. [12]

3   Benchmarking

Multiple datasets have been proposed for end-to-end Question Answering performance evaluation on open domain. Perhaps the most popular datasets are the TREC QA track, QALD [15] and WebQuestions [2].

There are many considerations that put a dataset on a scale from easy (single class of questions, clean, without required inference) to realistic (noisy with typos, requiring complex reasoning). Some datasets are highly biased for a particular knowledge base [2], or mix questions with typically entirely independent answering strategies (e.g. yes/no questions, which translate to a textual entailment, with factoid and paraphrasing questions).

To train and benchmark a system for answering factoid questions with answers that can be found in unstructured text corpora, we used the public QA benchmark from the main tasks of the TREC 2001 and 2002 QA tracks[2] with regular expression answer patterns,[3] extended by a set of questions asked to a YodaQA predecessor by internet users via an IRC interface. The dataset was further manually reviewed, questions deemed ambigous or outdated were removed, and the patterns were updated based on current data or Wikipedia phrasing.

The outcome is a dataset of 867 open domain factoid questions, randomly split to 430-question training (and development) and 430-question testing sets.[4]

---

[2] http://trec.nist.gov/data/qa/2001_qadata/main_task.html, or 2002.

[3] Similar datasets from TREC 1999 and TREC 2000 are also available, however are of lower quality and we lacked the resources required to clean them up — TREC 1999 contains large number of corpora-specific questions with many rephrasings, while TREC 2000 contains many paraphrasing questions, which are hard to match.

[4] The outstanding 7 questions are left unused for now.

We release this as a free-standing dataset `factoid-curated` (v1)[5] and invite researchers to use this system for performance measurements. To allow cross-system comparisons, the dataset also includes precise knowledge base versions to use; we offer their archived snapshots for download (and will run query endpoints for a time). We outline further plans for our common dataset initiative in Sec. 5.1.

4 YodaQA Question Answering System

To unite diverse approaches to Question Answering, we propose a new system **YodaQA**, which aims to provide an open source platform that can serve both as scientific research testbed and a practical system. It is composed from largely independent modules, allowing easy extension with better algorithms or novel approaches, while as a fundamental principle all modules share a common pipeline.

4.1 System Architecture

The YodaQA pipeline is implemented mainly in Java, using the Apache UIMA framework. YodaQA represents each artifact as a separate UIMA CAS, allowing easy parallelization and straightforward leverage of pre-existing NLP UIMA components (via the DKPro interface); as a corollary, we compartmentalize different tasks to interchangeable UIMA annotators. Extensive support tooling is included within the package. Detailed technical description of the pipeline is included in a technical report [1].

The system maps an input question to ordered list of answer candidates in a pipeline fashion, with the flow as in Fig. 1 (inspired by the DeepQA model of IBM Watson [6]), encompassing the following stages:[6]

- **Question Analysis** extracts natural language features from the input and produces in-system representations of the question.
- **Answer Production** generates a set of candidate answers based on the question, by performing a **Primary Search** in the knowledge bases according to the question clues and either directly using the results as candidate answers or selecting the relevant passages (the **Passage Extraction**) and generate candidate answers from these (the **Passage Analysis**).
- **Answer Analysis** generates answer features based on detailed analysis (most importantly, lexical type determination and coercion to question type).
- **Answer Merging and Scoring** consolidates the set of answers, removing duplicates and using a machine learned classifier to score answers by their features. Logistic regression is popular. [9]

---

[5] https://github.com/brmson/dataset-factoid-curated
[6] An extra **Successive refining** phase is available, but currently no-op in production.

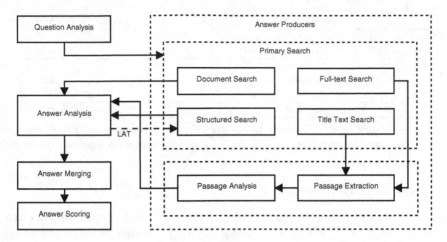

Fig. 1. The general architecture of the YodaQA pipeline. Present but unused final pipeline portions not shown.

4.2 Reference Baseline

The reference pipeline currently considers an English-language task of answering open domain factoid questions (in a style similar to the `factoid-curated` v1 dataset), producing a narrowly phrased answer. While [1] goes into technical details, here we just outline the aspects pertinent to our multi-approach paradigm.

Question Representation: Similar to DeepQA [13], we currently build just a naive representation of the question as bag-of-features. The most important characterization of the question is a set of clues (keywords, keyphrases, and concept clues crisply matching enwiki titles) and possible lexical answer types.

Knowledge Bases: So far, our system is optimized primarily to query unstructured corpora (English Wikipedia, *enwiki*). For informational retrieval, we use Apache Solr[7] and include the document and title-in-clue strategies described in DeepQA [5]. Full-text results are filtered for passages containing the most clues and answers are produced simply from all the named entities and noun phrases.

YodaQA can also query structured corpora (DBpedia, Freebase), so far by a simple baseline query generation approach that just generates an answer for each relation of a concept clue, using relation names as lexical answer types.

Our key design rule is avoidance of hand-crafted rules and heuristics, instead relying just on fully-learned universal mechanisms; we use just about 10 hard-coded rules at this point, mostly in question analysis.

---

[7] http://lucene.apache.org/solr/

System	Accuracy-at-1	Recall	F1	MRR
LLCpass03 [10] (hand-crafted system)	68.5%			
AskMSR [4] (web-search system)	61.4%			0.507
OpenEphyra [14] (hand-crafted OSS)	"above 25%"			
JacanaIR [16] (modern fully-learned OSS)				0.299*
OQA [7] (modern fully-learned OSS)			29%**	
YodaQA v1.0	25.1%	62.2%	35.8%	0.323

Fig. 2. Benchmark results of some relevant systems on the unmodified TREC dataset.
* answer-bearing sentence retrieval ** sub-sampled dataset with manual evaluation

4.3 System Performance

On the test set of the `factoid-curated` v1 dataset, the system achieved **accuracy-at-one of 32.6%**. When we consider all the generated answers, the **recall is 79.3% (F1 46.2%), accuracy-at-five is 52.7%** and the correct question **mean reciprocal rank is 0.420**.[8] In Fig. 2, we compare various performance measures with the most relevant previously published systems (on the TREC dataset, as reported in the respective papers), with ours benchmarked on non-curated version of the TREC 2002, 2003 dataset test split.

5 Conclusion and Future Work

We gave a bird eye's view of the Question Answering research landscape and presented the open source platform YodaQA that aims to bring together diverse approaches and allows to benchmark their contributions within a real-world portfolio of methods. We also discussed some common issues with QA datasets and proposed a new one.

While we invested large amount of software engineering effort to the YodaQA pipeline, it is algorithmically still fairly simple. Our work-in-progress efforts include an answer producer that uses a sequence tagging model [17] and extended question representations.

5.1 Benchmarking

By providing a free-standing dataset tracked on Github, we hope to kick-start an effort to build a larger, widely accepted benchmarking dataset. We also work on a web-based platform for crowd-sourcing both questions and correct answers.

One open problem is automatic answer verification, as a correct answer can typically have numerous paraphrases. The current approach of using regex patterns has many caveats (for example numerical quantities with varying formatting and units). While the problem seems ultimately QA-complete, we believe

---

[8] The system was configured to take 30s per answer on average without caching (most of it is spent in IR and dependency parsing of passages) on the author's machine; longer-time configurations can further improve the performance.

a satisfactory noise reduction could be achieved by specialized matching procedures for some question categories. Some datasets like WebQuestions side-step the issue by posing only questions asking for entity names, but could this bias mis-represent the scientific progress on QA?

References

1. Baudiš, P.: YodaQA: a modular question answering system pipeline. In: POSTER 2015–19th International Student Conference on Electrical Engineering (2015)
2. Berant, J., Chou, A., Frostig, R., Liang, P.: Semantic parsing on freebase from question-answer pairs. In: EMNLP, pp. 1533–1544 (2013)
3. Bordes, A., Chopra, S., Weston, J.: Question answering with subgraph embeddings (2014). arXiv preprint arXiv:1406.3676
4. Brill, E., Dumais, S., Banko, M.: An analysis of the AskMSR question-answering system. In: Proceedings of the ACL 2002 Conference on Empirical Methods in Natural Language Processing, vol. 10, pp. 257–264. Association for Computational Linguistics (2002)
5. Chu-Carroll, J., Fan, J., Boguraev, B., Carmel, D., Sheinwald, D., Welty, C.: Finding needles in the haystack: Search and candidate generation. IBM Journal of Research and Development **56**(3.4), 6:1–6:12 (2012)
6. Epstein, E.A., Schor, M.I., Iyer, B., Lally, A., et al.: Making watson fast. IBM Journal of Research and Development **56**(3.4), 15:1–15:12 (2012)
7. Fader, A., Zettlemoyer, L., Etzioni, O.: Open question answering over curated and extracted knowledge bases. In: Proceedings of the 20th ACM SIGKDD International Conference on Knowledge Discovery and Data Mining, pp. 1156–1165. ACM (2014)
8. Fader, A., Zettlemoyer, L.S., Etzioni, O.: Paraphrase-driven learning for open question answering. In: ACL (1), pp. 1608–1618 (2013)
9. Gondek, D., Lally, A., Kalyanpur, A., Murdock, J.W., Duboué, P.A., Zhang, L., et al.: A framework for merging and ranking of answers in DeepQA. IBM Journal of Research and Development **56**(3.4), 14:1–14:12 (2012)
10. Harabagiu, S.M., Moldovan, D.I., Clark, C., Bowden, M., Williams, J., Bensley, J.: Answer mining by combining extraction techniques with abductive reasoning. In: TREC, pp. 375–382 (2003)
11. Heilman, M., Smith, N.A.: Tree edit models for recognizing textual entailments, paraphrases, and answers to questions. In: Human Language Technologies: The Annual Conference of the North American Chapter of the ACL (2010), pp. 1011–1019. Association for Computational Linguistics (2010)
12. Iyyer, M., Boyd-Graber, J., Claudino, L., Socher, R., Daumé III, H.: A neural network for factoid question answering over paragraphs. In: Empirical Methods in Natural Language Processing (2014)
13. Lally, A., Prager, J.M., McCord, M.C., Boguraev, B., Patwardhan, S., Fan, J., Fodor, P., Chu-Carroll, J.: Question analysis: how watson reads a clue. IBM Journal of Research and Development **56**(3.4), 2:1–2:14 (2012)
14. Schlaefer, N., Gieselmann, P., Schaaf, T., Waibel, A.: A pattern learning approach to question answering within the ephyra framework. In: Sojka, P., Kopeček, I., Pala, K. (eds.) TSD 2006. LNCS (LNAI), vol. 4188, pp. 687–694. Springer, Heidelberg (2006)
15. Unger, C.: Multilingual question answering over linked data: Qald-4 dataset (2014)

16. Yao, X., Van Durme, B., Clark, P.: Automatic coupling of answer extraction and information retrieval. In: ACL (2), pp. 159–165. Citeseer (2013)
17. Yao, X., Van Durme, B., et al.: Answer extraction as sequence tagging with tree edit distance. In: HLT-NAACL, pp. 858–867 (2013)
18. Yu, L., Hermann, K.M., Blunsom, P., Pulman, S.: Deep learning for answer sentence selection. In: NIPS Deep Learning Workshop, December 2014

Unfair Means: Use Cases Beyond Plagiarism

Paul Clough[✉], Peter Willett, and Jessie Lim

Information School, University of Sheffield, Sheffield, UK
{p.d.clough,p.willett}@sheffield.ac.uk

Abstract. The study of plagiarism and its detection is a highly popular field of research that has witnessed increased attention over recent years. In this paper we describe the range of problems that exist within academe in the area of 'unfair means', which encompasses a wider range of issues of attribution, ownership and originality. Unfair means offers a variety of problems that may benefit from the development of computational methods, thereby requiring appropriate evaluation resources. This may provide further areas of focus for large-scale evaluation activities, such as PAN, and researchers in the field more generally.

1 Introduction

Plagiarism[1] and its detection has been a popular area of research for the past 25 years, particularly within academia [1, 2, 4, 12]. Factors, such as the increased availability of freely-accessible digital content, the emergence of online essay banks and writing services, and technological developments are resulting in a rise in plagiarism, particularly in education[2]. However, within the educational context plagiarism is just one example of cheating, which may also include [14]: (i) *collusion*: collaboration among students; (ii) *falsification*: student presenting another work as his own; and (iii) *replication*: student submitting same work again (i.e., self-plagiarism) inter alia. Plagiarism is also not restricted to students, but has also surfaced amongst academics [9]. For example, Citron & Ginsberg [3] analyze text reuse within ArXiv.org and Errami et al. [5] identify duplication in PubMed abstracts. In addition, plagiarism can, and does, occur in documents beyond text[3]. In this paper we discuss the range of problems commonly encountered in Higher Education that extend beyond typical examples of plagiarism and that may provide further case studies for research into computational methods for determining authorship, attribution and originality.

2 Related Work

Two aspects commonly discussed in the literature are *intent* and *extent*. The former captures whether the (re-)use of existing sources was intentional or unintentional

---

[1] Joy and Luck [8] (p. 129) define plagiarism as *"unacknowledged copying of documents or programs"*.

[2] http://www.bbc.co.uk/news/magazine-12613617 (site visited: 25/06/2015).

[3] https://www.plagiarismtoday.com/2015/03/05/plagiarism-is-more-than-just-text/ (site visited: 25/06/2015).

© Springer International Publishing Switzerland 2015
J. Mothe et al. (Eds.): CLEF 2015, LNCS 9283, pp. 229–234, 2015.
DOI: 10.1007/978-3-319-24027-5_21

(e.g., the result of poor academic writing skills); the latter notion captures the extent or degree to which an original source is edited and modified, ranging from verbatim cut-and-paste to substantial rewriting and obfuscation (e.g., paraphrasing). Two further aspects commonly discussed are 'type' of plagiarism and detection methods.

2.1   Types of Plagiarism

Several authors have attempted to categorize plagiarism into different forms or types [2, 7, 10, 12]. For example, Martin [10] lists several distinct forms of plagiarism: word-for-word plagiarism, paraphrasing plagiarism, plagiarism of secondary sources, plagiarism of the form of a source, plagiarism of ideas and plagiarism of authorship. These types get progressively harder to detect, both manually and automatically, as they go on. Harris [7] also categorizes different types of plagiarism, including buying a paper from a commercial paper mill, translating foreign language articles into English or another language, cutting and pasting text from several sources (patchwork plagiarism or *quilting*) and faking citations. Potthast et al. [11] propose a more formalized taxonomy of plagiarism types that also includes approaches to detect them. In this paper we provide a similar categorization scheme for unfair means, although at this stage less detailed and formalized than existing schemes.

2.2   Plagiarism Detection

Detecting plagiarism and making decisions about originality is a human process; however, automated tools can assist with this process [4]. Various factors can signal plagiarism, such as inconsistencies in writing style, unexpected use of advanced vocabulary, incorrect references and shared similarities with existing materials. In discussing problems of *text attribution,* Wilks [13] describes four general problems: identifying inconsistencies within a text that suggest it is unlikely to be written by the claimed author, finding the likely sources of an unoriginal text, identifying collaboratively-written texts (i.e., collusion) and identifying copying between texts (i.e., plagiarism). The notions of *intrinsic* and *extrinsic* have also been used as plagiarism detection tasks at the PAN series of evaluation activities: intrinsic relates to identifying stylistic inconsistencies within a text; extrinsic relates to identifying the possible sources of a plagiarized document [6]. Alzahrani et al. [1] summarize the range of approaches commonly used to detect plagiarism, ranging from simpler lexical methods to more complex authorship- and semantic-based methods. Potthast et al. [11] also describe different types of approaches for producing exact and modified copies.

3   Types of Unfair Means Problems

As previously stated plagiarism, particularly in Higher Education, is one of many problems encountered within a wider area known as *unfair means* or *unfair practice*. This refers to a student attempting to gain advantage over another student in assessment, or assisting someone else to gain an unfair advantage or qualification. This paper seeks to provide an initial review of the area, with the immediate aim of identifying the range of types of miscreant behavior that can occur. To this end, we have examined publicly available guidelines on academic misconduct provided by ten universities in the UK (Section 3.1), and conducted interviews with faculty involved in handling unfair means in departments in the University of Sheffield (Section 3.2).

3.1   Review of University Guidelines

Careful reading of the academic misconduct guidelines for the universities of Bangor, Cambridge, Lincoln, Manchester, Northumbria, Sheffield, Swansea, Brunel, Hull and York has identified the types of behavior summarized in Table 1. It will be seen that they have been divided into two main types, depending upon whether they are practiced by students in a formal unseen examination context, or in, e.g., coursework assignments that are carried out in the student's own time. The list contains the most frequently mentioned behaviors, but is certainly not fully inclusive; for example, the Bangor guidelines consider the presentation of false evidence of extenuating circumstances to an examination board, or failing to obtain informed consent from participants in research projects as examples of unfair practice. Further examples of academic misconduct in one of the ten include the selling, distributing, website posting, or publishing information provided by instructors (e.g., lecture notes), or using them for any commercial purpose without permission of the instructor.

3.2   Interviews with Staff in the University of Sheffield

Face-to-face interviews were conducted with the unfair means officers (hereafter UMOs) in ten departments that encompassed all five of the faculties (Arts & Humanities, Engineering, Medicine, Pure Science, and Social Science) in the University of Sheffield. The questions covered the responsibilities of their role, the procedures they followed when unfair means was suspected, the types of unfair means and of material with which they had to deal, the tools available to assist them, and the scale of the problem in their department. The interviews typically lasted about 30 minutes and were recorded for subsequent analysis. In a short paper such as this it is not possible to go into any great depth, and some of the responses are of only local interest but it is possible to draw some more general conclusions as to the types of problem that might benefit from the development of new types of computational support tool.

Straight-forward plagiarism was by far the most common type of occurrence and mentioned by all of the respondents, with collusion being the next-most common occurrence. All of the other types of behavior listed in Table 1 were mentioned at least once, with the sole exception of impersonation during an examination. Perhaps surprisingly, since it is arguably the most serious type of academic offence, the submission of bought or commissioned work was mentioned four times; that said, one respondent noted that this was very difficult to detect, with the implication that it might have happened more frequently than it had been identified. Also mentioned was what might be described as *translation plagiarism*: loading a plagiarized piece of coursework into an online translation program that converts the input English to another language, and then back-translating the resulting text to yield a submission typical of that which might be expected from a student whose first language was not English. Several comments suggested that the use of unfair means in general was more common with such students.

Table 1. A summary of types of unfair means behaviour

Non-examination conditions	Plagiarism (either intentional or unintentional)	Copying text or images without acknowledging the source, passing off someone else's work or ideas as the author's own
	Double submission or self-plagiarism	Work may have been previously submitted for a different assessment
	Collusion	Submitting assessed work meant to be your own on which others have collaborated
	Fabrication of data /results	Making up research data, presentation or inclusion in a piece of work of figures or data which have been made up or altered and which have no basis in verifiable sources
	Falsification of data /results	Falsifying signatures of others, e.g. on consent forms or transcripts, misrepresentation of results
	Submitting bought or commissioned work	Submitting work which has been produced by someone else, e.g. another student, an essay bank or a ghost writing service
Examination conditions	Impersonation	Impersonation of a student during an examination or allowing oneself to be impersonated
	Cheating	Cheating in an examination by possessing or using materials prohibited in the examination room, copying from others (or communicating) during an exam, being in possession of notes or text books during exam, unfair use of electronic devices, presentation of an examination script as one's own work when the script includes material produced by unauthorised means including collusion

All of the UMOs dealt with cases of textual unfair means; examples of other types of material included software code, database or website designs, and architectural drawings (although the person mentioning this noted that it could only be detected manually by the person marking the student submissions). The Turnitin system developed by iParadigms is used in all departments as the principal tool to support UMOs in their work. This can only handle textual material; therefore, the MOSS (Measure Of Software Similarity) tool is used when software plagiarism has been suspected. As one would expect, frequent mention was made of the fact that tools such as these should only be used as a precursor to a detailed inspection by the UMO. There were several comments on the time-consuming nature of these inspections, with the implication that substantial benefits in terms of time and effort could be achieved if more effective tools could be developed; that said, much of the time requirement relates to the administrative procedures necessary to ensure that students are treated fairly when the use of unfair means is suspected, especially in the case of more serious offences such as essay purchase or plagiarism in multiple assignments.

Specific types of example where new or improved tools could assist UMOs include translation plagiarism, the copying of images, cases of collusion where exactly the same material is presented but in different wordings, materials purchased from on-demand essay-writing services, and the citation of sources that on close inspection appear to have little or nothing to do with the content of the assignment. Although some of the activities at PAN deal with these issues (e.g., the plagiarism detection task at PAN@CLEF addresses intrinsic and extrinsic plagiarism detection and translation plagiarism; the author identification task at PAN@CLEF focuses on author identification and verification that is common in ghostwriting; and PAN@FIRE deals with source code plagiarism), there are still areas that could be explored in the area of unfair means as well as developing tools for UMOs. Understanding the domain and identifying areas for deploying new technologies are vital in developing realistic use cases to frame the development and evaluation of new tools.

4   Discussion

Further to our discussion of the findings in Section 3 further areas within Higher Education that may benefit from the use of computational methods include the following:

- **Identification of fabricated or falsified data/results:** for example identifying statistical anomalies within quantitative data, or identifying falsified documents, transcripts or language certificates.
- **Supporting 'proving' plagiarism[4]:** educators must be able to prove that unfair means has occurred. This could include, for example, developing techniques to compute deviations from 'normal' language distributions.
- **Citation and referencing analysis:** helping to identify fake (i.e., non existent) citations, referencing inconsistencies or the use of incorrect references (i.e., references that do not match the context of the citation text).
- **Analysis of authorship style of contract services:** identifying whether coursework was likely produced by third-party services would be highly useful. This could include profiling the authorship style of commonly-used essay banks and online translation systems.
- **Plagiarism detection beyond text:** although much focus has been English text, there are many other forms of resource that are dealt with by UMOs. For example, non-English texts, program code, HTML and web pages, designs (e.g., database designs), images, drawings, presentations, and music.
- **Online learning environments:** increasingly institutions are offering distance learning courses and using online learning environments. This presents challenges around establishing the identity and authorship of students.
- **Discipline-specific plagiarism detection:** although there are elements of unfair means that are common across disciplines, there are clearly unique aspects too that may require the use of bespoke tools. For example, plagiarism detection of laboratory notebooks within biomedical sciences or equations within mathematics.

---

[4] https://www.plagiarismtoday.com/2015/04/29/the-challenge-of-proving-plagiarism/

5   Summary

This paper discusses the notion of unfair means in Higher Education, a wider issue than plagiarism that deals with various types of academic misconduct, including falsification and fabrication. Through a preliminary review of university guidelines and interviews with staff responsible for handling academic misconduct at the University of Sheffield, we highlight the range of problems encountered in Higher Education today. In the longer term, we hope that the study will encourage researchers to develop new computational tools that can assist in the detection not just of plagiarism, but also of the other types of unfair means. Future work will include developing a more detailed and formalized framework or taxonomy for categorizing unfair means.

References

1. Alzahrani, S., et al.: Using structural information and citation evidence to detect significant plagiarism cases in scientific publications. Journal of the Association for Information Science and Technology **63**(2), 286–312 (2012)
2. Bretag, T., Mahmud, S.: A Model for Determining student plagiarism: electronic detection and academic judgement. Journal of University Teaching & Learning Practice **6**(1) (2009). http://ro.uow.edu.au/jutlp/vol6/iss1/6
3. Citron, D.T., Ginsparg, P.: Patterns of text reuse in a scientific corpus. PNAS **112**(1), 25–30 (2015)
4. Culwin, F., Lancaster, T.: Plagiarism issues for higher education. Vine **31**(2), 36–41 (2001)
5. Errami, M., et al.: Déjà vu: A study of duplicate citations in Medline. Bioinformatics **24**(2), 243–249 (2008)
6. Gollub, T., Potthast, M., Beyer, A., Busse, M., Rangel, F., Rosso, P., Stamatatos, E., Stein, B.: Recent trends in digital text forensics and its evaluation - Plagiarism detection, author identification, and author profiling. In: Forner, P., Müller, H., Paredes, R., Rosso, P., Stein, B. (eds.) CLEF 2013. LNCS, vol. 8138, pp. 282–302. Springer, Heidelberg (2013)
7. Harris, R.A.: The Plagiarism Handbook: Strategies For Preventing, Detecting, And Dealing With Plagiarism. Eyrczak Publishing, California (2001)
8. Joy, M., Luck, M.: Plagiarism in programming assignments. IEEE Transactions on Education **42**(1), 129–133 (1999)
9. Lesk, M.: How many scientific papers are not original? PNAS **112**(1), 6–7 (2015)
10. Martin, B.: Plagiarism: a misplaced emphasis. Journal of Information Ethics **3**(2), 36–47 (1994)
11. Potthast, M., et al.: Cross-language plagiarism detection. Language Resources and Evaluation **45**(1), 45–62 (2011)
12. Pupovac, V., Fanelli, D.: Scientists Admitting to Plagiarism: A Meta-analysis of Surveys. Journal of Science and Engineering Ethics 1–22 (2014)
13. Wilks, Y.: On the Ownership of Text. Computers and the Humanities **38**(2), 115–127 (2004)
14. Wood, G., Warnken, P.: Academic original sin: plagiarism, the Internet and librarians. Journal of Academic Librarianship **30**(3), 237–242 (2004)

Instance-Based Learning for Tweet Monitoring and Categorization

Julien Gobeill[1,2]([✉]), Arnaud Gaudinat[1], and Patrick Ruch[1,2]

[1] BiTeM Group, HEG/HES-SO, University of Applied Sciences,
7 rte de Drize, 1227 Carouge, Switzerland
`{julien.gobeill,arnaud.gaudinat,patrick.ruch}@hesge.ch`
[2] SIBtex Group, SIB Swiss Institute of Bioinformatics,
1 rue Michel-Servet, 1206 Genève, Switzerland

Abstract. The CLEF RepLab 2014 Track was the occasion to investigate the robustness of instance-based learning in a complete system for tweet monitoring and categorization based. The algorithm we implemented was a k-Nearest Neighbors. Dealing with the domain (automotive or banking) and the language (English or Spanish), the experiments showed that the categorizer was not affected by the choice of representation: even with all learning tweets merged into one single Knowledge Base (KB), the observed performances were close to those with dedicated KBs. Interestingly, English training data in addition to the sparse Spanish data were useful for Spanish categorization (+14% for accuracy for automotive, +26% for banking). Yet, performances suffered from an overprediction of the most prevalent category. The algorithm showed the defects of its virtues: it was very robust, but not easy to improve. BiTeM/SIBtex tools for tweet monitoring are available within the DrugsListener Project page of the BiTeM website (http://bitem.hesge.ch/).

1 Introduction

BiTeM/SIBtex has a long tradition of participating in large evaluation campaigns, such as TREC, NTCIR or CLEF [1-4]. The CLEF RepLab 2014 Track was the occasion to integrate several local tools into a complete system, and to evaluate a simple and robust statistical approach for tweet classification in competition. The goal of the first task was to perform text categorization on Twitter, i.e. to design a system able to assign a predefined category to a tweet. This category was one out of eight related to companies' reputations. All tweets dealt with entities from the automotive (20 entities) or the banking (11 entities) domain, and were in English (93%) or in Spanish (7%). For training and/or learning purposes, participants were provided with approximately 15,000 tweets labeled by human experts (the training set). Then, the systems had to predict the good categories for 32,000 unlabeled tweets (the test set).

In this task, the main difficulty was to efficiently preprocess the text, as standard Natural Language Processing strategies can fail to deal with the short, noisy, and strongly contextualised nature of the tweets. Another difficulty was to efficiently

© Springer International Publishing Switzerland 2015
J. Mothe et al. (Eds.): CLEF 2015, LNCS 9283, pp. 235–240, 2015.
DOI: 10.1007/978-3-319-24027-5_22

learn from unbalanced classes. Finally, this was a multilingual task, but the language distribution also was unbalanced, with less than 10% Spanish learning instances. We applied a simple and robust statistical approach in order to design our system, based on instance-based learning for categorization purposes.

Two particular questions were investigated during this study. Q_1 : is it better to build one Knowledge Base (KB) for each domain, or to merge automotive and banking into the same KB ? Q_2 : is it better to build one KB for each language, or to merge English and Spanish into the same KB ?

2   Methods

2.1   Overall Architecture of the System

Figure 1 illustrates the overall architecture of our system. The workflow is divided into two steps: the training phase (offline), and the test phase (online). Three independent components act cooperatively to preprocess data (component 1), to build the knowledge base (component 2) and to classify tweets (component 3).

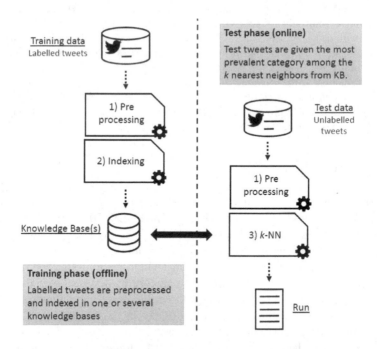

Fig. 1. Overall architecture of the system

During the training phase, all tweets belonging to the training set were preprocessed by component 1. Component 1 merges several standard Natural Language Processing treatments, along with a language detector. Then, they were indexed in one or several indexes by component 2, in order to make the KB. Component 2 is an Information Retrieval platform, which builds indexes for related documents retrieval.

During the test phase, all tweets belonging to the test set also were preprocessed by component 1. Then, for a given test tweet, the component 3 (k-NN) exploited the KB in order to retrieve the most similar tweets seen in the training data, and to infer a predicted category. Official runs were computed with the whole test set.

Tweets often contain metadata within tags, the most frequent being hyperlinks (<a>) and emphasis (<b>). Moreover, they often don't have proper punctuation.

2.2 Preprocessing

The goal of the component 1 was to preprocess the tweets in order to have proper and efficient instances to index (for the training phase) or search (for the test phase). For this purpose, a set of basic rules was applied. Tags were first discarded. Contents within an emphasis tag (<b>) were repeated in order to be overweighted. Contents within a hyperlink tag (<a>) also were repeated, and were preceded by the "HREF" mention.

For language detection purposes, we performed a simple N-Gram-Based Text Categorization, based on the Cavnar and Trenkle works [5]. This approach aims at comparing n-grams frequency profiles in a given text, with profiles observed in large English and Spanish corpus. This simple approach is reported to have an accuracy in the range of 92% to 99%. N-grams profiles were taken from [6].

2.3 Indexing

The goal of the component 2 was to build one or several indexes from the training data, in order to obtain a related documents search engine. For this purpose, we used the Terrier platform [7]. We used default stemming, stop words and a Poisson weighting scheme (PL2).

Dealing with Q_1 and Q_2, we investigated several strategies and built several indexes, mixing tweets from the cars or banks domains, and tweets in English or Spanish.

2.4 k-NN

The goal of the component 3 was to categorize tweets from the test set. For this purpose, we used a k-Nearest Neighbors, a remarkably simple algorithm which assigns to a new text the categories that are the most prevalent among the k most similar tweets contained in the KB [8]. Similar tweets were retrieved thanks to component 2. Then, a score computer inferred the category from the k most similar instances, following this formula:

$$predcat = \arg\max_{c \in \{c_1, c_2 \ldots c_m\}} \sum_{x_i \in K} E(x_i, c) \times RSV(x_i)$$

where *predcat* is the predicted category for a test tweet, $c_1, c_2 \ldots c_m$ are the possible categories, K is the set of the k nearest neighbors of the test tweet, $RSV(x_i)$ is the retrieval status value given by the component 2 (i.e. the similarity score) for the neighbor x_i, and $E(x_i, c)$ is 1 when x_i is of category c, 0 otherwise.

3   Results and Discussions

The Q_1 and Q_2 issues were addressed with the training data, thanks to a ten-fold cross validation strategy.

3.1   Q₁: Is It Better to Build One KB for Each Domain, or to Merge Automotive and Banking into the Same KB ?

First, we investigated Q_1, by exploiting KB with only bank tweets (*banks* index), only automotive tweets (*car* index), or both (*all* index). English and Spanish were merged into the same KB. Figure 2 shows the performances of the system for the banks test set, for different values of k.

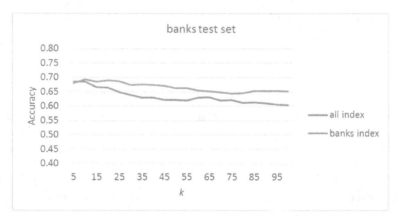

Fig. 2. Performances for the banks test set, using the *all* index (all training data merged) or the specific *banks* index (only banks training data), for different values of k.

Experiments showed that the optimal k for these data was around 10. They also showed that throughout the curves, it was better to use specific indexes (orange curve) versus a unique merged index (blue curve). Yet, the difference between best performances is not significant, with an accuracy of 0.69 for the *all* and the *banks* indexes for banks tweets (at $k=10$), and accuracies of 0.77 versus 0.76 for the *cars* index and the *all* index. We can say that, for categorizing tweets from a given domain, data from the other domain do not provide useful information, but do not degrade the optimal performances, thanks to the k-NN robustness.

3.2 Q_2: Is It Better to Build one KB for Each Language, or to Merge English and Spanish into the Same KB ?

Then, we investigated Q_2, especially for the Spanish language that represented less than 7% of the training data. We exploited the *cars, banks, cars_es and banks_es* indexes. Figure 3 shows the performances of the system for the cars test set, for different values of k.

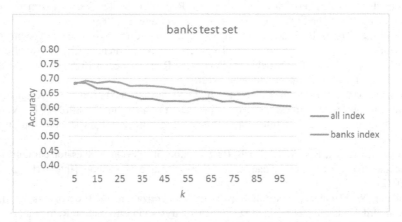

Fig. 3. Performances for the cars - Spanish test set, using the cars index (English and Spanish merged) or the specific cars - Spanish index (only Spanish data), for different values of k.

Experiments showed that the optimal k for Spanish data was around 30, significantly higher than the general case. This could be explained by the smaller set of Spanish instances. They also showed that it was better to use both languages indexes (orange curves) versus a Spanish-specific index (blue curves). We can say that, for categorizing tweets from Spanish, an additional amount of English data provides useful information and increases the top accuracy (from 0.69 to 0.79 for cars, from 0.57 to 0.72 for banks).

The same experiments with the English language showed no significant differences between the merged and the English-specific indexes. We have not tried any cross-language strategy [10,11].

4   Conclusion

We designed a complete system for tweet categorization according to predefined reputational categories. Dealing with the domain (automotive or banking) and the language (English or Spanish), the experiments showed that the k-NN was not very affected by the kind of representations: even with all data merged into one single KB, the observed performances are close to those observed with dedicated KB. Moreover, English training data were useful for Spanish categorization (+14% for accuracy for automotive, +26% for banking). Yet, the unbalanced labels make the k-NN to predict the most prevalent category more often than necessary; this issue needs to be investigated in future works. The k-NN showed the defects of its virtues: it was robust, but not easy to improve. BiTeM/SIBtex tools for tweet monitoring are available within the DrugsListener Project page of the BiTeM website [9].

References

1. Gobeill, J., Teodoro, D., Pasche, E., Ruch, P.: Report on the trec 2009 experiments: chemical IR track. In: The Eighteenth Text REtrieval Conference (2009)
2. Gobeill, J., Pasche, E., Teodoro, D., Ruch, P.: Simple pre and post processing strategies for patent searching in CLEF intellectual property track. In: Peters, C., Di Nunzio, G.M., Kurimo, M., Mandl, T., Mostefa, D., Peñas, A., Roda, G. (eds.) CLEF 2009. LNCS, vol. 6241, pp. 444–451. Springer, Heidelberg (2010)
3. Teodoro, D., Gobeill, J., Pasche, E., Ruch, P., Vishnyakova, D., Lovis, C.: Automatic IPC encoding and novelty tracking for effective patent mining. In: The 8th NTCIR Workshop Meeting on Evaluation of Information Access Technologies, Tokyo, Japan, pp. 309–317 (2010)
4. Vishnyakova, D., Pasche, E., Ruch, P.: Selection of relevant articles for curation for the comparative toxicogenomic database. In: BioCreative Workshop [Internet], pp. 31–38 (2012)
5. Cavnar, W., Trenkle, J.: N-gram-based text categorization. In: Proceedings of SDAIR-1994, 3rd Annual Symposium on Document Analysis and Information Retrieval (1994)
6. Practical cryptography. http://practicalcryptography.com/
7. Ounis, I., Amati, G., Plachouras, V., He, B., Macdonald, C., Lioma, C.: Terrier: A high performance and scalable information retrieval platform. In: Proceedings of ACM SIGIR 2006 Workshop on Open Source Information Retrieval (2006)
8. Manning, C., Schütze, H.: Foundations of Statistical Natural Language Processing. MIT Press, Cambridge (1999)
9. BiTeM website. http://bitem.hesge.ch/
10. Müller, H., Geissbühler, A., Ruch, P.: ImageCLEF 2004: combining image and multilingual search for medical image retrieval. In: Peters, C., Clough, P., Gonzalo, J., Jones, G.J., Kluck, M., Magnini, B. (eds.) CLEF 2004. LNCS, vol. 3491, pp. 718–727. Springer, Heidelberg (2005)
11. Müller, H., Geissbühler, A., Marty, J., Lovis, C., Ruch, P.: The use of medGIFT and easyIR for imageCLEF 2005. In: Peters, C., Gey, F.C., Gonzalo, J., Müller, H., Jones, G.J., Kluck, M., Magnini, B., de Rijke, M., Giampiccolo, D. (eds.) CLEF 2005. LNCS, vol. 4022, pp. 724–732. Springer, Heidelberg (2006)

Are Test Collections "Real"? Mirroring Real-World Complexity in IR Test Collections

Melanie Imhof[1,2]([✉]) and Martin Braschler[2]

[1] Université de Neuchâtel, Neuchâtel, Switzerland
imhf@zhaw.ch
[2] Zurich University of Applied Sciences, Winterthur, Switzerland
bram@zhaw.ch

Abstract. Objective evaluation of effectiveness is a major topic in the field of information retrieval (IR), as emphasized by the numerous evaluation campaigns in this area. The increasing pervasiveness of information has lead to a large variety of IR application scenarios that involve different information types (modalities), heterogeneous documents and context-enriched queries. In this paper, we argue that even though the complexity of academic test collections has increased over the years, they are still too structurally simple in comparison to operational collections in real-world applications. Furthermore, research has brought up retrieval methods for very specific modalities, such as ratings, geographical coordinates and timestamps. However, it is still unclear how to systematically incorporate new modalities in IR systems. We therefore propose a categorization of modalities that not only allows analyzing the complexity of a collection but also helps to generalize methods to entire modality categories instead of being specific for a single modality. Moreover, we discuss how such a complex collection can methodically be built for the usage in an evaluation campaign.

Keywords: Collection complexity · Modality categorization · Evaluation campaigns

1 Introduction

Evaluation campaigns such as TREC[1] and CLEF[2] have been a great success in bringing objective benchmarking to many areas of IR research. A fundamental problem of the approach of those campaigns however, is their reliance on the Cranfield paradigm or IR evaluation [4,8] and therefore the cost of producing test collections. Consequently, only a few test collections are created every year. In order to be cost-efficient and transferable to industrial applications, a common goal of those campaigns is to make the evaluations as realistic as possible. In the past years, the focus was mostly on increasing the variety of domains and tasks covered by the test collections as well as on the comprehension of the user's

---

[1] http://trec.nist.gov
[2] http://www.clef-initiative.eu

© Springer International Publishing Switzerland 2015
J. Mothe et al. (Eds.): CLEF 2015, LNCS 9283, pp. 241–247, 2015.
DOI: 10.1007/978-3-319-24027-5_23

role [2]. However, in reality, the increasing pervasiveness of information has not only lead to an ever increasing amount of information, but also to a much larger variety of IR application scenarios that leverage this information. This leads to an increasing complexity in the document collections that underlie these applications. The complexity evolved primarily from the increasing number of different information types (modalities) used in both the collections and the queries. The collections contain heterogeneous documents, from different sources with many different modalities, such as text and images, as well as the multimodal context. Hereby, the context can include user interactions with the system, such as ratings and click-paths. Further, the information needs are represented with more complex queries that additionally contain the personal and situational context, multimedia examples and many more.

The leading evaluation campaigns have reacted to this increase in complexity and this is reflected in the test collections they produce. Figure 1 shows how the complexity of the collections used at CLEF increased over the last sixteen years. Note that the average number of modalities in the collections has increased significantly in 2012 mostly due to the INEX track. However, our experience in working with practitioners has shown that the complexity of most academic collections has still not reached the complexity level of operational collections. Collections used in practice mostly not only include more different modalities but also modalities of different importance that are sometimes highly inter-dependent but at other times are complementary to each other. As a consequence, the performance of the participants of the existing evaluation campaigns does not necessarily indicate how to approach such collections and thus the developed methods are ultimately not transferable to real use cases.

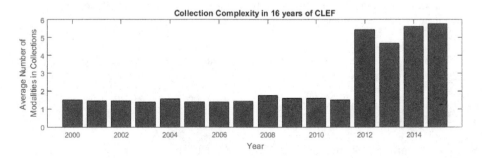

Fig. 1. Average number of modalities in the collections over the last sixteen years at CLEF.

Until now, it is often unclear how to best systematically incorporate upcoming new modalities into IR systems. Most retrieval methods have been developed for a single very specific modality, e.g. geographical coordinates, and have not been generalized to other modalities or modality categories. In practice, for complex collections, one is left with the challenging task to assemble a number of these methods and combine them in a meaningful way. As a first step to app-roach this problem more thoroughly, we propose a categorization of modalities which should help to generalize the methods for single modalities to the entire category. An example of how well the same methods work for different modalities is the usage of the TF-IDF and BM25 weighting schemes in both text retrieval and image retrieval.

In this paper, we compare academic collections as provided in evaluation cam-paigns and operational collections as found in IR applications in the industry and we propose a categorization of modalities that allows methods to be generalized to entire modality categories. Further, we show which properties a collection should fulfill to accurately mirror the complexity of real-world collections.

2 Status Quo and Related Work

In our work with practitioners we have seen that today's IR applications are unsurprisingly no longer limited to the traditional library scenario, but are used in various more complex use cases such as online shops and news streaming appli-cations. The documents and the queries in these applications consist of a larger and more diverse set of information that has to be considered. Also, studies about the relationships of task complexity and the use of information resources have shown that the more complex a task is the more information sources are used [7][3]. IR applications designed to handle complex tasks require more com-plex collections, since multiple information sources need to be incorporated. In our technology transfer projects, we have been challenged to create IR systems that can handle such complex collections.

The database research community [1] has identified the problem of managing structured, semi-structured and unstructured data from various sources as one of their long-term goals. Thus, they face a similar problem to the increasing collec-tion complexity in IR, to efficiently incorporate all aspects of this heterogeneous data. They appeal for collaboration with the IR community, for methods to query such complex collections and for creating corresponding data collections.

The lack of complexity we identified in academic test collections is not an entirely new observation, as evidenced by the following quote from Kekäläinen and Järvelin in 2002 [5]: "*The test collections, albeit nowadays large, are struc-turally simple (mainly unstructured text) and topically narrow (mainly news domain). The test documents mostly lack interesting internal structure that some real-life collections do have (e.g., field structure, XML, citations)*". Today, more than ten years later, this statement no longer accurately reflects the breadth of test collections available. Several new domains have been explored, e.g. patent retrieval, expert search and retrieval in the cultural heritage domain. Also, some collections with internal structure have arisen, most prominently represented by the Initiative for the Evaluation of XML Retrieval (INEX). However, we claim that even these collections, although they reflect progress in the march to more collection complexity, have not yet reached the complexity level of operational collections. In the following, will give examples of some of the most complex academic collections and describe their shortcomings with respect to operational collections.

GeoCLEF a collection from 2008 offers only two modalities - the textual description and geographical coordinates. The geographical coordinates are not available as a separate modality, but need to be extracted from the text. Thus, the main focus of the evaluation tasks using this collection lies in the extraction of the geographical coordinates rather than the combination of the two modalities.

The ImageCLEF collections mostly contain two modalities - the images and textual description thereof (captions, titles, etc.). Still, they are not ideal to study complex multimodal collections. This is not only due to the small number of modalities, but also because the two modalities mostly contain the same overall information; e.g. the caption of an image that shows a cat most likely contains the word "cat".

The Living Lab track of CLEF 2015 offers a collection that brings an online shop scenario to the academic community [2]. The live setting of an ad hoc search task in an online toy store offers for each product a limited amount of textual data together with a lot of structured modalities such as the recommended age, the brand, the availability and the price. We came across a similar setup in our transfer projects with the shopping app "Troffy", which allows users to search for products from different retailers in their area. In this project, an important aspect of the experimentation was to include the user's context such as his location and preferences. Since in the Living Lab no user information is provided it is not possible to personalize the result lists. In this case, the academic collection is as complex as in reality, but the query is a lot simpler. For many queries, the user preferences are however an important aspect. For example, consider the search for a tractor. The results should be quite different for a model vehicle fan than for a mother searching a present for her son.

The news domain has a long history in evaluation campaigns in IR; e.g. in the ad hoc track at CLEF. However, the focus so far was on multilingual retrieval of textual modalities. In a recent project, we worked on the noise canceling news feed application "Squirro" that collects documents from various sources such as public search engines, social networks and news feeds in general. The users of this application can create topics that not only consist of a textual description of the user's interests but also the user's preferences with respect to recency, language, popularity and source-quality of the documents. Again, we are not aware of academic test collections that mirror these aspects in comparable complexity.

3   Modality Categorization

We argue that in order to build test collections that reflect a desired complexity, it is important to start with a categorization of modalities; with the goal to uncover similarities between modalities. Methods developed for very specific modalities could then be generalized to these modality categories. Such a systematic structuring of the modalities also facilitates the uncovering of modalities that are inter-related.

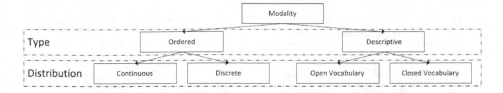

Fig. 2. Categorization of modalities into their types and distributions.

In order to come up with the categorization, we started with a huge set of different modalities that we have seen in evaluation campaigns and transfer projects of the past. The set included very specific descriptors for each modality, e.g. dates, ratings, geographical coordinates, terms, SIFT features, etc. We clustered the modalities that share similar characteristics into hierarchical modality categories. We identified the two top hierarchical levels of the categorization as shown in Figure 2. In the future, we assume that further levels will need to be introduced to handle more specific modality types.

We first distinguish between ordered and descriptive modalities. Ordered modalities such as ratings, dates, prices, number of clicks or likes have a natural order. Therefore, statements such as "which date is earlier" or "which item is more popular" can be made. We believe that the order of these modalities is important for the retrieval and needs to be considered. In contrast, descriptive modalities such as terms in text retrieval and SIFT features in image retrieval do not have an order that contains relevant information for the retrieval. Terms usually are sorted alphabetically; however it is not important for the retrieval process if two terms start with adjacent letters.

At first, it seems that all numerical modalities are ordered modalities, while all textual modalities are descriptive. However, a modality that contains a group id may be descriptive even though the group id is numerical. The group ids are probably arbitrarily chosen without an order in mind, therefore the numerical order of the group ids is not important and hence it is a descriptive modality. On the other side, a modality describing the reading level of a book such as "Ages 4-8", "Ages 9-12" and "Young Adult" are textual, but also ordered.

We subdivide the descriptive modalities into open and closed vocabulary. An open vocabulary modality is a free text with a variable length as we know them from years of traditional text retrieval and many ad hoc retrieval collections. In a closed vocabulary modality the values that can be used are a predefined finite set; e.g. the binding of a book. For the ordered modalities we suggest a similar subdivision into discrete and continuous, since the methods need to be able to distinguish between a finite and an infinite amount of values.

In Table 1, we use the INEX Social Book Search (SBS) collection [6] to show how the proposed categorization can be applied to a specific collection. The collection consists of ca. 2.8 million books from Amazon enriched with content information from Library Thing. The SBS collection is especially suited for such an assembly, since a lot of very different modalities are included.

Table 1. An excerpt of the modalities of the INEX Social Book Search collection with the associated type and distribution.

Name	Type	Distribution	Name	Type	Distribution
Id	descriptive closed vocabulary		Price	ordered continuous	
Title	descriptive open vocabulary		Reading Level	ordered discrete	
Binding	descriptive closed vocabulary		Release Date	ordered continuous	
Label	descriptive closed vocabulary		No. of Pages	ordered continuous	

4   Building Complex Collections

An ideal complex collection that mirrors the complexity of real-world IR applications should contain a large amount of modalities from different modality categories. Hence, it not only contains textual modalities from the category descriptive, open vocabulary as in traditional IR collections, but also non-textual and non-descriptive modalities such as images, ratings, prices and geographical coordinates. Moreover, both independent and inter-related modalities should appear in the collection. The independent modalities are important to provide preferably diverse information, while the inter-related modalities also coexist in the real-world collections and must be considered by the methods. The queries should likewise contain several modalities from different categories. Although it needs to be defined how each modality in the document contributes to the probability of relevance, not each modality needs to have a corresponding modality in the queries. It is also possible to define their contribution based on query independent factors; e.g. a higher number of likes usually leads to a higher probability of relevance. From our experience, we saw that most operational collections contain a substantial textual part and approximately ten non-textual modalities. For some applications, the non-textual modalities must be considered in the retrieval, since they may contain key information that is required to fulfill the task requirements; e.g. the date in a recent news search. For others, they can be used in order to improve the retrieval performance.

5   Conclusions

In this paper, we argue that even though the complexity of collections increased in the last decade, academic test collections do not yet reach the level of complexity of operational collections in real-world applications. We propose a categorization of modalities, which serves two purposes: firstly, the large number of diverse modalities in operational collections makes it necessary to have unified methods for many kinds of modality types. This allows us to generalize the methods that have been developed for specific modalities to a modality category. Secondly, we suggest thinking about how to methodologically build academic test collections of higher, more realistic complexity by deriving the right mix of modalities from the categorization. This task requires an explicit reflection on the inter-dependence of the different modalities, and their characteristics. Still open is the handling of multi-dimensional modalities in the context of the presented categorization (e.g. geographical coordinates).

References

1. Agrawal, R., Ailamaki, A., Bernstein, P.A., Brewer, E.A., Carey, M.J., Chaudhuri, S., Doan, A., Florescu, D., Franklin, M.J., Garcia-Molina, H., et al.: The claremont report on database research. Communications of the ACM **52**(6), 56–65 (2009)
2. Balog, K., Kelly, L., Schuth, A.: Head first: living labs for ad-hoc search evaluation. In: Proceedings of the 23rd ACM International Conference on Conference on Information and Knowledge Management, pp. 1815–1818. ACM (2014)
3. Byström, K., Järvelin, K.: Task complexity affects information seeking and use. Information Processing & Management **31**(2), 191–213 (1995)
4. Jones, K.S.: Readings in information retrieval. Morgan Kaufmann (1997)
5. Kekäläinen, J., Järvelin, K.: Evaluating information retrieval systems under the challenges of interaction and multidimensional dynamic relevance. In: Proceedings of the 4th CoLIS Conference, pp. 253–270 (2002)
6. Koolen, M., Kazai, G., Kamps, J., Preminger, M., Doucet, A., Landoni, M.: Overview of the inex 2012 social book search track, p. 77 (2012)
7. Saastamoinen, M., Kumpulainen, S., Järvelin, K.: Task complexity and information searching in administrative tasks revisited. In: Proceedings of the 4th Information Interaction in Context Symposium, pp. 204–213. ACM (2012)
8. Voorhees, E.M.: The philosophy of information retrieval evaluation. In: Peters, C., Braschler, M., Gonzalo, J., Kluck, M. (eds.) CLEF 2001. LNCS, vol. 2406, pp. 355–370. Springer, Heidelberg (2002)

Evaluation of Manual Query Expansion Rules on a Domain Specific FAQ Collection

Mladen Karan[✉] and Jan Šnajder

Text Analysis and Knowledge Engineering Lab, Faculty of Electrical Engineering
and Computing, University of Zagreb, Unska 3, 10000 Zagreb, Croatia
{mladen.karan,jan.snajder}@fer.hr

Abstract. Frequently asked question (FAQ) knowledge bases are a convenient way to organize domain specific information. However, FAQ retrieval is challenging because the documents are short and the vocabulary is domain specific, giving rise to the *lexical gap* problem. To address this problem, in this paper we consider rule-based query expansion (QE) for domain specific FAQ retrieval. We build a small test collection and evaluate the potential of QE rules. While we observe some improvement for difficult queries, our results suggest that the potential of manual rule compilation is limited.

1 Introduction

Organizing information into frequently asked questions (FAQ) knowledge bases (KB) has some notable advantages over traditional information retrieval (IR) from document collections. Because each FAQ is focused on a single (typically a problem-oriented) topic, the user can get an answer that directly addresses her information need. While construction of FAQ KBs takes some effort, for closed domains (e.g., services of a telecom company) this effort is often manageable.

The task of FAQ retrieval is to retrieve the most relevant question-answer pairs for a user's query. FAQ retrieval lies between classic IR and question answering. The main challenge of FAQ retrieval is that text are short and domain specific, increasing the chance of a *lexical gap*. E.g., the query *"Can't connect to the net"* should map to the question *"Why is my internet down?"* although the two queries share no common words. A number of FAQ retrieval systems have been proposed in the literature [1,9,10].

One way to tackle the lexical gap problem is to perform query expansion (QE). The main idea behind QE is to add additional words to the query to improve the likelihood of a query-document match. One variant of QE is rule-based QE, in which each term is associated with a list of related terms (synonyms or lexically/semantically related terms) inserted at query time.

In this paper we focus on rule-based QE for domain specific FAQ retrieval. As QE has been found to be useful for IR [2], we hypothesize that rule-based QE can also improve the performance of FAQ IR systems. We are interested in situations when relevance judgments are not available and the KBs are small, rendering machine learning inapplicable but manual QEs rule construction feasible. We

© Springer International Publishing Switzerland 2015
J. Mothe et al. (Eds.): CLEF 2015, LNCS 9283, pp. 248–253, 2015.
DOI: 10.1007/978-3-319-24027-5_24

build a small domain-specific FAQ collection and conduct experimental evaluation to answer two research questions: (1) to what extent an optimal set of QE rules can improve retrieval performance and (2) can human annotators produce an optimal set of QE rules. Contrary to our intuition, the rules hurt overall performance, but do help for difficult cases. Our analysis indicates that in this setting manual construction of effective QE rules is a much more difficult task than expected.

2   Related Work

A number of FAQ retrieval systems have been proposed in the literature [1,9,10]. The model of Surdeanu et al. [10] is one of the most elaborate, as it combines similarity, translation, frequency, and web correlation features to rank documents. The model is trained on a large collection of FAQs obtained from Yahoo Answers.

Carpineto and Romano [2] give an overview of QE and describe methods to identify good expansion rules for large KBs. Automated QE rule acquisition has been studied in [3,11]. All mentioned approaches require a large, general-domain collection, limiting their applicability in our setting. Sneiders [9] tackle the lexical gap by defining 'question templates' that cover the ontological, lexical, morphological, and syntactical variations of questions. The templates, which can be thought of as sophisticated QE rules, were defined manually by inspecting query logs obtained during the course of several months.

3   Test Collection

For the experiments in this paper, we built a small, domain specific FAQ test collection from scratch. We first crawled a publicly available FAQ collection of a big telecom company.[1] From this data we sampled 500 FAQ pairs for our collection. These constitute the target documents in our retrieval experiments.

To obtain the queries, we asked three human annotators to produce question paraphrases for each of the 500 FAQ pairs. The paraphrases will be treated as queries for which the original FAQ pair is the target document. The annotators were instructed to produce realistic paraphrases that could be genuine queries submitted by real users. One annotator produced three paraphrases for each FAQ. After removing some unclear cases, we ended up with a dataset of 486 FAQ pairs and 1450 queries. Examples from the test collection are given in Table 1.

Table 1. Examples of FAQ questions and question paraphrases used as queries

Question	Query
What other refill options are available through my prepaid device?	What are the possible ways of refilling with a prepaid device?
How soon will I be able to use an added feature?	The timespan from adding a feature to using it.
What is local number portability?	Can I keep my phone number when changing service providers?

---

[1] http://www.verizon.com

4   Methodology

4.1   Retrieval Models

We use two underlying retrieval models for our QE experiments: (1) the widely-used BM25 model and (2) a vector-based model based on the recently proposed neural word embeddings. We perform basic preprocessing: stop words removal and stemming using the Porter stemmer [7].

The **BM25 model** [8] is an extension of the probabilistically motivated query likelihood model [4]. While simple to implement, it has been shown to be a fairly competitive retrieval model. In BM25, each document D is scored against a query Q containing words $\{q_1, \dots, q_n\}$, as follows:

$$score(Q, D) = \sum_{i=1}^{n} idf(q_i) \cdot \frac{f(q_i, D) \cdot (k+1)}{f(q_i, D) + k \cdot (1 - b + b \cdot \frac{|D|}{avg})} \tag{1}$$

where $idf(q_i)$ is the inverse document frequency of term q_i, $f(q_i, D)$ is the frequency of term q_i in document D, $|D|$ is the length of document D, and avg is the average length of the document. Parameters k and b can be fine-tuned, but we simply set them to recommended values proposed in [8].

The **word2vec** [5] based model relies on semantic vectors of words obtained by training a neural network on a large corpus using the `word2vec` tool.[2] The vectors have been shown to perform exceptionally well in a variety of lexico-semantic tasks. For our purposes, we require vector representations of units larger than single words, namely queries and FAQ pairs, i.e., we need to semantically compose the vectors of the individual words. In [6] it has been shown that semantic composition of word embeddings of short phrases can be modeled via simple vector addition. Although we do not work with short phrases, in this preliminary work we follow this approach and construct vector representations of queries and FAQ pairs by simply summing the vectors of the individual content words. Once the query and FAQ vectors are generated, the score of FAQ pair D for query Q is defined as the cosine of their corresponding vector representations.

4.2   Query Expansion Rules

In this work we focus on manual QE rules compiled by the annotators but not the end user. Consequently, we must limit ourselves to global techniques [12], which do not take into account the set of retrieved documents. In this work, QE is performed by constructing a global set of expansion rules. A QE rule is a set of words $R = \{r_1, \dots, r_n\}$ such that, if any word from R appears in the user query, all other words from R will be added to the query.

Gold QE Rules. To evaluate the optimal QE rules performance, we construct a gold set of rules by inspecting the errors on the test set and manually crafting the rules that bridge the lexical gap where possible. We assume that the gold rules

---

[2] http://code.google.com/p/word2vec/

are universal, thus we create them only for the BM25 model. Our results tend to justify this assumption, but further research is warranted to confirm it.

Human-Crafted QE Rules. We also create a set of QE rules annotated by humans, with no reference to the actual errors of the system. Given a list of words, three annotators were asked to add appropriate (in the subjective view of the annotator) expansion words for each word. E.g., given the word *pay*, an annotator might add words like *charge, rate, cost*, etc.

One interesting problem here is how to generate the list of words to be presented to the annotators, i.e., how to pick those words out of the vocabulary that will yield useful expansion rules after annotation. After trying different strategies, we decided to simply rank words by frequency. A set of top ranked 300 words (a feasible amount for the annotators) obtained by this approach had a recall of 95% when compared to words from the gold rules.

The three annotators each produced a different set of expansion rules and we considered several ways of combining their results. We got the best performance using the intersection, which yielded 24 rules. Examples of rules include {*broadband, internet, connection*}, {*customer, buyer, client*}, and {*number, phone, telephone, mobile, digit*}.

5   Evaluation

5.1   QE Rules Accuracy

Not all of the words in the lists given to the annotators yield useful expansions, while for the words that warrant an expansion the annotators might not provide useful expansions. We evaluate both aspects: the ability of the annotators to select the words that warrant an expansion, and the quality of the expansion. For the former, we consider all the words in the annotators list. Only those words present in the gold QE rules are considered to belong to the positive class, and the annotation is counted as positive if the annotator expanded the word.

To evaluate the quality of the expansion, we treat each expansion as a word cluster and compare the cluster produced by the annotator against the gold cluster. We evaluate the clustering quality in terms of pairwise binary decisions, thereby ignoring the words not found in the gold clusters.

Table 2 presents the results. Selection precision is very low because gold rules are specifically engineered to solve particular cases of the test set. Consequently, a large number of rules that might generally be useful is missing from the gold rules. On the other hand, recall is very high for two out of three annotators. These results indicate that, while expanding more words than necessary, the annotators did not fail to expand the words from the gold rules.

A different picture emerges when looking at the word clusters. Precision is fairly high, indicating that annotators make correct expansions. However, recall is rather low, indicating that the expansions are incomplete. This suggest that it is easy to omit expansions that address very specific lexical gap problems.

Table 2. QE rules accuracy of human-crafted rules with respect to selecting which words to expand (left) and word expansion viewed as a clustering problem (right).

	Selection			Clustering		
	P	R	F_1	P	R	F_1
Annotator 1	8.2	95.0	**15.1**	75.0	9.4	16.6
Annotator 2	6.2	65.0	11.3	85.0	9.4	16.9
Annotator 3	6.9	95.0	12.9	62.5	15.6	**25.0**

5.2 Retrieval Evaluation

For the final evaluation, we perform retrieval on our test collection. We report mean reciprocal rank (MRR) and R@1 for both BM25 and the word2vec model, for different QE strategies. As the target document, we used (1) only the question part of a FAQ pair ("Q only") and (2) the entire FAQ pair ("Q+A").

The models performance on the entire collection was quite high, potentially masking the QE effects. We therefore created a "hard" version of the collection by leaving only those queries for which the relevant FAQ was not ranked first (e.g., the third query from Table 1). This was done separately for all combinations of retrieval models (BM25 / word2vec) and target document types (question only / FAQ pair). Results are presented in Table 3.

Table 3. Results of retrieval for all models and data set variants (MRR/R@1).

	Q only		Q+A	
	All	Hard	All	Hard
BM25	92.9/88.9	38.7/0.0	90.4/84.6	38.0/0.0
BM25 + gold	93.2/89.5	43.1/10.6	88.4/81.5	39.9/3.6
BM25 + annotators	92.6/88.4	36.8/2.5	90.0/84.2	39.5/4.5
word2vec	89.5/86.1	25.0/0.0	79.5/71.1	29.0/0.0
word2vec + gold	88.0/83.6	27.8/3.5	77.8/69.1	31.8/5.2
word2vec + annotators	86.6/82.4	23.7/1.0	74.8/66.0	28.0/4.0

Without QE, the BM25 model performs the best, with word2vec being competitive in the "Q only" setup, but falling behind in the "Q+A" setup. The reason for this might be that in the latter case a large number of answer words is included in the computation of the FAQ pair vector, introducing a lot of noise.

QE rules in general tend to decrease the performance on the entire collection, but improve performance on hard queries. Gold rules were engineered for the BM25 with "Q only" scenario, where they bring improvement. Interestingly, gold rules also help on some of the other hard queries for which they were not made (though different hard sets can have some queries in common). Human-crafted rules tend to work slightly worse than gold rules, which is expected. On hard queries, on which the gold rules were not fit, the difference is less pronounced. While slightly decreasing MRR, all rules consistently improve R@1.

6 Conclusion

On our domain specific FAQ test collection, manually compiled QE rules slightly decreased the performance. When considering only the difficult queries, we observed some improvements, particularly in R@1. The reason behind this is that the annotators read the questions before rephrasing them. Consequently, the paraphrased questions tend to have many words in common with the original questions. This setup favors simple word matching models, as confirmed by very high MRR. Inspecting the few errors shows that many of them are not caused merely by the lexical gap (e.g., some require inference or specific knowledge). To better validate our results, further experiments on other collections are required.

Future work will focus on creating a more realistic test collection by having annotators autonomously create questions instead of just rephrasing them. Another possibility is to experiment in different domains. Finally, we could enhance our rule set by allowing n-grams and domain specific multi-word expressions.

References

1. Burke, R.D., Hammond, K.J., Kulyukin, V., Lytinen, S.L., Tomuro, N., Schoenberg, S.: Question answering from frequently asked question files: Experiences with the FAQ Finder system. AI magazine **18**(2), 57 (1997)
2. Carpineto, C., Romano, G.: A survey of automatic query expansion in information retrieval. ACM Computing Surveys (CSUR) **44**(1), 1 (2012)
3. Latiri, C.C., Yahia, S.B., Chevallet, J., Jaoua, A.: Query expansion using fuzzy association rules between terms. Proceedings of JIM (2003)
4. Manning, C.D., Raghavan, P., Schütze, H.: Introduction to Information Retrieval, vol. 1. Cambridge university press, Cambridge (2008)
5. Mikolov, T., Chen, K., Corrado, G., Dean, J.: Efficient estimation of word representations in vector space. In: Workshop at ICLR (2013)
6. Mikolov, T., Sutskever, I., Chen, K., Corrado, G.S., Dean, J.: Distributed representations of words and phrases and their compositionality. In: Advances in Neural Information Processing Systems, pp. 3111–3119 (2013)
7. Porter, M.F.: Snowball: A language for stemming algorithms (2001)
8. Robertson, S.E., Walker, S., Jones, S., Hancock-Beaulieu, M.M., Gatford, M., et al.: Okapi at TREC-3. NIST Special Publication SP, pp. 109–109 (1995)
9. Sneiders, E.: Automated FAQ answering with question-specific knowledge representation for web self-service. In: HSI, pp. 298–305. IEEE (2009)
10. Surdeanu, M., Ciaramita, M., Zaragoza, H.: Learning to rank answers on large online QA collections. In: ACL, pp. 719–727 (2008)
11. Wei, J., Bressan, S., Ooi, B.C.: Mining term association rules for automatic global query expansion: methodology and preliminary results. In: Proceedings of WISE, vol. 1, pp. 366–373. IEEE (2000)
12. Xu, J., Croft, W.B.: Query expansion using local and global document analysis. In: Proceedings of ACM SIGIR, pp. 4–11. ACM (1996)

Evaluating Learning Language Representations

Jussi Karlgren[1,2], Jimmy Callin[1], Kevyn Collins-Thompson[3],
Amaru Cuba Gyllensten[1], Ariel Ekgren[1], David Jurgens[4]([✉]), Anna Korhonen[5],
Fredrik Olsson[1], Magnus Sahlgren[1], and Hinrich Schütze[6]

[1] Gavagai, Stockholm, Sweden
[2] Kungl Tekniska Högskolan, Stockholm, Sweden
[3] University of Michigan, Ann Arbor, USA
[4] McGill University, Montréal, Canada
jurgens@cs.mcgill.ca
[5] University of Cambridge, Cambridge, UK
[6] Ludwig-Maximilians-Universität, München, Germany

Abstract. Machine learning offers significant benefits for systems that
process and understand natural language: (a) lower maintenance and
upkeep costs than when using manually-constructed resources, (b) easier portability to new domains, tasks, or languages, and (c) robust and
timely adaptation to situation-specific settings. However, the behaviour
of an adaptive system is less predictable than when using an edited,
stable resource, which makes quality control a continuous issue. This
paper proposes an evaluation benchmark for measuring the quality, coverage, and stability of a natural language system as it learns word meaning. Inspired by existing tests for human vocabulary learning, we outline
measures for the quality of semantic word representations, such as when
learning word embeddings or other distributed representations. These
measures highlight differences between the types of underlying learning
processes as systems ingest progressively more data.

Keywords: Language representations · Semantic spaces · Word embeddings · Machine learning · Evaluation

1 Introduction and Motivation

For language technologies that need to represent and understand the meaning
of text, machine learning provides a crucial tool for supporting new terminology or semantic interpretations. Learning allows systems to adapt without the
need to manually curate knowledge bases, thereby lowering maintenance costs,
and to quickly retrain for new domains. Indeed, new genres and communication
channels make the requirements for an adaptable system all the more greater
[6]. However, learning comes at a risk: The behaviour of an adaptive resource
is less predictable than that of an edited stable resource, and quality control
thus becomes a continuous issue, rather than something which is done when a
knowledge resource is deployed.

© Springer International Publishing Switzerland 2015
J. Mothe et al. (Eds.): CLEF 2015, LNCS 9283, pp. 254–260, 2015.
DOI: 10.1007/978-3-319-24027-5_25

Table 1. An example TOEFL synonym-selection item

probe item	correct answer	confounder items
haphazardly	randomly	linearly densely dangerously

Currently, many existing natural language and information retrieval systems that employ learned semantic representations are evaluated after learning completes. While these tests are effective at measuring performance on a specific task, application, or domain, they capture only the outcome of learning while providing little insight into the learning process itself. Thus, a tailored solution may be able to achieve high scores on an outcome-oriented test without measuring the advantage of introducing learning. While this outcome-based evaluation does reflect the motivation for performing a task well, it does not measure the specific aspects which might make a particular learning technique worth re-using.

We propose a new evaluation benchmark aimed at measuring the process of learning, which enables capturing phenomena such as adaptability to new data, sensitivity to the order of example data, and the rate of learning. As a case study, we outline three tests for evaluating the learning process when creating semantic word representation, e.g., the word embeddings produced by word2vec [8]. Such representation are widely used in language technology and must capture a wide variety of meanings [9]. Our evaluation builds upon existing outcome-oriented metrics to illuminate the role and impact of learning.

2   Testing Outcome Versus Process

Techniques for learning word meaning typically process many examples of a word's usage to arrive at a representation of its meaning. While many representations are opaque to direct interpretation (e.g., dimensionally-reduced vectors), the quality of these representations may nonetheless be evaluated by comparing the representations themselves, where words with similar meanings are expected to have similar representations. Thus, the most common tests involve testing various aspects of synonymy between terms, with a frequent benchmark being the TOEFL test [7] which consists of a set of target words and a multiple-choice set of options for each from which the best synonym should be chosen, as shown in Table 1. The TOEFL test is typically applied by presenting a respondent with a probe item and some candidates from which the correct item is chosen. This means that the system may be able to answer correctly without ever having established any relationship between the probe item and the correct answer and that the test does not measure the quality of the semantic neighbourhood or semantic field the system has learnt.

Later and more fine-grained tests have included multiple relationship types. For example, the BLESS test divides up the general relation of semantic association into specific relationships such as synonymy, hyponymy, or meronymy between the probe word and the test items. This allows for more detailed analyses of semantic similarity. The authors explicitly state that their intention was to enable testing on specific and intrinsic characteristics of the testable representations under consideration [1,5].

While these types of outcome-based tests offer valuable contributions for differentiating the qualities of semantic representations, we propose a different but complementary objective that assesses qualities of the *learning process*, not only the final learning outcome. Such *process-based testing* would evaluate *how* various models progress toward learning representations with the qualities that they are intended to capture. At their simplest, process-based tests could be performed by applying an outcome test at intervals throughout a learning process to track the progress of learning the set of probe terms; more sophisticated designs may incorporate insights from developmental psychology or learning theory when creating test items.

Process-based testing would detect potential differences between representation-learning approaches. For example, one model might be designed to learn representations that capture all the diversity of a word's meanings, whereas another may be designed to converge to a representation for the most-frequently seen meaning as quickly as possible; whereas the final representations of both models may produce similar results with outcome-based testing, process-based testing may highlight cases where one model would be preferred over the other, e.g., quicker convergence. Furthermore, given the recent interest in computationally-intensive models such as word2vec [8], an evaluation benchmark which assesses the learning process itself will be of practical utility for understanding the learning rate and representation robustness as more training data is seen.

3 Existing Tests for Human Language Learning

In designing a process-based evaluation for automated language learning, we can draw on recent related progress in cognitive psychology that has developed methods for evaluating the human language learning process - and more specifically, on tracking how people acquire new vocabulary. The human learning process for vocabulary is incremental: it involves knowledge of individual words that is often passive, unstable, and partial [3]. Human vocabulary competence has been tested in a variety of settings that include reading comprehension, synonym judgment, synonym generation, gap filling and cloze exercises, acceptability assessment, paired analogies, and translation or paraphrasing. However, traditionally there had been little work on sensitive assessment measures that could detect the partial and incremental aspects of the word learning process. Thus, a key inspiration for our computational work is a recently-developed line of research in contextual word learning that tracks incremental changes and improvements in word knowledge as people are exposed to words in different contexts over time [4]. The resulting assessment methods include a form of lexical learning test that controls for numerous characteristics of the sample probe terms and contexts given, most notably the semantic constraints imposed by the context. Probe items are sample sentences of infrequent words, which are presented to human subjects who are then asked to self-assess knowledge of them, verify synonyms or to generate synonym items. Example words are given in Table 2 with contexts of varying semantic constraint levels. The type and level of these constraints can be computed and calibrated via crowdsourcing of cloze assessments or other semantic judgment tasks.

Table 2. Test items shown to human subjects for word substitution under varying semantic constraints [4].

Constraint	Target	Test item
High		In winter the dogs frolic and ..... in the snow.
Medium	*cavort*	The monkeys hooted as they ..... in the branches.
Low		Ida and Peggy meet after work to ..... outside.
High		Joanne likes being alone and doesn't trust people because she's a ..... .
Medium	*recluse*	Mandy has twenty cats and no family, a typical ..... .
Low		We weren't able to tell if the man was a(n) ..... or not.

4 Requirements for a Learning-Focused Evaluation

As an initial case study in how to design process-based tests, we examine the evaluation requirements for the task of learning word-based semantic representations. Here, test items consist of comparisons between vocabulary items and measuring the appropriateness of a particular word usage. In addition to the standard requirements when designing lexical tests, such as test items being balanced for word frequency, part of speech, polysemy, and distributional qualities, we propose four desiderata for the items comprising the test set.

1. A test should be robust across the domains and datasets used during learning and not require a specific dataset to be used for training; ideally, such test items should be recruited from the core vocabulary of the language.
2. A test should be sensitive to the task of learning a new meaning for an item it already knows, as well as to learning how a particular item's meaning has adapted over time. This requires the test to be able to show that a representation can handle seeing usages of a known item in a new domain, upholding the distinction between when an item has acquired a new sense versus when it has not changed.
3. Test items should not be biased towards learning a specific kind of representation in order to compare systems with complementary goals, such as rapid or one-shot learning, learning multiple representations for a word's meanings, or learning representations that encode multiple relationships.
4. The intrinsic properties of the test items should be quantified. For example, recording the difficulty of test items (e.g., as measured by human performance) enables assessing whether systems correctly answer easy items first during learning or whether mistakes occur randomly across the dataset.

Following, we propose three tests and then outline the general testing procedure.

Table 3. Example test items for the word *coconut* from the Plausible Utterance Test drawn from human-generated text (top) and term substitution (bottom).

health benefits of *coconut* oil include hair care, skin care, and proper digestion and metabolism
the *coconut* tree is a member of the palm family
in the rendang beef stew from sumatra, chunks of beef are cooked in *coconut* milk along with other spices
thanks to a promotion from the airline you can now book a *coconut* to frankfurt for 100 off
he looks dapper in a *coconut* as he arrives for the emporio armani show during milan fashion week
it's on the 28th floor of the *coconut* and it's got all the charms of a corporate headquarters

Paradigmatic Usage Test. The first test consists of evaluating context-independent paradigmatic usage, similar to TOEFL [7] and BLESS [1]. Test items are constructed by giving a probe word for which the system must identify which word has the desired semantic relation from a list. Underlying this test is the notion that as a model learns the representation for a word, those words that are semanticly similar would begin to have similar representations, i.e., appear in the word's semantic field. To control for the effects of polysemy and relationship interpretation, we propose selecting probes from relatively closed semantic fields: colour names, names of months, names of countries, professional roles, categories of animals. These probe items' linguistic properties, e.g., relative frequency and polyseymy, can then be measured to create a representative test set where confounder items have similar properties.

Plausible Utterance Test. The second test embeds the same lexical items of the first test in contexts, some of which have been found in naturally occurring text and some of which have been generated through replacing some unrelated word with a probe word, in effect generating implausible contexts of use. The target task is to rank the samples in order of plausibility, ideally ranking confounder items as least plausible. Table 3 shows an example of this question type.

Representational Stability and Agility Test. The third test measures the ability of a model to update its meaning representation when observing new data in two condiditions. In the Stability condition, a model is tested on its ability to maitain a self-consistent representation of a word when observing new contexts for that word that have the same meaning but differ in their contextual features, e.g., examples from a new domain; here the representation should not change drastically, as the underlying meaning has not changed. However, in the second Agility condition, a model is tested on how quickly it can adapt a word's representation when the nex contexts contain a new meaning not seen in training contexts, e.g., a novel sense appears. One possibility for creating these test items would be extending tests on identifying novel word senses [2] with confounding words whose meaning does not change but whose surrounding context does.

Test Procedure and Reporting. All three evaluations follows a similar testing procedure. For all tests, a target system is provided with examples of a targeted word, drawn from a corpus according to specific, desired properties (e.g., corpus domain, number of example instances). An evaluation may have the system learn different representations from multiple corpora in order to control for the effect of the corpus itself. During the learning process, the model is tested at desired testing intervals, e.g., after seeing k examples of the a probe item in training.

For the Paradigmatic Usage test, the model is queried for the semantic field of each probe term and given a target set of k related words, a system is scored according to the fraction of items in the semantic field are in the set. For the Plausibility test, the system ranks contexts for the probe word in order of plausibility; scoring calculates how many of the naturally-occurring contexts are ranked higher than the artificially-generated ones. The Stability and Agility tests are measured according to changes in the semantic field of probe words between testing intervals; Stability measures the degree of similarity in the field, whereas Agility measures the percentage of words associated with the probe's new meaning now in the semantic field. Each test's performance is measured with respect to the testing interval of the probe item and reported as learning curves.

5   Conclusion

We advocate the creation of a shared benchmark for lexical learning which evaluates the process of achieving a learning outcome rather than the outcome itself. The proposed benchmark builds upon existing outcome-based tests by controlling for the conditions in which learning occurs, which allows for extending the benchmark to new semantic objectives (e.g., representing antonymy) or to new domains by incorporating additional datasets under the same conditions.

Acknowledgments. This paper reports results from a workshop on Evaluating Learning Language Models which in part was supported by the European Science Foundation, through its ELIAS project for Evaluating Information Access Systems. Parts of this research (Collins-Thompson) were supported by the Institute of Education Sciences, U.S. Department of Education, through Grant R305A140647 to the University of Michigan. The opinions expressed are those of the authors and do not represent views of the Institute or the U.S. Department of Education.

References

1. Baroni, M., Lenci, A.: How we BLESSed distributional semantic evaluation. In: Proceedings of the 2011 Workshop on GEometrical Models of Natural Language Semantics, pp. 1–10. ACL (2011)
2. Cook, P., Lau, J.H., McCarthy, D., Baldwin, T.: Novel word-sense identification. In: Proceedings of COLING, pp. 1624–1635 (2014)
3. Frishkoff, G.A., Collins-Thompson, K., Perfetti, C.A., Callan, J.: Measuring incremental changes in word knowledge: Experimental validation and implications for learning and assessment. Behavior Research Methods 40(4), 907–925 (2008)
4. Frishkoff, G.A., Perfetti, C.A., Collins-Thompson, K.: Predicting robust vocabulary growth from measures of incremental learning. Scientific Studies of Reading 15(1), 71–91 (2011)

5. Hill, F., Reichart, R., Korhonen, A.: Simlex-999: Evaluating semantic models with (genuine) similarity estimation (2014). arXiv preprint arXiv:1408.3456
6. Karlgren, J. (ed.): Proceedings of the EACL workshop on New Text: Wikis and blogs and other dynamic text sources, EACL 2006
7. Landauer, T., Dumais, S.: A solution to plato's problem: The latent semantic analysis theory of acquisition, induction and representation of knowledge. Psychological Review **104**(2), 211–240 (1997)
8. Mikolov, T., Sutskever, I., Chen, K., Corrado, G.S., Dean, J.: Distributed representations of words and phrases and their compositionality. In: Proceedings of NIPS, pp. 3111–3119 (2013)
9. Turney, P.D., Pantel, P.: From Frequency to Meaning: Vector Space Models of Semantics. Journal of Artificial Intelligence Research **37**, 141–188 (2010)

Automatic Segmentation and Deep Learning of Bird Sounds

Hendrik Vincent Koops$^{(\boxtimes)}$, Jan van Balen, and Frans Wiering

Department of Information and Computing Sciences,
Utrecht University, Utrecht, The Netherlands
{h.v.koops,j.m.h.vanbalen,f.wiering}@uu.nl

Abstract. We present a study on automatic birdsong recognition with deep neural networks using the BIRDCLEF2014 dataset. Through deep learning, feature hierarchies are learned that represent the data on several levels of abstraction. Deep learning has been applied with success to problems in fields such as music information retrieval and image recognition, but its use in bioacoustics is rare. Therefore, we investigate the application of a common deep learning technique (deep neural networks) in a classification task using songs from Amazonian birds. We show that various deep neural networks are capable of outperforming other classification methods. Furthermore, we present an automatic segmentation algorithm that is capable of separating bird sounds from non-bird sounds.

Keywords: Deep learning · Feature learning · Bioacoustics · Segmentation

1 Introduction

Features are predominantly handcrafted in audio information retrieval research. For a successful translation from heuristics to algorithmic methods, a significant amount of domain- and engineering knowledge is needed. Creating features from heuristics depends on the assumption that the feature designer can know what a good representation of a signal must be to solve a problem. Feature design is thus constrained by what a designer can conceive and comprehend. Furthermore, manual optimization of handcrafted features is a slow and costly process.

A research area that tries to solve some of the aforementioned problems in feature design is called *deep learning*, in which multilayer architectures are used to learn *feature hierarchies*. The more abstract features that are higher up in the hierarchy are formed by the composition of less abstract features on lower levels. These multi-level representations allow a deep architecture to learn the complex functions that map the input (such as digital audio) to output (e.g. classes), without the need of dependence on handcrafted features [11].

Related Work. Feature learning has been succesfully applied in music information retrieval tasks such as musical genre [5], and emotion recognition [6]. Deng and Yu [7] argue that automatic learning of feature hierarchies, and high level

© Springer International Publishing Switzerland 2015
J. Mothe et al. (Eds.): CLEF 2015, LNCS 9283, pp. 261–267, 2015.
DOI: 10.1007/978-3-319-24027-5_26

features in particular, will become more important as the amount of data and range of machine learning applications continues to grow. Therefore, we investigate the application of deep neural networks (DNN) in classification of a large birdsong corpus. This paper extends previous work [12] with network strategies to prevent overfitting.

Contribution. The contribution of this paper is threefold. First, it provides the first results of applying DNN in classification of bird songs. Secondly, this paper provides a novel algorithm to automatically segment noisy bird sounds into bird- and non-bird sounds. Thirdly, this paper sets a baseline towards the application of state of the art feature learning algorithms in bioacoustics.

The remainder of this paper is structured as follows. Section 2 details bird sound segmentation. Section 3 describes classification using DNN. Section 4 presents classification results. Concluding remarks can be found in Section 5.

2 Automatic Segmentation of Noisy Bird Sounds

Often, a substantial part of a birdsong recording contains background noise. Therefore, we create a segmentation algorithm that is based on the assumption that the loudest parts of a signal are the most relevant. The algorithm consists of three parts: 1: decimating and filtering, 2: segmenting and 3: clustering.

Decimating and Filtering. Decimation of a signal is common practice in speech recognition, as it reduces the amount of information by removing the top part of the spectrum that we know cannot hold the most important information. The spectrum energy in song birds is typically concentrated on a very narrow area in the range of 1 to 6 kHz [2]. Therefore, we down-sample birdsong recordings by a factor 4, resulting in a maximum signal frequency of 5.5125 KHz for signals with a sample rate of 44100 Hz. Although some bird song frequencies could exist beyond this limit, this is never the loudest frequency. After decimation, the signal is passed through a 10th order high pass filter with a passband frequency of 1kHz and a stop band attenuation of 80 dB to filter unwanted low frequency noise. Finally, the signal is passed through another 10th order high pass filter to account for sounds that occur below the bird sound in the spectrogram. This filter varies its passband frequency to $0.6 * f_m$ per signal, where f_m is the the maximum value of the signal's spectrogram.

Segmentation. We segment a recording into bird sounds and non-bird sounds by finding the maximum sections of a spectrogram using a an energy-based algorithm somewhat similar to [3]. In the spectrogram of a signal f, the peak of f at time t_n is found. From this peak, a left and right wise trace is performed until the value at the trace position falls below a threshold φ dB, which indicates the boundary of a segment. Tracing is repeated until no untraced peak above the threshold is found, resulting in n segments per recording. In a manual inspection, $\varphi = 17$ was found to create the best segments.

Clustering. An unwanted artifact of the aforementioned segmentation is the creation of a large number of small segments of only a few milliseconds (ms) in length. Bird songs are better described at a higher temporal level, which is richer in information. Therefore, we merge segments by analyzing the distances between sections and combining subsequent segments with distances smaller than m ms. Segmentation is evaluated in an experiment where handcrafted segments are compared to automatically generated segments [10]. $m = 800$ms was found to create segments that closely match human annotations.

3   Deep Neural Network Classification

Figure 1 shows an example of a DNN. We use a multilayer neural network that is fully connected between layers, also called a *deep belief network* [13]. The networks are initialized using a greedy layer-wise unsupervised pre-training phase, thereby initializing the network closer to a good solution than random initialization. This avoids local minima when using supervised gradient descent [14]. After pre-training, gradient descent learning is used to train and fine-tune the networks. To explore the effects of hidden layer size on classification, we create two types of networks: one in which the hidden layer size is smaller or equal to the input layer, and one where the hidden layer is larger than the input layer. The classification layer is always of a fixed size in every network, corresponding to the number of species classes in a dataset. We also experiment with *dropout*, [1] to avoid overfitting. In dropout, half of the nodes of the hidden layers of the neural networks are randomly omitted on each training case, by setting their value to 0 with a probability of 0.5 on each training iteration. This prevents complex co-adaption in which hidden layer activation is only helpful in the context of other specific hidden layer activation.

Batch Optimization. To update the parameters of the networks, we use *mini-batch optimization*. With this method, the parameters of the networks are updated using the summed gradients measured on a rotating subset of size n

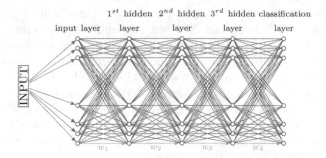

Fig. 1. Example of a Deep Neural Network with three hidden layers.

Table 1. Contents of three different MFCC datasets.

	Mean	Variance	Speed	Acceleration	Means of three subsections
$\mathcal{D}_{48}$	✓				
$\mathcal{D}_{96}$	✓	✓			
$\mathcal{D}_{240}$	✓	✓	✓	✓	✓

of a training set. During early testing and implementation, it was found that a batch size of $n = 250$ returned favorable results.

Voting. The input to the networks are segments of recordings, and the networks therefore perform *segment based* classification. To be able to classify individual *recordings*, we use voting to combine the classifications of segments of a recording. We use an approach that uses the classification layer activations as probabilities, thereby taking advantage of the network's classification uncertainty. For each segment in a recording, a vector is created in which the classes are added proportionally to their activation in the classification layer (e.g. a class with activation 0.1 is added 1 time, 0.4 is added 4 times, etc). Finally, the mode over the vectors of all segments is chosen as the class for the recording.

4   Results

The BirdCLEF2014 ($\mathcal{BC}_{14}$) [4] dataset is used for evaluation. $\mathcal{BC}_{14}$ was released for the 2014 BirdCLEF task and contains around 14000 audio recordings of 501 South American bird species. The segments created by our algorithm are used to select Mel-Frequency Cepstrum Coefficients (MFCC) features from a MFCC dataset that was included in the $\mathcal{BC}_{14}$. MFCC are coefficients that together represent the power spectrum of a sound on a scale that tries to mimic human perception of pitch. Originally designed for speech processing applications, they have since been successfully used in bioacoustics research [8,9].

Using the segments, we create three MFCC datasets ($\mathcal{D}_{48}$, $\mathcal{D}_{96}$ and $\mathcal{D}_{240}$), of which the contents is listed in Table 1. Each dataset contains 46799 segments (4.83 segments per recording). The datasets are shuffled per recording and divided into a 80% train and 20% test set, and together with their classes used as input for several DNN. The classification results of several network topologies are presented in Table 2. Network topologies are notated as a series of layer sizes. "48-(40×2)-501" denotes a DNN with 48 input nodes, two layers of hidden nodes with 40 nodes and an output layer of 501 nodes. 48-networks are trained and tested with $\mathcal{D}_{48}$, 96-networks with $\mathcal{D}_{96}$ and 240-networks with $\mathcal{D}_{240}$.

We find that classification accuracy increases with the size of the network, except for the 48-networks. In the 96-networks, a big jump in accuracy is observed with regard to the 48-networks, to around 10% in the 96-networks without dropout and around 6% accuracy with dropout. Training accuracy is high in the 96-networks without dropout, while the testing accuracy is low. The training and testing accuracy of the 96-networks with dropout are lower, but closer together, showing that dropout was effective in preventing overfitting.

Table 2. Train and test results of various network topologies. In the columns on the right "+d" denotes drop-out, "+v" denotes voting. Best performance is highlighted.

Network topology	Train (segments)	Test (segments)	Test+v (recordings)	Network topology	Train (segments)	Test (segments)	Test+v (recordings)
48-(40×2)-501	45.6%	0.5%	0.32%	48-(40×3)-501 +d	4%	0.27%	0.13%
48-(48×2)-501	52%	0.34%	0.27%	48-(48×3)-501 +d	3%	0.30%	0.11%
96-(64×2)-501	77.6%	9.34%	10.05%	96-(64×3)-501 +d	10%	5.97%	5.05%
96-(84×2)-501	85%	10.55%	11.35%	96-(84×3)-501 +d	17%	8.10%	7.40%
240-(128×2)-501	15.0%	10.03%	11.25%	240-(128×3)-501 +d	22%	9.51%	9.11%
240-(350×2)-501	10.0%	11.03%	12.08%	240-(350×3)-501 +d	51%	13.83%	13.23%

Table 3. Results of two non-neural network classifiers. Best performance is highlighted.

Classifier	Dataset	Train accuracy	Test accuracy
Rotation Forest (RF)	$\mathcal{D}_{48}$	99.979%	0.24%
Rotation Forest (RF)	$\mathcal{D}_{96}$	26.686%	8.99%
Rotation Forest (RF)	$\mathcal{D}_{240}$	100%	8.25%
Support Vector Machines (SVM)	$\mathcal{D}_{48}$	7.086%	1.03%
Support Vector Machines (SVM)	$\mathcal{D}_{96}$	29.75%	10.17%
Support Vector Machines (SVM)	$\mathcal{D}_{240}$	29.64%	10.06%

$\mathcal{D}_{240}$ supplements the $\mathcal{D}_{96}$ with the means of three equal subsections of a segment. This extra information improves only a little bit in the 240-networks with a hidden layer of size 350 without dropout. In the networks without dropout, the 240-network with hidden layer size 128 performs worse than the 96-network with hidden layer size 84, but better than the 96-network with hidden layer size 64. The 240-networks outperform other networks with dropout. The difference between test and train accuracy in the dropout networks increases with the size of the networks, but this is not observed in the networks without dropout. Overall, the largest network (240-(350×3)-501) with dropout the best classifier.

Other Classification Methods. Table 3 shows the classification accuracies of the $\mathcal{D}_{48}$, $\mathcal{D}_{96}$ and $\mathcal{D}_{240}$ on two non-neural network classifiers. Again it is found that using only the mean of the MFCC in a segment ($\mathcal{D}_{48}$) produces classification accuracies close to random classification. This holds for both Rotation Forest (RF) and Support Vector Machines SVM, with the former accurately classifying only 0.235% of the examples and the latter 1.026% of the examples. RF performs below random classification and SVM above the random baseline of 0.3%. A big jump in classification accuracy with both methods is observed when adding the variance ($\mathcal{D}_{96}$). Additionally adding the means of three subsections by using the $\mathcal{D}_{240}$-set decreases the classification accuracy of RF, compared to $\mathcal{D}_{96}$, but outperforms the $\mathcal{D}_{48}$. Overall, SVM produces best result for this task (10.17%).

5   Discussion and Conclusions

The results from the Table 2 and 3 show that DNN are capable of outperforming RF and SVM, when taking into account all datasets. The BirdClef committee reported that the random baseline in this task was 0.3%, which is comparable to the the smallest DNN used in the experiments. Using $\mathcal{D}_{96}$, DNN outperform the other tested classification methods. The best 96-network (96-(84×2)-501) outperforms SVM by 1.2% and RF by 2.4%. Comparing the results of the 96-networks with those of the 48-networks shows that important information of birdsong is contained in the variance of the MFCC, indicating that how coefficients vary over time is important in discriminating species. The best results are obtained using the 240-set on DNN with and without dropout. Overall, these results show that adding time-varying information is vital to the classification of birdsongs using MFCC. Furthermore, is is shown that DNN are capable of outperforming SVM and RF on several MFCC datasets. The results of this paper show that deep learning is valuable to bioacoustics research and bird song recognition.

Acknowledgments. Hendrik Vincent Koops is supported by the Netherlands Organization for Scientific Research, through the NWO-VIDI-grant 276-35-001 to Anja Volk. Frans Wiering is supported by the FES project COMMIT/. Jan Van Balen is supported by Cogitch (NWO CATCH project 640.005.004).

References

1. Hinton, G.E., Srivastava, N., Krizhevsky, A., Sutskever, I., Salakhutdinov, R.R.: Improving neural networks by preventing co-adaptation of feature detectors. CoRR abs/1207.0580 (2012)
2. Harma, A.: Automatic identification of bird species based on sinusoidal modeling of syllables. In: Proceedings of the 2003 IEEE International Conference on Acoustics, Speech, and Signal Processing (ICASSP 2003), vol. 5 (2013)
3. Somervuo, P., Harma, A.: Bird song recognition based on syllable pair histograms. In: 2004 Proceedings of the IEEE International Conference on Acoustics, Speech, and Signal Processing (ICASSP 2004), vol. 5, p. V–825. IEEE (2004)
4. Goëau, H., Glotin, H., Vellinga, W.-P., Rauber, A.: LifeCLEF bird identification task 2014. In: CLEF Working Notes 2014 (2014)
5. Hamel, P., Eck, D.: Learning features from music audio with deep belief networks. In: Proceedings of the 11th International Society for Music Information Retrieval Conference (ISMIR 2010), pp. 339–344. Utrecht, The Netherlands (2010)
6. Schmidt, E., Scott, J., Kim, Y.: Feature learning in dynamic environments: modeling the acoustic structure of musical emotion. In: Proceedings of the 13th International Society for Music Information Retrieval Conference, Porto, Portugal, October 8–12, 2012
7. Deng, L., Yu, D.: Deep learning: Methods and applications. Technical Report MSR-TR-2014-21, Microsoft, January 2014
8. Lee, C.-H., Lee, Y.-K., Huang, R.-Z.: Automatic recognition of bird songs using cepstral coefficients. Journal of Information Technology and Applications 1(1), 17–23 (2006)
9. Chou, C.-H., Ko, H.-Y.: Automatic birdsong recognition with MFCC based syllable feature extraction. In: Hsu, C.-H., Yang, L.T., Ma, J., Zhu, C. (eds.) Ubiquitous Intelligence and Computing. LNCS, vol. 6905, pp. 185–196. Springer, Heidelberg (2011)
10. Koops, H.V.: A Deep Neural Network Approach to Automatic Birdsong Recognition. Master's Thesis, Utrecht University (2014)

11. Bengio, Y.: Learning deep architectures for AI. In: Foundations and trends® in Machine Learning, pp. 1–127. Now Publishers Inc. (2009)

12. Koops, H.V., Van Balen, J., Wiering, F.: A deep neural network approach to the LifeCLEF 2014 bird task. In: CLEF 2014 Working Notes, vol. 1180, pp. 634–642 (2014)

13. Hinton, G.E., Osindero, S., Teh, Y.-W.: A fast learning algorithm for deep belief nets. Neural Computation **18**(7), 1527–1554 (2006). MIT Press

14. Bengio, Y., Lamblin, P., Popovici, D., Larochelle, H.: Greedy layer-wise training of deep networks. In: Advances in Neural Information Processing Systems 19, pp. 153–160. MIT Press (2007)

The Impact of Noise in Web Genre Identification

Dimitrios Pritsos[✉] and Efstathios Stamatatos

University of the Aegean, 83200 Karlovassi, Samos, Greece
{dpritsos,stamatatos}@aegean.gr

Abstract. Genre detection of web documents fits an open-set classification task. The web documents not belonging to any predefined genre or where multiple genres co-exist is considered as noise. In this work we study the impact of noise on automated genre identification within an open-set classification framework. We examine alternative classification models and document representation schemes based on two corpora, one without noise and one with noise showing that the recently proposed RFSE model can remain robust with noise. Moreover, we show how that the identification of certain genres is not practically affected by the presence of noise.

1 Introduction

The genre of web documents refer to their form, communicative purpose and it is associated with style rather than content. The ability to automatically recognize genre of web documents can enhance modern information retrieval systems by providing genre-based grouping/filtering of search results or intuitive hierarchies of web page collections. However, research in web genre identification (WGI), a.k.a automated genre identification (AGI), is limited mainly due to an inherent difficulty of defining the notion of genre and how many different genres (and sub-genres) exist [5,10,11,17].

Traditionally, WGI has been viewed as a closed-set classification problem. Recently, it has been suggested that WGI better fits an open-set classification task since in any practical application it would not be easy to predefine the whole set of possible genres [13]. All web documents not belonging to a predefined genre taxonomy or documents where multiple (known or unknown) genres co-exist can be viewed as noise in WGI [11]. It is necessary to study in detail how such noise affects the effectiveness of WGI in an open-set scenario [1].

In this paper we focus on measuring and analysing the impact of noise in open-set WGI. In particular, similar to [13], we are testing two open-set models *Random Feature Subspacing Ensembles* (RFSE) and *One-Class Support Vector Machines* (OC-SVM). We are applying these models to a corpus without noise and another corpus with noise and we are examining differences in performance. The experiments indicate that both models are affected, RFSE still outperforms OC-SVM while the extracted results are more realistic. Other contributions of this paper are the examination of alternative text representation schemes for both WGI models and the use of MinMax similarity in RFSE that seems to be helpful to improve performance on certain genres.

© Springer International Publishing Switzerland 2015
J. Mothe et al. (Eds.): CLEF 2015, LNCS 9283, pp. 268–273, 2015.
DOI: 10.1007/978-3-319-24027-5_27

2   Previous Work

Most of the previous work on WGI view this problem as a closed-set classification task [5,6,10,11,17]. There is still lack of consensus about the definition of the genre itself and the web genre palette. This is due to the core characteristics of the genre notion, i.e. form, function, purpose, which are very abstract and even in the user agreement level the results are discouraging [14].

However, there is significant amount of work on several aspects of WGI, including *document representation* (e.g. character n-grams, words, part-of-speech features etc.), *term weighting schemas* (e.g. TF, TF-IDF, Binary, etc.) *feature selection methods* (e.g. frequency-based, chi-square, information gain, mutual information) and *classification models* (e.g., SVM, decision trees, aNN, etc.). Additionally, the contribution of the textual and/or the structural information has been investigated where textual information proven to be mostly useful [2,3, 5,9,10,15,17]. As an exception, in [12], the structural information was yielding excellent results in blog/non-blog classification.

Santini in [11] defines *noise-set* as a collection of web-pages having *no genre* or *multiple genres* same as the non-noise genres of the corpus. Similarly, noise is defined as the set of web pages not belonging to any of the known genres of the corpus in [2,6]. In these works noise was used as negative examples for training binary classifiers or as an additional ("Don't know") class rather than examining the robustness of classification models to deal with noise.

There are a couple of published studies that apply WGI on an open-set classification framework [13,18]. However, noise-free corpora were used in their evaluation. Recently, Asheghi showed that WGI on the noisy web is more challenging as compared to noise-free corpora[1].

3   Experiments

In this paper, we use two corpora already used in previous work in WGI:

1. *7-GENRE* [15]: This is a collection of 1,400 English web pages evenly distributed into 7 genres (blogs, e-shops, FAQs, on-line front pages, listing, personal home pages, search pages).
2. *SANTINIS* [11]: This is a corpus comprising 1,400 English web pages evenly distributed into 7 genres (blogs, e-shops, FAQs, online front pages, listing, personal home pages, search pages), 80 documents evenly categorized to 4 additional genres taken from BBC web pages (DIY, editorial, bio, features) and a random selection of 1,000 English web pages taken from the SPIRIT corpus [4]. The latter can be viewed as noise in this corpus.

We are using only textual information from web pages excluding any structural information, URLs, etc. Based on the good results reported in [13,17] as well as some preliminary experiments, the following document representation schemes are examined: *Character 4-grams, Words uni-grams.*

In our experiments, we do not use the noisy pages at all in the training phase. We only use them in evaluation phase. To obtain results comparable with previous studies, we followed the practice of performing 10-fold cross-validation with these corpora. In all cases, we use the Term-Frequency (TF) weighting scheme and the vocabulary only comprises the terms of the training set. Together with the RFSE model's random feature selection characteristic and the parameters selection (as explained later), the over-fitting has been prevented for the RFSE.

As concerns OC-SVM, two parameters have to be tuned: the number of features fs and ν. For the former, we used $fs =\{1k,\ 5k,\ 10k,\ 50k,\ 90k\}$, of most frequent terms of the vocabulary. Following the reports of previous studies [16] and some preliminary experiments, we examined $\nu=\{0.05,\ 0.07,\ 0.1,\ 0.15,\ 0.17,\ 0.3,\ 0.5,\ 0.7,\ 0.9\}$. In comparison to [13], this set of parameter values is more extended.

With respect to RFSE, four parameters should be set: the vocabulary size V, the number of feature used in each iteration f, the number of iterations I, and the threshold σ. We examined $V=\{5k,\ 10k,\ 50k,\ 100k\}$, $f=\{1k,\ 5k,\ 10k,\ 50k,\ 90k\}$, $I=\{10,\ 50,\ 100\}$ (following the suggestion in [7] that more than 100 iterations does not improve significantly the results) and $\sigma_s=\{0.5,\ 0.7,\ 0.9\}$ (based on some preliminary tests). Additionally, in this work we are testing two document similarity measures: cosine similarity (similar to [13]) and MinMax similarity (used also in a similar task by [8]).

Based on suggestions from previous work [7] and some preliminary experiments we used the following parameter values for RFSE: 100k *available Vocabulary*, 5k *Random Features per Iteration*, 0.5 σ threshold and 100 as *Iterations parameter*. It should be noted that these settings do not optimize the performance of RFSE models. They can be viewed as general settings to test the performance of RFSE in any given corpus.

On the contrary, we selected the parameters that optimize the performance of *OC-SVM* to be used as baseline in the following experiments. The optimal performance was achieved for character 4-grams in both corpora and parameter values: *50000 Features*, $\nu = 0.1$ for 7Genres and *5000 Features*, $\nu = 0.5$ for SANTINIS. The performance of these models in the following figures are referred as *baseline*.

We first applied the WGI models to noise-free 7Genres corpus. Figure 1 shows the precision-recall curves based on the parameters sets as explained above. It is evident that RFSE models are more effective than the *baseline*, although the later is optimized exactly on the 7Genre corpus. Another important observation is that all models seem to lose their effectiveness for high levels of recall. The results based on this corpus seems particularly encouraging since very high precision can be achieved for most of the standard recall values. Character n-grams seem to be more effective than word unigrams for this corpus.

Next, we applied the WGI models to the SANTINIS corpus which comprises a big part of pages belonging to unknown genres (noise). Again, we show the precision-recall curves of the best OC-SVM model (baseline) and the RFSE models on the SANTINIS corpus in figure 2. As can be seen, both WGI approaches

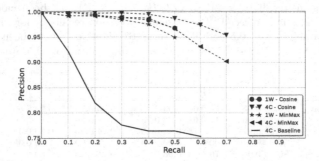

Fig. 1. Precision-Recall Curves of RFSE ensemble based on most occurred parameters found in preliminary cross-validation experiments, i.e. Vocabulary size 100k, Feature set 5k, simga threshold 0.5, Iterations 100. Corpus: 7Genres

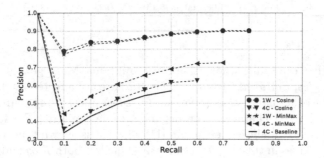

Fig. 2. Precision-Recall Curves of RFSE ensemble based on most occurred parameters found in preliminary cross-validation experiments, i.e. Vocabulary size 100k, Feature set 5k, simga threshold 0.5, Iterations 100. Corpus: SANTINIS

are heavily affected by the introduction of noise. Precision suddenly falls at low recall levels and then it increases quasi-linearly. This sudden fall is caused by the noisy pages and their incorrect classification to some of the known genres. It should be underlined that after that point, at standard recall level of 0.10, models with word unigrams are quite robust and achieve to maintain very high precision at high recall levels which indicates that the examined models are generally tolerant to noise. On the other hand, character n-gram models seem to be much more affected by the presence of noise. Again, RFSE is generally better than the baseline approach.

One important parameter for RFSE is the similarity measure. In figure 1 RFSE with *Cosine similarity* gives in general higher precision compared to Min-Max. On the contrary, when noise is included in the corpus MinMax helps character n-gram models to improve. Word unigram models do not seem to be affected so much by the similarity measure.

Table 1 provides a closer look to precision and recall per genre of the SANTINIS corpus. As can be viewed, the identification of the *OTHER* class, corresponding to

Table 1. Precision-Recall table of *SANTINI'S corpus*, F1 has been calculated by macro-precision and macro-recall. The baseline precision-recalls is for character 4-grams with parameters $\nu = 0.5$ and 5k features RFSE models have been calculated with parameters: Vocabulary size 100k, Feature set 5k, σ threshold 0.5, Iterations 100.

	1W Cos P R	4C Cos P R	1W MinMax P R	4C MinMax P R	BASELINE P R
OTHER	0.93 0.95	0.96 0.60	0.93 0.95	0.95 0.73	0.90 0.60
Blog	0.32 0.96	0.17 0.98	0.33 0.96	0.18 0.99	0.28 0.50
Eshop	0.93 0.32	0.56 0.78	0.94 0.15	0.74 0.49	0.30 0.43
FAQs	1.00 0.64	1.00 0.65	0.99 0.89	0.95 0.99	1.00 0.35
Front Page	0.96 0.96	0.76 1.00	0.98 0.92	0.21 1.00	1.00 0.10
Listing	0.77 0.05	0.04 0.60	0.58 0.04	0.07 0.26	0.03 0.47
Per. Home P.	0.56 0.14	0.48 0.47	0.93 0.06	0.56 0.23	0.30 0.34
Search Page	0.76 0.54	0.74 0.82	0.56 0.51	0.64 0.79	0.86 0.41
DIY Guides	1.00 1.00	1.00 1.00	1.00 1.00	0.34 1.00	0.26 0.50
Editorial	0.72 0.90	0.53 1.00	0.35 1.00	0.09 1.00	1.00 0.25
Features	1.00 1.00	1.00 1.00	1.00 1.00	0.87 1.00	1.00 0.25
Short Bio	1.00 1.00	1.00 1.00	0.45 1.00	0.23 1.00	1.00 0.20
	F1 = .0.76	F1 = .75	F1 = .73	F1 = .60	F1 = .47

noise, is effective, especially when using word unigrams. Many genres (e.g., *Front Page, DIY Guides, Editorial, Features, Short Bio*) are not affected by the presence of noise. On the other hand, we observe that for *Blogs* and *Listing* genres precision is significantly low for character 4-grams and Cosine similarity. This is justified from the qualitative analysis reported in [11] where it is shown that a significant amount of web pages in this corpus could be assigned to both *Blog* and *Listing*, in the Spirit1000 (noise) part.

4   Conclusion

In this paper we focused on the impact of noise in WGI. This is necessary from a practical point of view since in any given application of WGI, it is impossible to predefine a complete genre palette. There will always be some web pages not belonging to the predefined genres. To test the robustness of WGI models, we used a corpus where a significant number of web pages does not belong to any of the known genres. Moreover, we examine appropriate classification models in an open-set scenario which is more realistic taking into account the lack of a consensus on genre palette and the constantly evolving web genres. Experimental results show that the precision of both RFSE and OC-SVM models are affected by noise, especially in low levels of recall, but in general RFSE based on word unigrams remains robust. MinMax seems to significantly improve the performance of character n-gram models in the presence of noise. Moreover, certain genres are not affected by the introduction of noise and their identification remains relatively easy.

References

1. Asheghi, N.R.: Human Annotation and Automatic Detection of Web Genres. Ph.D. thesis, University of Leeds (2015)
2. Dong, L., Watters, C., Duffy, J., Shepherd, M.: Binary cybergenre classification using theoretic feature measures (2006)
3. Meyer zu Eissen, S., Stein, B.: Genre classification of web pages. In: Biundo, S., Frühwirth, T., Palm, G. (eds.) KI 2004. LNCS (LNAI), vol. 3238, pp. 256–269. Springer, Heidelberg (2004)
4. Joho, H., Sanderson, M.: The spirit collection: an overview of a large web collection. In: ACM SIGIR Forum, vol. 38, pp. 57–61. ACM (2004)
5. Kanaris, I., Stamatatos, E.: Learning to recognize webpage genres. Information Processing & Management 45(5), 499–512 (2009)
6. Kennedy, A., Shepherd, M.: Automatic identification of home pages on the web. In: Proceedings of the 38th Annual Hawaii International Conference on System Sciences, HICSS 2005, pp. 99c–99c. IEEE (2005)
7. Koppel, M., Schler, J., Argamon, S.: Authorship attribution in the wild. Language Resources and Evaluation 45(1), 83–94 (2011)
8. Koppel, M., Winter, Y.: Determining if two documents are written by the same author. Journal of the Association for Information Science and Technology 65(1), 178–187 (2014)
9. Lim, C.S., Lee, K.J., Kim, G.C.: Multiple sets of features for automatic genre classification of web documents. Information Processing and Management 41(5), 1263–1276 (2005)
10. Mason, J., Shepherd, M., Duffy, J.: An n-gram based approach to automatically identifying web page genre. In: HICSS, pp. 1–10. IEEE Computer Society (2009)
11. Mehler, A., Sharoff, S., Santini, M.: Genres on the Web: Computational Models and Empirical Studies. Text, Speech and Language Technology. Springer (2010)
12. Pardo, F.M.R., Padilla, A.P.: Detecting blogs independently from the language and content. In: 1st International Workshop on Mining Social Media (MSM09-CAEPIA09). Citeseer (2009)
13. Pritsos, D.A., Stamatatos, E.: Open-set classification for automated genre identification. In: Serdyukov, P., Braslavski, P., Kuznetsov, S.O., Kamps, J., Rüger, S., Agichtein, E., Segalovich, I., Yilmaz, E. (eds.) ECIR 2013. LNCS, vol. 7814, pp. 207–217. Springer, Heidelberg (2013)
14. Roussinov, D., Crowston, K., Nilan, M., Kwasnik, B., Cai, J., Liu, X.: Genre based navigation on the web. In: Proceedings of the 34th Annual Hawaii International Conference on System Sciences, 2001, p. 10. IEEE (2001)
15. Santini, M.: Automatic identification of genre in web pages. Ph.D. thesis, University of Brighton (2007)
16. Scholkopf, B., Platt, J., Shawe-Taylor, J., Smola, A., Williamson, R.: Estimating the support of a high-dimensional distribution. Technical Report MSR-TR-99-87 (1999)
17. Sharoff, S., Wu, Z., Markert, K.: The web library of babel: evaluating genre collections. In: Proceedings of the Seventh Conference on International Language Resources and Evaluation, pp. 3063–3070 (2010)
18. Stubbe, A., Ringlstetter, C., Schulz, K.U.: Genre as noise: Noise in genre. International Journal of Document Analysis and Recognition (IJDAR) 10(3–4), 199–209 (2007)

On the Multilingual and Genre Robustness of EmoGraphs for Author Profiling in Social Media

Francisco Rangel[1,2](✉) and Paolo Rosso[1]

[1] NLE Lab, Universitat Politècnica de València, Valencia, Spain
prosso@dsic.upv.es
[2] Autoritas Consulting, S.A., Madrid, Spain
francisco.rangel@autoritas.es

Abstract. Author profiling aims at identifying different traits such as age and gender of an author on the basis of her writings. We propose the novel EmoGraph graph-based approach where morphosyntactic categories are enriched with semantic and affective information. In this work we focus on testing the robustness of EmoGraphs when applied to age and gender identification. Results with PAN-AP-14 corpus show the competitiveness of the representation over genres and languages. Finally, some interesting insights are shown, for example with topic and emotion bounded genres such as hotel reviews.

Keywords: Author profiling · Age identification · Gender identification · Emotion-labeled graphs · EmoGraph

1 Introduction

Author profiling aims at identifying different traits such as age and gender of an author on the basis of her writings. Profiling an author is very important from a forensic and security viewpoint due to the possibility of profiling possible delinquents as well as from a marketing perspective due to the possibility of improving users segmentation. The growing interest in age and gender identification is notable in the scientific community. A shared task on author profiling has been organised at PAN Lab[1] of the CLEF initiative. The interest of PAN 2015 remains on identifying age and gender together with personality.

Pioneer investigations on author profiling were carried on by Pennebaker [4], who divided features into content and style-based. Similarly, in [1] authors approached the task of gender identification by combining function words with parts-of-speech (POS). A high variety of different approaches were used at PAN

The research has been carried out in the framework of the European Commission WIQ-EI IRSES (no. 269180) and DIANA - Finding Hidden Knowledge in Texts (TIN2012-38603-C02) projects. The work of the first author was partially funded by Autoritas Consulting SA and by Spanish Ministry of Economics under grant ECOPORTUNITY IPT-2012-1220-430000.

[1] http://pan.webis.de

© Springer International Publishing Switzerland 2015
J. Mothe et al. (Eds.): CLEF 2015, LNCS 9283, pp. 274–280, 2015.
DOI: 10.1007/978-3-319-24027-5_28

shared tasks [6,7]. Participants used combinations of style-based features such as frequency of punctuation marks, capital letters, quotations, etc., joint POS tags and content-based features such as bag-of-words, TF-IDF of words, dictionary-based words, topic-based words, entropy-based words, or content-based features obtained with Latent Semantic Analysis. Few authors used emotions as features [3], but none of them focused on how users convey verbal emotions. Also, there are no investigations on graph-based representations to tackle author profiling. We approached the task of age and gender identification in Spanish with EmoGraphs in [5], obtaining competitive results and interesting insights on how people convey verbal emotions in their discourse. In this paper we are interested in investigating further the robustness of EmoGraphs from multilingual and genre perspectives in social media texts.

The rest of the paper is structured as follows. In Section 2 we introduce EmoGraphs. In Section 3 we explain the evaluation framework, presenting and discussing experimental results in Section 4. Finally, in Section 5 we draw some conclusions.

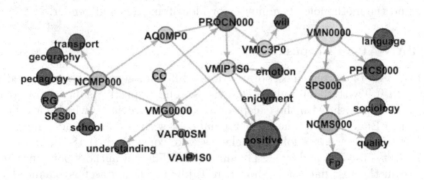

Fig. 1. EmoGraph of "He estado tomando cursos en línea sobre temas valiosos que disfruto estudiando y que podrían ayudarme a hablar en público" (*"I have been taking online courses about valuable subjects that I enjoy studying and might help me to speak in public"*).

2   Emotion-Labelled Graphs

Emotion-labeled Graphs (EmoGraphs) [5] obtains morphosyntactic categories with the Freeling library[2] for each word in all texts of an author. Each POS is modeled as a node in the graph and each edge defines a POS sequence in the text. The graph obtained is enriched with semantic and affective information. Adjectives, adverbs and verbs are annotated with their polarity and the Spanish Emotion Lexicon [8] and Wordnet Affect [9] are used to identify their associated

---

[2] http://nlp.lsi.upc.edu/freeling/

emotions in Spanish and English respectively. WordNet Domains[3] is used to obtain the topics of nouns. On the basis of what was investigated in [2], verbs are annotated with one of the following semantic categories: i) perception (see, listen, smell...); ii) understanding (know, understand, think...); iii) doubt (doubt, ignore...); iv) language (tell, say, declare, speak...); v) emotion (feel, want, love...); vi) and will (must, forbid, allow...). We can see an example in Figure 1.

Once the graph is built, our objective is to use a machine learning approach to classify texts into the right age and gender. We obtain two kind of features on the basis of graph analysis: i) general properties of the graph describing the overall structure of the modelled texts, such as nodes-edges ratio, average degree, weighted average degree, diameter, density, modularity, cluster coefficient or average path length; ii) and specific properties of its nodes and how they are related to each other, such us eigenvector and betweenness values.

3   Evaluation Framework

In the following sections we describe the PAN-AP-14 corpus of the PAN Lab at CLEF and the methodology employed for identifying age and gender.

3.1   PAN-AP-14 Corpus

The PAN-AP-14 corpus incorporates four different genres: *i*) social media; *ii*) blogs; *iii*) Twitter; *iv*) and hotel reviews. The respective subcorpora cover English and Spanish, with the exception of the hotel reviews, which have been provided in English only. The author is labeled with age and gender information. For labeling age, the following classes were considered: *i*) 18-24; *ii*) 25-34; *iii*) 35-49; *iv*) 50-64; *v*) and 65+ . The number of different authors per genre and language in the test dataset is shown in Table 1. The dataset is balanced by gender. In the overview paper on the shared task [6] more details are given on how the different subcorpora were built.

Table 1. Distribution of the number of authors with respect to age classes per language in test set.

	Social Media		Blogs		Twitter		Reviews
	English	Spanish	English	Spanish	English	Spanish	English
18-24	680	150	10	4	12	4	74
25-34	900	180	24	12	56	26	200
35-49	980	138	32	26	58	46	200
50-64	790	70	10	10	26	12	200
65+	26	28	2	2	2	2	147
Σ	3376	566	78	54	154	90	821

---

[3] http://wndomains.fbk.eu/

3.2 Methodology

Our final representation is a combination of the presented EmoGraph with the 1,000 most frequent character 6-grams[4]. For training we used the training dataset of the PAN-AP-14 corpus. Several machine learning algorithms were evaluated with the training set and selected the best ones: *i*) Simple logistic in Englih Twitter for gender identification; *ii*) Support Vector Machines in Spanish blogs, English reviews and English social media for both gender and age, and Spanish Twitter for age identification; *iii*) and AdaBoost with Decision Stump for all the rest. To compare our results with the ones of the participants in the PAN 2014 task, we evaluated our models on the test set.

4 Experimental Results

In this section results are presented and discussed. The first subsection presents the overall accuracy obtained in the task and compare them to the best method presented at PAN 2014 for each corpus and task. The second subsection shows the analysis of the impact of EmoGraphs.

4.1 Age and Gender Identification

As can be seen in Figure 2, results for Spanish are better than for English, except maybe in blogs. This may be due to the highest variety in the morphological information obtained with Freeling for both languages. The Eagles group[5] proposed a series of recommendations for the morphosyntactic annotation of corpora. Freeling obtains 247 different annotations for Spanish whereas it obtains 53 for English. For example, in the Spanish version[6] the word "cursos" (courses) for the given example in Figure 1 is returned as NCMP000 where NC means common noun, M means male, P means plural, and 000 is a filling until 7 chars; in the English version, the word "courses" is annotated as NNS.

Contrary to what we obtained in the PAN-AP-13 corpus for Spanish [5], results for gender are better than for age. This is in line with the rest of participants of 2014 which improved more in gender than in age identification with respect to the results obtained in 2013. This was due to the highest number of classes (3 classes in 2013 vs. 5 continuous ones in 2014). Results for blogs and Twitter are better than for social media and reviews. We may explain this because both blogs and Twitter datasets were manually annotated, ensuring that the gender and age of each author is true. On the contrary, in social media and reviews what the authors reported was assumed to be true. Furthermore, in blogs there are enough texts per author in order to obtain a better profile.

---

[4] We combine our representation with n-grams due to the good results of other participants by using them in the task [6]. We selected n=6 due to experimental results on the training set.

[5] http://www.ilc.cnr.it/EAGLES96/intro.html

[6] http://nlp.lsi.upc.edu/freeling/doc/tagsets/tagset-es.html

278   F. Rangel and P. Rosso

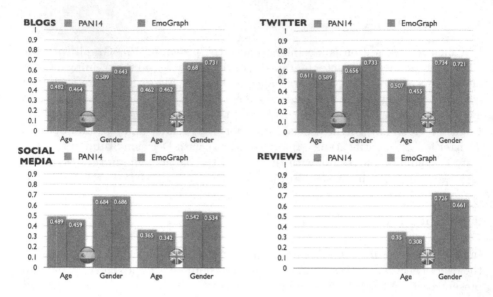

Fig. 2. Accuracies of the best PAN14 team vs. EmoGraph on different languages and genres.

In fact, although in Twitter each tweet is short (as much 140 characters), there are hundreds of tweets per author. On the other hand, although the quality of social media with respect to the previous year was improved, the data remain with more noise than in blogs. Reviews, where EmoGraphs obtained the worst results, need a special mention. Besides the short texts and the possibility of deceptive information regarding age and gender, reviews are bounded to hotel domain and to the expression of two kinds of emotions: complain or praise.

4.2 The Impact of EmoGraphs

We merged the EmoGraph method with the 1,000 more frequent character 6-grams as described previously. In Figure 3 the contribution of EmoGraph to the overall accuracy is presented.

It is noteworthy that, in general, EmoGraph obtains the best results without the need of combination with character n-grams in the Spanish language. This may be due to the lower number of morphosyntactic labels in English. With respect to the performance for gender identification in blogs and Twitter in English, contrary to the one in these social media in Spanish, character n-grams may have helped to capture the missing information due to the lack of detailed morphosyntactic annotation.

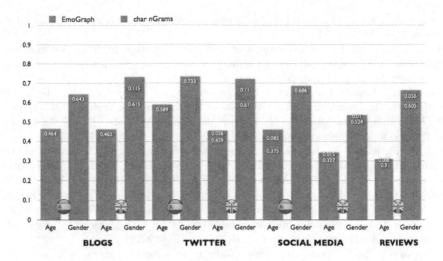

Fig. 3. Contribution to the global accuracy of the EmoGraph representation.

5   Conclusions

We have investigated the robustness of the EmoGraph representation for the age and gender identification in several social media genres and different language (Spanish and also English). We showed that our method remains competitive, although it obtains better results in Spanish. In our opinion this is due to the coarse-grained morphosyntactic annotation of English. Results for reviews are very insightful because they are much worse than other genres. We believe this is due to the more bounded topics and emotions.

The performance at age identification in some cases, such as for Spanish blogs, is not much higher than majority class. This is due to the skew in the age distribution.[7] In this sense, it would be interesting to investigated further the application of cost-sensitive machine learning techniques.

References

1. Argamon, S., Koppel, M., Fine, J., Shimoni, A.: Gender, genre, and writing style informal written texts. TEXT **23**, 321–346 (2003)
2. Levin, B.: English Verb Classes and Alternations. University of Chicago Press, Chicago (1993)
3. Mohammad, S.M., Yang, T.: Tracking sentiment in mail: how gender differ on emotional axes. In: Proceedings of the 2nd Workshop on Computational Approaches to Subjectivity and Sentiment Analysis (2011)

---

[7] The skew in the distribution is representative of the real use of social media in the different stages of life: http://jetscram.com/blog/industry-news/social-media-user-statistics-and-age-demographics-2014/

4. Pennebaker, J.W.: The Secret Life of Pronouns: What Our Words Say About Us. Bloomsbury Press (2011)
5. Rangel, F., Rosso, P.: On the impact of emotions on author profiling. Information Processing & Management, Special Issue on Emotion and Sentiment in Social and Expressive Media (in press, 2015)
6. Rangel, F., Rosso, P., Chugur, I., Potthast, M., Trenkmann, M., Stein, B., Verhoeven, B., Daelemans, W.: Overview of the 2nd author profiling task at pan 2014. In: Cappellato L., Ferro N., Halvey M., Kraaij, W. (eds.) CLEF 2014 Labs and Workshops, Notebook Papers. CEUR-WS.org, vol. 1180 (2014)
7. Rangel, F., Rosso, P., Koppel, M., Stamatatos, E., Inches, G.: Overview of the author profiling task at pan 2013. In: Forner, P., Navigli, R., Tufis, D. (eds.) Notebook Papers of CLEF 2013 LABs and Workshops. CEUR-WS.org, vol. 1179 (2013)
8. Sidorov, G., Miranda-Jimnez, S., Viveros-Jimnez, F., Gelbukh, F., Castro-Snchez, N., Velsquez, F., Daz-Rangel, I., Surez-Guerra, S., Trevio, A., Gordon-Miranda, J.: Empirical study of opinion mining in spanish tweets. In: 11th Mexican International Conference on Artificial Intelligence, MICAI, pp. 1–4 (2012)
9. Strapparava, C., Valitutti, A.: Wordnet-affect: an affective extension of wordnet. In: Proceedings of the 4th International Conference on Language Resources and Evaluation, Lisbon (2004)

Is Concept Mapping Useful
for Biomedical Information Retrieval?

Wei Shen and Jian-Yun Nie[✉]

DIRO, University of Montreal, C.P. 6128, Succursale Centre-ville,
Montreal, QC H3C 3J7, Canada
{shenwei,nie}@iro.umontreal.ca

Abstract. Concepts have been extensively used in biomedical information retrieval (BIR); but the experimental results have often showed limited or no improvement compared to a traditional bag-of-words method. In this paper, we
analyze the problems in concept mapping, and show how they can affect the results of BIR. This suggests a flexible utilization of the identified concepts.

Keywords: Biomedical information retrieval · Concept · MetaMap · UMLS

1 Introduction

The biomedical area is rich in domain resources. MeSH [7], SNOMED [12] and
UMLS Metathesaurus [2] etc. have been created to store concepts and their various
expressions. For example, "hypertension" and "High blood pressure" are associated
with the same concept "D006973" in UMLS Metathesaurus. In addition, specific tools
(e.g. MetaMap [1]) have been developed to recognize concepts from texts, a process
often called *concept mapping*. Intuitively, such resources are valuable for biomedical
information retrieval (BIR): a document about "hypertension" can match a query on
"high blood pressure", thus alleviating the vocabulary mismatch problem.

However, the experimental results have been mitigated. While some studies (e.g.
[13]) found concept mapping useful for BIR, in ShARe/eHealth CLEF 2013 task 3
[3], it has been difficult for an approach based on concepts to compete against a BOW
approach. The underlying reasons of such results are still unclear. In this paper, we
examine the experimental results on several test collections, and show the problems of
concept mapping with respect to BIR. Our analysis shows that a number of concept
mapping errors, granularity, and inconsistency, may affect the BIR effectiveness. In
such a situation, an appropriate approach is to use the concepts as flexible phrases.

2 Related Work

The mapped concepts using a tool (e.g. MetaMap) can be used in several ways in
BIR: The mapped concepts or their IDs can be used to form an additional conceptual
representation (e.g. [5] [10] [6]). This approach is often called bag-of-concepts (BOC)

© Springer International Publishing Switzerland 2015
J. Mothe et al. (Eds.): CLEF 2015, LNCS 9283, pp. 281–286, 2015.
DOI: 10.1007/978-3-319-24027-5_29

approach. It relies on the correctness and coverage of the concept-mapping tool – mis-mapped concepts or unmapped concepts will deteriorate the quality of the conceptual representation. An alternative is to use the recognized concepts in a query as phrases – the terms forming a phrase are required to appear in the same form or at proximity. Using the latter approach, the principle is similar to Markov Random Field model [8]. The only difference is that in MRF model, no concept mapping is required and adjacent words in a query are assumed to form a phrase. MRF has been used for BIR in several experiments (e.g. [13]). It is however unclear how the MRF model compares to the one that uses concept mapping. We will compare them in our experiments.

3 Experiments Using Concepts

We run experiments on three test collections: OHSUMED, CLEF 2013 and CLEF 2014. Table 1 shows some statistics[1].

Table 1. Statistics of the test collections

Collection	# Docs	# Queries	# Rel. docs
OHSUMED	348,566	106	2,252
CLEF 2013	110,1228	50	6,218
CLEF 2014	110,1228	50	6,800

The traditional BOW is used as the baseline method, which is a language model with Dirichlet smoothing (Dirichlet prior 2000). We use Indri as the search platform. MetaMap [1] is used to identify concept ID (Concept Unique Identifier – CUI) from documents and queries.

3.1 Bag-of-Concepts vs. Bag-of-Words

We first compare the BOC and BOW approaches in Table 2. We can observe that the BOC method alone always underperforms the BOW method. When BOW and BOC are combined (by linearly combining their retrieval scores, with the combination parameter manually tuned), we observe some improvements over BOW. However, only the improvements on OHSUMED are statistically significant.

At this point, it is interesting to analyze why the BOC method cannot leverage the expected advantage of concept mapping. The answer may lie in the accuracy of the concept-mapping tool. In an analysis [9], MetaMap is reported to have a precision of 84% and a recall of 70%. However, this analysis was done with respect to the general concept-mapping task. Here, we analyze the set of CLEF 2014 queries and examine how well the mapped concepts are matched against documents. From the 50 short queries, MetaMap recognized 85 concepts. We manually examined the mapping results.

---

[1] Notice that the original document collection of CLEF 2013 contained some more documents, which have been removed from CLEF 2014 collection. In our experiments, we use the same CLEF 2014 collection for CLEF 2013 queries.

Table 2. Results with BOW and BOC (* and ** mean statistical significance with t-test at p<0.05 and p<0.01)

Method	OHSUMED		CLEF13 short		CLEF13 long		CLEF14 short		CLEF14 long	
	MAP	P@10	MAP	P@10	MAP	P@10	MAP	P@10	MAP	P@10
BOW	0.1607	0.2099	0.2844	0.4940	0.2709	0.4680	0.3945	0.7180	0.4026	0.6680
BOC	0.1474	0.1823	0.1677	0.3220	0.1745	0.3160	0.2276	0.4920	0.2494	0.5260
BOW + BOC	0.1838 **	0.2495 **	0.2512	0.4360	0.2205	0.3960	0.3325	0.6280	0.2913	0.5320

Only 61 of the 85 concepts are correct. The overall precision is 71.8%. On the other hand, the queries contain 182 meaningful words (non stopwords). 161 of them appear in the identified concepts and 21 are left alone. However, only 125 of the 161 words are covered by correct concepts, leading to a coverage rate of 68.7%. This figure is consistent with the previous observation. The main concept mapping problems are as follows:

1. 14 concepts have been mapped to incorrect CUIs or to CUIs inconsistently with respect to documents (Table 3).
   - An expression may correspond to more than one CUI (e.g. "Myocardial infarction" may correspond to C2926063 or C0027051). MetaMap may select one for the query and another one for the document.
   - The surface form similarity used in MetaMap may lead to errors. For example, "C1963154 (Renal Failure Adverse Event)" is preferred to "C0035078 (Kidney Failure)" for the query "renal failure".
   - MetaMap may map a concept to a more specific one ("foramen ovale" to "cranial foramen ovale" or to "diac foramen ovale") or to a more general concept ("dobhoff tube" to "biomedical tube device").
2. 5 concept expressions in the queries are not recognized, or only partially recognized, by MetaMap (Table 4).
3. 5 errors are due to misspelling or unrecognized variations of words in queries, for example, repiratory (for respiratory), hemorrage (for hemorrhage).

Table 3. Examples of incorrect and inconsistent concept mapping

Query	CUI identified in query	CUI identified in rel. doc.
Myocardial infarction	C2926063 (Myocardial infarction: Finding: Point in time: Patient: Ordinal)	C0027051 (Myocardial Infarction)
renal failure	C1963154 (Renal Failure Adverse Event)	C0035078 (Kidney Failure)
Right upper lobe pneumonia with cavitary lesion	C0032285 (Pneumonia) and C0221198 (Lesion)	C0746131 (lung lesion cavitary)
aspiration pneumonia due to misplacement of dobhoff tube	C0175730 (biomedical tube device)	C3204189 (Dobhoff Tubes)
foramen ovale	C1110599 (cranial foramen ovale)	C1110599 (cranial foramen ovale) and C0016521 (diac foramen ovale)

Table 4. Examples of unrecognized or partially recognized concepts

Query	CUI identified in query	CUI identified in rel. doc.
Right upper lobe pneumonia with cavitary lesion	C0032285 (Pneumonia) and C0221198 (Lesion)	C0746131 (lung lesion cavitary)
advices for patient with acute infarctus myocardi	C0205178 (Acute)	C0155626 (Acute myo-cardial infarction)
Bilateral pulmonary contu-sions and safety belt	C0238767 (Bilateral) and C0347625 (Contusion of lung)	C2836276 (Contusion of lung, bilateral)

These problems of concept mapping indicate clearly that one cannot heavily rely on the recognized concepts for BIR, and a more flexible way to match concepts is required.

3.2 Concepts as Phrases

A more flexible method is to consider the expressions of the concepts identified in a query as phrases. At the retrieval step, the words in a phrase should preferably appear together or at proximity. In addition, Metathesaurus contains many synonym expressions of concepts. They can naturally be used to expand the original concept expressions of the query (using Indri's #syn operator). More formally, document score is determined as follows:

$$Score(D,Q) = w_1 Score_{BOW}(D,Q) + w_2 Score_{Phrase}(D,Q) + w_3 Score_{Prox}(D,Q) + w_4 Score_{Exp}(D,Q)$$

where $Score_{BOW}(D,Q)$, $Score_{Phrase}(D,Q)$, $Score_{Prox}(D,Q)$ and $Score_{Exp}(D,Q)$ are respectively the scores obtained using the BOW of the initial query, using the concept expressions and their synonyms as contiguous phrases, requiring these words of a concept expression to be at proximity within a text window, and using the BOW formed by all the concept expressions. Below, we give an example to illustrate the approach. Assume a query "Anoxic brain injury", which is identified as a concept by MetaMap. The concept has 9 different expressions in Metathesaurus. Each of these expressions is wrapped into a #1 operator for strict phrase matching, or a #uwN operator for flexible proximity matching, which requires the terms of a phrase to appear within N words. We set N to be the number of words in a phrase + 1 (which is found to work well). In addition to these phrase matches, we also use all the words in the concept expressions to form a new BOW. This leads to the following Indri query:

```
#combine(w1 #combine(anoxic brain damage)
    w2 #syn( #1(anoxic brain damage) #1(anoxic brain injury) #1(anoxic
    disorder dup encephalopathy) ... )
    w3 #syn( #uw4(anoxic brain damage) #uw4(anoxic brain injury)
    #uw5(anoxic disorder dup encephalopathy) ... )
    w4 #combine(anoxic brain damage   anoxic brain injury   anoxic
    disorder dup encephalopathy ... ) )
```

where w1, ..., w4 are weights which we set at 0.8, 0, 0.1, 0.1. This setting is trained on CLEF 2013 short queries. It does not produce the best results on all the collections, but the results are close to the best. We only show the results with this setting in Table 5. This method has been used in our participation [11] at ShARe/eHealth CLEF 2014 task 3a [4] and we obtained the best result.

We can observe that using concept expressions as phrases is a much better strategy than BOC. It is also interesting to see that the weight assigned to exact phrase matching is turned to 0. This suggests that the exact phrase match may be less useful when the other components are used. Indeed, we observed that many occurrences of concepts have slightly different forms (e.g. an adjective is inserted in the phrase). Such occurrences require a more flexible match.

In Table 5 we also include the results with MRF sequential model, which considers any two adjacent words as a phrase. The weights of the three components in MRF - the BOW model, the ordered phrase model and the unordered phrase model are set at 0.8, 0.1 and 0.1 as suggested in [8]. Compared with the method that uses identified concepts as phrases, we can see that MRF usually performs worse, except for P@10 on OHSUMED and CLEF 2014 short queries. This result confirms the usefulness of concept mapping.

Table 5. Results with concept as phrase and MRF (* and **, M and MM means statistical significance with respect to BOW and MRF, at p<0,05 and p<0.01)

Method	OHSUMED		CLEF13 short		CLEF13 long		CLEF14 short		CLEF14 long	
	MAP	P@10	MAP	P@10	MAP	P@10	MAP	P@10	MAP	P@10
Concept as phrase	0.1815 **	0.2267 **	0.2908 * M	0.4960 M	0.2838*	0.4700	0.4137 * MM	0.7580 *	0.4316 ** MM	0.7180 * M
MRF	0.1729 *	0.2297 **	0.2750	0.4680	0.2735	0.4560	0.3904	0.7620	0.4099	0.6760

4 Conclusions

In this paper, we compared several ways to incorporate concepts in BIR. Our experiments showed that concepts should not be used as rigid representation units, but as phrases, in BIR. The latter approach can significantly outperform the BOW method. In addition, we also showed that the MRF model that does not use concepts underperforms our method. Our results confirm the usefulness of concepts, even though they may contain errors. The key lies in the flexibility in concept matching.

References

1. Aronson, A.R.: Effective mapping of biomedical text to the UMLS Metathesaurus: the MetaMap program. In: Proc. of the AMIA Symposium, pp. 17–21 (2001)
2. Bodenreider, O.: The unified medical language system (UMLS): integrating biomedical terminology. Nucleic Acids Research 32(Suppl. 1), D267–D270 (2004)

3. Goeuriot, L., Jones, G., Kelly, L., Leveling, J., Hanbury, A., Müller, H., Salanterä, S., Suominen, H., Zuccon, G.: ShARe/CLEF eHealth Evaluation Lab 2013, Task 3: Information Retrieval to Address Patients' Questions when Reading Clinical Reports. In: Proc. of CLEF 2013 (2013)
4. Goeuriot, L., Kelly, L., Li, W., Palotti, J., Pecina, P., Zuccon, G., Hanbury, A., Jones, G., Müller, H.: ShARe/CLEF eHealth Evaluation Lab 2014, Task 3: User-centred health information retrieval. In: Proc. of CLEF 2014 (2014)
5. Hersh, W., Hickam, D., Leone, T.: Words, concepts, or both: optimal indexing units for automated information retrieval. In: Proc. of 16th Annual Symposium on Computer Applications in Medical Care, pp. 644–648 (1992)
6. Koopman, B., Zuccon, G., Nguyen, A., Vickers, D., Bruza, P.: Exploiting SNOMED CT concepts and relationships for clinical information retrieval: Australian e-Health Research Centre and Queensland University of Technology at the TREC 2012 Medical Track (2012)
7. Lipscomb, C.E.: Medical subject headings (MeSH). Bulletin of the Medical Library Association **88**(3), 265–266 (2000)
8. Metzler, D., Croft, W.B.: A Markov random field model for term dependencies. In: Proceedings of SIGIR, pp. 472–479 (2005)
9. Pratt, W., Yetisgen-Yildiz, M.: A study of biomedical concept identification: MetaMap vs. people. In: Proc. of AMIA Annual Symposium, pp. 529–533 (2003)
10. Qi, Y., Laquerre, P.-F.: Retrieving Medical Records with sennamed: NEC Labs America at TREC 2012 Medical Records Track (2012)
11. Shen, W., Nie, J.Y., Liu, X., Liu, X.: An investigation of the effectiveness of concept-based approach in medical information retrieval GRIUM@CLEF2014 eHealth Task 3. In: Proc. of the ShARe/CLEF eHealth Evaluation Lab (2014)
12. Spackman, K.A., Campbell, K.E., Côté, R.A.: SNOMED RT: a reference terminology for health care. In: Proc. AMIA Annual Fall Symp., pp. 640–644 (1997)
13. Zhu, D., Carterette, B.: Improving health records search using multiple query expansion collections. In: Proceedings of IEEE International Conference on Bioinformatics and Biomedicine (BIBM), pp. 1–7 (2012)

Using Health Statistics to Improve Medical and Health Search

Tawan Sierek[✉] and Allan Hanbury

Institute of Software Technology and Interactive Systems (ISIS),
Vienna University of Technology, Vienna, Austria
tawan@sierek.at, hanbury@ifs.tuwien.ac.at

Abstract. We present a probabilistic information retrieval (IR) model
that incorporates epidemiological data and simple patient profiles that
are composed of a patient's sex and age. This approach is intended to
improve retrieval effectiveness in the health and medical domain. We
evaluated our approach on the TREC Clinical Decision Support Track
2014. The new approach performed better than a baseline run, however
at this time, we cannot report any statistically significant improvements.

1 Introduction

Healthcare professionals often find additional information by consulting IR systems when treating a patient. But they face an ever growing amount of scientific literature, which makes it harder to find the relevant citations or articles for a given clinical case [4]. Laypeople now commonly seek information about health on their own, often starting at a web search engine [2]. Without a medical background, a layperson is vulnerable to unnecessary concerns about rare, serious diseases. This problem is referred to as Cyberchondria by White and Horvitz, who presented a log–based study on this subject [15]. We think that both user types, professionals and laypeople, would benefit if the ranking process considers disease frequencies as an additional relevance signal when assessing medical documents. Furthermore, health search can potentially be personalized. Independent of any symptoms, the probability of having a disease differs from person to person with regard to personal traits such as the age and sex of a person. The main contribution of this work is a probabilistic IR approach that incorporates data from epidemiological studies and patient profiles that are composed of the patient's sex and age. It is based on work presented in the master's thesis by Sierek [10]. Evaluation of the proposed approach is done on the TREC Clinical Decision Support Track 2014 [11].

2 Probabilistic Model for Personalized Health Search

This section introduces the Personalized Probabilistic Health Search (PPHS) model that we propose. The PPHS model is based on the work of Sontag et al. [13], who presented probabilistic models to personalize web search. The authors

© Springer International Publishing Switzerland 2015
J. Mothe et al. (Eds.): CLEF 2015, LNCS 9283, pp. 287–292, 2015.
DOI: 10.1007/978-3-319-24027-5_30

introduced a modular personalization framework that is able to integrate many different data sources. Sontag et al. also conducted a large scale evaluation of their framework which showed to increase retrieval effectiveness, especially for one word- and acronym queries. Since the model is indifferent to the data sources, as the authors suggest, we adapted it to the health domain. Our approach incorporates data from epidemiological studies and patient profiles which are composed of the patient's sex and age. We hypothesize that incorporating these two data sources leads to more accurate estimations of relevance probabilities if the following constraints hold:

1. Documents from the collection provide information about diseases or health disorders.
2. A document's prior relevance probability correlates positively with the incidence rate of the disease that it covers.
3. The search was initiated by a specific medical case. Therefore, a single patient of known age and sex is given.
4. Diseases have different incidence rates for persons of different age and sex.

Let the search be placed in a setting which satisfies these constraints. Then a single search use case can be described by a document collection $\mathcal{D}$, where each document $d \in \mathcal{D}$ provides information about medical conditions such as specific diseases and health disorders. The patient u has a medical condition C from a finite set of medical conditions $\mathcal{C}$. The patient is modeled with a patient profile θ_u which is composed of the age and the sex of the patient. The conditional probability distribution of medical conditions $C \in \mathcal{C}$ being present, is denoted as $\Pr(C \mid \theta_u)$. The probability that a document provides information about a condition is also modeled as a conditional distribution with $\Pr(C \mid d)$. A discrete random variable $\mathrm{rel}(d, q)_u \in \{0, 1\}$ takes on the value 1 if a document d is relevant to query q, and the value 0 otherwise. A scoring value which is obtained from a ranking process that does not incorporate health statistics is denoted with $\psi(d, q)$ (we use the same notation as Sontag et al., where it is sensible). We follow the Probability Ranking Principle [8] and rank documents according to this formula:

$$\Pr(\mathrm{rel}_u(d, q) = 1 \mid \theta_u, q, d, \psi(d, q)) = \psi(d, q) \sum_{C \in \mathcal{C}} \Pr(C \mid d) \Pr(C \mid \theta_u, q) \ .$$

$$(1)$$

We calculate the distribution $\Pr(C \mid \theta_u, q)$ by estimating $\Pr(C \mid \theta_u)$ and $\Pr(C \mid d)$ separately and applying Bayes' Rule:

$$\Pr(C \mid \theta_u, q) = \frac{\Pr(C \mid \theta_u) \Pr(q \mid C)}{\sum_{C' \in \mathcal{C}} \Pr(C' \mid \theta_u) \Pr(q \mid C')} \ . \tag{2}$$

We suggest to estimate the distribution $\Pr(C \mid \theta_u)$ based on disease frequencies which are inferred from epidemiological studies.

2.1   Epidemiological Measures of Occurrence

We considered three different epidemiological measures, namely (1) the incidence proportion, (2) the incidence rate and (3) the prevalence of a disease. The incidence proportion of a disease states how many new cases occurred in a specified period in relation to the size of the population at risk. The prevalence of a disease tells us how many cases of a disease were present at a specific point in time, without taking into account when the onset of the disease occurred. The incidence rate is the number of onsets of the disease, divided by the cumulative time of people being at risk [7,9].

We argue here that the incidence rate is the most suitable measure when estimating $\Pr(C \mid \theta_u)$. We employed Belkin's conceptual framework which describes a user's anomalous state of knowledge (ASK). An ASK initiates the search for information in order to resolve it. The onset of an ASK is triggered by observations of the world that the user cannot incorporate into the user's current state of knowledge [1]. In a clinical scenario, we assume that the recent onset of a disease is the reason for the user's ASK. The onset's recency is essential, therefore we rule out the prevalence measure, since it does not reflect the onset of diseases. In contrast, the incidence proportion explicitly considers only new cases but the length of the period in question is arbitrary. The incidence rate, on the other hand, allows us to specify a time frame t, into which we assume that the onset of the disease of the patient falls.

2.2   Estimating Probability Distributions

Let $\kappa(C, \theta_u)$ denote the incidence rate of a disease for a given patient profile, then $t\kappa(C, \theta_u)$ provides the number of new cases in the subpopulation, described by θ_u, for any given time frame t. Under the premise that the patient has developed a medical condition for sure, and therefore $\Pr(C) = 1$, we can show that:

$$\widehat{\Pr}(C \mid \theta_u) = \frac{t\kappa(C, \theta)}{\sum\limits_{C' \in \mathcal{C}} t\kappa(C', \theta)} . \tag{3}$$

The time frame t can be canceled out and therefore becomes obsolete.

In order to estimate $\Pr(C \mid d)$, we train a text classifier with medical documents that have been annotated manually. We denote the classifier as $\phi(C, d)$ in the PPHS model. Equation 2 also depends on the distribution $\Pr(q \mid C)$. Sontag et al. suggest a language model approach in the general case. We suggest to use the same text classifier ϕ to facilitate practical applications in a first step. We can replace the probability distributions with these estimators and calculate the patient dependent relevance of a document as:

$$\Pr(\mathrm{rel}_u(d, q) = 1 \mid \theta_u, q, d, \psi(d, q)) = \psi(d, q) \sum_{C \in \mathcal{C}} \phi(C, d) \frac{\kappa(C, \theta_u) \phi(C, q)}{\sum\limits_{C' \in \mathcal{C}} \kappa(C', \theta_u) \phi(C', q)} .$$

$$\tag{4}$$

3   Evaluation

We developed a reference implementation of the PPHS model and evaluated it on the TREC Clinical Decision Support Track 2014. This track's goal is to advance the development of tools that retrieve relevant information for medical cases. The users of such systems would be physicians in need of information when presented with a medical case narrative.

A baseline run was conducted with the Apache Solr 4.10.2 open source search engine[1]. The configuration for the baseline run was the default scoring method of Apache Solr, which is a VSM with TFIDF weighting. In order to evaluate the PPHS model we re–ranked the top 150 results of the result produced with the baseline configuration. Our experimental setup controls for all constraints mentioned in Section 2 except for the assumption that a document's prior probability correlates with the incidence rate of the disease that it covers.

3.1   Experimental Setup

We briefly present how we implemented the PPHS model and conducted the runs on the evaluation track. The document collection is indexed by a Solr instance. HTML tags, XML tags and stop words are removed. Tokens are normalized to lower case and possessives are removed as well. We also employed the Porter stemming algorithm. This Solr instance was used to produce the baseline run, and it also provided the scores which are referred to with $\psi(d, q)$.

Incidence Rate Estimation $\kappa(C, \theta_u)$. In order to estimate incidence rates of diseases, we processed the data from the National Hospital Discharge Survey (NHDS) from 2007 [6]. One sample record includes, among many other attributes, the age, the sex and up to eight diagnoses encoded in ICD–9–CM. We imported the records into a relational database. The NHDS data set allows only to estimate a hospitalization rate. But we regarded each primary diagnosis of a discharge as an incidence (onset) of the diagnosed disease. We exported from the relational database the data in a CSV file format, which was further processed by an R script. The R script performed a nonparametric regression with local polynomials. We used the locfit function with its default parameters from the package with the same name [3,5].

Text Classifier $\phi(C, d)$. To train the text classifier, which we refer to as $\phi(C, d)$ in the PPHS model, we obtained the Wikipedia pages that list ICD–9–CM codes for links to articles that cover the corresponding concepts. These pages were merged to build "ICD–9–CM documents" for the ICD–9–CM codes at the three digits hierarchy level. These documents were indexed by another Solr instance. In order to classifiy a piece of text into a ICD–9–CM three digit code, the text is sent this Solr instance as a query. The "ICD–9–CM documents" are scored, again with the default scoring method of Solr, and these scores serve

---

[1] http://lucene.apache.org/solr/

as a confidence estimation on how likely this piece of text is affiliated with the disease class of the corresponding ICD–9–CM code. This approach was inspired by the work of Trieschnigg et al. who studied classifiers that annotate documents with MeSH concepts [14].

Re–ranking. The test query is processed by the Solr instance that also produces the baseline results. The document titles of each result of the top 150 are classified by the ICD–9–CM classifier, as well as the query itself. The incidence rate estimations have been calculated in an off–line step for patient profiles which have been extracted manually from the track's topic descriptions. The text classifier results and the incidence rate estimates are combined according to the PPHS model. This score is added to the baseline score and the top 150 results are re–ranked accordingly.

3.2 Results

We conducted a baseline run and five runs with variations of the PPHS model. The variations include a non–personalized approach, which we refer to as Probabilistic Health Search (PHS). This approach estimates incidence rates without taking a patient profile into account. Furthermore, we conducted a run which does not incorporate the sex of a patient, a Probabilistic Age–specific Health Search (PAHS) model. We also conducted a run that uses a model that is only sex–specific, without age information (PSHS). Finally, we conducted a control run, which is identical to the run with the complete PPHS model, but the incidence rates of all diseases are set to 1.

Table 1. The results in bold indicate the best result with regard to a single measure.

Measure	Baseline	PHS	PPHS	PSHS	PAHS	Control
MAP	0.1208	**0.1222**	0.1221	0.1221	**0.1222**	0.1215
NDCG@5	0.3188	**0.3308**	0.3286	**0.3308**	0.3286	0.321
NDCG@10	0.2732	**0.2885**	0.2863	**0.2885**	0.2864	0.2836
P@5	0.3667	**0.3733**	0.3667	**0.3733**	0.3667	0.3667
P@10	0.3033	**0.3167**	0.3133	**0.3167**	0.3133	**0.3167**

4 Discussion and Future Work

All probabilistic models performed better than the baseline. However, the absolute improvements are minimal with regard to every measure. The non–personalized run performed well in comparison to all measures. The control run performed worse with regard to all measures except P@10. But it is interesting that it still produced better results than baseline. For this reason, the text classification step appears to have a positive influence. We performed a statistical test for significance. Unfortunately, after performing a randomized test, as suggested by Smucker et al. [12], we cannot report any statistically significant improvements with the present results.

Our implementation maps documents to ICD–9–CM codes automatically, but relies only on Wikipedia articles serving as the ground truth. Due to this sparseness of training data, we cannot evaluate this crucial step and, therefore, our results are biased. We suggest conducting further research based on our formal model, but with test collections of manually annotated documents.

References

1. Belkin, N.: Anomalous states of knowledge as a basis for information retrieval. Canadian Journal of Information Science (5), 133–143 (1980)
2. Fox, S., Duggan, M.: Health online 2013. Health (2013)
3. Hens, N., Shkedy, Z., Aerts, M., Faes, C., Damme, P.V., Beutels, P.: Modeling Infectious Disease Parameters Based on Serological and Social Contact Data: A Modern Statistical Perspective. Springer Science & Business Media, October 2012
4. Hersh, W.: Information Retrieval: A Health and Biomedical Perspective, 2009 edn. Springer, New York (2010) (softcover reprint of hardcover, 3rd edn.)
5. Loader, C.: Local regression and likelihood, vol. 47. Springer, New York (1999)
6. National Center for Health Statistics. National Hospital Discharge Survey (2007). Public-use data file and documentation: ftp://ftp.cdc.gov/pub/Health_Statistics/NCHS/Datasets/NHDS/
7. Porta, M.S., Greenland, S., Hernán, M., Silva, I.D.S., Last, J.M.: A Dictionary of Epidemiology. Oxford University Press (2014)
8. Robertson, S.E.: The probability ranking principle in IR. Journal of Documentation 33(4), 294–304 (1977)
9. Rothman, K.J., Greenland, S., Lash, T.L.: Modern Epidemiology. Lippincott Williams & Wilkins (2008)
10. Sierek, T.: Using Health Statistics to Improve Medical and Health Search. Master's Thesis, Vienna University of Technology, Vienna, Austria (2015)
11. Simpson, M.S., Voorhees, E., Hersh, W.: Overview of the trec 2014 clinical decision support track. In: Proc. 23rd Text Retrieval Conference (TREC 2014). National Institute of Standards and Technology (NIST) (2014)
12. Smucker, M.D., Allan, J., Carterette, B.: A comparison of statistical significance tests for information retrieval evaluation. In: Proceedings of the Sixteenth ACM Conference on Conference on Information and Knowledge Management, pp. 623–632. ACM (2007)
13. Sontag, D., Collins-Thompson, K., Bennett, P.N., White, R.W., Dumais, S., Billerbeck, B.: Probabilistic models for personalizing web search. In: Proceedings of the Fifth ACM International Conference on Web Search and Data Mining, WSDM 2012, pp. 433–442. ACM, New York (2012)
14. Trieschnigg, D., Pezik, P., Lee, V., de Jong, F., Kraaij, W., Rebholz-Schuhmann, D.: MeSH Up: effective MeSH text classification for improved document retrieval. Bioinformatics 25(11), 1412–1418 (2009)
15. White, R.W., Horvitz, E.: Cyberchondria: Studies of the escalation of medical concerns in web search. ACM Trans. Inf. Syst. 27(4), 23:1–23:37 (2009)

Determining Window Size from Plagiarism Corpus for Stylometric Features

Šimon Suchomel[(✉)] and Michal Brandejs

Faculty of Informatics, Masaryk University, Brno, Czech Republic
{suchomel,brandejs}@fi.muni.cz

Abstract. The sliding window concept is a common method for computing a profile of a document with unknown structure. This paper outlines an experiment with stylometric word-based feature in order to determine an optimal size of the sliding window. It was conducted for a vocabulary richness method called 'average word frequency class' using the PAN 2015 source retrieval training corpus for plagiarism detection. The paper shows the pros and cons of the stop words removal for the sliding window document profiling and discusses the utilization of the selected feature for intrinsic plagiarism detection. The experiment resulted in the recommendation of setting the sliding windows to around 100 words in length for computing the text profile using the average word frequency class stylometric feature.

1 Problem Statement

In automated plagiarism detection, the task for the computer system is to highlight potentially plagiarized passages from input suspicious documents and ideally, to match the highlighted passage with the original document from a set of all documents. This style of detection is referred as external plagiarism and one needs a reference corpus of source documents in order to match the suspicious document with the original document [1].

If no reference corpus is available, the task shifts into the detection of anomalies inside the text itself. This is called intrinsic plagiarism detection [9], which in this case can be viewed as a one-class classification problem [2]. The text portion is either classified as written by the same author or classified as not written by the same author and therefore, suspicious. In this concept the task is closely related to the author identification problem [8].

It is generally believed that each writer has a specific writing style and if a text contains copied passages, they would probably deviate from the writing style of the putative author. The various methods used for this task try to detect changes in the writing style of the text being analyzed and are called stylometric features [6]. Such features are based on statistical likelihood estimation, therefore, the more statistical data they compute with, the more precision they can achieve. This means that generally the longer the analyzed text is the better the feature distinguishes between text characteristics. However, in plagiarism detection there is often a need for detection of relatively short passages, which is a hard problem to achieve without a reference corpus for text comparison.

© Springer International Publishing Switzerland 2015
J. Mothe et al. (Eds.): CLEF 2015, LNCS 9283, pp. 293–299, 2015.
DOI: 10.1007/978-3-319-24027-5_31

In general document analysis there is usually no prior information about the position and the length of which different passage should be detected, which comprises the most challenging part of the plagiarized passage detection. This problem is usually addressed by the moving or shifting window computation concept.

The most widespread method is to compute the feature for the whole document as a reference value. Thereafter, the feature is computed for the portion of the document defined by the window size and compared with the reference value. If the current window-size feature differs significantly from the reference value, that part is said to be suspicious according to the feature description. However, this method has several difficulties. The moving windows should ideally, precisely overlap with the plagiarized passage in order to produce unbiased characteristics of that passage. Any misalignment in this manner produces more biased results towards the surrounding text.

The right setting of the moving window size and position is important for the stylometric feature to produce accurate results. While moving the window through the document, the adjacent windows can be overlapping in order to minimize the probability of a misplaced window. Small shifting intervals ensure that the beginning of some windows will be close enough to the beginning of the plagiarized passage. The maximum deviation from the optimal placement is half of the window shifting interval.

Moreover, the size of the window is more important and more difficult to set. In order to compute some text features, a sufficient amount of statistical data is needed, therefore a bigger window size might seem advantageous. On the other hand, if the plagiarized text is shorter than the window size, the calculated feature from that part would be distorted by the redundant text contained in that window .Various window sizes can be used, it may depend on many variables such as stylometric features used, input data type, or purpose of analysis. Examples can be less than 200 words [3,12], 250 words [10], 500 words [2], 1000 characters [7].

Window feature comparison against the reference value from the whole document assumes that the reference value describes the whole document correctly, and relatively small textual anomalies inside the document could be detected. However, if the document contains lot of plagiarism the reference value is too affected of it and the feature would then describe a mashup created from plagiarism and from the original text of the alleged writer. In such cases the values obtained from moving window should be compared only to each other, while the character of the document is determined by changes among those values.

For our experiment we have chosen a lexical word-based feature called 'Average Word Frequency Class' (AWFC), which is a statistical vocabulary richness method [3]. This method is supposed to be accurate for short text passages and is also said to be consistent with the length of passages, which makes it suitable for plagiarism detection. We wanted to extrapolate an optimal window size for the AWFC. The experiment was conducted on training corpus for PAN competition on a plagiarism detection [4] for source retrieval subtask. Another contribution is to analyse whether this feature is suitable for intrinsic plagiarism detection within the PAN source retrieval corpus.

The PAN 2015 source retrieval corpus is a set of intentionally plagiarized documents by semiprofessional writers [5]. The task of source retrieval is part of the automated plagiarism detection process [11], which is conducted before actual textual similarities computation within the reference corpus of all known documents. If a plagiarized passage can be detected in this stage, it could be used as a template for search engine queries for original document retrieval.

2   Methodology

The PAN source retrieval corpus contained 98 plagiarized documents written manually on a random topic and each document followed only one theme. The corpus were based on texts retrieved from ClueWeb[1] corpus by querying a search engine for topic related documents. The size of the plaintexts were 30 KB on average and each document contained around five thousand words on average. The plagiarism in the corpus was wide spread, which results in understanding this corpus as a simulation of highly plagiarized seminar papers or similar types of documents.

The plagiarism cases were annotated with the assigned *id* of the case and also with some metadata, such as the URL of the original document. Each case, according to its *id*, referred to one source, therefore, the assumption is that texts from one source should hold a common textual feature.

From each document in the corpus all passages under a given *id* were extracted and concatenated. Resulting texts from all plagiarism cases in each document formed a base for calculations of a feature result.

The AWFC feature is defined as follows [3]: Let C be a reference text corpus, and let $f(w)$ be the frequency of a word w in that corpus. The class of each word w in the suspicious document is defined as:

$$c(w) = \lfloor log_2 \frac{f(w^*)}{f(w)} \rfloor, \ w \in C \ , \tag{1}$$

where w^* denotes the most frequent word in C. Finally, the averaged word frequency class for a text passage (chunk) u is calculated as an averaged value of classes $c(w)$ of all words $w \in u$:

$$\text{AWFC}(u) = \frac{\sum\limits_{i=1}^{|u|} c(w_i)}{|u|} \ . \tag{2}$$

For all based texts the referencing AWFC were also calculated. Each text was subsequently divided into smaller chunks, simulating the length of the resulting text window. All smaller chunks were of the same size and not overlapping over

---

[1] http://lemurproject.org/clueweb09.php

the based text in order not to average the feature among the chunks. A resulting length for each plagiarism case was calculated as follows: Divide based text into the chunks $u \in U$ of length n in words. Find the minimal windows size n for which chunks u_i and u_j have the same AWFC value for all i and j:

$$\forall i, j : \text{AWFC}(u_i) = \text{AWFC}(u_j), \ |U| > 1 \ . \tag{3}$$

The division process was considered successful, if all the chunks AWFC values were equal to the referencing AWFC, so the feature held for the whole passage and for all the windows of size n within the passage. The experiment was carried out for both the texts with removed stop words and for the unchanged texts.

3 Analysis and Results

Table 1 shows plagiarism cases and their portion of success and failure. Only cases for which the extracted text was at least 20 words long were considered. Unsuccessful cases were those for which no n complying with (3) was found. Cases labelled inconsistent didn't comply with the reference AWFC value, despite their successful division and meeting the (3) requirements.

Figure 1 depicts resulting chunk sizes of successful cases. The x axis shows $|U|$, which is the number of chunks into which the text was divided. The resulting chunk lengths for stop words clean texts depicted in the left plot of Fig. 1 were lower, which results in the fact that AWFC converges faster for vocabulary richer texts. However, the stop words removal significantly reduces the size of an original text passage. In terms of word count, for the PAN corpus, it was a reduction of 69% from the original size.

The final recommended window size was calculated as a weighted arithmetic mean from chunk sizes of successful cases. The higher weight was assigned to

Table 1. Plagiarism cases.

plagiarism cases	unchanged text	without stop words
in total	1263	1101
successful	75.3%	77.3%
unsuccessful	13.9%	13.5%
inconsistent	10.8%	9.2%

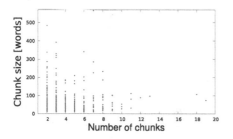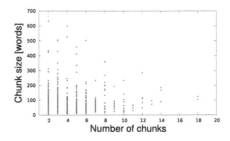

Fig. 1. Sizes of chunks, left with removed stop words.

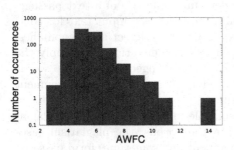

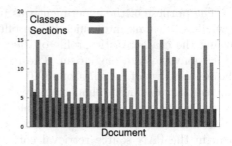

Fig. 2. Occurrences of classes.

Fig. 3. Number of different plagiarism sections vs. number of different classes.

sizes which stem from higher chunk count of divided text. For example, one of the most statistical data, which Fig. 1 shows in the right plot, contains the two cases, which based texts were successfully divided into 18 chunks of length 105 and 125 words, while complying with (3). Let X be the sorted sequence in descending order of defined chunk sizes ($|U_j|$). The average size $\bar{n}$ of all chunks of all successful cases were calculated as:

$$\bar{n} = \frac{\sum_{i=1}^{n} n_i w_i^2}{\sum_{i=1}^{n} w_i^2}, \quad w \in (0,1\rangle, \quad w = (1 - \frac{X.\mathrm{index}(|U_j|)}{|X|}) \tag{4}$$

For the original text, the average size was **101.67**, for the stop words clean text it was **62.28** words, which makes a window size decrease of 39%.

In terms of average word frequency class, the most frequent of successful classifications for unchanged text was in class 5, with 40% of all occurrences, and for stop words clean text in class 7, occupying 30% of all classifications. Figure 2 shows class distribution of the unchanged texts, please note that the scale of the y axis is logarithmic, thus showing a single occurrence of classes 11 and 14. Figure 3 shows only 30 selected documents from the input corpus with the highest diversity of occurred classes. The number of different classes is compared with the number of different plagiarism cases in each document. Due to the fact that AWFC has a relatively sparse classification domain, it hardly distinguishes among all plagiarism cases in largely plagiarized documents.

4   Conclusion

This paper presented an experiment with a stylometric statistical vocabulary richness method called 'Average Word Frequency Class' (AWFC) conducted on PAN source retrieval training corpus for plagiarism detection, with both the stop words removed and not removed texts. The benefit of the corpus is that the documents were written manually and not automatically generated, thus creating quality testing environment.

The purpose of the experiment was to determine the size of a text passage, a window, a chunk into which it is profitable to divide the input text for computing the characteristic profile of the text in order to detect style anomalies, which may indicate plagiarism. The resulting recommendation is to apply the sliding windows of length around 100 words, on unchanged text. If stop words are removed, one needs chunks nearly twice as long[2] than the original document for the method to produce comparable results.

However, the AWFC seems not to be suitable for detecting intrinsic plagiarism in the PAN source retrieval corpus. In the corpus, the plagiarism cases are usually distributed across the whole document and sometimes form passages shorter than 100 words. The number of plagiarism cases outnumbers the number of different classes into which a text is classified. On the other hand, if a class change between two neighbouring plagiarized passages is detected the intrinsic plagiarism detection is successful, and so there is no need for the classification method to have a different class for each plagiarism case inside one document. The main purpose of the AWFC is to detect a change of writing style in an otherwise consistent text, for example, to distinguish a brilliant passage that has been copied, in otherwise average seminar work. The performance of the method on the PAN corpus is a matter of future work.

References

1. Kasprzak, J., Brandejs, M., Křipač, M.: Finding Plagiarism by Evaluating Document Similarities. In: Hersh, B., Callan, J., Maarek, Y., Sanderson, M. (eds.) SEPLN 2009 Workshop on Uncovering Plagiarism, Authorship and Social Software Misuse, pp. 24–28. CEUR Workshop Proceedings, August 2009
2. Koppel, M., Schler, J.: Authorship Verification as a One-class Classification Problem. In: Proceedings of the Twenty-First International Conference on Machine Learning (ICML 2004), Banff, Alberta, Canada, July 4–8 (2004)
3. Meyer zu Eissen, S., Stein, B., Kulig, M.: Plagiarism Detection Without Reference Collections. In: Advances in Data Analysis, Proceedings of the 30th Annual Conference of the Gesellschaft für Klassifikation e.V., Freie Universität Berlin, pp. 359–366 (2006)
4. Potthast, M., Hagen, M., Beyer, A., Busse, M., Tippmann, M., Rosso, P., Stein, B.: Overview of the 6th International Competition on Plagiarism Detection. In: Working Notes for CLEF 2014 Conference, Sheffield, UK, September 15–18, pp. 845–876 (2014)
5. Potthast, M., Hagen, M., Völske, M., Stein, B.: Crowdsourcing Interaction Logs to Understand Text Reuse from the Web. In: ACL (1), pp. 1212–1221. The Association for Computer Linguistics (2013)
6. Stamatatos, E.: A Survey of Modern Authorship Attribution Methods. Journal of the American Society for Information Science and Technology 60(3), 538–556 (2009)

---

[2] By stop words removal, the original text's word count is reduced to 31%, but the resulting windows size of stop words clean experiment were reduced to 61% of the unchanged text window size.

7. Stamatatos, E.: Intrinsic Plagiarism Detection Using Character n-gram Profiles. In: Proceedings of the SEPLN 2009 Workshop on Uncovering Plagiarism, Authorship and Social Software Misuse, pp. 38–46 (2009)
8. Stamatatos, E., Daelemans, W., Verhoeven, B., Stein, B., Potthast, M., Juola, P., Sánchez-Pérez, M.A., Barrón-Cedeño, A.: Overview of the Author Identification Task at PAN 2014. In: Working Notes for CLEF 2014 Conference, Sheffield, UK, September 15–18, pp. 877–897 (2014)
9. Stein, B., Lipka, N., Prettenhofer, P.: Intrinsic Plagiarism Analysis. Language Resources and Evaluation 45(1), 63–82 (2011)
10. Stein, B., Meyer zu Eissen, S.: Intrinsic Plagiarism Analysis with Meta Learning. In: Proceedings of the SIGIR 2007 International Workshop on Plagiarism Analysis, Authorship Identification, and Near-Duplicate Detection, Amsterdam, Netherlands, July 27 (2007)
11. Suchomel, Š., Brandejs, M.: Approaches for Candidate Document Retrieval. In: 2014 5th International Conference on Information and Communication Systems (ICICS), pp. 1–6. IEEE, Irbid (2014)
12. Suchomel, Š., Kasprzak, J., Brandejs, M.: Three Way Search Engine Queries with Multi-feature Document Comparison for Plagiarism Detection. In: CLEF 2012 Evaluation Labs and Workshop, Online Working Notes, Rome, Italy (2012)

Effect of Log-Based Query Term Expansion on Retrieval Effectiveness in Patent Searching

Wolfgang Tannebaum[1(✉)], Parvaz Mahdabi[2], and Andreas Rauber[1]

[1] Institute of Software Technology and Interactive Systems,
Vienna University of Technology, Vienna, Austria
{tannebaum,rauber}@ifs.tuwien.ac.at
[2] Idiap Research Institute, Martigny, Switzerland
parvaz.mahdabi@idiap.ch

Abstract. In this paper we study the impact of query term expansion (*QTE*) using synonyms on patent document retrieval. We use an automatically generated lexical database from USPTO query logs, called *PatNet*, which provides synonyms and equivalents for a query term. Our experiments on the CLEF-IP 2010 benchmark dataset show that automatic query expansion using *PatNet* tends to decrease or only slightly improve the retrieval effectiveness, with no significant improvement. An analysis of the retrieval results shows that *PatNet* does not have generally a negative effect on the retrieval effectiveness. Recall is drastically improved for query topics, where the baseline queries achieve, on average, only low recall values. But we have not detected any commonality that allows us to characterize these queries. So we recommend using *PatNet* for semi-automatic *QTE* in Boolean retrieval, where expanding query terms with synonyms and equivalents with the aim of expanding the query scope is a common practice.

Keywords: Patent searching · Query term expansion · Query log analysis

1 Introduction

Patent search is the task of finding relevant patent information in patent databases to judge the validity of an applied or granted patent based on novelty and inventiveness. This task is usually performed by examiners in a patent office and patent searchers in private companies. For searching the patent databases the patent searchers commonly formulate complex Boolean queries, which are easy for patent experts to manipulate and which provide a record of what documents were searched. Query terms are expanded with synonyms or equivalents, co-occurring terms and keyword phrases [1,2]. Especially the expansion of the query terms with synonyms is particularly common in Boolean patent retrieval, as shown in [7]. In this paper, we want to measure the effect of query expansion using synonyms on retrieval effectiveness in patent searching, in particular when used in a fully automatic manner. We use the lexical database *PatNet* automatically generated from USPTO query logs, which provides synonyms and equivalents for a query term [8].

© Springer International Publishing Switzerland 2015
J. Mothe et al. (Eds.): CLEF 2015, LNCS 9283, pp. 300–305, 2015.
DOI: 10.1007/978-3-319-24027-5_32

2   Related Work

Currently, fully automatic query expansion in patent search is mostly based on computing co-occurring terms in a patent corpus [1,4]. Additional query terms are extracted automatically from the query documents, the feedback documents or from the
cited documents, for example based on statistical measures, such as term frequencies
(tf) and a combination of term frequencies and inverted document frequencies (tfidf)
[4,10]. Also, whole documents or whole sections of the query documents are used for
query generation and query expansion [9]. One approach, which uses synonyms for
automatic query expansion in the patent domain is described in [4]. The standard
dictionary *WordNet* and a lexical database extracted from a European Patent Office
(*EPO*) patent collection, called *SynSet*, was used to improve the retrieval effectiveness. Experiments show better retrieval precision over the baseline queries, but not for
recall. So for recall-oriented patent searching, this result is negative. Contrary to the
usage of synonyms from standard dictionaries and extracted from patent documents,
as indicated in [4], we propose to use query logs as presented in [6] and in particular
query logs of patent examiners as suggested in [7,8] for automatic query expansion.
This allows us to use specific terms for query expansion, in particular the query and
expansion terms to the patent applications used by the patent examiners for searching.

3   Experiments

For our experiments, we use the data set of the CLEF-IP initiative[1], namely the
CLEF-IP 2010 data set. To evaluate the performance of IR approaches we use the test
set of the CLEF-IP data set, which is based on 1,348 English patent topics, and the
metrics Precision, Recall, Average Precision (AP) and Mean Average Precision
(MAP). In addition, we use the Patent Retrieval Evaluation Score (PRES), which
combines recall and the user's search effort in one single score [3].

3.1   Baseline Runs

The first query model (*QS-BL*) estimates the importance of each term according to a
weighted log-likelihood based approach comparing the foreground (query patent) and
background (collection) language models. Terms with high similarity to the foreground language model and low similarity to the background language model are
used as query terms representing the specific terminology of the query patent. Top k
terms with higher weights are selected as query terms from this query model. All
fields of the query patents are considered in the query estimation process and k is
experimentally set to 100. Initial query *QS-BL* is expanded using the information
available in the citations of the query patent. Two different weighting algorithms are
used for calculating query weights while taking into account the citation information.
The first approach (*QS-PR*) uses PageRank scores to identify influential documents in
the citation graph of a query patent and then uses those documents for drawing expan-

---

[1] http://ifs.tuwien.ac.at/ clef-ip/

sion terms. The second approach (*QS-TPR*) uses a time-aware decay function to give importance to newer documents in the citation graph and penalize older documents. Further explanations on baseline queries can be found in [5]. We also combined all the query lists above and we refer to this combined list as (*QS-MQL*). Table 1 shows the evaluation results using the CLEF-IP 2010 corpora in terms of MAP, Recall, and PRES at cut-off value of 1000.

Table 1. Retrieval Results of the baseline runs.

| Query | MAP | | Recall | | PRES | |
Model	value	change	value	change	value	change
QS-BL	0.1368	NA	**0.6215**	NA	**0.5067**	NA
QS-PR	**0.1392**	+1.7%	0.6302	+1.4%	0.5121	+2.1%
QS-TPR	0.1391	+1.7%	0.6305	+1.4%	0.5123	+1.1%
QS-MQL	**0.0815**	-40%	**0.6761**	+8.8%	**0.5484**	+8.2%

The results show that the expanded query sets obtain better performance compared to the baseline query set in view of recall and PRES. Further, the citation query model, which is based on citation information together with the publication dates, and the citation query model using Page Rank scores achieve similar performance in view of recall and PRES. Compared to the previous approaches tested on CLEF-IP 2010, the runs can be considered as the second best methods in terms of recall and PRES.[2]

3.2   Using *PatNet* for Query Term Expansion

We use *PatNet* to expand the query and expansion terms of the baseline query sets with synonymous expansion terms (*ET*). We use the most likely *ETs*, which are commonly used by patent examiners of the USPTO for *QTE*. For each expansion we use the highest ranked, in particular the most frequent, *ET* provided by *PatNet* for a query and expansion term. Specifically, we replace the terms in the baseline query sets with synonyms for which *PatNet* suggests *ETs*. So we generate four additional query sets for the query topics. Table 2 shows the evaluation results in terms of MAP, Recall, and PRES at cut-off value of 1000 when using *PatNet* for *QTE*.

Table 2. Retrieval Results of the expanded query sets.

| Query | MAP | | Recall | | PRES | |
Model	value	change	value	change	value	change
QS-BLE	0.0848	-38%	0.4983	-19%	0.3835	-24%
QS-PRE	**0.1390**	-0.1%	**0.6307**	+0.1%	**0.5123**	+0.1%
QS-TPRE	**0.0066**	-95%	**0.1871**	-70%	**0.1238**	-76%
QS-MQLE	0.0132	-84%	0.2033	-70%	0.1478	-73%

[2] http://www.ifs.tuwien.ac.at/clef-ip/pubs/CLEF-IP-2010-IRF-TR-2010-00003.pdf

The results show that, when querying *QS-BL* in combination with *QS-BLE*, the retrieval performance drastically decreases. In particular, recall goes down (-19%) from 62% to 50%. Further, PRES decreases by 24% from 51% to 38% and MAP decreases from 14% to 8% (-38%). Further, recall and precision can be slightly improved, while precision decreases slightly (-0.1%), when using *PatNet* with *QS-PR*. In combination with the second and third expansion approach the retrieval performance drastically decreases.

4   Analysis of the Retrieval Results

The experiments show that there was no significant improvement in the retrieval effectiveness, when using *PatNet* for fully-automatic *QTE*. We now analyze the results per topic (1348 topics) to validate whether there are certain characteristics that indicate when the approach comes in useful. Table 3 shows the percentage of topics for which the retrieval performance is improved, remains unchanged, or is degraded.

Table 3. Improved, unchanged, and degraded query topics.

QS-BLE	Recall	MAP	PRES
improved	**13.96%**	23.46%	24.20%
unchanged	36.90%	**2.52%**	**2.52%**
degraded	**49.15%**	**74.02%**	**73.27%**

Table 3 shows that expanding *QS-BL* with synonyms results in improving the recall of 14% of query topics. For about 49% of the topics recall decreases. As expected through the expansion of the query scope, precision decreases for large number of topics (74%). A lot of additional non-relevant documents are retrieved. But Table 4 shows that recall can be significantly improved (+34%) for query topics, which achieve, on average, only low recall (44%). Otherwise, recall drastically degrades (from 64% to 35%) when queries, which still provide good recall measures, are expanded with *PatNet* (initially retrieved relevant documents are lost from the rank list). To see if the differences were statistically relevant, we run a *t*-test (p=0.05).

Table 4. Recall achieved for improved, unchanged and degraded query topics.

Recall	QS-BL	QS-PR	QS-TPR	QS-BLE
Avg.	0.6215	0.6302	0.6305	0.4983
improved	**0.4407**	**0.5263**	**0.5298**	**0.5911**
unchanged	0.6635	**0.6726**	**0.6724**	0.6635
degraded	**0.6411**	0.6289	0.6285	**0.3478**

Further, *PatNet* significantly outperform the related expansion approaches *QS-PR* and *QS-TPR,* which achieve for these query topics compared to their avg. recall performance and values achieved for the unchanged and degraded query topics, on average, only moderate recall. The retrieval performance of these query topics are apparently difficult to improve with the related expansion approaches.

To characterize for which queries the expansion performs better, we now try to detect commonalities. At first, we consider the patent classifications of the query topics and the cited documents, and the classes *PatNet* was extracted from. We measure the overlap of the classes based on the queries for which the retrieval performance is improved, remains unchanged, or is degraded. The analysis shows for the query topics as well as for the citations that in each case (for improved, unchanged or degraded topics) about half of the query patents and citations are classified in the same classes as *PatNet* was extract from. So the patent classification is no criterion to detect queries for which the expansion performs better. Next, we evaluate whether the performance of the lexical database depends on the number of provided *ETs (n)*, the query topic length *(l)* or on the number of retrieved relevant documents *(c)*.

Table 5. Query topic, query and citation characteristics.

QS-BL		Avg.	Max.	Min.
	n	51	74	28
improved	l	14,959	133,762	1,280
	c	13	76	0
	n	56	75	26
unchanged	l	11,174	110,506	1,513
	c	11	57	0
	n	56	77	19
degraded	l	12,370	102,371	1,509
	c	16	85	1

Table 5 shows that the performance of *PatNet* is independent from the number of provided *ETs* and from the query topic length. We consider the number of character strings of each query patent. For improved, unchanged or degraded query topics virtually the same number of *ETs* are used for query expansion. Further, query topics have, on average, virtually equivalent topic lengths showing that *PatNet* can be used both for shorter topics and for longer query topics. Also the number of retrieved relevant documents is no criterion to detect when *PatNet* comes in useful. Table 6 shows the rank positions of the relevant documents provided by the baseline query set to detect whether it is an issue of being too generic or not found via the given query terms. The latter would argue for extending the query scope using synonyms.

Table 6. Rank positions of the retrieved relevant documents provided by *QS-BL*.

QS-BL	1 - 250	251 - 500	501 - 750	751 - 1000
improved	65%	16%	11%	8%
unchanged	79%	12%	6%	3%
degraded	63%	18%	11%	8%

As shown more than two-thirds of the retrieved relevant documents appear in the rank lists among the top 250 documents. Less than 8% appear in the last 250 documents. These distributions of the documents speaks for extending the query scope using synonyms. But the experiments indicate just the opposite. Finally, we consider the patent conventions and countries the relevant documents have been filed to detect, whether it is an issue that *PatNet* was extracted only from US patents. In each case about half of the relevant documents are *EP* or *WO* patents and about one third of the topics are US patents. There is no increase of US patents for improved query topics.

5   Conclusions and Future Work

In this paper we used the lexical database *PatNet* for automatic *QTE* in patent searching. The experiments show that the retrieval performance of the query generation and expansion models presented in this work is decreased or only marginally improved, when using *PatNet* for *QTE*. No significant improvement is recognized. But the analysis of the retrieval results shows that the query log-based *QTE* method does not have generally a negative effect on the retrieval effectiveness. Recall is drastically improved for query topics, where the baseline queries achieve, on average, only low recall values. But we have not detected any commonality that allows us to characterize these queries. So we recommend to use *PatNet* as a lexical resource for semi-automatic *QTE* in Boolean patent retrieval, where synonym expansion is particularly common to improve recall. In our future work we will focus on semi-automatic *QTE* to assist patent searchers in assembling complex Boolean queries.

References

1. Jochim, C., Lioma, C., Schütze, H.: Expanding queries with term and phrase translations in patent retrieval. In: Hanbury, A., Rauber, A., de Vries, A.P. (eds.) IRFC 2011. LNCS, vol. 6653, pp. 16–29. Springer, Heidelberg (2011)
2. Kim, Y., Seo, J., Croft, W.B.: Automatic Boolean query suggestion for professional search. In: Proc. of the 34th Int. ACM SIGIR Conf. on Research and Development in Inf. Retrieval (SIGIR 2011), Beijing, China, pp. 825–834 (2011)
3. Magdy, W., Jones, G.J.F.: PRES: a score metric for evaluating recall-oriented information retrieval applications. In: Proc. of the 33rd Int. ACM SIGIR Conf. on Research and Development in Inf. Retrieval (SIGIR 2010), Geneva, Switzerland, pp. 611–618 (2010)
4. Magdy, W., Jones, G.J.F.: A study of query expansion methods for patent retrieval. In: Proc. of PaIR 2011, Glasgow, Scotland, pp. 19–24 (2011)
5. Mahdabi, P., Crestani, F.: Patent Query Formulation by Synthesizing Multiple Sources of Relevance Evidence. Trans. on Inf. Systems 32(4), Article No. 4 (2014)
6. Silvestri, F.: Mining Query Logs: Turning Search Usage Data into Knowledge. Foundations and Trends in Information Retrieval 4(1–2), 1–174 (2010)
7. Tannebaum, W., Rauber, A.: Mining query logs of USPTO patent examiners. In: Forner, P., Müller, H., Paredes, R., Rosso, P., Stein, B. (eds.) CLEF 2013. LNCS, vol. 8138, pp. 136–142. Springer, Heidelberg (2013)
8. Tannebaum, W., Rauber, A.: *PatNet*: a lexical database for the patent domain. In: Hanbury, A., Kazai, G., Rauber, A., Fuhr, N. (eds.) ECIR 2015. LNCS, vol. 9022, pp. 550–555. Springer, Heidelberg (2015)
9. Xue, X., Croft, W.: Transforming patents into prior-art queries. In: Proc. of the 32nd Int. ACM SIGIR Conf. on Research and Development in Inf. Retrieval, USA, pp. 808–809 (2009)
10. Xue, X., Croft, W.: Automatic query generation for patent search. In: Proc. of CIKM 2009, Hong Kong, China, pp. 2037–2040 (2009)

Integrating Mixed-Methods for Evaluating Information Access Systems

Simon Wakeling[✉] and Paul Clough

Information School, University of Sheffield, Sheffield, UK
{s.wakeling,p.d.clough}@sheffield.ac.uk

Abstract. The evaluation of information access systems is increasingly making use of multiple evaluation methods. While such studies represent forms of mixed-methods research, they are rarely acknowledged as such. This means that researchers are potentially failing to recognise the challenges and opportunities offered by multi-phase research, particularly in terms of data integration. This paper provides a brief case study of how one framework – Bazely & Kemp's metaphors for integrated analysis – was employed to formalise data integration for a large exploratory evaluation study.

1 Introduction

The evaluation of an information access system can take many forms. This can involve both system-oriented and user-oriented approaches, the latter falling within the area of interactive information retrieval and the focus of this paper. Kelly [7] has offered one way of conceptualising information retrieval evaluation studies, suggesting a continuum ranging from system to user focus along which different methods can be placed. In attempting more holistic evaluations of information systems, researchers may utilise multiple methods from varying points on this continuum.

We argue that when taken together, such multi-phase evaluations essentially constitute mixed-methods research, an area that has received intense study within the social sciences. As Fidel [5] notes, such research within the IR field frequently does not self-identify as mixed-methods. While this has implications for the quality and clarity of research design and implementation, this paper focuses on the benefits of adopting a more formalised approach to integrating data from multiple research phases. In practice this means identifying the most appropriate and effective strategies for combining results from different forms of evaluation, and identifying areas of research that will benefit most from this integration. We therefore present a case study describing how data from a mixed-methods evaluation of WorldCat.org were integrated according to a framework developed by Bazely & Kemp [1].

In the following sections we provide a summary of data integration methods for mixed-methods research (Section 2), introduce a case study based on WorldCat.org (Section 3), then demonstrate integrating multiple methods for studying an information access system (Section 4). Finally, Section 5 concludes the paper.

© Springer International Publishing Switzerland 2015
J. Mothe et al. (Eds.): CLEF 2015, LNCS 9283, pp. 306–311, 2015.
DOI: 10.1007/978-3-319-24027-5_33

2   Related Work

While the research literature of many disciplines abounds with discussions of mixed-methods research, relatively little attention has been paid to the theory and practice of integrating the results of mixed-methods research [6]. Several authors have noted the prevalence of published works which claim to present integrated results of mixed-methods research projects, but which either fail to adequately assimilate findings from the attendant methodological strands, or do not properly discuss the techniques employed to achieve integration [2], [9].

Perhaps the most commonly cited theoretical underpinning to mixed-methods integration is *triangulation*. The use of the term as a methodological concept dates back to the 1960s, when Webb et al., building on earlier work by Campbell & Fiske, noted that "the most persuasive evidence comes through a triangulation of measurement processes" [8]. Initially this argument was most usually applied to quantitative forms of research, and therefore closer in spirit to the original meaning of the term as a surveying methodology involving the taking of multiple measurement readings. Later however the concept was popularised as a mixed-methods approach by Denzin [3], who outlined four modes of triangulation: data triangulation (capturing data from diverse subjects at diverse points in time and space), investigator triangulation (the use of more than one researcher to collect data), theory triangulation (utilising multiple theoretical constructs to interpret the data) and methodological triangulation (using different methods to collect data).

Table 1. Overview of Bazeley & Kemp's metaphors for integrated analysis [1]

Complementary Approaches	Description
Completion: Bricolage, Mosaics, and Jigsaws	Constructing a "patchy" aggregate based on the available data, or more carefully amalgamating all findings into a unified whole.
Enhancement: Sprinkling and Mixing/Stirring	Augmenting meaning by incorporating small data points, or mingling diverse but complementary findings together.
Detailing a More Significant Whole: Triangulation and Archipelago	Revealing unknowns through the combination of known points, or reveal a broader picture through snapshots of evidence.
Generative Approaches	Description
Exploration Through Transformation Involving Blending, Morphing, or Fusion of Data Elements	Developing new variables, or otherwise transforming or combining data
Conversation and DNA as Iterative Exchange	Re-assessing initial interpretations in light of subsequent findings, and identifying and linking "sense strands"

Of these by far the most influential in social sciences research is methodological triangulation, where it is frequently cited as a justification for and conceptual underpinning of mixed-methods research. A difficulty arises though in the extension of triangulation to a point where it is cited as a model for integrating qualitative and quantitative data. As Denzin himself has noted [4], this interpretation is somewhat beyond the defined scope of his earlier work. The primary purpose of methodological triangulation is to use multiple data sources as a means of validating findings [6], rather than a method of integrating complementary findings.

Bazeley & Kemp's metaphors for integrative analysis [1] offer an attempt to address this deficit. Their work systematically combines ideas taken from a review of the methodological literature into a set of approaches to data integration, which they express as metaphors. These are presented in Table 1. The result is a framework of methods which the authors encourage researchers to interpret imaginatively. The metaphors describe a set of principles and strategies for integrating data obtained through different methods in order to maximize the analytical potential of multi-phase research projects.

3   Case Study: WorldCat.org

Bazely & Kemp's metaphors were used as a framework for the integration of data collected during a multi-phase mixed methods research project investigating the use of WorldCat.org. Managed by OCLC, WorldCat.org is a publically accessible online aggregate catalogue of the holdings of OCLCs member libraries. The project sought to address a series of research questions relating to use of the system, including the extent to which it supported record retrieval in a variety of information-seeking contexts. Data were collected and analysed between April 2011 and September 2014. The four phases of the research can be summarised as follows:

Phase 1: Focus Groups (Qualitative): 21 focus groups undertaken with users in four countries. The sessions aimed to explore how and why the system is used, and elicit perspectives on system strengths and weaknesses. Transcripts of the focus groups were analyzed using Qualitative Content Analysis.

Phase 2: Survey (Quantitative): A pop-up survey was implemented on WorldCat.org, which generated 2,918 responses. The survey asked respondents about their use of the system and its various features.

Phase 3: Transaction Log Analysis (Quantitative): Analysis was performed on log files generated from two months of traffic to WorldCat.org, identifying common patterns of user behavior and use of various system features. Some manual analysis of sample sessions was also undertaken.

Phase 4: Lab based User Study (Quantitative and Qualitative): A task-based laboratory study in which participants' interactions with WorldCat.org were measured, and compared to the use of Amazon.co.uk. A post-session interview was also conducted, and this interview data analysed using Qualitative Content Analysis.

4   Data Integration

While consideration was paid to the potential methods and breadth of data integration at the planning stages of the project, these initial strategies were revised and improved at each stage of data collection as the quality and scope of data became better understood. By the end of the project, seven instances of integration had been identified and completed, some constituting more than one type. These are represented diagrammatically in **Figure 1**.

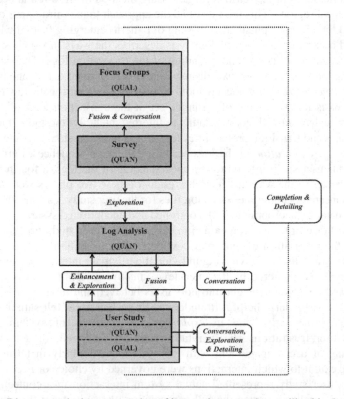

Fig. 1. Diagrammatical representation of integration metaphors utilised in the study

The first instance represented the integration of data from the first two phases of the research – the Focus Groups and Survey. Here two of the metaphors were employed, *fusion* and *conversation*. While the focus groups provided a rich source of anecdotal evidence relating to use of the system, they could not provide a reliable means of determining the extent to which participants' use cases were typical, or the degree to which those participants represented larger or smaller user groups. Fusing this data with the survey data allowed for a richer understanding of the relative importance of individuals' perspectives, and the generation of new ideas about the types of tasks that the system need support most. Initial interpretations of the data from each of the first two phases were also re-assessed collectively. In practice this conversational approach meant both better understanding how respondents were likely to have interpreted questions asked in the survey, and appreciating how users' own limited requirements might have blinded them to beneficial aspects of system functionality for others.

How findings from the first two phases informed the *exploration* of the transaction logs represented the second instance of integrated analysis. Differences in purpose and behavior from users arriving at WorldCat.org via a search engine referral, as opposed to actively seeking out the service, were clearly apparent from survey and focus groups responses, and this proved a fruitful means of approaching the analysis of the logs. Similarly, differences in the reasons for accessing the system were found across different geographical regions. This too informed the approach to the third phase of research, and allowed for a more sophisticated reading of patterns emerging from the logs.

The third occurrence of integrated analysis describes the ways in which results of the user study served to influence understanding of the transaction logs. The rich data collected during the user study for two distinct and clearly defined tasks (one exploratory, one fact-finding) allowed for the creation of unambiguous surrogate log files. These formed the basis for the coding of a sample set of the transaction logs, allowing these samples to be enhanced with codes relating to inferred intent. Furthermore, the computation of n-grams and transition probabilities for the user study sessions provided an empirical basis for the *exploration* of the logs according to action sequences. Furthermore, in addition to the user study informing the understanding of the logs, a fourth example of integration comes in the way in which the results of these two phases were *fused* into a whole. This meant obtaining the actual log files for the user study sessions, thereby creating a single data set incorporating both controlled and uncontrolled system interactions.

A fifth instance of integration came in analysis of the user study post-session interviews, and the integration of that interview data with the quantitative data collected from the user study itself. By viewing individual participant interactions in light of the detailed perspectives offered by the interviews, a *conversational* process was enacted which allowed for greater insight into how users behaved and interacted with the system. This was particularly helpful in understanding when users felt satisfied that they had completed the tasks, and in *exploring* how patterns of system interaction represented user frustration. The qualitative data also allowed for a more *detailed* understanding of user engagement with the system, particularly in terms of understanding the extent to which interactions were governed by choice or necessity.

Since the user study represented actual system interaction in a controlled setting, the findings naturally informed the full appreciation of results from the other strands. This sixth example of integration represented a *conversation* between the data collected throughout the first three phases, and the user study findings. The focus groups, survey and log analysis provided a rich picture of who was using the system and why, while the user study investigated how the system supported these tasks. These results could then be viewed holistically to better understand how system functionality influenced perceptions of system performance, and identify ways in which the system could better support its users.

The final instance of analytic integration came at the end of the project. Reviewing data from each phase led to the discovery of *details* beyond the scope of the original project – in this case the differing perspectives of intermediation by librarians and students. The findings from all four phases could also be aggregated into a *complete* whole, with the research questions addressed in a robust and comprehensive manner.

5   Conclusions

Evaluations of information access systems that incorporate more than one method can reasonably be viewed as representing mixed-methods research, and offer huge potential for providing a rich understanding of system performance. In order to maximise the potential benefits of these multi-phase studies, we suggest that researchers should attempt to formalise the relationship between each distinct method, and the key modes and strategies of integration. Bazely & Kemp's metaphors for integrated analysis offer a flexible framework for this process which can ensure researchers get the most out of their data.

References

1. Bazeley, P., Kemp, L.: Mosaics, Triangles, and DNA: Metaphors for Integrated Analysis in Mixed Methods Research. J. Mix. Methods Res. **6**(1), 55–72 (2012)
2. Bryman, A.: Why do researchers integrate/combine/mesh/blend/mix/merge/fuse quantitative and qualitative research? In: Bergman, M.M. (ed.) Advances in Mixed Methods Research, pp. 87–100. SAGE, London (2008)
3. Denzin, N.K.: The research act: A theoretical introduction to sociological methods. McGraw-Hill, New York (1978)
4. Denzin, N.K.: Triangulation 2.0. J. Mix. Methods Res. **6**(2), 80–88 (2012)
5. Fidel, R.: Are we there yet?: Mixed methods research in library and information science. Library & Information Science Research **30**, 265–272 (2008)
6. Greene, J.C.: Mixed methods in social inquiry. Jossey-Bass, San Francisco (2007)
7. Kelly, D.: Methods for Evaluating Interactive Information Retrieval Systems with Users. Foundations and Trends in Information Retrieval **3**, 1–224 (2009)
8. Webb, E.J., Campbell, D.T,, Schwartz, R.D., Sechrest, L.: Unobtrusive measures: Nonreactive research in the social sciences. Rand McNally, Chicago (1966)
9. Woolley, C.M.: Meeting the Mixed Methods Challenge of Integration in a Sociological Study of Structure and Agency. J. Mix. Methods Res. **3**(7), 7–25 (2009)

Teaching the IR Process Using Real Experiments Supported by Game Mechanics

Thomas Wilhelm-Stein[✉] and Maximilian Eibl

Technische Universität Chemnitz, 09107 Chemnitz, Germany
{wilt,eibl}@hrz.tu-chemnitz.de

Abstract. We present a web-based tool for teaching and learning the information retrieval process. An interactive approach helps students gain practical knowledge. Our focus is the arrangement and configuration of IR components and their evaluation. The incorporation of game mechanics counteracts an information overload and motivates progression.

Keywords: Information retrieval · Teaching · Learning · Web application · Components · Game mechanics

1 Motivation

An information retrieval system can be described as a pipeline of different components for indexing and retrieval like stemmers, indexing, search algorithms, and blind relevance feedback. Experienced researchers know which components work well together and which components do not. They developed a mental model through experimentation with a system and its components [1]. A lecturer can provide a conceptual model, but the learners still need to develop and refine their own mental model of how an information retrieval system works.

2 State-of-the-Art

Fernández-Luna et al. [2] gave an overview of the state-of-the-art for teaching and learning in information retrieval. They discuss various, existing systems focused on different aspects of IR and learning.

The key aspects of IR Game [3] are query formulation and processing. A user can test different queries and review their retrieval results. Different result presentations help him to understand how changes to a query alter the performance of the system. They conducted thorough studies with very good results, which led all teachers involved in IR instruction at the University of Tampere to include this tool into their lessons [4].

IR Toolbox [5] covers the whole retrieval process, i.e. document analysis, indexing, retrieval, and evaluation. Users configure the creation of indices and how they are searched. The evaluation relies on treceval, but does not deliver visualisations like IR Game.

© Springer International Publishing Switzerland 2015
J. Mothe et al. (Eds.): CLEF 2015, LNCS 9283, pp. 312–317, 2015.
DOI: 10.1007/978-3-319-24027-5_34

More recent approaches try to improve these systems or allow an in-depth study of certain components.

SulaIR [6] is based on the concepts of the IR Toolbox, but chose another way of visual presentation. As a desktop application, it covers basic IR elements like document pre-processing, indexing, retrieval and relevance feedback. A major difference to IR Toolbox was the goal to support custom components, which can be created and shared by the students.

VIRlab [7], a web-based platform, addresses especially retrieval models by providing easy access to term and document statistics. Users can write and test their own retrieval models without dealing with parsing the collection and calculating evaluation metrics.

Some systems, like IR Toolbox, scratch the surface of components as an integral part of the information retrieval process. SulaIR recognizes the importance of components, but focuses on a desktop application. However all systems fall short when it comes to motivate the learners.

3   System Overview

Our web application enables learners to select, configure, and arrange IR components. Using evaluation corpora learners see the impact of their changes on the retrieval quality. Thereby, learners gain insight in the dependencies of retrieval components without the necessity of programming.

The system covers three main aspects:

1. Managing and inspection of collections,
2. Selection, configuration and arrangement of components, and
3. Exploration of indices and results.

Many aspect are customizable. For example the evaluation measures and how they are calculated relies on JavaScript functions, which can be modified by users with appropriate permissions.

As a single-page web application, we rely on a RESTful API. Jersey[1] is used as backend and AngularJS[2] as frontend. Students are able to access and use it with a modern web browser.

Currently, the indexing and retrieval part is done by Apache Lucene[3], but it is not restricted to it. The Xtrieval framework as an abstraction layer allows the use of other frameworks as well, like Terrier[4]. Even a mixing of these frameworks is possible as the pipeline does not rely on any of them.

---

[1] http://jersey.java.net/
[2] https://angularjs.org/
[3] http://lucene.apache.org/
[4] http://terrier.org/

4   Conducting Experiments

Experiments are set up by configuring two processes: Indexing and retrieval. The user has to choose from a variety of components to create an index and search it.

- Lower case filter,
- Snowball stemmer,
- n-Gram stemmer, and
- Stop words removal

After each change, a preview (see figure 1) of a single document is created to track the changes induced by each component. It is intended to supply the user with direct feedback about how the components modify a document. The preview can be customized to show the content of a single field and to highlight changes, like insertion (green) and removals (red).

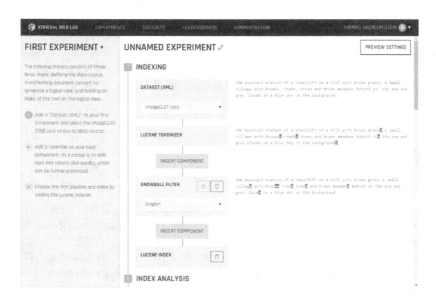

Fig. 1. Experiment configuration and preview

Once the user has set up his experiment, he can conduct the experiment for the whole collection. Each experiment is actually conducted on the server and all results, including details of the index and result lists, are submitted to the browser. Currently, Recall and Precision metrics and graphs are provided for the whole experiment and each topic.

The user can inspect the results for each topic and display the content of the retrieved documents. To gain more insight he can access statistics about the index, like total number of occurences of a term or number of documents containing a term.

The setup and results of every conducted experiment are stored in a database for later investigation and for creating the leaderboards.

Privileged users are allowed to supply their own collections. All necessary files can be uploaded and necessary metadata entered. Each collection is accompanied with at least one set of topics and the corresponding relevance assessments.

As some collections are restricted in their usage, we supply the IAPR TC-12 collection [8] from ImageCLEF as a default. It consists of 20,000 photographs from a variety of locations, which are annotated in English, German and Spanish. Topics and relevance assessments are available for a total of 30 languages. Furthermore it is free of charge and without any copyright restrictions.

5   Gamification

By incorporating game mechanics, we hope to counteract an information over-load and motivate progression.

With the help of assignments (see the left side of figure 1), users get a set of tasks to complete and a direct feedback, when they have completed it. Through assignments we can provide the user with additional information about the infor-mation retrieval process and how he can use our system.

Achievements [9, p.233] are a virtual representation of having accomplished something, like the first working experiment. They are also a representation of users experience with the different IR components. In Xtrieval Web Lab some achievements have different levels (shown by the small numbers on top of a

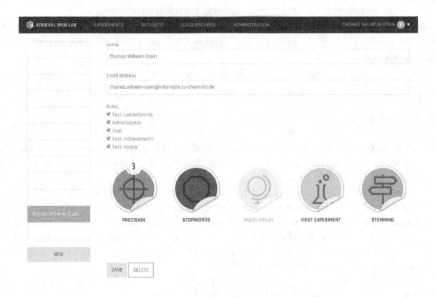

Fig. 2. User profile with achievements

badge), which designates what extend this achievement was mastered. For example the "precision" achievement has a total of three levels, which are obtained by scoring particular values for mean average precision.

Through earning achievements (see figure 2) a user unlocks new, more complex components, comparable to the Cascading Information Theory [10]. Thus, newbies are not overwhelmed by all components and gradually gain access to them.

With Leaderboards users can track the performance of their experiments and their overall performance [9, p.34]. They allow users to compare their results to other user's. A variety of leaderboards are possible, for example we already show the best experiment regading the Mean Average Precision and the users with best performing experiments. Since the leaderboards are generated from all experiments stored in the database, new ones can be added easily and use all data stored in an experiment, like all calculated metrics, properties of the experiment or of the user. With this approach a leaderboard showing the scores of students from the same course is possible, too.

6   Conclusions and Future Work

The results of a pre-test within a university course on information retrieval were very promising. Without further instructions all students were able to set up their first experiment and to include basic IR components like stemmers. In persuit of a better score they dealt with the settings of these components and kept adjusting them until they reached the goal. We are planning to conduct a more comprehensive evaluation with a larger group of students.

With the feedback collected during our pre-test we made considerable changes to the user interface. For example the concept of assignments is a direct result of this feedback.

There is a working prototype at http://mytuc.org/xdht.

References

1. Borgman, C.L.: The user's mental model of an information retrieval system: An experiment on a prototype online catalog. International Journal of Man-Machine Studies **24**(1), 47–64 (1986)
2. Fernández-Luna, J.M., Huete, J.F., MacFarlane, A., Efthimiadis, E.N.: Teaching and learning in information retrieval. Information Retrieval **12**(2), 201–226 (2009)
3. Sormunen, E., Laaksonen, J., Keskustalo, H., Kekäläinen, J., Kemppainen, H., Laitinen, H., Pirkola, A., Järvelin, K.: The ir game-a tool for rapid query analysis in cross-language ir experiments. In: PRICAI 1998 Workshop on Cross Language Issues in Artificial Intelligence, pp. 22–32 (1998)
4. Airio, E., Sormunen, E., Halttunen, K., Keskustalo, H.: Integrating standard test collections in interactive ir instruction. In: Proceedings of the First International Conference on Teaching and Learning of Information Retrieval, p. 10. British Computer Society (2007)

5. Efthimiadis, E.N., Freier, N.G.: Ir-toolbox: an experiential learning tool for teaching IR. In: Kraaij, W., de Vries, A.P., Clarke, C.L.A., Fuhr, N., Kando, N. (eds.): SIGIR 2007: Proceedings of the 30th Annual International ACM SIGIR Conference on Research and Development in Information Retrieval, Amsterdam, The Netherlands, July 23–27, p. 914. ACM (2007)
6. Fernández-Luna, J., Huete, J., Rodríguez-Cano, J., Rodríguez, M.: Teaching and learning information retrieval based on a visual and interactive tool: Sulair. In: EDULEARN12 Proceedings, pp. 6634–6642 (2012)
7. Fang, H., Wu, H., Yang, P., Zhai, C.: Virlab: a web-based virtual lab for learning and studying information retrieval models. In Geva, S., Trotman, A., Bruza, P., Clarke, C.L.A., Järvelin, K. (eds.) The 37th International ACM SIGIR Conference on Research and Development in Information Retrieval, SIGIR 2014, Gold Coast, QLD, Australia, July 06–11, pp. 1249–1250. ACM (2014)
8. Grubinger, M., Clough, P., Müller, H., Deselaers, T.: The iapr tc-12 benchmark: A new evaluation resource for visual information systems. In: International Workshop OntoImage, pp. 13–23 (2006)
9. Kapp, K.M.: The gamification of learning and instruction: game-based methods and strategies for training and education. John Wiley & Sons (2012)
10. Dorogan, V., Mic, T.: Enhancing organizational socialization through the player journey. Res. & Sci. Today **6**, 108 (2013)

Tweet Contextualization Using Association Rules Mining and DBpedia

Meriem Amina Zingla[1,2]($\boxtimes$), Chiraz Latiri[3], and Yahya Slimani[1]

[1] INSAT, LISI Research Laboratory, University of Carthage, Tunis, Tunisia
{zinglameriem,yahya.slimani}@gmail.com
[2] Faculty of Sciences of Tunis, University of Tunis El Manar, Tunis, Tunisia
[3] Faculty of Sciences of Tunis, LIPAH Research Laboratory,
University of Tunis El Manar, Tunis, Tunisia
chiraz.latiri@gnet.tn

Abstract. Tweets are short 140 characters-limited messages that do not always conform to proper spelling rules. This spelling variation makes them hard to understand without some kind of context. For these reasons, the tweet contextualization task was introduced, aiming to provide automatic contexts to explain the tweets. We present, in this paper, two tweet contextualization approaches. The first is an inter-term association rules mining-based method, the second one, however, makes use of the DBpedia ontology. These approaches allow us to augment the vocubulary of a given tweet with a set of thematically related words. We conducted an experimental study on the INEX2014 collection to prove the effectiveness of our approaches, the obtained results are very promising.

Keywords: Information retrieval · Tweet contextualization track · Query expansion · DBpedia · Association rules

1 Introduction

Twitter is an online social networking service that enables users to send and read short textual messages, called "tweets". Limited to 140 characters, a tweet's size exacerbates the well-known vocabulary mismatch problem, rendering the tweet hard to understand. To make it understandable by readers, it is necessary to find out its contexts.

The aim of the tweet contextualization INEX (Initiative for the Evaluation of XML retrieval) task is the following: given a tweet and a related entity, the system must provide some context about the subject of the tweet from the perspective of the entity, in order to help the reader answer questions of the form "why this tweet concerns the entity? should it be an alert?". In order to get this aim, two systems are combined, an Information Retrieval System (IRS) and an Automatic Summarization System (ASS). While the IRS extracts, from the Wikipedia document collection, a set of relevant documents for a given tweet, the ASS selects the most relevant passages from the extracted documents. The general process involves three steps:

© Springer International Publishing Switzerland 2015
J. Mothe et al. (Eds.): CLEF 2015, LNCS 9283, pp. 318–323, 2015.
DOI: 10.1007/978-3-319-24027-5_35

- Tweet analysis.
- Passage and/or XML elements retrieval, using an information retrieval system (IRS) based on the Indri1 search engine.
- Construction of the answer, using an automatic summarization system (ASS) based on an efficient summarization algorithm created by TermWatch.

A baseline system composed of an IRS and an ASS has been made available online[1]. Despite the fact that the idea to contextualize tweets is quite recent, there are several works in this field. Recently, authors of [5] used Latent Dirichlet Analysis (LDA) to obtain a representation of the tweet in a thematic space. This representation allows the finding of a set of latent topics covered by the tweet, this approach gives good results for the tweet contextualization task. Whereas, in [3], authors added a hashtag performance prediction component to the Wikipedia retrieval step. They used all available tweet features including web links which were not allowed by INEX's organisers. Finally, in [6], authors developed three statistical summarizer systems the first one called Cortex summarizer, that uses several sentence selection metrics and an optimal decision module to score sentences from a document source, the second one called Artex summarizer, that uses a simple inner product among the topic-vector and the pseudo-word vector and the third one called Reg summarizer which is a performant graph-based summarizer.

In this paper, we define the tweet contextualization task as a query expansion issue, we consider tweets as queries. The aim is to enhance the quality of a tweet (query) for the baseline system, since it has a direct impact on the context quality. Hence, we propose two approaches to extend the initial query, namely: A Statistical Approach based on Association Rules inter-Terms (ARE), and a Semantic Approach based on DBpedia as an external knowledge source (DBE). While the first is based on association rules mining [1,4], the second is based on the DBpedia ontology. Our proposed approach ARE for the tweet contextualization offers an interesting solution to obtain relevant context. This mainly relies on an accurate choice of the added terms to an initial query. Interestingly enough, tweet contextualization takes advantage of large text volumes provided by Wikipedia articles by extracting statistical information. The advantage of the insight gained through association rules is in the contextual nature of the discovered inter-term correlations. The use of such dependencies in a query expansion process should significantly increase the quality of the derived context. The advantage of the use of DBpedia in our DBE approach is its ability to provide vast amounts of structured knowledge, hence, allowing to augment query representation with massive amounts of related information.

The remainder of this paper is organized as follows: Section 2 details our proposed approaches for tweet contextualization. Section 3 describes our different submitted runs as the experimental results. The conclusion and future work are finally presented in Section 4.

---

[1] http://qa.termwatch.es/data

2   The Proposed Approaches for Tweet Contextualization

The tweet contextualization system serves to expand a given tweet and to elaborate the corresponding query, which is sent in order to retrieve its related context. To address tweet contextualization in an efficient manner, we propose two approaches ARE and DBE. Our proposed approaches for the tweet contextualization offer an interesting solution to obtain relevant context. This mainly relies on an accurate choice of the added terms to an initial query since they have a direct impact on the context quality.

2.1   Statistical Approach Based on Inter-Terms Association Rules (ARE)

The main idea is to extract a set of non redundant rules, representing inter-terms correlations in a contextual manner. We use these rules that convey the most interesting correlations amongst terms to extend the initial queries. Then, we send the extended queries to the baseline system to extract their contexts. The contextualization tweet process is performed in the following steps:

1. Selection of a sub-set of articles, according to the tweet's entity, from the INEX 2014 documents collection, using an algorithm based on the TF-IDF measure [7].
2. Annotation of the selected Wikipedia articles with part-of-speech and lemma information using TreeTagger [2].
3. Extraction of nouns from the annotated Wikipedia articles, and removal of the most frequents nouns.
4. Generation of the association rules using an efficient algorithm CHARM[3] for mining all the closed frequent termsets [8]. We adapted the algorithm CHARM, because it allows to generate non-redundant association rules. As an input, CHARM takes a corpus in the basic ascii format, where each line or row (article) is a list of terms, and as parameters, it takes *minsup* as the relative minimal support and *minconf* as the minimal threshold to derive valid association rules and gives as output, a set of association rules with their appropriate support and confidence.
5. Projection of the queries on the set of the association rules in order to obtain the thematic space of each query. This is done by projecting the terms of the query on the premises of the association rules and enriching the query using their conclusions.
6. Creating the query from the terms of the initial tweet (entity, topic and content) and the thematic space.
   This query is then transformed to its Indri [4] format as follow:
   #weight(0.6 #combine(initial tweet's terms) 0.4 #combine (thematic space))

---

[2] http://www.cis.uni-muenchen.de/~schmid/tools/TreeTagger/
[3] http://www.cs.rpi.edu/~zaki/www-new/pmwiki.php/Software/Software
[4] http://www.lemurproject.org/indri.php

7. Send of the query to the baseline system, composed of an Information Retrieval System (IRS) and an Automatic Summary System (ASS) offered by the organizers of INEX 2014, to extract from a provided Wikipedia corpus a set of sentences representing the tweet context that should not exceed 500 words.

2.2 Semantic Approach Based on DBpedia (DBE)

DBpedia is a project aiming to represent Wikipedia content in RDF triples. It plays a central role in the Semantic Web, due to the large and growing number of resources linked to it.

The main idea of this approach is to extract for each term in the initial query a set of related concepts from the DBpedia ontology, this is done using a simple SPARQL query. For example for the term *"volvo"* we extract the following related informations: *Organisation, Business, Car, Manufacturer, Company, Institution...etc.*, then we add these related informations to the initial query in order to augment its presentation by a massive amounts of related information. Like in the last steps of the previous approach, we transform the query to its Indri format, then, we send it to the baseline system, to extract the context of the tweet.

3 Experiments and Results

We validated our approach over INEX 2014 collection which contains:

- A collection of articles, that has been rebuilt based on a dump of the English Wikipedia from November 2012. It is composed of 3 902 346 articles, where all notes and bibliographic references that are difficult to handle are removed and only non-empty Wikipedia pages (pages having at least one section) are kept.
- A collection of English tweets, composed of 240 tweets selected from the CLEF RepLab 2013. To focus on content analysis alone, urls are removed from the tweets.

We released two runs, namely :

Run-ARE: This run is based on our ARE approach, we applied CHARM with the following parameters : $minsup = 5$, and $minconf = 0.7$.

Run-DBE: This run is based on our DBE approach.

We have evaluated our runs according to the **Informativeness metric** [2], this latter is proposed by the INEX organizers, it aims at measuring how well the summary helps a user understand the tweets content. Therefore, for each tweet, each passage will be evaluated independently from the others, even in the same summary. the results are based on a thorough manual run on 1/5 of the 2014 topics using the baseline system. From this run two types of references were extracted, namely:

- a list of relevant sentences per topic.
- extraction of Noun Phrases from these sentences together with the corresponding Wikipedia entry.

We have compared our runs with the following different runs submitted by INEX 2014 participants:

- In run-Cortex participants [6] used a statistical summarizer system called Cortex, which is based on the fusion process of several different sentence selection metrics.
- In run-Artex participants [6] used a statistical summarizer system called Artex, which is based on the inner product of a main topic and pseudo-words vectors.

Tables 1 and 2 describe our obtained results where the lowest scores represent the best runs.

Table 1. Informativeness based on sentences

Run Id	Unigram	Bigram	Skip
run-ARE	**0.7632**	**0.8689**	**0.8702**
run-DBE	**0.7940**	**0.8822**	**0.8831**
run-Cortex	0.8415	0.9696	0.9702
run-Artex	0.8539	0.9700	0.9712

Table 2. Informativeness based on noun phrases

Run Id	Unigram	Bigram	Skip
run-ARE	**0.7903**	**0.9273**	**0.9461**
run-DBE	**0.8202**	**0.9373**	**0.9530**
run-Cortex	0.8477	0.971	0.9751
run-Artex	0.8593	0.9709	0.9752

The obtained informativeness evaluation results shed light that our proposed approaches offer interesting results and help ensure that context summaries contain adequate correlating information with the tweets and avoid inclusion of non-similar information in them as much as possible. However, we noticed that the run-ARE performed better than run-DBE (*cf.* Table1 and 2). This is justified by the fact that the association rules allowed us to find the terms having a strong correlation with the tweet's terms. The DBE results could be more competitive with some improvements on the queries sent to the baseline system by integrating a disambiguation phase.

4 Conclusion

In this paper, we proposed to use statistical and semantic approaches for the tweet contextualization task. while the statistical one is based on the association rules mining, the semantic one uses DBpedia as an external knowledge source.The experimental study was conducted on the INEX 2014 collection. The results we obtained through the different performed runs showed a significant improvement in the informativeness of the contexts. In our future work we intend to add a disambiguation phase to improve the quality of the extended tweets. We also propose to use other structured and semantically enriched data sources, such as UMBEL, Freebase, WordNet etc, as external resources.

Acknowledgments. This work is partially supported by the French-Tunisian project PHC-Utique RIMS-FD 14G 1404.

References

1. Agrawal, R., Imielinski, T., Swami, A.N.: Mining association rules between sets of items in large databases. In: Proceedings of the 1993 ACM SIGMOD International Conference on Management of Data, Washington, D.C., May 26–28, 1993, pp. 207–216 (1993). http://doi.acm.org/10.1145/170035.170072
2. Bellot, P., Moriceau, V., Mothe, J., SanJuan, E., Tannier, X.: Overview of INEX tweet contextualization 2013 track. In: Working Notes for CLEF 2013 Conference, Valencia, September 23–26, 2013 (2013). http://ceur-ws.org/Vol 1179/CLEF2013wn-INEX-BellotEt2013.pdf
3. Deveaud, R., Boudin, F.: Effective tweet contextualization with hashtags performance prediction and multi-document summarization. In: Working Notes for CLEF 2013 Conference, Valencia, Spain, September 23–26, 2013 (2013)
4. Latiri, C.C., Haddad, H., Hamrouni, T.: Towards an effective automatic query expansion process using an association rule mining approach. J. Intell. Inf. Syst. **39**(1), 209–247 (2012). http://dx.doi.org/10.1007/s10844-011-0189-9
5. Morchid, M., Dufour, R., Linéars, G.: Lia@inex2012: combinaison de thèmes latents pour la contextualisation de tweets. In: 13e Conférence Francophone sur l'Extraction et la Gestion des Connaissances. Toulouse (2013)
6. Torres-Moreno, J.: Three statistical summarizers at CLEF-INEX 2013 tweet contextualization track. In: Working Notes for CLEF 2014 Conference, Sheffield, September 15–18, 2014, pp. 565–573 (2014). http://ceur-ws.org/Vol-1180/CLEF2014wn-Inex-TorresMoreno2014.pdf
7. Xia, T., Chai, Y.: An improvement to TF-IDF: term distribution based term weight algorithm. JSW **6**(3), 413–420 (2011). http://dx.doi.org/10.4304/jsw.6.3.413-420
8. Zaki, M., Hsiao, C.J.: An efficient algorithm for closed itemset mining. In: Second SIAM International Conference on Data Mining (2002)

Best of the Labs

Search-Based Image Annotation: Extracting Semantics from Similar Images

Petra Budikova, Michal Batko$^{(\boxtimes)}$, Jan Botorek, and Pavel Zezula

Masaryk University, Brno, Czech Republic
{budikova,batko,botorek,zezula}@fi.muni.cz

Abstract. The importance of automatic image annotation as a tool for handling large amounts of image data has been recognized for several decades. However, working tools have long been limited to narrow-domain problems with a few target classes for which precise models could be trained. With the advance of similarity searching, it now becomes possible to employ a different approach: extracting information from large amounts of noisy web data. However, several issues need to be resolved, including the acquisition of a suitable knowledge base, choosing a suitable visual content descriptor, implementation of effective and efficient similarity search engine, and extraction of semantics from similar images. In this paper, we address these challenges and present a working annotation system based on the search-based paradigm, which achieved good results in the 2014 ImageCLEF Scalable Concept Image Annotation challenge.

1 Introduction

Acquiring and storing images is very easy nowadays – anyone with a decent mobile phone can take a picture and upload it to a web gallery in a few seconds. However, organizing and retrieving such data remains a challenging task. The most natural way of accessing data is a text search, but a lot of images are not associated with any text information. Therefore, automatic image annotation methods are being developed to improve the accessibility of visual information.

The image annotation task can be formalized as follows: given an *input image*, which may or may not be accompanied by *input metadata*, select suitable descriptive words from a given *vocabulary*. Depending on the target application, the annotation vocabulary may contain a few labels, or all words from a given language. In this paper, we focus on the problem of broad-domain annotation with no input metadata and large vocabularies, which applies to the above-mentioned task of annotating web images.

To address this problem, we have developed a search-based annotation system which exploits labeled web images to determine the annotation of an arbitrary input image. Such approach is not useful for narrow-domain classification tasks with few candidate classes, which are better served by traditional machine learning techniques. However, the search-based solution can be successfully used for broad-domain annotation tasks with sparse training data, as demonstrated by the success of our system in the ImageCLEF 2014 Image Annotation challenge.

© Springer International Publishing Switzerland 2015
J. Mothe et al. (Eds.): CLEF 2015, LNCS 9283, pp. 327–339, 2015.
DOI: 10.1007/978-3-319-24027-5_36

The search-based annotation paradigm is based on techniques for content-based data retrieval. Visual similarity of image content is exploited to search for images similar to the picture being annotated, and textual metadata of the resulting images are used to form the annotation. While the idea of search-based annotation is rather straightforward, it is not easy to achieve satisfactory results. The challenges that need to be solved are several: acquisition of suitable image set for similarity searching, choosing a suitable visual content descriptor, implementation of effective and efficient search engine, and extraction of semantics from similar images. In the following sections, we address all these issues and propose a novel technique for analysis of image semantics.

The rest of the paper is organized as follows. In Section 2, we review recent work in the field of image annotation. Next, we introduce our annotation system and describe its components. The ImageCLEF 2014 annotation task is introduced in Section 4 and our results from the competition are analyzed in Section 5. Section 6 concludes the paper and outlines our future work.

2   Related Work

Recent work in the field of image annotation can be divided into two categories – model-based and search-based. Model-based techniques, which are surveyed in more detail e.g. in [21], require a training dataset consisting of reliably annotated images, which are used compute a statistical model for each concept. The state-of-the art model-based solution is represented by the neural network classifier developed by Alex Krizhevsky for the 2012 ImageNet challenge, which defeated other participants of the contest by a significant margin and achieved impressive results [12]. However, any model-based solution is limited in terms of vocabulary scalability: the classifiers can be created only for concepts for which reliable training data is available, and every new concept requires costly re-training.

On the other hand, search-based solutions sacrifice precision for broad applicability and attempt to utilize the voluminous but potentially erroneous information available in web image collections and social networks. The authors of [14] presented a simple solution based on this idea, which straightforwardly takes the tags from the most similar images and assigns them to the input image. The Arista system [20] exploits efficient duplicate search over a very large reference data set to select the most relevant images for annotation mining. In [1], a learning procedure is proposed which projects both visual and textual words into a latent meaning space, and the learned mapping is used to find nearest neighbors for annotation. Many works focus on advanced methods of extracting relevant keywords for visual-neighbor annotations, which include web search [22], analysis of co-occurring words [10], or concept ranking by random walks in similarity graphs [22]. Recently, several authors have also proposed to utilize semantic knowledge sources such as ontologies for improving annotation quality [11,18]. In our approach, we combine the basic strategy of [14] with semantic knowledge bases and co-occurrence analysis similar to [10,18]. The main improvement over existing work is a novel semantics-aware keyword selection process.

3   Semantic Search-Based Image Annotation

The annotation task may take many forms, as it appears in diverse applications that have different requirements on annotation vocabulary, efficiency, or flexibility. While most existing solutions focus on a single instance of the annotation problem, we believe that a more universal system can be designed that would be capable of adapting to diverse requirements. In our previous paper [2], we proposed a modular architecture for such system which allows to flexibly combine different image- and text-processing components.

In this paper, we present an instance of this architecture developed for broad-domain image annotation. Its fundamental modules and the flow of the data among them are schematically depicted in Figure 1 starting with a plain input image and finishing with the automatically generated annotation. There are four main phases of the annotation process. In the first phase, the annotation tool retrieves visually similar images from a suitable image collection. Then, the textual descriptions from the retrieved similar images are processed. Resulting sets of candidate keywords are analyzed using the WordNet lexical database and other sematic resources. Finally, the most probable concepts from the annotation vocabulary are selected as the final image description. In the following, we provide more details about the specific implementations of the respective parts and discuss different parameters of the annotation system that influence the overall performance.

3.1   Retrieval of Similar Images

The search-based approach to image annotation is based on the assumption that in a sufficiently large collection, images with similar content to any given query image are likely to appear. If these can be identified by a suitable content-based retrieval technique, their metadata such as accompanying texts, labels, etc. can be exploited to obtain text information about the query image. Important factors that influence the performance of search-based annotation are the reference collection size, reliability of reference image annotations, the quality of visual similarity measure, and the implementation of the similarity search engine.

Datasets. The choice of image collection(s) over which the content-based retrieval is evaluated is a crucial factor of the whole annotation process. There should be as many images as possible in the chosen collection, the images should be relevant for the domain of the queries, and their descriptions should be rich and precise. Naturally, these requirements are in a conflict – while it is relatively easy to obtain large collections of image data (at least in the domain of general-purpose images appearing in personal photo-galleries), it is very difficult to automatically collect images with high-quality descriptions.

At the moment, our annotation system uses the Profiset image collection [5] as the baseline reference dataset. If additional training images are available for a specific task, they are added to this collection. The Profiset collection is freely

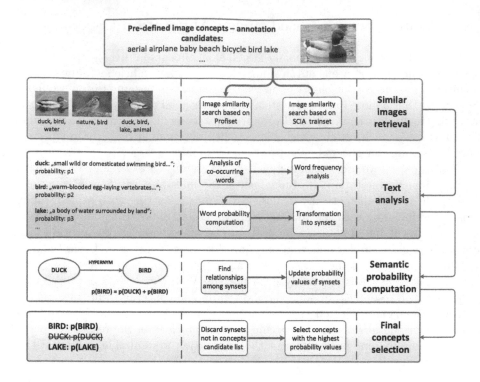

Fig. 1. Annotation tool architecture

available for research purposes and contains 20M high-quality images with rich annotations (about 20 keywords per image in average) obtained from a photostock website. The Profiset annotations have no fixed vocabulary and their quality is not centrally supervised, however the authors of annotations were interested in selling their photos and thus motivated to provide relevant keywords.

Visual Descriptors. Visual content descriptors and associated similarity function are used to evaluate the visual similarity of images. The content-based retrieval engine we employ can work with any descriptors that satisfy the metric space postulates, i.e. the similarity function is reflexive, symmetric, and satisfies the triangle inequality. Historically, the MPEG7 [15] multimedia standard defined several global visual features which were known to provide reasonably effective results with high efficiency. The annotation tool thus, as one option, uses a combination of five MPEG7 visual descriptors according to the best configuration provided in [13].

Recently, new visual descriptors called DeCAF features were proposed in [8]. Based on the successful image classifier developed by Krizhevsky [12], these features have been shown to perform promisingly in various image processing tasks. Therefore, we decided to use them as another option for our similarity search module. Specifically, we utilize the $DeCAF_7$ feature, which is produced by the last hidden layer of the neural network classifier. The DeCAF$_7$ representation of a single image consists of a 4096-dimensional vector of real numbers and its extraction is a rather heavy computational task [8]. However, once the descriptors are extracted from a dataset, they can be efficiently indexed and searched. To compute the distance of two DeCAF$_7$ features, we utilize the Euclidean distance.

Indexing and Searching. In our solution, we utilize the MUFIN similarity search system [3] to index and search images. The MUFIN system exploits state-of-the-art metric indexing structures and enables fast retrieval of similar images from very large collections. For the combination of the five MPEG7 descriptors, we employ the M-Index technique [16]. For the bigger DeCAF descriptors, which need to read more data from the disk, we use the PPP-Codes technique [17]. Both indexing structures allows us to search a collection of 20M images in 1-2 seconds.

For each image to be annotated, a fixed number k of most similar images is selected and used for further processing. The number k needed to be chosen carefully, as it influences the quality of results. If we could suppose that all found objects are relevant for the query, a high k would be advantageous. However, this is often not the case in similarity-based image retrieval, where semantically irrelevant images are likely to be evaluated as visually similar to the query. It is therefore necessary to determine such k that the selected images provide sufficient amount of information but do not introduce too much noise.

3.2   Text Processing

In the second phase of the annotation process, the descriptions of images returned by content-based retrieval need to be analyzed in order to select the most probable concepts from target vocabulary. During this phase, we utilize various semantic resources to reveal the common topics depicted in the images. In the current implementation, our solution relies mainly on the WordNet semantic structure. The following sections explain how we link keywords from similar images' annotations to WordNet synsets, how the probability of individual synsets is computed, and how the synsets are transformed into the final annotation.

Selection of Initial Keywords. Having retrieved the set of similar images, we first divide their text metadata into separate words and compute the frequency of each word. This way, we obtain a set of *initial keywords*. For each keyword, we compute its *initial probability*, which depends on the frequency of the keyword in descriptions of similar images. Only the n most probable keywords are kept for further processing.

Matching Keywords to WordNet. The set of keywords with their associated probabilities contains rich information about query image content, but it is difficult to work with this representation since we have no information about semantic connections between individual words. Therefore, we need to transform the keywords into semantically connected objects. We have decided to base our furter analysis on the WordNet lexical database [9], which is a comprehensive semantic tool interlinking dictionary, thesaurus and language grammar book. The basic building block of WordNet hierarchy is a *synset*, an object which unifies synonymous words into a single item. On top of synsets, different semantic relations are encoded in the WordNet structure.

Each initial keyword is therefore mapped to a corresponding WordNet synset. Since there are often more possible meanings of a given word and thus more candidate synsets, we use a probability measure based on the cntlist[1] frequency values to select the most probable synset for each keyword. The cntlist measure is based on the frequency of words in a particular sense in semantically tagged corpora and expresses a relative frequency of a given synset in general text. To avoid false dismissals, several highly probable synsets may be selected for each keyword. Each selected synset is assigned a probability value computed as a product of the WordNet normalized frequency and the respective keyword's initial probability.

Exploitation of WordNet Relationships. By transforming keywords into synsets, we are able to group words with the same meaning and thus increase the probability of recognizing a significant topic. Naturally, this can be further improved by analyzing semantic relationships between the candidate synsets. In our solution, we exploit four WordNet relationships to create a *candidate synset graph*: *hypernymy* – the generalization, is-a relationship; *hyponymy* – the specialization relationship, the opposite of hypernymy; *holonymy* – the has-parts relationship, upward direction in the part/whole hierarchy; and *meronymy* – the is-a-part-of relationship, the opposite of holonymy.

To build the candidate synset graph, we first apply the upward-direction relationships (i.e. hypernymy and holonymy) in a so-called *expansion mode*, when all synsets that are linked to any candidate synset by these relationships are added to the graph; this way, the candidate graph is enriched by upper level synsets in the potentially relevant WordNet subtrees. However, we are not interested in some of the upper-most levels that contain very general concepts such as *entity, physical entity*, etc. Therefore, we also utilize the Visual Concept Ontology (VCO) [4] in this step, which was designed as a complementary tool to WordNet and provides a more compact hierarchy of concepts related to image content. Synsets not covered by the VCO are considered to be too general and therefore are not included in the candidate graph.

After the expansion, the other two relationships are utilized in an *enhancement mode* that adds new links to the graph using relationships between synsets that already are in the graph. Finally, the candidate graph is submitted to an iterative algorithm that updates the probabilities of individual synsets so that synsets with high number of links receive higher probabilities and vice versa.

---

[1] https://wordnet.princeton.edu/wordnet/man/cntlist.5WN.html

Final Concept Selection. At the end of the candidate graph processing, the system produces a set of candidate synsets with updated probabilities. If the annotation vocabulary is unlimited, the m most probable synsets are displayed as the final annotation. Otherwise, the synsets are confronted with the annotation vocabulary and the m most probable concepts from the intersection are displayed. The parameter m can be provided by the user, otherwise an experimentally determined value is used that provides the optimal trade-off between annotation precision and recall.

4   ImageCLEF 2014 Annotation Challenge

In 2014, we entered the ImageCLEF Scalable Concept Image Annotation (SCIA) challenge [19] to compare our annotation system to other state-of-the-art solutions. This section briefly introduces the task and describes the necessary adjustments of our annotation system.

4.1   Scalable Concept Image Annotation Task

The SCIA challenge is a standard annotation task, where relevant concepts from a fixed set of candidate concepts need to be assigned to an input image. The *input images* are not accompanied by any descriptive metadata, so only the visual image content serves as annotation input. For each test image, there is a *list of SCIA concepts* from which the relevant ones need to be selected. Each concept is defined by one keyword and a link to relevant WordNet nodes.

As the 2014 SCIA challenge focused especially on the concept-wise scalability of annotation techniques, the participants were not provided with hand-labeled training data and were not allowed to use resources that require significant manual preprocessing. Instead, they were encouraged to exploit data that can be crawled from the web or otherwise easily obtained, so that the proposed solutions should be able to adapt easily when the list of concepts is changed. Accordingly, the training dataset provided by organizers consisted of 500K images downloaded from the web, and the accompanying web pages. The raw images and web pages were further preprocessed by competition organizers to ease the participation in the task, resulting in several visual and text descriptors as detailed in [19].

The actual competition task consisted of annotating 7291 images with different concept lists. Altogether, there were 207 concepts, with the size of individual concept lists ranging from 40 to 207 concepts. Prior to releasing the test image set, participants were provided with a development set of query images and concept lists, for which a ground truth of relevant concepts was also published. The development set contained 1940 images and only 107 concepts.

4.2   DISA Participation

Our annotation system entered the competition under the name DISA, referring to the name of our lab. The DISA solution consisted of the system described in

Section 3 with one minor extension – the 500K set of training images provided by SCIA organizers (the SCIA trainset) was used as a second collection of images for similarity searching. In comparison to Profiset, the SCIA trainset is smaller and the quality of text data is much lower; on the other hand, it has been designed to contain images for all keywords from the SCIA task concept lists, which makes it a very good fallback for topics not sufficiently covered in Profiset.

5   Evaluation

Participation in the SCIA challenge allowed us to compare our system to other solutions and also to evaluate the performance of various settings of our system. As explained in Section 3, the annotation tool has multiple components that have various parameters. The following sections describe the most interesting findings, more details can be found in the reports on DISA participation in SCIA 2014 [6,7]. Let us also mention that the implementation with DeCAF descriptors was not ready before the SCIA competition deadline, therefore it did not enter the competition. However, the organizers kindly agreed to evaluate the DeCAF implementation for us afterward (out of the contest).

The quality of annotations was measured in terms of precision (P), recall (R), F-measure (F), and mean average precision (MAP). All these measures can be computed from two different perspectives: concept-based and sample-based. A concept-based precision (or any other measure) is computed for each concept, whereas sample-based precision is computed for each image to annotate. In both cases, the arithmetic mean was used as a global measure of performance. More details about the measures can be found in [19].

Visual Descriptors. As expected, the choice of visual descriptors used in the similarity searching phase is crucial for the overall performance of the annotation system. Using the cutting-edge $DeCAF_7$ features, the quality of results was 10-20 % higher than with older MPEG7 features. The values of individual measures are provided in Table 1.

Knowledge Base Size and Quality. To analyze the influence of dataset size and quality on the annotation system performance, we utilized several test image collections that were employed in the similarity search phase. Apart from the SCIA 500K dataset and Profiset 20M, we created random subsets of Profiset with 500K, 2M and 5M images. The performance of the annotation system on individual datasets is depicted in Figure 2. For each set of experiments, optimal settings of the semantic analysis phase were chosen so that the influence of similarity search parameters is clearly visible.

The first two groups of results compare the performance of DeCAF on SCIA 500K and Profiset 500K. We can clearly see that the higher-quality Profiset database provides better results in all three metrics. For both collections, the result quality grows with number k of similar images taken into consideration.

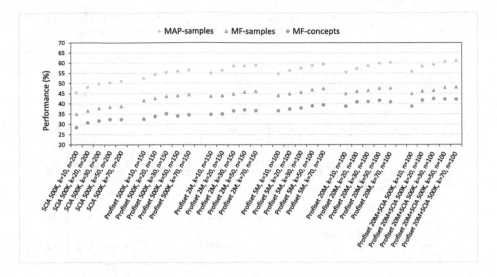

Fig. 2. Influence of the dataset quality and size on the annotation performance.

The following result groups provide comparison of DeCAF performance on high-quality datasets of different sizes. We can observe that increasing dataset size continually improves the result quality, so we can assume that even better results could be achieved if we had a larger reference dataset with high-quality data. Again, better results are generally achieved for larger k.

Finally, the last group of results depicts the results achieved by combination of Profiset 20M and SCIA 500K data. The slight improvement over Profiset 20M is caused by the fact that the SCIA 500K dataset covers all topics considered in the annotation task. This increases the chance of correctly identifying less common concepts that do not appear in the Profiset collection.

Semantic Analysis. Next, we focus on the semantic analysis part of our annotation process that utilizes WordNet relationships. Table 1 compares MPEG7-based and DeCAF-based similarity search combined with different levels of semantic analysis.

The base semantic analysis uses only the frequency of the words occurring in the retrieved similar images. In the next step, we have used WordNet synsets instead of the original words. Therefore, synonyms present the similar images keywords are grouped together (see Section 3.2) thus increasing their probability to enter the final annotation. The two final steps then utilize the relationships between to synsets to find the most probable words for the annotation (see Section 3.2). We can observe that for both the MPEG and DeCAF data, adding semantic analysis steps consistently increases the final result quality.

Efficiency. The annotation of a single image requires on average about 4-5 seconds. The overall processing time is determined by the costs of four

Table 1. Experiments on SCIA development dataset: MPEG and DeCAF similarity search over 20M Profiset combined with different levels of semantic analysis.

Semantic analysis	MP-c	MR-c	MF-c	MP-s	MR-s	MF-s	MAP-s
MPEG, basic word frequency analysis	18.2	32.9	19.0	23.8	40.8	27.6	34.7
MPEG, mapping words to synsets, synset frequency analysis	29.1	29.2	22.4	28.3	39.5	30.3	38.4
MPEG, semantic probability computation using hypernymy, hyponymy	29.2	26.7	21.2	30.1	44.2	33.1	42.1
MPEG, full semantic probability comp. (hypernymy, hyponymy, meronymy, holonymy)	29.5	27.5	21.8	30.4	45.2	33.5	42.7
DeCAF, basic word frequency analysis	32.5	46.8	33.6	37.4	49.9	39.6	49.5
DeCAF, mapping words to synsets, synset frequency analysis	48.9	48.8	40.6	42.7	55.6	44.9	55.6
DeCAF, semantic probability computation using hypernymy, hyponymy	48.0	48.5	41.5	44.6	61.0	48.1	60.8
DeCAF, full semantic probability comp. (hypernymy, hyponymy, meronymy, holonymy)	47.7	49.0	41.7	44.7	61.5	48.3	61.1

computationally intensive phases: 1) extraction of visual features from the query image, 2) the similarity search, 3) retrieval of words for similar images (these are not stored in the similarity index to minimize its size), and 4) the computation of synset probabilities over the candidate synset graph.

The annotation tool with the parameter setup as described above needed about 1 second for extraction of DeCAF descriptor from a common size image. The similarity search in 20M images took about 1-2 seconds, the retrieval of the words from the 70 similar images needed about half a second and the semantic analysis restricted to 100 most probable synsets required another 0.5-1 second.

SCIA Task Results. After fine-tuning the various annotation parameters on SCIA development data, the DISA team submitted several competition runs. The results of the ImageCLEF 2014 SCIA Task are summarized in Table 2, more details can be found in [7, 19]. Altogether, the DISA team ranked fifth out of eleven participating teams.

In comparison with other competing groups, our best solution ranked rather high in both sample-based mean F-measure and sample-based MAP. Especially the sample-based MAP achieved by the run DISA_04 was very close to the overall best result (DISA_04 – MAP 34.3, best result kdevir_09 – MAP 36.8). The results for concept-based mean F-measure were less competitive, which did not come as a surprise. In general, the search-based approach works well for frequent terms, whereas concepts for which there are few examples are difficult to recognize. Furthermore, the MPEG7 similarity is more suitable for scenes and dominant objects rather than details which were sometimes needed by SCIA.

Table 2 also shows that with the DISA DeCAF run, the DISA team would rank as close second while outperforming the winner in most sample-based quality measures. However, it is clear that the KDEVIR solution still significantly outperforms ours in terms of concept-based MF. The evaluation results also

Table 2. The SCIA competition results table from [19] with a new line for DISA DeCAF results. Only the best result for each group is given. The systems are ranked by overall performance as defined in [19].

System	MAP-samples				MF-samples				MF-concepts				
	all	ani.	food	207	all	ani.	food	207	all	ani.	food	207	unseen
KDEVIR 9	36.8	33.1	67.1	28.9	37.7	29.9	64.9	32.0	54.7	67.1	65.1	31.6	66.1
DISA DeCAF	48.7	51.0	67.1	32.3	39.9	44.4	48.5	26.7	41.1	45.3	42.1	22.4	44.9
MIL 3	36.9	30.9	68.6	23.3	27.5	20.6	53.1	18.0	34.7	34.7	50.4	16.9	36.7
MindLab 1	37.0	43.1	63.0	22.1	25.8	17.0	45.2	18.3	30.7	35.1	35.3	16.7	34.7
MLIA 9	27.8	18.8	53.6	16.7	24.8	12.1	46.0	16.4	33.2	32.7	37.3	16.9	34.8
DISA 4	34.3	46.6	39.6	19.0	29.7	40.6	31.2	16.9	19.1	23.0	22.3	7.3	19.0
RUC 7	27.5	25.2	44.2	15.1	29.3	28.0	28.2	20.7	25.3	20.1	23.1	10.0	18.7
IPL 9	23.4	30.0	48.5	18.9	18.4	20.2	29.8	17.5	15.8	15.8	33.3	12.5	22.0
IMC 1	25.1	35.7	35.6	12.9	16.3	14.3	21.0	10.9	12.5	10.2	15.1	6.1	11.2
INAOE 5	9.6	6.9	15.0	8.5	5.3	0.4	0.5	6.4	10.3	1.0	0.8	17.9	19.0
NII 1	14.7	23.2	22.0	4.6	13.0	18.9	18.7	4.9	2.3	3.0	2.1	0.9	1.8
FINKI 1	6.9	N/A	N/A	N/A	7.2	8.1	12.3	4.1	4.7	6.3	9.0	2.9	4.7

show that DISA DeCAF achieved better results than some other groups who also employed the neural network approach. This confirms the importance of the semantic analysis step developed by our group.

6   Conclusions and Future Work

In this paper, we have described our approach to general image annotation task. The presented tool applies similarity-based retrieval on annotated image collections to retrieve images similar to a given query, and then utilizes semantic resources to detect dominant topics in the descriptions of similar images. We have presented experimental results with various settings of our tool as well as the tool performance in 2014 Scalable Concept Image Annotation challenge. The results show that the search-based approach to annotation can be successfully used to identify dominant concepts in images. As opposed to training-based annotators that can provide better results for a limited set of pre-trained concepts, the strength of the similarity-search approach lies in the fact that it requires minimum training and easily scales to new concepts.

The experiments and the competition revealed several directions in which the system can be further improved. First, we plan to extend the set of semantic relationships exploited in the annotation process, using e.g. specialized ontologies or Wikipedia. We also intend to develop a more sophisticated method of the final selection of concepts. Furthermore, we would like to improve the response times of our implementation. In particular, the feature extraction can be made faster by introducing GPU processing, while SSD disks can be used for keyword data storage. We will also focus on a more efficient implementation of the semantic analysis phase.

Acknowledgments. This work was supported by the Czech national research project GBP103/12/G084. The hardware infrastructure was provided by the METACentrum under the programme LM 2010005.

References

1. Ballan, L., Uricchio, T., Seidenari, L., Bimbo, A.D.: A cross-media model for automatic image annotation. In: International Conference on Multimedia Retrieval (ICMR), pp. 73–80 (2014)
2. Batko, M., Botorek, J., Budikova, P., Zezula, P.: Content-based annotation and classification framework: a general multi-purpose approach. In: 17th International Database Engineering & Applications Symposium (IDEAS 2013), pp. 58–67 (2013)
3. Batko, M., Falchi, F., Lucchese, C., Novak, D., Perego, R., Rabitti, F., Sedmidubský, J., Zezula, P.: Building a web-scale image similarity search system. Multimedia Tools and Applications **47**(3), 599–629 (2010)
4. Botorek, J., Budíková, P., Zezula, P.: Visual concept ontology for image annotations. CoRR abs/1412.6082 (2014). http://arxiv.org/abs/1412.6082
5. Budikova, P., Batko, M., Zezula, P.: Evaluation platform for content-based image retrieval systems. In: Gradmann, S., Borri, F., Meghini, C., Schuldt, H. (eds.) TPDL 2011. LNCS, vol. 6966, pp. 130–142. Springer, Heidelberg (2011)
6. Budíková, P., Botorek, J., Batko, M., Zezula, P.: DISA at imageclef 2014 revised: Search-based image annotation with decaf features. CoRR abs/1409.4627 (2014). http://arxiv.org/abs/1409.4627
7. Budikova, P., Botorek, J., Batko, M., Zezula, P.: DISA at Image CLEF 2014: The search-based solution for scalable image annotation. In: CLEF 2014 Evaluation Labs and Workshop, Online Working Notes (2014)
8. Donahue, J., Jia, Y., Vinyals, O., Hoffman, J., Zhang, N., Tzeng, E., Darrell, T.: DeCAF: A Deep Convolutional Activation Feature for Generic Visual Recognition. In: International Conference on Machine Learning, pp. 647–655 (2014)
9. Fellbaum, C. (ed.): WordNet: An Electronic Lexical Database. The MIT Press (1998)
10. Hu, J., Lam, K.M.: An efficient two-stage framework for image annotation. Pattern Recognition **46**(3), 936–947 (2013)
11. Ke, X., Li, S., Chen, G.: Real web community based automatic image annotation. Computers & Electrical Engineering **39**(3), 945–956 (2013)
12. Krizhevsky, A., Sutskever, I., Hinton, G.E.: ImageNet classification with deep convolutional neural networks. In: Advances in Neural Information Processing Systems (NIPS 2012), pp. 1106–1114 (2012)
13. Lokoč, J., Novák, D., Batko, M., Skopal, T.: Visual image search: feature signatures or/and global descriptors. In: Navarro, G., Pestov, V. (eds.) SISAP 2012. LNCS, vol. 7404, pp. 177–191. Springer, Heidelberg (2012)
14. Makadia, A., Pavlovic, V., Kumar, S.: A new baseline for image annotation. In: Forsyth, D., Torr, P., Zisserman, A. (eds.) ECCV 2008, Part III. LNCS, vol. 5304, pp. 316–329. Springer, Heidelberg (2008)
15. MPEG-7: Multimedia content description interfaces. Part 3: Visual. ISO/IEC 15938-3:2002 (2002)
16. Novak, D., Batko, M., Zezula, P.: Large-scale similarity data management with distributed metric index. Inf. Processing & Management **48**(5), 855–872 (2012)

17. Novak, D., Zezula, P.: Rank aggregation of candidate sets for efficient similarity search. In: Decker, H., Lhotská, L., Link, S., Spies, M., Wagner, R.R. (eds.) DEXA 2014, Part II. LNCS, vol. 8645, pp. 42–58. Springer, Heidelberg (2014)
18. Tousch, A.M., Herbin, S., Audibert, J.Y.: Semantic hierarchies for image annotation: A survey. Pattern Recognition **45**(1), 333–345 (2012)
19. Villegas, M., Paredes, R.: Overview of the ImageCLEF 2014 Scalable Concept Image Annotation Task. In: CLEF 2014 Evaluation Labs and Workshop, Online Working Notes (2014)
20. Wang, X.J., Zhang, L., Ma, W.Y.: Duplicate-search-based image annotation using web-scale data. Proceedings of the IEEE **100**(9), 2705–2721 (2012)
21. Zhang, D., Islam, M.M., Lu, G.: A review on automatic image annotation techniques. Pattern Recognition **45**(1), 346–362 (2012)
22. Zhang, X., Li, Z., Chao, W.H.: Improving image tags by exploiting web search results. Multimedia Tools and Applications **62**(3), 601–631 (2013)

NLP-Based Classifiers to Generalize Expert Assessments in E-Reputation

Jean-Valère Cossu[1]([✉]), Emmanuel Ferreira[1], Killian Janod[1,2], Julien Gaillard[1], and Marc El-Bèze[1]

[1] LIA/Université d'Avignon Et des Pays de Vaucluse, 39 Chemin des Meinajaries, Agroparc, BP 91228, 84911 Avignon Cedex 9, France
{jean-valere.cossu,emmanuel.ferreira,
julien.gaillard}@alumni.univ-avignon.fr, marc.elbeze@univ-avignon.fr
[2] ORKIS, Aix En Provence, France
kjanod@orkis.com

Abstract. *Online Reputation Management*(ORM) is currently dominated by expert abilities. One of the great challenges is to effectively collect annotated training samples, especially to be able to generalize a small pool of expert feedback from area scale to a more global scale. One possible solution is to use advanced *Machine Learning* (ML) techniques, to select annotations from training samples, and propagate effectively and concisely. We focus on the critical issue of understanding the different levels of annotations. Using the framework proposed by the RepLab contest we present a considerable number of experiments in Reputation Monitoring and Author Profiling. The proposed methods rely on a large variety of *Natural Language Processing* (NLP) methods exploiting tweet contents and some background contextual information. We show that simple algorithms only considering tweets content are effective against state-of-the-art techniques.

1 Introduction

Analyzing a company's and an individual's reputation is a difficult end-user oriented problem, requiring complex modeling. Experts involved in this modeling might generate features that computers are not able to differentiate or capture. ORM has become a key component for an entity's communication strategy with the growing influence of information available on social networks [1]. Reputation managers still have to monitor and analyze social data related to their brand for alarm signals manually and take immediate action to avoid damages on the reputation of their clients on key issues. Hybrid approaches have been proposed in works such as [2,3] for automatic annotation under expert supervision and estimation of the gain in using support tools. However, as the field is relatively new, the algorithmic support for ORM is still limited.

Last RepLab[1] [4,5] and TASS[2] [6] evaluations have shown significant algorithmic advances in several aspects related to ORM tasks such as filtering,

---

[1] http://www.limosine-project.eu/events/replab2013
[2] http://www.daedalus.es/TASS2013/about.php

© Springer International Publishing Switzerland 2015
J. Mothe et al. (Eds.): CLEF 2015, LNCS 9283, pp. 340–351, 2015.
DOI: 10.1007/978-3-319-24027-5_37

polarity for reputation (*Sentiment Analysis*) and clustering (the so-called '*Topic Detection*' by the organizers of RepLab). It became quite clear that systems have achieved high classification results ([7–9]) that may not reflect annotators' assessments variety. Nevertheless, other aspects such as *polarity analysis* at politics-entity level, *tweets ranking*, *dimensions detection, socioeconomic classification* for *Author Profiling* (with the PAN contest [10]) still require further progress. This is mainly because these aspects are vague, subjective and may depend on each expert. Then, it becomes harder to automatically predict an exact class when the models are difficult to understand and subject to diversity.

We proposed experiments for all the tasks in the 2013 and 2014 editions of RepLab. In this paper, we deal with *Reputation Alert Detection*, *Reputation Dimension Assignment* and *Author Profiling* (AP). We will not focus on the remaining tasks since the issues have been considered as partially solved [7–9]. Our main objective is to extract sets of textual contents requiring a particular attention from a reputation manager. By doing so, we aim at guiding reputation experts to understand why a decision should be taken after these tweets. For this purpose we also need to determine the importance of an author and its type with regard to its '*bag-of-tweets*'. We use *NLP-based classifiers* to project each tweet in a *multidimensional reputation* space to generalize the expert's point-of-view. Then, we determine whether this expertise concerns the topic of a particular message or the Influence of an author.

The rest of this paper is organized as follows: Section 2 gives an overview of related work and establishes further motivation for our work. In Sections 3 - 4, we provide details of our approaches to tackle *E-Reputation tasks* and *Author Profiling*. A discussion of our results is provided in Section 5. Finally, Section 6 give our conclusions on our work and open several perspectives.

2   Related Work

To our knowledge, most of the contributions on ORM were proposed in the last editions of RepLab [4,5] and TASS [6]. Others contributions took place in the context of major national elections in Mexico [11], France and Spain respectively on the behalf of the Imagiweb project [12,13] and TASS campaign [14].

RepLab'2014's reputation dimensions classification task is a complement to the *Topic Detection* of the previous edition. It also comparable to the *Target-Oriented Opinion* defined in the Imagiweb [12,13] project as it is nearer to a stress classification of the aspects of the entity under public scrutiny. Where these stresses are defined by experts (stakeholders, reputation managers, communication adviser or scientists) and only reflect their own interest, which may differ from the real information carried in the tweets (topic, event...). All these works mainly rely on supervised classification methods based on tweet content and its more or less complex pre-processing [7,15]. Moreover, ORM issues are tackled at a different granularity level: global approaches, domain or entity specific models. There are also three sub-levels of approach: the use of meta-data, the human involvement in the systems (so-called hybrid categorization approaches) and the use of additional lexical or linguistic resources. In this light, *SibTex* [16] investigated both domain and language specific approaches. They reported a slight improvement in using domain or language dedicated knowledge bases in their *k-NN* approach. This statement may confirm that any information deemed important should be considered to feed systems (in some way it can be considered as a form of enrichment) rather than focusing on a single entity. It then requires a huge amount of annotated data to provide stable hypotheses.

PAN [10] provides a nice overview of AP recent progress. More generally in RepLab *Social Network Analysis* techniques were used for both tweets and user ranking [15,17,18]. Assuming that *Influencers* tweet mainly about '*Hot Topics*' *UTDBRG* group obtained the best performance by using *Trending Topics Information*. Some works investigated extended tweet-representation to consider information beyond the tweet textual content such as pseudo-relevant term expansion [19] as well as Wikipedia-concept term expansion [20] to enrich the tweets and improve a *Random Forest classifier*. These works imply a heavy involvement to induce rules or to build the resources used. We also experimented a joint work linking *Tweet Clustering* [21] and *Dimensions Classification* [22] to *Priority Detection* over a *NLP-based Classification*.

Nevertheless, according to RepLab organizers [4,5], it remains difficult to find a correspondence between performances and algorithm or features used. Moreover, the amount of research dedicated to understanding the experts' stress effects on mis-classified tweets is very limited.

3   Reputation Monitoring

The RepLab [4,5] framework propose a complete Reputation Monitoring challenge for more than 61 entities drawn from four domains: Automotive, Banking, Music and University. We approach Reputation Monitoring as the following cascade: for a given set of tweets in a certain time span, we have to identify opinions in key topics whatever the entity concerned as it could be done manually by reputation management experts just in reading the tweets stream. Then systems have to identify tweet clusters (each cluster represents a topic/event/issue/conversation). As these aspects are not know *a-priori* we are far from a typical categorization task or standard Topic Detection problem. The clusters are then ranked into Priority level (*Alert, Important, Unimportant*). Additionally systems have to look for positive or negative implications of the contents on the entity's reputation and finally tweets are categorized according to their *Reputation Dimensions* using standards given by the Reputation Institute's Reptrak framework[3]. From the perspective of reputation management, '*Reputation Alerts*' which have immediate and negative effects on the entity's reputation must be clearly identified and detected early enough to prevent the number of tweets growth over these topics.

---

[3] http://www.reputationinstitute.com/about-reputation-institute/
the-reptrak-framework

In this paper, we intend to extend the work done in the RepLab context. We aim to observe the effect of tweet content and its engineering on ORM and ML methods. Our main contribution is the assessment of tweet content efficiency for E-Reputation Analysis.

3.1   Approaches

A short description and preliminary results obtained in each task with our approaches have been presented in [23,24]. Class hypotheses are generated by the following systems:

- Cosine is considered as a more or less lightweight statistical baseline;
- SVM is used as a state-of-the-art classification baseline;
- We also propose a CRF-based approach to extend the bag-of-words.

Within those systems we use a Word2Vec models as generalization engine.

Terms Weighting. The features used by our baselines proposals are words, bi-grams and tri-grams. They compose the tweet discriminant bag-of-words representation. We use Term Frequency-Inverse Document Frequency (TF-IDF) [25] combined with the Gini purity criteria, as several works reported improvements using this association [26]. Purity of a word G_i is defined with the Gini criterion as follows (1):

$$G_i = \sum_{c \in \mathbb{C}} \mathbb{P}^2(i|c) = \sum_{c \in \mathbb{C}} \left(\frac{DF_i(c)}{DF_{(i)}} \right)^2 \tag{1}$$

where C is the set of classes, $DF_{(i)}$ is the # of tweets in the training set containing the word i and $DF_i(c)$ is the # of tweets of the training set annotated with class c containing word i. This factor is used to weight the contribution $\omega_{i,d}$ of each term i in document d as (2):

$$\omega_{i,d} = TF_{i,d} \times log(\frac{N}{DF_{\mathbb{C}}(i)}) \times G_i \tag{2}$$

Where N is the number of tweets in the training set and the contribution $\omega_{i,c}$ of each term i in class c by replacing the word # of occurrences $TF_{i,d}$ by $DF_{i,c}$:

Baselines. We propose two baselines approaches. The first one consists in computing similarities between the tweet BoW and each class BoW as follows (3):

$$cos(d,c) = \frac{\sum\limits_{i \in d \cap c} \omega_{i,d} \times \omega_{i,c}}{\sqrt{\sum\limits_{i \in d} \omega_{i,d}^2 \times \sum\limits_{i \in c} \omega_{i,c}^2}} \tag{3}$$

The second one consists in training linear multi-class Support Vectors Machine [27] with the objective of classifying multiple classes. Classifiers have been trained with default parameters and the BoW vectorial representation of each tweet d (each term weight is computed as (2) but with DF_i instead of $TF_{i,d}$).

Multi-word Expression. In order to take into account the sequence of words in the tagging issue, we consider Conditional Random Fields(CRFs) [28], more exactly Linear CRFs. They represent log-linear models, normalized at the entire tweet level, where each word has an output class associated to it. Thus, CRFs can localize specific positions in tweets that carry information and highlight continuous contextual information. In this setup the probability between words and classes for the whole tweet (of N words) is defined as follows:

$$P(c_1^N|w_1^N) = \frac{1}{Z} \prod_{n=1}^{N} \sum_{m=1}^{M} \lambda_m \cdot h_m(c_{n-1}, c_n, s)) \tag{4}$$

Log-linear models are based on M feature functions h_m computed at each position from the previous class c_{n-1}, current class c_n and the whole observation sequence s (tweet). λ_m are the weights estimated during the training process and Z is a normalization term given by:

$$Z = \sum_{c_1^N} \prod_{n=1}^{N} \sum_{m=1}^{M} \lambda_m \cdot h_m(c_{n-1}, c_n, s)) \tag{5}$$

The tweets from the training set were used to train our CRF tagger with unigram (neighborhood window of length 2 around the current word) and bi-gram features. Then a CRF tagged each word in every tweets and decision for the final tweet's label is made by majority.

Lexical Context. RepLab test set vocabulary size is twice as big as the one of the annotated set. In order to reduce the impact of the information loss carried by out of vocabulary words (OOV), we project OOV into the known vocabulary in a Continuous distributed words representation [29] (considered as a generalization engine). We used a Word2Vec [30] model which is learn by a Skip-gram neural-network. This network try to maximize the following log probability [30]:

$$\frac{1}{N} \sum_{n=1}^{N} \sum_{-c<j<c, j\neq 0} log(\frac{exp(i_{w_{t+j}}^T o_{w_t}))}{\sum_{w=1}^{N} exp(i_w^T o_{w_t})}) \tag{6}$$

where N is the number of words in the training corpus, $w_0..w_N$ the sequence of training words, c the size of the context. Word2vec models where proved being able to capture syntactic and semantic relationship between words [30]. It allows us to measure similarity with simple geometric operations like sum and angle metrics. We trained a 600 dimensions,10 context windows, multilingual (English+Spanish) Skip-gram model over RepLab's background messages [4] which we added a large amount of easily available corpora[4]. This trained

---

[4] enwik9, One Billion Word Language Modelling Benchmark, the Brown corpus, English GigaWord from 1 to 5, eswik, parallel es-en europarl.

model is then used as a generalization engine by other classifier i.e.: it finds for each OOV in the test sample the closest word in the Continuous distributed words representation which exists in the training vocabulary and has a sufficient purity as defined with (1).

4   Author Profiling

As far as the author of the messages plays a key role in determining the *Reputation Alerts* we have to profile authors. Besides their type, the number of comments and followers are also important aspects that determine the influence of an author in Twitter in a potential reputation-dangerous perspective. These tasks are usually addressed as Community Detection or Complex Network issues. This means that systems should define profile according to social meta-data (followers' graphs, numbers of favorites, followers or comments and so on). It then puts the need on complete relations graphs which may not be possible to extract in Twitter with private/deleted account and with queries limitations from Twitter's API. We understand *Author Profiling* as the following issue: using tweet contents that Twitter-users produced, systems have to reproduce experts' evaluations: ranking users according to their influence level and detecting the socioeconomic category users belong to.

4.1   Approaches

We investigate AP using different NLP-based profile representations. We made the same assumption of specific vocabulary that can differentiate opinion-makers from non opinion-makers[5] and users from separate socioeconomic categories. In our official submissions [24] we considered *k-NN* classification for *Influence Detection* and *Socioeconomic Categorization* (for this last task we also considered the Cosine described above (3)). We investigate the following user-profile definitions: *'User-as-document'* [12] and *'Bag-of-tweets'* (respectively noted *'UaD'* and *'BoT'*):

- *'UaD'* consists in merging all tweets from a profile to create one document and computing a similarity between each document and each class;
- *'BoT'* considers a binary classification problem for each tweet. Classification is achieved by counting the number of tweets tagged for the considered user.

The *'UaD'* *k-NN* consists in matching each user BoW to the most similar ones in the training set which are voting for the class they are belonging to according to the similarity index (here Jaccard). For the *'BoT'* Cosine, a user is deemed the belong to a socioeconomic category if a majority of his tweets are themselves considered to belong to this socioeconomic category. In both cases, ranking is achieved with the probability of being an *'Influencer'*.

---

[5] According to [10] influential Twitter authors in the economic domains considered in RepLab tend to be male in the 35-49 age range.

5   Experimental Evaluation and Results

5.1   Evaluation

We compare our proposal to RepLab baselines[6] and best submitted systems in both tasks. We report our results using RepLab official metrics. Although Accuracy (Acc) is a standard metric easy to understand, it has nevertheless a drawback when it comes to compare non-informative systems on unbalanced data-sets. RepLab organizers previously proposed a F-Measure (FM) based on Reliability and Sensitivity [31]. This metric compares the gold-standard with system produced priority relationship (in the case of the Alert Detection task). In addition, we compute an average F-Score (AvgF), based on Precision and Recall for each class which gives an overview of the system's ability to recover information from each class. Author Ranking is viewed as a Search problem, having the domain as query, systems have to return a ranking of the most relevant users. Evaluation is done according to Mean Average Precision (MAP) which compares ordered vectors based on a binary reference. Nevertheless with only two domains it is not possible to conclude that MAP improvements are significant.

5.2   Reputation Monitoring

We chose to tackle the classification issues with a global approach. Our experiments in using entity's or domain's specific training process shown no significant improvement.

Reputation Dimensions. Experts proposed the following Reputation Dimensions taxonomy: *Citizenship, Governance, Innovation, Leadership, Performance, Product&Services, WorkPlace* with an additional Undefined concept (see [5] for more details). As the *'Undefined'* class is excluded from the RepLab evaluation process, we first chose to investigate it as a filtering issue. That is to say, when systems are not able to significantly predict a dimension for a given tweet they tag this tweet as related to an *'Undefined'* Dimension. This experiment has shown no significant improvements for contextualized CRF (noted w/ Context in table 1), even if it simplifies the models' complexity (from 8 to 7 classes). Then, better than withdrawing the *'Undefined'* class in our evaluation (-U), we made additional experiments pulling back *'Undefined'* tweets (+U). Cosine is then significantly improved by the lexical context. All our proposal then performed competitively with respect to the best official submissions (noted Best_Acc and

---

[6] The organizers provided two baselines in the Reputation Dimension detection task and Author Categorization. A Naive one that assigns the most frequent class to each tweet. A ML-based classification using a linear SVM for each entity with Bag-of-Word's (BoW) binary representation. For the Priority Detection task the baseline consists in tagging the tweets of the test set with the label of the closest tweet (Jaccard similarity) in the training set. The Ranking baseline ranks authors by descending number of followers.

Best_F in table 1) and baselines. And that neither using generalization and considering the *'Undefined'* as part of the classification issue or not. Finally, the *'Undefined'* class shows interesting results. SVM as a discriminative method is the most perturbed by the novelty provided from this class. While additional context tend to reinforce Cosine and CRF robustness in generalizing new vocabulary, it has no effect on SVM performances.

Table 1. Dimensions detection performances ordered according to Accuracy(-U). Best performances are highlighted in bold. Statistical significant improvements (averaged across entities) over the SVM(-U) (two-sided pairwise t-test $p < 0.05$) are denoted *

Method	AvgF (-U)	Acc (-U)	AvgF(+U)	Acc(+U)
CRF w/ Context	.492	**.771***	.481	.761
CRF	.491	.769*	.483	.762
Cosine w/ Context	**.505**	.739	.494	.707
Cosine	.491	.736	.500	.693
SVM	.469	.732	.461	.679
SVM w/ Context	.468	.732	.456	.679
Best_Acc	.473	.731	-	-
Best_F	.489	.695	-	-
SVM Baseline	.38	.622	-	-
Naive Baseline	.152	.560	-	-

Priority Detection. We proposed during RepLab'2013 a kNN-based classification method [23] (noted Lia_Prio_5 in table 2) and obtained the best *FM (R,S)* reported up to our knowledge in this task. Other performances ranked with regards to FM are noted in Table 2. Both SVM and Cosine approaches are competitive according to *Acc* but their *AvgF* remain lower and the Cosine even stays lower than the Replab2013 baseline according to FM (R,S). Given the relatively limited number of *'Alerts'*, an alternative evaluation reconsidering the classification issue as search problem (ranking) should provide interesting additional information.

Our experimental evaluations establish that tweet lexical content is sufficient for simple ML approaches to tackle the tasks of identifying the reputation alerts

Table 2. Priority detection performances ordered by F-Measure (R,S).

Method	AvgF	Acc	FM (R,S)
Lia_Prio_5	**.571**	.636	**.335**
SVM	.563	.644	.304
CRF	.554	.633	0.318
SVM w/ Context	.564	**.645**	.304
CRF w/ Context	.551	.631	0.318
Baseline	.512	.570	.274
Cosine w/ Context	.562	.634	.260
Cosine	.561	.633	.260

and dimensions. Our experiments with generalization shown that lexical context can be useful and efficient in dimension assignment but not for reputation alerts.

5.3 Author Profiling

We chose to process English and Spanish messages separately to reduce the models complexity for the *'UaD'* approach. We supposed that profiles have particular influence or socioeconomic characteristics in their vocabulary regardless the domain they are mainly associated with.

Author Ranking. As the experts did not rank the authors, we first have considered a binary classification problem for each author. The ranking can be tackled as a post processing applied on the binary classification output [24]. We have chosen to rank the authors according to their probability of being *'Influencers'*. As it can be seen in table 3, our proposal (noted Lia_AR_1) got an Average MAP under the best system, but it was globally better than the Baseline approach. In the Banking domain, which seems to be a difficult one, Lia_AR_1 performed better than both of them.

Since this system was optimized on a development set in order to maximize the AvgF and not the MAP (used for evaluation), there was clearly some room for improvement. We then chose to estimate the parameter values of a *k-NN* for each language with the purpose to maximize the MAP[7] on the development set. For instance, with k=16 for English, (17 for Spanish) on the development. It can been observed in table 3 (row LIA_NEW) that on the test set, the results are better than the ones obtained by all submitted systems. It is nevertheless impossible to verify that improvements are statistically significant.

Table 3. Author Ranking performances ordered according to Average MAP.

Method	Automotive	Banking	Average MAP
Lia_NEW (UaD)	**.764**	**.652**	**.708**
Best	.721	.410	.565
Lia_AR_1 (UaD)	.502	.450	.476
Baseline	.370	.385	.378
Cosine (BoT)	.207	.194	.200

Author Categorization. Organizers reported that only one approach [24] (noted Lia_AC_1 in the left part of table 3) performed as well as *'most frequent class'* and ML SVM baselines according to *Acc*. Cosine_RA uses a re-affectation post-process over the Cosine output (described in the next section) in order to fit class distribution of the training set but it shown no performances improvements. The SVM baseline reaches the best *AvgF* and stay far above all proposals when considering the *'Undecidable'* class as part of the evaluation process. When we

---

[7] This way, there is no need to introduce any offset or to penalize a class as done previously in [24].

ignore the *'Undecidable'* (the right part of table 3) from the evaluation process the re-affectation post-process allows small *AvgF* improvements with limited losses in *Acc* but it remains unsatisfactory. Author Categorization is still an open problem. The availability of more data will surely allow to propose a deeper results analysis.

Table 4. Author Categorization performances ordered by Average Accuracy.

Method	Average Acc	AvgF	Method	Average Acc	AvgF
Lia_AC_1 (UaD)	.471	.269	Cosine (BoT)	**.486**	.244
Baseline-SVM	.460	**.302**	Cosine_RA (BoT)	.481	.294
MF-Baseline	.435	-	Lia_AC_1 (UaD)	.393	.253
Cosine (BoT)	.346	.185			
Cosine_RA (BoT)	.341	.221			

5.4 Classes Distribution Issue and Perspectives

With regard to a large variety of label distribution in the *Author Categorization* and *Dimensions Detection* training sets, we decided to have a harmonization post-process of our systems output. For each output the post-process consists in considering the second hypothesis of the system (fill small classes despite having a better confidence in a bigger class) in the following case:

– The best hypothesis is an over-populated class [8]
– The second hypothesis is an under-populated class
– The score differential between the two hypotheses is not significant.

Another approach, taking root in the field of game theory, could also be considered. In [32], the author applies a matching game algorithm to a ranking problem in the context of movie recommendations. This method lie in the fact that both movies and users have preferences and both of them are involved in the recommendation process. In other words, the system does not simply recommend the best movie based on the user's preferences, but also takes into account the movie point of view, by somehow selecting the best candidates. If we transpose this idea to our classification problem, we could consider a matching game in which the players would be authors (or tweets) and classes. Each author would have its preferred class and each class its preferred author. More precisely, both would have a list ordered by preferences which means regarding each class we would be able to select the most representative tweets.

6 Conclusions

RepLab contests allowed us to perform a large number of experiments with state-of-the-art evaluation. Our experimental evaluations establish that discriminating textual features inferred from expert assessments coupled with simple

---

[8] The notion of over or under population is considered with regards to the class distribution in the training set.

ML approaches is sufficient to expand these feedback to unlabeled data. However, while the results remain lower in term of *Author Profiling*, they prepare the ground for further experiments using additional data.

In future work, we plan to examine relations between classes and in a broader sense tasks to discover latent hierarchies. Since *Lexical Context* provided interesting results we also intend to study an interesting *Lexical Expansion* simulating, *Active Learning* over non-annotated provided tweets. In this way, tweets which do not correspond to expert stresses could be filtered or manually checked before being re-injected as supplementary training material. Since the mass of data has caused many problems, we will consider automatic summarizations of tweet clusters and user profiles to reduce class spaces and perform a more rapid classification.

Acknowledgments. This work is funded by ImagiWeb ANR-2012-CORD-002-01. Thanks to Judith Cuinier for proofreading this paper.

References

1. O'Connor, B., Balasubramanyan, R., Routledge, B.R., Smith, N.A.: From tweets to polls: Linking text sentiment to public opinion time series. In: ICWSM 11 (2010)
2. Peetz, M.H., Spina, D., Gonzalo, J., De Rijke, M.: Towards an active learning system for company name disambiguation in microblog streams. In: CLEF 2013
3. Carrillo-de Albornoz, J., Amigó, E., Spina, D., Gonzalo, J.: Orma: A semi-automatic tool for online reputation monitoring in twitter. In: Advances in IR
4. Amigó, E., Carrillo de Albornoz, J., Chugur, I., Corujo, A., Gonzalo, J., Martín, T., Meij, E., de Rijke, M., Spina, D.: Overview of RepLab 2013: evaluating online reputation monitoring systems. In: Forner, P., Müller, H., Paredes, R., Rosso, P., Stein, B. (eds.) CLEF 2013. LNCS, vol. 8138, pp. 333–352. Springer, Heidelberg (2013)
5. Amigó, E., Carrillo-de-Albornoz, J., Chugur, I., Corujo, A., Gonzalo, J., Meij, E., de Rijke, M., Spina, D.: Overview of RepLab 2014: author profiling and reputation dimensions for online reputation management. In: Kanoulas, E., Lupu, M., Clough, P., Sanderson, M., Hall, M., Hanbury, A., Toms, E. (eds.) CLEF 2014. LNCS, vol. 8685, pp. 307–322. Springer, Heidelberg (2014)
6. Villena Román, J., Lana Serrano, S., Martínez Cámara, E., González Cristóbal, J.C.: Tass-workshop on sentiment analysis at SEPLN (2013)
7. Hangya, V., Farkas, R.: Filtering and polarity detection for reputation management on tweets. In: CLEF 2013
8. Gârbacea, C., Tsagkias, M., de Rijke, M.: Detecting the reputation polarity of microblog posts. In: ECAI (2014)
9. Spina, D., Gonzalo, J., Amigó, E.: Learning similarity functions for topic detection in online reputation monitoring. In: Proc. of the 37th SIGIR conference on Research & development in IR (2014)
10. Rangel, F., Rosso, P., Chugur, I., Potthast, M., Trenkmann, M., Stein, B., Verhoeven, B., Daelemans, W.: Overview of the author profiling task at pan (2014)
11. Sandoval-Almazan, R.: Using twitter in political campaigns: The case of the pri candidate in mexico. International Journal of E-Politics (IJEP) **6** (2015)

12. Kim, Y.M., Velcin, J., Bonnevay, S., Rizoiu, M.A.: Temporal multinomial mixture for instance-oriented evolutionary clustering. In: Advances in IR (2015)
13. Velcin, J., Kim, Y., Brun, C., Dormagen, J., SanJuan, E., Khouas, L., Peradotto, A., Bonnevay, S., Roux, C., Boyadjian, J., et al.: Investigating the image of entities in social media: Dataset design and first results. In: LREC (2014)
14. Pla, F., Hurtado, L.F.: Political tendency identification in twitter using sentiment analysis techniques. In: Proc. of COLING (2014)
15. Vilares, D., Hermo, M., Alonso, M.A., Gómez-Rodrıguez, C., Vilares, J.: Lys at clef replab 2014: Creating the state of the art in author influence ranking and reputation classification on twitter. In: CLEF (2014)
16. Gobeill, J., Gaudinat, A., Ruch, P.: Instance-based learning for tweet categorization in clef replab 2014. In: CLEF (2014)
17. Berrocal, J.L.A., Figuerola, C.G., Rodríguez, Á.Z.: Reina at replab2013 topic detection task: Community detection. In: CLEF (2013)
18. Ramírez-de-la Rosa, G., Villatoro-Tello, E., Jiménez-Salazar, H., Sánchez-Sánchez, C.: Towards automatic detection of user influence in twitter by means of stylistic and behavioral features. In: Human-Inspired Computing and Its Applications
19. McDonald, G., Deveaud, R., McCreadie, R., Macdonald, C., Ounis, I.: Tweet enrichment for effective dimensions classification in online reputation management. In: Ninth International AAAI Conference on Web and Social Media (2015)
20. Qureshi, M.A., ORiordan, C., Pasi, G.: Exploiting wikipedia for entity name disambiguation in tweets. In: NLP and Information Systems (2014)
21. Cossu, J.V., Bigot, B., Bonnefoy, L., Senay, G.: Towards the improvement of topic priority assignment using various topic detection methods for e-reputation monitoring on twitter. In: NLP and Information Systems (2014)
22. Cossu, J.-V., Sanjuan, E., Torres-Moreno, J.-M., El-Bèze, M.: Automatic classification and PLS-PM modeling for profiling reputation of corporate entities on twitter. In: Biemann, C., Handschuh, S., Freitas, A., Meziane, F., Métais, E. (eds.) NLDB 2015. LNCS, vol. 9103, pp. 282–289. Springer, Heidelberg (2015)
23. Cossu, J., Bigot, B., Bonnefoy, L., Morchid, M., Bost, X., Senay, G., Dufour, R., Bouvier, V., Torres-Moreno, J., El-Bèze, M.: Lia@replab 2013. In: CLEF (2013)
24. Cossu, J.V., Janod, K., Ferreira, E., Gaillard, J., El-Bèze, M.: Lia@ replab 2014: 10 methods for 3 tasks. In: CLEF (2014)
25. Jones, K.S.: A statistical interpretation of term specificity and its application in retrieval. Journal of Documentation 28, 11–21 (1972)
26. Torres-Moreno, J., El-Beze, M., Bellot, P.: Bechet, opinion detection as a topic classification problem in textual information access Chapter 9 (2013)
27. Crammer, K., Singer, Y.: On the algorithmic implementation of multiclass kernel-based vector machines. Journal of Machine Learning Research 2, 265–292 (2002)
28. Lafferty, J., McCallum, A., Pereira, F.C.: Conditional random fields: Probabilistic models for segmenting and labeling sequence data (2001)
29. Bengio, Y., Ducharme, R., Vincent, P.: A neural probabilistic language model. Journal of Machine Learning Research 3, 1137–1155 (2003)
30. Mikolov, T., Sutskever, I., Chen, K., Corrado, G.S., Dean, J.: Distributed representations of words and phrases and their compositionality. In: Advances in Neural Information Processing Systems, pp. 3111–3119 (2013)
31. Amigó, E., Gonzalo, J., Verdejo, F.: A general evaluation measure for document organization tasks. In: Proc. of the 36th SIGIR conference on Research & development in IR (2013)
32. Gaillard, J.: Recommendation Systems: Dynamic Adaptation and Argumentation. PhD thesis, University of Avignon, France (2014)

A Method for Short Message Contextualization: Experiments at CLEF/INEX

Liana Ermakova[1,2](✉)

[1] Institut de Recherche en Informatique de Toulouse, Toulouse, France
ermakova@irit.fr
[2] Perm State National Research University, Perm, Russia

Abstract. This paper presents the approach we developed for automatic multi-document summarization applied to short message contextualization, in particular to tweet contextualization. The proposed method is based on named entity recognition, part-of-speech weighting and sentence quality measuring. In contrast to previous research, we introduced an algorithm from smoothing from the local context. Our approach exploits topic-comment structure of a text. Moreover, we developed a graph-based algorithm for sentence reordering. The method has been evaluated at INEX/CLEF tweet contextualization track. We provide the evaluation results over the 4 years of the track. The method was also adapted to snippet retrieval and query expansion. The evaluation results indicate good performance of the approach.

Keywords: Information retrieval · Tweet Contextualization · Summarization · Snippet · Sentence extraction · Readability · Topic-comment structure

1 Introduction

The efficient communication tends to follow the principle of the least effort. According to this principle, using a given language interlocutors do not want to work any harder than necessary to reach understanding. This fact led to the extreme compression of texts especially in electronic communication, e.g. microblogs, SMS, search queries. However, sometimes these texts are not self-contained and need to be explained since understanding of them requires knowledge of terminology, named entities (NE) or related facts. The idea to contextualize short texts like micro-blogs or tweets is quite recent. Meij et al. mapped a tweet into a set of Wikipedia articles but in their work, no summary is provided to the user, rather a set of related links [6]. San Juan et al. went a step further and introduced Tweet Contextualization (TC) as an INEX task which became the CLEF lab in 2012 [2,9].

The main motivation of this research is to help a user to better understand a short message by extracting a context from an external source like the Web or the

---

L. Ermakova—Ambassade de France en Russie, bourse de thèse en cotutelle.

J. Mothe et al. (Eds.): CLEF 2015, LNCS 9283, pp. 352–363, 2015.
DOI: 10.1007/978-3-319-24027-5_38

Wikipedia by means of text summarization. A summary is either an "extract", if it consists in the most important passages extracted from the original text, or an "abstract", if these sentences are re-written, generating a new text. In this paper we focus on extracts. Extraction implies two steps: (1) searching for relevant sentences and (2) organizing them into a readable text. In previous summarization approaches sentence retrieval is based on the similarity to the query [10]. We also use this principle. In addition, we assume that part-of-speech (POS) tagging can ameliorate results since in general some POS provide more information than others (e.g. nouns are more informative that adverbs or functional words). As in [5], we integrated POS weights into the TF-IDF measure. The application of NE recognition may improve information retrieval (IR) performance, including tweet study [8], therefore we introduced NE similarity measure. Not all sentences are suitable for summarization purpose (e.g. headers, labels etc.). To avoid trash passages we enriched our method by sentence quality measure based on Flesch reading ease test, lexical diversity, meaningful word ratio and punctuation ratio. Thus, the proposed approach is based on NE recognition, POS weighting and sentence quality measuring.

Usually, a sentence is viewed as a unit in summarization task. However, often a single sentence is not sufficient to catch its meaning and even human beings need a context. In contrast to [13], we believe that a context does not provide redundant information, but allows to precise and extend sentence meaning. Therefore, we introduce an algorithm to smooth a candidate sentence by its local context, i.e. the neighboring sentences from the source document. Neighboring sentences influence the sentence of interest, but this influence decreases as the remoteness of the context increases, which differs from the previous approaches where the dependence is considered to be binary (i.e. a neighboring sentence influences the sentence of interest or not) [7]. The binary understanding of the influence of the context assumes that the influence is the same for all sentences.

Moreover, our algorithm takes advantage of topic-comment structure of sentences. The topic-comment structure have already got the attention of linguists in the 19-th century, however, it is hardly applied in IR tasks. To our knowledge, the topic-comment analysis was never exploited in the summarization task.

As Barzilay et al. showed, sentence order is crucial for readability [1]. Moreover, sentence reordering is the only way to improve the readability of a text produced by an extraction system. Barzilay et al. proposed to order the sentences by searching for the Hamiltonian path of maximal length in a directed graph where vertices are themes and edges corresponds to the number of times a theme precedes the other one. This approach requires a training corpus. In contrast to this, we hypothesized that in a coherent text neighboring sentences should be somehow similar to each other and the total distance between them should be minimal. Therefore, we propose an approach to increase global coherence of text on the basis of its graph model, where the vertices correspond to the extracted passages and the edges represent the similarity measure between them. Under these assumptions, sentence ordering implies searching for the minimal path that visits each vertex exactly once. This task is known as the traveling salesman problem. However, this method does not consider chronological constraints therefore we introduce another method based on the sequential ordering problem. In contrast to [1], our approach is not restricted by the news articles on the same topic and it takes advantages of the similarity between sentences.

The proposed approach demonstrated better performance than other systems like Cortex, Enertex, REG, etc. Cortex combines such metrics as word frequency, overlap with query terms, entropy of the words, shape of text etc. [11]. In Enertex sentence score is calculated from text energy matrix [11]. REG is an enhancement of Cortex which uses query expansion (QE) [12].

The rest of the paper is organized as follows. Section 2 presents our method. Section 3 contains the results and their analysis. Section 4 suggests the application of the proposed sentence retrieval method to snippet generation and QE. Section 5 concludes the paper.

2   Method Description

We participated in the INEX TC Track that aims at evaluating systems providing a context to a tweet. A context should be a readable summary of a limited size (up to 500 words) extracted from the Wikipedia dump. In this section we present our approach and its evolution over four-year period. The proposed method aims at contextualizing short messages by extracting passages from an external text collection. In this case contextualization task can be considered as query-biased multi-document summarization where a short message corresponds to a query. Our approach includes three steps: (1) preprocessing of the queries and the corresponding documents; (2) sentence scoring; and (3) sentence re-ordering.

Query preprocessing involves hashtag and reply treatment as well as combining different query parts. We put higher weight to words occurring in hashtags. We split hashtags and replies by capitalized letters. An initial tweet is expanded by the words obtained from tweet hashtags and replies as stated above. Thus, a tweet *RT StateDept: #SecKerry: Europe is strong, and stronger together. Europe and the US together have an opportunity to create jobs, build a stronger future* is expanded by *State, Dept, Sec, Kerry.* We assume that relevant sentences come from relevant documents. Documents are retrieved by the Terrier platform[1]. We apply a DFR (divergence from randomness) model InL2c1.0 which is a default retrieval model in Terrier based on TF-IDF measure with L2 term frequency normalization. 5 top-ranked documents are considered. Queries and documents are parsed by Stanford CoreNLP[2] which integrates such tools as POS tagger and NE recognizer. Parser annotation is merged with Wikipedia tags.

2.1   Sentence Scoring

In 2011 we introduced a system based on TF-IDF cosine similarity measure, special weighting for POS, NE, structural elements of a document, definitional

---

[1] terrier.org/
[2] nlp.stanford.edu/software/corenlp.shtml

sentences and the algorithm for smoothing from local context. Prior scores of sentence r_i was a product of the cosine similarity measure sim_{uni} between the sentence and the query that included IDF and POS weight and the NE similarity sim_{NE}:

$$r_i = sim_{uni} \times sim_{NE} \qquad (1)$$

$$sim_{NE} = \frac{NE_{common} + NE_{weight}}{NE_{query} + 1} \qquad (2)$$

where NE_{common} is the number of NE appearing in both query and sentence, NE_{query} is the number of NE appearing in the query, NE_{weight} is positive floating point parameter that allows not to reject sentence without NE which can be still relevant. We add 1 to the denominator to avoid division by zero.

We introduced an algorithm for smoothing from the local context. We assumed that the neighboring sentences influence the sentence of interest, but this influence decreases as the remoteness of the context increases. In other words, the nearest sentences should produce more effect on the target sentence sense than others. We choose the simplest dependence model, namely the linear function. In this case, the smoothed relevance $R(S)$ is calculated by the formulas:

$$R(S) = \sum_{i=-k}^{k} w_i \times r_i, \quad \sum_{i=-k}^{k} w_i = 1 \qquad (3)$$

$$w_i = \begin{cases} \frac{1-w(S)}{k+1} \times \frac{k-|i|}{k} & 0 < |i| \leq k \\ w(S), & i = 0 \end{cases} \qquad (4)$$

where $w(S)$ is the weight of the sentence S set by a user, w_i and r_i are respectively the weights and the prior scores of the sentences from the context of S of k length. If the sentence number in left or right context is less than k, their weights are added to the target sentence weight $w(S)$. This allows keeping the sum equal to one since otherwise a sentence with a small number of neighbors (e.g. the first or last sentences) would be penalized.

In 2011 our system showed the best results according the relevance judgment (see [3] for details). In 2012 we modified our method by adding bigram similarity, anaphora resolution, hashtag processing, redundancy treatment and sentence reordering. However, we obtained lower results than in the previous year. Therefore, in 2013 we decided to not consider bigram similarity, anaphora resolution, nor redundancy treatment. We also used generalized POS (e.g. we merge regular adverbs, superlative and comparative into a single adverb group). To avoid trash passages we enriched our method by sentence quality measure based on Flesch reading ease test, lexical diversity, meaningful word ratio and punctuation ratio. Lexical diversity allows avoiding sentences that do not contain terms except those from the query. We define it as the number of different lemmas used within a sentence divided by the total number of tokens in this sentence. Meaningful word ratio over the total number of tokens in the sentence is aimed at penalizing sentences that either have no sense at all or are not comprehensible without large context. The punctuation score penalizes sentences containing many punctuation marks. Thus, we believe that a good sentence should have high ratio of different meaningful words and reasonable ratio of punctuation.

The sentence score $score(S)$ is estimated as the product of its quality $Q(S)$, smoothed relevance $R(S)$ and the score of the document $DocRel(d)$ from which it is extracted:

$$score(S) = DocRel(d) \times Q(S) \times R(S) \tag{5}$$

We define sentence quality $Q(S)$ as the product of the lexical diversity $Div(S)$, Flesch index $F(S)$, meaningful word ratio $M(S)$ and punctuation score $P(S)$:

$$Q(S) = Div(S) \times M(S) \times P(S) \times F(S) \tag{6}$$

$$P(S) = 1 - \frac{PM(S)}{T(S)} \tag{7}$$

where $PM(S)$ is the number of punctuation marks in S, and $T(S)$ is the number of tokens in S. $P(S)$ shows the ratio of tokens that are not punctuation marks.

2.2   Topic-Comment Relationship in Contextualization Task

Linguistics establishes the difference between the clause-level topic and the discourse-level topic. The discourse-level topic refers to the notion of aboutness. While most IR models make the assumption that relevant documents are about the query and that aboutness can be captured considering bags of words only, we rather consider a clause-level topic-comment structure. The topic (or theme) is the phrase in a clause that the rest of the clause is understood to be about, and the comment (also called rheme or focus) is what is being said about the topic. In most languages the common means to mark topic-comment structure are word order, intonation and special constructions. In simple English clause the topic usually coincides with the subject. Therefore, topic identification in our approach is performed under assumption of topic fronting, i.e. the tendency to place topic at the beginning of a clause. We simplify this hypothesis by assuming that topic should be place at the sentence beginning. Sentence beginning is viewed as the first half of the sentence.

In 2014 participants should provide a context to tweets from the perspective of the related entities. Tweets are at least 80 characters long and do not contain URLs. A tweet has the following annotation types: the category (4 distinct), an entity name from the Wikipedia (64 distinct) and a manual topic label (235 distinct) (see an example Table 1). The context has to explain the relationship between a tweet and an entity. As in previous years it should be a summary extracted from a Wikipedia dump. We hypothesize that topic-comment relationship identification is useful for this task. Quick query analysis provides evidence

Table 1. Tweet example 2014

tweet_id	category	entity	topic	content
213051315880869888	automotive	Fiat	sales	Seeing a lot of #Fiat cars downtown these days. #Traffic

that an entity may be considered as a topic, while tweet content refers rather to comment, i.e. what is said about the entity. In order to link an entity to a tweet we combined the fields entity, topic and content into a single search query. Moreover, we assumed that providing the context to an entity implies that this context should be about the entity, i.e. the entity is the topic, while the retrieved context presents the comment. We used these assumptions for candidate sentence scoring. We doubled the weight of sentences in which the topic contains the entity under consideration.

2.3   Sentence Re-ordering

Although sentence ordering was not evaluated at INEX, we propose an approach to increase global coherence of text based on its graph model. The hypothesis is that neighboring sentences should be somehow similar to each other and the total distance between them should be minimal since word repetition is one of the formal indicators of text coherence. In our approach vertices represent sentences and edges correspond to the distances between adjacent sentences estimated as $1 - sim_{uni}$. If two relevant sentences are neighbors in the original text, they are considered as a single vertex. Thus, we reduced sentence ordering task to traveling salesman problem (TSP). TSP is an NP-hard problem in combinatorial optimization. Given a graph, the task is to find the shortest path that visits each vertex exactly once and returns to the start vertex. Algorithms to find the exact solution have exponential complexity. Therefore, we chose the greedy nearest neighbor algorithm with minor changes. Since sentence ordering does not request to return to the start vertex and the start vertex is arbitrary, we tried every vertex as the start one and chose the best result, i.e. the start vertex giving the path of the minimal length.

However, this method does not consider chronological constraints. Sentences with time stamps (e.g. date and time) should be ordered chronologically. Other sentences are not restricted by the chronological constraints but the coherence of text should be the maximal. As in the TSP approach, we believe that text coherence increases as the total sum of the distances between neighboring sentences decreases, i.e. the similarity between adjacent sentences should be maximal. So, we modified the task and it gave us sequential ordering problem (SOP). SOP "is a version of the asymmetric traveling salesman problem where precedence constraints on the vertices must also be observed" [4]. SOP is stated as follows. Given a directed graph, find a Hamiltonian path of the minimal length from the start vertex to the terminal vertex observing precedence constraints. Usually SOP is solved by the means of integer programming. Integer programming is NP-hard and these methods achieved only limited success. Therefore, we solved the problem as follows. Firstly, we ordered sentences with time stamps assigned by a parser $s_1 - s_2 - ... - s_n$. Sentences without time stamp were added to the set $P = \{p_j\}_{j=\overline{1,m}}$. For each pair $s_i - s_{i+1}$ we searched for the shortest path passing through vertices from P. These vertices were removed from P and $i = i + 1$. If $i = n$, we searched for the shortest path passing through the vertices that remained in P and the edge with the maximal weight was removed.

3   Evaluation

In this paper we focus on the results demonstrated at INEX in the two last years. Summaries were evaluated according to their informativeness and readability.

Informativeness was estimated as the lexical overlap (*uni, big* and *skip* representing the proportion of shared unigrams, bigrams and bigrams with gaps of two tokens respectively) of a summary with the pool of relevant passages extracted from the runs submitted by all participants [2]. Official ranking was based on decreasing score of divergence with the gold standard estimated by *skip*:

$$Dis(S,T) = \sum_{t \in T} \frac{f_{T(t)}}{f_T} \times \left(1 - \frac{\min \log P, \log Q}{\max \log P, \log Q} \right) \tag{8}$$

where $P = \frac{f_{T(t)}}{f_T} + 1$ and $Q = \frac{f_{S(t)}}{f_S} + 1$, T is the set of terms in the pool of relevant passages, $f_{T(t)}$ is the frequency of a term t (*uni, big* or *skip*) in the pool, $f_{S(t)}$ is the frequency of a term t in a summary.

In 2013 the informativeness was estimated as the overlap of a summary with 3 pools of relevant passages: (1) prior set (PRIOR) of relevant pages selected by organizers (40 tweets, 380 passages); (2) pool selection (POOL) of the most relevant passages (1 760) from participant submissions for 45 selected tweets; and (3) all relevant texts (ALL) merged together with extra passages from a random pool of 10 tweets (70 tweets, 2 378 relevant passages) [2]. The system was evaluated with three parameter sets. In our run 273 each sentence is smoothed by its local context and first sentences from Wikipedia article which it is taken from. The run 274 has the same parameters except it does not have any smoothing. In our best run 275 punctuation score is not taken into account, it has slightly different formula for NE comparison and no penalization for numbers. Among automatic runs our best run 275 was ranked first (PRIOR and POOL) and second (ALL) over 24 runs submitted by all participants. Table 2 provides results of the best automatic systems presented by the participants. Our results are marked by *. The best results are set off in bold. According to bigrams and skip bigrams, our best run is 275, while according to unigrams the best run is 273. So, we can conclude that smoothing improves Informativeness. Another conclusion is that ranking is sensitive to the pool selection as well as to the choice of divergence.

In 2014 there were 240 tweets in English collected by the organizers of CLEF RepLab 2013. 2 gold standards (1/5 of the topics) were used: (1) pool of relevant sentences per topic (SENT); and (2) pool of noun phrases (NOUN) extracted from these sentences together with the corresponding Wikipedia entry. The first run (ETC) was performed by the system developed in 2013. Three fields (entity, topic and content) were treated as a query. An entity was treated as a single phrase. The second run (ENT) differed from ETC by double weight for sentences where the entity represented the topic. The third run (RESTR) was based on document set retrieved for the tweet and filtered by the results obtained for the entity. Thus, the document retrieved by using the field content as a query were rejected if they did not coincide with top-ranked documents retrieved by using

Table 2. Informativeness evaluation 2013

Run	All.skip	All.big	All.uni	Pool.skip	Pool.big	Pool.uni	Prior.skip	Prior.big	Prior.uni
258	**0,894**	**0,891**	**0,794**	0,880	0,877	0,792	0,929	0,923	0,799
275*	0,897	0,892	0,806	**0,879**	**0,875**	0,794	**0,917**	**0,911**	0,790
273*	0,897	0,892	0,800	0,880	0,875	**0,792**	0,924	0,916	**0,786**
274*	0,897	0,892	0,801	0,881	0,875	0,793	0,923	0,915	0,787

the field entity. According to the evaluation performed on the pool of sentences, our runs ETC, ENT and RESTR were ranked 3-rd, 4-nd and 6-th; while according to the evaluation based on noun phrases, they got slightly better ranks, namely 2, 3 and 5 respectively. Thus, the best results among our runs were obtained by the system that merges fields entity, topic and content into a single query. The run #360 is better than our runs according to sentence evaluation; nevertheless, it showed worse results according to noun phrase evaluation. Our system is targeted at nouns and especially NEs. This could provoke the differences in ranking with respect to sentences and noun phrases. The run based on entity restriction showed worst results. This could be explained by the fact that filtering out the documents that are considered irrelevant to the entity may cause a big loss of relevant documents if they are not top-ranked according to entities. The results of ETC and ENT are very close. However, topic-subject identification slightly decreased the performance of the system. Yet we believe that finer topic-comment identification procedure may ameliorate the results.

Table 3. Informativeness evaluation 2014

Run	SENT.uni	SENT.big	SENT.skip	NOUN.uni	NOUN.big	NOUN.skip
361	**0.7632**	**0.8689**	**0.8702**	**0.7903**	**0.9273**	**0.9461**
360	0.782	0.8925	0.8934	0.8104	0.9406	0.9553
ETC*	0.8112	0.9066	0.9082	0.8088	0.9322	0.9486
ENT*	0.814	0.9098	0.9114	0.809	0.9326	0.9489
RESTR*	0.8152	0.9137	0.9154	0.8131	0.936	0.9513

Readability was estimated as mean average (MA) scores per summary over relevancy (T), soundness (no unresolved anaphora) (A), non-redundancy (R) and syntactical correctness (S) among relevant passages of the ten tweets having the largest text references. The score of a summary was the average normalized number of words in valid passages. Sentence order was not judged at INEX/CLEF.

In 2013 according to all metrics except redundancy our approach was the best among all participants (see Table 4). Runs were officially ranked according to mean average scores. Readability evaluation also showed that the run 275 is the best by relevance, soundness and syntax. However, the run 274 is much better in terms of avoiding redundant information. The runs 273 and 274 are close according readability assessment as well.

In 2014 we received very low score for diversity and structure. This may be related to the fact that we decide not to treat this problem since in previous years their impact was small. Despite we retrieved the entire sentences from the Wikipedia, unexpectedly we received quite low score for syntactical correctness.

Table 4. Readability evaluation 2013

Rank	Run	MA	T	R	A	S
1	275	**72.44%**	**76.64%**	67.30%	**74.52%**	**75.50%**
2	274	71.71%	74.66%	**68.84%**	71.78%	74.50%
3	273	71.35%	75.52%	67.88%	71.20%	74.96%

4   Other Applications of the Sentence Retrieval

Our approach is generic enough to be applied for various tasks. Here, we consider two of them: snippet retrieval and query expansion.

4.1   Snippet Retrieval

A search engine returns a larger number of results that a user cannot examine all. Therefore, a search engine provides a user with snippets (small text passages appearing under a search result extracted from the document) to help in evaluating web page relevance before browsing it.We slightly modified the method applied for TC for the INEX Snippet Retrieval Track 2012-2013: (1) nominal sentences were not penalized; (2) sentences were not re-ordered; (3) we did not treat redundancy since in the single-document summarization the probability of redundant information is much lower, and snippets are short and should be generated fast. We used two algorithms for the candidate passage selection: dynamic programming approach to solve the knapsack problem and the moving window (MW) algorithm.

A snippet is limited up to 1-2 sentences (150-300 symbols) but it should provide as much information about the underlying document as possible. Therefore, snippet retrieval can be viewed as a task of selecting passages of the maximal total importance under the restriction of the total weight. This task is known as a knapsack problem stated as follow: given a set of items (sentences), each with a weight (number of symbols) and a value (score), find the subset of this set to pack the rucksack so that the total weight is less than or equal to a given capacity and the total value is as large as possible. We solve this problem by the basic dynamic programming algorithm $DP - 1$.

However, this algorithm has pseudo-polynomial time. Moreover, if each sentence within a document were greater than a predefined threshold, the snippet would be an empty string. Therefore, we used a MW algorithm to find the best scored passage. At each step the first token is removed from a candidate passage and the tokens following the candidate passage are added while its total weight is no greater than a predefined threshold. The passage with the maximal score is selected as a snippet. Despite the most relevant information may occur in the too long sentences, snippets beginning in the middle of a sentence have lower readability. That is why, we penalize them.

Evaluation was performed manually by the organizers of INEX Snippet Retrieval Track 2013 [2]. The relevance of the documents was judged apart from the relevance of the snippets. Then these judgments were integrated by the following measures: Mean prediction accuracy (MPA), Mean normalized prediction accuracy (MNPA), Recall, Negative recall (NR), Positive agreement (PA), Negative agreement (NA), and Geometric mean (GM). The official ranking was based on GM. The results are given in the Table 5 (our results are marked by *, the best values are set off in bold). Our approach demonstrated the highest performance. As we hypothesized, the knapsack algorithm provided better results since it searches for the most valuable information regardless its position.

Table 5. Snippet evaluation 2013

Rank	Run	MPA	MNPA	Recall	NR	PA	NA	GM
1	knapsack*	**0.8300**	**0.6834**	**0.4190**	0.9477	**0.4921**	0.8673	**0.5352**
2	Focused	0.8171	0.6603	0.3507	0.9700	0.4210	0.8675	0.4774
3	Focused_Split	0.8214	0.6549	0.3684	0.9413	0.4358	0.8624	0.4732
4	MW*	0.8300	0.6459	0.3852	0.9067	0.4283	0.8572	0.4605
5	Baseline	0.8171	0.6414	0.2864	**0.9964**	0.3622	**0.8711**	0.4025

4.2   Query Expansion

QE in a search engine may be also viewed as contextualization of the initial query. The key idea of the proposed method is to search the most appropriate candidates for QE by ranking terms and sentences from the pseudo-relevance feedback. Our approach is underlain by the following hypotheses: (1) good expansion terms come from quality sentences relevant to the query; (2) they should have appropriate POS and high IDF; and (3) the terms lying in the neighborhood of query terms are closer related to them than the remote ones. Candidate terms are ranked according to the following metric:

$$w_{total}(t) = score(S) \times w_{pos}(t) \times IDF(t) \times importance(t, Q) \qquad (9)$$

$$importance(t, Q) = wd(t, Q) \times cooccurrence(t, Q) \qquad (10)$$

where $score(S)$ is score of the sentence S containing t computed by (5), $w_{pos}(t)$ is the weight of the POS of t, $IDF(t)$ is the inverse document frequency of the candidate term, $wd(t, Q)$ is a function of the distance from the candidate terms to the query Q and their weights, and $coocurence(t, Q)$ shows the likelihood of the candidate term to occur not by chance with the query terms in the top documents ranked according to the initial query. Our approach outperformed the baseline InL2c1.0 and DFR models for QE (KL, CS, Bo1, Bo2) implemented in Terrier according to MAP, NDCG, R-precision, P@5, P@10, and P@100 on TREC Ad Hoc 6-8 collection and WT10g. The differences between the our approach and other evaluated methods are significant at the level $p < 0.05$ for TREC Ad Hoc 6-8. On WT10g the differences with Bo2 and KL models are not significant.

5   Conclusion

In this paper we presented an approach for short message contextualization from an external source based on query-biased summarization. Our approach implies sentence retrieval and re-ordering. Sentence retrieval is based on NE recognition, POS weighting and sentence quality measuring. We introduced an algorithm of smoothing from the local context. We also integrated the knowledge of topic-comment structure into the sentence retrieval model. Moreover, we developed a graph-based algorithm for sentence re-ordering. The method has been evaluated at INEX/CLEF TC track. We obtained the best results in 2011 according to informative evaluation. In 2013 according to informative evaluation our system was ranked first (PRIOR and POOL) and second (ALL) over all automatic systems that participated. At the same time in terms of readability it was the best among all participants according to all metrics except redundancy. Run comparison showed that smoothing improves informativeness. Another conclusion is that ranking is sensitive to the pool selection as well as to the choice of divergence. Despite the topic-comment analysis did not improve results, we believe that small changes in implementation may produce positive effect on the system performance. In 2014 the worst results among our runs were shown by the run based on entity restriction that could be explained by the loss of the recall. Although sentence ordering was not evaluated at INEX campaign, we believe that it is crucial for readability. The sentence retrieval method was also adapted to snippet retrieval and QE. In 2013 our system showed the best results in the INEX Snippet Retrieval Track.

References

1. Barzilay, R., Elhadad, N., McKeown, K.R.: Inferring strategies for sentence ordering in multidocument news summarization. Journal of Artificial Intelligence Research **17**, 35–55 (2002)
2. Bellot, P., Doucet, A., Geva, S., Gurajada, S., Kamps, J., Kazai, G., Koolen, M., Mishra, A., Moriceau, V., Mothe, J., Preminger, M., SanJuan, E., Schenkel, R., Tannier, X., Theobald, M., Trappett, M., Wang, Q.: Overview of INEX 2013. In: Forner, P., Müller, H., Paredes, R., Rosso, P., Stein, B. (eds.) CLEF 2013. LNCS, vol. 8138, pp. 269–281. Springer, Heidelberg (2013)

3. Ermakova, L., Mothe, J.: IRIT at INEX: question answering task. In: Geva, S., Kamps, J., Schenkel, R. (eds.) INEX 2011. LNCS, vol. 7424, pp. 219–226. Springer, Heidelberg (2012)
4. Hernádvölgyi, I.T.: Solving the sequential ordering problem with automatically generated lower bounds. In: Proceedings of Operations Research 2003, pp. 355–362 (2003)
5. Lioma, C., Blanco, R.: Part of speech based term weighting for information retrieval. In: Boughanem, M., Berrut, C., Mothe, J., Soule-Dupuy, C. (eds.) ECIR 2009. LNCS, vol. 5478, pp. 412–423. Springer, Heidelberg (2009)
6. Meij, E., Weerkamp, W., de Rijke, M.: Adding semantics to microblog posts. In: Proceedings of the Fifth ACM International Conference on Web Search and Data Mining, WSDM 2012, pp. 563–572. ACM, New York (2012)
7. Murdock, V.G.: Aspects of sentence retrieval. Dissertation (2006)
8. de Oliveira, D.M., Laender, A.H., Veloso, A., da Silva, A.S.: FS-NER: a lightweight filter-stream approach to named entity recognition on twitter data. In: Proceedings of the 22Nd International Conference on Arabic named entity recognition World Wide Web Companion, WWW 2013 Companion, pp. 597–604. International World Wide Web Conferences Steering Committee, Republic and Canton of Geneva, Switzerland (2013)
9. SanJuan, E., Moriceau, V., Tannier, X., Bellot, P., Mothe, J.: Overview of the INEX 2011 question answering track (QA@INEX). In: Geva, S., Kamps, J., Schenkel, R. (eds.) INEX 2011. LNCS, vol. 7424, pp. 188–206. Springer, Heidelberg (2012)
10. Shen, C., Li, T.: Learning to rank for query-focused multi-document summarization, pp. 626–634. IEEE (2012)
11. Torres-Moreno, J.-M., Velázquez-Morales, P., Gagnon, M.: Statistical summarization at QA@INEX 2011 track using cortex and enertex systems. In: Geva, S., Kamps, J., Schenkel, R. (eds.) INEX 2011. LNCS, vol. 7424, pp. 247–256. Springer, Heidelberg (2012)
12. Vivaldi, J., da Cunha, I.: QA@INEX track 2011: question expansion and reformulation using the REG summarization system. In: Geva, S., Kamps, J., Schenkel, R. (eds.) INEX 2011. LNCS, vol. 7424, pp. 257–268. Springer, Heidelberg (2012)
13. Yang, Z., Cai, K., Tang, J., Zhang, L., Su, Z., Li, J.: Social context summarization. In: Proceedings of the 34th International ACM SIGIR Conference on Research and Development in Information Retrieval, pp. 255–264. ACM, Beijing (2011)

Towards Automatic Large-Scale Identification of Birds in Audio Recordings

Mario Lasseck[✉]

Animal Sound Archive, Museum für Naturkunde, Berlin, Germany
Mario.Lasseck@mfn-berlin.de

Abstract. This paper presents a computer-based technique for bird species identification at large scale. It automatically identifies multiple species simultaneously in a large number of audio recordings and provides the basis for the best scoring submission to the LifeCLEF 2014 Bird Identification Task. The method achieves a Mean Average Precision of 51.1% on the test set and 53.9% on the training set with an Area Under the Curve of 91.5% during cross-validation. Besides a general description of the underlying classification approach a number of additional research questions are addressed regarding the choice of features, selection of classifier hyperparameters and method of classification.

Keywords: Bird Identification · Information retrieval · Biodiversity · Spectrogram segmentation · Median Clipping · Template matching · Decision trees

1 Introduction

Automatic identification of species from their sound is a promising computational tool for assessing biodiversity. It has many potential applications in ecology, bioacoustic monitoring and behavioral science [1]. Examples of previous studies on species identification of birds are given in [2,3,4]. Many approaches however suffer from different drawbacks. Some only work on clean recordings without overlapping sounds others require significant levels of human intervention or are restricted to a limited number of species.

The here proposed method is a combination of algorithms designed to identify a large number of species simultaneously without manual intervention under a wide range of recording conditions. Robustness, scalability and generalization power of the method are evaluated with the dataset of the LifeCLEF 2014 Bird Identification Task. In this task participants have to automatically identify 501 different species in 4339 audio recordings with undetermined content. For training, 9688 audio files paired with metadata including dominant and background species are provided. A recording may contain only one or up to 11 simultaneously vocalizing birds. What makes this challenge unique but also quite difficult is the large amount of data, the high variability of the recordings, both in quality and content and of course the very large number of different species to be identified. The all in all 14,027 audio files, if added together

© Springer International Publishing Switzerland 2015
J. Mothe et al. (Eds.): CLEF 2015, LNCS 9283, pp. 364–375, 2015.
DOI: 10.1007/978-3-319-24027-5_39

33.3 GB of data with over 4.5 days of acoustic material, are provided by Xeno-Canto (http://www.xeno-canto.org). The files were recorded between 1979 and 2013 in over 2000 different locations centered on Brazil by almost 250 amateur and expert ornithologists using different combinations of microphones and portable recorders. The duration of the recordings varies from half a second to several minutes. Also the quality of the audio files is quite diverse and challenging. One has to deal with all kinds of background noise and in some cases artifacts due to lossy mp3 data compression. An overview and further details about the LifeCLEF Bird Identification Task is given in [5]. The task is among others part of the CLEF 2014 evaluation campaign [6].

The features extracted for each audio file are introduced in section 2 followed by methods for feature selection in section 3. In section 4 different training approaches are presented and in section 5 classification results are compared regarding choice of features, method of classification and variation of hyperparameters. Final conclusions are drawn and possible improvements in classification performance are discussed in section 6.

2   Feature Engineering

The features used for classification are taken from three different sources briefly described in the following sections.

2.1   Metadata

The first source for feature extraction is the provided metadata. Each audio file is paired with additional contextual information about date, time, location and author of the recording. This information is used to extract 8 features per file: Year, Month, Time, Latitude, Longitude, Elevation, Locality Index and Author Index. To use the provided metadata a few steps had to be taken for preparation. From the recording date, only year and month were extracted and considered as relevant features. The recording time was converted to minutes. Since only numeric values can be used as features, for locality and author a look up table was created and the corresponding index was used. All missing or none numeric values were replaced by the mean value of its category.

2.2   openSMILE

The openSMILE feature extraction tool [7] was used to extract a large number of features per audio recording. The framework was configured with the *emo_large.conf* configuration file written by Florian Eyben. It was originally designed for emotion detection in speech signals but was also recently applied in the field of audio scene analysis [8]. The configuration file used here first calculates 57 so-called low-level descriptors (LLDs) per frame, adds delta (velocity) and delta-delta (acceleration) coefficients to each LLD and finally applies 39 statistical functionals after smoothen (moving average) the feature trajectories. The all in all 57 LLDs consist of: 1 time domain signal feature (zero crossing rate), 34 spectral features (Mel-Spectrum bins 0-25; 25%, 50%, 75% and 90% spectral roll-off points; spectral flux; spectral centroid; relative position of spectral minimum and maximum), 13 cepstral features (MFCC 0-12), 6 energy features (logarithmic energy; energy in frequency bands 0-250 Hz, 0-650 Hz, 250-650 Hz, 1000-4000 Hz and 3010-9123 Hz) and 3 voicing-related features (F0; F0 envelope; voicing probability).

To describe an entire audio recording, statistics are calculated from all LLD, velocity and acceleration trajectories by 39 functionals including e.g. means, extremes, moments, percentiles and linear as well as quadratic regression. This sums up to 6669 (57×3×39) features per recording. Further details regarding openSMILE and the extracted features can be found in the openSMILE 1.0.1 manual and the *emo_large.conf* configuration file (http://opensmile.sourceforge.net).

2.3   Segment-Probabilities

The idea of using the matching probabilities of segments as features or more precisely the maxima of the normalized cross-correlation [9] between segments, also referred to as region of interests (ROIs) or templates, and spectrogram images was previously used by Nick Kriedler in The Marinexplore and Cornell University Whale Detection Challenge, Gábor Fodor in the MLSP 2013 Bird Classification Challenge [10] and Ilyas Potamitis in the NIPS 2013 Bird Song Classification Challenge [4].

For the current task an adaptation of this method was used which was already very successfully applied also in the NIPS 2013 Challenge [11]. It differs mainly in the way segments are extracted and which subsets of segments and their probabilities are used during classification. It turned out that proper preprocessing and segmentation of the spectrogram images is a key element to improve classification performance. The number of segments should be rather small but still representative, capturing typical elements and combinations of sounds of the species to be identified.

The following sections give a brief overview of the feature extraction steps regarding Segment-Probabilities. Some additional details can be found in [11].

Preprocessing and Segmentation. As mentioned above the way of preprocessing and segmentation is crucial to gather a good repertoire of segments especially when dealing with unknown content and noisy recordings. Methods and parameters were chosen as in [11]. They were tested and optimized during the NIPS4B 2013 Challenge and proved to work well for a wide range of recording conditions. The following steps were performed for each audio file in the training set:

- resample to 22050 Hz
- get spectrogram via STFT (512 samples, Hann window, 75% overlap)
- normalize spectrogram to 1.0
- remove 4 lowest and 24 highest spectrogram rows

- get binary image via *Median Clipping* per frequency band and time frame by setting each pixel to 1, if it is above 3 times the median of its corresponding row AND 3 times the median of its corresponding column, otherwise to 0
- apply closing, dilation and median filter for further noise reduction
- label all connected pixels exceeding a certain spatial extension as a segment
- define its size and position by a rectangle with a small area added (12 pixel) to each direction

Different stages of the preprocessing and segmentation process are illustrated in Fig. 1 to 5. The audio example is taken from the training set [MediaId: 86] containing simultaneously vocalizing birds in different frequency bands. The final segmentation result is given in Fig. 6 visualizing size and position of each segment to be extracted for template matching.

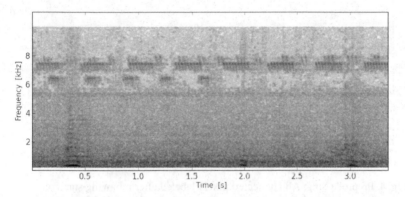

Fig. 1. Preprocessing: 4 lowest and 24 highest spectrogram rows removed

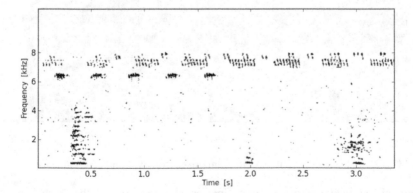

Fig. 2. Preprocessing: Binarization via *Median Clipping*

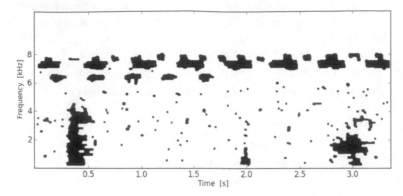

Fig. 3. Preprocessing: Closing, Dilation and Median Filter

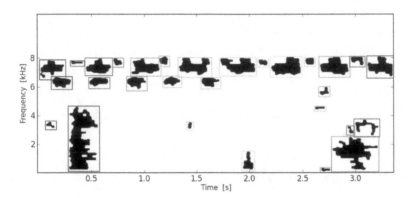

Fig. 4. Preprocessing: All connected pixels labeled after removing small objects

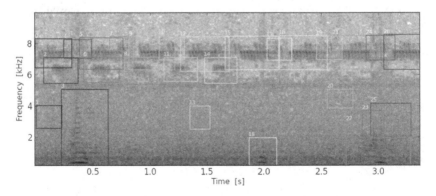

Fig. 5. Segmentation result: spectrogram image (log) with marked segments

Selection of Typical Segments per Species. In contrast to the Metadata and openSMILE feature sets that are species respectively class independent, Segment-Probabilities form individual feature sets for each species. In order to get a small but representative set of features per species, only segments from files without background species and very good quality (metadata: Quality = 1) were selected. For some species this condition was too strict, leading to none or too few segments. The following queries were applied successively for every target species until there was at least one file that met the conditions and the number of retrieved segments was greater than a given threshold (40 segments per species):

Select all segments of files WHERE: Species = target species AND:

1. BackgroundSpecies = { } AND Quality = 1
2. BackgroundSpecies = { } AND (Quality = 1 OR Quality = 2)
3. BackgroundSpecies = { } AND (Quality = 1 OR Quality = 2 OR Quality = 3)
4. Quality = 1 OR Quality = 2

The number of segments retrieved this way sums up to 492,753 for all training files with an average of approximately 984 segments per species.

Template Matching. After selecting a set of segments for each species, template matching was performed to get an individual feature set per species. The highest matching probability was determined using normalized cross-correlation after applying a Gaussian blur to segment and target image. Due to the large number of audio files and segments used as templates, the method described in [11] was way too time consuming and had to be modified. In order to speed up the process the following changes were applied:

- segments and target spectrogram images were calculated via STFT using only 50% overlap (instead of 75%)
- search range for segments within the target images along the frequency axes was set to ± 3 pixel (instead of 4 pixel)
- segments and target spectrogram images were converted to 8 bit unsigned integer before the template matching procedure (instead of 32 bit floating point)

Even with these modifications, the process of template matching (sliding almost half a million templates over 14,027 target images) took very long and kept four computers with regular hardware quite busy for several days.

3   Feature Selection

To cope with the large number of features and to improve and speed up the classification process a reduction of features was inevitable. It was performed in two phases before and during classification.

The openSMILE features were reduced from 6669 to 1277 features per file before the actual classification step. This was done by recursive feature elimination with the scikit-learn [12] RFECV selector [13] and a support vector machine with linear kernel and 2-fold cross-validation. For this preselection only a small subset from the training data consisting of 50 species and good quality files (metadata: Quality = 1 or Quality = 2) was used.

During classification, furthermore the k highest scoring features were individually selected per species using univariate feature selection. This was done separately for each fold during classifier training with cross-validation. Different values for k were tested, ranging from 150 to 400 features per class.

4   Training and Classification

Since it was optional to use the information about background species, single- and multi-label approaches were tested. In both cases the classification problem was split up into 501 independent classification problems using one classifier for each species following the one-vs.-rest or binary relevance method. For the single-label approach only dominant species were considered as targets. In case of the multi-label approach background species (BS), if assigned, were also considered for each training file but were set to lower probabilities compared to the dominant species. The classification was done with the scikit-learn library (ExtraTreesRegressor) by training ensembles of randomized decision trees [14] with probabilistic outputs. Following variations were used for training:

- classification methods
  - o single-label
  - o multi-label with probabilities of dominant species set to 1.0
    - probabilities of BS set to 0.3
    - probabilities of BS set to 0.7
    - probabilities of BS set to 1.0 (equally weighted as dominant species)

- feature sets & feature set combinations
  - o Meatadata Only
  - o openSMILE Only
  - o Segment-Probabilities[1] (Seg.Probs.)
  - o Metadata + openSMILE
  - o Metadata + openSMILE + Seg.Probs.
  - o openSMILE + Seg.Probs. (Audio Only)

- number of features (univariate feature selection per species in each fold)
  - o 150, 170, 180, 200, 250, 300, 400

- number of folds for cross-validation
  - o 10, 12, 15

---

[1]   By the time of the submission deadline Segment-Probabilities were extracted for 485 species. The remaining 16 species used Metadata + openSMILE features for classification.

Variations of classifier parameters and tree-specific hyperparameters:

- number of estimators (trees in the forest)
    - 300, 400, 500

- max_features (number of features to consider when looking for the best split)
    - 4, 5, 6, 7

- min_sample_split (minimum number of samples required to split an internal node)
    - 1, 2, 3, 4, 5

During cross-validation using stratified folds the probability of each species in all test files was predicted and averaged. Additionally each species was predicted in the held-out training files for validation. This way it was possible to choose a variation and/or parameter set separately per species and to increase the MAP score on the test files by optimizing the MAP score on the training files.

5   Results

In Table 1 the results of the four submitted runs are summarized using evaluation measures: the mean of the Area Under the Curve (AUC) calculated per species and the Mean Average Precision (MAP) on the public training and the private test set. All four runs outperformed the runs of the other participating teams.

Table 1. Performance of submitted runs (without / with background species)

	Public Training Set		Private Test Set
Run	Mean AUC [%]	MAP [%]	MAP [%]
1	91.4 / 85.0	53.7 / 48.6	50.9 / 45.1
2	91.1 / 84.9	49.4 / 44.6	49.2 / 43.7
3	91.5 / 85.1	53.9 / 48.7	51.1 / 45.3
4	91.4 / 85.3	50.1 / 45.3	50.4 / 44.9

For the first and the best performing third run a mix of parameter sets individually selected per species was used. As mentioned above the selection was based on how a particular set of training parameters was able to increase the overall MAP on the held-out training files during cross-validation. None of the test data was used to optimize the parameters. A higher mean AUC score might be a hint of a generally good selection of training parameters but it is still possible that for some classes (species) a different selection works better. To give an example, in Fig. 6 AUC scores are visualized per species using one of the three different feature sets exclusively during training. On average the use of Segment-Probabilities outperforms the other feature sets but for some species the openSMILE and in rare cases even the Metadata feature set is a better choice.

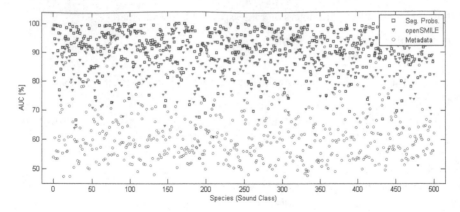

Fig. 6. AUC scores per species for individual feature sets calculated on held-out training files during cross-validation (without background species)

For the best performing third run a list of the parameters and feature sets used for each species, together with their individually achieved AUC scores can be download-ed from http://www.animalsoundarchive.org/RefSys/LifeCLEF2014. Here one can also find additional figures visualizing the preprocessing, segmentation and the most important segments used for classification.

To give an impression how different parameter settings used during training influ-ence classification performance, run 4 was altered in several ways and corresponding evaluation statistics were summarized over the entire training set and visualized in Fig. 7 and 8.

Parameters used for Run 4:

- classification method: single-label
- feature set: Segment-Probabilities
- number of features: 150
- number of folds: 15
- number of estimators: 500
- max_features: 7
- min_sample_split: 4

Parameter variations of Run 4:

- Run 2 → max_features: 6 & min_sample_split: 3
- Run 5 → feature set: Metadata
- Run 6 → feature set: openSMILE
- Run 7 → feature set: openSMILE + Segment-Probabilities (Audio Only)
- Run 8 → method: multi-label and background species weighted with 0.3
- Run 9 → method: multi-label and background species weighted with 0.7
- Run 10 → method: multi-label and background species weighted equally

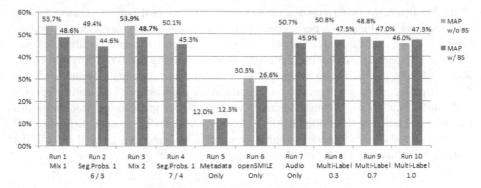

Fig. 7. Mean Average Precision (MAP) of Runs

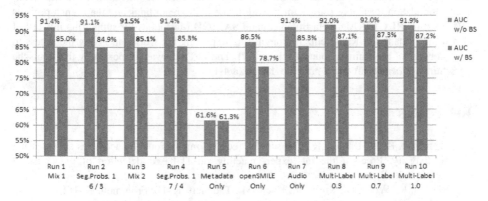

Fig. 8. Area Under the Curve (AUC) of Runs

6 Discussion

To train separate classifiers per sound class with individual parameter tuning for each species produces better classification results than training one single classifier. It also addresses the long tail curse e.g. as described by Joly et al. [15] and appears to be more "biodiversity-friendly". By training different classifiers for each species, parameters are not as much tuned in favor of the most common and therefore more populated species as they usually are in case of training just one classifier.

To use matching probabilities of segments as features was once again a good choice. One drawback of this method is that the template matching procedure involved to calculate the feature sets is quite time consuming especially if the number of species and audio files is as large as in the current challenge. The use of image-pyramids [16] could help to speed up the process and would be worth investigating. The features derived from metadata and the ones calculated by openSMILE did not perform as well. Nevertheless, they could increase the overall classification performance by improving the results for individual species. Considering the use of the openSMILE tool there is still a lot of room for improvement. The configuration file could be altered to better capture the characteristics of bird sounds. Furthermore a preselection of features on a per species basis to get individually designed feature sets for each sound class, as was done for Segment-Probabilities, could be advantageous. Another approach is windowing the audio files, classifying the fixed length sections and combining the results via averaging. Other interesting attempts to improve identification performance are hierarchical classification approaches that identify species with fairly simple calls or song structures very quick but spend more time and effort on species known to be rather hard to classify. A classification on different time scales might also help to better capture temporal song structures as well as call and syllable repetition rates and their changes over time.

Acknowledgments. I would like to thank Hervé Glotin, Hervé Goëau, Andreas Rauber and Willem-Pier Vellinga for organizing the LifeCLEF 2014 Bird Identification Task, the Xeno-Canto foundation for nature sounds for providing the audio recordings and the French projects Pl@ntNet (INRIA, CIRAD, Tela Botanica) and SABIOD Mastodons for supporting this task. I also want to thank Dr. Karl-Heinz Frommolt for supporting my work and giving me access to the resources of the Animal Sound Archive [17]. The research was supported by the Deutsche Forschungsgemeinschaft (DFG grant no. FR 1028/4-1).

References

1. Frommolt, K.-H., Bardeli, R., Clausen, M. (eds.) Computational bioacoustics for assessing biodiversity. Proc. of the int. expert meeting on IT-based detection of bioacoustical patterns (2008)
2. Bardeli, R., Wolff, D., Kurth, F., Koch, M., Tauchert, K.-H., Frommolt, K.-H.: Detecting bird sounds in a complex acoustic environment and application to bioacoustic monitoring. Pattern Recognition Letter **31**(23), 1524–1534 (2009)
3. Briggs, F., Lakshminarayanan, B., Neal, L., et al.: Acoustic classification of multiple simultaneous bird species: A multi-instance multi-label approach. The Journal of the Acoustical Society of America **131**(6), 4640–4650 (2012). doi:10.1121/1.4707424
4. Potamitis, I.: Automatic Classification of Taxon-Rich Community Recorded in the Wild. PLoS ONE **9**(5), e96936 (2014). doi:10.1371/journal.pone.0096936
5. Glotin, H., Goëau, H., Vellinga, W-P., Rauber, A.: LifeCLEF bird identification task 2014. In: CLEF working notes (2014)
6. Cappellato, L., Ferro, N., Halvey, M., Kraaij, W. (eds.) CLEF 2014 Labs and Workshops, Notebook Papers. CEUR Workshop Proceedings. (CEUR-WS.org), ISSN 1613-0073, (2014). http://ceur-ws.org/Vol-1180/
7. Eyben, F., Wöllmer, M., Schuller, B.: openSMILE - the munich versatile and fast open-source audio feature extractor. In: Proc. ACM Multimedia (MM), pp. 1459–1462. ACM, Florence, Italy (2010). ISBN 978-1-60558-933-6, doi:10.1145/1873951.1874246
8. Geiger, J.T., Schuller, B., Rigoll, G.: Large-scale audio feature extraction and svm for acoustic scenes classification. In: IEEE Workshop on Applications of Signal Processing to Audio and Acoustics (WASPAA), 2013. IEEE (2013)
9. Lewis, J.P.: Fast Normalized Cross-Correlation. Industrial Light and Magic (1995)
10. Fodor, G.: The ninth annual MLSP competition: first place. In: 2013 IEEE International Workshop on Machine Learning for Signal Processing (MLSP), pp. 1–2 (2013). doi:10.1109/MLSP.2013.6661932

11. Lasseck, M.: Bird song classification in field recordings: winning solution for NIPS4B 2013 competition. In: Glotin, H. et al. (eds.) Proc. of int. symp. Neural Information Scaled for Bioacoustics, sabiod.org/nips4b, joint to NIPS, Nevada, pp. 176–181 (2013)
12. Pedregosa, F., et al.: Scikit-learn: Machine learning in Python. JMLR **12**, 2825–2830 (2011)
13. Guyon, I., Weston, J., Barnhill, S., et al.: Gene selection for cancer classification using support vector machines. Machine Learning **46**(1–3), 389–422 (2002)
14. Geurts, P., Ernst, D., Wehenkel, L.: Extremely randomized trees. Machine Learning **63**(1), 3–42 (2006)
15. Joly, A., Goëau, H., Bonnet, P. et al.: Are multimedia identification tools biodiversity-friendly? In: Proceedings of the 3rd ACM International Workshop on Multimedia Analysis for Ecological Data (2014). doi:10.1145/2661821.2661826
16. Adelson, E.H., Anderson, C.H., Bergen, J.R., et al.: Pyramid Method in Image Processing. RCA Engineer **29**(6), 33–41 (1984)
17. Animal Sound Archive Berlin. http://www.animalsoundarchive.org

Optimizing and Evaluating Stream-Based News Recommendation Algorithms

Andreas Lommatzsch[1]($\boxtimes$) and Sebastian Werner[2]

[1] Agent Technologies in Business Applications and Telecommunication Group
(AOT), Technische Universität Berlin, Ernst-Reuter-Platz 7, 10587 Berlin, Germany
andreas.lommatzsch@tu-berlin.de
[2] Database Systems and Information Management Group (DIMA), Technische
Universität Berlin, Einsteinufer 17, 10587 Berlin, Germany
sebastian.werner@campus.tu-berlin.de

Abstract. Recommender algorithms are powerful tools helping users to
find interesting items in the overwhelming amount available data. Classic recommender algorithms are trained based on a huge set of user-item
interactions collected in the past. Since the learning of models is computationally expensive, it is difficult to integrate new knowledge into the
recommender models. With the growing importance of social networks,
the huge amount of data generated by the real-time web (e.g. news portals, micro-blogging services), and the ubiquity of personalized web portals stream-based recommender systems get in the focus of research.

In this paper we develop algorithms tailored to the requirements
of a web-based news recommendation scenario. The algorithms address
the specific challenges of news recommendations, such as a context-
dependent relevance of news items and the short item lifecycle forcing the
recommender algorithms to continuously adapt to the set of news articles. In addition, the scenario is characterized by a huge amount of messages (that must be processed per second) and by tight time constraints
resulting from the fact that news recommendations should be embedded
into webpages without a delay. For evaluating and optimizing the recommender algorithms we implement an evaluation framework, allowing
us analyzing and comparing different recommender algorithms in different contexts. We discuss the strength and weaknesses both according
to recommendation precision and technical complexity. We show how
the evaluation framework enables us finding the optimal recommender
algorithm for a specific scenarios and contexts.

1 Introduction

Recommender algorithms efficiently support users in finding interesting items
matching the individual user preferences. Traditionally, recommender algorithms
are trained based on huge sets of user-item interactions collected over a long
period of time. In recent years, social networks, news portals and micro-blogging
services (e.g. Twitter) get in the focus of interest. In contrast to most "traditional" recommender scenarios, the real-time web is characterized by fast changes

© Springer International Publishing Switzerland 2015
J. Mothe et al. (Eds.): CLEF 2015, LNCS 9283, pp. 376–388, 2015.
DOI: 10.1007/978-3-319-24027-5_40

in the user interests and in the set of items. The context and current trends have a strong influence on the relevance of recommendations. In addition, stream-based recommendation scenario often suffer from a steady "cold-start problem"[10] induced by the continuous changes in the set of users and items. That is the reason why stream-based recommender scenarios need optimized algorithms able to handle new data efficiently adapting to changes in the context. Additional challenges in many stream-recommendation scenarios are tight time-constraints limiting the complexity of the recommender algorithms. Due to the continuous changes of data, batch-based pre-computed recommender models often do not match the requirements of the scenario.

In this paper we present algorithms tailored to the specific requirements of the news recommendation scenario. In addition, we discuss our framework enabling the context-aware evaluation and optimization of recommender algorithms and explain how the framework supports us handling the specific challenges of stream-based recommender algorithms.

The remaining paper is organized as follows. In Section 2 we review existing frameworks and recommender algorithms optimized for computing recommendations based on user-item streams. In Section 3 we discuss the analyzed news recommendation scenario in detail and explain the requirements for the algorithms and the evaluation framework. In Section 4 we describe the implemented framework and the recommender algorithms. We explain the evaluation framework and discuss its strengths and weaknesses. In Section 5, the evaluation results are presented. We discuss advantages and disadvantages of the algorithms with respect to different benchmarking metrics. Finally a conclusion and an outlook on future work is given in Section 6.

2   Related Work

Recommender algorithms have been developed to suggest users potentially interesting items matching the individual preferences. Traditionally, recommender systems are based on collaborative filtering [2]: User-based collaborative filtering [8] searches for users similar to the current user based on the actions and explicit ratings in the past. In a second step, the algorithm suggests items users with similar preferences liked. Item-based collaborative filtering algorithms [7] compute the similarity between items based on the user ratings ("user who liked this item also liked that item") and suggest the items most similar to the items the user liked in the past. Collaborative filtering (CF) algorithms are often implemented based on a user-item matrix describing how a user rated specific items. Due to the small number of ratings compared to the size of the user-item matrix, the matrix is usually very sparse resulting in a poor recommendation quality [6]. In order to overcome the sparsity low-rank approximations (e.g. based on a Singular Value Decomposition of the matrix) or clustering approaches can be applied [5]. These approaches are computational expensive and time consuming. Thus, these approaches are not well-suited for scenarios characterized by rapidly changing user-items sets requiring a continuous re-calculation of the model.

In order to prevent problems with the re-calculation of recommender models and to be able considering current trends memory-based recommender approaches are applied [1].

For computing news recommendations, algorithms are applied that rank articles incrementally based on user feedback. The number of feedback events (e.g. thumb up, thumb down, number of comments) and the freshness of the articles are used for computing ratings for news articles. Popular web portals applying this approach are REDDIT[1] and SLASHDOT[2]. Studies conducted by Google show that Bayesian models trained on large scale user click data can be used for improving the suggestion found at Google News [4]. In order to get high quality recommendations the recommendation algorithms must be optimized for the specific properties of the news portal such as the amount of messages and the number of users per day.

For the development of recommendation services several frameworks exist, such as MAHOUT[9] and LENSKIT[3]. These frameworks also provide components for the evaluation of recommender algorithms. Unfortunately, these frameworks are built for static datasets and do not provide support for stream-based recommendation scenarios.

The adaptation and optimization of recommender algorithms for news portals is an interesting research topic. The specific characteristics of the scenario require adaptive recommender algorithms and tools supporting the fine-grained, context-aware optimization and evaluation of algorithms.

3   Approach

We develop algorithms optimized for providing recommendations for a stream of news articles and user-item interactions. The algorithms are evaluated using an offline testing framework simulating streams based on data recorded by several different news portals. In this section we start with a detailed scenario description. Subsequently, we present our evaluation framework and explain the implemented algorithms.

3.1   The Analyzed Scenario

We analyze the task of online news recommendation. In order to increase the time users spend on a news portal, the recommender system should suggest news articles matching the individual user preferences. Figure 1 visualizes the analyzed task. Next to the news article requested by the user, up to six news recommendation are presented, typically in a box labeled with "also interesting". The user may accept the recommendations by clicking on one of the specific suggestion forwarding the user to the recommended news item.

---

[1] http://www.reddit.com/
[2] http://www.slashdot.org

Fig. 1. The graphic shows schematically the structure of a news portal and the placement of news recommendations.

The development of online news recommender systems leads to several challenges:

i. Since news articles have a short lifetime, the recommender system faces a continuous "cold-start problem": Comprehensive collaborative knowledge (user-item interaction statistics) is usually not available for "new" articles. This fact is a special challenge since a news recommender system should suggest "new" articles. In addition, the recommender system must remove outdated articles ensuring the suggested items are not too old.

ii. Online news portals have only a limited user tracking accuracy. Since the users do not have to login, the user tracking is based on implicit indicators such as the IP address and browser specific data. Thus, the recommender system must be able to provide recommendations also for new users or users who cannot be matched with an existing profile.

iii. There are several challenging technical requirements for news recommendation systems. On the one hand, the recommendations should be provided very fast (typically within 100 milliseconds) in order to ensure that the recommendations can be embedded seamlessly into a requested news article. On the other hand, the recommender system must be able to handle a large number of messages per second ("throughput"). The algorithms should scale well both with the number of users and the number of news items.

While analyzing the user behavior the system can collect feedback for the provided recommendations. Since clicking on a recommendation results in loading a new article and new recommendations, typically only one of the recommendations is clicked by a user (even though several of the suggestions may match the user's interests).

3.2   The Evaluation Framework

The evaluation of stream recommender algorithms can be done either online or offline.

Online Evaluation. The CLEF NewsREEL challenge[3] gives participants the opportunity to evaluate recommender algorithms online (in cooperation with the PLISTA GMBH[4]). When a user requests an article from a news portal (part

---

[3] http://www.clef-newsreel.org/, http://clef2015.clef-initiative.eu/

[4] http://www.plista.com

of the NewsREEL challenge) a recommendation request is sent to one of the registered recommender teams. The recommendations provided by the team are embedded in the requested web page. If the user clicks on a recommended item, the recommendation is counted as correct.

From the scientific perspective the online evaluation has several weaknesses. On the one hand, the evaluation is not reproducible: The news items and the contexts are changing continuously making it impossible to compare different algorithms in an exactly identical setting. The changes in the environment also complicate the parameter optimization since changes in the context may overlay the effect of optimized parameters. On the other hand the analysis of technical dependencies (required CPU, RAM, scalability) needs a detailed examination of a complex set of parameters which cannot be done if tight time constraints must be ensured. In addition, technical restrictions correlating with recommendation quality prevent the separation of technical and recommendation precision related concerns.

Offline Evaluation. In order to overcome the problems of an online evaluation approach, we focus on an offline evaluation for stream-based recommender. Based on a stream (recorded in the online scenario) we simulate a stream of messages and recommendation requests. This allows us analyzing different algorithms and parameter configurations based on exactly the same stream (in a reproducible manner). Special events (e.g. floating holidays or the final game in a championship) can be analyzed in detail as well as the effect of changes in the computing environment (e.g. with respect to limited CPU resources).

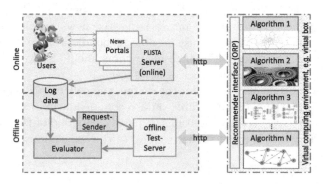

Fig. 2. The graphic shows the architecture of the NewsREEL challenge.

Figure 2 visualizes the architecture of our evaluation framework. The messages (article creates, article update, user-item interactions) captured in the online recommendation scenario are stored in a database. Based on the timestamps, the recorded stream can be used for benchmarking the recommender algorithms. The recorded messages are sent to the recommender algorithms which must provide a set of recommendations. The recommendations are then compared with the user actions (present in the recorded log file) in order to compute the CTR.

4   The Recommender Algorithms

We adapt several different recommender strategies in order to match the requirements of the news recommendation scenario. We optimize the algorithms for handling continuously changing sets of users and items. Instead of using a static set of user-item interactions, the recommender algorithms implement a sliding windows approach considering only the most recent users and items. Old articles are handled as outdated and are not considered when computing recommendations. The parameters (such as number of considered items and users) are optimized using the offline evaluation framework.

4.1   The Implemented Algorithms

We discuss the algorithms implemented and optimized for the news recommendation scenario.

Most Popular Items. News articles read by a large number of users are potentially more relevant than rarely requested articles. We use this idea for implementing a recommender creating a statistic that describes how often news articles have been accessed. Requests are answered by returning the most frequently read news articles. For ensuring that only "fresh" articles are delivered, the recommender considers only the N most recently created news articles. When a new article is added to the popularity statistic, the oldest article in the statistic is removed. Technically, the recommender is implemented using a size-bounded Map, automatically deleting the oldest entries when a new item is added. In order to be able to handle several requests concurrently, adequate synchronization methods for the item statistic must be applied.

Most Popular Item Sequence. In order to improve the recommendation precision, we refine the most popular recommender by creating a most-popular statistic for every news item. This allows us considering the articles currently requested by the user (a "context attribute"). In addition this reduces the probability of concurrent changes in the statistics for an article.

Time-weighted Popularity. We describe the REDDIT-like ranking strategy that computes the ranking of the recommendations based on the quotient of the number of positive user feedback and the lifetime of the item. News items requested by many users even though the item is only several minutes old are seen as most relevant. In contrast to a most popular recommender the ranking is continuously since articles are ranked down as the lifetime of a news items grows.

User-based Collaborative Filtering. The best-known recommender approach is used-based Collaborative Filtering. The algorithm is built based on the observation that users who showed similar preferences in the past will also like the same items in the future. Thus, the Collaborative Filtering algorithm computes in a first step the users most similar to the current user and recommends the items theses similar users liked. In order to adapt this algorithm to be capable with streams, we apply a sliding window approach. For determining users most similar with the current user, we also consider the last n users who requested news articles. The same time window is also used for determining the articles most requested by similar users.

Item-based Collaborative Filtering. An alternative version of collaborative filtering is item-based CF. Instead of analyzing the similarity between users, item-based CF computes the similarity between items ("users who bought this item also bought that item"). In contrast to user-based CF, item-based CF is robust against noisy user-IDs. Similar to our user-based CF algorithms, we implement the algorithm using a sliding window, considering only the last n user-item interactions while computing the similarity between news articles.

Baseline: Most Recently Requested News Items. The algorithms discussed in the previous paragraphs are based on comprehensive statistics describing the user-item interactions. As a baseline strategy, we use an algorithm that recommends the news articles most recently requested by other users. We implement this algorithm using a ring buffer storing the articles requested in the last minutes. Duplicates as well as articles requested by the current user are filtered out. The advantage of the strategy is that it needs little resources but gives a higher probability to item popular during the time of the request.

4.2   Implementation Details

We implemented the recommendation algorithms as well as the evaluation components in JAVA version 1.8. Since the news recommendation is characterized by high load demands, the recommender algorithms support the concurrent handling for recommendation requests. The recommender algorithms apply different approaches for synchronizing the access to global data structures such as traditional `synchronized` maps as well as concurrent maps and unsynchronized maps (which may cause dirty read operations). The used techniques usually do not change the algorithms; but the implementation highly influences the runtime complexity and the amount of required resources.

4.3   Discussion

In this section we presented several recommender algorithms optimized for the stream-based news scenario ensuring that only "fresh" articles are recommended and the algorithms adapt to new user preferences and items. All the discussed algorithms have several parameters that need to be optimized, such as the "sliding windows size" and what synchronization strategy should be used dependent from the number of requests per second. There is a need for an evaluation and optimization framework enabling the detailed comparison of different algorithms and parameter settings considering the context and the specific characteristics of different news domains.

5   Evaluation

We evaluate the performance of the recommender algorithms based on the recommendation precision and the technical complexity. Both aspects have a high influence on the business models. In general, more complex algorithms (that may lead to an improved recommendation quality) need more computational power resulting in higher costs for operating the recommender framework. In this section, we first explain the metrics used for benchmarking the recommender algorithms. Then, we describe the evaluation setup and present the evaluation results. We discuss our findings and show how to optimize the algorithms towards the requirements of specific scenarios.

5.1   Metrics

We benchmark the recommender algorithms both according to recommendation precision and the amount of required resources.

Recommendation Precision. We compute the recommendation precision based on the simulated Click-Through-Rate (CTR). Since we analyze the precision offline based on a previously recorded stream, there is no direct user feedback available. We assume that a recommendation for a user u is correct, if the user will have requested the recommended article (either by clicking on the recommendation or by using the news portal's navigation) within the next 5 minutes after the recommendation. If a recommendation is counted as valid, the article is marked as already considered in the evaluation for the user u. Thus, recommending repeatedly the same article for one user is not rewarded.

Resource Focused Evaluation. In addition to the CTR we benchmark the recommender algorithms also according to the amount for required resources. This question can be addressed from two different perspectives. (1) We measure the CPU cycles and the average amount of memory used for completing the recommendation task. In order to ensure an exact measurement, we execute the recommender algorithms in a virtual machine enabling us to measure the amount of resources used for a task. (2) We measure how many requests a pre-defined computing environment ("virtual machine") can handle. The "throughput" (measured in requests per second) describes whether an algorithm uses the provided resources efficiently. In multi-threaded environment an inadequate synchronization strategy may result in a low throughput and idling CPUs. Since in the news recommendation scenario there are strict limits for completing recommendations requests we also measure the average service response time and the fraction of requests successfully completed within 200ms (for different load levels characterized by the number of concurrent requests).

The evaluation of different implementations of one algorithm often gives helpful insights what implementation works best in a specific setting and how to optimize the algorithms.

Discussion. The evaluation of recommender algorithms is usually focused on academic measures such as RMSE or MAP computed using a cross-validation setting. For the evaluation of recommender algorithms optimized for a news stream we adapt these measures in order to meet the requirements of our recommendation scenario. In addition, our evaluation considers the "technical complexity" (amount of required resources, expected throughput, and average response time). Both aspects (precision and complexity) are important for a commercially successful recommender. A fine-grained evaluation and optimization provides the basis for figuring out a configuration working best in the analyzed scenario.

5.2 Evaluation Setup

We evaluate our recommender algorithms based on a stream of messages (item creates, item updates, user-item interactions) recorded by the PLISTA GMBH for three different news portals in July 2014. The dataset is structured in JSON and available from the NewsREEL webpage[5]. In total, the July 2014 dataset consists of 53,323,934 messages. 8,809,138 of these messages are marked as request each asking for six recommendations. 63% of the messages belong to a sport newspaper (ID: 596); 32% to a regional daily newspaper (ID: 1677), and 5% of the messages to a discussion board (ID: 694). The size of the dataset ensures the significance of the evaluation results.

The evaluation framework consists of a component creating the stream based on the dataset files and the evaluator component computing the CTR and the response time statistic[6]. The recommender algorithms run in VAGRANT-build virtual machines enabling us controlling the computational resources available to the recommender algorithms.

5.3 Evaluation Results

We evaluate the recommendation precision of the implemented algorithms. Table 1 shows the measured CTR for the different domains. The results show that the performance of the algorithms highly varies dependent from the specific news portal. The CTR for the sport news portal is notably higher than for the other portals. Comparing the CTR for the analyzed algorithms, we find that the item sequence-based recommender outperforms all other algorithms.

We compare the CTR of the implemented algorithms with the two baseline strategies. Baseline 1 computes recommendations based on the recently requested algorithms strategy (see Sec. 4); baseline 2 is defined based on the recommendations originally presented to the user while recording the dataset. Almost all of the implemented algorithms outperform the baseline strategies.

In the next step, we study the strength and weaknesses of the implemented algorithms in detail. For this purpose we analyze how the CTR depends on context parameters such as time and user device. Figure 3 visualizes the CTR of the recommender algorithms at the first weekend in July 2014 (Friday, July 4th - Sunday, July 6th) for the local news domain (domainID 1677). The results show that the

---

[5] http://www.clef-newsreel.org/
[6] The source code is available at
   https://github.com/andreas-dai/NewsREEL-Template

Table 1. The table shows the CTR for the implemented recommender algorithms measured on the offline dataset.

Recommender algorithm	sport newspaper (596)	discussion board (694)	regional daily newspaper (1677)	all news portals [aggregated]
item sequence-based CF	3.2%	2.2%	1.4%	2.6%
item-based CF	0.7%	1.2%	0.8%	0.8%
user-based CF	2.7%	1.8%	1.1%	2.1%
most popular	2.7%	1.7%	1.1%	2.2%
most polular and creation time	2.8%	1.5%	0.9%	2.1%
baseline 1: Most recently requested	2.0%	1.2%	0.7%	1.5%
baseline 2: Return the online suggested items	1.6%	0.7%	0.5%	1.2%

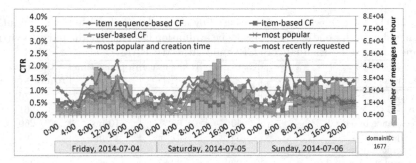

Fig. 3. The graph visualizes the CTR for the first July weekend (Friday, July 4th - Sunday, July 6th) for the local news domain (domainID 1677).

amount of requests and the CTR reached by the recommender algorithms strongly depends on the time. For instance, the most-popular algorithm only reaches a good CTR in the hours characterized by a big number of messages. This can be explained by the fact, that the prediction what items are most popular is the more reliable the higher the number of messages.

In addition to the definition of context based on the time, we analyze the recommendation performance with respect to the device that has been used. Figure 4 visualizes the CTR dependent from the user devices. The results show that the device highly influences the CTR. For all recommender algorithms the CTR is notably lower for users having a phone than for users using a tablet or a desktop pc. The item sequence-based recommender performs best for all devices. The most popular algorithm is the second best algorithm for phone and tablet users; user-based CF performs well for desktop users. This indicates that desktop users have longer sessions giving the CF-based algorithm the chance to better adapt to the individual user preferences. News-portal readers using mobile devices seem to be more interested in the top news.

5.4 Complexity Dependent Evaluation

We benchmark the algorithms with respect to technical aspects. At first we compare the amount of resources used for processing the dataset. Table 2 shows

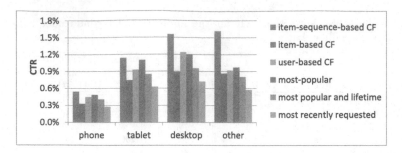

Fig. 4. The graph visualizes the CTR dependent on the user's device (domain: 1677 [local news], July 2014).

Table 2. The table shows the resources used by the analyzed algorithms for computing recommendations for one day [July 1st]. The evaluation has been conducted on a virtual machine having a 2 GHz dual core CPU and 2048 MB RAM.

Recommender algorithm	CPU usage [%]	RAM usage [%]	response time [ms]	throughput [requests per sec]
Item-based CF	38 %	46 %	12 ms	270
User-based CF	44 %	68 %	12 ms	261
Item sequence based CF	40 %	65 %	10 ms	266
Most popular	39 %	27 %	15 ms	264
User interaction and creation time	38 %	28 %	15 ms	274
Most recently requested	29 %	26 %	8 ms	347

the average CPU usage, the amount of allocated RAM, and the average time needed for processing a request. The results show that the baseline strategy requires only a minimum of resources. There is no direct correlation between the CTR and the amount of needed resources.

The amount of resources needed by an algorithm also strongly depends on the concrete implementation. Increasing the RAM an algorithm can allocate for caching data, often improves the throughput. In the analyzed scenario a bottleneck of the recommender algorithms is the statistic describing what news article has been requested by which user. For studying this problem, we use our evaluation framework for benchmarking three different implementations of the most-popular recommender algorithm. We analyze the throughput of the most-popular recommender algorithm dependent from the map implementation used for storing the number of requests per news item. The results show that different synchronization strategies perform best dependent from the number of concurrent requests (Fig. 5). For scenarios characterized by a large number of concurrent requests the maps classes from the GUAVA library perform best; for small number of concurrent request simpler synchronization strategies such as provided by the standard JAVA classes outperform the more complex libraries.

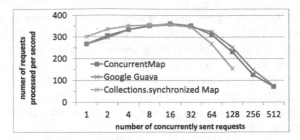

Fig. 5. The figure visualizes the throughput of different implementation of the `Most-popular` recommender. We tested three different strategies for implementing a `map` storing the number of requests per news item. The results show that different synchronization strategies perform best dependent from the number of concurrent requests.

5.5 Discussion

Our framework allows us benchmarking the recommender algorithms and the implementations of the algorithms in detail. We do not only consider the recommendation precision (measured based on CTR) but also technical aspects such as the amount of required resources. Our experiments show that the framework enables the fine-grained benchmarking of algorithm taking into account different definitions of context (e.g. time or user's device). Compared with the online evaluation, the offline stream recommender evaluation framework supports the identification of bottlenecks and enables the parameter tuning. Since the framework allows replaying pre-recorded streams the effect changes in the implementation of an algorithm can be systematically studied in a reproducible way. In addition, the framework helps us studying problems induced by concurrent threads that can only be observed at specific load levels. Analyzing the behavior of the algorithms for different numbers of concurrent request enabled us detecting bugs that can be observed in rare situations (e.g. in extreme load peaks).

Our evaluation of the algorithms shows that the analyzed algorithms have different strengths and weaknesses. The comprehensive testing of the algorithms enables us selecting the most appropriate algorithm for a specific context.

6 Conclusion

In this paper we have presented a framework enabling the analysis and optimization of stream-based recommender algorithms. We have shown how recommender algorithms can be evaluated considering different context parameters (e.g. time and user device). The framework allows us detecting the strengths and weaknesses of different algorithms and optimizing the parameters with respect to a specific scenario. In our evaluation we also consider technical aspects such as CPU time, average response time, and throughput (measured using VAGRANT script-created virtual machines).

The evaluation shows that there is not one best algorithm; the recommendation quality highly depends on the context and the specific news domain. The technical complexity is an aspect needing fine-grained optimization. The offline evaluation framework is a powerful tool since it enables us analyzing various different parameter settings for interesting scenarios in a reproducible way.

As future work we plan to support additional computation environments (such as AMAZON EC2) and to automize the parameter tuning for the recommender algorithms. In addition we will implement additional recommender algorithms and define ensembles based on the algorithms allowing us adapting to the requirements for specific contexts.

Acknowledgments. The research leading to these results was performed in the CrowdRec project, which has received funding from the European Union Seventh Framework Program FP7/2007-2013 under grant agreement n. 610594.

References

1. Adomavicius, G., Tuzhilin, A.: Toward the next generation of recommender systems: A survey of the state-of-the-art and possible extensions. IEEE Trans. on Knowledge and Data Engineering **17**(6) (2005)
2. Herlocker, J.L., Konstan, J.A., Terveen, L.G., Riedl, J.T.: Evaluating collaborative filtering recommender systems. ACM Trans. Inf. Syst. **22**(1), 5–53 (2004)
3. Kluver, D., Konstan, J.A.: Evaluating recommender behavior for new users. In: Proc. of the 8th ACM Conf. on Recommender Systems, pp. 121–128. ACM, NY (2014)
4. Liu, J., Pedersen, E., Dolan, P.: Personalized news recommendation based on click behavior. In: 2010 International Conference on Intelligent User Interfaces (2010)
5. Lommatzsch, A., Plumbaum, T., Albayrak, S.: A linked dataverse knows better: Boosting recommendation quality using semantic knowledge. In: Proc. of the 5th Intl. Conf. on Advances in Semantic Processing, pp. 97–103, Wilmington, DE, USA (2011)
6. Rendle, S.: Learning recommender systems with adaptive regularization. In: Proc. of the 5th ACM Intl. Conf. on Web Search and Data Mining, pp. 133–142. ACM, NY (2012)
7. Sarwar, B., Karypis, G., Konstan, J., Riedl, J.: Item-based collaborative filtering recommendation algorithms. In: Proc. of the 10th Conf. on WWW, pp. 285–295, NY, USA (2001)
8. Su, X., Khoshgoftaar, T.M.: A survey of collaborative filtering techniques. Advances in Artificial Intelligence, January 2009
9. Walunj, S.G., Sadafale, K.: An online recommendation system for e-commerce based on apache mahout framework. In: Proceedings of the 2013 Annual Conference on Computers and People Research, SIGMIS-CPR 2013, pp. 153–158. ACM, New York (2013)
10. Zhang, Z.-K., Liu, C., Zhang, Y.-C., Zhou, T.: Solving the cold-start problem in recommender systems with social tags. EPL (Europhysics Letters) **92**(2), 28002 (2010)

Information Extraction from Clinical Documents: Towards Disease/Disorder Template Filling

Veera Raghavendra Chikka[1]([✉]), Nestor Mariyasagayam[2], Yoshiki Niwa[3],
and Kamalakar Karlapalem[1]

[1] International Institute of Information Technology, Hyderabad, India
`raghavendra.ch@research.iiit.ac.in, kamal@iiit.ac.in`
[2] Research and Development Centre, Hitachi India Pvt Ltd, Bangalore, India
`nestor@hitachi.co.in`
[3] Central Research Laboratory, Hitachi, Ltd., Kokubunji, Japan
`yoshiki.niwa.tx@hitachi.com`

Abstract. In recent years there has been an increase in the generation of electronic health records (EHRs), which lead to an increased scope for research on biomedical literature. Many research works have been using various NLP, information retrieval and machine learning techniques to extract information from these records. In this paper, we provide a methodology to extract information for understanding the status of the disease/disorder. The status of disease/disorder is based on different attributes like temporal information, severity and progression of the disease. Here, we consider ten attributes that allow us to understand the majority details regarding the status of the disease/disorder. They are Negation Indicator, Subject Class, Uncertainty Indicator, Course Class, Severity Class, Conditional Class, Generic Class, Body Location, DocTime Class, and Temporal Expression. In this paper, we present rule-based and machine learning approaches to identify each of these attributes and evaluate our system on attribute level and system level accuracies. This project was done as a part of the ShARe/CLEF eHealth Evaluation Lab 2014. We were able to achieve state-of-art accuracy (0.868) in identifying normalized values of the attributes.

Keywords: NLP · Information extraction · Unified Medical Langugae System (UMLS) · Apache cTAKES · Relation extraction · Machine learning

1 Introduction

Electronic Health Records (EHRs) have known to be rich sources of patient information. These records are largely available in unstructured text format. So,

© Springer International Publishing Switzerland 2015
J. Mothe et al. (Eds.): CLEF 2015, LNCS 9283, pp. 389–401, 2015.
DOI: 10.1007/978-3-319-24027-5_41

there is a need of extracting valuable information which can be utilized to assist professionals, researchers or even patients in providing better health care [17].

In biomedical literature, text mining has been an active research area focused on extracting varied information. One such approach to effectively extract and structure complex information from text is Template filling[1] [20].

In this paper we extract the information that helps in understanding the status of a disease/disorder. The status of disease/disorder (DD) relies on diverse aspects like temporal information, body location, severity and progression of the disease. We coalesce this information in the form of a template with ten attributes adopted from ShARe/CLEF2014 eHealth 2014 task 2 challenge[2]. We have built a pipeline architecture to extract the information of each of these attributes using rule based and machine learning approaches. This paper is an extension of our participation in CLEF eHealth 2014 task2 [14].

Problem

We have a corpus of de-identified healthcare reports along with an empty template for each disorder mentioned in the report. The template consists of disorder UMLS[3] CUI (Concept Unique Identifier), its span offset (character boundary of the disorder) and a list of default values for each of the 10 attributes: Negation Indicator (NI), Subject Class (SC), Uncertainty Indicator (UI), Course Class (CC), Severity Class (SV), Conditional Class (CO), Generic Class (GC), Body Location (BL), DocTime Class (DT), and Temporal Expression (TE). Table 1 provides details of these attributes. The problem was divided into two sub-tasks, Task **a** is to identify the normalization value for each attribute from a list of possible predefined norm values and Task **b** is to identify the cue slot value (span offset of each attribute) [18]. We have a template of the following format:

DD DocName|DD Spans|DD CUI|Norm NI|Cue NI|Norm SC|Cue SC|Norm UI|Cue UI|Norm CC|Cue CC|Norm SV|Cue SV|Norm CO|Cue CO|Norm GC|Cue GC|Norm BL|Cue BL|Norm DT|Norm TE|Cue TE

For example, the following sentence, "The patient has an extensive thyroid history.", was represented following disorder template with default normalization and cue values given in Table 1:

09388-093839-DISCHARGE SUMMARY.txt|30-36|C0040128|*no|*NULL| patient|*NULL|*no|*NULL|*false|*NULL|unmarked|*NULL| *false|*NULL|*false|*NULL|NULL|*NULL|*Unknown|*None| *NULL

---

[1] Template filling is a task of filling a predefined schema, often called template, to gather information related to specific domain.

[2] http://clefehealth2014.dcu.ie/task-2

[3] http://www.nlm.nih.gov/research/umls/

After Task a, for the example sentence, the template changes to:

09388-093839-DISCHARGE SUMMARY.txt|30-36|C0040128|*no|*NULL|
patient|*NULL|*no|*NULL|*false|*NULL|unmarked|*NULL|
severe|*NULL|*false|*NULL|**C0040132**|*NULL|
Before|*None|*NULL

After Task b, for the example sentence, the template changes to:

09388-093839-DISCHARGE SUMMARY.txt|30-36|C0040128|*no|*NULL|
patient|*NULL|*no|*NULL|*false|*NULL|unmarked|*NULL|
severe|**20-28**|*false|*NULL|C0040132|**30-36**|Before|
*None|*NULL

Table 1. Disease/Disorder Attribute details

Disease/Disorder (DD) Attribute Types	Definitions from ShARe guidelines: A span of text that ..	Norm Slot Values (possible values)	Cue Slot Value (spanOffsets of lexical cue)
Negation Indicator (NI)	indicates a disease/disorder was negated.	*no, yes	span offset of lexical cue
Subject Class (SC)	indicates who experienced a disease/disorder.	*patient, family-member, donor_family_member, donor_other, null, other	span offset of lexical cue
Uncertainity Indicator (UI)	indicates a measure of doubt into a statement about a · disease/disorder.	*no, yes	span offset of lexical cue
Course Class (CC)	indicates progress or decline of a disease/disorder.	*unmarked, changed, increased, decreased, improved, worsened, resolved	span offset of lexical cue
Severity Class (SV)	indicates how severe a disease/disorder is.	*unmarked, slight, moderate, severe	span offset of lexical cue
Conditional Class (CO)	indicates conditional existence of disease/disorder under certain circumstances.	*false, true	span offset of lexical cue
Generic Class (GC)	indicates a generic mention of a disease/disorder.	*false, true	span offset of lexical cue
Body Location (BL)	represents an anatomical location.	*NULL, CUI, CUI-less	span offset of lexical cue
DocTime Class (DT)	indicates temporal relation between a disease/disorder and document authoring time.	before, after, overlap, before-overlap, *unknown	−No cue annotated/no slot−
Temporal Expression (TE)	represents any TIMEX (TimeML) temporal expression related to the disease/disorder.	*none, date, time, duration set	span offset of lexical cue

The remaining paper is organized as follows: in section 2 we review related work, in section 3 the different approaches we have used are discussed; section 4 presents evaluation details and performance of the system and we finally present our conclusion in section 5.

2   Related Work

Early works on biomedical literature was focused on rule based approaches. As the clinical information is growing at rapid pace, researchers have moved towards machine learning (ML) approaches like Conditional Random Fields (CRF) [3], Support Vector Machines (SVM) [1] for information extraction.

There have been various works of extracting information like identifying symptoms, medications, tests, procedures [8], protein names [6], enzyme Interactions, protein structures [10][13], the names of Genes and Gene products [5] from biomedical literature. Other kinds of information extraction includes generation of disease-drug association rules [23][11] and summarization of medical documents to a tabular format [2].

Even data mining techniques were used for identifying medical terms [25] and their relationships [24]. In [9], the author combines clinical informatics with protein profiles to evaluate the disease-specific, severity-associated, duration-related biomarkers. In clinical documents the progression of disease/disorder is recorded in chronological fashion and this information captures a lot of significant hidden patterns regarding the condition of illness [22].

Biomedical Natural Language Processing (BioNLP) community have organized various shared tasks/challenges have been organized over the past 10 years [12]. Few BioNLP clinical challenges include Informatics for Integrating Biology and the Bedside[4] (i2b2), TREC Medical[5] (Text REtrieval Conference), SemEval[6], ShARe/CLEF eHealth, etc. In 2014, ShARe/CLEF eHealth evaluation lab organized a unique clinical template filling task targeting rich semantic attributes [18]. The same task was later adopted by SemEval 2015 to encourage and accelerate the research on the template filling.

3   Methodology

We approached the task by building a baseline system using Apache clinical Text Analysis and Knowledge Extraction System (cTAKES) [21]. Although few cTAKES[7] modules are still under development, we followed its clinical pipeline for development of our baseline system.

3.1   System Architecture

Our system adopted four modules (Assertion, Relation Extraction, Temporal Extraction and DocTime Extraction) from Apache cTAKES, an NLP framework specifically built for processing medical text. The assertion module is used to

---

[4] https://www.i2b2.org/NLP/
[5] http://trec.nist.gov/
[6] http://alt.qcri.org/semeval2015/
[7] http://ctakes.apache.org/

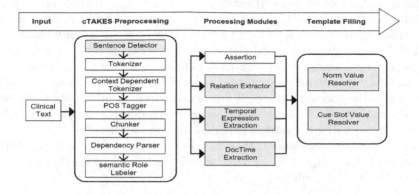

Fig. 1. System Architecture and Processing Pipeline built upon Apache cTAKES. The grey components are modified or rebuilt where as other components remained unchanged from original cTAKES framework.

examine the implications of disease/disorder, attributes of assertion: NI, UI, CO, SC and GC. The task of BL, SC and CC comes under relation extraction module [7]. Figure 1 depicts our system's architecture (built upon Apache cTAKES v3.1). It takes clinical text as input, applies preprocessing steps followed by individual module's process and finally supplies the generated result to Template Filler which ultimately resolves norm values and identifies cue slot values of attributes.

3.2   Pipeline Processing of Individual Modules

3.2.1   Assertion

Assertion attributes are determined using machine learning as well as rule based approach. We evaluate both of these approaches separately.

Rule Based Assertion: In rule based assertion, the polarity of sentence is predicted using NegEx algorithm [4]. It requires predefined negation phrases which have been divided into two groups *pseudo-negation* and *actual-negation*. Pseudo negation consists of phrases that indicate negation but instead identify double negative (*"not ruled out"*) and ambiguous phrasing (*"unremarkable"*). For instance, in the sentence *"Ambulating without difficulty, chest pain free, and without further evidence of bleeding"*, all diseases *ambulating*, *chest pain* and *bleeding* are negated by pseudo negation phrases *without difficulty*, *free* and *without further evidence of*, respectively. On the other hand, actual negation phrase denies disease or finding when used in a window of +/- 5 tokens. The window size is decided based on empirical evaluation. For example, in the sentence *"Ext: No clubbing, cyanosis or edema"* all the findings are negated by *No* phrase.

In order to predict the uncertainty and conditional classes, the assertion module first extracts phrases using POS tags and token entries present in the left window of mentioned disease. These target phrases are then scored using list of words with predefined uncertainty/conditional values. For example, *if, risk, evaluate, when* are some typical words with high conditional score. Similarly, *uncertain, differentiate, suspect* are tokens having high uncertainty score.

The feature set used in subject class identification includes token, SRL argument, dependency path and SRL dependent token of all the persons who appeared in the sentence mentioning disease/disorder. A rule based approach is applied over the selected features. If donor and family member both features are true, the subject will be *donor_family_member*. Similarly other cases have been introduced to predict the subject experiencing disease/disorder.

As per the training dataset, there is no entry asserting generic attribute in the whole dataset. However, we used generic classifier of assertion module to classify the generic attribute.

Machine Learning Assertion: In machine learning assertion, we used ClearTK [19] framework for feature extraction and trained separate models for each assertion attribute on training data.

All assertion attributes have a common feature list which includes word, word-stem, tokens within -/+ 5 window, bag of words within -/+ 3 window of disorder mention and word score. Word score is derived by taking mean of contextual token distance from the mentioned disease/disorder. In addition to common feature list, NI uses negation dependency features and SC uses features of rule based approach along with the outcomes.

Table 2. Sample stem dictionary for assertion attributes

Subject	Negation Indicator	Uncertainty	Conditional	Generic
father	no evidence of	differentia	if	recommended
mother	no sign of	uncertain	Concern	consult
family	negative	potential	protect	sign
parent	absent	probab	when	service
paternal	without	suspec	indicat	mention

3.2.2   Relation Extraction

Body Location Extraction: This involves two steps: extraction of the body location and its normalization to CUI. the extraction of Body Location is the most critical attribute in this template filling task concerning CUI ambiguity of clinical concepts. For example, in a sentence *"intact in all four extremities to LT, PP, cold"*, *extremities* has CUIs C0015385 and C0278454 but the correct CUI in the context of given sentence is C0278454. Figure 2 depicts a typical sequence of algorithms applied for body location finding.

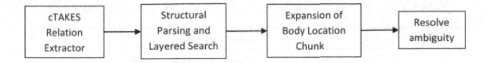

Fig. 2. Sequence of algorithms applied for body location finding

As a preprocessing step in body location identification, we built a Lucene [16] based dictionary comprising all UMLS concepts of body parts falling into different semantic types defined by CLEF eHealth 2014 [15]. We indexed first term as well as full text of concept in order to implement a layered search approach.

Structural Parsing and Layered Search: We apply dictionary based lookup over NP chunks to extract entity mentions (body part, anatomical sites and their associated CUIs). We used SVM model to extract the pair of disease and entity mentions. For example, in the sentence *"patient has severe pain in left shoulder while right shoulder is normal"*, *pain* is disease and *left shoulder* and *right shoulder* are two body locations. In this case, two training instances *pain .. left shoulder* and *pain .. right shoulder* (true and false respectively) are generated to find the relationship between these pairs.

Expansion of Body Chunks: After extracting relationship between body part and disease, we expand body part text chunks to +/- 5 token windows. For example, in the sentence *"EGD showed food compaction in the lower third of the esophagus and gastroesophageal junction "*, structural parsing and layer search finds *esophagus* which is expanded to *lower third of the esophagus* and hence overlapping results are transformed into strict results resolving CUI ambiguity to some extent.

Resoving CUI Ambiguity: Finally ambuity among CUIs is resolved by preparing a separate dictionary for each report type. Each dictionary includes anatomical sites pertaining to the report type. For example, ECG dictionary includes heart, chambers and other heart components. However, dictionaries have been created from supplied training data and CUI ambiguity has been resolved by considering most frequent CUI.

Severity Class. Our system extracts the mentions which describes the severity of the disease. However, a specific mention may not be able to express the degree of the severity. For this reason, we have a predefined classes to describe the *degree_of* severity namely severe, slight and moderate. The extracted mentions are then normalized into one of these three classes.

To identify the severity class mentions, we built a CRF model with feature set including tokens covered and POS tags. After annotating severity class using CRF, features are generated for all possible pairs of disease mention and severity class mentions, SVM models are trained for relation.

Table 3. Sample list of severity and course modifiers with synonym stems

Modifier type	Class	Synonym stems
Severity Modifier	severe	advanc, bad, dart, elevat,
	slight	small, little, minimal, niggl
	moderate	check, control, mild, moderat
Course Modifier	increased	increas, high, advanc, ascend, addition
	improved	improv, normal, better, come-back, well
	resolved	recover, regain, block-up, ceas, clear
	decreased	decreas, contract, declin, degenerat, dim
	changed	chang, evolv, moving, transform
	worsened	worse, spoil, swell, tough, wretch

Once relationship is determined, normalization of the mention is determined using synonym stem dictionaries. We collected all the nearest synonyms of norm values and prepared a dictionary comprising stem of severity class and their synonyms.

Course Class. Severity class depicts the current state of the condition, whereas course class indicates the progress/decline of the disease/disorder. The normalized values used for course class are: changed, increased, decreased, improved, worsened and resolved. We followed the same approach used in severity class for course class identification. Table 3 shows sample stem dictionaries of severity and course classes.

Temporal Expression Extraction

Temporal expression (TE) represents any TIMEX (TimeML) expression related to the disease/disorder. The normalized values used for TE are: date, time and duration.

We found two types of temporal expressions in our dataset, namely numerical date/time (Ex: 24-11-1990, 11:40 PM, 23:20 A.M etc) and textual temporal expresion (Ex: "evening of postoperative day three", "3 days ago", 1day, x1 yr, 12p.m).

We built finite state machines (FSM) for numerical date and time patterns. Besides FSM, we also developed an algorithm to find textual temporal expressions.

Firstly, we used regular expressions to extract the time patterns from time classes (*PartOfDay, DayOfWeek, MonthOfYear, SeasonOfYear, today,* etc.,) and derived classes (*1day before, hd2, x1 yr, 5am, 12p.m*). Then we expand these patterns by using adjusters and modifiers (few, ago, each, postoperative, etc). For example, in the sentence "*On the evening of day three, the patient had another short 7-beat run of ventricular tachycardia*", *evening* has class PartOfDay and *day* has Unit, so it is expanded to *evening of day three*. Finally, we relate disease/disorder to the nearest temporal expression when multiple temporal expressions are found in a sentence.

Once temporal expression is found, it has to be classified into one of the three norm values DATE, TIME or DURATION. Table 4 shows the classes and corresponding dictionary categories and keywords.

Table 4. Temporal expression class, their categories and keywords

Class	Categories	Keywords
DURATION	DUR_UNIT, Duration, SeasonOfYear,	year, month, day, week, year, wk, period, century, Past, over, within, since, throughout, through, several
TIME	TIME_UNIT, PartOfDay, TimeAnnotation	ago, before, after, prior, earlier, hour, min, sec, am, pm
DATE	Prepost, DATE_UNIT, Date, MonthOfYear, Year, DayOfWeek, DateAnnoation	postoperative, pod, day, date

DocTime Extraction

DocTime class indicates temporal relation between a disease/disorder and document authoring time. We build a CRF model with feature set comprising of tokens and POS tags within +/-3 window of mentioned disease/disorder, tense of nearby verb, section heading and closest verb. Along with these features, we also integrated time expression features found during temporal expression extraction phase.

4 Evaluation

4.1 Dataset

ShARe/CLEF eHealth 2014 was organized and provided a shared dataset for information extraction from clinical documents: disease/disorder template filling task. The training dataset consists of 4 types of healthcare reports: Discharge summary, Radiology report, ECHO report and ECG report, while test data has only Discharge summaries. Table 5 describes corpus statistics.

Table 5. Statistics of training and test data

Report type	Training dataset		Test dataset	
	#reports	#annotations	#reports	#annotations
DISCHARGE SUMMARY	136	9098	133	8003
RADIOLOGY REPORT	54	831	0	0
ECHO REPORT	54	1429	0	0
ECG REPORT	54	196	0	0

Our system was developed on a training set (298 reports) and evaluated on a test set (133 reports). All machine learning models are optimized using 10-fold cross validation on the training data; however no additional annotations are used throughout the development.

4.2   Evaluation Metric

Evaluation focuses on accuracy for Normalization value detection (Task a) and F1-score for Cue slot identification (Task b), defined as strict F1-score (span is identical to the gold standard span) and relaxed F1-score (span overlaps with the gold standard span). Each task has been evaluated on each attribute type and overall system performance.

4.3   Results and Discussion

We have evaluated our system on two runs: TeamHitachi.1 which uses rule based methods and TeamHITACHI.2 which uses machine learning algorithms (CRF and SVM) for assertion module. Table 6 shows the official ranking result of our system on Task a. Out of 10 teams participated in the task, 7 teams used both rule-based and machine learning approaches and other 3 teams have dealt only with rule-based approaches.

Table 6. Overall performance of our system on Task a on overall average of attributes

System ID ({team}.{system})	Accuracy (Overall Average)
TeamHITACHI.2	0.868
TeamHITACHI.1	0.854
RelAgent.2	0.843
RelAgent.1	0.843
TeamHCMUS.1	0.827
DFKI-Medical.2	0.822
LIMSI.1	0.804
DFKI-Medical.1	0.804
TeamUEvora.1	0.802
LIMSI.2	0.801
ASNLP.1	0.793
TeamCORAL.1.add	0.790
TeamGRIUM.1	0.780
HPI.1	0.769

As shown in the evaluation results, our system outperformed in overall system evaluation. In Task a, our system (0.868) achieved an improvement of 0.025 in overall accuracy benchmarking with respect to second best team (0.843). On the other hand, in Task b, our system's performance is best among all the submitted systems [18]. Even in attribute wise evaluation, our system obtained the highest accuracy in 7 out of 10 attributes. In body location identification, our system achieved the highest accuracy 0.797 in mapping body location to

UMLS CUI. The difference between strict F1-score 0.735 and relaxed F1-score 0.874 for body location cue slot identification suggests amendment of dictionaries and optimization of dictionary lookup algorithm. Another concerning attribute which achieved least accuracy 0.328 is DocTime class, albeit highest among all the systems. One possible feature enhancement for DocTime relation could be inclusion of section features other than sentence.

5   Conclusions

In this paper we define a template filling task with template comprising of ten semantic attributes to analyze the status of disease/disorder. We built a clinical pipeline system over Apache cTAKES to extract these ten predefined attributes. We developed several wrappers comprising machine learning and rule based techniques for normalization and cue slot value detection. Finally, we evaluate our system on ShARe/CLEF eHealth 2014 dataset. The results depicts that our system achieved the best accuracy in both norm and cue slot value identification, indicating promising enhancement over baseline system. We conclude with the fact that healthcare relies on diverse information and combining such relevant information can help in better analysis of healthcare.

Acknowledgments. We would like to thank the task organizers of ShARe/CLEF eHealth 2014 task 2 which was partially supported by the CLEF Initiative, the ShARe project funded by the United States National Institutes of Health (R01GM090187), the US Office of the 37National Coordinator of Healthcare Technology, Strategic Health IT Advanced Research Projects (SHARP) 90TR0002, and the Swedish Research Council (350-2012-6658).

References

1. Andrade, M.A., Valencia, A.: Automatic extraction of keywords from scientific text: application to the knowledge domain of protein families. Bioinformatics **14**(7), 600–607 (1998)
2. Aramaki, E., Miura, Y., Tonoike, M., Ohkuma, T., Mashuichi, H., Ohe, K.: Text2table: medical text summarization system based on named entity recognition and modality identification. In: Proceedings of the Workshop on Current Trends in Biomedical Natural Language Processing, BioNLP 2009, pp. 185–192 (2009)
3. Bodnari, A., Deleger, L., Lavergne, T., Neveol, A., Zweigenbaum, P.: A supervised named-entity extraction system for medical text. In: Online Working Notes of the CLEF 2013 Evaluation Labs and Workshop, September 2013
4. Chapman, W.W., Bridewell, W., Hanbury, P., Cooper, G.F., Buchanan, B.G.: A simple algorithm for identifying negated findings and diseases in discharge summaries. Journal of Biomedical Informatics **34**(5), 301–310 (2001)
5. Collier, N., Nobata, C., Tsujii, J.I.: Extracting the names of genes and gene products with a hidden markov model. In: Proceedings of the 18th conference on Computational Linguistics, vol. 1, pp. 201–207 (2000)

6. Dingare, S., Nissim, M., Finkel, J., Manning, C., Grover, C.: A system for identifying named entities in biomedical text: How results from two evaluations reflect on both the system and the evaluations. Comparative and Functional Genomics 6(1–2), 77–85 (2005)
7. Dligach, D., Bethard, S., Becker, L., Miller, T.A., Savova, G.K.: Discovering body site and severity modifiers in clinical texts. JAMIA 21(3), 448–454 (2014)
8. Doan, S., Xu, H.: Recognizing medication related entities in hospital discharge summaries using support vector machine. In: Proceedings of the 23rd International Conference on Computational Linguistics: Posters, pp. 259–266 (2010)
9. Fang, X., Bai, C., Wang, X.: Bioinformatics insights into acute lung injury/acute respiratory distress syndrome. Clinical and Translational Medicine 1(1), 9 (2012)
10. Gaizauskas, R., Demetriou, G., Humphreys, K.: Term recognition and classification in biological science journal articles. In: Proc. of the Computional Terminology for Medical and Biological Applications Workshop of the 2nd International Conference on NLP (2000)
11. Hara, A., Ichimura, T., Yoshida, K.: Discovering multiple diagnostic rules from coronary heart disease database using automatically defined groups. Journal of Intelligent Manufacturing 16(6), 645–661 (2005)
12. Huang, C.C., Lu, Z.: Community challenges in biomedical text mining over 10 years: success, failure and the future. Briefings in Bioinformatics, bbv024 (2015)
13. Humphreys, K., Demetriou, G., Gaizauskas, R.: Two applications of information extraction to biological science journal articles: enzyme interactions and protein structures. In: Proceedings of the Pacific Symposium on Biocomputing (PSB-2000), pp. 505–516, January 2000
14. Johri, N., Niwa, Y., Chikka, V.R.: Optimizing apache ctakes for disease/disorder template filling: team HITACHI in the share/clef 2014 ehealth evaluation lab. In: Cappellato, L., Ferro, N., Halvey, M., Kraaij, W. (eds.) Working Notes for CLEF 2014 Conference, Sheffield, UK, September 15–18, 2014. CEUR Workshop Proceedings, vol. 1180, pp. 111–123. CEUR-WS.org (2014)
15. Kelly, L., et al.: Overview of the ShARe/CLEF ehealth evaluation lab 2014. In: Kanoulas, E., Lupu, M., Clough, P., Sanderson, M., Hall, M., Hanbury, A., Toms, E. (eds.) CLEF 2014. LNCS, vol. 8685, pp. 172–191. Springer, Heidelberg (2014)
16. Lucene, A.: Apache lucene. http://lucene.apache.org/core/
17. Mittal, P., Gill, N.S.: Article: Study and analysis of predictive data mining approaches for clinical dataset. International Journal of Computer Applications 63(3), 35–39 (2013)
18. Mowery, D.L., Velupillai, S., South, B.R., Christensen, L., Martinez, D., Kelly, L., Goeuriot, L., Elhadad, N., Pradhan, S., Savova, G., et al.: Task 2: share/clef ehealth evaluation lab 2014. In: Proceedings of CLEF 2014 (2013)
19. Ogren, P.V., Wetzler, P.G., Bethard, S.J.: Cleartk: a framework for statistical natural language processing. Unstructured Information Management Architecture Workshop at the Conference of the German Society for Computational Linguistics and Language Technology, 9 (2009)
20. Raja, K., Subramani, S., Natarajan, J.: Template filling, text mining. In: Dubitzky, W., Wolkenhauer, O., Cho, K.H., Yokota, H. (eds.) Encyclopedia of Systems Biology, pp. 2150–2154. Springer, New York (2013)
21. Savova, G.K., Masanz, J.J., Ogren, P.V., Zheng, J., Sohn, S., Kipper-Schuler, K.C., Chute, C.G.: Mayo clinical text analysis and knowledge extraction system (ctakes): architecture, component evaluation and applications. Journal of the American Medical Informatics Association 17(5), 507–513 (2010)

22. Sun, W., Rumshisky, A., Uzuner, O.: Temporal reasoning over clinical text: the state of the art. Journal of Biomedical Informatics **20**(5), 814–823 (2013)
23. Wang, X., Hripcsak, G., Friedman, C.: Characterizing environmental and phenotypic associations using information theory and electronic health records. BMC Bioinformatics **10**(Suppl. 9), S13 (2009)
24. Yoo, I., Alafaireet, P., Marinov, M., Pena-Hernandez, K., Gopidi, R., Chang, J.F., Hua, L.: Data mining in healthcare and biomedicine: A survey of the literature. Journal of Medical Systems **36**(4), 2431–2448 (2012)
25. Yoo, I., Song, M.: Biomedical ontologies and text mining for biomedicine and healthcare: A survey. Journal of Computing Science and Engineering, 109–136, June 2008

Adaptive Algorithm for Plagiarism Detection: The Best-Performing Approach at PAN 2014 Text Alignment Competition

Miguel A. Sanchez-Perez[(⊠)], Alexander Gelbukh, and Grigori Sidorov

Centro de Investigacin en Computacin, Instituto Politcnico Nacional,
Mexico City, Mexico
masp1988@hotmail.com, gelbukh@gelbukh.com, sidorov@cic.ipn.mx

Abstract. The task of (monolingual) text alignment consists in finding similar text fragments between two given documents. It has applications in plagiarism detection, detection of text reuse, author identification, authoring aid, and information retrieval, to mention only a few. We describe our approach to the text alignment subtask of the plagiarism detection competition at PAN 2014, which resulted in the best-performing system at the PAN 2014 competition and outperforms the best-performing system of the PAN 2013 competition by the cumulative evaluation measure Plagdet. Our method relies on a sentence similarity measure based on a tf-idf-like weighting scheme that permits us to consider stopwords without increasing the rate of false positives. We introduce a recursive algorithm to extend the ranges of matching sentences to maximal length passages. We also introduce a novel filtering method to resolve overlapping plagiarism cases. Our system is available as open source.

1 Introduction

Plagiarism detection, and more generally, text reuse detection, has become a hot research topic given the increasing amount of information being produced as the result of easy access to the Web, large databases and telecommunication in general, which poses a serious problem for publishers, researchers, and educational institutions [8]. Plagiarism detection techniques are also useful in applications such as content authoring systems, which offer fast and simple means for adding and editing content and where avoiding content duplication is desired [1]. Hence, detecting text reuse has become imperative in such contexts.

Our approach outperforms the best-performing systems of both PAN 2013 [14] and PAN 2014 [13] competitions. PAN[1] is a CLEF Lab on uncovering plagiarism, authorship, and social software misuse. In 2013 and 2014, the PAN competition consisted of three tasks: plagiarism detection, author verification, and author profiling. The plagiarism detection task was divided into source retrieval and text alignment subtasks. In the text alignment subtask, the systems

---

[1] http://pan.webis.de

© Springer International Publishing Switzerland 2015
J. Mothe et al. (Eds.): CLEF 2015, LNCS 9283, pp. 402–413, 2015.
DOI: 10.1007/978-3-319-24027-5_42

were required to identify all contiguous maximal-length passages of reused text between a given pair of documents. At the PAN 2014 competition, our approach showed the best result out of ten participating systems. Our system is available open source.[2]

The rest of the paper is organized as follows. Section 2 explains the general steps to build a text alignment model with some related work, and the main problems to solve when building one. Section 3 describes in detail our approach. Section 4 discusses the experimental experiments. Finally, Section 5 gives conclusions and future work.

2 Text Alignment

The text alignment task consists in the following: given a pair of documents, to identify contiguous passages of reused text between them. Most of the text alignment models follow a three-step approach: seeding, extension, and filtering [13]. The first step consists in finding relations (so-called "seeds") between features extracted from the documents. At this stage, it is important to determine which type of features to use and what kind of relation to look for. For example, the features could be word n-grams with several implementations like Context n-grams [9,16–18], Context skip n-gram [18], Stopwords n-grams [16,17] and Named entity n-grams [16]; all of them looking for exact match. In our approach, we extracted sentences and compared them in a Vector Space Model (VSM) using the cosine similarity alike [6]. We also used the Dice coefficient as in [7] given that this measure look for a basic and equal distributions of the terms in the passages to compare.

Taking into account only the seeds extracted, some passages that do not show high similarity but are part of a plagiarism case could be missed. This due to the presence of noise and also because a specific type of feature or similarity measure does not necessarily identify all possible types of obfuscation techniques.[3]

Accordingly, the extension step consists in joining these seeds into larger fragments. This is the core of a text alignment model. The basic idea here is to cluster together nearby seeds. A plagiarism case will be defined by the edges of a cluster: if we draw a rectangle around the cluster, the plagiarism case is the fragment of text in the suspicious document and its corresponding counterpart in the source document, as shown in Fig. 1. Defining a cluster by its edges and not as a set of seeds allows for small gaps in the range of seeds that can be part of the plagiarism case even if our seeding process did not detect them; for example, see cluster 1 in the figure.

However, the greater the distance allowed between seeds in a cluster, the greater the probability of including passages that do not really belong to the plagiarism case. Measuring the quality of a plagiarism case includes computing

---

[2] http://www.gelbukh.com/plagiarism-detection/PAN-2014
[3] Obfuscation techniques refers to the changes done to the plagiarized passages like sentence reordering, changing words with synonyms, using summaries, among others.

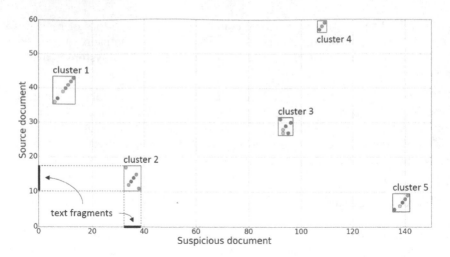

Fig. 1. Clusters obtained after the extension step. The fragments of text (ranges of sentences) corresponding to cluster 2 are shown

the similarity between the two fragments of text. Thus, the challenge for an extension algorithm is to find a balance between the dispersion in a clusters and the similarity of the fragments of text this cluster correlates. A problem that arises in finding this balance in our approach is that the sentences do not necessarily have the same length, so a distance good for one cluster is not necessarily good for another cluster given the resulting similarity between the fragments of text. Therefore, balancing should be done for each cluster independently after the initial iteration of clustering is done.

Another important problem when building an extension method is to determine what type of measure of distance should be used, and this is not a trivial problem. From the dots in Fig. 1, it is expected to have clusters such as those represented, which relate a fragment of text in the suspicious document with a fragment of text in the source document. However, a Euclidean distance clustering algorithm as in [9] will fail to detect cluster 2, because two of its points are far from the rest of the group using this distance. These seeds in cluster 2 represent just a reordering of sentences: for instance, changing the last sentence in the source document to the first one in the suspicious document. Another way to compute distance could be using a function that returns the minimum distance in either dimension. This would result in correct detection of cluster 2, but also would join together clusters 2 and 5, because they are close on the source document axis. Given that the two measures mentioned above compute the distance taking into account both dimensions at the same time. We used a method that computes the distance in one dimension at a time, alternating between them until no more division is needed. Several participants used algorithms in this direction taking into consideration the distance in character [7, 16–18] or sentences [6].

Table 1. Main ideas used in the systems participating in PAN 2012 and 2013

Stage	Method	[6]	[18]	[17]	[16]	[9]	[7]	Our
	Special character removal	+	–	–	–	–	–	+
	Number removal	–	–	–	–	+	–	–
Preprocessing	Stopword removal	+	+	–	–	–	–	–
	Case folding	+	+	+	+	+	–	+
	Stemming	+	+	–	–	+	–	+
	Bag of words	+	–	–	–	–	+	+
	Context n-grams	–	+	+	+	+	–	–
Seeding	Context skip n-grams	–	+	–	–	–	–	–
	Stopword n-grams	–	–	+	+	–	–	–
	Named entity n-grams	–	–	–	+	–	–	–
	Bilateral Alternating Sorting	+	–	–	–	–	–	–
Extension	Distance between seeds	+	+	+	+	–	+	+
	Euclidean distance clusters	–	–	–	–	+	–	–
	Extension with multiple features	–	+	–	+	–	–	–
	Passage similarity	+	–	–	–	–	–	+
Filtering	Small passage removal	–	+	+	–	+	–	+
	Overlapping removal	–	–	+	+	–	–	+
	Nearby passage joining	–	–	–	+	–	–	–

The final step in the text alignment task is responsible for filtering out those clusters that do not meet certain criteria. Usually this includes removing too short plagiarism cases or treating overlapping cases. The main problem we found using the PAN 2013 training corpus was that some plagiarism cases are contained inside larger cases in any of the two sides. To solve this problem we introduced a measure of quality that compares overlapped cases, to decide which one to keep and which one to discard.

Finally, given that the three-step model for text alignment uses many parameters, it is impossible to find one optimal setting for all types of obfuscation. Therefore, the model should be adaptive: it should use heuristics to decide which type of obfuscation it deals with in a given document and choose the corresponding settings optimized for each type of obfuscation.

Table 1 summarizes the main ideas employed by the systems participating in PAN 2012 and 2013 [4,6,7,9,16–18], classified by the four main stages of a typical alignment process as suggested in [14].

3   Our Approach

We describe our approach using the three-steps model: seeding, extension, and filtering. Before these steps, we pre-process the documents applying sentence splitting and tokenization, removing all tokens ("words") that do not start in a letter or digit, reducing all letters to lowercase, applying stemming, and joining small sentences (shorter than $minsentlen = 3$ words) with the next one (if the new joint "sentence" was still small, we join it with the next one, etc.). In the following sections, we describe our processes of seeding, extension, and filtering.

3.1 Seeding

Given a suspicious document and a source document, the task of the seeding stage is to construct a large set S of short similar passages called *seeds*. Each seed is a pair that consists of a small fragment of the suspicious document and a small fragment of the source document that are in some sense similar. In our case, the fragments to form the pairs were sentences, which may be joined as described above. Constructing these pairs required to measure similarity between sentence vectors, for which we had to choose a weighting scheme.

To measure the similarity between two sentences, we represented individual sentences with a tf-idf vector space model (VSM), as if each sentence were, in terminology of VSM, a separate document and all sentences in the pair of original document formed a document collection. The idf measure calculated in this way is called *isf measure* (inverse sentence frequency) to emphasize that it is calculated over sentences as units and not documents:

$$tf\,(t, s) = f\,(t, s)\,,$$

$$isf\,(t, D) = \log \frac{|D|}{|\{s \in D : t \in s\}|}\,,$$

$$w\,(t, s) = tf\,(t, s) \times isf\,(t, D)\,,$$

where for term frequency $tf(t, s)$ we simply used the number of occurrences $f(t, s)$ of the term t in the sentence s; D is the set of all sentences in both given documents, and $w(t, s)$ is the final weight of a term t of the sentence s in our VSM representation.

After we defined the weighting scheme and transformed all sentences into vectors in both documents we compared each sentence in the suspicious document to each sentence in the source document.

Now we construct the desired set S as

$$S = \{(i, j) \mid \cos\,(susp_i, src_j) > mincos \wedge dice\,(susp_i, src_j) > mindice\}\,,$$

where the two sentences are represented as vectors, cos is the cosine similarity, *dice* is the Dice coefficient:

$$\cos\,(susp_i, src_j) = \frac{susp_i \cdot src_j}{|susp_i| \times |src_j|}\,,$$

$$dice\,(susp_i, src_j) = \frac{2\,|\delta\,(susp_i) \cap \delta\,(src_j)|}{|\delta\,(susp_i)| + |\delta\,(src_j)|}\,,$$

$\delta(x)$ is the set of non-zero coordinates of a vector x, $|*|$ is the Euclidean length of a vector or the cardinality of a set, respectively, and *mincos* and *mindice* are some thresholds determined experimentally.

3.2 Extension

Given the set of seeds S, defined as the pairs (i, j) of similar sentences, the task of the extension stage is to form larger text fragments that are similar between two documents. For this, the sentences i are joint into maximal contiguous fragments of the suspicious document and sentences j into maximal contiguous fragments of the source document, so that those large fragments be still similar.

We divide the extension process into two steps: (1) Clustering and (2) Validation. In the clustering step we create text fragments grouping seeds that are not separated by more than a *maxgap* number of sentences. In our implementation, an easier way to proceed is to sort and cluster the set of seeds by i (left or suspicious document) such that $i_n - i_{n+1} \leq maxgap$. Then, for each of the resulting clusters, sort and cluster by j (right or source document), and thereby alternate by i and j until no new clusters are formed. Each cluster should have at least *minsize* seeds or will be discarded. Since we use the parameter *maxgap* to cluster seeds into larger text fragments, some sentences in these fragment may have no similarity to any of the sentences in the corresponding fragment. Therefore in order to avoid adding to much noise in the clustering step we validate that the similarity between the text fragments of the remaining clusters exceed some threshold. If the similarity is less than the given threshold we apply the extension stage using $maxgap - 1$ for this particular cluster. We will reduce *maxgap* at most to a *min_maxgap* value. If the *min_maxgap* value is reached and the validation condition is not met then the cluster is discarded.

A text fragment is defined as the collection of all the sentences comprised in the seeds of a particular cluster. Given a cluster integrated by seeds of the form (i, j), then the text fragment in the suspicious document F_{susp} is the collection of all the sentences from the smallest i to the largest i in the cluster, similarly the corresponding text fragment in the source document F_{src} is the collection of all the sentences from the smallest j to the largest j in the cluster.

We measured the similarity between text fragments F_{susp} and F_{src} computing the cosine between their vectors:

$$ similarity\,(F_{susp}, F_{src}) = \cos\left(\sum_{v \in F_{susp}} v, \sum_{v \in F_{src}} v \right), $$

where the vector representation of the fragments is done adding together the vectors corresponding to all sentences of F_{susp} and F_{src} respectively.

For details of our method, see Algorithm 1. The variable *side* indicates by which side the pairs are clustered: $+1$ means clustering by sentences of the suspicious document (i) and -1, by sentences of the source document (j). The output of the Extension stage is a set of pairs of similar text fragments $\{(F_{susp}, F_{src}), \dots\}$ taken from the resulting clusters.

3.3   Filtering

Given the set $\{(F_{susp}, F_{src}), \dots\}$ of plagiarism cases, the task of the filtering stage is to improve precision (at the expense of recall) by removing some "bad" plagiarism cases. We did the filtering in two stages: first, we resolved overlapping fragments; then, we removed too short fragments (in what follows we only refer

---

Algorithm 1. Extension algorithm

---

    const *minsize, minsim*
    Function extension(*seeds, maxgap*)
1   *clusters* ← clustering(*seeds,maxgap,*+1)
2   *clusters* ← validation(*clus,maxgap*)
3   **return** *clusters*
    Function clustering(*seeds, maxgap, side*)
1   *clusters* ← clusters of *seeds* such that in each cluster, *side*-hand sentences
       form in the document fragments with at most *maxgap*-sentence gaps
2   discard all $c \in$ *clusters* such that $|c| <$ *minsize*
3   **if** $|clusters| \leq 1$ **then**
4 | **return** *clusters*
    else
5 | *result* ← ∅
6 | **foreach** $c \in$ *clusters* **do**
7 | | *result* ← *result* ∪ clustering(*c,maxgap,−side*)
8   **return** *result*
    Function validation(*clusters, maxgap*)
1   *result* ← ∅
2   **foreach** $c \in$ *clusters* **do**
3 | **if** $similarity(F_{susp}(c), F_{src}(c)) <$ *minsim* **then**
4 | | **if** $maxgap > min\_maxgap$ **then**
5 | | | *result* ← *result* ∪ extension(*c,maxgap* − 1)
     | | **else**
6 | | | *result* ← *result* ∪ { *c* }
7   **return** *result*

---

to fragments that represent plagiarism cases, not to arbitrary fragments of the documents).

Resolving Overlapping Cases. We call two plagiarism cases $\left(F'_{susp}, F'_{src}\right)$ and $\left(F''_{susp}, F''_{src}\right)$ overlapping if the fragments F'_{susp} and F''_{susp} share (in the suspicious document) at least one sentence. We assume that the same source fragment can be used several times in a suspicious document, but not vice versa: each sentence can be plagiarized from only one source and thus can only belong to one plagiarism case. To simplify things, instead of re-assigning only the overlapping parts, we simply discarded whole cases that overlapped with other cases. Specifically, we used the following algorithm:

1. While exists a case P ("pivot") that overlaps with some other case
   (a) Denote $\Psi(P)$ be the set of cases $Q \neq P$ overlapping with P
   (b) For each $Q \in \Psi(P)$, compute the quality $q_Q(P)$ and $q_P(Q)$; see (1)
   (c) Find the maximum value among all obtained $q_y(x)$
   (d) Discard all cases in $\Psi(P) \cup \{P\}$ except the found x

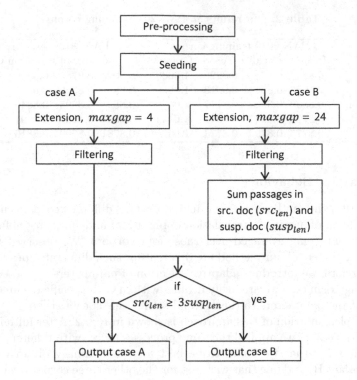

Fig. 2. Adaptive behavior

In our implementation, at the first step we always used the first case from the beginning of the suspicious document. We compute the quality function $q_y(x)$ of the case x with respect to an overlapping case y as follows. The overlapping cases $x = \left(F_{susp}^x, F_{src}^x\right)$ and $y = \left(F_{susp}^y, F_{src}^y\right)$ are pairs of corresponding fragments. Let $O = F_{susp}^x \cap F_{susp}^y$ be the overlap and $N = F_{susp}^x/O$ be the non-overlapping part. Then the quality

$$q_y(x) = sim_{F_{src}^x}(O) + \left(1 - sim_{F_{src}^x}(O)\right) \times sim_{F_{src}^x}(N), \qquad (1)$$

where sim is a non-symmetric similarity of a fragment F_{susp} (in the suspicious document) to a reference fragment F_{src} (in the source document):

$$sim_{F_{src}}(F_{susp}) = \frac{1}{|F_{susp}|} \sum_{s \in F_{susp}} \max_{r \in F_{src}} \left(\cos\left(s, r\right)\right).$$

Formula (1) combines the similarity of the overlapping part and of the non-overlapping part of suspicious fragment to the source counterpart.

Removing Small Cases. We also discard the plagiarism cases that relate too small fragments: if either suspicious or source fragment of a case has the length in characters less than $minplaglen$, then the case is discarded.

Table 2. Our results on PAN 2013 training corpus

Obfuscation	PAN 2013 training corpus				PAN 2013 test corpus			
	Plagdet	Recall	Precision	Granul.	Plagdet	Recall	Precision	Granul.
None	0.8938	0.9782	0.8228	1.0000	0.9003	0.9785	0.8336	1.0000
Random	0.8886	0.8581	0.9213	1.0000	0.8841	0.8606	0.9101	1.0008
Translation	0.8839	0.8902	0.8777	1.0000	0.8865	0.8895	0.8846	1.0008
Summary	0.5772	0.4247	0.9941	1.0434	0.5607	0.4127	0.9991	1.0588
Entire	0.8773	0.8799	0.8774	1.0021	0.8781	0.8790	0.8816	1.0034

3.4 Adaptive Behavior

At PAN-2014, the methods were evaluated on four different corpora: no obfuscation, random obfuscation, translation obfuscation, and summary obfuscation, the final result being averaged over those four corpora. We observed that the optimal parameters of our method are different for such different types of plagiarism. Therefore, we introduce adaptive selection of parameters: we detect which type of plagiarism case we are likely dealing with in each specific document pair, and adjust the parameters to the optimal set for this specific type.

Our implementation of this approach is shown in Fig. 2. After initial preprocessing and seeding, we applied the same processes twice, with different $maxgap$ values: one value that we found to be best for the summary obfuscation subcorpus (variant B) and one that was best for the other three corpora (variant A). After we obtain the plagiarism cases using these two different settings, we decide whether those cases are likely to represent summary obfuscation or not, judging by the relative length of the suggested suspicious fragments with respect to the source fragments, and depending on this, choose to output the results of one of the two variants. Our results at PAN-2014 were obtained with:

$$mincos = 0.33 \qquad minsim = 0.4 \qquad minsize = 1 \quad minsentlen = 3$$
$$mindice = 0.33 \qquad minplaglen = 150 \quad min\_maxgap = 2$$

We used equal values for $mincos$ and $mindice$; however, later we obtained better results (not reported here) when their values were different.

Specifically, the decision is made based on the variables src_{len} and $susp_{len}$, which correspond to the total length of all passages, in characters, in the source document and the suspicious document, respectively: when $susp_{len}$ is much smaller than src_{len}, then we are likely dealing with summary obfuscation.

4 Experimental Results

The evaluation framework for plagiarism detection referring to the Precision, Recall, Granularity and Plagdet measures on this specific task was introduced by Potthast in [15]. We trained our system using the corpus provided for PAN 2014 competition (pan13-text-alignment-training-corpus-2013-01-21) [13].

Table 3. Comparative results according to the Plagdet measure on PAN 2013 test corpus. Performance of the systems was published in [14]

Team	Year	Entire corpus	None	Random	Translation	Summary
Sanchez-Perez (our)	–	**0.8781**	0.9003	**0.8841**	**0.8865**	0.5607
Torrejn	2013	0.8222	0.9258	0.7471	0.8511	0.3413
Kong	2013	0.8189	0.8274	0.8228	0.8518	0.4339
Suchomel	2013	0.7448	0.8176	0.7527	0.6754	**0.6101**
Saremi	2013	0.6991	0.8496	0.6566	0.7090	0.1111
Shrestha	2013	0.6955	0.8936	0.6671	0.6271	0.1186
Palkovskii	2013	0.6152	0.8243	0.4995	0.6069	0.0994
Nourian	2013	0.5771	0.9013	0.3507	0.4386	0.1153
Baseline	2013	0.4219	**0.9340**	0.0712	0.1063	0.0446
Gillam	2013	0.4005	0.8588	0.0419	0.0122	0.0021
Jayapal	2013	0.2708	0.3878	0.1814	0.1818	0.0594

Table 4. PAN 2014 official results reported in [13] using TIRA [5]

Team	PlagDet	Recall	Precision	Granularity	Runtime
Sanchez-Perez (our)	**0.8781**	**0.8790**	0.8816	1.0034	00:25:35
Oberreuter	0.8693	0.8577	0.8859	1.0036	00:05:31
Palkovskii	0.8680	0.8263	0.9222	1.0058	01:10:04
Glinos	0.8593	0.7933	**0.9625**	1.0169	00:23:13
Shrestha	0.8440	0.8378	0.8590	1.0070	69:51:15
R. Torrejn	0.8295	0.7690	0.9042	1.0027	**00:00:42**
Gross	0.8264	0.7662	0.9327	1.0251	00:03:00
Kong	0.8216	0.8074	0.8400	1.0030	00:05:26
Abnar	0.6722	0.6116	0.7733	1.0224	01:27:00
Alvi	0.6595	0.5506	0.9337	1.0711	00:04:57
Baseline	0.4219	0.3422	0.9293	1.2747	00:30:30
Gillam	0.2830	0.1684	0.8863	**1.0000**	00:00:55

We also evaluated our model on the test corpus of PAN 2013 (pan13-text-alignment-test-corpus2-2013-01-21) in order to compare our approach with existing approaches. Table 2 shows our results on the training corpus of PAN 2014, which was the same as the training corpus of PAN 2013, and on the test corpus of PAN 2013. Table 3 compares our results using the cumulative Plagdet measure with those of the systems submitted to PAN 2013. Column shows the system results on each sub-corpus built using different types of obfuscation.

We experimented with each one of our improvements separately and verified that they do boost the cumulative Plagdet measure. Both the use of the tf-isf measure and our recursive extension algorithm considerably improved recall without a noticeable detriment to precision. On the other hand, resolution of overlapping cases improved precision without considerably affecting recall. Finally, the dynamic adjustment of the gap size improved Plagdet on the summary sub-corpus by 35%, without considerably affecting other corpora.

We participate in the Text Alignment task of the PAN 2014 Lab outperforming all 10 participants as shown in Table 4. The official results showed that recall is the measure where we excel but need to improve the precision of the model by identifying and adjusting to other types of obfuscation rather than just summary obfuscation. Regarding the system runtime, even our goal is not aiming at efficiency, out software performed at an average level.

5   Conclusions and Future Work

We have described our approach to the task of text alignment in the context of PAN 2014 competition, with which our system showed the best result of ten participating systems, as well as outperformed the state-of-art systems that participated in PAN 2013 on the corresponding corpus [14]. Our system is available open source.

Our main contributions are: (1) the use of the tf-isf (inverse sentence frequency) measure for "soft" removal of stopwords instead of using a predefined stopword list; (2) a recursive extension algorithm, which allows to dynamically adjust the tolerance of the algorithm to gaps in the fragments that constitute plagiarism cases; (3) a novel algorithm for resolution of overlapping plagiarism cases, based on comparison of competing plagiarism cases; (4) dynamic adjustment of parameters according to the obfuscation type of plagiarism cases (summary vs. other types). Each of these improvements contributes to improve the performance of the system.

In our future work, we plan to use linguistically motivated methods to address possible paraphrase obfuscation [2] and test it on the P4P corpus.[4] We also plan to build a meta-classifier that would guess which obfuscation type of plagiarism case we deal with at each moment and dynamically adjust the parameters. Finally, we plan to apply concept-based models for similarity and paraphrase detection [10–12].

Acknowledgments. Work done under partial support of FP7-PEOPLE-2010-IRSES: Web Information Quality – Evaluation Initiative (WIQ-EI) European Commission project 269180, Government of Mexico (SNI, CONACYT), and Instituto Politcnico Nacional, Mexico (SIP 20152100, 20151406, BEIFI, COFAA).

References

1. Bär, D., Zesch, T., Gurevych, I.: Text reuse detection using a composition of text similarity measures. In: Kay, M., Boitet, C. (eds.) COLING 2012, 24th International Conference on Computational Linguistics, Proceedings of the Conference: Technical Papers, December 8–15, Mumbai, India, pp. 167–184. Indian Institute of Technology Bombay (2012)
2. Barrón-Cedeño, A., Vila, M., Martí, M.A., Rosso, P.: Plagiarism meets paraphrasing: Insights for the next generation in automatic plagiarism detection. Computational Linguistics **39**(4), 917–947 (2013)

---

[4] http://clic.ub.edu/corpus/en/paraphrases-en

3. Forner, P., Navigli, R., Tufis, D., Ferro, N. (eds.): Working Notes for CLEF 2013 Conference. CEUR Workshop Proceedings, Valencia, Spain, September 23–26, vol. 1179. CEUR-WS.org (2013)
4. Gillam, L.: Guess again and see if they line up: surrey's runs at plagiarism detection notebook for PAN at CLEF 2013. In: Forner et al. [3]
5. Gollub, T., Stein, B., Burrows, S.: Ousting ivory tower research: towards a web framework for providing experiments as a service. In: Hersh, B., Callan, J., Maarek, Y., Sanderson, M. (eds.) 35th International ACM Conference on Research and Development in Information Retrieval (SIGIR 2012), pp. 1125–1126. ACM, August 2012
6. Kong, L., Qi, H., Du, C., Wang, M., Han, Z.: Approaches for source retrieval and text alignment of plagiarism detection notebook for PAN at CLEF 2013. In: Forner et al. [3]
7. Küppers, R., Conrad, S.: A set-based approach to plagiarism detection. In: Forner, P., Karlgren, J., Womser-Hacker, C. (eds.) CLEF 2012 Evaluation Labs and Workshop, Online Working Notes. CEUR Workshop Proceedings, Rome, Italy, September 17–20, vol. 1178. CEUR-WS.org (2012)
8. Maurer, H., Kappe, F., Zaka, B.: Plagiarism – A survey. Journal of Universal Computer Science **12**(8), 1050–1084 (2006)
9. Palkovskii, Y., Belov, A.: Using hybrid similarity methods for plagiarism detection notebook for PAN at CLEF 2013. In: Forner et al. [3]
10. Poria, S., Agarwal, B., Gelbukh, A., Hussain, A., Howard, N.: Dependency-based semantic parsing for concept-level text analysis. In: Gelbukh, A. (ed.) CICLing 2014, Part I. LNCS, vol. 8403, pp. 113–127. Springer, Heidelberg (2014)
11. Poria, S., Cambria, E., Ku, L.W., Gui, C., Gelbukh, A.: A rule-based approach to aspect extraction from product reviews. In: Proceedings of the Second Workshop on Natural Language Processing for Social Media (SocialNLP), pp. 28–37. Association for Computational Linguistics and Dublin City University, Dublin, August 2014
12. Poria, S., Cambria, E., Winterstein, G., Huang, G.: Sentic patterns: Dependency-based rules for concept-level sentiment analysis. Knowl.-Based Syst. **69**, 45–63 (2014)
13. Potthast, M., Hagen, M., Beyer, A., Busse, M., Tippmann, M., Rosso, P., Stein, B.: Overview of the 6th international competition on plagiarism detection. In: Cappellato, L., Ferro, N., Halvey, M., Kraaij, W. (eds.) Working Notes for CLEF 2014 Conference. CEUR Workshop Proceedings, Sheffield, UK, September 15–18, vol. 1180, pp. 845–876. CEUR-WS.org (2014)
14. Potthast, M., Hagen, M., Gollub, T., Tippmann, M., Kiesel, J., Rosso, P., Stamatatos, E., Stein, B.: Overview of the 5th international competition on plagiarism detection. In: Forner et al. [3]
15. Potthast, M., Stein, B., Barrón-Cedeño, A., Rosso, P.: An evaluation framework for plagiarism detection. In: Huang, C., Jurafsky, D. (eds.) COLING 2010, 23rd International Conference on Computational Linguistics, Posters Volume, August 23–27, Beijing, China, pp. 997–1005. Chinese Information Processing Society of China (2010)
16. Shrestha, P., Solorio, T.: Using a variety of n-grams for the detection of different kinds of plagiarism notebook for PAN at CLEF 2013. In: Forner et al. [3]
17. Suchomel, S., Kasprzak, J., Brandejs, M.: Diverse queries and feature type selection for plagiarism discovery notebook for PAN at CLEF 2013. In: Forner et al. [3]
18. Torrejón, D.A.R., Ramos, J.M.M.: Text alignment module in CoReMo 2.1 plagiarism detector notebook for PAN at CLEF 2013. In: Forner et al. [3]

Question Answering via Phrasal Semantic Parsing

Kun Xu[1]([✉]), Yansong Feng[1], Songfang Huang[2], and Dongyan Zhao[1]

[1] Institute of Computer Science & Technology, Peking University, Beijing, China
{xukun,fengyansong,zhaodongyan}@pku.edu.cn
[2] China Research Lab, Beijing, China
huangsf@cn.ibm.com

Abstract. Understanding natural language questions and converting them into structured queries have been considered as a crucial way to help users access large scale structured knowledge bases. However, the task usually involves two main challenges: recognizing users' query intention and mapping the involved semantic items against a given knowledge base (KB). In this paper, we propose an efficient pipeline framework to model a user's query intention as a phrase level dependency DAG which is then instantiated regarding a specific KB to construct the final structured query. Our model benefits from the efficiency of linear structured prediction models and the separation of KB-independent and KB-related modelings. We evaluate our model on two datasets, and the experimental results showed that our method outperforms the state-of-the-art methods on the Free917 dataset, and, with limited training data from Free917, our model can smoothly adapt to new challenging dataset, WebQuestion, without extra training efforts while maintaining promising performances.

1 Introduction

As very large structured knowledge bases have become available, e.g.,YAGO [2], DBpedia [3] and Freebase [4], answering natural language questions over structured knowledge facts has attracted increasing research efforts. Different from keyword based information retrieval, the structure of query intentions embedded in a user's question can be represented by a set of predicate-argument structures, e.g., <*subject, predicate, object*> triples, and effectively retrieved by a database search engine. Thereby, the main challenge of understanding the query intention in a structural form is to solve two tasks: recognizing the predicate-argument structures and then instantiating these structures against a given KB.

Take the question in Figure 1 as an example, the structure of the query intention consists of multiple predicate-argument pairs, involving an named entity *france* mapping to a KB entity "France", a word *country* mapping to a KB type "Country" and a verb *colonise* possibly indicating a KB relation "**colonise**" with domain and range "Country". Previous works solved these subtasks in a joint framework, e.g., [5] proposed a PCFG-based semantic parser to simultaneously learn the combination rules among words or phrases and the mappings to

© Springer International Publishing Switzerland 2015
J. Mothe et al. (Eds.): CLEF 2015, LNCS 9283, pp. 414–426, 2015.
DOI: 10.1007/978-3-319-24027-5_43

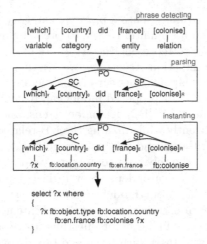

Fig. 1. An example of converting a natural language question into a structured query via phrasal semantic parsing.

specific KB components. However, given the size of existing KBs (usually thousands of predicates, millions of entities and billions of knowledge facts), it is still difficult to jointly train such a PCFG-based parser (the model of [5] takes several days to train only with 3,000 sentences), and even more difficult to adapt to other KBs, let alone retrieving multiple KBs within one query, e.g., some queries in the QALD task[6] are mixed with predicates from both DBpedia and Yago. In contrast, we find that recognizing the query intention structure is usually KB-independent. Look at the example question again, even without grounding to a knowledge base, we can still guess that a location called *france* has some relationship, indicated by the verb *"colonise"*, with some *countries*, (the queried objects), which can be learned directly without reliance on a specified KB. On the other hand, the task of mapping natural language phrases from the intention structures to items in a given KB and producing the final structured queries is KB-dependent, since one has to solve these mappings according to the schema of a specified KB.

Given the observations above, we thus assume that the structure of a question's query intention can be learned independent from a specific knowledge base, while instantiating a query intention into a structured query is dependent on a knowledge base. Our assumption will naturally lead to a pipeline paradigm to translating a natural language question into a structured query, which can then be directly retrieved by a structured database query engine, e.g., Virtuoso [1].

In this paper, we deal with the task of understanding natural language questions in a pipeline paradigm, involving mainly two steps: recognizing the query intention structure inherent in the natural language questions, and then instantiating the query intention structures by mapping the involved semantic items into existing KBs. In the first phase, we build a phrase detector to detect possible

---

[1] http://www.virtuoso.com

semantic phrases, e.g., variables, entity phrases, category phrases and relation phrases. We then develop a semantic parser to predict the predicate-argument structures among phrases to represent the structure of query intentions. In the second phase, given the intention structures, we are then able to adopt a Naive Bayes model to solve the mappings between semantic phrases and KB items. By taking a two-phase format, our proposed model can benefit from the separation of KB related components and KB independent steps, and recognize the intention structures more efficiently while making the KB-related component flexible, e.g., we can only retrain the second phase when adapting to new KBs, which is similar in sprite with [7], who rely on a combinatory categorial grammar (CCG) parser to produce an ontological-independent logical representation to express users' intention. We evaluate our model on two datasets, and show that our model can effectively learn the structures of query intentions, and outperform the state-of-the-art methods in terms of question-answering accuracy. Specifically, by testing on a new dataset with large and broad-coverage KB predicates, our model can still perform comparably to the state of the arts without any extra training on the new datasets.

2   Related Work

Question answering is a long-standing problem in the field of natural language processing and artificial intelligence. Previous research is mainly dominated by keyword matching based approaches, while recent advancements in the development of structured KBs and structured query engines have demanded the research of translating natural language questions into structured queries, which can then be retrieved using a structured query engine. Existing methods can be roughly categorized into two streams, pattern/template-based models [8,9,10] and semantic parsing-based models [11,12,7,5,13].

Frank et al. [8] use lexical-conceptual templates for query generation but do not address the disambiguation of constituents in the question. Unger et al. [14] rely on a manually created ontology-driven grammar to directly map questions onto the underlying ontology, where the grammars are hard to adapt or generalize to other large scale knowledge bases. They further develop a template-based approach to map natural language questions into structured queries [10]. Yahya et al. [9] collect the mapping between natural language expressions and Yago2 predicates using a set of predefined patterns over dependency parses, and find an optimal mapping assignments for all possible fragments in the questions using an Integer Linear Programming (ILP) model. Those methods are mainly reply on a set of manually created templates or patterns to collect lexicons or represent the structure of query intentions, therefore are difficult to scale in practice due to the manual efforts involved.

Krishnamurthy et al. [11] use distant supervision to collect training sentences as well as manual rules to construct CCG lexicons from dependency parses in order to train a semantic parser. Cai et al. [12] develop a probabilistic CCG-based semantic parser, FreeParser, where questions are automatically mapped to logical forms grounded in the symbols of certain fixed ontology or relational database. They take a similar distant supervision approach to automatically construct CCG lexicon and induce combination rules [15], though with inadequate coverage, for example, their parser will fail if any phrase in the question is not included in the lexicon of the PCCG parser. Berant et al. [5] develop a PCFG-based semantic parser, where a *bridge* operation is proposed to improve coverage and they utilize a set of manual combination rules as well as feature-simulated *soft rules* to combine predicates and produce logical forms.

To handle the *mismatch* between language and the KB, Kwiatkowski et al. [7] develop a PCCG parser to build an ontology-independent logical representation, and employ an ontology matching model to adapt the output logical forms for each target ontology. Berant et al. [13] first generate candidate canonical utterances for logical forms, then utilize paraphrase models to choose the canonical utterance that best paraphrases the candidate utterance, and thereby the logical form that generated it.

In contrast, we focus on translating natural language questions into structured queries by separating the KB independent components from the KB-related mapping phase. Like [12], our model takes question-phrase dependency Directed Acyclic Graph (DAG) pairs as input for our structure recognition phase, but relies far less training data than [12] towards a open domain parser, since we do not learn KB related mappings during structured predictions. We then learn a joint mapping model to instantiate the phrase dependency DAG with a given KB. Our model is simple in structure but efficient in terms of training, since we have a much smaller search space during structure prediction with respect to the query intention, and still hold the promise for further improvement, for example, taking question-answer pairs as training data after initializing with some question-DAG training samples.

3   The Task

We define the task of using a KB to answer natural language questions as follows: given a natural language question q_{NL} and a knowledge base KB, our goal is to translate q_{NL} into a structured query in certain structured query language, e.g., SPARQL, which consists of multiple triples: a conjunction of <subject, predicate, object> search conditions.

4   Recognizing the Structure of Query Intention

Our framework first employs a pipeline of phrase detection and phrase dependency parsing to recognize the inherent structure of user's query intention, which is then instantiated regarding a specific KB.

4.1   Phrase Detection

We first detect phrases of interest that potentially correspond to semantic items, where a detected phrase is assigned with a label $l \in \{entity, relation,$

category, *variable*}. Entity phrases may correspond to entities of KB, relation phrases correspond to KB's predicates and category phrases correspond to KB's categories. This problem can be casted as a sequence labeling problem, where our goal is to build a tagger to predict labels for a sentence. For example:

what   are   the sub-types   of   coal
V-B none R-B   R-I   R-I E-B

(Here, we use *B-I* scheme for each phrase label: *R-B* represents the beginning of a relation phrase, *R-I* represents the continuation of a relation phrase). We use structured perceptron [17] to build our phrase tagger. Structured perceptron is an extension to the standard linear perceptron for structured prediction. Given a question instance $x \in X$, which in our case is a sentence, the structured perceptron involves the following *decoding problem* which finds the best configuration $z \in Y$, which in our case is a label sequence, according to the current model **w**:

$$z = \arg\max_{y' \in Y} w \cdot f(x, y')$$

where $f(x, y')$ represents the feature vector for instance x along with configuration y'. We use three types of features: lexical features, POS tag features and Named Entity Recognition (NER) features. Table 1 summarizes the feature templates we used in the phrase detection.

Table 1. Set of feature templates for phrase detection

p = pos tag; n = ner tag; w = word; t = phrase type tag; i = current index

1	unigram of POS tag	p_i
2	bigram of POS tag	$p_i p_{i+1}$, $p_{i-1}p_i$
3	trigram of POS tag	$p_i p_{i+1} p_{i+2}$, $p_{i-1}p_i p_{i+1}$, $p_{i-2}p_{i-1}p_i$
4	unigram of NER tag	n_i
5	bigram of NER tag	$n_i n_{i+1}$, $n_{i-1}n_i$
6	trigram of NER tag	$n_i n_{i+1} n_{i+2}$, $n_{i-1}n_i n_{i+1}$, $n_{i-2}n_{i-1}n_i$
7	unigram of word	w_i
8	bigram of word	$w_i w_{i+1}$, $w_{i-1}w_i$
9	trigram of word	$w_i w_{i+1} w_{i+2}$, $w_{i-1}w_i w_{i+1}$, $w_{i-2}w_{i-1}w_i$
10	previous phrase type	t_{i-1}
11	conjunction of previous phrase type and current word	$t_{i-1}w_i$

4.2 Phrase Dependency Parsing with Multiple Heads

As shown in Figure 1, query intention can be represented by dependencies between *"country"*, *"france"* and *"colonise"*, forming a phrase dependency DAG, we thus introduce a transition-based DAG parsing algorithm to perform a structural prediction process and reveal the inherent structures.

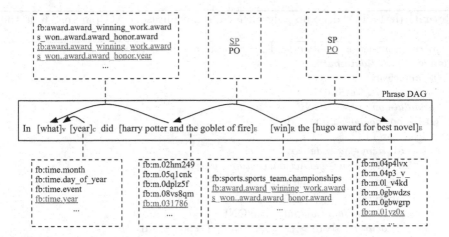

Fig. 2. An example of phrasal semantic DAG, where the dashed boxes list the mapping candidates for all phrases and the underlined are the gold-standard mappings.)

Phrase Dependency DAG. We propose to use the predicate-argument dependencies to capture the query intention, that is, the arguments of a predicate are dependents of that predicate. Here, each predicate is either a unary predicate (characterize its only argument) or a binary predicate (represents the semantic relation between its two arguments). For example, in Figure 2, the category phrase *"year"* indicates the variable is one specific year, and the relation phrase *"win"* indicates that the award *"hugo award for best novel"* is won by *"harry potter and the goblet of fire"*.

Phrase Dependency Parsing. Note that, in our setup, one phrase can have more than one head, as in Figure 2, variable node *what* has two heads in the resulting dependency DAG. We thus use the framework proposed by [18], i.e., extending traditional arc-eager shift-reduce parsing with multiple heads to find a DAG directly. Specifically, given a question with sequence of phrases, our parser uses a stack of partial DAGs, a queue of incoming phrases, and a series of actions to build a dependency DAG. We assume that each input phrase has been assigned a POS-tag and a semantic label.

Our semantic parser uses four actions: SHIFT, REDUCE, ARCRIGHT and ARCLEFT.

The SHIFT action follow the standard definitions that just pushes the next incoming phrase onto the stack.

The REDUCE action pops the stack top. Note that, the standard REDUCE action which is taken on the condition that the stack top has at least one head. This precondition ensures the dependency graph is a connected graph. However, our phrase dependency parser only concerns the predicate-argument structures, and we add a dependency only between the predicate and argument of our interest. In our case, the dependency graph can be a unconnected directed graph.

Algorithm 1. The decoding algorithm for the phrase DAG parsing; K is the beam size

Require: sentence x; *agenda*: hold the K-best candidate items
Ensure: *candidate_output*
1: *agenda*.clear()
2: *agenda*.insert(GetStartItem(x))
3: *candidate_output* = NONE
4: **while** not *agenda*.empty() **do**
5:    *list*.clear()
6:    **for all** *item* ∈ *agenda* **do**
7:       **for all** *action* ∈ *getActions*(*actions*, *item*) **do**
8:          *item*$'$ = *item*.apply(*action*)
9:          **if** *item*$'$.F == TRUE **then**
10:             **if** *candidate_output* == NONE
                or *item*$'$.score > *candidate_output*.score **then**
11:                *candidate_output* = *item*$'$
12:             **end if**
13:          **else**
14:             *list*.append(*item*$'$)
15:          **end if**
16:       **end for**
17:    **end for**
18:    *agenda*.clear()
19:    *agenda*.insert(*list*.best(K))
20: **end while**

The ARCRIGHT action adds a dependency edge from the stack top to the first phrase of the incoming queue, where the phrase on the stack is the head and the phrase in the queue is the dependent (the stack and queue are left untouched), as long as a left arc does not already exist between these two phrases.

The ARCLEFT action adds a dependency edge from the first phrase on the queue to the stack top, where the phrase in the queue is the head and the phrase on the stack is the dependent (again, the stack and queue are left untouched), as long as a right arc does not already exist between the two phrases.

The Decoding Algorithm for Phrase DAG Parsing. We apply the standard beam-search along with early-update to perform inexact decoding [19] during training. To formulate the decoding algorithm, we define a *candidate item* as a tuple <S,Q,F>, where S represents the stack with partial derivations that have been built, Q represents the queue of incoming phrases that have not been processed, and F is a boolean value that represents whether the candidate item has been finished. A candidate item is finished if and only if the queue is empty, and no more actions can be applied to a candidate item after it reaches the finished status. Given an input sentence x, we define the start item as the unfinished item with an empty stack and the whole input sentence as the incoming phrases(line 2). A derivation is built from the start item by repeated applications of actions (SHIFT, REDUCE, ARCLEFT and ARCRIGHT) until the item is finished.

Pseudocode for the decoding algorithm is shown in Algorithm 1. To apply beam-search, an agenda is used to hold the K-best partial (unfinished) candidate items at each parsing step. A separate *candidate output* is used to record the current best finished item that has been found, since candidate items can be finished at different steps. Initially the agenda contains only the start item, and the candidate output is set to none(line 3). At each step during parsing, a temporary list is clear(line 5) so that to hold the possible extended candidate items. Each candidate item from the agenda is extended in all possible ways by applying one action according to the current status(line 7), and a number of new candidate items are generated(line 8). If a newly generated candidate is finished(line 9), it is compared with the current *candidate output*. If the candidate output is none(line 10) or the score of the newly generated candidate is higher than the score of the *candidate output*, the *candidate output* is replaced with the newly generated item(line 11); otherwise the newly generated item is discarded (line 14). If the newly generated candidate is unfinished, it is appended to a list of newly generated partial candidates. After all candidate items from the agenda have been processed, the agenda is cleared(line 18) and the K-best items from the list are put on the agenda(line 19). Then the list is cleared and the parser moves on to the next step. This process repeats until the agenda is empty (which means that no new items have been generated in the previous step), and the candidate output is the final derivation.

Table 2. The set of feature templates used in our phrase DAG parser

p = phrase; t = POS-tag; s = phrase type

Category	Description	templates
lexical features	stack top	$STpt$; STp; STt;
	current phrase	N_0pt; N_0p; N_0t
	next phrase	N_1pt; N_1p; N_1t;
	ST and N0	$STptN_0pt$; $STptN_0p$;
	POS bigram	N_0tN_1t
	POS trigrams	$N_0N_1tN_2t$;
	N0 phrase	$N_0pN_1tN_2t$;
semantic features	Conjunction of phrase label and pos tag	N_0s; N_0ts; N_0ps; N_1s;N_1ts;$STtN_0s$; $STsN_0t$; $STpN_0s$; $STtN_0t$; $STsN_0s$;
structural features	Indicates whether exists an arc between the stack top item and next input item, and if so what type of arc	ArcLeft(STs, N_0s); ArcRight(STs, N_0s)

Features. Features play an important role in transition-based parsing. Our parser takes three types of features: lexical, semantic and structure-related features. We summarize our feature templates in Table 2, where ST represents the top node in the stack, N_0, N_1, N_2 represent the three incoming phrases from the incoming queue, subscript t indicates POS tags, subscript p indicates lexical surface forms and subscript s represent the semantic label of the phrase (*entity, relation, category* and *variable*).

Lexical features include features used in traditional word level dependency parsing with some modifications: all co-occurrences are built on phrase nodes and the POS tag of a phrase is defined as the concatenation of each token's POS tag in the phrase.

To guide the ARCLEFT and ARCRIGHT actions, we introduce semantic features indicating the semantic label of a phrase. Since our parser allows one phrase to have multiple heads, we modify the ARCLEFT and ARCRIGHT actions so that they can create new dependency arcs without removing the dependent from further consideration for being a dependent of other heads. And we introduce structure-related features to indicate whether an arc already exists between the top phrase on the stack and the next phrase on the queue.

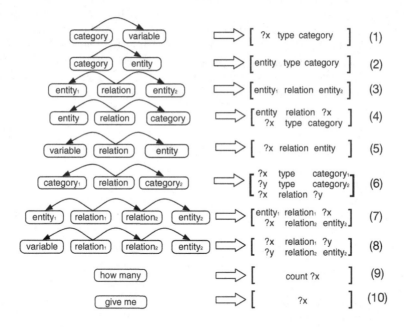

Fig. 3. Rules for converting dependency graph into structured queries.

5   Converting Phrase Dependency Graph into Structured Queries

We convert the phrase dependency graph into structured queries relying on the rules shown in Figure 3, where the left and the right of each rule correspond to the dependency graph pattern and the relative query triples, respectively.

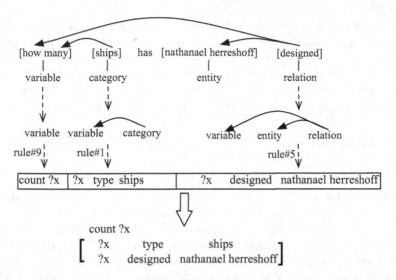

Fig. 4. A running example for converting phrase dependency graph into structured queries.

By comparing the graph patterns with those of rules, we convert the proper subgraphs of the dependency graph into query triples, which compose the final structured query. Figure 4 is a running example.

6   Instantiating Query Intention Regarding Existing KBs

We instantiated the ungrounded structured query Q_{ind} by mapping the NL phrases to semantic items of the *KB*, which has been widely addressed by previous works. Here, we follow simple but effective stream of work to simplify the process. Specifically, we break down the joint mappings into two main independent parts, i.e., mapping entities and relations. For entities, we use the Freebase search API[2] to compute the probabilities of mapping entity phrases. Given an entity phrase, the API will return a ranked list of entity candidates, each of which is assigned with a confidence score. We directly adopt the confidence scores to evaluate the possibilities of mapping entity phrases to candidates. And for relation phrases, we use a mixture of resources [16], as well as type constraints, to build a Naive Bayesian model. All these will give the final model as:

$$\overline{P}(Q_d|Q_{ind}) = \prod_i \overline{P}(e_{d_i}|e_{ind_i}) \prod_j \overline{P}(p_{d_j}|p_{ind_j})$$

where e_{ind_i}, p_{ind_j} denotes an entity phrase and a relation phrase, respectively, e_{d_j}, p_{d_j} represents a KB entity, a KB predicate, respectively.

---

[2] https://developers.google.com/freebase/

One question of interest is that what is necessary to port our system to another KB such as DBpedia. We practically map the types, entities and relations of Freebase to the ones of DBpedia in two steps. First, we use the wikipedia ids to identify the entities so that the ones that own the same ids can be naturally mapped together. Second, the types and relations that charactered the same entities and entity pairs are thought to be semantically same.

7   Experiments

7.1   Datasets

The Free917 dataset [12] contains 917 questions annotated with logical forms grounded to Freebase. Note that in all of our experiments, we only use the training set of Free917 as our training data. To prepare the training data for our parser, we first parse these questions with CCG parser and accordingly replace the KB items in the gold-standard logical forms with natural language phrases, which we manually assign a semantic label to. Following [12], we held out 30% of the data for the final test, and perform 3 random 80%-20% splits of the training set for development.

The WebQuestions dataset [5] contains 5,810 question-answer pairs, with the same training/testing split with previous work. This dataset was created by crawling questions through the Google Suggest API, and then obtaining answers through Amazon Mechanical Turk. We directly employ the parser trained on the Free917 to test on the test set of WebQuestions and retrieve the answers by executing the queries against a copy of Freebase using the Virtuoso engine.

7.2   Main Results

We evaluate our model on two datasets, Free917 and WebQuestions, using the F1 value. On Free917, our model can obtain a F1 of 69.0%, outperforming the state-of-the art. Since the Free917 dataset covers only 635 Freebase predicates, we also evaluate our model on a more natural dataset, WebQuestions, introduced by [5]. Because the WebQuestions only include the weak supervised data, i.e., question answer pairs, we do not train our model from the WebQuestions, but instead directly use the trained parser from Free917, and experiment on the test set. Interestingly, our system is able to achieve a relative higher accuracy of 39.1%, indicating that the KB-independent structured predictions can be learned separately from the KB-related mappings, while maintaining a comparable performance. In other words, these experiments show that regardless of the topics people are asking, their way of presenting the questions are still similar, which can be captured by learning the structures of phrases of semantic meanings.

8   Conclusion and Future Work

In this paper, we propose a novel framework to translate natural language questions into structural queries, which can be effectively retrieved by structured query engines and return the answers according a KB. The novelty of our framework lies in modeling the task in a KB-independent and KB-related pipeline paradigm, where we use phrasal semantic DAG to represent users' query intention, and develop a KB-independent shift-reduce DAG parser to capture the structure of the query intentions, which are then grounded to a given KB via joint mappings. This gives the advantages to analyze the questions independent from a KB and easily adapt to new KBs without much human involvement. The experiments on two datasets showed that our model outperforms the state-of-the-art methods in Free917, and performs comparably on a new challenging dataset without any extra training or resources.

Acknowledgments. We would like to Sheng Zhang, Weiwei Sun and Liwei Chen for their helpful discussions. This work was supported by National High Technology R&D Program of China (Grant No. 2015AA015403, 2014AA015102), Natural Science Foundation of China (Grant No. 61202233, 61272344, 61370055) and the joint project with IBM Research. Any correspondence please refer to Yansong Feng.

References

1. Fader, A., Soderland, S., Etzioni, O.: Identifying Relations for Open Information Extraction. EMNLP, 1535–1545 (2011)
2. Suchanek, F.M., Kasneci, G., Weikum, G.: Yago: a core of semantic knowledge. In: WWW, pp. 697–706 (2007)
3. Auer, S., Bizer, C., Kobilarov, G., Lehmann, J., Cyganiak, R., Ives, Z.G.: DBpedia: a nucleus for a web of open data. In: Aberer, K., et al. (eds.) ASWC 2007 and ISWC 2007. LNCS, vol. 4825, pp. 722–735. Springer, Heidelberg (2007)
4. Bollacker, K.D., Evans, C., Paritosh, P., Sturge, T., Taylor, J.: Freebase: a collaboratively created graph database for structuring human knowledge. SIGMOD, 1247–1250 (2008)
5. Berant, J., Chou, A., Frostig, R., Liang, P.: Semantic Parsing on Freebase from Question-Answer Pairs. EMNLP, 1533–1544 (2013)
6. Cimiano, P., Lopez, V., Unger, C., Cabrio, E., Ngonga Ngomo, A.-C., Walter, S.: Multilingual question answering over linked data (QALD-3): lab overview. In: Forner, P., Müller, H., Paredes, R., Rosso, P., Stein, B. (eds.) CLEF 2013. LNCS, vol. 8138, pp. 321–332. Springer, Heidelberg (2013)
7. Kwiatkowski, T., Choi, E., Artzi, Y., Zettlemoyer, L.S.: Scaling Semantic Parsers with On-the-Fly Ontology Matching. EMNLP, 1545–1556 (2013)
8. Frank, A., Krieger, H.-U., Xu, F., Uszkoreit, H., Crysmann, B., Jörg, B., Schäfer, U.: Question answering from structured knowledge sources. J. Applied Logic, 20–48 (2007)
9. Yahya, M., Berberich, K., Elbassuoni, S., Ramanath, M., Tresp, V., Weikum, G.: Natural Language Questions for the Web of Data. EMNLP-CoNLL, 379–390 (2012)
10. Unger, C., Bühmann, L., Lehmann, J., Ngonga Ngomo, A.-C., Gerber, D., Cimiano, P.: Template-based question answering over RDF data. In: WWW, pp. 639–648 (2012)
11. Krishnamurthy, J., Mitchell, T.: Weakly Supervised Training of Semantic Parsers. EMNLP-CoNLL, 754–765 (2012)

12. Cai, Q., Yates, A.: Semantic Parsing Freebase: Towards Open-domain Semantic Parsing. SEM (2013)
13. Berant, J., Liang, P.: Semantic Parsing via Paraphrasing. ACL (2014)
14. Unger, C., Cimiano, P.: Pythia: compositional meaning construction for ontology-based question answering on the semantic web. In: Muñoz, R., Montoyo, A., Métais, E. (eds.) NLDB 2011. LNCS, vol. 6716, pp. 153–160. Springer, Heidelberg (2011)
15. Kwiatkowski, T., Zettlemoyer, L.S., Goldwater, S., Steedman, M.: Inducing Probabilistic CCG Grammars from Logical Form with Higher-Order Unification. EMNLP, 1223–1233 (2010)
16. Tao, X., Van Durme, B.: Information Extraction over Structured Data: Question Answering with Freebase. ACL (2014)
17. Collins, M.: Discriminative Training Methods for Hidden Markov Models: Theory and Experiments with Perceptron Algorithms. EMNLP, 1–8 (2002)
18. Sagae, K., Tsujii, J.: Shift-Reduce Dependency DAG Parsing. COLING, 753–760 (2008)
19. Collins, M., Roark, B.: Incremental Parsing with the Perceptron Algorithm. ACL, 111–118 (2004)

Labs Overviews

Overview of the CLEF eHealth Evaluation Lab 2015

Lorraine Goeuriot[1]([✉]), Liadh Kelly[2], Hanna Suominen[3,4,5,6], Leif Hanlen[3,4,5], Aurélie Névéol[7], Cyril Grouin[7], João Palotti[8], and Guido Zuccon[9]

[1] LIG, Université Grenoble Alpes, Grenoble, France
Lorraine.Goeuriot@imag.fr
[2] ADAPT Centre, Trinity College, Dublin, Ireland
Liadh.Kelly@tcd.ie
[3] NICTA, Canberra, ACT, Australia
{hanna.suominen,leif.hanlen}@nicta.com.au
[4] The Australian National University, Canberra, ACT, Australia
[5] University of Canberra, Canberra, ACT, Australia
[6] University of Turku, Turku, Finland
[7] LIMSI CNRS UPR 3251, Orsay, France
{aurelie.neveol,cyril.grouin}@limsi.fr
[8] Vienna University of Technology, Vienna, Austria
palotti@ifs.tuwien.ac.at
[9] Queensland University of Technology, Brisbane, Australia
g.zuccon@qut.edu.au

Abstract. This paper reports on the 3rd CLEFeHealth evaluation lab, which continues our evaluation resource building activities for the medical domain. In this edition of the lab, we focus on easing patients and nurses in authoring, understanding, and accessing eHealth information. The 2015 CLEFeHealth evaluation lab was structured into two tasks, focusing on evaluating methods for information extraction (IE) and information retrieval (IR). The IE task introduced two new challenges. Task 1a focused on clinical speech recognition of nursing handover notes; Task 1b focused on clinical named entity recognition in languages other than English, specifically French. Task 2 focused on the retrieval of health information to answer queries issued by general consumers seeking information to understand their health symptoms or conditions.

The number of teams registering their interest was 47 in Tasks 1 (2 teams in Task 1a and 7 teams in Task 1b) and 53 in Task 2 (12 teams) for a total of 20 unique teams. The best system recognized $4,984$ out of $6,818$ test words correctly and generated $2,626$ incorrect words (i.e., 38.5% error) in Task 1a; had the F-measure of 0.756 for plain entity recognition, 0.711 for normalized entity recognition, and 0.872 for entity normalization in Task 1b; and resulted in P@10 of 0.5394 and nDCG@10 of 0.5086 in Task 2. These results demonstrate the substantial community interest and capabilities of these systems in addressing challenges

---

In alphabetical order, LG & LK co-chaired the lab. In order of contribution, HS & LH led Task 1a. In order of contribution, AN & CG led Task 1B. In alphabetical order, JP & GZ led Task 2.

© Springer International Publishing Switzerland 2015
J. Mothe et al. (Eds.): CLEF 2015, LNCS 9283, pp. 429–443, 2015.
DOI: 10.1007/978-3-319-24027-5_44

faced by patients and nurses. As in previous years, the organizers have made data and tools available for future research and development.

Keywords: Evaluation · Information retrieval · Information extraction · Medical informatics · Nursing records · Patient handoff/handover · Speech recognition · Test-set generation · Text classification · Text segmentation · Self-diagnosis

1   Introduction

This paper presents an overview of the CLEFeHealth 2015 evaluation lab[1], organized within the Conference and Labs of the Evaluation Forum (CLEF)[2] to support development of approaches, which support patients, their next-of-kins, and clinical staff in understanding, accessing and authoring health information. This third year of the evaluation lab aimed to build upon the resource development and evaluation approaches offered in the first two years of the lab, which focused on patients and their next-of-kins' ease in understanding and accessing health information.

The first CLEFeHealth lab [1] contained three tasks: Task 1 on named entity recognition and/or normalization of disorders [2]; Task 2 on acronyms/ abbreviations [3] in clinical reports; Task 3 health-focused web information retrieval, supporting laypeople's information needs stemming from clinical reports [4].

The second CLEFeHealth [5] expanded our year-one efforts and again organized three tasks. Specifically, Task 1 aimed to help patients (or their next-of-kin) by addressing visualisation and readability issues related to their hospital discharge documents and related information search on the Internet [6]. Task 2 continued the IE work of the 2013 CLEFeHealth lab, specifically focusing on IE of disorder attributes from clinical text [7]. Task 3 further extended the 2013 IR task, with a cleaned version of the 2013 document collection being produced and the introduction of a new query generation method, as well as multilingual queries [8].

The 2015 lab was split into two tasks focusing on information extraction and information retrieval. The IE task introduced two new challenges: Task 1a focused on clinical speech recognition (SR) of nursing shift changes [9]; Task 1b focused on named entity recognition in clinical reports in languages other than English, specifically French clinical reports [10]. The IR task focused on a new type of queries people issue to obtain information on the web [11]; Task 2a considered English queries, while Task 2b considered multilingual queries obtained through expert translation of the English queries[3].

---

[1] https://sites.google.com/site/clefehealth2015/

[2] http://www.clef-initiative.eu/

[3] In the remaining we will refer to Task 2a as Task 2; we will use Task 2b to refer to the multilingual queries only when this specific case was considered. Note that only one team submitted runs for multilingual queries.

In total the 2015 edition of the CLEFeHealth lab attracted 20 teams to submit 4 submissions[4] to Task 1a, 38 to Task 1b, and 97 to Task 2; demonstrated the capabilities of these systems in contributing to patients and nurses' understanding and information needs; and made data, guidelines, and tools available for future research and development. The lab workshop was held at CLEF in September 2015.

2   Tasks Motivations

2.1   Task 1

Laypeople find health related documents to be difficult to understand; clinicians have also problems in understanding the jargon of other professional groups even though policies and regulations emphasise the need to document care in a comprehensive manner and provide further information on health conditions to help their understanding. An example from a US discharge document is *"AP: 72 yo f w/ ESRD on HD, CAD, HTN, asthma p/w significant hyperkalemia & associated arrythmias"*. Another example from a French hospital stay report is *"FOGD sous A.G. + dilatation chez un patient porteur d'un carcinome épidermoide du 1/3 supérieur de l'oesophage T2N0M0 opéré en 97"*. However, authors of both care documents and consumer leaflets are overloaded with information and face many challenges in the timely and efficient generation, processing and sharing of such information. One example here is clinical handover between nurses, where verbal handover and note taking can lead to loss of information. As described in [1], there is much need for techniques, which support individuals in understanding such clinical documents including in languages other than English. This edition of the CLEF eHealth lab answers the call for biomedical shared tasks in languages other than English [12] by introducing a task addressing clinical named entity recognition and normalization in biomedical documents in French.

In addition, auto-converting a verbal nursing handover to text and then highlighting important information within the transcription — or even filling out a structured handover form — for the next nurse would aid care documentation and release nurses time to, for example, discuss these resources and provide further information for a longer time with the patients. Task 1a aims at tackling this challenge.

2.2   Task 2

The use of the Web as source of health-related information is a wide-spread phenomena. Search engines are commonly used as a means to access health information available online. The 2013 and 2014 CLEFeHealth lab Task 3 aimed at evaluating the effectiveness of search engines to support people when searching

---

[4] Note that in this paper, we refer to submissions, systems, experiments, and runs as *submissions*.

for information about known conditions, e.g. to answer queries like "thrombo-cytopenia treatment corticosteroids length" [4,8,13]. Other types of searches for health related information are for self-diagnosis purposes, often issued before attending a medical professional (or to help the decision of attending) [14]. Previous research has shown that exposing people with no or scarce medical knowledge to complex medical language may lead to erroneous self-diagnosis and self-treatment and that access to medical information on the Web can lead to the escalation of concerns about common symptoms (e.g., cyberchondria) [15,16]. Research has also shown that current commercial search engines are yet far from being effective in answering such queries [17]. We thus decided to investigate this type of queries in the 2015 CLEFeHealth lab Task 2. We expected these queries to pose a new challenge to the participating teams; a challenge that, if solved, would lead to significant contributions towards improving how current commercial search engines answer health queries.

3   Materials and Methods

3.1   Speech and Text Documents

The NICTA Synthetic Nursing Handover Data was used in Task 1a [9,18]. This set of 200 synthetic patient cases (i.e., 100 for training and another 100 for testing) was developed for SR and IE related to nursing shift-change handover in 2012–2015. Each case consisted of a patient profile; a written, free-form text paragraph (i.e., the written handover document) to be used as a reference standard in SR; and its spoken (i.e., the verbal handover document) and speech-recognized counterparts.

For Task 1b, two types of biomedical documents were used: a total of 1,668 titles of scientific articles indexed in The MEDLINE database, and 6 full text drug monographs published by the European Medicines Agency (EMEA).

For Task 2, the CLEFeHealth 2014 Task 3 large crawl of health resources on the Internet was used. It contained about one million documents [19] and originated from the Khresmoi project[5]. The crawled domains were predominantly health and medicine sites, which were certified by the HON Foundation as adhering to the HONcode principles (appr. 60–70 per cent of the collection), as well as other commonly used health and medicine sites such as Drugbank, Diagnosia and Trip Answers.[6] Documents consisted of pages on a broad range of health topics and were targeted at both the general public and healthcare professionals. They were made available for download on the Internet in their raw HTML format along with their URLs to registered participants on a secure password-protected server.

---

[5] Medical Information Analysis and Retrieval, http://www.khresmoi.eu

[6] Health on the Net, http://www.healthonnet.org, http://www.hon.ch/HONcode/Patients-Conduct.html, http://www.drugbank.ca, http://www.diagnosia.com, and http://www.tripanswers.org

3.2   Human Annotations, Queries, and Relevance Assessments

For Task 1b, the annotations covered ten types of entities of clinical interest, defined by Semantic Groups in the Unified Medical Language System (UMLS) [20]: *Anatomy, Chemicals & Drugs, Devices, Disorders, Geographic Areas, Living Beings, Objects, Phenomena, Physiology, Procedures.* The annotations marked each relevant entity mention in the documents, and assigned the corresponding semantic type(s) and Concept Unique Identifier(s) or CUIs. Each document was annotated by one professional annotator (two annotators participated in total) according to detailed guidelines [21]. The annotations were then validated and revised by a senior annotator to ensure annotation consistency and correctness throughout the corpus. The corpus was split evenly between training data supplied to the participants at the beginning of the lab, and an unseen test set used to evaluate participants' systems.

For Task 2, queries were obtained by showing images and videos related to medical symptoms to users, who were then asked which queries they would issue to a web search engine if they or their next-of-kins were exhibiting such symptoms and thus wanted to find more information to understand these symptoms or which condition they were affected by. This methodology for eliciting circumlocutory, self-diagnosis queries was shown to be effective by Stanton et al. [22]; Zuccon et al. [17] showed that current commercial search engines are yet far from being effective in answering such queries.

Following the methodology in [17,22], 23 symptoms or conditions that manifest with visual or audible signs (e.g. ringworm or croup) were selected to be presented to users to collect queries. A cohort of 12 volunteer university students and researchers based in the organisers' institutions was used to generate the queries. A total of 266 possible unique queries were collected; of these, 67 queries (22 conditions with 3 queries and 1 condition with 1 query) were selected to be used in this year's task. In addition, we developed translations of this query set into Arabic (AR), Czech (CS), German (DE), Farsi (FA), French (FR), Italian (IT) and Portuguese (PT); these formed the multilingual query sets which were made available to participants for submission of multilingual runs. Queries were translated by medical experts available at the organisers institutions.

Relevance assessments were collected by pooling participants' submitted runs as well as baseline runs. Assessment was performed by four paid medical students who had access to the query the document was retrieved for, as well as the target symptom or condition that was used to obtained the query during the query generation phase. Along with relevance assessments, readability judgements were also collected for the assessment pool. Assessments were provided on a four point scale: 0, It is very technical and difficult to read and understand; 1, It is somewhat technical and difficult to read and understand; 2, It is somewhat easy to read and understand; 3, It is very easy to read and understand.

3.3   Evaluation Methods

In Task 1a, the participants needed to submit their processing results. Submissions that developed the SR engine itself were evaluated separately from those that studied post-processing methods for the speech-recognized text. Also a separate submission category was assigned to solutions based on both SR and text post-processing. Each participant was allowed to submit up to two systems to the first category and up to two systems to the second category. If addressing both these categories, the participant was asked to submit all possible combinations of these systems as their third category submission. Final submission then consisted of the processing outputs for each method on the 100 training and 100 test documents.

In Task 1b, teams could submit up to two runs for three subtasks that were evaluated separately on the two types of text supplied (MEDLINE and EMEA): 1/for **plain entity recognition**, raw text was supplied to participants who had to submit entity annotations comprising entity offsets and entity types. 2/for **normalized entity recognition**, raw text was supplied to participants who had to submit entity annotations comprising entity offsets, entity types, and entity normalization (UMLS CUIs). 3/for **entity normalization**, raw text and plain entity annotations were supplied to participants who had to submit entity normalization (UMLS CUIs). For each of the subtasks, the system output on the unseen test set was compared to the gold standard annotations and precision recall and F-measure was computed.

In Task 2, teams could submit up to ten runs for the English queries, and an additional ten runs for each of the multilingual query languages. Teams were required to number runs such as that run 1 was a baseline run for the team; other runs were numbered from 2 to 10, with lower numbers indicating higher priority for selection of documents to contribute to the assessment pool (i.e. run 2 was considered of higher priority than run 3).

Teams received data from November 2014 to April 2015. In Task 1a, teams could access the training documents on 15 November 2014 and test documents on 23 April 2015. In Tasks 1b, data was divided into training and test sets; the evaluation for these tasks was conducted using the blind, withheld test data (documents for Task 1b). Teams were asked to stop development as soon as they downloaded the test data. The training set and test set for Tasks 1b and the 5 example queries and the test queries for Task 2 were released from December 2014 and April 2015 respectively. For Task 1b, the test set was released in two steps because the plain entity gold standard was needed as an input for the normalization subtask. Participants had to submit their runs for the entity recognition subtasks before the entity gold standard was released. Evaluation results were announced to the participants for the three tasks in May.

In Task 2, for each query, the top 10 documents returned in runs 1, 2 and 3 produced by the participants[7] were pooled to form the relevance assessment pool. In addition, the organisers also generated baseline runs using BM25, TF-IDF and Dirichlet Language model, as well as a set of benchmark systems that

---

[7] With the exclusion of multilingual submissions, for which runs were not pooled due to the larger assessment effort pooling these runs would have required. Note that only one team submitted multilingual runs.

ranked documents by estimating both (topical) relevance and readability[8]; these were pooled with the same methodology used for participants runs. A total of 8,713 documents were assessed.

The system performance in the different tasks was evaluated against task-specific criteria. In Task 1a, we challenged the participants to minimize the number of incorrectly recognized words on the independent test set. This correctness was evaluated on the entire test set using the primary measure of the percentage of incorrect words (aka the error rate percentage E) as defined by the Speech Recognition Scoring Toolkit (SCTK), 2.4.0 without punctuation as a differentiating feature. This measure sums up the percentages of substituted (S), deleted (D), and inserted (I) words (i.e., $E = S+D+I$). As secondary measures, we reported the percentage of correctly detected words (C) on the entire test set together with the breakdown of E to D, I, and S. We also documented the raw word numbers behind these percentages, provided more details on performance differences across the individual handover documents, and assessed the resubstitution performance on the training set. We used two baseline systems in Task 1a, namely Dragon Medical 11.0 and Majority, which assumed that the right number of words is detected and recognized every word as the most common training word with the correct capitalization. Statistical differences between the error rate percentages of the two baselines and participant submissions were evaluated using the Wilcoxon signed-rank test (W) [23]. After ranking the baselines and submissions based on their error rate percentage on the entire dataset for testing, W was computed for the paired comparisons from the best and second-best system to the second-worst and worst system. The resulting p value and the significance level of 0.05 was used to determine if the median performance of the higher-ranked method was significantly better than this value for the lower-ranked method. All statistical tests were computed using R 3.2.0.

Tasks 1b system performance was evaluated using precision, recall and F-measure. The official primary measure was exact match F-measure.

In Task 2, system evaluation was conducted using precision at 10 (p@10) and normalised discounted cumulative gain [24] at 10 (nDCG@10) as the primary and secondary measures, respectively. Precision was computed using the binary relevance assessments; nDCG was computed using the graded relevance assessments. A separate evaluation was conducted using both relevance assessments and readability assessments following the methods in [25]. For all runs, Rank biased precision (RBP)[9] was computed along with readability-biased modifications of RBP, namely uRBP (using the binary readability assessments) and uRBPgr (using the graded readability assessments). More details on the readability-based evaluation are provided in the Task overview paper [11].

---

[8] Run 1: linear interpolation of BM25 scores (weight 0.9) and Dale Chall readability score (weight 0.1); run 2: multiplication of BM25 scores and log of word frequency extracted from Wikipedia; run 3: TF-IDF and Flesh-Kincaid readability scores combined via an inverse logarithmic function. See [11] for details.

[9] The persistence parameter p in RBP was set to 0.8.

The organizers provided the following evaluation tools on the Internet. To supplement the usage guidelines of SCTK, we provided the Task 1a participants with some helpful tips. More specifically, we released an example script for removing punctuation and formatting text files; a formatted reference file and Dragon baseline for the training set; overall and document-specific evaluation results for this file pair; and commands to perform these evaluations and ensure the correct installation of SCTK. For Task 1b, results were computed using the `brateval` [26] program which we extended to cover the evaluation of normalized entities. The updated version of `brateval` was supplied to task participants along with the training data. For Task 2, precision and nDCG were computed using `trec_eval`; while the readability-biased evaluation was performed using `ubire`[10].

4   Results

The number of people who registered their interest in Tasks 1 and 2 was 47 and 53, respectively, and in total 20 teams with unique affiliations submitted to the

Table 1. Participating teams

ID	Team	Affiliation	Location
1	CISMeF	CISMeF, LITIS	France
2	CUNI	Institute of Formal and Applied Linguistics	Czech Republic
3	ECNU-ICA	Shanghai Key Laboratory of Multidimensional Information Processing	China
4	Erasmus	Erasmus Mc	Netherlands
5	FDUSGinfo	Fudan University	China
6	GRIUM	RALI, DIRO, University of Montreal	Canada
7	HCMUS	Vietnam National University	Vietnam
8	HIT-W	Harbin Institute of Technology	China
9	IHS-RD	IHS Inc	Belarus
10	KISTI	KISTI	Korea
11	KU-CS	Kasetsart University	Thailand
12	LIMSI-ILES	LIMSI	France
13	Miracl	Miracl Lab, IRIT	Tunisia, France
14	TUC-MI/MC	Technische Universität Chemnitz	Germany
15	UBML	University of Botswana	Botswana
16	UC	University of Canberra	Australia
17	UPF	Universitat Pompeu Fabra, Universidad de Buenos Aires	Spain, Argentina
18	USST	University of Shanghai for science and technology	China
19	Watchdogs	Dhirubhai Ambani Institute of Information and Communication Technology	India
20	YorkU	York University	Canada

---

[10] https://github.com/ielab/ubire, [25].

shared tasks (Tables 1 and 2). No team participated in all tasks. Two teams participated in Tasks 1b and 2 (Table 2). Teams represented Argentina, Australia, Belarus, Botswana, Canada, China, Czech Republic, France, Germany, India, Korea, Spain, The Netherlands, Thailand, Tunisia, and Vietnam.

In total 209 systems were submitted to the challenge (Table 2).

Table 2. The tasks that the teams participated in

ID	Team	Number of submitted systems per task				
		1a	1b	2a	2b	
1	CISMeF		4			
2	CUNI			10	70 (10 runs per language)	
3	ECNU-ICA			10		
4	Erasmus		12			
5	FDUSGinfo			10		
6	GRIUM			7		
7	HCMUS			8		
8	HIT-W		6			
9	IHS-RD		8			
10	KISTI			8		
11	KU-CS			4		
12	LIMSI-ILES		2	5		
13	Miracl			5		
14	TUC-MI/MC	4				
15	UBML			10		
16	UC	Rejected				
17	UPF		2			
18	USST			10		
19	Watchdogs		4			
20	YorkU			10		
	Systems:	4	38	97	70	*Total: 209*
	Teams:	1	7	12	1	

Task 1a opened in both verbal and written formats the total of 200 synthetic clinical documents that can be used for studies on nursing documentation and informatics. It attracted 48 team registrations with 21 teams confirming their participation through email. Two interdisciplinary teams submitted two SR methods each. Unfortunately, UC.2 submission was incomplete and thus was rejected by the organizers.

The Dragon baseline had clearly the best performance (i.e., $E = 38.5$) on the Task 1a test documents, followed by the TUC_MI/MC.2 ($E = 52.8$), TUC_MI/MC.1 ($E = 52.3$), UC.1 ($E = 93.1$), and the Majority baseline ($E = 95.4$). The performance of the Dragon baseline on the test set was significantly better than that of the second-best system (i.e., TUC_MI/MC.2, $W = 302.5$, $p < 10^{-12}$). However, this rank-2 system was not significantly better than the third-best method (i.e., TUC_MI/MC.1), but this rank-3 system was significantly better than the fourth-best system (i.e., UC.1, $W = 0$, $p < 10^{-15}$). Finally, the performance of the lowest-ranked system (i.e., the Majority baseline) was significantly worse than that of this rank-4 system ($W = 1,791.5$, $p < 0.05$). See the Task 1a [9] for more detailed evaluation results.

In total, seven teams submitted systems for Task 1b. For the plain entity recognition subtask, seven teams submitted a total of 10 runs for each corpus (EMEA and MEDLINE). For the normalized entity recognition task, four teams submitted a total of 5 runs for each corpus. For the normalization task, three teams submitted a total of 4 runs for each corpus. The best system had an F-measure of 0.756 for plain entity recognition, 0.711 for normalized entity recognition and 0.872 for entity normalization. See Tables 3, 4, 5, 6, 7 and 8 for details.

Twelve teams participated in Task 2 with result submissions for the English queries (only one of these teams submitted results for the multilingual queries). On average, teams submitted 8 runs each (the total number of submitted runs by participating teams was 97). Run 3 from Team ECNU performed best under all measures, achieving improvements of up to about 62% and 54% over the best task baseline and the best task benchmark, respectively, and 60% over the second best run from another team. Table 9 summarises the retrieval effectiveness of the best system runs for each participating team and it includes the evaluation

Table 3. Task 1b system performance for plain entity recognition on the EMEA test corpus. Data shown in *italic font* presents versions of the official runs that were submitted with format corrections after the official deadline. The **official** median and average are computed using the official runs while the *fix* median and average are computed using the late-submission corrected runs

Team	TP	FP	FN	Precision	Recall	F-measure
Erasmus-run1	1720	570	540	0.751	0.761	**0.756**
Erasmus-run2	1753	716	507	0.710	**0.776**	0.741
IHS-RD-run1-fix	*1350*	*223*	*910*	*0.858*	*0.597*	*0.704*
Watchdogs-run1	1238	203	1022	**0.859**	0.548	0.669
IHS-RD-run2-fix	*1288*	*328*	*972*	*0.797*	*0.570*	*0.665*
HIT-WI Lab-run1-fix	*971*	*234*	*1289*	*0.806*	*0.430*	*0.561*
LIMSI-run1	945	644	1315	0.595	0.418	0.491
Watchdogs-run2	1309	2361	951	0.357	0.579	0.442
UPF-run1-fix	*113*	*2147*	*704*	*0,050*	*0,138*	*0,073*
HIT-WI Lab-run1	12	1137	2248	0.010	0.005	0.007
CISMeF-run1	9	4124	2251	0.002	0.004	0.003
IHS-RD-run1	0	0	2260	0.000	0.000	0.000
IHS-RD-run2	0	1616	2260	0.000	0.000	0.000
UPF-run1	0	1067	2260	0.000	0.000	0.000
average (official)				0.328	0.309	0.311
average-fix				0.573	0.468	0.503
median (official)				0.184	0.212	0.224
median-fix				0.731	0.559	0.613

Table 4. Task 1b system performance for plain entity recognition on the MEDLINE test corpus. Data shown in *italic font* presents versions of the official runs that were submitted with format corrections after the official deadline. The **official** median and average are computed using the official runs while the *fix* median and average are computed using the late-submission corrected runs

Team	TP	FP	FN	Precision	Recall	F-measure
Erasmus-run1	1861	756	1116	0.711	0.625	**0.665**
Erasmus-run2	1912	886	1065	0.683	**0.642**	0.662
IHS-RD-run1-fix	*1195*	*1782*	*376*	*0.761*	*0.401*	*0.526*
IHS-RD-run2	1188	383	1789	**0.756**	0.399	0.522
Watchdogs-run1	1215	490	1762	0.713	0.408	0.519
LIMSI-run1	1121	834	1856	0.573	0.377	0.455
HIT-WI Lab-run1	1068	671	1909	0.614	0.359	0.453
Watchdogs-run2	1364	2069	1613	0.397	0.458	0.426
CISMeF-run1	680	4412	2297	0.134	0.228	0.169
IHS-RD-run1	75	168	2902	0.309	0.025	0.047
UPF-run1	82	888	2895	0.085	0.028	0.042
average (official)				0.498	0.355	0.396
average-fix				0.543	0.393	0.444
median (official)				0.594	0.388	0.454
median-fix				0.649	0.400	0.487

Table 5. Task 1b system performance for normalized entity recognition on the EMEA test corpus. Data shown in *italic font* presents versions of the official runs that were submitted with format corrections after the official deadline. The **official** median and average are computed using the official runs while the *fix* median and average are computed using the late-submission corrected runs

Team	TP	FP	FN	Precision	Recall	F-measure
CISMeF-run1	10	2255	4128	0.004	0.002	0.003
Erasmus-run1	1637	655	678	**0.714**	**0.707**	**0.711**
Erasmus-run2	1627	680	866	0.705	0.653	0.678
IHS-RD-run1	0	2260	1616	0.000	0.000	0.000
IHS-RD-run1-fix	*923*	*17264*	*710*	*0.051*	*0.565*	*0.093*
HIT-WI Lab-run1	8	2252	1112	0.003	0.007	0.005
HIT-WI Lab-run1-fix	*432*	*1828*	*735*	*0.191*	*0.370*	*0,252*
average (official)				0.286	0.274	0.279
average-fix				0.333	0.460	0.347
median (official)				0.004	0.007	0.005
median-fix				0.191	0.565	0.252

Table 6. Task 1b system performance for normalized entity recognition on the MED-LINE test corpus. Data shown in *italic font* presents versions of the official runs that were submitted with format corrections after the official deadline. The **official** median and average are computed using the official runs while the *fix* median and average are computed using the late-submission corrected runs

Team	TP	FP	FN	Precision	Recall	F-measure
CISMeF-run1	1020	2434	4461	0.295	0.186	0.228
Erasmus-run1	1660	1376	957	**0.547**	**0.634**	**0.587**
Erasmus-run2	1677	1363	1121	0.552	0.599	0.575
IHS-RD-run1	634	15170	938	0.040	0.403	0.073
IHS-RD-run1-fix	*927*	*17495*	*644*	*0.050*	*0.590*	*0.093*
HIT-WI Lab-run1	515	2460	1223	0.173	0.2963	0.219
average (official)				0.321	0.424	0.336
average-fix				0.323	0.461	0.340
median (official)				0.295	0.403	0.228
median-fix				0.295	0.590	0.228

Table 7. Task 1b system performance for entity normalization on the EMEA test corpus

Team	TP	FP	FN	Precision	Recall	F-measure
Erasmus-run1	1734	526	0	0.767	**1.000**	0.868
Erasmus-run2	1748	512	0	**0.774**	**1.000**	**0.872**
IHS-RD-run1	1578	26642	715	0.056	0.688	0.103
HIT-WI Lab-run1	1266	994	1027	0.560	0.552	0.556
average (official)				0.532	0.896	0.615
median (official)				0.767	1.000	0.868

Table 8. Task 1b system performance for entity normalization on the MEDLINE test corpus

Team	TP	FP	FN	Precision	Recall	F-measure
Erasmus-run1	1780	1328	398	0.573	**0.817**	**0.674**
Erasmus-run2	1787	1321	433	**0.575**	0.805	0.671
IHS-RD-run1	1712	38213	1264	0.043	0.575	0.080
HIT-WI Lab-run1	1386	1589	1590	0.466	0.466	0.466
average (official)				0.397	0.733	0.475
median (official)				0.573	0.805	0.671

Table 9. Task 2 system effectiveness. For each participant teams, only the best run (according to p@10) is reported; systems are ranked by p@10. Best retrieval effectiveness are highlighted in bold; task baseline and benchmark effectiveness are reported in italics. Average and median system effectiveness are computed over all (English-only) submitted runs

Run	p@10	nDCG@10	RBP	uRBP	uRBPgr
ECNU_EN_Run.3	**0.5394**	**0.5086**	**0.5339**	**0.3877**	**0.4046**
KISTI_EN_RUN.6	0.3864	0.3464	0.3332	0.2607	0.2695
CUNI_EN_Run.7	0.3803	0.3465	0.3946	0.3422	0.3312
HCMUS_EN_Run.1	0.3636	0.3323	0.3715	0.3017	0.3062
readability_run.2	*0.3606*	*0.3299*	*0.3756*	*0.3154*	*0.3117*
USST_EN_Run.2	0.3379	0.3000	0.3557	0.2659	0.2727
baseline_run.1	*0.3333*	*0.3151*	*0.3567*	*0.2990*	*0.2933*
Miracl_EN_Run.1	0.3212	0.2787	0.3287	0.2546	0.2631
UBML_EN_Run.2	0.3197	0.2909	0.3305	0.2709	0.2735
GRIUM_EN_Run.6	0.3182	0.2944	0.3306	0.2791	0.2761
YorkU_EN_Run.7	0.3015	0.2766	0.3125	0.2470	0.2523
FDUSGInfo_EN_Run.1	0.2970	0.2718	0.3134	0.2572	0.2568
LIMSI_EN_run.3	0.2621	0.1960	0.2417	0.2036	0.2060
KUCS_EN_Run.1	0.2545	0.2205	0.2785	0.2312	0.2251
average (all runs)	0.2771	0.2529	0.2806	0.2228	0.2247
median (all runs)	0.2970	0.2718	0.3095	0.2394	0.2426

results for the most effective task baseline and benchmark systems. Note that average and median system effectiveness are below the task baseline effectiveness, and only five teams achieved results that are more effective than the best task baseline.

5   Conclusions

In this paper we provided an overview of the third year of the CLEF eHealth evaluation lab. The lab aimed to support the continuum of care by developing methods and resources that make health documents easier to understand, access and author for patients and nurses. Building on the first and second years of the lab, which contained three tasks focusing on IE from clinical reports, information visualization and both mono-lingual and multi-lingual IR, this year's edition featured clinical speech recognition, French IE, and a new mono- and multi-lingual IR challenge. Specifically this year's tasks comprised: 1) Clinical speech recognition related to converting verbal nursing handover to written free-text records; 2) Named entity recognition in clinical reports; and 3) health-focused web search. The lab attracted much interest with 20 teams from around the world submitting a combined total of 174 systems to the shared tasks. Given the significance of the tasks, all test collections and resources associated with the lab have been made available to the wider research community.

Acknowledgments. The CLEF eHealth 2015 evaluation lab has been supported in part by (in alphabetical order) ANR, the French National Research Agency, under grant CABeRneT ANR-13-JS02-0009-01; NICTA, funded by the Australian Government through the Department of Communications and the Australian Research Council through the Information and Communications Technology (ICT) Centre of Excellence Program; PhysioNetWorks Workspaces; the CLEF Initiative; and the Khresmoi and Kconnect projects, funded by the European Union Seventh Framework Programme (FP7/2007-2013) under grant agreement no 257528 and Horizon 2020 program (H2020-ICT-2014- 1) no 644753, respectively. We express our gratitude to Maricel Angel, Registered Nurse at NICTA, for helping us to create the Task 1a dataset, to Dr. Johannes Bernhardt-Melischnig (Medizinische Universität Graz) for coordinating the recruitment and management of the paid medical students that participated in the relevance assessment exercise, and to the volunteering students and researchers at the organisers' universities for participating to the query generation exercise. Last but not least, we gratefully acknowledge the participating teams' hard work. We thank them for their submissions and interest in the lab.

References

1. Suominen, H., et al.: Overview of the ShARe/CLEF eHealth evaluation lab 2013. In: Forner, P., Müller, H., Paredes, R., Rosso, P., Stein, B. (eds.) CLEF 2013. LNCS, vol. 8138, pp. 212–231. Springer, Heidelberg (2013)
2. Pradhan, S., Elhadad, N., South, B., Martinez, D., Christensen, L., Vogel, A., Suominen, H., Chapman, W., Savova, G.: Task 1: ShARe/CLEF eHealth evaluation lab 2013. In: Online Working Notes of CLEF, CLEF (2013)
3. Mowery, D., South, B., Christensen, L., Murtola, L., Salanterä, S., Suominen, H., Martinez, D., Elhadad, N., Pradhan, S., Savova, G., Chapman, W.: Task 2: ShARe/CLEF eHealth Evaluation Lab 2013. In: Online Working Notes of CLEF, CLEF (2013)
4. Goeuriot, L., Jones, G., Kelly, L., Leveling, J., Hanbury, A., Müller, H., Salanterä, S., Suominen, H., Zuccon, G.: ShARe/CLEF eHealth evaluation lab 2013, task 3: information retrieval to address patients' questions when reading clinical reports. In: Online Working Notes of CLEF, CLEF (2013)
5. Kelly, L., Goeuriot, L., Schreck, T., Leroy, G., Mowery, D.L., Velupillai, S., Chapman, W., Martinez, D., Zuccon, G., Palotti, J.: Overview of the ShARe/CLEF eHealth evaluation lab 2014. In: Kanoulas, E., Lupu, M., Clough, P., Sanderson, M., Hall, M., Hanbury, A., Toms, E. (eds.) CLEF 2014. LNCS, vol. 8685, pp. 172–191. Springer, Heidelberg (2014)
6. Suominen, H., Schreck, T., Leroy, G., Hochheiser, H., Goeuriot, L., Kelly, L., Mowery, D., Nualart, J., Ferraro, G., Keim, D.: Task 1 of the CLEF eHealth Evaluation Lab 2014: visual-interactive search and exploration of eHealth data. In: CLEF 2014 Evaluation Labs and Workshop: Online Working Notes, Sheffield, UK (2014)
7. Mowery, D., Velupillai, S., South, B., Christensen, L., Martinez, D., Kelly, L., Goeuriot, L., Elhadad, N., Pradhan, S., Savova, G., Chapman, W.: Task 2 of the CLEF eHealth Evaluation Lab 2014: Information extraction from clinical text. In: CLEF 2014 Evaluation Labs and Workshop: Online Working Notes, Sheffield, UK (2014)
8. Goeuriot, L., Kelly, L., Lee, W., Palotti, J., Pecina, P., Zuccon, G., Hanbury, A., Gareth, J.F., Jones, H.M.: ShARe/CLEF eHealth Evaluation Lab 2014, Task 3: User-centred health information retrieval. In: CLEF 2014 Evaluation Labs and Workshop: Online Working Notes, Sheffield, UK (2014)

9. Suominen, H., Hanlen, L., Goeuriot, L., Kelly, L., Jones, G.J.: Task 1a of the CLEF eHealth evaluation lab 2015: Clinical speech recognition. In: CLEF 2015 Online Working Notes, CEUR-WS (2015)
10. Névéol, A., Grouin, C., Tannier, X., Hamon, T., Kelly, L., Goeuriot, L., Zweigenbaum, P.: CLEF eHealth evaluation lab 2015 task 1b: clinical named entity recognition. In: CLEF 2015 Online Working Notes, CEUR-WS (2015)
11. Palotti, J., Zuccon, G., Goeuriot, L., Kelly, L., Hanburyn, A., Jones, G.J., Lupu, M., Pecina, P.: CLEF eHealth evaluation lab 2015, task 2: Retrieving information about medical symptoms. In: CLEF 2015 Online Working Notes, CEUR-WS (2015)
12. Névéol, A., Dalianis, H., Savova, G., Zweigenbaum, P.: Didactic panel: clinical natural language processing in languages other than English. In: Proc AMIA Annu. Symp. (2014)
13. Goeuriot, L., Kelly, L., Jones, G.J., Zuccon, G., Suominen, H., Hanbury, A., Mueller, H., Leveling, J.: Creation of a new evaluation benchmark for information retrieval targeting patient information needs. In: The Fifth International Workshop on Evaluating Information Access (EVIA 2013), vol. 18 (2013)
14. Fox, S.: Health topics: 80% of internet users look for health information online. Pew Internet & American Life Project (2011)
15. Benigeri, M., Pluye, P.: Shortcomings of health information on the internet. Health Promotion International 18(4), 381–386 (2003)
16. White, R.W., Horvitz, E.: Cyberchondria: studies of the escalation of medical concerns in web search. ACM TOIS 27(4), 23 (2009)
17. Zuccon, G., Koopman, B., Palotti, J.: Diagnose this if you can. In: Hanbury, A., Kazai, G., Rauber, A., Fuhr, N. (eds.) ECIR 2015. LNCS, vol. 9022, pp. 562–567. Springer, Heidelberg (2015)
18. Suominen, H., Zhou, L., Hanlen, L., Ferraro, G.: Benchmarking clinical speech recognition and information extraction: New data, methods and evaluations. JMIR Medical Informatics 3(2), e19 (2015)
19. Hanbury, A., Müller, H.: Khresmoi - multimodal multilingual medical information search. In: MIE Village of the Future (2012)
20. Bodenreider, O., McCray, A.T.: Exploring semantic groups through visual approaches. J. Biomed. Inform. 36(6), 414–432 (2003)
21. Névéol, A., Grouin, C., Leixa, J., Rosset, S., Zweigenbaum, P.: The QUAERO French medical corpus: A resource for medical entity recognition and normalization. In: Proc. of BioTextMining Work., pp. 24–30 (2014)
22. Stanton, I., Ieong, S., Mishra, N.: Circumlocution in diagnostic medical queries. In: Proceedings of the 37th International ACM SIGIR Conference on Research & Development in Information Retrieval, pp. 133–142. ACM (2014)
23. Wilcoxon, F.: Individual comparisons by ranking methods. Biometrics Bulletin 1(6), 80–83 (1945)
24. Järvelin, K., Kekäläinen, J.: Cumulated gain-based evaluation of IR techniques. ACM Transactions on Information Systems 20(4), 422–446 (2002)
25. Zuccon, G., Koopman, B.: Integrating understandability in the evaluation of consumer health search engines. In: Medical Information Retrieval Workshop at SIGIR 2014, p. 32 (2014)
26. Verspoor, K., Yepes, A.J., Cavedon, L., McIntosh, T., Herten-Crabb, A., Thomas, Z., Plazzer, J.P.: Annotating the biomedical literature for the human variome. Database (Oxford), bat019-bat019 (2013)

General Overview of ImageCLEF at the CLEF 2015 Labs

Mauricio Villegas[1]([✉]), Henning Müller[2], Andrew Gilbert[3], Luca Piras[4],
Josiah Wang[5], Krystian Mikolajczyk[3], Alba G. Seco de Herrera[2],
Stefano Bromuri[2], M. Ashraful Amin[6], Mahmood Kazi Mohammed[7],
Burak Acar[8], Suzan Uskudarli[8], Neda B. Marvasti[8], José F. Aldana[9],
and María del Mar Roldán García[9]

[1] Universitat Politècnica de València, Valencia, Spain
mauvilsa@upv.es
[2] University of Applied Sciences Western Switzerland (HES-SO),
Delémont, Switzerland
[3] University of Surrey, Guildford, UK
[4] University of Cagliari, Cagliari, Italy
[5] University of Sheffield, Sheffield, UK
[6] Independent University, Dhaka, Bangladesh
[7] Sir Salimullah Medical College, Dhaka, Bangladesh
[8] Bogazici University, Istanbul, Turkey
[9] University of Malaga, Malaga, Spain

Abstract. This paper presents an overview of the ImageCLEF 2015
evaluation campaign, an event that was organized as part of the CLEF
labs 2015. ImageCLEF is an ongoing initiative that promotes the evaluation of technologies for annotation, indexing and retrieval for providing
information access to databases of images in various usage scenarios and
domains. In 2015, the 13th edition of ImageCLEF, four main tasks were
proposed: 1) automatic concept annotation, localization and sentence
description generation for general images; 2) identification, multi-label
classification and separation of compound figures from biomedical literature; 3) clustering of x-rays from all over the body; and 4) prediction
of missing radiological annotations in reports of liver CT images. The
x-ray task was the only fully novel task this year, although the other
three tasks introduced modifications to keep up relevancy of the proposed
challenges. The participation was considerably positive in this edition of
the lab, receiving almost twice the number of submitted working notes
papers as compared to previous years.

1 Introduction

In the current age of the Internet and the proliferation of increasingly cheaper
devices to capture, amongst others, visual information, developing technologies
for the storage of this ever growing body of information and providing means
to access these huge databases is and will be a requirement. As part of this
development, it is of great importance to organise campaigns for evaluating the

© Springer International Publishing Switzerland 2015
J. Mothe et al. (Eds.): CLEF 2015, LNCS 9283, pp. 444–461, 2015.
DOI: 10.1007/978-3-319-24027-5_45

emerging problems and for fairly comparing the proposed techniques for solving them. Motivated by this, now in its 13th edition, ImageCLEF has been an initiative aimed at evaluating multilingual or language independent annotation and retrieval of images [14]. The main goal of ImageCLEF is to support the advancement of the field of visual media analysis, classification, annotation, indexing and retrieval, by proposing novel challenges and developing the necessary infrastructure for the evaluation of visual systems operating in different contexts and providing reusable resources for benchmarking.

To meet its objectives, ImageCLEF organises tasks that benchmark the annotation, classification and retrieval of diverse images such as the heterogeneous images found on web pages as well as imagery used in specialised fields such as medicine. These tasks aim to support and promote research that addresses key challenges in the field. ImageCLEF has had a significant influence [20] on the visual information retrieval field by benchmarking various retrieval, classification and annotation tasks and by making available the large and realistic test collections built in the context of its activities. Many research groups have participated over the years in its evaluation campaigns and even more have acquired its datasets for experimentation. The impact of ImageCLEF can also be seen by its significant scholarly impact indicated by the substantial numbers of its publications and their received citations [19]. One offspring of ImageCLEF is LifeCLEF [9] that includes besides images of leaves (a former ImageCLEF task) now also videos of fish that need to be identified and sounds of birds, making it a real multimedia retrieval task. Another CLEF lab linked to ImageCLEF is CLE-FeHealth [6] that deals with information retrieval from health-related documents. Also the eHealth lab is coordinated in close collaboration with ImageCLEF, as there is an overlap with the medical task.

This paper presents a general overview of the ImageCLEF 2015 evaluation campaign[1], which as usual was an event organised as part of the CLEF labs[2]. The remainder of this paper is organised as follows. Section 2 starts with a general description of the 2015 edition of ImageCLEF, commenting about the overall organisation and participation in the lab. Followed by this are subsections dedicated to the four main tasks that were organised this year, Section 2.1 for the image annotation task, Section 2.2 for the medical classification task, Section 2.3 for the medical clustering task and Section 2.4 for the liver CT annotation task. Finally, the paper concludes with Section 3 giving an overall discussion, and pointing towards the challenges ahead and possible new directions for Image-CLEF 2016.

2   ImageCLEF 2015: The Tasks, the Data and the Participation

The 2015 edition of ImageCLEF consisted of four main tasks that covered challenges in diverse fields and usage scenarios. Similar to the 2014 edition [2],

---

[1] http://imageclef.org/2015/
[2] http://clef2015.clef-initiative.eu/

all of the tasks addressed topics related to processing the images in order to automatically assign meta-data to them, not directly evaluating retrieval, but techniques that produce valuable annotations that can be used for subsequent image database indexing, mining or analysis. The four tasks organised were the following:

- **Image Annotation:** aims at developing systems for automatic annotation of concepts, their localization within the image, and generation of sentences describing the image content in a natural language.
- **Medical Classification:** addresses the identification, multi-label classification and separation of compound figures commonly found in the biomedical literature.
- **Medical Clustering:** is a task of which the objective is to cluster a dataset of x-rays from all over the body in order to group them according to the body part that is visible.
- **Liver CT Annotation:** has as goal the prediction of missing radiological annotations in structured radiology reports of liver CT images based on a new ontology of liver cases LiCO.

In order to participate in the evaluation campaign, the groups first had to register either on the CLEF website or from the ImageCLEF website. To actually get access to the datasets, the participants were required to submit by email a signed End User Agreement (EUA). Table 1 presents figures that summarize the participation in ImageCLEF 2015, including the number of registrations and number of signed EUAs, indicated both per task and for the overall lab. The table also includes the number of groups that submitted results (also called runs) and the ones that submitted a working notes paper describing the techniques used.

The number of registrations could be interpreted as the initial interest that the community has for the evaluation. However, it is a bit misleading because several people from the same institution might register, even though in the end they would count as a single group participation. The EUA explicitly requires all groups that get access to the data to participate. Unfortunately, the percentage of groups that take part is relatively small. Nevertheless, as observed in studies of scholarly impact [19], in subsequent years the datasets and challenges provided by ImageCLEF do get used quite often, which in part is due to the researchers that for some reason were unable to participate in the original event.

A very positive result for the 2015 edition of ImageCLEF was the number of working notes paper submissions, which can be considered the most important outcome, since this indicates the number of evaluated techniques that get properly reported in the literature. In total 25 papers were submitted, which in comparison to the previous two years (11 papers for 2013 and 13 papers for 2014), the participation has almost doubled.

The following four subsections are dedicated to each of the tasks. Only a short overview is reported, including general objectives, description of the tasks and datasets and a short summary of the results. For more detais please refer to the corresponding task overview papers [1,5,8,13].

Table 1. Key figures of participation in ImageCLEF 2015.

Task	Online registrations	Signed EUA	Groups that subm. results	Submitted working notes
Image Annotation	92	47	14	11
Medical Classification	79	34	8	7
Medical Clustering	72	36	8	6
Liver CT Annotation	51	27	1	1
Overall	148	72	31*	25*

* Total for all tasks, not unique groups.

2.1   The Image Annotation Task

Every day, users struggle with the ever-increasing quantity of data available to them. Trying to find that photo they took on holiday last year, the image on Google of their favourite actress or band, or the images of the news article someone mentioned at work. There is a large number of images that can be cheaply found and gathered from the Internet. However, more valuable is mixed modality data, for example, web pages containing both images and text. A large amount of information about the image is present on these web pages and vice-versa. However, the relationship between the surrounding text and images varies greatly, with much of the text being redundant and/or unrelated. Despite the obvious benefits of using such information in automatic learning, the very weak supervision it provides means that it remains a challenging problem. The scalable concept annotation, localization and sentence generation task aims to develop techniques to allow computers to reliably describe images, localize the different concepts depicted in the images and generate a description of the scene. This year the task was split into three related subtasks using a single mixed modality data source of 500,000 web page items.

Past Editions. The Scalable Concept annotation, localization and sentence generation task is a continuation of the general image annotation and retrieval task that has been part of ImageCLEF since its very first edition in 2003. In the early years the focus was on retrieving relevant images from a web collection given (multilingual) queries, while from 2006 onwards annotation tasks were also held, initially aimed at object detection, but more recently also covering semantic concepts. In its current form, the 2015 Scalable Concept Image Annotation task

448   M. Villegas et al.

(a) Images from a search query of "rainbow".

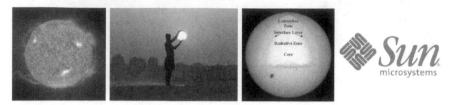

(b) Images from a search query of "sun".

Fig. 1. Examples of images retrieved by a commercial image search engine.

is its fourth edition, having been organized in 2012 [21], 2013 [23] and 2014 [22]. In light of recent interest in annotating images beyond just concept labels, we introduced two new subtasks this year where participants developed systems to describe an image with a textual description of the visual content depicted in the image.

Objective and Task for the 2015 Edition. Image concept annotation, localization and natural sentence generation generally has relied on training data that has been manually, and thus reliably annotated, an expensive and laborious endeavour that cannot easily scale, particularly as the number of concepts grow. However, images for any topic can be cheaply gathered from the web, along with associated text from the webpages that contain the images. The degree of relationship between these web images and the surrounding text varies greatly, i.e., the data are very noisy, but overall these data contain useful information that can be exploited to develop annotation systems. Figure 1 shows examples of typical images found by querying search engines. As can be seen, the data obtained are useful and furthermore a wider variety of images is expected, not only photographs, but also drawings and computer generated graphics. Likewise there are other resources available that can help to determine the relationships between text and semantic concepts, such as dictionaries or ontologies.

The goal of this task was to evaluate different strategies to deal with the noisy data so that it can be reliably used for annotating, localizing, and generating natural sentences from practically any topic. There were 3 sub tasks available to participants, which all use the common 500,000 web pages of images and text training data. Unlike previous years the test set was also the training set.

1. **SubTask 1:** The image annotation task continues in the same line of past years. The objective required the participants to develop a system that receives as input an image and produces as output a prediction of which concepts are present in that image, selected from a predefined list of concepts and starting this year, where they are located within the image.
2. **SubTask 2:** *Clean track.* In light of recent interest in annotating images beyond just concept labels, this subtask required the participants to describe images with a textual description of the visual content depicted in the image. It is thought of as an extension of SubTask 1. Aimed primarily at those interested only in the Natural Language Generation aspects of the subtask, therefore a gold standard input (bounding boxes labelled with concepts) was provided to develop systems that generate sentence, (natural language based) descriptions based on these gold standard annotations as input.
3. **SubTask 3:** *Noisy Track* This track was geared towards participants interested in developing systems that generated textual descriptions directly from images, e.g. by using visual detectors to identify concepts and generating textual descriptions from the detected concepts. This had a large overlap with sub task 1.

The concepts this year were chosen to be visual objects that are localizable and that are useful for generating textual descriptions of visual content of images. They include animate objects such as person, dogs and cats, inanimate objects such as houses, cars and balls, and scenes such as city, sea and mountains. The concepts were mined from the texts of our large database of image-webpage pairs. Nouns that are subjects or objects of sentences are extracted and mapped onto WordNet synsets. These were then filtered to 'natural', basic-level categories ('dog' rather than a 'yorkshire terrier'), based on the WordNet hierarchy and heuristics from a large-scale text corpora. The final list of concepts were manually shortlisted by the organizers such that they were (i) visually concrete and localizable; (ii) suitable for use in image descriptions; (iii) at a suitable 'every day' level of specificity that were neither too general nor too specific.

The data used in this task was similar to the one from last year [22]. The training and test set was composed of 500,000 samples each of which included: the raw image, pre-computed visual features and textual features. These training images were obtained from the web by querying popular image search engines. The development and sub task 1 and 3 test sets were both taken from the "training set" and had 1,979 and 3,070 samples, and the clean sub task 2 track had 500 and 450 samples. For further details, please refer to the task overview paper [5].

Participation and Results. This year 14 groups participated in the task, submitting a total of 122 runs across the 3 sub tasks and 11 of the participants also submitted working notes papers. Further details on the specific sub tasks is shown below. Sub task 1 was well received despite the additional requirement of labeling and localizing all 500,000 images. The ground truth used for the evaluation of the approaches used an unknown small subset of the 500,000 images.

Table 2. Sub task 1 results.

Group	0% Overlap	50% Overlap
SMIVA	0.79	0.66
IVANLPR	0.64	0.51
Multimedia Comp Lab	0.62	0.50
RUC	0.61	0.50
CEA	0.45	0.29
Kdevir	0.39	0.23
ISIA	0.25	0.17
CNRS-TPT	0.31	0.17
IRIP-iCC	0.61	0.12
UAIC	0.27	0.06
MLVISP6	0.06	0.02
REGIM	0.03	0.02
Lip6	0.04	0.01

Localization of Sub task 1 was evaluated using the PASCAL style metric of intersection over union (IoU), the area of intersection between the foreground in the output segmentation and the foreground in the ground-truth segmentation, divided by the area of their union. The final results are presented in table 2 in terms of mean average precision (MAP) over all images of all concepts, with both 0% overlap (i.e. no localization) and 50% overlap. It can be seen that four groups have achieved over 50 MAP across the evaluation set with 50% overlap with the ground-truth. This seems an excellent result given the challenging nature of the images used and the wide range of concepts provided. SMIVA used a deep learning framework with additional annotated data, while IVANLPR implemented a two-stage process, initially classifying at an image level with an SVM classifier, and then applying deep learning feature classification to provide localization. The Multimedia Comp Lab gathered high-quality training examples from the Web, then per concept, an ensemble of linear SVMs is trained by Negative Bootstrap, with CNN features as image representation. A shortcoming of the overall challenge however is the difficulty of ensuring the ground truth has 100% of concepts labelled, thus allowing a recall measure to be used. With the current crowd source based hand labelling of the ground truth it was found not to achieve this and so a recall measure isn't evaluated.

The pilot sub tasks on sentence generation received a reasonably good amount of participation, with two groups participating in sub task 2 and four in sub task 3. We observed a variety of approaches used to tackle these sub tasks, including top-down approaches, deep learning methods and joint image-text retrieval. Both sub tasks were evaluated using the Meteor evaluation metric [3]. We have also pioneered an additional fine-grained metric for sub task 2, which is the average F1 score across 450 test images on how well the sentence generation system selects the correct concepts to be described against gold standard image descriptions. Table 3 shows the results of the best run for each participant. For sub task 2, both groups achieved comparable results for both evaluation metrics. For sub task 3,

Table 3. Sub task 2 and 3 results

Group	Sub task 2		Sub task 3
	F1 score	Meteor	Meteor
ISIA	–	–	0.1687 ± 0.0852
MindLab	–	–	0.1403 ± 0.0564
RUC	0.5310 ± 0.2327	0.2393 ± 0.0865	0.1875 ± 0.0831
UAIC	0.5030 ± 0.1775	0.2097 ± 0.0660	0.0813 ± 0.0513

three groups achieved Meteor scores of over 0.10. The encouraging participation rates and promising results in these pilot sub tasks are sufficient motivations for the sub tasks to be included in future editions of this challenge.

For the complete results and a more detailed analysis, the reader should refer to the task overview paper [5].

2.2 The Medical Classification Task

This task is motivated by the fact that an estimated 40% of the figures in PubMed Central are compound figures (images consisting of several sub figures) [7]. Examples of compound figures can be seen in Figure 2. When data of articles are made available digitally, often the compound images are not available separated but made available in a single block. Information retrieval systems for images should be capable of distinguishing the parts of compound figures that are potentially relevant to a given query. A major step for making the content of the compound figures accessible is the detection of compound figures and then their separation into sub figures that can subsequently be classified into modalities and made available for research via their visual content. More information about this task can also be found in [8].

Past Editions. The medical image retrieval and classification task has been held every year at ImageCLEF since 2004, apart from 2014 [10]. The goal has been to promote biomedical image retrieval by combining text and images for more effective multimodal retrieval. It is also possible to use image modality classification to filter retrieval result lists or rerank them to improve and focus the retrieval. Therefore, in 2010, a modality classification task was introduced. The classification hierarchy has evolved over the years to an improved ad hoc hierarchy with 31 classes in 2012. It includes sections of diagnostic images, generic biomedical illustrations and compound or multipane images [15]. In 2013, the same hierarchy as in ImageCLEF 2012 was used. However, a larger number of compound figures than in ImageCLEF 2012 were provided in the training and test sets. The distribution of compound vs. non-compound figures corresponds to that in the PubMed Central data set[3] that the traing and test set are part of.

---

[3] http://www.ncbi.nlm.nih.gov/pmc

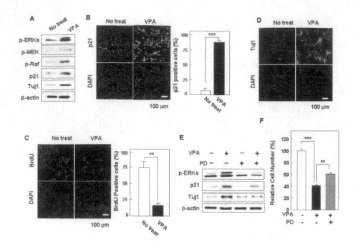

(a) Mixed modalities in a single figure.

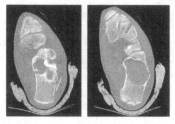

(b) Two images from the same modality in a single figure.

Fig. 2. Examples of compound figures found in the biomedical literature.

Making the content of the compound figures accessible for targeted search can improve retrieval accuracy. For this reason the detection of compound figures and their separation into subfigures was introduced in 2013 [7].

Objective and Task for the 2015 Edition. In 2015, the task focused only on the compound figures and not on potential retrieval steps after the compound figure analyis. There are four subtasks in 2015:

- *Compound Figure Detection* – Compound figure identification is a required first step to separate compound images from images only containing a single type of content. Therefore, the goal of this subtask is to identify whether a figure is a compound figure or not. The task makes training data available containing compound and non compound figures from the biomedical literature that are labelled and then a test set with similar images.
- *Multi-label Classification* – Characterization of compound figures is difficult, as they may contain subfigures from various imaging modalities or image types. This task aims to label each compound figure with each of the modalities (of the 31 classes of a defined hierarchy) of the subfigures contained

without knowing where the separation lines are. Differently from previous years, in which we focused on separating the subfigures to classify them on their own, we decided to consider the entire compound figure as having multiple labels simultaneously. We expect that this approach may help identifying the classes in the subfigures by taking into consideration the relationships occurring among the classes during the training of the model.

- *Figure Separation* – This subtask was first introduced in 2013. The task makes available training data with separation labels of the figures and then a test data set where the labels are made available after the submission of the results. In 2015, a larger number of compound figures was distributed compared to the previous subtask.
- *Subfigure Classification* – Similar to the modality classification task organized in 2011-2013 this subtask aims to classify images into the 31 classes of the hierarchy. The images are the subfigures extracted from the compound figures distributed for the figure separation subtask.

Participation and Results. Over seventy groups registered for the medical classification tasks and 8 groups submitted at least one run and a working notes paper. 40 runs were submitted in this task in total.

The FHDO Biomedical Computer Science Group [16] obtained best results on the compound figure detection and subfigure classification subtasks achieving 85% and 68% of accuracy respectively. In the multi-label classification, the MindLab group[4] obtained the best result with a Hamming loss of 0.05, while the IIS [17] group obtained a very close result to MindLab with a 0.671 in terms of Hamming loss. Finally, the National Library of Medicine (NLM) [18] submitted the best run in the figure separation subtask achieving an accuracy of 85%.

A more detailed analysis of the medical classification tasks is presented in the task overview paper of the working notes [8].

2.3 The Medical Clustering Task

At our research centre we are developing a diagnostic imaging teaching and learning system for medical students of Bangladesh [4]. As part of this project, a large collection of digital x-ray images was created from data obtained at a local hospital. These data are being used to build our teaching and learning system. However, during this development process the archiving and retrieving of x-ray images from a large database was found to be a challenging problem. Thus we decided to open up this challenge to the community by organising it as an evaluation under the framework of ImageCLEF.

Objective and Task for the 2015 Edition. The primary objective of this task is to group digital x-ray images into four major clusters: head-neck, upper-limb, body, and lower-limb. The secondary goal of this task is to partition the initial

---

[4] https://sites.google.com/a/unal.edu.co/mindlab

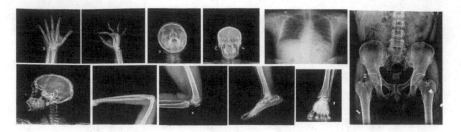

Fig. 3. Example images from the training data set.

clusters into sub-clusters, for example the upper-limb cluster can be farther divided into: Clavicle, Scapula, Humerus, Radius, Ulna, and Hand. However, due to the time constraint and difficulty level of the task, this year we decided to go only with the primary objective.

All together there are 500 digital x-ray images in the training dataset, of which 100 are from each of the four desired clusters: head-neck, upper-limb, body, and lower-limb, and the remaining 100 are true negative images that are taken by the same digital x-ray camera for calibration purpose. Some example images are given in Figure 3. A point to be noted about the assigned classification information for an x-ray image is that a single image can belong to multiple classes. For example, if a full body x-ray image for a child is given, then the associated classes are: head-neck, upper-limb, body, and lower-limb and the associated output is a 4-bit string that should have the value [1 1 1 1]. 250 test images were made available to the participants to check the performance of their system. At this moment, the task organizers have made the 750 samples available. They intend to make all 5000 images available in high resolution as '.dcm' format for non-commercial use at[5] soon after the CLEF 2015 conference.

Participation and Results. 71 groups from all 6 continents of the world participated in the initial level and acquired data from the ImageCLEF website. Though it is primarily a European event, 15 groups from EU, 14 from North America, 6 from Australia and 29 from Asia participated in the initial event. Among all EU countries there were 5 German groups and in Asia China had 5 groups which is highest in their region. Finally, participants were given the test data and a month time to submit their results on the test data. Only, 8 groups submitted their final results. There were 2 submissions from Australia, 2 from USA, 1 from each of the countries Republic of Korea, Israel, China and none from the EU. One group withdrew their runs (submitted results) as their method was semi-automatic. 7 groups submitted 29 runs and the best results for each group are selected and provided in Table 4. Finally, 6 groups were able to submit working note papers describing the methods used to implement their x-ray clustering system.

---

[5] http://www.cvcrbd.org

Table 4. Final Results of the Digital X-Ray Image clustering task.

Group	Exact Match Score	Any Match Score	Hamming Similarity
IBM MMAFL	0.752	0.864	0.863
SNUMedInfo	0.709	0.856	0.895
AmrZEGY	0.646	0.780	0.868
NLM	0.613	0.740	0.849
CASMIP	0.606	0.732	0.843
BMET	0.497	0.596	0.816
db Lab	0.219	0.264	0.664

To solve this multiclass classification problem of grouping digital x-ray image in to four clusters, participants have taken different approaches. For feature extraction they utilized: Intensity Histogram (IH), Gradient Magnitude Histogram (GM), Shape Descriptor Histogram (SD), Curvature Descriptor Histogram (CD), Histogram of Oriented Gradient (HOG), Local Binary Pattern (LBP), Color Layout Descriptor (CLD), Edge Histogram Descriptor (EHD) from MPEG-7 standard, Color and Edge Direction Descriptor (CEDD), Fuzzy Color and Texture Histogram (FCTH), Tamura texture descriptor, Gabor texture feature, primitive length texture features, edge frequency texture features, autocorrelation texture features, Bag of Visual Words (BoVW), Scale invariant feature transform (SIFT), Speeded up robust features (SURF), Binary robust independent elementary features Brief (BRIEF), Oriented fast and rotated BRIEF (ORB), Multi-scale LBP Histogram with Spatial Pyramid, Sparse Coding with Max-pooling and Spatial Pyramid, Fisher Kernel Feature Coding, Global mean of rows and columns, Local Mean of rows and columns, and Gray Level Co-occurrence Matrix (GLCM).

Classification was performed using Backpropagation Neural Networks (BPNN), Logistic Regression (LR), K Nearest Neighbors (KNN) and Deep Belief Network (DBN), Convolution Neural networks (CNN), Decision Tree, Support Vector Machine (RBF Kernel, Poly kernel, Normalized Ploy kernel and Puk kernel), Random Forest, Logistic Model Tree (LMT), Naive Bayesian, and Ensemble Neural Network.

Because one input can belong to multiple classes, we have tested the performance based on three different methods. The most conventional one is the Hamming similarity calculation. However, a stricter version of classification accuracy checking is also used, that we are calling exact matching, which basically checks, for a given input how many of its multiple possible classes are correctly identified. We also checked the accuracies using another method that we call any match. For an input image if the predicted class matches with any of the actual class of that image then it is considered a correct classification. Best result for exact match was 0.752; for any match was 0.864; and for Hamming similarity was 0.895. Final score for all seven groups is provided in Table 4.

It is very likely that participants are using similar feature extraction and classification techniques. It is accepted that some features are used by most of the participants, those are the so-called state of the art techniques. However, for this problem of clustering x-ray images into 4 clusters 6 participants have employed 27 different image feature extraction techniques. Different characteristics of the feature extractors are revealed. One interesting observation is that while exploring the famous HoG features one group claims it has poor discriminating capacity and, on the other hand, another group is providing an accuracy above 0.90 using HoG features. Another interesting observation is that, even though, x-ray images are gray scale, color features like CEDD, FCTH show good discriminating ability [1]. Most interesting yet obvious observation is the use of Convolution Neural Network (CNN). Recently, CNN were made popular by GoogLeNet. Out of seven, four groups used or experimented with Neural Networks. It is good news for the neural network researchers. We believe people have already started (rather restarted) to explore enormous ability of CNN and other computational learners other than SVMs.

2.4   The Liver CT Annotation Task

Medical and more specifically radiological databases present challenges due to the exponential increase in data volumes. Radiological images contain a rich source of meta-data associated with the images. A significant part of the medical image analysis is based on the subtle differences between a set of similar images, such as abdominal CT images. In a conventional setting, these critical differences, such as the parenchyma texture of a liver, are manually observed by experts and are translated into the medical vocabulary. Domain-specific radiological structured-reporting is useful in accurately reflecting the interpretation of medical images. Such reporting can improve the clinical workflow by means of facilitating standardized reports as well as boost the performance of search and retrieval from radiological databases for the purpose of comparative diagnosis, medical education, etc. Despite its advantages, an expert annotation is a labour intensive task, which can be performed by qualified individuals only and must be consistent among different individuals, sites, countries, etc. Computer-aided automatic annotation is a challenging task, which facilitates filling in a structured radiology report. Several standard terminologies are being developed/used for medical annotation, such as SNOMED-CT (Systemized Nomenclature in Medicine), RadLex (Radiology Lexicon), NCBO, UMLS (Unified Medical Language System), LOINC (Logical Observation Identifiers Names and Codes), etc. An annotation is performed via a high-level processing of the medical evidence derived from the images. Hence, a key challenge in expert annotation is to translate computer generated objective low-level image observations (CoG) to high level semantic descriptions (i.e., annotations) that comply with a standard terminology of choice. The "Liver CT Annotation Task", aims at filling structured reports by facilitating the computer aided annotation of liver CT images.

Past Edition. The Liver CT Annotation task was introduced for the first time in ImageCLEF 2014 [12], which focused on the annotation of the liver

Table 5. Results of the runs of Liver CT annotation task.

Run	Completeness	Accuracy	Total Score
Run1	0.990909	0.825688	0.904534
Run2	0.990909	0.822630	0.902857
Run3	0.990909	0.836391	0.910378

CT images and filling structured reports generated using the ontology called ONLIRA (ONtology of Liver for Radiology) [11]. ONLIRA describes the imaging observations of the liver itself as well as vessel and lesions inside. Every term in the given structured report is defined by an ontology property (object/data).

Objective and Task for the 2015 Edition. In 2015 [13], the ontology was enriched by adding patient and study level information to ONLIRA. The new ontology is called LiCO (Liver Case Ontology)[6]. Patient level contains general information about the current patient, which includes name, age, gender, regular drugs, surgeries, and diseases. Study level consists of nonregular drugs, different diagnosis, physical examination, and laboratory results. The participants were given a training set of 50 cropped liver CT images together with the liver masks, and a bounding box defining the lesion area, a set of semantic annotations regarding the patient, study and imaging observations generated automatically from structures reports based on LiCO. Imaging observations contain the liver, vessels and one selected lesion. The semantic features were generated by an expert radiologist as part of the CaReRa[6] (Case Retrieval in Radiology) project, using the open source LiCO. The test set had 10 cases, with all types of data available in the training set except the semantic features in RDF format. The participants were asked to estimate the missing 65 imaging observations (UsE features). They were allowed to use any feature extraction method to generate low-level imaging observations from the CT images. The evaluation was based on the completeness (defined as the percentage of all 65 UsE features that were estimated) and accuracy (defined as the percentage of the estimated UsE features that were correct), and geometric mean of which was used as the total Score. Ideally, all metrics are 1.00.

Participation and Results. In 2015, there was 1 participant from Tlemcen University, who submitted 3 runs and 1 working note paper. Table 5 lists the results of all runs submitted. It can be seen that the third run outperforms the other two. Table 6 compares the results of different runs in predicting different groups of UsE features. We divide UsE features into 5 groups: liver, vessels and three lesion groups with area, lesion and component concepts. Results show that all methods have predicted the vessel UsE features completely. Also all runs have the same performance over liver features. The only difference is on lesion specified features, in which the third run outperforms the other. The first run is

---

[6] http://www.vavlab.ee.boun.edu.tr/pages.php?p=research/CARERA/carera.html

Table 6. Total score of the runs of Liver CT annotation task for different groups of features.

Group	Run1	Run2	Run3
Liver	0.925	0.925	0.925
Vessel	1.000	1.000	1.000
LesionArea	0.730	0.746	0.753
LesionLesion	0.470	0.470	0.480
LesionComponent	0.870	0.844	0.889

using a random forest classifier with liver texture and shape features, the second run is performed with the same method as the first run, except it employs the texture and shape features of the lesion. The third run is completed using the specific signature of the liver, which is done in 2D space on the slice located in the centre of the lesion. First, in order to forbid the imaging inconsistencies, they normalized the image into a rectangular block with constant dimensions, which is then divided into small blocks. Then, the 1D Log-Gabor filter is applied to each block and the dominant phase data is selected and quantized to 4 levels to encode the pattern of the liver. Finally, The similarity is calculated by Hamming distance and majority voting is then employed to assign the annotation.

For more details on the task and the results, the reader should refer to the task overview paper [13].

3   Conclusions

This paper presents a general overview of the activities and outcomes of the 2015 edition of the ImageCLEF evaluation campaign. Four main tasks were organised covering challenges in: automatic concept annotation, localization and sentence description generation for web images; identification, multi-label classification and separation of compound figures from biomedical literature; clustering of x-rays from all over the body; and prediction of missing radiological annotations in reports of liver CT images.

The interest in the lab was outstanding, receiving signed End User Agreements requesting access to the datasets from over seventy groups world wide. The participation in terms of submission of results was also quite satisfactory, receiving system runs from about thirty groups. In total 25 working notes papers were submitted describing the systems that were evaluated in all tasks, this being almost double than the previous years.

Even though the x-ray clustering task was in its first edition, several groups showed interest and submitted results. On the other hand, the Liver CT task in its second edition had a lower than expected participation. In part this can be due to the difficulty of the problem, although it is possible that there was not enough advertising or the audience targeted was not fully appropriate. For the next editions of ImageCLEF a greater effort must be made to assure that all tasks are well advertised so that they all have good participation.

The other two tasks that have run for several years both introduced important modifications that seemed to be heading in the right directions. The compound figure task addressed all aspects of dealing with compound figures in the literature and the participants obtained good performances. On the other hand, the image annotation task introduced the requirements of locating the concepts within the image and generating a natural language description. The added difficulty did not hinder the participation, in fact it can be said that there was a renewed interest. The sentence description generation had fewer participants although it has a great potential so it should continue in future editions.

Acknowledgments. The Scalable Concept image annotation, localization and sentence generation task is co-organized by the ViSen consortium under the EU CHIST-ERA D2K Programme, supported by EPSRC Grants EP/K01904X/1 and EP/K019082/1. The medical clustering task at the 2015 ImageCLEF is supported by the Independent University Bangladesh and European Science Foundations (ESF) Research Networking Programmes (RNPs). The Liver CT Annotation task is supported by TÜBİTAK Grant # 110E264 (CaReRa project) and in part by COST Action IC1302 (KEYSTONE).

References

1. Amin, M.A., Mohammed, M.K.: Overview of the ImageCLEF 2015 medical clustering task. In: CLEF2015 Working Notes. CEUR Workshop Proceedings, CEUR-WS.org, Toulouse, France, September 8–11, 2015
2. Caputo, B., Müller, H., Martinez-Gomez, J., Villegas, M., Acar, B., Patricia, N., Marvasti, N., Üsküdarlı, S., Paredes, R., Cazorla, M., Garcia-Varea, I., Morell, V.: ImageCLEF 2014: overview and analysis of the results. In: Kanoulas, E., Lupu, M., Clough, P., Sanderson, M., Hall, M., Hanbury, A., Toms, E. (eds.) CLEF 2014. LNCS, vol. 8685, pp. 192–211. Springer, Heidelberg (2014). doi:10.1007/978-3-319-11382-1_18
3. Denkowski, M., Lavie, A.: Meteor universal: language specific translation evaluation for any target language. In: Proceedings of the EACL 2014 Workshop on Statistical Machine Translation (2014)
4. Faruque, M.S.S., Banik, S., Mohammed, M.K., Hasan, M., Amin, M.A.: Teaching and learning system for diagnostic imaging phase i: X-ray image analysis and retrieval. In: Proceedings of the 6th International Conference on Computer Supported Education (2015)
5. Gilbert, A., Piras, L., Wang, J., Yan, F., Dellandrea, E., Gaizauskas, R., Villegas, M., Mikolajczyk, K.: Overview of the ImageCLEF 2015 scalable image annotation, localization and sentence generation task. In: CLEF2015 Working Notes. CEUR Workshop Proceedings, CEUR-WS.org, Toulouse, France, September 8–11, 2015
6. Kelly, L., Goeuriot, L., Suominen, H., Schreck, T., Leroy, G., Mowery, D.L., Velupillai, S., Chapman, W.W., Martinez, D., Zuccon, G., Palotti, J.: Overview of the ShARe/CLEF eHealth evaluation lab 2014. In: Kanoulas, E., Lupu, M., Clough, P., Sanderson, M., Hall, M., Hanbury, A., Toms, E. (eds.) CLEF 2014. LNCS, vol. 8685, pp. 172–191. Springer, Heidelberg (2014)

7. García Seco de Herrera, A., Kalpathy-Cramer, J., Demner Fushman, D., Antani, S., Müller, H.: Overview of the ImageCLEF 2013 medical tasks. In: Working Notes of CLEF 2013 (Cross Language Evaluation Forum), September 2013. http://ceur-ws. org/Vol-1179/CLEF2013wn-ImageCLEF-SecoDeHerreraEt2013b.pdf

8. García Seco de Herrera, A., Müller, H., Bromuri, S.: Overview of the ImageCLEF 2015 medical classification task. In: Working Notes of CLEF 2015 (Cross Language Evaluation Forum). CEUR Workshop Proceedings, CEUR-WS.org, September 2015

9. Joly, A., Goëau, H., Glotin, H., Spampinato, C., Bonnet, P., Vellinga, W.-P., Planque, R., Rauber, A., Fisher, R., Müller, H.: LifeCLEF 2014: multimedia life species identification challenges. In: Kanoulas, E., Lupu, M., Clough, P., Sanderson, M., Hall, M., Hanbury, A., Toms, E. (eds.) CLEF 2014. LNCS, vol. 8685, pp. 229–249. Springer, Heidelberg (2014)

10. Kalpathy-Cramer, J., de Herrera, A.G.S., Demner-Fushman, D., Antani, S., Bedrick, S., Müller, H.: Evaluating performance of biomedical image retrieval systems -an overview of the medical image retrieval task at imageclef 2004–2014. Computerized Medical Imaging and Graphics 39, 55–61 (2015). doi:10.1016/j.compmedimag.2014.03.004

11. Kokciyan, N., Turkay, R., Uskudarli, S., Yolum, P., Bakir, B., Acar, B.: Semantic description of liver ct images: An ontological approach. IEEE Journal of Biomedical and Health Informatics PP(99), 1–1 (2014). doi:10.1109/JBHI.2014.2298880

12. Marvasti, N., Kökciyan, N., Türkay, R., Yazıcı, A., Yolum, P., Üsküdarlı, S., Acar, B.: ImageCLEF liver CT image annotation task 2014. In: CLEF 2014 Evaluation Labs and Workshop, Online Working Notes (2014). http://ceur-ws.org/Vol-1180/CLEF2014wn-Image-MarvastiEt2014.pdf

13. Marvasti, N.B., del Mar Roldán García, M., Uskudarli, S., Aldana, J.F., Acar, B.: Overview of the ImageCLEF 2015 liver CT annotation task. In: CLEF2015 Working Notes. CEUR Workshop Proceedings, CEUR-WS.org, Toulouse, France, September 8–11, 2015

14. Müller, H., Clough, P., Deselaers, T., Caputo, B.: ImageCLEF: experimental evaluation in visual information retrieval. Springer, Heidelberg (2010). doi:10.1007/978-3-642-15181-1

15. Müller, H., García Seco de Herrera, A., Kalpathy-Cramer, J., Demner Fushman, D., Antani, S., Eggel, I.: Overview of the ImageCLEF 2012 medical image retrieval and classification tasks. In: Working Notes of CLEF 2012 (Cross Language Evaluation Forum), September 2012. http://ceur-ws.org/Vol-1178/CLEF2012wn-ImageCLEF-MullerEt2012.pdf

16. Pelka, O., Friedrich, C.M.: FHDO biomedical computer science group at medical classification task of ImageCLEF 2015. In: Working Notes of CLEF 2015 (Cross Language Evaluation Forum). CEUR Workshop Proceedings, CEUR-WS.org, September 2015

17. Rodríguez-Sánchez, A., Fontanella, S., Piater, J., Szedmak, S.: IIS at imageclef 2015: multi-label classification task. In: Working Notes of CLEF 2015 (Cross Language Evaluation Forum). CEUR Workshop Proceedings, CEUR-WS.org, September 2015

18. Santosh, K.C. and Xue, Z., Antani, S., Thoma, G.: NLM at imageCLEF2015: biomedical multipanel figure separation. In: Working Notes of CLEF 2015 (Cross Language Evaluation Forum). CEUR Workshop Proceedings, CEUR-WS.org, September 2015

19. Tsikrika, T., de Herrera, A.G.S., Müller, H.: Assessing the scholarly impact of Image-CLEF. In: Forner, P., Gonzalo, J., Kekäläinen, J., Lalmas, M., de Rijke, M. (eds.) CLEF 2011. LNCS, vol. 6941, pp. 95–106. Springer, Heidelberg (2011). doi:10.1007/978-3-642-23708-9_12

20. Tsikrika, T., Larsen, B., Müller, H., Endrullis, S., Rahm, E.: The scholarly impact of CLEF (2000–2009). In: Forner, P., Müller, H., Paredes, R., Rosso, P., Stein, B. (eds.) CLEF 2013. LNCS, vol. 8138, pp. 1–12. Springer, Heidelberg (2013)

21. Villegas, M., Paredes, R.: Overview of the ImageCLEF 2012 scalable web image annotation task. In: Forner, P., Karlgren, J., Womser-Hacker, C. (eds.) CLEF 2012 Evaluation Labs and Workshop, Online Working Notes. Rome, Italy, September 17–20, 2012. http://ceur-ws.org/Vol-1178/CLEF2012wn-ImageCLEF-VillegasEt2012.pdf

22. Villegas, M., Paredes, R.: Overview of the ImageCLEF 2014 scalable concept image annotation task. In: CLEF2014 Working Notes. CEUR Workshop Proceedings. CEUR-WS.org, Sheffield, UK, vol. 1180, pp. 308–328, September 15–18, 2014. http://ceur-ws.org/Vol-1180/CLEF2014wn-Image-VillegasEt2014.pdf

23. Villegas, M., Paredes, R., Thomee, B.: Overview of the ImageCLEF 2013 scalable concept image annotation subtask. In: CLEF 2013 Evaluation Labs and Workshop, Online Working Notes. Valencia, Spain, September 23–26, 2013. http://ceur-ws.org/Vol-1179/CLEF2013wn-ImageCLEF-VillegasEt2013.pdf

LifeCLEF 2015: Multimedia Life Species Identification Challenges

Alexis Joly[1](✉), Hervé Goëau[2], Hervé Glotin[3], Concetto Spampinato[4],
Pierre Bonnet[5], Willem-Pier Vellinga[6], Robert Planqué[6], Andreas Rauber[7],
Simone Palazzo[4], Bob Fisher[8], and Henning Müller[9]

[1] Inria, LIRMM, Montpellier, France
alexis.joly@inria.fr
[2] Inria, Montpellier, France
[3] IUF & University de Toulon, Toulon, France
[4] University of Catania, Catania, Italy
[5] CIRAD-Amap, Montpellier, France
[6] Xeno-canto Foundation, Drachten, The Netherlands
[7] Vienna University of Technology, Vienna, Austria
[8] University of Edinburgh, Edinburgh, UK
[9] HES-SO, Sierre, Switzerland

Abstract. Using multimedia identification tools is considered as one of
the most promising solutions to help bridging the taxonomic gap and
build accurate knowledge of the identity, the geographic distribution
and the evolution of living species. Large and structured communities of
nature observers (e.g. eBird, Xeno-canto, Tela Botanica, etc.) as well as
big monitoring equipments have actually started to produce outstanding
collections of multimedia records. Unfortunately, the performance of the
state-of-the-art analysis techniques on such data is still not well understood and is far from reaching the real world's requirements. The Life-
CLEF lab proposes to evaluate these challenges around 3 tasks related to
multimedia information retrieval and fine-grained classification problems
in 3 living worlds. Each task is based on large and real-world data and
the measured challenges are defined in collaboration with biologists and
environmental stakeholders in order to reflect realistic usage scenarios.
This paper presents more particularly the 2015 edition of LifeCLEF. For
each of the three tasks, we report the methodology and the data sets as
well as the raw results and the main outcomes.

1 LifeCLEF Lab Overview

1.1 Motivations

Building accurate knowledge of the identity, the geographic distribution and the
evolution of living species is essential for a sustainable development of humanity
as well as for biodiversity conservation. Unfortunately, such basic information
is often only partially available for professional stakeholders, teachers, scientists
and citizens, and more often incomplete for ecosystems that possess the highest

© Springer International Publishing Switzerland 2015
J. Mothe et al. (Eds.): CLEF 2015, LNCS 9283, pp. 462–483, 2015.
DOI: 10.1007/978-3-319-24027-5_46

diversity, such as tropical regions. A noticeable cause and consequence of this sparse knowledge is that identifying living plants or animals is usually impossible for the general public, and often a difficult task for professionals, such as farmers, fish farmers or foresters, and even also for the naturalists and specialists themselves. This taxonomic gap [57] was actually identified as one of the main ecological challenges to be solved during Rio's United Nations Conference in 1992.

In this context, using multimedia identification tools is considered as one of the most promising solutions to help bridge the taxonomic gap [9,18,37,54] [1,17,30,50,53]. With the recent advances in digital devices, network bandwidth and information storage capacities, the collection and production of multimedia data has indeed become an easy task. In parallel, the emergence of citizen science and social networking tools has fostered the creation of large and structured communities of nature observers (e.g. eBird[1], Xeno-canto[2], Tela Botanica[3], etc.) that have started to produce outstanding collections of multimedia records. Unfortunately, the performance of the state-of-the-art multimedia analysis techniques on such data is still not well understood and is far from reaching the real world's requirements in terms of identification tools [30]. Most existing studies or available tools typically identify a few tens or hundreds of species with moderate accuracy whereas they should be scaled-up to take one, two or three orders of magnitude more, in terms of number of species (the total number of living species on earth is estimated to be around 10K for birds, 30K for fish, 300K for flowering plants (cf. The Plant list[4]) and more than 1.2M for invertebrates [5].

1.2   Evaluated Tasks

The LifeCLEF lab[5] originally evaluated these challenges in the continuity of the image-based plant identification task [31] that was run within the ImageCLEF labs[6] [43] during the last three years with an increasing number of participants. It recently however radically enlarged the evaluated challenge towards multimodal data by (i) considering birds and fish in addition to plants, (ii) considering audio and video content in addition to images, and (iii) scaling-up the evaluation data to hundreds of thousands of life media records and thousands of living species. More concretely, the lab is organized around three tasks:

---

[1] http://ebird.org/
[2] http://www.xeno-canto.org/
[3] http://www.tela-botanica.org/
[4] http://www.theplantlist.org/
[5] http://www.lifeclef.org/
[6] http://www.imageclef.org//

PlantCLEF: an image-based plant identification task

 BirdCLEF: an audio-based bird identification task

 FishCLEF: a video-based fish identification task

As described in more detail in the following sections, each task is based on big and real-world data and the measured challenges are defined in collaboration with biologists and environmental stakeholders so as to reflect realistic usage scenarios. For this year, the three tasks are mainly concerned with species identification, i.e., helping users to retrieve the taxonomic name of an observed living plant or animal. Taxonomic names are actually the primary key to organize life species and to access all available information about them either on the web, or in herbariums, in scientific literature, books or magazines, etc. Identifying the taxon observed in a given multimedia record and aligning its name with a taxonomic reference is therefore a key step before any other indexing or information retrieval task. More focused or complex challenges (such as detecting species duplicates or ambiguous species) could be evaluated in coming years.

The three tasks are primarily focused on content-based approaches (i.e. on the automatic analyses of the audio and visual signals) rather than on interactive information retrieval approaches involving textual or graphical morphological attributes. The content-based approach to life species identification has several advantages. It is first intrinsically language-independent and solves many of the multi-lingual challenges related to the use of classical text-based morphological keys that are strongly language dependent and understandable only by few experts in the world. Furthermore, an expert of one region or a specific taxonomic group does not necessarily know the vocabulary dedicated to another group of living organisms. A content-based approach can then be much more easily generalizable to new flora or fauna contrary to knowledge-based approaches that require building complex models manually (ontologies with rich descriptions, graphical illustrations of morphological attributes, etc.). On the other hand, the LifeCLEF lab is inherently cross-modal through the presence of contextual and social data associated to the visual and audio content. This includes geo-tags or location names, time information, author names, collaborative ratings or comments, vernacular names (common names of plants or animals), organ or picture type tags, etc. The rules regarding the use of these meta-data in the evaluated identification methods will be specified in the description of each task. Overall, these rules are always designed so as to reflect real possible usage scenarios while offering the largest diversity in the affordable approaches.

1.3   Main Contributions

The main outcomes of LifeCLEF evaluation campaigns are the following:

- give a snapshot of the performance of state-of-the-art multimedia techniques towards building real-world life species identification systems,
- provide large and original data sets of biological records, and then allow comparison of multimedia-based identification techniques,
- boost research and innovation on this topic in the next few years and encourage multimedia researchers to work on trans-disciplinary challenges involving ecological and environmental data,
- foster technological bridges from one domain to another and exchanges between the different communities (information retrieval, computer vision, bio-acoustic, machine learning, ornithology, botany, etc.),
- promote citizen science and nature observation as a way to describe, analyse and preserve biodiversity.

In 2015, more than 160 research groups and companies worldwide registered to at least one task of the lab. Of course, as in any evaluation campaign, only a small fraction of this raw audience did cross the finish line by submitting runs (actually 15 of them). Still, this shows the high attractiveness of the proposed data sets and challenges as well as the potential emergence of a wide community interested in life media analysis.

2   Task1: PlantCLEF

2.1   Context

Image-based plant identification methods are one of the most promising solution to bridge the botanical taxonomic gap, as illustrated by the proliferation of research work on the topic [27], [10], [33], [42], [28], [3] as well as the emergence of dedicated mobile applications such as LeafSnap [34] or Pl@ntNet [30]. Beyond the raw identification performance achievable by state-of-the-art computer vision algorithms, the visual search approach actually offers much more efficient and interactive ways of browsing large floras than standard field guides or online web catalogs. The first noticeable progress in this way was achieved by the US consortium at the origin of LeafSnap[7]. This popular iPhone application allows a fair identification of 227 common American plant species by simply shooting a cut leaf on a uniform background (see [34] for more details). A step beyond was achieved recently by the Pl@ntNet project [30] which released a cross-platform application (iPhone [21], android[8] and web [9]) allowing (i) to query the system with pictures of plants in their natural environment and (ii) to contribute to

---

[7] http://leafsnap.com/
[8] https://play.google.com/store/apps/details?id=org.plantnet
[9] http://identify.plantnet-project.org/

the dataset thanks to a collaborative data validation workflow involving Tela Botanica[10] (i.e. the largest botanical social network in Europe).

As promising as these applications are, their performances are however still far from the requirements of a real-world participatory ecological surveillance scenario. Allowing the mass of citizens to produce accurate plant observations requires to equip them with much more accurate identification tools. Measuring and boosting the performances of content-based identification tools is therefore crucial. This was precisely the goal of the ImageCLEF[11] plant identification task organized since 2011 in the context of the worldwide evaluation forum CLEF[12]. In 2011, 2012, 2013 and 2014 respectively 8, 10, 12 and 10 international research groups crossed the finish line of this large collaborative evaluation by benchmarking their images-based plant identification systems (see [22], [23], [31] and [32] for more details). The evaluation data set was enriched each year with the new contributions and progressively diversified with other input feeds (annotation and cleaning of older data, contributions made through Pl@ntNet mobile applications). The plant task of LifeCLEF 2015 is directly in the continuity of this effort. The main novelties compared to the previous year are the following: (i) the doubling of the number of species, i.e. 1000 species instead of 500, (ii) the possibility to use external training data in order to foster the use of transfer learning methods (at the condition that the experiment is entirely re-producible).

2.2   Dataset

The PlantCLEF 2015 dataset is composed of 113,205 pictures belonging to 41,794 observations of 1000 species of trees, herbs and ferns living in Western European regions. This data was collected by 8,960 distinct contributors of the Tela Botanica social network in the context of the Pl@ntNet project [30]. Each picture belongs to one and only one of the 7 types of views reported in the meta-data (entire plant, fruit, leaf, flower, stem, branch, leaf scan) and is associated with a single plant observation identifier allowing to link it with the other pictures of the same individual plant (observed the same day by the same person). It is noticeable that most image-based identification methods and evaluation data proposed in the past were based on leaf images (e.g. in [34],[4],[10]) whereas leaves are far from being the only discriminating visual key between species but, due to their shape and size, they have the advantage to be easily observed, captured and described. More diverse parts of the plants however have to be considered for accurate identification. As an example, the 6 species depicted in Figure 1 share the same French common name of *"laurier"* even though they belong to different taxonomic groups (4 families, 6 genera). The main reason is that these shrubs, often used in hedges, share leaves with more or less the same-sized elliptic shape. Identifying a *laurel* can be very difficult for a novice by just observing leaves, while it is indisputably easier with flowers.

---

[10] http://www.tela-botanica.org/
[11] http://www.imageclef.org/
[12] http://www.clef-initiative.eu/

Fig. 1. 6 plant species sharing the same common name for laurel in French, belonging to distinct species.

Another originality of the PlantCLEF dataset is that its social nature makes it closer to the conditions of a real-world identification scenario: (i) images of the same species are coming from distinct plants living in distinct areas, (ii) pictures are taken by different users that might not use the same protocol to acquire the images, and (iii) pictures are taken at different periods in the year. Each image of the dataset is associated with contextual meta-data (author, date, locality name, plant id) and social data (user ratings on image quality, collaboratively validated taxon names, vernacular names) provided in a structured XML file. The GPS geo-localization and the device settings are available only for some of the images.

Figure 2 gives some examples of pictures with decreasing average users ratings for the different types of views. Note that the users of the specialized social network creating these ratings (Tela Botanica) are explicitly asked to rate the images according to their plant identification ability and their accordance to the pre-defined acquisition protocol for each view type. This is not an aesthetic or general interest judgement as in most social image sharing sites.

2.3   Task Description

The task was evaluated as a plant species retrieval task based on multi-image plant observations queries. The goal is to retrieve the correct plant species among the top results of a ranked list of species returned by the evaluated system. Contrary to previous plant identification benchmarks, queries are not defined as single images but as *plant observations*, meaning a set of one to several images depicting the same individual plant, observed by the same person, the same day. Each image of a query observation is associated with a single view type (entire plant, branch, leaf, fruit, flower, stem or leaf scan) and with contextual meta-data (data, location, author). Semi-supervised and interactive approaches were allowed but as a variant of the task and therefore evaluated independently from the fully automatic methods. None of the participants, however, used such approaches in the 2015 campaign.

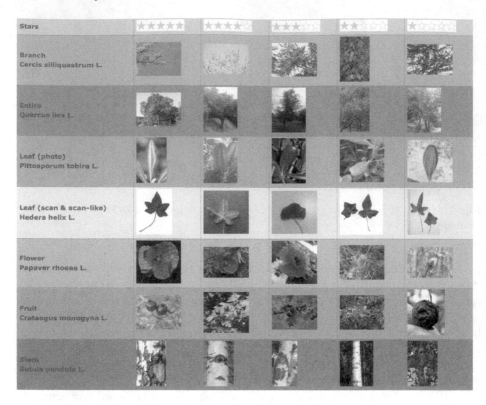

Fig. 2. Examples of PlantCLEF pictures with decreasing averaged users ratings for the different types of views.

In practice, each candidate system was evaluated through the submission of a *run*, i.e. a file containing the set of ranked lists of species (each list corresponding to one query observation and being sorted according to the confidence score of the system in the suggested species). The metric used to evaluate the submitted runs is an extension of the mean reciprocal rank [56] classically used in information retrieval. The difference is that it is based on a two-stage averaging rather than a flat averaging such as:

$$S = \frac{1}{U} \sum_{u=1}^{U} \frac{1}{P_u} \sum_{p=1}^{P_u} \frac{1}{r_{u,p}} \tag{1}$$

where U is the number of users (within the test set), P_u the number of individual plants observed by the u-th user (within the test set), $r_{u,p}$ is the rank of the correct species within the ranked list of species returned by the evaluated system (for the p-th observation of the u-th user). Note that if the correct species does not appear in the returned list, its rank $r_{u,p}$ is considered as infinite. Overall, the proposed metric allows compensating the long-tail distribution of the data. As any social network, few people actually produce huge quantities of data whereas a vast majority of users (the long tail) produce much less data. If, for instance, only one person did collect an important percentage of the images, the classical mean reciprocal rank over a random set of queries will be strongly influenced by the images of that user to the detriment of the users who only contributed with few pictures. This is a problem for several reasons: (i) the persons who produce the more data are usually the most expert ones but not the most representative of the potential users of the automatic identification tools, (ii) the large number of the images they produce makes the classification of their observations easier because they tend to follow the same protocol for all their observations (same device, same position of the plant in the images, etc.), (iii) the images they produce are also usually of better quality so that their classification is even easier.

2.4 Participants and Results

123 research groups worldwide registered to LifeCLEF plant challenge 2015 and downloaded the dataset. Among this large raw audience, 7 research groups succeeded in submitting runs (from 1 to 4 depending on the participant). Details of the participants and the methods used in the runs are synthesised in the overview working note of the task [26] and further developed in the individual working notes of the participants for those who submitted one (EcoUAN [46], Inria ZENITH [11], Mica [36], QUTRV [19], Sabanci [41], SNUMED [13]). We here only report the official scores of the 18 collected runs and discuss the main outcomes of the task.

Figure 3 therefore shows the identification score S obtained by each run submitted to the challenge. It is noticeable that the top-9 runs which performed the best were based on the GoogLeNet [52] convolutional neural network which clearly confirmed the supremacy of deep learning approaches over hand-crafted features as well as the benefit of training deeper architecture thanks to the improved utilization of the computing resources inside the network. The score's deviations between these 9 runs are however still interesting (actually 10 points of MAP between the worst and the best one). A first source of improvement was the fusion strategy allowing to combine the classification results at the image level into classification scores at the observation level. In this regard, the best performing algorithm was a SoftMax function [6] as shown by the performance of QUT RV Run 2 compared to INRIA ZENITH run1 based on max pooling, or SNUMED INFO run1 based on a Borda count, or QUT RV run1 based on a sum pooling. The other source of improvement, which allowed the SNUMED group to get the best results, was to use a bootstrap aggregating (bagging) strategy [7] to improve the stability and the accuracy of the GoogLeNet Convolutional Neural Network. In SNUMED INFO Run 3 and SNUMED INFO Run 4, they actually randomly partitioned the PlantCLEF training set into five-fold so as to train 5 complementary CNN classifiers. Bagging is a well known strategy for reducing variance and avoiding overfitting, in particular in the case of decision trees, but it is interesting to see that it is also very effective in the case on deep learning.

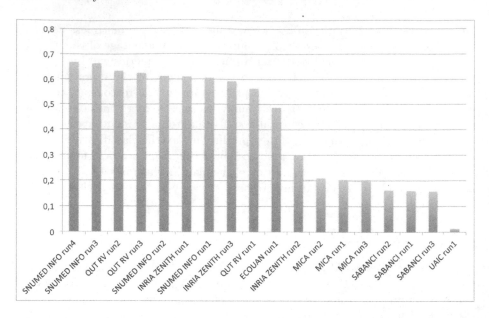

Fig. 3. Results of LifeCLEF 2015 Plant Identification challenge.

The second best approach that did not rely on deep learning (i.e. INRIA ZENITH run 2) was based on the Fisher Vector model [44] on top of a variety of hand-crafted visual features. It is important to note that this method did not not make use of any additional training data other than the one provided in the benchmark (contrary to the CNN's that were all previously trained on the large-scale ImageNet dataset). Within the previous PlantCLEF challenge in 2014 [32], in which using external training data was not allowed, the Fisher Vector approach was performing the best, even compared to CNN's. But still, the huge performance gap confirms that learning visual features through deep learning is much more effective than sticking on hand-crafted visual features. Interestingly, the third run of the INRIA ZENITH team was based on a fusion of the fisher vector run and the GoogLeNet one which allows assessing in which measure the two approaches are complementary or not. The results show that the performance of the merged run was not better than the GoogLeNet alone. This indicates that the hand-crafted visual features encoded in the fisher vectors did not bring sufficient additional information to be captured by the fusion model (based on Bayesian inference).

A last interesting outcome that can be derived from the raw results of the task is the relative low performance achieved by the runs of the SABANCI research group which were actually based on the recent PCANet method [12]. PCANet is a very simple deep learning network which comprises only basic data processing components, i.e. cascaded principal component analysis (PCA), binary hashing, and block-wise histograms. The learned visual features are claimed by the authors to be on par with the state of the art features, either prefixed, highly hand-crafted or carefully learned (by DNNs). The results of our challenge do not confirm this assertion. All the runs of SABANCI did notably have lower performances than the hand-crafted visual features used by MICA runs or INRIA ZENITH Run 2, and much lower performances than the features learned by all other deep learning methods. This conclusion should however be mitigated by the fact that the PCANet of SABANCI was only trained on PlantCLEF data and on a large-scale external data such as ImageNet. Complementary experiments in this way should therefore be conducted to really conclude on the competitiveness of this simple deep learning technique.

Further analysis of the raw results are provided in the overview working note of the task [26], in particular a study of the contribution of the different plant organs.

3   Task2: BirdCLEF

3.1   Context

The bird and the plant identification tasks share similar usage scenarios. The general public as well as professionals like park rangers, ecology consultants, and of course, the ornithologists themselves might actually be users of an automated bird identifying system, typically in the context of wider initiatives related to ecological surveillance or biodiversity conservation. Using audio records rather than bird pictures is justified by current practices [9],[54],[53],[8]. Birds are actually not easy to photograph as they are most of the time hidden, perched high in a tree or frightened by human presence, and they can fly very quickly, whereas audio calls and songs have proved to be easier to collect and very discriminant.

Only three noticeable previous initiatives on bird species identification based on their songs or calls in the context of worldwide evaluation took place, in 2013. The first one was the ICML4B bird challenge joint to the International Conference on Machine Learning in Atlanta, June 2013. It was initiated by the SABIOD MASTODONS CNRS group[13], the University of Toulon and the National Natural History Museum of Paris [20]. It included 35 species, and 76 participants submitted their 400 runs on the Kaggle interface. The second challenge was conducted by F. Brigs at MLSP 2013 workshop, with 15 species, and 79 participants in August 2013. The third challenge, and biggest in 2013, was organised by University of Toulon, SABIOD and Biotope, with 80 species from the Provence, France. More than thirty teams participated, reaching 92% of average AUC. The description of the ICML4B best systems are given in the on-line book [2], including for some of them references to some useful scripts.

In collaboration with the organizers of these previous challenges, BirdCLEF 2014 & 2015 challenges went one step further by (i) significantly increasing the species number by an order of magnitude, (ii) working on real-world social data built from thousands of recordists, and (iii) moving to a more usage-driven and

---

[13] http://sabiod.org

system-oriented benchmark by allowing the use of meta-data and defining information retrieval oriented metrics. Overall, the task is much more difficult than previous benchmarks because of the higher confusion risk between the classes, the higher background noise and the higher diversity in the acquisition conditions (devices, recordists uses, contexts diversity, etc.). It therefore produces substantially lower scores and offer a better progression margin towards building real-world generalist identification tools.

3.2   Dataset

The training and test data of the challenge consists of audio recordings collected by Xeno-canto (XC)[14]. Xeno-canto is a web-based community of bird sound recordists worldwide with about 2400 active contributors that have already collected more than 240,000 recordings of about 9350 species (numbers for june 2015). Nearly 1000 (in fact 999) species were used in the BirdCLEF dataset, representing the 999 species with the highest number of recordings in october 2014 (14 or more) from the combined area of Brazil, French Guiana, Surinam, Guyana, Venezuela and Colombia, totalling 33,203 recordings produced by thousands of users. This dataset also contains the entire dataset from the 2014 BirdCLEF challenge [25], which contained about 14,000 recordings from 501 species.

To avoid any bias in the evaluation related to the used audio devices, each audio file has been normalized to a constant bandwidth of 44.1 kHz and coded over 16 bits in wav mono format (the right channel is selected by default). The conversion from the original Xeno-canto data set was done using ffmpeg, sox and matlab scripts. The optimized 16 Mel Filter Cepstrum Coefficients for bird identification (according to an extended benchmark [15]) have been computed with their first and second temporal derivatives on the whole set. They were used in the best systems run in ICML4B and NIPS4B challenges.

All audio records are associated with various meta-data including the species of the most active singing bird, the species of the other birds audible in the background, the type of sound (call, song, alarm, flight, etc.), the date and location of the observations (from which rich statistics on species distribution can be derived), some textual comments of the authors, multilingual common names and collaborative quality ratings. All of them were produced collaboratively by Xeno-canto community.

3.3   Task Description

Participants were asked to determine the species of the most active singing birds in each query file. The background noise can be used as any other meta-data, but it was forbidden to correlate the test set of the challenge with the original annotated Xeno-canto data base (or with any external content as many of them are circulating on the web). More precisely and similarly to the plant task, the whole BirdCLEF dataset was split in two parts, one for training (and/or

---

[14] http://www.xeno-canto.org/

indexing) and one for testing. The test set was built by randomly choosing 1/3 of the observations of each species whereas the remaining observations were kept in the reference training set. Recordings of the same species done by the same person the same day are considered as being part of the same observation and cannot be split across the test and training set. The XML files containing the meta-data of the *query* recordings were purged so as to erase the taxon name (the ground truth), the vernacular name (common name of the bird) and the collaborative quality ratings (that would not be available at query stage in a real-world mobile application). Meta-data of the recordings in the training set were kept unaltered.

The groups participating to the task were asked to produce up to 4 runs containing a ranked list of the most probable species for each query records of the test set. Each species was associated with a normalized score in the range [0; 1] reflecting the likelihood that this species is singing in the sample. The primary metric used to compare the runs was the Mean Average Precision averaged across all queries.

3.4 Participants and Results

137 research groups worldwide registered for the bird challenge and downloaded the data but only 6 of them finally submitted runs notably because the scale of the data prevent many groups to complete a full experiment. Details on the participants and the methods used in the runs are synthesised in the overview working note of the task [24] and further developed in the individual working notes of the participants (Golem [38], Inria [29], MARF [39], MNB TSA [35], QMUL [51]). We here only report the official scores of the 17 collected runs and discuss the main outcomes of the task. Figure 4 therefore displays the two distinct measured mean Average Precision (MAP) for each run, the first one (MAP 1) considering only the foreground species of each test recording and the other (MAP 2) considering additionally the species listed in the *Background species* field of the metadata.

The main outcome of the evaluation was that the use of matching-based scores as high-dimensional features to be classified by supervised classifiers (as done by MNB TSA and INRIA ZENITH) provides the best results, with a MAP value up to 0.454 for the fourth run of the MNB TSA group. These approaches notably outperform the unsupervised feature learning framework of the QMUL group as well as the baseline method of the Golem group. The matching of all the audio recordings however remains a very time-consuming process that had to be carefully designed in order to process a large-scale dataset such as the one deployed within the challenge. The MNB TSA group notably reduced as much as possible the number of audio segments to be matched thanks to an effective audio pre-processing and segmentation framework. They also restricted the extraction of these segments to the files having the best quality according to the user ratings and that do not have background species. On the other side, the INRIA ZENITH group did not use any segmentation but attempted to speed-up the matching though the use of a hash-based approximate k-nearest neighbors

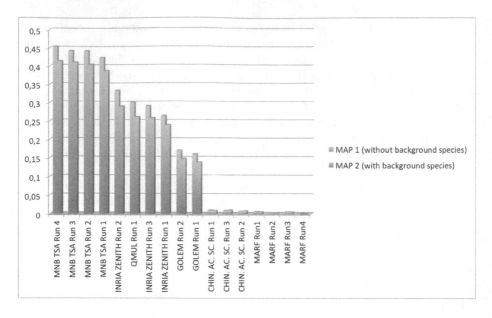

Fig. 4. Official scores of the LifeCLEF Bird Identification Task. MAP 2 is the Mean Average Precision averaged across all queries taking into account the background species (while MAP 1 is considering only the foreground species).

search scheme (on top of MFCC features). The better performance of the MNB TSA runs shows that cleaning the audio segments vocabulary before applying the matching is clearly beneficial. But using a scalable knn-based matching as the one of the INRIA ZENITH runs could be a complementary way to speed up the matching phase.

It is interesting to notice that the first run of the MNB TSA group is roughly the same method than the one they used within the BirdCLEF challenge of the previous year [25] and which achieved the best results (with a MAP1 equals to 0.511 vs. 0.424 this year). This shows that the impact of the increasing difficulty of the challenge (with twice the number of species) is far from negligible. The performance loss is notably not compensated by the bagging extension of the method which resulted in a MAP1 equals to 0.454 for MNB TSA run 4.

As a final comment on this evaluation study, it is worth noting that none of the participants attempted to evaluate deep learning approaches such as using deep convolutional neural networks (CNN) that have been recently shown to achieve excellent classification performance on both image and audio contents. The most likely reason is that the use of external training data was not allowed. It was consequently not possible to employ transfer learning mechanisms such as specializing a CNN previously trained on a large generalist training set. Without using such strategy, the provided training data might be insufficiently large to train the millions of parameters of the deep networks.

4   Task3: FishCLEF

4.1   Context

The goal of the fish identification task is to identify fish occurrences in video segments. The typical usage scenario of automated underwater video analysis tools is to support marine biologists in studying thoroughly the marine ecosystem and fish biodiversity. Also, scuba divers, marine stakeholders and other marine practitioners may benefit greatly from this kind of tools. Recently, underwater video and imaging systems, able to continuously record the underwater environment, have gained a lot of interest as opposed to the traditional techniques used for studying fish populations, such as casting nets or human manned photography. Indeed, they do not affect fish behavior and may provide large amounts of visual data at the same time. However, manual analysis as performed by human operators is largely impractical, and requires automated methods. Nevertheless, the development of automatic video analysis tools is challenging because of the complexities of underwater video recordings in terms of the variability of scenarios and factors that may degrade the video quality such as water clarity and/or depth.

Despite some preliminary work, mainly carried out in controlled environments (e.g., labs, cages, etc.) [40],[50],[16], the most important step in the automated visual analysis has been done in the EU-funded Fish4Knowledge (F4K)[15] project, where computer vision methods were developed to extract information about fish density and richness from videos taken by underwater cameras installed at coral reefs in Taiwan [48],[48]. Since the Fish4Knowledge project, many researchers have directed their attention towards underwater video analysis [45],[47], including some recent initiatives by the National Oceanographic and Atmospheric Administration (NOAA) [49] and the fish identification task at LifeCLEF 2014 [14]. Although there are recent advances in the underwater computer vision field, the problem is still open and needs several (joint) efforts to devise robust methods able to provide reliable measures on fish populations.

4.2   Dataset

Training and test data of the fish task consists of several underwater video sequences collected by NCHC in Taiwan and used in the Fish4Knowledge project.

The training set is built up of 20 manually annotated videos, a list of 15 fish species and for each species, a set of sample images to support learning of fish appearance models. Each video is manually labelled and agreed by two expert annotators and the ground truth consists of a set of bounding boxes (one for each instance of the given fish in the species list) together with the fish species. In total, the training dataset contains more than 9000 annotations (bounding boxes with species) and more than 20000 sample images (see Fig. 5). The training set is unbalanced in the number of instances of fish species: for

---

[15] www.fish4knowledge.eu

instance, it contains 3165 instances of *Dascyllus Reticulate* and only 72 instances of *Zebrasoma Scopas*. This has been done so as to not favour nonparametric methods over model-based methods. For each considered fish species, its fishbase. org link is also provided. In order to make the identification process independent from tracking, temporal information has not be exploited. This means that the annotators only labelled fish for which the species was clearly identifiable, i.e., if at time t the species of fish A was not clear, it was not labelled, no matter if the same fish instance was observed at time $t - 1$.

Fish Species ID	Fish Species Name	Occurences in the GT
1	Abudefduf Vaigiensis	132
2	Acanthurus Nigrofuscus	294
3	Amphiprion Clarkii	363
4	Chaetodon Lunulatus	1217
5	Chaetodon Speculum	138
6	Chaetodon Trifascialis	335
7	Chromis Chrysura	275
8	Dascyllus Aruanus	894
9	Dascyllus Reticulatus	3165
10	Hemigymnus Melapterus	242
11	Myripristis Kuntee	214
12	Neoglyphidodon Nigroris	85
13	Pempheris Vanicolensis	999
14	Plectrogly-Phidodon Dickii	737
15	Zebrasoma Scopas	72

Fig. 5. Fish species occurrences in the training set.

The test set contains 73 underwater videos and an overview, in terms of fish species occurrences, is shown in Fig 6. For some fish species, there were no occurrences in the test set. Also some video segments contain no fish. This has been done to test the method's capability to reject false positives.

4.3   Task Description

The main goal of the video-based fish identification task is to count automatically fish per species in video segments (e.g., video X contains $N1$ instances of fish of species 1, ..., N_n instances of fish species N). However, participants were also asked to identify fish bounding boxes. The ground truth for each video (provided as an XML file) contains information on fish species and location as shown in Fig. 7.

The participants were asked to provide up to three runs. Each run had to contain all the videos included in the set and for each video the frame where the fish was detected together with the bounding box, and species name (only the most confident species) for each detected fish.

Fish Species ID	Fish Species Name	Occurrences in the GT
1	Abudefduf vaigiensis	93
2	Acanthurus nigrofuscus	129
3	Amphiprion clarkii	517
4	Chaetodon lunulatus	1876
5	Chaetodon speculum	0
6	Chaetodon trifascialis	1317
7	Chromis chrysura	24
8	Dascyllus aruanus	1985
9	Dascyllus reticulatus	5016
10	Hemigymnus melapterus	0
11	Myripristis kuntee	118
12	Neoglyphidodon nigroris	1531
13	Pempheris vanicolensis	0
14	Plectrogly-phidodon dickii	700
15	Zebrasoma scopas	187

Fig. 6. Fish species occurrences in the test set.

```xml
<?xml version="1.0" encoding="utf-8"?>
<video id="0b21f0579d247c855e05405d3ed805c1#201205251240" location="NPP3" camera="4">
   <frame id="0">
      <object fish_species="Dascyllus Aruanus" h="68" w="87" x="322" y="233"/>
   </frame>
   <frame id="1">
      <object fish_species="Dascyllus Aruanus" h="68" w="87" x="319" y="230"/>
   </frame>
   <frame id="2">
      <object fish_species="Dascyllus Aruanus" h="68" w="87" x="342" y="231"/>
   </frame>
   <frame id="391">
      <object fish_species="Plectrogly-Phidodon Dickii" h="50" w="35" x="271" y="336"/>
      <object fish_species="Plectrogly-Phidodon Dickii" h="41" w="29" x="339" y="375"/>
   </frame>
</video>
```

Fig. 7. An example of XML ground truth file. It contains information on fish species as well as bounding box coordinates.

As metrics, we used the "**counting score (CS)**" and the "**normalized counting score (NCS)**", defined as:

$$CS = e^{-\frac{d}{N_{gt}}} \tag{2}$$

with d being the difference between the number of occurrences in the run (per species) and, N_{gt}, the number of occurrences in the ground truth. To define NCS we needed to compute precision (Pr) as

$$Pr = \frac{TP}{TP + FP} \tag{3}$$

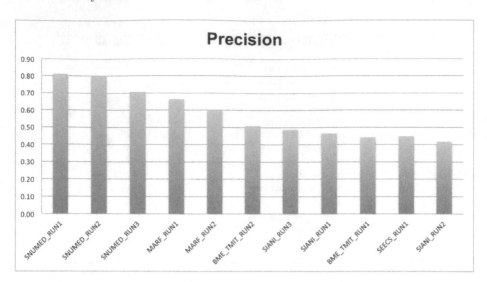

Fig. 8. Official precision scores of the LifeCLEF 2015 -Fish Identification Task.

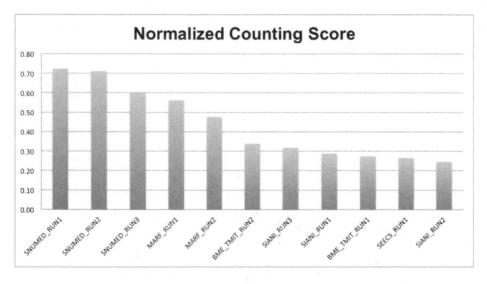

Fig. 9. Official normalized counting scores of the LifeCLEF 2015 -Fish Identification Task.

with TP and FP being, respectively, the true positive and the false positive. As detection was considered a true positive if the intersection over union score of its bounding box and the ground truth was over 0.5 and the fish species was correctly identified. Finally, the normalised counting score (NCS) is computed as:

$$NCS = CS \times Pr \tag{4}$$

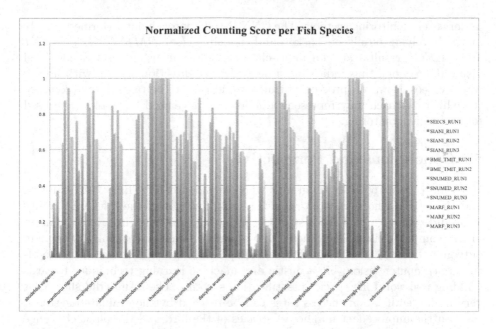

Fig. 10. Official normalized counting scores per species of the LifeCLEF 2015 -Fish Identification Task.

4.4   Participants and Results

89 research groups registered for the fish challenge while only five of them finally submitted runs. This, however, is a notable increase with respect to the first FishCLEF edition in 2014. Thorough details on the employed methods for video-based fish identification can be found in the task overview working note [14] as well as in the participants' working notes. The official scores achieved by the five teams (overall, 12 submitted runs) are given in the following. More specifically, figure 8 and 9 show, respectively, average (per video and species) precision and normalized counting score for all the 12 runs.

As with the Plant task, the best evaluated system was the one by the SNUMED INFO research group based on the GoogLeNet convolutional neural network [52] for classifying fish instances. Potential fish instances were previously segmented from the video through a stationary foreground detection using background subtraction and a selective search strategy [55]. Producing the final output counts was finally achieved by grouping the temporally connected video segments classified by the CNN. Thanks to this framework, the monitoring performance of the 15 considered species is on average very effective, with a normalized counting score of about 80% for the best run SNUMED_RUN1. As illustrated in Figure 10, showing the scores by species, the strength of the GoogLeNet approach is notably to provide good results for all species whereas most other methods fail on some of them. Scaling this experiment to more species is, however, required to validate the applicability of the approach in real-life underwater monitoring systems. The CNN-based approach outperformed greatly methods relying purely on background modelling (see BME_TMIT, $SIANI$ and $SEECS$ results) and on multi-class classification using a set of low-level visual descriptors, thus indicating a new effective direction to deal with underwater videos. However, processing times would need to be taken into account to see which approach may represent a good accuracy-speed trade-off to be used for real-time monitoring.

5   Conclusions and Perspectives

With more than 160 research groups who downloaded LifeCLEF 2015 datasets and 15 of them who submitted runs, the second edition of the LifeCLEF evaluation did confirm a high interest of the proposed challenges in several communities (computer vision, multimedia, bio-accoustic, machine learning). The main outcome of this collaborative effort is a snapshot of the performance of state-of-the-art computer vision, bio-acoustic and machine learning techniques towards building real-world life species identification systems. The results did show that very high identification success rates can be reached by the evaluated systems, even on the unprecedent number of species of the bird and the plant challenge (actually 1000 species). The most noticeable progress came from the deployment of deep Convolutional Neural Networks which definitely confirmed their ability to learn effective content specific features by transferring knowledge from generalist training sets. In this perspective, collecting and building appropriate training data continues being one of the most central problem and we believe it is essential to continue the LifeCLEF effort in the next years if we would like to use such tools for automatically monitoring real-world ecosystems.

References

1. MAED 2012: Proceedings of the 1st ACM International Workshop on Multimedia Analysis for Ecological Data. ACM, New York (2012). 433127
2. Proc. of the first workshop on Machine Learning for Bioacoustics (2013)
3. Aptoula, E., Yanikoglu, B.: Morphological features for leaf based plant recognition. In: Proc. IEEE Int. Conf. Image Process., Melbourne, Australia, p. 7 (2013)
4. Backes, A.R., Casanova, D., Bruno, O.M.: Plant leaf identification based on volumetric fractal dimension. International Journal of Pattern Recognition and Artificial Intelligence 23(6), 1145–1160 (2009)
5. Hilton-Taylor, C., Baillie, J.E.M., Stuart, S.: 2004 iucn red list of threatened species: a global species assessment. IUCN, Gland, Switzerland and Cambridge, UK (2004)
6. Bishop, C.M., et al.: Pattern recognition and machine learning, vol. 4. Springer New York (2006)
7. Breiman, L.: Bagging predictors. Machine Learning 24(2), 123–140 (1996)
8. Briggs, F., Lakshminarayanan, B., Neal, L., Fern, X.Z., Raich, R., Hadley, S.J., Hadley, A.S., Betts, M.G.: Acoustic classification of multiple simultaneous bird species: A multi-instance multi-label approach. The Journal of the Acoustical Society of America 131, 4640 (2012)

9. Cai, J., Ee, D., Pham, B., Roe, P., Zhang, J.: Sensor network for the monitoring of ecosystem: bird species recognition. In: 3rd International Conference on Intelligent Sensors, Sensor Networks and Information, ISSNIP 2007, pp. 293–298, December 2007

10. Cerutti, G., Tougne, L., Vacavant, A., Coquin, D.: A parametric active polygon for leaf segmentation and shape estimation. In: Bebis, G., Boyle, R., Parvin, B., Koracin, D., Wang, S., Kyungnam, K., Benes, B., Moreland, K., Borst, C., Di Verdi, S., Yi-Jen, C., Ming, J. (eds.) ISVC 2011, Part I. LNCS, vol. 6938, pp. 202–213. Springer, Heidelberg (2011)

11. Champ, J., Lorieul, T., Servajean, M., Joly, A.: A comparative study of fine-grained classification methods in the context of the lifeclef plant identification challenge 2015. In: Working Notes of CLEF 2015 Conference (2015)

12. Chan, T.-H., Jia, K., Gao, S., Lu, J., Zeng, Z., Ma, Y.: Pcanet: a simple deep learning baseline for image classification? arXiv preprint arXiv:1404.3606 (2014)

13. Choi, S.: Plant identification with deep convolutional neural network: Snumedinfo at lifeclef plant identification task 2015. In: Working Notes of CLEF 2015 Conference (2015)

14. Concetto, S., Palazzo, S., Fisher, B., Boom, B.: Lifeclef fish identification task 2014. In: CLEF Working Notes 2015 (2015)

15. Dufour, O., Artieres, T., Glotin, H., Giraudet, P.: Clusterized mel filter cepstral coefficients and support vector machines for bird song idenfication (2013)

16. Evans, F.: Detecting fish in underwater video using the em algorithm. In: Proceedings of the 2003 International Conference on Image Processing, ICIP 2003, vol. 3, pp. III-1029-32 vol. 2, September 2003

17. Farnsworth, E.J., Chu, M., Kress, W.J., Neill, A.K., Best, J.H., Pickering, J., Stevenson, R.D., Courtney, G.W., VanDyk, J.K., Ellison, A.M.: Next-generation field guides. BioScience 63(11), 891–899 (2013)

18. K. J. Gaston and M. A. O'Neill. Automated species identification: why not? 359(1444), 655–667 (2004)

19. Ge, Z., Mccool, C., Corke, P.: Content specific feature learning for fine-grained plant classification. In: Working Notes of CLEF 2015 Conference (2015)

20. Glotin, H., Sueur, J.: Overview of the first international challenge on bird classification (2013)

21. Goëau, H., Bonnet, P., Joly, A., Bakić, V., Barbe, J., Yahiaoui, I., Selmi, S., Carré, J., Barthélémy, D., Boujemaa, N., et al.: Pl@ ntnet mobile app. In: Proceedings of the 21st ACM International Conference on Multimedia, pp. 423–424. ACM (2013)

22. Goëau, H., Bonnet, P., Joly, A., Boujemaa, N., Barthélémy, D., Molino, J.-F., Birnbaum, P., Mouysset, E., Picard, M.: The ImageCLEF 2011 plant images classification task. In: CLEF Working Notes (2011)

23. Goëau, H., Bonnet, P., Joly, A., Yahiaoui, I., Barthelemy, D., Boujemaa, N., Molino, J.-F.: The imageclef 2012 plant identification task. In: CLEF Working Notes (2012)

24. Goëau, H., Glotin, H., Vellinga, W.-P., Planque, R., Rauber, A., Joly, A.: Lifeclef bird identification task 2015. In: CLEF Working Notes 2015 (2015)

25. Goëau, H., Glotin, H., Vellinga, W.-P., Rauber, A.: Lifeclef bird identification task 2014. In: CLEF Working Notes 2014 (2014)

26. Goëau, H., Joly, A., Bonnet, P.: Lifeclef plant identification task 2015. In: CLEF Working Notes 2015 (2015)

27. Goëau, H., Joly, A., Selmi, S., Bonnet, P., Mouysset, E., Joyeux, L., Molino, J.-F., Birnbaum, P., Bathelemy, D., Boujemaa, N.: Visual-based plant species identification from crowdsourced data. In: ACM Conference on Multimedia, pp. 813–814 (2011)
28. Hazra, A., Deb, K., Kundu, S., Hazra, P., et al.: Shape oriented feature selection for tomato plant identification. International Journal of Computer Applications Technology and Research 2(4), 449–454 (2013)
29. Joly, A., Champ, J., Buisson, O.: Shared nearest neighbors match kernel for bird songs identification - lifeclef 2015 challenge. In: Working Notes of CLEF 2015 Conference (2015)
30. Joly, A., Goëau, H., Bonnet, P., Bakić, V., Barbe, J., Selmi, S., Yahiaoui, I., Carré, J., Mouysset, E., Molino, J.-F., et al.: Interactive plant identification based on social image data. Ecological Informatics 23, 22–34 (2014)
31. Joly, A., Goëau, H., Bonnet, P., Bakic, V., Molino, J.-F., Barthélémy, D., Boujemaa, N.: The imageclef plant identification task 2013. In: International Workshop on Multimedia Analysis for Ecological Data, Barcelone, Espagne, October 2013
32. Joly, A., Müller, H., Goëau, H., Glotin, H., Spampinato, C., Rauber, A., Bonnet, P., Vellinga, W.-P., Fisher, B.: Lifeclef 2014: multimedia life species identification challenges
33. Kebapci, H., Yanikoglu, B., Unal, G.: Plant image retrieval using color, shape and texture features. The Computer Journal 54(9), 1475–1490 (2011)
34. Kumar, N., Belhumeur, P.N., Biswas, A., Jacobs, D.W., Kress, W.J., Lopez, I.C., Soares, J.V.B.: Leafsnap: a computer vision system for automatic plant species identification. In: Fitzgibbon, A., Lazebnik, S., Perona, P., Sato, Y., Schmid, C. (eds.) ECCV 2012, Part II. LNCS, vol. 7573, pp. 502–516. Springer, Heidelberg (2012)
35. Lasseck, M.: Improved automatic bird identification through decision tree based feature selection and bagging. In: Working Notes of CLEF 2015 Conference (2015)
36. Le, T.-L., Dng, D.N., Vu, H., Nguyen, T.-N.: Mica at lifeclef 2015: multi-organ plant identification. In: Working Notes of CLEF 2015 Conference (2015)
37. Lee, D.-J., Schoenberger, R.B., Shiozawa, D., Xu, X., Zhan, P.: Contour matching for a fish recognition and migration-monitoring system. In: Optics East, pp. 37–48. International Society for Optics and Photonics (2004)
38. Meza, I., Espino-Gamez, A., Solano, F., Villarreal, E.
39. Mokhov, S.A.: A marfclef approach to lifeclef 2015 tasks. In: Working Notes of CLEF 2015 Conference (2015)
40. Morais, E., Campos, M., Padua, F., Carceroni, R.: Particle filter-based predictive tracking for robust fish counting. In: 18th Brazilian Symposium on Computer Graphics and Image Processing, SIBGRAPI 2005. pp. 367–374, October 2005
41. E. A. O. M. Mostafa Mehdipour Ghazi, Yanikoglu, B., Ozdemir, M.C.: Sabanci-okan system in lifeclef 2015 plant identification competition. In: Working Notes of CLEF 2015 Conference (2015)
42. Mouine, S., Yahiaoui, I., Verroust-Blondet, A.: Advanced shape context for plant species identification using leaf image retrieval. In: ACM International Conference on Multimedia Retrieval, pp. 49:1–49:8 (2012)
43. Müller, H., Clough, P., Deselaers, T., Caputo, B. (eds.): ImageCLEF – Experimental Evaluation in Visual Information Retrieval. The Springer International Series on Information Retrieval, vol. 32. Springer, Heidelberg (2010)
44. Perronnin, F., Sánchez, J., Mensink, T.: Improving the fisher kernel for large-scale image classification. In: Daniilidis, K., Maragos, P., Paragios, N. (eds.) ECCV 2010, Part IV. LNCS, vol. 6314, pp. 143–156. Springer, Heidelberg (2010)

45. Ravanbakhsh, M., Shortis, M.R., Shafait, F., Mian, A., Harvey, E.S., Seager, J.W.: Automated fish detection in underwater images using shape-based level sets. The Photogrammetric Record **30**(149), 46–62 (2015)

46. Reyes, A.K., Caicedo, J.C., Camargo, J.E.: Fine-tuning deep convolutional networks for plant recognition. In: Working Notes of CLEF 2015 Conference (2015)

47. Rodriguez, A., Rico-Diaz, A.J., Rabuñal, J.R., Puertas, J., Pena, L.: Fish monitoring and sizing using computer vision. In: Vicente, J.M.F., Álvarez-Sánchez, J.R., López, F.P., Toledo-Moreo, F.J., Adeli, H. (eds.) Bioinspired Computation in Artificial Systems. LNCS, vol. 9108, pp. 419–428. Springer, Heidelberg (2015)

48. Shortis, M.R., Ravanbaksh, M., Shaifat, F., Harvey, E.S., Mian, A., Seager, J.W., Culverhouse, P.F., Cline, D.E., Edgington, D.R.: A review of techniques for the identification and measurement of fish in underwater stereo-video image sequences. In: SPIE Optical Metrology 2013, pp. 87910G–87910G. International Society for Optics and Photonics (2013)

49. Sigler, M., DeMaster, D., Boveng, P., Cameron, M., Moreland, E., Williams, K., Towler, R.: Advances in methods for marine mammal and fish stock assessments: Thermal imagery and camtrawl. Marine Technology Society Journal **49**(2), 99–106, 2015-03-01T00:00:00

50. Spampinato, C., Chen-Burger, Y.-H., Nadarajan, G., Fisher, R.B.: Detecting, tracking and counting fish in low quality unconstrained underwater videos. In: VISAPP (2), pp. 514–519. Citeseer (2008)

51. Stowell, D.: Birdclef 2015 submission: unsupervised feature learning from audio. In: Working Notes of CLEF 2015 Conference (2015)

52. Szegedy, C., Liu, W., Jia, Y., Sermanet, P., Reed, S., Anguelov, D., Erhan, D., Vanhoucke, V., Rabinovich, A.: Going deeper with convolutions. arXiv preprint arXiv:1409.4842 (2014)

53. Towsey, M., Planitz, B., Nantes, A., Wimmer, J., Roe, P.: A toolbox for animal call recognition. Bioacoustics **21**(2), 107–125 (2012)

54. Trifa, V.M., Kirschel, A.N., Taylor, C.E., Vallejo, E.E.: Automated species recognition of antbirds in a mexican rainforest using hidden markov models. The Journal of the Acoustical Society of America **123**, 2424 (2008)

55. Uijlings, J.R., van de Sande, K.E., Gevers, T., Smeulders, A.W.: Selective search for object recognition. International Journal of Computer Vision **104**(2), 154–171 (2013)

56. Voorhees, E.M., et al.: The trec-8 question answering track report. In: TREC, vol. 99, pp. 77–82 (1999)

57. Wheeler, Q.D., Raven, P.H., Wilson, E.O.: Taxonomy: Impediment or expedient? Science **303**(5656), 285 (2004)

Overview of the Living Labs for Information Retrieval Evaluation (LL4IR) CLEF Lab 2015

Anne Schuth[1]([✉]), Krisztian Balog[2], and Liadh Kelly[3]

[1] University of Amsterdam, Amsterdam, The Netherlands
anne.schuth@uva.nl
[2] University of Stavanger, Stavanger, Norway
krisztian.balog@uis.no
[3] ADAPT Centre, Trinity College, Dublin, Ireland
liadh.kelly@tcd.ie

Abstract. In this paper we report on the first Living Labs for Information Retrieval Evaluation (LL4IR) CLEF Lab. Our main goal with the lab is to provide a benchmarking platform for researchers to evaluate their ranking systems in a live setting with real users in their natural task environments. For this first edition of the challenge we focused on two specific use-cases: product search and web search. Ranking systems submitted by participants were experimentally compared using interleaved comparisons to the production system from the corresponding use-case. In this paper we describe how these experiments were performed, what the resulting outcomes are, and conclude with some lessons learned.

Keywords: Information retrieval evaluation · Living labs · Product search · Web search

1 Introduction

Evaluation is a central aspect of information retrieval (IR) research. In the past few years, a new evaluation paradigm known as living labs has been proposed, where the idea is to perform experiments in situ, with real users doing real tasks using real-world applications [12]. The need for more realistic evaluation, involving real users, was reiterated at recent IR workshops [11,1,3]. This type of evaluation, however, has so far been available only to (large) industrial research labs [23,15]. Our main goal with the Living Labs for IR Evaluation (LL4IR) CLEF Lab is to provide a benchmarking platform for researchers to evaluate their ranking systems in a live setting with real users in their natural task environments, similar to the living labs for IR instances proposed in [2,13]. The lab acts as a proxy between commercial organizations (live environments) and lab participants (experimental systems), facilitates data exchange, and makes comparison between the participating systems. The first edition of the lab focuses on two use-cases and one specific notion of what a living lab is (with a view to

© Springer International Publishing Switzerland 2015
J. Mothe et al. (Eds.): CLEF 2015, LNCS 9283, pp. 484–496, 2015.
DOI: 10.1007/978-3-319-24027-5_47

expanding to other use-cases and other interpretations of living labs in subsequent years). Use-cases for the first lab are: product search (on an e-commerce site) and web search (through a commercial web search engine).

The LL4IR CLEF Lab contributes to the understanding of online evaluation as well as an understanding of the generalization of retrieval techniques across different use-cases. Most importantly, it promotes IR evaluation that is more realistic, by allowing researches to have access to historical search and usage data and by enabling them to validate their ideas in live settings with real users. This initiative is a first of its kind for IR. CLEF Newsreel [6][1] is a similar initiative, but for a different problem domain: news recommendation. By contrast we are focusing on the very different space of information retrieval, which contains its own unique use-cases, approaches, challenges, and researchers. Major differences between the labs include the presence of a query and, importantly, that our API lifts the real time processing requirements on the part of participants, lowering the participation threshold significantly.

This paper reports on the results obtained during the official CLEF evaluation round that took place between May 1 and May 15, 2015. The positive feedback and growing interest from participants motivated us to organize a subsequent second evaluation round. As this second round is still ongoing at the time of writing, we provide more detailed results and analysis, including those of the second round, in an extended version of this overview paper [21].

In the next section we describe our API architecture and evaluation methodology. We then describe each of the two use-cases of the first edition of the lab in turn in Sections 2 and 4, and provide details and analysis of the submissions received. Finally, in Section 5, we conclude the paper.

2   Living Labs for IR

For the LL4IR CLEF Lab, evaluation is done primarily through an API. We first describe the workings of our API, followed by the setup of our evaluation divided into training and test phases. We then describe how we compute evaluation metrics using interleaved comparisons. Finally, we describe how we aggregate interleaving outcomes.

2.1   Living Labs API

For each of the use-cases, described in Sections 2 and 4, challenge participants take part in a live evaluation process. For this they use a set of frequent queries as training queries and a separate set of frequent queries as test queries. Candidate documents are provided for each query and historical information associated with the queries. When participants produce their rankings for each query, they upload these to the commercial provider use-case through the provided LL4IR API. The commercial provider then interleaves a given participant's ranked list

---
[1] http://www.clef-newsreel.org/

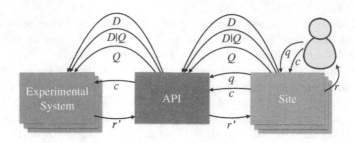

Fig. 1. Schematic representation of interaction with the LL4IR API, taken from [4].

with their own ranking, and presents the user with the interleaved result list. Participants take turns in having their ranked list interleaved with the commercial providers ranked list. This process of interleaving a single experimental system with the production system at a time is orchestrated by the LL4IR API, such that each participant gets about the same number of impressions. The actions performed by the commercial providers' system users are then made available to the challenge participant (whose ranking was shown) through the API; i.e., the interleaved ranking, resulting clicks, and (aggregated) interleaving outcomes.

Figure 1 shows the Living Labs architecture and how the participant interacts with the use-cases through the LL4IR provided API. As can be seen, frequent queries (Q) with candidate documents for each query $(D|Q)$ are sent from a site through the API to the experimental systems of participants. These systems upload their rankings (r') for each query to the API. When a user of the site issues one of these frequent queries (q), then the site requests a ranking (r') from the API and presents it interleaved with r to the users. Any interactions (c) of the user with this ranking are sent back to the API. Experimental systems can then obtain these interactions (c) from the API and update their ranking (r') if they wish. We provided participants with example code and guidelines to ease the adaptation to our setup.[2] Our evaluation methodology, including reasons for focusing on frequent queries, is described in more detail in [4].

Training Phase. During the training phase, participants are free to update their rankings using feedback information. This feedback information is made available to them as soon as it arrives at the API. Their rankings can be updated at any time and as often as desired. Both click feedback and aggregated outcomes are made available directly and are updated constantly.

Test Phase. In the test phase, challenge participants receive another set of frequent queries as test queries. Again, the associated historical click information as well as candidate results for these queries are made available. After downloading the test queries, participants could only upload their rankings until the test phase started or only once after it started. These rankings are then treated

---

[2] http://doc.living-labs.net/en/latest/guide-participant.html

in the same way as training queries. That is, they are interleaved with the commercial providers' rankings for several weeks. As for the training phase, in the test phase each challenge participant is given an approximately equal number of impressions. A major difference is that for the test queries, the click feedback is not made available. Aggregated outcomes are provided only after the test phase ends.

2.2 Evaluation Metric

The overall evaluation of challenge participants is based on the final system performance, and additionally on how the systems performed at each query issue. The primary metric used is aggregated interleaving outcomes, and in particular we are interested in the fractions of winning system comparisons. There are two reasons for using interleaved comparisons. Firstly, interleaved comparisons ensure that at least half the ranking shown to users comes from the production system. This reduces the risk of showing bad rankings to users. Secondly, interleaved comparisons were shown to be two orders of magnitude more sensitive than other ways of performing online evaluation such as A/B testing [23,7]. This means that far fewer query impressions are required to make informed decisions on which ranker is better.

Interleaved Comparisons. Many interleaving approaches have been proposed over the past few years (for instance [10,19,9,18,24,22]). By fare the most frequently used interleaving algorithm to date is Team Draft Interleaving (TDI) [19] which is also what is used in our living labs. Given a user query q, TDI produces an interleaved result list as follows. The algorithm takes as input two rankings. One ranking from the participant $r' = (a_1, a_2, \ldots)$ and one from the production system $r = (b_1, b_2, \ldots)$. The goal is to produce a combined, interleaved ranking $L = (a_1, b_2, \ldots)$. This is done analogue to how sports teams may be constructed in a friendly sports match. The two team captains take turns picking players. They can pick available documents (players) from the top of the rankings r' and r, these top ranked document are deemed to be the best documents. Documents can only be picked once (even if they are listed in both r and r'). And the order in which the documents are picked determines ranking L. In each round, the team captains flip a coin to determine who goes first. The algorithm remembers which team each documents belong to. If a document receives a click from a user, credit is assigned to the team the document belongs to. The team (participant or production system) with most credit wins the interleaved comparison. This process is repeated for each query. For more details see the original paper describing TDI by [19] and a large scale comparison of interleaving methods by [7].

Aggregated Outcomes. We report the following aggregated interleaving metrics, where *Outcome* serves as the primary metric for comparing participants rankings. These aggregations are constantly updated for training queries. For the test phase they are only computed after the phase is over.

#Wins is defined as the number of wins of the participant against the production system, where a *win* is defined as the experimental system having more clicks on results assigned to it by TDI than clicks on results assigned to the production system;

#Losses is defined as the number of losses against the production system;

#Ties is defined as the number of ties with the production system;

#Impressions is the total number of times when rankings (for any of the test queries) from the participant have been displayed to users of the production system; and

Outcome is defined as the fraction of wins, so $\#Wins/(\#Wins+\#Losses)$.

An *Outcome* value below the *expected outcome* (typically 0.5) means that the participant system performed worse than the production system (i.e., overall it has more losses than wins). Significance of outcomes is tested using a two-sided binomial test which uses the expected outcome, p-values are reported.

Note that using these metrics, we are in theory only able to say something about the relationship between the participant's system and the production system. However, [19] show experimentally that it is not unreasonable to assume transitivity. This allows us to also draw conclusions about how systems compare to each other. Ideally, instead of interleaving, we would have used multileaved comparison methods [24,22] which would directly give a ranking over rankers by comparing them all at once for each query.

3   Use-Case 1: Product Search

3.1   Task and Data

The *product search* use-case is provided by REGIO Játék (REGIO Toy in English), the largest (offline) toy retailer in Hungary with currently over 30 stores. Their webshop[3] is among the top 5 in Hungary. The company is working on strengthening their online presence; improving the quality of product search in their online store is directed towards this larger goal. An excerpt from the search result page is shown in Figure 2.

As described in Section 2, we distinguish between training and test phases. Queries are sampled from the set of frequent queries; these queries are very short (1.18 terms on average) and have a stable search volume. For each query, a set of candidate products (approximately 50 products per query) and historical click information (click-through rate) is made available. For each product a structured representation is supplied (see below). The task then is to rank the provided candidate set.

Product Descriptions. For each product a fielded document representation is provided, containing the attributes shown in Table 1. The amount of text available for individual products is limited (and is in Hungarian), but there are structural and semantic annotations, including:

---

[3] http://www.regiojatek.hu/

Fig. 2. Screenshot of REGIO, our product search use-case.

- Organization of products into a two-level deep topical categorization system;
- Toy characters associated with the product (Barbie, Spiderman, Hello Kitty, etc.);
- Brand (Beados, LEGO, Simba, etc.);
- Gender and age recommendations (for many products);
- Queries (and their distribution) that led to the given product.

Table 1. Fielded document representation of products in the product search use-case.

Field	Description
age_max	Recommended maximum age (may be empty, i.e., 0)
age_min	Recommended minimum age (may be empty, i.e., 0)
arrived	When the product arrived (first became available); only for products that arrived after 2014-08-28
available	Indicates if the product is currently available (1) or not (0)
bonus_price	Provided only if the product is on sale; this is the new (sales) price
brand	Name of the brand (may be empty)
category	Name of the (leaf-level) product category
category_id	Unique ID of the (leaf-level) product category
characters	List of toy characters associated with the product (may be empty)
description	Full textual description of the product (may be empty)
main_category	Name of the main (top-level) product category
main_category_id	Unique ID of the main (top-level) product category
gender	Gender recommendation. (0: for both girls and boys (or unclassified); 1: for boys; 2: for girls)
photos	List of photos about the product
price	Normal price
product_name	Name of the product
queries	Distribution of (frequent) queries that led to this product (may be empty)
short_description	Short textual description of the product (may be empty)

Candidate Products. The candidate set, to be ranked, contains all products that were available in the (recent) past. This comprises all products that are considered by the site's production search engine (in practice: all products that contain any of the query terms in any of their textual fields). One particular challenge for this use-case is that the inventory (as well as the prices) are constantly changing; however, for challenge participants, a single ranking will be used throughout the entire test period of the challenge, without the possibility of updating it. The candidate set therefore also includes products that may not be available at the moment (but might become available again in the future). Participating systems were strongly encouraged to consider all products from the provided candidate set. Those that were unavailable at a given point in time were not displayed to users of the REGIO online store. Further, it may happen (and as we show in [21] it indeed does happen) during the test period that new products arrive; experimental systems are not able to include these in their ranking (this is the same for all participants), while the production system might return them. This can potentially affect the number of wins against the production system (to the advantage of the production system), but it will not affect the comparison across experimental systems.

3.2   Submissions and Results

Two organizations submitted a total of four runs. In addition, a simple baseline provided by the challenge organizers is also included for reference. Table 2 presents the results.

Approaches. The organizers' baseline (BASELINE in Table 2) ranks products based on historical click-through rate. Only products that were clicked for the given query are returned; their attributes are not considered. In case historical clicks are unavailable (this happened for a single query R-q97), (all) candidate products are returned in an arbitrary order (in practice, in the same order as they were received from the API via the `doclist` request).

The University of Stavanger [8] employed a fielded document retrieval approach based on language modeling techniques. Specifically, building upon the Probabilistic Retrieval Model for Semistructured Data by [14], they experimented with three different methods (UIS-*) for estimating term-field mapping probabilities. Their results show that term-specific field mapping in general is beneficial, but their attempt at estimating field importance based on historical click-through information has met with limited success.

Team GESIS [20] also used a fielded document representation. They used Solr for ranking products and incorporated historical click-through rates, if available, as a weighting factor.

Dealing with Inventory Changes. As mentioned in Section 3.1, the product inventory is subject to changes. Not all products that were part of the candidate set were available at all times. If all products were available, the expected probability of winning an interleaved comparison (assuming a randomly clicking user) would be 0.5. However, on average, 44% of the products were actually unavailable. These products were only ever present in the participants ranking (the site's ranking never considered them). And, only *after* interleaving were these products removed from the resulting interleaved list. We note that this is undesired behavior, as they should have been filtered out *before* interleaving. The necessary adjustments have been made to the implementation for the next round of the challenge. As for interpreting the current results, this means that the chances for products from the participants ranking to be clicked were reduced. This in turn reduces the expected probability to win to:

$$P(participant > site) = (1 - 0.44) \cdot 0.5 = 0.28.$$

Consequently, if a participant's system wins more than in 28% of the impressions, then this is more than expected. And thus the participant's system can be said to be better than the site's system if the outcome is (significantly) more than 28%.

492   A. Schuth et al.

Table 2. Results for the product search use-case. The expected outcome under a randomly clicking user is 0.28. P-values are computed using a binomial test.

Submission	Outcome	#Wins	#Losses	#Ties	#Impressions	p-value
BASELINE	0.4691	91	103	467	661	< 0.01
UIS-MIRA [8]	0.3413	71	137	517	725	0.053
UIS-JERN [8]	0.3277	58	119	488	665	0.156
UIS-UIS [8]	0.2827	54	137	508	699	0.936
GESIS [20]	0.2685	40	109	374	523	0.785

Results. We find that at least 3 submissions are likely to have improved upon the production system's ranking. Somewhat surprisingly, the simple baseline performed by far the best, with an outcome of 0.4691. This was also the only system that significantly outperformed the production system. The best performing participant run is UIS-MIRA, with an outcome of 0.3413. A more in-depth analysis of the results is provided in the extended lab overview paper [21].

4   Use-Case 2: Web Search

4.1   Task and Data

The *web search* use-case is provided by Seznam,[4] a very large web search engine in the Czech Republic. See Figure 3 for a screenshot of the user interface.

Seznam serves almost half the country's search traffic and as such has very high site traffic. Queries are the typical web search queries, and thus are a mixed bag of transactional, navigational and transactional [5]. In contrast to the product search use-case, apart from the scale and the query types, Seznam does not make raw document and query content available, rather features computed for documents and queries. This is much like any learning to rank dataset, such as Letor [17]. Queries and documents are only identified by a unique identifier and for each query, the candidate documents are represented with sparse feature vectors. Seznam provided a total of 557 features. These features were not described in any way. The challenge with this use-case then is a learning to rank challenge [16].

As described in Section 2, the web search use-case also consists of a training and test phase. For the test phase, there were 97 queries, for the training phase 100 queries were provided. On average, for each query there were about 179 candidate documents. In total, there were 35,322 documents.

4.2   Results

The web search use-case attracted 6 teams that submitted runs for the training queries. However, none of them submitted runs for the test queries. Therefore,

---
[4] http://search.seznam.cz/

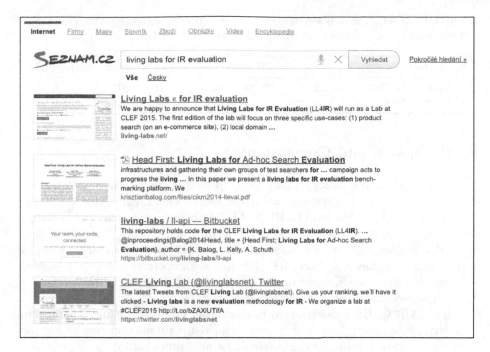

Fig. 3. Screenshot of Seznam, our web search use-case.

we can only report on two baseline systems, provided by the challenge organizers. Baseline 1, titled EXPLOITATIVE BASELINE in Table 3, uses the original Seznam ranking and was therefore expected to produce an outcome of 0.5.[5] Baseline 2, titled UNIFORM BASELINE in Table 3, assigned uniform weights to each feature and ranked by the weighted sum of feature values. This baseline was expected to not perform well.

Over the past months, there have been over 440K impressions on Seznam through our Living Labs API. On average this amounts to 2,247 impressions for each query. Approximately 6% of all impressions were used for the testing period. As can be seen in Table 3, the EXPLOITATIVE BASELINE outperformed the production system. An outcome (outcome measure described in Section 2) of 0.5527 was achieved, with 3,030 wins and 2,452 losses against the production system, and 19,055 ties with it. As expected, the UNIFORM BASELINE lost many more comparisons than it won. Both outcomes were statistically significant according to a binomial test. Again, we refer to the extended lab overview paper [21] for full details.

---

[5] If use-cases uploaded their candidate documents in the order that represented their own ranking, then this was available to participants. We plan to change this in the future.

Table 3. Results for the web search use-case. The expected outcome under a randomly clicking user is 0.5. P-values were computed using a binomial test.

Submission	Outcome	#Wins	#Losses	#Ties	#Impressions	p-value
EXPLOITATIVE BASELINE	0.5527	3030	2452	19055	24537	< 0.01
UNIFORM BASELINE	0.2161	430	1560	1346	3336	< 0.01

5 Discussion and Conclusions

The living labs methodology offers great potential to evaluate information retrieval systems in live settings with real users. The Living Labs for Information Retrieval Evaluation (LL4IR) CLEF Lab represents the first attempt at a shared community benchmarking platform in this space. The first edition of LL4IR focused on two use-cases, product search and web search, using a commercial e-commerce website, REGIO, and a commercial web search engine, Seznam. A major contribution of the lab is the development of the necessary API infrastructure, which is made publicly available.

The LL4IR CLEF Lab attracted interest from dozens of teams. There were 12 active participants, but only 2 teams ended up submitting results for the official evaluation (excluding the baseline systems, provided by the organizers). We found that, while many researchers expressed and showed their interest in the lab, our setup with an API, instead of a static test collection, was a hurdle for many. We plan to ease this process of adapting to this new evaluation paradigm by providing even more examples and by organizing tutorials where we demonstrate working with our API.

Overall, we regard our effort successful in showing the feasibility and potential of this form of evaluation. For both use-cases, there was an experimental system that outperformed the corresponding production system significantly. It is somewhat unfortunate that in both cases that experimental system was a baseline approach provided by the challenge organizers, nevertheless, it demonstrates the potential benefits to use-case owners as well. One particular issue that surfaced and needs addressing for the product search use-case is the frequent changes in inventory. This appears to be more severe than we first anticipated and represents some challenges, both technical and methodological.

The API infrastructure developed for the LL4IR CLEF Lab offers the potential to host ongoing IR evaluations in a live setting. As such, it is planned that these "challenges" will continue on an ongoing basis post-CLEF, with an expanding number of use-cases as well as refinements to the existing use-cases.[6] In fact, a second round of our evaluation challenge is already underway at the time of writing, with some modifications to the initial setup. A more detailed analysis of the use-cases, including results from the second evaluation round, and a discussion of ideas and opportunities for future development is provided in the extended lab overview paper [21].

---

[6] See http://living-labs.net/ for details.

Acknowledgments. We would like to acknowledge the support of (in alphabetical order): the CLEF Initiative; the Dutch national program COMMIT; the REGIO Játék online toy store; and the Seznam commercial search engine. We would also like to thank the participants for their submissions and interest in the lab.

References

1. Allan, J., Croft, B., Moffat, A., Sanderson, M.: Frontiers, challenges, and opportunities for information retrieval: Report from SWIRL 2012 the second strategic workshop on information retrieval in lorne. SIGIR Forum **46**(1), 2–32 (2012)
2. Azzopardi, L., Balog, K.: Towards a living lab for information retrieval research and development. A proposal for a living lab for product search tasks. In: Forner, P., Gonzalo, J., Kekäläinen, J., Lalmas, M., de Rijke, M. (eds.) CLEF 2011. LNCS, vol. 6941, pp. 26–37. Springer, Heidelberg (2011)
3. Balog, K., Elsweiler, D., Kanoulas, E., Kelly, L., Smucker, M.D.: Report on the CIKM workshop on living labs for information retrieval evaluation. SIGIR Forum **48**(1), 21–28 (2014)
4. Balog, K., Kelly, L., Schuth, A.: Head first: living labs for ad-hoc search evaluation. In: CIKM 2014 (2014)
5. Broder, A.: A taxonomy of web search. SIGIR Forum **36**(2), 3–10 (2002)
6. Brodt, T., Hopfgartner, F.: Shedding light on a living lab: the CLEF NEWSREEL open recommendation platform. In: IIiX 2014 (2014)
7. Chapelle, O., Joachims, T., Radlinski, F., Yue, Y.: Large-scale validation and analysis of interleaved search evaluation. ACM Transactions on Information Systems (TOIS) **30**, 1–41 (2012)
8. Ghirmatsion, A.B., Balog, K.: Probabilistic field mapping for product search. In: CLEF 2015 Online Working Notes (2015)
9. Hofmann, K., Whiteson, S., de Rijke, M.: A probabilistic method for inferring preferences from clicks. In: CIKM 2011, p. 249 (2011)
10. Joachims, T.: Evaluating retrieval performance using clickthrough data. In: Franke, J., Nakhaeizadeh, G., Renz, I. (eds.) Text Mining, pp. 79–96. Physica/Springer (2003)
11. Kamps, J., Geva, S., Peters, C., Sakai, T., Trotman, A., Voorhees, E.: Report on the SIGIR 2009 workshop on the future of IR evaluation. SIGIR Forum **43**(2), 13–23 (2009)
12. Kelly, D., Dumais, S., Pedersen, J.O.: Evaluation challenges and directions for information-seeking support systems. Computer **42**(3), 60–66 (2009)
13. Kelly, L., Bunbury, P., Jones, G.J.F.: Evaluating personal information retrieval. In: Baeza-Yates, R., de Vries, A.P., Zaragoza, H., Cambazoglu, B.B., Murdock, V., Lempel, R., Silvestri, F. (eds.) ECIR 2012. LNCS, vol. 7224, pp. 544–547. Springer, Heidelberg (2012)
14. Kim, J., Xue, X., Croft, W.B.: A probabilistic retrieval model for semistructured data. In: Boughanem, M., Berrut, C., Mothe, J., Soule-Dupuy, C. (eds.) ECIR 2009. LNCS, vol. 5478, pp. 228–239. Springer, Heidelberg (2009)
15. Kohavi, R.: Online controlled experiments. In: SIGIR 2013 (2013)
16. Liu, T.-Y.: Learning to rank for information retrieval. Found. Trends Inf. Retr. **3**(3), 225–331 (2009)
17. Liu, T.-Y., Xu, J., Qin, T., Xiong, W., Li, H.: LETOR: benchmark dataset for research on learning to rank for information retrieval. In: LR4IR 2007 (2007)

18. Radlinski, F., Craswell, N.: Optimized interleaving for online retrieval evaluation. In: WSDM 2013 (2013)
19. Radlinski, F., Kurup, M., Joachims, T.: How does clickthrough data reflect retrieval quality? In: CIKM 2008 (2008)
20. Schaer, P., Tavakolpoursaleh, N.: GESIS at CLEF LL4IR 2015. In: CLEF 2015 Online Working Notes (2015)
21. Schuth, A., Balog, K., Kelly, L.: Extended overview of the living labs for information retrieval evaluation (LL4IR) CLEF lab 2015. In: CLEF 2015 Online Working Notes (2015)
22. Schuth, A., Bruintjes, R.-J., Büttner, F., van Doorn, J., Groenland, C., Oosterhuis, H., Tran, C.-N., Veeling, B., van der Velde, J., Wechsler, R., Woudenberg, D., de Rijke, M.: Probabilistic multileave for online retrieval evaluation. In: SIGIR 2015 (2015)
23. Schuth, A., Hofmann, K., Radlinski, F.: Predicting search satisfaction metrics with interleaved comparisons. In: SIGIR 2015 (2015)
24. Schuth, A., Sietsma, F., Whiteson, S., Lefortier, D., de Rijke, M.: Multileaved comparisons for fast online evaluation. In: CIKM 2014 (2014)

Stream-Based Recommendations:
Online and Offline Evaluation as a Service

Benjamin Kille[1], Andreas Lommatzsch[1], Roberto Turrin[2], András Serény[3],
Martha Larson[4], Torben Brodt[5], Jonas Seiler[5], and Frank Hopfgartner[6](✉)

[1] TU Berlin, Berlin, Germany
{benjamin.kille,andreas.lommatzsch}@dai-labor.de
[2] ContentWise R&D - Moviri, Milan, Italy
roberto.turrin@moviri.com
[3] Gravity R&D, Budapest, Hungary
sereny.andras@gravityrd.com
[4] TU Delft, Delft, The Netherlands
m.a.larson@tudelft.nl
[5] Plista GmbH, Berlin, Germany
{torben.brodt,jonas.seiler}@plista.com
[6] University of Glasgow, Glasgow, UK
frank.hopfgartner@glasgow.ac.uk

Abstract. Providing high-quality news recommendations is a challenging task because the set of potentially relevant news items changes continuously, the relevance of news highly depends on the context, and there are tight time constraints for computing recommendations. The CLEF NewsREEL challenge is a campaign-style evaluation lab allowing participants to evaluate and optimize news recommender algorithms online and offline. In this paper, we discuss the objectives and challenges of the NewsREEL lab. We motivate the metrics used for benchmarking the recommender algorithms and explain the challenge dataset. In addition, we introduce the evaluation framework that we have developed. The framework makes possible the reproducible evaluation of recommender algorithms for stream data, taking into account recommender precision as well as the technical complexity of the recommender algorithms.

Keywords: Recommender systems · News · Evaluation · Living lab · Stream-based recommender

1   Introduction

When surveying research advances in the field of recommender systems, it becomes evident that most research hypotheses are studied under the premise that the existence and the relevance of recommendable items are constant factors that remain the same throughout the whole recommendation task. The reasons underlying these assumptions can be traced to the use by the research community of shared datasets with static content for the purposes of system development

© Springer International Publishing Switzerland 2015
J. Mothe et al. (Eds.): CLEF 2015, LNCS 9283, pp. 497–517, 2015.
DOI: 10.1007/978-3-319-24027-5_48

and evaluation. An example is the well-known MovieLens dataset [12], which is used extensively to benchmark movie recommendations. A multitude of experiments have pointed out that recommendation algorithms, such as collaborative filtering, developed under such a premise can provide good recommendations. However, these techniques are inherently limited by the fact that they cannot easily be applied in more dynamic domains, in which new items continuously emerge and are added to the data corpus, while, at the same time, existing items become less and less relevant [4]. An example where recommendation of dynamic data is required can be found in the news domain where new content is constantly added to the data corpus. CLEF NewsREEL[1] addresses this news recommendation scenario by asking participants to recommend news articles to visitors of various news publisher web portals. These recommendations are then embedded on the same news web page. The news content publishers constantly update their existing news articles, or add new content. Recommendations are required in real-time whenever a visitor accesses a news article on one of these portals. We refer to this constant change of the data corpus as streamed data, and the task of providing recommendations as stream-based recommendations. This news recommendation scenario provides ground to study several research challenges:

1. In contrast to traditional recommender systems working with a static set of users and items, the set of valid users and items is highly dynamic in the news recommendation scenario. New articles must be added to the recommender model; outdated news articles must be demoted in order to ensure that the recommended articles are timely. Thus, one big challenge of the news recommender system is the continuous cold-start problem: New articles potentially more relevant than old articles are only sparsely described by meta-data or collaborative knowledge. The system has not observed sufficiently many interactions to determine these articles' relevance.

2. Noisy user references pose an additional challenge in the analyzed web-based news recommendation scenario. Since users do not need to register explicitly on the news portals, these systems lack consistent referencing. They seek to overcome this issue by tracking users with cookies and JavaScript. Some of the users may apply obfuscating tools (such as Ad-Blocker) leading to noisy user references. The implemented recommender algorithms be aware of the challenge and should apply algorithms providing highly relevant recommendations even if the user tracking is noisy.

3. The user preferences in news highly depend on the domain and on the hour of the day. In the morning, users usually do not have much time. For this reason, at this time, users are interested in the top news from the domains of politics and sports. In the evening users usually spend more time reading and engaging in longer, more detailed news articles from diverse domains. Therefore, news recommender algorithms must consider different aspects of context such as the news domain, the time of the day and the users' devices.

---

[1] http://clef-newsreel.org/

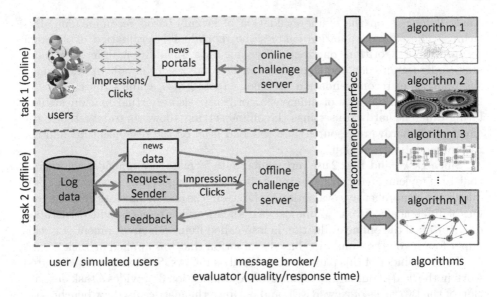

Fig. 1. The figure visualizes the similarities and differences between the online and the offline task. In task 1 (online) the impressions and recommendation requests are initiated by real users. The quality of the recommendations is evaluated based on the fraction of recommendations clicked by the users ("click-through-rate"). Task 2 (offline) simulates users based on the user behavior recorded in the online scenario. The recommender algorithms are similar in the online and the offline evaluation tasks. The recommender API ensures that all recommender algorithms use a similar interface and ensures that new strategies can be integrated in the system.

4. In the online news recommendation scenario, the requests must be answered within a short period of time. The response time constraint is defined as publishers require suggestions to be seamlessly integrated in their web page.

Regarding these challenges, CLEF NewsREEL 2015 aims to promote benchmarking of recommendation techniques for streamed data in the news domain. As depicted in Figure 1 the lab consists of two separate tasks targeting the benchmarking challenges from two different directions:

Task 1 focuses on the online evaluation. The participating teams register with the online system (ORP). Whenever a user visits a news web page assigned to the NewsREEL challenge, a recommendation request is sent to a randomly selected registered team. The team has to provide a list of up to 6 recommendations. The time constraint for completing the recommendation request is 100ms. In addition to the recommendation requests, there are messages describing the creation, removal, or update of news articles. The performance of the recommender algorithms is measure based on the click-through-rate (CTR) recorded in four pre-defined time frames. The scenario can be seen as an example of evaluation-as-a-service [19,13] where a service API is provided rather than a dataset.

Task 2 focuses on the offline evaluation of stream-based recommender algorithms. The offline evaluation enables the reproducible evaluation of different recommender algorithms on exactly the same data. In addition, different parameter configurations for one algorithm can be analyzed in detail. In addition to the analysis of recommendation precision, Task 2 also enables the analysis of the technical complexity of different algorithms. Using virtual machines simulating different hardware settings the offline setting allows us to investigate the effect of the hardware resources and the load level on the response time and the recommendation precision.

Since Task 1 and Task 2 use very similar data formats recommender algorithms that are implemented can be tested in both online and offline evaluation. This allows the comprehensive evaluation of the strengths and weaknesses of the strategies of different algorithms. While last year's lab overview paper provided a detailed description of the online evaluation in a so-called living lab environment [14], this paper focuses on the simulation based evaluation that was applied in Task 2.

The remainder of this paper is structured as follows. Section 2 surveys related work in the field of online and offline evaluation. Section 3 provides a task description of the two tasks of NewsREEL and outlines the metrics used for benchmarking the different recommendation algorithms. Focusing on Task 2, Section 4 introduces the Idomaar benchmarking framework. Section 5 provides an overview of NewsREEL 2015. A discussion and conclusion is provided in Section 6.

2   Related Work

In this section we discuss related evaluation initiatives. In addition we focus on recommender algorithms able to take into account dynamic contexts and evaluations using a living lab approach.

2.1   Benchmarking Using Static Datasets

CLEF NewsREEL is a campaign-style evaluation lab that focuses on benchmarking news recommendation algorithms. Benchmarking has been one of the main driving forces behind the development of innovative advances in the field. In the context of recommender systems evaluation, the release of the first MovieLens dataset[2] in 1998 can be seen as an important milestone. Since then, four different MovieLens datasets have been released. As of June 2015, 7500+ references to "movielens" can be found on Google Scholar, indicating its significance in education, research, and industry. The datasets consist of movie titles, ratings for these movies provided by users of the MovieLens system, and anonymized user identifiers. The ratings are stored as tuples in the form ⟨user, item, rating, timestamp⟩. While MovieLens focuses on movie recommendation, various datasets for other domains (e.g., [10]) have been released by now following a similar data structure.

---

[2] http://movielens.org/

Using these *static* datasets, a typical benchmarking task is to predict withheld ratings. The most important event that triggered research in the field is the Netflix Challenge where participants could win a prize for beating the baseline recommender system of a on-demand video streaming service by providing better predictions. Other benchmarking campaigns are organized as challenges in conjunction with Academic conferences such as the Annual ACM Conference Series on Recommender Systems (e.g., [2,25]), and the European Semantic Web Conference (e.g., [22]), or as Kaggle competition (e.g., [21]).

Apart from providing static datasets and organizing challenges to benchmark recommendation algorithms using these datasets, the research community has been very active in developing software and open source toolkits for the evaluation of static datasets. Examples include Lenskit[3], Mahout[4], and RiVal[5].

2.2   Recommendations in Dynamic Settings

The research efforts that have been presented above have triggered innovation in the field of recommender systems, but the use of static datasets comes with various drawbacks.

Various research exists focusing on the use of non-static datasets, referred to as streamed data that showcase some of these drawbacks. Chen et al. [5] performed experiments on recommending microblog posts. Similar work is presented by Diaz-Aviles et al. [7]. Chen et al. [6] studied various algorithms for real-time bidding of online ads. Garcin et al. [9] and Lommatzsch [20] focus on news recommendation, the latter in the context of the scenario presented by NewsREEL.

All studies deal with additional challenges widely overlooked in a static context. In particular, research based on static databases does not take external factors into account that might influence users' rating behavior. In the context of news, such external factors could be emerging trends and news stories. In the same context, the freshness of items (i.e., news articles) plays an important role that needs to be considered. At the same time, computational complexity is out of focus in most academic research scenarios. Quick computation is of uttermost importance for commercial recommender systems. Differing from search results provided by an information retrieval system, recommendations are provided proactively without any explicit request by the user. Another challenge is the large number of requests and updates that online systems have to deal with.

Offline evaluation using a static dataset conducts an exact comparison between different algorithms and participating teams. However, offline evaluation requires assumptions, such as that past rating or consumption behavior is able to reflect future preferences. The benchmarking community is just starting to make progress in overcoming these limitations. Notable efforts from the Information Retrieval community include the CLEF Living Labs task [1], which uses

---

[3] http://lenskit.org/
[4] http://mahout.apache.org/
[5] http://rival.recommenders.net/

real-world queries and user clicks for evaluation. Also, the TREC Live Question Answering task[6] involves online evaluation, and requires participants to focus on both response time and answer quality.

NewsREEL addresses the limitations of conventional offline evaluation in the area of recommender systems running an online evaluation. It also offers an evaluation setting that attempts to add the advantages of online evaluation, while retaining the benefits of offline evaluation. An overview of the NewsREEL recommendation scenario is provided in the next section.

3   Task Descriptions

As mentioned earlier, NewsREEL 2015 consists of two tasks in which news recommendation algorithms of streamed data can be evaluated in an online, and an offline mode, respectively. The online evaluation platform used in Task 1 enables participants to provide recommendations and observe users' responses. While this scenario has been described in detail by Hopfgartner et al. [14], Section 3.1 provides a brief overview of the underlying system and the evaluation metrics used. Task 2 is based on a recorded dataset providing the ground truth for the simulation-based evaluation. The dataset is presented in Section 3.2.

3.1   Task 1: Benchmark News Recommendations in a Living Lab

Researchers face different challenges depending on whether they work in industry or academia. Industrial researchers can access vast data collections. These collections better reflect actual user behavior due to their dimensionality. Industry requires researchers to quickly provide satisfactory solutions. Conversely, academia allows researchers to spend time on fundamental challenges. Academic research often lacks datasets of sufficiently large size to reflect populations such as internet users. The Open Recommendation Platform (ORP) [3] seeks to bridge this gap by enabling academic researchers to interactively evaluate their algorithms with actual users' feedback.

Participants connect their recommendation service to an open interface. Users visiting a selection of news portals initiate events. ORP randomly selects among all connected recommendation services and issues a request for recommendations. The selected recommendation service returns an ordered list of recommended items. This list must arrive within, at most, 100ms. In case of delayed responses, ORP forwards a pre-computed default list as fall back.

In addition, participants receive notifications. These notifications either signal interactions between visitors and articles or articles being created or updated. ORP provides two types of interactions. Impressions refer to visitors accessing articles. 'Clicks' occur whenever visitors click on recommendations. Participants may use these data to implement their recommendation algorithms. Further, participants may exploit additional information sources to boost their performances.

---

[6] https://sites.google.com/site/trecliveqa2015/

The evaluation focuses on maximizing the visitors click on recommended items. Since the number of requested recommendations limits the number of clicks, ORP uses the ratio between the clicks and the number of requests for measuring the recommendation quality. This quantity is also known as Click-Through-Rate (CTR). A higher CTR indicates a superior ability to suggest relevant items. In real-life settings the CTR is often low ($\approx 1\%$) sufficient number of requests must be taken into account for ensuring the significance of the computed CTR scores.

We observe how users interact with news articles offered by various publishers. Publishers provide news articles with a headline, optionally an image, and a snippet of text. We interpret users clicking on such snippets as positive feedback. This assumption may not hold in all instances. For instance, users may fail to click on articles that match their interest. Similarly, users may misinterpret the title and ultimately find the article irrelevant. Dwell times could offer a more accurate picture of users' preferences. Unfortunately, we cannot measure dwell times reliably. Most web sessions tend to be short and include only few articles. We cannot assure that users actually read the articles. Nonetheless, we expect users not to click on articles whose snippets they deem irrelevant.

The ORP provides four types of data for each participant:

- *Clicks:* Clicks refer to users clicking on an article recommended by the participant. Generally, we assume clicks to reflect positive feedback. The underlying assumption, as stated above, is that users avoid clicking on irrelevant articles.
- *Requests:* Requests refer to how often the participant received a recommendation request. The ORP delegates requests randomly to active, connected recommendation engines. Recommendation engines occasionally struggle to respond under heavy load. For this reason, the ORP temporarily reduces the volume of request under such circumstances. Participants with similar technical conditions should obtain approximately equal numbers of requests.
- *Click-through Rate:* The CTR relates clicks and requests. It represents the ratio of requests which led to a click to the total number of requests. Hypothetically, a recommender could achieve a CTR of 100.0%. Each recommendation would have to be clicked to achieve such a perfect score. Humans have developed a blindness for contents such as advertisements. Frequently, publishers embed recommendations alongside advertisements. For this reason, there is a chance that users fail to notice the recommendations leading to fewer clicks than might have otherwise occurred. Historically, we observe CTR in the range of $0.5 - 5.0\%$.
- *Error Rate:* ORP reports the error rate for each participant. Errors emerge as recommendation engines fail to provide recommendations. The error rate denotes the proportion of such events within all requests. Ideally, a systems would have an error rate of 0.0%.

As a result, we can measure performance with respect to four criteria. First, we can determine the algorithm that received the most clicks. This might favor algorithms receiving a high volume of requests. Participants who lack access to powerful servers may fall short. Second, we can determine the algorithm that handles the largest volume of requests. Operating news recommenders have to handle enormous volumes of requests. This objective can be addressed by further optimizing the algorithms or by adding additional hardware. In the NewsREEL challenge we ought to avoid penalizing participants lacking hardware resources. Third, we can determine the algorithm obtaining highest CTR. The CTR reflects the system's ability to accurately determine users' preferences. As a drawback, we might not grasp how algorithms scale by analyzing CTR. A system might get a high CTR by chance on a small number of requests. Finally, we can determine how stably an algorithm performs in terms of the error rate. Although, a system may respond in time with inadequate suggestions and still obtain a perfect error rate. We chose CTR as decisive criteria. Additionally, we award the participants handling the largest volume of requests.

3.2 Task 2: Benchmark News Recommendations in a Simulated Environment

The NewsREEL challenge provides access to streams of interactions. Still, ORP routes requests to individual recommendation engines. Consequently, recommendation engines serve different groups of users in different contexts. We recorded interaction streams on a set of publishers. The stream-based evaluation issues these streams to different recommendation engines. Each engine faces the identical task. As a result, the stream-based evaluation improves comparability as well as reproducibility.

The dataset used in the offline evaluation has been recorded between July 1st, 2014 and August 31st, 2014. A detailed overview of the general content and structure of the dataset is provided by Kille et al. [15]. The dataset describes three different news portals: One portal providing general as well as local news, the second portal provides sport news; the third portal is a discussion board providing user generated content. In total, the dataset contains approximately 100 million messages. Messages are chronologically ordered. Thereby, participants could reduce the data volume by selecting subsets to explore larger parameter spaces.

We evaluate the quality of news recommendation algorithms by chronologically re-iterating interactions on news portals. Thereby, we simulate the situation which the system had faced while data recording. Unfortunately, we only obtain positive feedback and lack negative feedback. Unless the actual recommender had included the recommended items, we cannot tell how the user would have reacted. Nevertheless, we can obtain meaningful results as Li et al. [18] pointed out.

Table 1. Data set statistics for Task 2.

	item create/update	user-item interactions	sum
July 2014	618,487	53,323,934	53,942,421
August 2014	354,699	48,126,400	48,481,099
sum	973,186	101,450,334	102,423,520

The evaluation of recommender algorithms online in a living lab leads to results that are difficult to reproduce since the set of users and items as well as the user preferences change continuously. This hampers the evaluation and optimization of algorithms due to the fact that different algorithms or different parameter settings cannot be tested in an exactly repeatable procedure. We seek to ensure reproducible results and to make sure that algorithms implemented by different teams are evaluated based on the same ground truth; the NewsREEL challenge also provides a framework for evaluating recommender algorithms offline using a well-defined, static dataset. The basic idea behind the offline evaluation is recording a stream in the online scenario that can be replayed in exactly the same way ensuring that all evaluation runs are based on the same dataset. Since the offline evaluation framework creates a stream that is based on the offline dataset, the adaptation of the recommender algorithms is not required. For the benchmarking of the recommender algorithms offline, we rely on similar metrics to those used in the online evaluation. Since there is no direct user feedback in the offline evaluation, the metrics must be slightly modified.

CTR. Instead of the *Click-Through-Rate* computed based on clicks in the live news portal, a simulated CTR is used that is computed based on a stream of recorded user interactions. In the offline evaluation, we assume that a recommendation is correct if the recommended item is requested by the user up to 5 minutes after the recommendation has been presented. This measure allows us to compute the CTR based on recorded data without requiring additional information. We do not have to adapt the definition of CTR since the offline CTR is still computed as the ratio between the recommended news items explicitly accessed by the user and the total number of computed recommendations. A disadvantage of the offline CTR is that the recorded user behavior is slightly influenced by the originally presented recommendation as well as by the presentation of news in the portal.

Computational Resources. We analyze the amount of computational resources required for providing recommendations. In order to have a controlled computation environment we use virtual machines. This ensures that the number of CPUs and the amount of RAM that can be used by the benchmarked algorithms is similar in all the evaluation runs. The measurement of the required resources is done using the management tools of the virtual machine.

In the NewsREEL offline evaluation we focus the benchmarking of the "computational complexity" in terms of the throughput. We analyze how effectively recommendations for the dataset can be computed based on the resources that are provided. The throughput can be measured by determining the number of recommendation that can be served by the system. In order to reach a maximal throughput, we have to ensure that the recommender algorithms are able to use multiple CPUs and an efficient management and synchronization strategy for concurrent threads is applied.

Response Time. One requirement in the news recommendation scenario is the provision of recommendation within the time limit of 100ms. For this reason, we analyze of response time distribution of the recommender algorithms that are implemented. Based on the idea of a service level agreement we calculate the relative frequency of cases in which the recommender cannot meet the time constraints.

Benchmarking recommender algorithms offline allows NewsREEL participants detailed insights in the characteristics of the implemented algorithms. Using exactly the same stream for comparing different parameter settings or recommender implementations ensures that the algorithms are benchmarked in the same setting. In addition, the offline evaluation supports the debugging of algorithms since the number of messages in the stream can be adapted. Furthermore, load peaks as well as special situation that can only rarely observed in the live evaluation. Even though the results obtained in the offline evaluation may not completely correlate with the online evaluation, the offline evaluation is very useful for understanding and optimizing recommender algorithms with respect to different aspects.

4   The Offline Evaluation Framework

Offline evaluation has been performed using *Idomaar*[7], a recommender system reference framework developed in the settings of the European Project CrowdRec[8] that addresses the evaluation of stream recommender systems. The key properties of Idomaar are:

- **Architecture independent**. The participants can use their preferred environments. Idomaar provides an evaluation solution that is independent of the programming language and platform. The evaluation framework can be controlled by connecting to two given communication interfaces by which data and control messages are sent by the framework.
- **Effortless integration**. The interfaces required to integrate the custom recommendation algorithms make use of open-source, widely-adopted technologies: Apache Spark and Apache Flume. Consequently, the integration can take advantage of popular, ready-to-use clients existing in almost any languages.
- **Consistency and reproducibility**. The evaluation is fair and consistent among all participants as the full process is controlled by the reference framework, which operates independently from the algorithm implementation.
- **Stream management**. Idomaar is designed to manage, in an effective and scalable way, a stream of data (e.g., users, news, events) and recommendation requests.

4.1   Idomaar Architecture

The high-level architecture of Idomaar is sketched in Figure 2 and it is composed of four main components: Data container, Computing environment, Orchestrator, and Evaluator.

---

[7] http://rf.crowdrec.eu/
[8] http://www.crowdrec.eu/

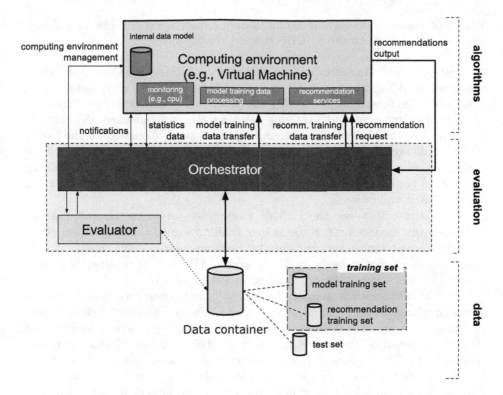

Fig. 2. The figure visualizes the architecture of the Idomaar framework used in the offline evaluation (Task 2).

Data Container. The Data container contains the datasets available for experiments. The data format is composed by entities (e.g., users, news) and relations (e.g., events) represented by 5 tab-separated fields: object type (e.g., user, news, event, etc.), object unique identifier, creation timestamp (e.g., when the user registers with the system, when a news is added to the catalog, when the user reads a news, etc.), a set of JSON-formatted properties (e.g., the user name, the news category, the rating value, etc.), and a set JSON-formatted linked entities (e.g., the user and the news, respectively, subject and object of an event). Further details are described in [23].

Computing Environment. The Computing environment is the environment in which the recommendation algorithms are executed. Typically, for the sake of reproducibility and fair comparison, it is a virtual machine automatically provisioned by the Orchestrator by means of tools such as Vagrant[9] and Puppet[10]. The Computing environment communicates with the Orchestrator to (i) receive

---

[9] https://www.vagrantup.com/
[10] http://www.puppetlabs.com/

stream of data and (ii) serve recommendation requests. Future releases will also provide system statistics (e.g., CPU times, i/o activity).

Orchestrator. The Orchestrator is in charge of initializing the Computing environment, providing training and test data at the right time, requesting recommendations, and eventually collecting the results to compute evaluation metrics. The Orchestrator may send a training dataset to the recommender algorithm in order to allow the algorithm to optimize on the dataset. Actually, for the News-REEL challenge, there is no separate training data in order to keep the offline evaluation very similar to the online evaluation. However, additional training sets are supported by the Orchestrator enabling also traditional static training-, test-set based evaluations.

The Orchestrator uses the Kafka[11] messaging system to transmit data to the computing environment. Kafka is specifically designed to handle linear event sequences, and training and test data for recommender systems consist of such event sequences. Kafka has a relatively simple API and offers superior performance (for which strict delivery guarantees are sacrificed).

The Orchestrator has support for Flume[12], a plugin-based tool to collect and move large amounts of event data from different sources to data stores. In Idomaar, it provides flexibility: Flume has a couple of built-in sources and sinks for common situations (e.g., file-based, HTTP-based, HDFS) and it is straightforward to implement and use new ones if the need arises. Notably, there is a Flume source (and a Flume sink) that reads data from Kafka (and writes data to Kafka), meaning that Flume can serve as an integration layer between Kafka and a range of data sources.

Kafka and Flume are automatically installed on the Orchestrator virtual machine by Vagrant provisioning (using packages from Cloudera). At runtime, the Orchestrator is able to configure and bring up Flume by generating Flume property files and starting Flume agents. For instance, the Orchestrator can instruct Flume to write recommendation results to plain files or HDFS.

Computing environments have the option to receive control messages and recommendation requests from the Orchestrator via ZeroMQ[13] or HTTP, and data via Kafka. In the NewsREEL competition, recommendation engines implement an HTTP server, so Idomaar is used in its pure HTTP-mode. The HTTP interface in Idomaar is implemented as a Flume plugin.

Evaluator. The Evaluator contains the logic to (i) split the dataset according to the evaluation strategy and (ii) compute the quality metrics on the results returned by the recommendation algorithm. As for NewsREEL, the data is a stream of timestamped user events; the Computing environment is flooded with such events that can be used to constantly train the recommendation models. Randomly, some events are selected and, in addition to the new information,

---

[11] http://kafka.apache.org/
[12] https://flume.apache.org/
[13] http://zeromq.org/

the Orchestrator sends a recommendation request for the target user. All news consumed by such user in the upcoming 5 minutes form the groundtruth for such recommendation request. The quality of results is measures in terms of CTR, as described in Section 3.2.

Splitting and evaluations are implemented as Apache Spark scripts, so that they can be easily customized and run in a scalable and distributed environment.

4.2 Idomaar Data Workflow

The data workflow implemented in Idomaar complies with the following three sequential phases: (i) data preparation, (ii) data streaming, and (iii) result evaluation.

Phase 1: Data Preparation. The first phase consists in reading the input data (entities and relations) and preparing them for experimenting with the recommendation algorithms. The Evaluator is used to split the data, creating a training set and ground truth data ("test set"). In the case that the data preparation is already done by explicit markers in the dataset (as it is done in NewsREEL Task 2), this phase can be skipped.

Phase 2: Data Streaming. Initially, once the Computing environment has booted, the recommendation models can be optionally bootstrapped with an initial set of training data. Afterwards, the Orchestrator floods the computing environment with both information messages (e.g., new users, news, or events) and recommendation requests. The second phase terminates when the Computing environment has processed all messages. The output of the Computing environment is stored in an extended version of the Idomaar format, composed by an additional column where the recommendation response for a given recommendation request is saved.

Phase 3: Result Evaluation. The last phase is performed by the Evaluator that compares the results returned by the computing environment with the created ground truth in order to estimate some metrics related to the recommendation quality (i.e., CTR).

In addition, the Orchestrator is seated in a position that makes it possible to measure metrics related to the communication between the Orchestrator (which simulates the final users) and the computing environment (which represents the recommender system), such as the response time.

4.3 Discussion

In this section, we have presented the evaluation framework supporting the efficient, reproducible evaluation of recommender algorithms. Idomaar is a powerful tool allowing users to abstract from concrete hardware or programming languages by setting up virtual machine having exactly defined resources. The evaluation platform allows a high degree of automatization for setting up the runtime environment and for initializing the evaluation components. This ensures the easy reproducibility of evaluation runs and the comparability of results obtained with different recommender algorithms. Idomaar supports the set-based as well as the stream-based evaluation of recommender algorithms.

In NewsREEL Task 2, the steam-based evaluation mode is used. In contrast to most existing evaluation frameworks Idomaar can be used out of the box and, for evaluation, considers not only the recommendation precision but also the resource demand of the algorithms.

5   Evaluation

The NewsREEL challenge 2015 attracted teams from 24 countries to develop and evaluate recommender algorithms. In this section, we provide details about the registered teams and the implemented algorithms. In addition, we explain the provided baseline recommender algorithm. Finally, we report the performance scores for the different algorithms and discuss the evaluation results. A more detailed overview can be found in [16].

5.1   Participation

A total of 42 teams registered for NewsREEL 2015. Of these, 38 teams signed up for both tasks. Figure 3 illustrates the spread of teams around the Globe. Central Europe, Iran, India, and the United States of America engaged most. Network latency may negatively affect the performance in Task 1 of team located far from Europe. Five teams received virtual machines to run their algorithms and alleviate latency issues. In the final evaluation phase of Task 1, we observed 8 actively competing teams. Each team could run several algorithms. Some teams explored a larger segment of algorithms. This led to a total of 19 algorithms competing during the final evaluation round of Task 1.

5.2   The Baseline Algorithm

The NewsREEL challenge provides a baseline algorithm implementing a simple, but powerful recommendation strategy. The strategy recommends users the items most recently requested by other users. The idea behind this strategy is that items currently interesting to users might also be interesting for others. Thereby, the strategy assumes that users are able to determine relevant articles for others.

Implementation of the Baseline Recommender. The most recently requested recommender is implemented based on a ring buffer. Whenever a user requests a new item, the system adds the item to the ring buffer. In order to keep insertion as simple as possible, duplicate entries in the buffer are allowed. If the ring buffer is completely filled, a new newly added item overwrites the oldest entry

Number of participants ■ 1 ■ 2 ■ 3 ■ 4 ■ 5

Fig. 3. The figure shows the participation around the world. Countries colored gray had no participation. Lighter blue colors indicate more participants than darker shades.

in the buffer. Upon receiving a recommendation request, we search for n distinct items starting at the most recently added. The process iterates in reverse order through the buffer until we collected n distinct items. Since the buffer may contain duplicate entries, the size of the ring buffer must be large enough that for all request at least n distinct items can be found. In addition, items may be blacklisted (e.g., because they are already known to the user) and excluded from the result set.

Properties of the Baseline Recommender. The provided baseline recommender has several advantages. Since the recommender only considers the item requested by other users during the last few minutes, the recommendation usually fits well with respect to the time-based context. In addition, the recommendations are biased towards popular items requested by many different users. Since users typically request news items from different fields of interest, the suggestions provided by the least-recently requested recommender are often characterized by a certain level of diversity, which supports recommendation of serendipitous news items.

Recommendation Precision. The baseline recommender has been tested in the online and the offline evaluation. Due to the limited memory used by the algorithm, the recommender quickly adapts to new users and items. The cold-start phase of the algorithm is short; as soon as there are sufficient distinct entities in the ring buffer, the recommender works correctly. Comparing the least-recently requested algorithms with alternative recommender strategies, the baseline

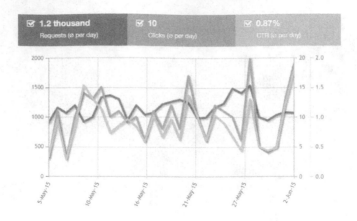

Fig. 4. The plot shows the CTR of the baseline recommender algorithm for the News-REEL's evaluation period (May–June 2015).

recommender behaves similarly to a most-popular recommender with a short "window" used for computing the most popular items.

Figure 4 shows the CTR of the baseline recommender observed during the final evaluation period of NewsREEL 2015. The figure shows that the CTR typically varies between 0.5% and 1.5% reaching an average CTR of 0.87%.

Required Computation Resources. The implementation of baseline recommender uses a ring buffer allocating a fixed amount of memory. This prevents problems with allocating and releasing memory while running the recommender. Concurrent threads accessing the ring buffer can be handled in a simple way allowing dirty read and write operations, since we do not require strong consistency of items contained in the buffer. The avoidance of locks and synchronized blocks simplifies the implementation and ensures that active threads are not blocked due to synchronization purposes. Due to the limited amount of memory required for the ring buffer, the baseline recommender keeps all necessary data in the main memory and does not require hard drive access. The small number of steps for computing recommendations and the simple (but dirty) synchronization strategy leads to a very short response time ensure that the time constraints are reliably fulfilled.

The baseline recommender is a simple, but powerful recommender reaching a CTR of $\approx 0.9\%$ in the online evaluation.

5.3   Evaluated Algorithms

Last year's NewsREEL edition produced a variety of ideas to create recommendation algorithms. We highlight three contributions. Castellanos et al. [11] created a content-based recommender. Their approach relies on a Formal Concept Analysis Framework. They represent articles in a concept space. As users interact with articles, their method derives preferences. The system projects these preferences onto a lattice and determines the closest matches. They report that content-based methods tend to struggle under heavy load. Doychev et al. [8] analyzed strategies with different contextual features. These features include time, keywords, and categories. They show that combining different methods yields performance increases. Finally, Kuchar and Kliegr [17] applied association rule mining techniques to news recommendation. Association rule mining seeks to discover regularities in co-occurring events. For instance, we may observe users frequently reading two particular articles in rapid sequence. Consequently, as we recognize a user reading one of them, we may consider recommending the remaining one. In this year's installment of NewsREEL, participants explored various ideas. The Team "cwi" investigated the potential improvement through considering geographic locations of news readers. Team "artificial intelligence" used time context and device information to build a meta recommender. Based on contextual factors, the system picked the most promising algorithm from a set of existing recommenders. Team "abc" extends the approach of team "artificial intelligence" by considering trends with respect to success of individual recommenders [20]. The remaining participants have not yet revealed their approaches. More details will be added to the working notes overview paper. Apart from Task 1 related approaches, we received some insights concerning Task 2. The team "irs" applied the Akka[14] framework to the task of news recommendation. They paid particular attention toward ensuring response time constraints and handling of request peaks. Akka allows concurrently running processes on multiple machines and CPUs for the purpose of load balancing. Team "7morning" tried to identify characteristic patterns in the data stream. Subsequently, they extrapolated these patterns to accurately predict future interactions between users and news articles.

5.4   Evaluation Results

Task 1 challenged participants to suggest news articles to visitors of publishers. The more visitors engaged with their suggested, the better we deemed their performances. The Open Recommendation Platform (ORP) seeks to balance the volume of requests. Generally, each participating recommendation service ought to receive a similar proportion of requests. Still, this requires all recommendation services to be available at any time. We observed some teams exploring various algorithms. As a result, some algorithms were partly active throughout the evaluation time frame. Consequently, they received fewer requests compared to algorithms running the full time span. Figure 5 related the volume of requests and the number of clicks for each recommendation service. We congratulate the teams "artificial intelligence" (CTR = 1.27%), "abc" (CTR = 1.14%), and "riadi-gdl" (CTR = 0.91%) on their outstanding performance. We ran two baselines varying in available resources. The baselines are "riemannzeta" and "gaussiannoise". We observe that both baselines achieve competitive CTR results.

---

[14] http://akka.io/

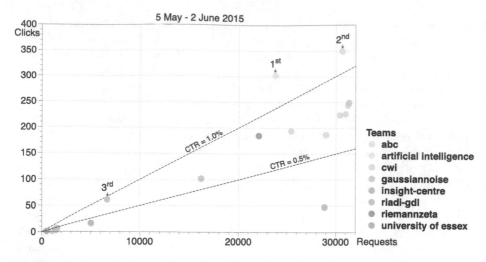

Fig. 5. Results of the final evaluation conducted from May 5 to June 2, 2015. The figure shows the volume of requests on the x-axis, and the number of clicks on the y-axis. Each point refers to the click-through-rate of an individual recommendation service. Colors reflect which team was operating the service. The closer to the top left corner a point is located, the higher the resulting CTR. Dashed lines depict CTR levels of 1.0% and 0.5%. The best performances have labels indicating their place assigned.

5.5   Discussion

The NewsREEL challenge gives participating teams the opportunity for evaluating individual algorithms for recommending news articles. Analyzing the implemented strategies and discussing with the researchers, we find a wide variety of approaches, ideas, and programming languages. The performance as well as the response time of the algorithms varies with the algorithms and contexts. Thus, the performance ranking may change during the course of a single day. In order to compute a reliable ranking, the challenge uses a comprehensive evaluation period (4 weeks in Task 1) and a huge dataset (consisting of $\approx$ 100 million messages in Task 2) respectively. The baseline recommender performs quite successfully, being always among the best 8 recommender algorithms.

6   Conclusion and Outlook

In this paper, we have presented the CLEF NewsREEL 2015 challenge that requires participants to develop algorithm capable of processing a stream of data, including news items, users, and interaction events, and generating news item recommendations. Participants can choose between two tasks, Task 1, in which their algorithms are tested online, and Task 2, in which their algorithms are tested offline using a framework that 'replays' data streams. The paper has devoted particular attention to the framework, called Idomaar, which makes use of open source technologies designed for straightforward usage. Idomaar enables a fair and consistent evaluation of algorithms, measuring the quality of the recommendations, while limiting or tracking the technical aspects, such as throughput, required CPU resources, and response time.

The NewsREEL 2015 challenge supports recommender system benchmarking in making a critical step towards wide-spread adoption of online benchmarking (i.e., "living lab evaluation"). Further, the Idomaar framework for offline evaluation of stream recommendation is a powerful tool that allowing multi-dimensional evaluation of recommender systems "as a service". Testing of stream-based algorithms is important for companies who offer recommender systems services, or provide recommendations directly to their customers. However, until now, such testing has occurred in house. Consistent, open evaluation of algorithms across the board was frequently impossible. Because NewsREEL provides a huge dataset and enables reproducible evaluation of recommender system algorithms, it has the power to reveal underlying strengths and weaknesses of algorithms across the board. Such evaluation provide valuable insights that help to drive forward the state of the art.

We explicitly point out that the larger goal of both Task 1 and Task 2 of the NewsREEL 2015 challenge is to evaluate stream-based recommender algorithms not only with respect to their performance as measured by conventional user-oriented metrics (i.e., CTR), but also with respect to their technical aspects (i.e., response time). As such, the NewREEL challenge takes a step towards realizing the paradigm of 3D benchmarking [24].

We face several major challenges as we move forward. These challenges must be addressed by a possible follow-up NewsREEL challenge, but also by any benchmark that aspires to evaluate stream recommendations with respect to both user and technical aspects. First, stream-based recommendation is a classic big data challenge. In order to ensure that a benchmark addresses a state-of-the-art version of the problem, it is necessary to continuously monitor new tools that are developed. Here, we are particularly interested in keeping up with the developments of key open source tools for handling data streams. Allowing the reference framework to track these developments requires a significant amount of engineering effort. Second, it is necessary to keep the threshold for participating in the benchmark low. In other words, new teams should be able to test their algorithms with a minimal of prior background knowledge or set up time. In 2015, we notice that it requires an investment for teams to be able to understand the complexities of stream-based recommendation, and how they are implemented within Idomaar. Again, a considerable amount of engineering effort is needed to ensure that Idomaar is straightforward to understand and easy to use. Finally, additional work is needed to fully understand the connection between online evaluation and the "replayed" stream used in offline evaluation. The advantage of offline testing is clear: on-demand exact repeatability of experiments. However, it also suffers from particular limitations. In the future, we will continue to work to understand the potential of using offline testing in place of online testing.

Acknowledgments. The research leading to these results was performed in the CrowdRec project, which has received funding from the European Union Seventh Framework Program FP7/2007-2013 under grant agreement No. 610594.

References

1. Balog, K., Kelly, L., Schuth, A.: Head first: Living labs for ad-hoc search evaluation. In: Proceedings of the 23rd ACM International Conference on Conference on Information and Knowledge Management, CIKM 2014, New York, NY, USA, pp. 1815–1818. ACM (2014)
2. Blomo, J., Ester, M., Field, M.: Recsys challenge 2013. In: Proceedings of the 7th ACM Conference on Recommender Systems, RecSys 2013, pp. 489–490 (2013)
3. Brodt, T., Hopfgartner, F.: Shedding Light on a living lab: the CLEF NEWSREEL open recommendation platform. In: Proceedings of the Information Interaction in Context conference, IIiX 2014, pp. 223–226. Springer-Verlag (2014)
4. Campos, P.G., Díez, F., Cantador, I.: Time-aware recommender systems: a comprehensive survey and analysis of existing evaluation protocols. User Model. User-Adapt. Interact. **24**(1–2), 67–119 (2014)
5. Chen, J., Nairn, R., Nelson, L., Bernstein, M.S., Chi, E.H.: Short and tweet: experiments on recommending content from information streams. In: Proceedings of the 28th International Conference on Human Factors in Computing Systems, CHI 2010, Atlanta, Georgia, USA, April 10–15, 2010, pp. 1185–1194 (2010)
6. Chen, Y., Berkhin, P., Anderson, B., Devanur, N.R.: Real-time bidding algorithms for performance-based display ad allocation. In: Proceedings of the 17th ACM SIGKDD International Conference on Knowledge Discovery and Data Mining, KDD 2011, pp. 1307–1315 (2011)
7. Diaz-Aviles, E., Drumond, L., Schmidt-Thieme, L., Nejdl, W.: Real-time top-n recommendation in social streams. In: Proceedings of the Sixth ACM Conference on Recommender Systems, RecSys 2012, pp. 59–66 (2012)
8. Doychev, D., Lawlor, A., Rafter, R.: An analysis of recommender algorithms for online news. In: Working Notes for CLEF 2014 Conference, Sheffield, UK, September 15–18, 2014, pp. 825–836 (2014)
9. Garcin, F., Faltings, B., Donatsch, O., Alazzawi, A., Bruttin, C., Huber, A.: Offline and online evaluation of news recommender systems at swissinfo.ch. In: Eighth ACM Conference on Recommender Systems, RecSys 2014, Foster City, Silicon Valley, CA, USA - October 06–10, 2014, pp. 169–176 (2014)
10. Goldberg, K., Roeder, T., Gupta, D., Perkins, C.: Eigentaste: A constant time collaborative filtering algorithm. Inf. Retr., **4**(2), July 2001
11. Gonzáles, Á.C., García-Serrano, A.M., Cigarrán, J.: UNED @ clef-newsreel 2014. In: Working Notes for CLEF 2014 Conference, Sheffield, UK, September 15–18, 2014, pp. 802–812 (2014)
12. GroupLens Research. MovieLens data sets, October 2006. http://www.grouplens.org/node/73
13. Hopfgartner, F., Hanbury, A., Mueller, H., Kando, N., Mercer, S., Kalpathy-Cramer, J., Potthast, M., Gollup, T., Krithara, A., Lin, J., Balog, K., Eggel, I.: Report of the evaluation-as-a-service (eaas) expert workshop. SIGIR Forum **49**(1), 57–65 (2015)

14. Hopfgartner, F., Kille, B., Lommatzsch, A., Plumbaum, T., Brodt, T., Heintz, T.: Benchmarking news recommendations in a living lab. In: Kanoulas, E., Lupu, M., Clough, P., Sanderson, M., Hall, M., Hanbury, A., Toms, E. (eds.) CLEF 2014. LNCS, vol. 8685, pp. 250–267. Springer, Heidelberg (2014)

15. Kille, B., Hopfgartner, F., Brodt, T., Heintz, T.: The plista dataset. In: NRS 2013: Proceedings of the International Workshop and Challenge on News Recommender Systems, pp. 14–21. ACM, 10 2013

16. Kille, B., Lommatzsch, A., Turrin, R., Serny, A., Larson, M., Brodt, T., Seiler, J., Hopfgartner, F.: Overview of clef newsreel 2015: News recommendation evaluation labs. In: 6th International Conference of the CLEF Initiative (2015)

17. Kuchar, J., Kliegr, T.: Inbeat: Recommender system as a service. In: Working Notes for CLEF 2014 Conference, Sheffield, UK, September 15–18, 2014, pp. 837–844 (2014)

18. Li, L., Chu, W., Langford, J., Wang, X.: Unbiased offline evaluation of contextual-bandit-based news article recommendation algorithms. In: Proceedings of the Forth International Conference on Web Search and Web Data Mining, WSDM 2011, Hong Kong, China, February 9–12, 2011, pp. 297–306 (2011)

19. Lin, J., Efron, M.: Evaluation as a service for information retrieval. SIGIR Forum 47(2), 8–14 (2013)

20. Lommatzsch, A., Albayrak, S.: Real-time recommendations for user-item streams. In: Proc. of the 30th Symposium On Applied Computing, SAC 2015, New York, NY, USA, pp. 1039–1046. ACM (2015)

21. McFee, B., Bertin-Mahieux, T., Ellis, D.P., Lanckriet, G.R.: The million song dataset challenge. In: Proceedings of the 21st International Conference Companion on World Wide Web, WWW 2012 Companion, pp. 909–916 (2012)

22. Di Noia, T., Cantador, I., Ostuni, V.C.: Linked open data-enabled recommender systems: ESWC 2014 challenge on book recommendation. In: Presutti, V., Stankovic, M., Cambria, E., Cantador, I., Di Iorio, A., Di Noia, T., Lange, C., Reforgiato Recupero, D., Tordai, A. (eds.) SemWebEval 2014. CCIS, vol 475, pp. 129–143. Springer, Heidelberg (2014)

23. Said, A., Loni, B., Turrin, R., Lommatzsch, A.: An extended data model format for composite recommendation. In: Poster Proceedings of the 8th ACM Conference on Recommender Systems, RecSys 2014, Foster City, Silicon Valley, CA, USA, October 6–10, 2014 (2014)

24. Said, A., Tikk, D., Stumpf, K., Shi, Y., Larson, M., Cremonesi, P.: Recommender systems evaluation: A 3D benchmark. In: Proceedings of the Workshop on Recommendation Utility Evaluation: Beyond RMSE, RUE 2012, Dublin, Ireland, September 9, 2012, pp. 21–23. CEUR (2012)

25. Tavakolifard, M., Gulla, J.A., Almeroth, K.C., Hopfgartner, F., Kille, B., Plumbaum, T., Lommatzsch, A., Brodt, T., Bucko, A., Heintz, T.: Workshop and challenge on news recommender systems. In: Seventh ACM Conference on Recommender Systems, RecSys 2013, Hong Kong, China, October 12–16, 2013, pp. 481–482 (2013)

Overview of the PAN/CLEF 2015 Evaluation Lab

Efstathios Stamatatos[1]([⊠]), Martin Potthast[2], Francisco Rangel[3,4],
Paolo Rosso[4], and Benno Stein[2]

[1] Department of Information & Communication Systems Engineering,
University of the Aegean, Mytilene, Greece
stamatatos@aegean.gr
[2] Web Technology & Information Systems,
Bauhaus-Universität Weimar, Weimar, Germany
[3] Autoritas Consulting, S.A., Madrid, Spain
[4] Natural Language Engineering Lab,
Universitat Politècnica de València, Valencia, Spain
pan@webis.de
http://pan.webis.de

Abstract. This paper presents an overview of the PAN/CLEF evaluation lab. During the last decade, PAN has been established as the main
forum of text mining research focusing on the identification of personal
traits of authors left behind in texts unintentionally. PAN 2015 comprises three tasks: plagiarism detection, author identification and author
profiling studying important variations of these problems. In plagiarism
detection, community-driven corpus construction is introduced as a new
way of developing evaluation resources with diversity. In author identification, cross-topic and cross-genre author verification (where the texts
of known and unknown authorship do not match in topic and/or genre)
is introduced. A new corpus was built for this challenging, yet realistic,
task covering four languages. In author profiling, in addition to usual
author demographics, such as gender and age, five personality traits
are introduced (openness, conscientiousness, extraversion, agreeableness,
and neuroticism) and a new corpus of Twitter messages covering four languages was developed. In total, 53 teams participated in all three tasks of
PAN 2015 and, following the practice of previous editions, software submissions were required and evaluated within the TIRA experimentation
framework.

1 Introduction

Nowadays, huge volumes of electronic texts are produced daily and the need to
automatically handle this information significantly increases. Topic, genre, and
sentiment can be used to assign texts into predefined categories by exploiting
their word usage, form and structure. Beyond such general characteristics, personal traits of authors left behind in texts unintentionally can also be used to
extract useful information from texts.

© Springer International Publishing Switzerland 2015
J. Mothe et al. (Eds.): CLEF 2015, LNCS 9283, pp. 518–538, 2015.
DOI: 10.1007/978-3-319-24027-5_49

Uncovering Plagiarism, Authorship, and Social Software Misuse (PAN), a series of evaluation labs, focuses on that direction. During the last decade, PAN has been established as the main forum of innovative research in textual plagiarism detection and authorship analysis by producing large volumes of challenging corpora and introducing novel evaluation frameworks. PAN/CLEF 2015 edition comprises 3 tasks:

- *Plagiarism detection*: Given a document, identify all plagiarized sources and boundaries of re-used passages.
- *Author identification*: Given a document, identify its author.
- *Author profiling*: Given a document, extract information about the author (e.g. gender, age).

The last editions of PAN also focused on the same tasks [13,44]. However, every year important novelties are introduced. In more detail, in plagiarism detection community-driven corpus construction is introduced as a new way of developing evaluation resources characterized by diversity. This helps to drive the plagiarism detection task toward a truly community-driven evaluation.

The author identification task focuses on the authorship verification problem. Given a set of documents all by the same author and another questioned document, the task is to determine whether the author of the known documents is also the author of the questioned document. In contrast to most previous work in this area (including PAN-2013 and PAN-2014 editions), it is not assumed that all documents within a problem belong to the same genre/topic [21,64]. New corpora in several languages are built to enable the evaluation of submitted methods in challenging, yet realistic, cross-genre and cross-topic conditions.

The author profiling task at PAN-2015 enriches the author's demographics that are extracted from texts. In addition to gender and age (similar to PAN-2013 and PAN-2014 editions), personality traits are introduced. More specifically, the Big Five personality traits of Twitter users are examined (openness, conscientiousness, extraversion, agreeableness, and neuroticism). New corpora are produced for this task covering several European languages.

In total, 53 submissions were received for the three tasks (13, 18, and 22, respectively). Following the successful practice of PAN-2014, all participants were requested to submit their software to be evaluated within the TIRA experimentation platform [14] where participants are able to remotely run their software and evaluate its output [44]. The role of task organizers is then reduced to review evaluation results and assist participants to solve execution errors. TIRA ensures credibility and reproducibility of the reported results and supports continuous experimentation of the submitted methods using new corpora.

The remainder of this paper is organized as follows. Sections 2, 3, and 4, comprise relevant work, the evaluation setup, and results of plagiarism detection, author identification, and author profiling tasks, respectively. Finally, section 5 summarizes the main conclusions of the evaluation lab.

2   Plagiarism Detection

This section gives a brief report on the results of the plagiarism detection task at PAN 2015. An extended version of this report can be found in [15,46], where a more in-depth analysis of the obtained results is given. This year marks the beginning of a complete task overhaul, introducing community-driven corpus construction as a new way of developing evaluation resources with diversity. This lays the groundwork to drive the plagiarism detection task toward a truly community-driven evaluation, where ideally all aspects of the task are self-organized. This complements our previous efforts to improve the reproducibility of shared tasks by means of software submission using the TIRA experimentation platform.

2.1   Related Work

Research on plagiarism detection has a long history, both within PAN and without. Within PAN, we have been the first to organize shared tasks on plagiarism detection [50], whereas since then, we have introduced a number of variations of the task as well as new evaluation resources: the first shared task in 2009 focused on two sub-problems of plagiarism detection, namely the traditional external plagiarism detection [67], where a reference collection is used to identify plagiarized passages, and intrinsic plagiarism detection [32,66], where no such reference collection is at hand and plagiarism has to be identified from writing style changes within a document. For the first shared task in 2009, we have created the first standardized, large-scale evaluation corpus for plagiarism detection [49]. As part of this effort, we have devised the novel performance measures which for the first time took into account task-specific characteristics of plagiarism detection, such as detection granularity. Finally, in the first three years of PAN, we have also introduced cross-language plagiarism detection as a sub-task of plagiarism detection for the first time [40], and introduced corresponding problem instances into the corpus. Altogether, in the first three years, we successfully acquired and evaluated the plagiarism detection approaches of 42 research teams from around the world, some participating more than once. Many insights have been gained from this experience which informed our subsequent activities [39,41,50].

Starting in 2012, we have completely overhauled our evaluation approach to plagiarism detection based on the insights gained from the previous years [42]. Since then, we have separated external plagiarism detection into the two tasks of source retrieval and text alignment. The former task deals with information retrieval approaches to retrieve potential sources for a suspicious document from a large text collection, such as the web, which has been indexed with traditional retrieval models. The latter task of text alignment focuses on the problem of extracting matching passages from pairs of documents, if there are any. Both tasks have never been studied in this way before, whereas most of the existing body of work can be considered to deal mostly with text alignment.

For source retrieval, we went to considerable lengths to set up a realistic evaluation environment: we have obtained and indexed the entire English portion of the ClueWeb09 corpus, building the research search engine ChatNoir [47]. ChatNoir served two purposes, namely as an API for plagiarism detectors for those who cannot afford to index the ClueWeb themselves, but also as an end user search engine for authors which were hired to construct a new, realistic evaluation resource for source retrieval. We have hired 18 semi-professional authors from the crowdsourcing platform oDesk (now Upwork) and asked them to write essays of length at least 5000 words on pre-defined topics obtained from the TREC web track. To write their essays, the authors were asked to conduct research using ChatNoir, reusing text from the web pages they found. This way, we have created realistic information needs which in turn lead the authors to use our search engine in a realistic way to fulfill their task. This has lead to new insights into the nature of how humans reuse text, some building up a text as they go, whereas others first collect a lot of text and then boil it down to the final essay [48]. Finally, we have devised and developed new evaluation measures for source retrieval that for the first time take into account the retrieval of near-duplicate results when calculating precision and recall [43, 45].

Regarding text alignment, we focus on the text reuse aspects of the task by boiling down the problem to its very core, namely comparing two text documents to identify reused passages of text. In this task, we have started in 2012 to experiment with software submissions for the first time, which lead to the development of the TIRA experimentation platform [14]. We have continued to employ this platform as a tool to collect softwares also for source retrieval and the entire PAN evaluation lab as of 2013, thus improving the reproducibility of PAN's shared tasks for the foreseeable future [13, 44]. Altogether, in the second three-year cycle of this task, we have acquired and evaluated the plagiarism detection approaches of 20 research teams on source retrieval and 31 research teams on text alignment [42, 43, 45].

2.2 Community-Driven Construction of Evaluation Resources

Traditionally, the evaluation resources required to run a shared task are created by its organizers—but the question remains: why? Several reasons come to mind:

- *Seniority.* Senior community members may have the best vantage point in order to create representative evaluation resources.
- *Closed data access.* Having access to an otherwise closed data source (e.g., from a company) gives some community members an advantage over others in creating evaluation resources with a strong connection to the real world.
- *Task inventorship.* The inventor of a new task (i.e., a task that has not been considered before), is in a unique position to create normative evaluation resources, shaping future evaluations.
- *Being first to the table.* The first one to pick up the opportunity may take the lead in constructing evaluation resouces (e.g., because a task has never been organized before, or, to mitigate a lack of evaluation resources).

All of the above reasons are sufficient for an individual or a small group of researchers to become organizers of a shared task, and, to create corresponding evaluation resources. However, from reviewing dozens of shared tasks that have been organized in the human language technologies, we can conclude that neither of them is a necessary condition [44].

We question the traditional connection of shared task organization and evaluation resource creation, since this imposes several limitations on scale and diversity and therefore the representativeness of the evaluation resources that can be created:

- *Scale.* The number of man-hours that can be invested in the creation of evaluation resources is limited by the number of organizers and their personal commitment. This limits the scale of the evaluation resources. Crowdsourcing may be employed as a means to increase scale in many situations, however, this is mostly not the case where task-specific expertise is required.
- *Diversity.* The combined task-specific capabilities of all task organizers may be limited regarding the task's domain. For example, the number of languages spoken by task organizers is often fairly small, whereas true representativeness across languages would require evaluation resources from at least all major language families spoken today.

By involving participants in a structured way into the creation of evaluation resources, task organizers may build on their combined expertise, man-power, and diversity.

2.3 Text Alignment Corpus Construction

In text alignment, given a pair of documents, the task is to identify all contiguous passages of reused text between them. The challenge with this task is to identify passages of text that have been obfuscated, sometimes to the extent that, apart from stop words, little lexical similarity remains between an original passage and its reused counterpart. Consequently, for task organizers, the challenge is to provide a representative corpus of documents that emulate this situation.

For the previous editions of PAN, we have created such corpora ourselves, whereas obfuscated text passages have been generated automatically, semi-automatically via crowdsourcing [5], and by collecting real cases. Until now, however, we neglected participants of our shared task as potential helpers in creating evaluation resources. Given that a stable community has formed around this task in previous years, and that the corpus format has not changed in the past three years, we felt confident to experiment with this task and to switch from algorithm development to corpus construction.

Corpus Construction Task.   The task was to construct an evaluation corpus for text alignment, where two possibilities to accomplish this task were given as follows:

- *Corpus collection.* Gather real-world instances of text reuse or plagiarism, and annotate them.

- *Corpus generation.* Given pairs of documents, generate passages of reused or plagiarized text between them. Apply a means of obfuscation of your choosing.

The task definition is cast as open as possible, imposing no particular restrictions on the way in which participants approach this task, which languages they consider, or which kinds of obfuscation they collect or generate. To ensure compatibility among each other and with previous corpora, however, the format of all submitted corpora had to conform with that of the existing corpora. By fixing the corpus format, future editions of the text alignment task may build on the evaluation resources created within this task without further effort, and the softwares that have been submitted in previous editions of the text alignment task and are now available at the TIRA experimentation platform may be re-evaluated on the new corpora. The latter in fact forms part of the analysis of the submitted corpora. To ensure compatibility, we handed a corpus validation tool that checked all format restrictions.

Corpus Validation and Analysis.   The creation of new evaluation corpora must be done with the utmost care, since corpora are barely double-checked or questioned again once they have been accepted as authoritative. This presents the organizers of a corpus construction task with the new challenge of evaluating submitted corpora, where the evaluation of a corpus should aim at establishing its validity.

Unlike with traditional shared tasks, the validity of a corpus can not only be established via an automatically computed performance measure, but requires manual reviewing effort. As part of their participation, all participants who submitted a corpus therefore had to peer-review the corpora submitted by other participants. Furthermore, we also publicly invited community members of PAN to volunteer to review submitted corpora. The following instructions were handed out to the reviewers:

The peer-review is about dataset validity, i.e. the quality and realism of the plagiarism cases. Conducting the peer-review includes:

- *Manual* review of as many examples as possible from all datasets and all obfuscation strategies therein
- Make observations about how the dataset has been constructed
- Make observations about potential quality problems or errors
- Make observations on the realism of each dataset and each obfuscation strategy
- Write about your observations in your notebook (make sure to refer to examples from the datasets for your findings).

Handing out the complete submitted corpora for peer-review, however, is out of the question, since this would defeat the purpose of subsequent shared task evaluations by revealing the ground truth prematurely. Therefore, the organizers of a corpus construction task serve as mediators, splitting submitted corpora into training and test datasets, and handing out only the training portion for peer-review. The participants who submitted a given corpus, however, may never be reliably evaluated based on their own corpus. Also, colluding participants may not be ruled out entirely.

Finally, when a shared task has previously invited software submission, this creates ample opportunity to re-evaluate the existing softwares on the submitted corpora. This allows for evaluating submitted corpora in terms of difficulty of detecting enclosed plagiarism cases: the performances of existing software on submitted corpora, when compared to their respective performances on previously used corpora, allow for a relative assessment of corpus difficulty. In our case, more than 30 text alignment softwares have been submitted since 2012.

Submitted Corpora. A total of 8 corpora have been submitted to the PAN 2015 text alignment corpus construction task. The corpora are of varying sizes and diversity: some corpora feature languages, such as Chinese, Persian, and Urdu, which were previously unobtainable to us. Some corpora feature real plagiarism cases, other automatically generated plagiarism.

A survey of the peer-reviews conducted by participants as well as the outlined evaluation of corpus difficulty based on software submitted to previous editions of the PAN text alignment task is forthcoming and will form part of the task overview paper [46].

3   Author Identification

The main idea behind author identification is that it is possible to reveal the author of a text given a set of candidate authors and undisputed text samples for each one of them [19,61]. The most crucial information for this task refers to writing style and it is essential to be able to quantify stylistic choices in texts and measure stylistic similarity between texts. Author identification is associated with important forensic applications (e.g. revealing the author of harassing messages in social media, linking terrorist proclamations by their author, etc.) and literary applications (e.g., verifying the authorship of disputed novels, identifying the author of works published anonymously, etc.) [10,20]

The author identification task has several variations depending mainly on the number of candidate authors and whether the set of candidate authors is closed or open. One particular variation of the task is authorship verification where there is only one candidate author for whom there are undisputed text samples and we have to decide whether an unknown text is by that author or not [16,24,29]. In more detail, the authorship verification task corresponds to a one-class classification problem where the samples of known authorship by the author in question form the positive class. All texts written by other authors can be viewed as the negative class, a huge and heterogeneous class from which it is not easy to find representative samples. However challenging, authorship verification is a very significant task since any given author identification problem can be decomposed into a set of authorship verification problems. The verification task is a fundamental problem in authorship analysis and provides an excellent research field to examine competitive approaches aiming at the extraction of reliable and general conclusions [25].

Previous PAN/CLEF editions have focused on the authorship verification task and achieved to produce appropriate evaluation corpora covering several natural languages and genres [21,64]. Moreover, a suitable evaluation framework was developed highlighting the ability of methods to leave problems unanswered when there is high uncertainty as well as to assign probability scores to their answers. However, most previous work in this field assumes that all texts within a verification problem match for both genre and thematic area. This assumption makes things easier since style is affected by genre in addition to the personal style of each author. Moreover, low frequency stylistic features are heavily affected by topic nuances.

PAN/CLEF 2015 also focuses on authorship verification but it no longer makes the assumption that all texts within a problem match for genre and thematic area. This cross-genre and cross-topic variation of the verification task corresponds to a more realistic view of the issue at hand since in many applications it is not possible to require undisputed text samples by certain authors in specific genres and topics. For instance, when one wants to verify the authorship of a suicide note it does not make sense to look for samples of suicide notes by the suspects [10]. In addition, the author of a crime fiction novel published anonymously could be a famous author of child fiction [20].

3.1   Related Work

Most of previous work in authorship verification (and more general in authorship analysis) only concern the case where the examined documents match for genre and topic [16,25,29,65]. A notable exception is reported in [24] where the *unmasking* method was applied to author verification problems where multiple topics were covered producing very reliable results. Kestemont *et al.* used the same method in a cross-genre experiment based on a corpus of prose and theatrical works by the same authors demonstrating that unmasking (with default settings) is not so effective in such difficult cases.

Stamatatos [62] presents a study focusing on cross-genre and cross-topic authorship attribution where a closed-set of candidate authors is used (a simpler case in comparison to authorship verification). A corpus of opinion articles covering multiple topics and book reviews all published in a UK newspaper was used and experimental results revealed that character n-gram features are more robust with respect to word features in cross-topic and cross-genre conditions. More recently, it was shown that character n-grams corresponding to word affixes and including punctuation marks are the most significant features in cross-topic authorship attribution [57]. In addition, Sapkota *et al.* demonstrated that using training texts from multiple topics (instead of a single topic) can significantly help to correctly recognize the author of texts on another topi [58].

3.2   Evaluation Setup

The evaluation setup for this task is practically identical to the one used in PAN-2014. Given a set of known documents all written by the same author and exactly one questioned document, the task is to determine whether the questioned document was written by that particular author or not. Text length varies from a few hundred to a few thousand words, depending on genre. The only difference with PAN-2014 is that texts within a problem do not match for genre and/or thematic area.

Participants are asked to submit their software that should provide a score, a real number in [0,1], corresponding to the probability of a positive answer (i.e., the known and the questioned documents are by the same author) for each verification problem. It is possible to leave some problems unanswered by assigning a probability score of exactly 0.5. The evaluation of the provided answers is based on two scalar measures: the Area Under the *Receiver Operating Characteristic* Curve (AUC) and c@1 [37]. The former tests the ability of methods to rank scores appropriately assigning low values to negative problems and high values to positive problems. The latter rewards methods that leave problems unanswered rather than providing wrong answers. Finally, the participant teams are ranked by the final score (AUC · c@1).

Baselines. One of the advantages of using TIRA for the evaluation of software submissions is that it supports the continuous evaluation of software in newly developed corpora. This enables us to apply methods submitted in previous editions of PAN to the cross-genre and cross-topic corpora of PAN-2015. That way, we can avoid the use of simplistic random-guess baselines (corresponding to final score = 0.25) and establish more challenging baselines that can be adapted to the difficulty of the corpus. In more detail, one of the best performing methods submitted to the author verification task at PAN-2013 (the winner approach when AUC is considered) [18] is also applied to evaluation corpora. In the reminder this approach is called PAN13-BASELINE. In addition, the second winner [12] and the third winner [6] of the corresponding PAN-2014 task are also used as baseline methods. For the rest of this paper, these two methods are called PAN14-BASELINE-1 and PAN14-BASELINE-2, respectively. It should be underlined that these methods have been trained and fine-tuned using different corpora and under the assumption that all documents within a problem match for genre and topic. Therefore, their performance on cross-genre and cross-topic author verification corpora is by no means optimized.

3.3   Corpus

Although it is relatively simple to compile a corpus of texts by different authors belonging to different genres/topics (negative instances of the verification task) it is particularly challenging to populate the corpus with appropriate positive instances (texts in different genres/topics by the same author). A new corpus was built that matches the volume of PAN-2014 and covers the same four languages: Dutch, English, Greek, and Spanish. The corpus is divided into a training part and an evaluation part as can be seen in Table 1. There are important differences between the sub-corpora for each language. In Dutch part, the known and unknown documents within a problem differ in genre while in English, Greek,

Table 1. The new cross-genre and cross-topic author identification corpus.

Language	Type	#problems	#docs	Known docs/ problem (avg.)	Words/doc (avg.)
Training					
Dutch	cross-genre	100	276	1.76	354
English	cross-topic	100	200	1.00	366
Greek	cross-topic	100	393	2.93	678
Spanish	mixed	100	500	4.00	954
Evaluation					
Dutch	cross-genre	165	452	1.74	360
English	cross-topic	500	1000	1.00	536
Greek	cross-topic	100	380	2.80	756
Spanish	mixed	100	500	4.00	946
Σ		1,265	3,701	1.93	641

and Spanish parts they differ in topic. In the English part only one known document per problem is provided. In Dutch and Greek parts the number of known documents per problem varies while in the Spanish part four known texts per problem are available. In all parts of the corpus, positive and negative instances are equally distributed.

The Dutch corpus is a transformed version of the *CLiPS Stylometry Investigation* corpus that includes documents written by language students at the University of Antwerp between 2012 and 2014 in two genres: essays and reviews [69]. The English corpus is a collection of dialogue from plays where the lines spoken by actors on the stage were extracted. Character names, stage directions, lists of characters, and so forth, were all removed. All positive verification instances comprise parts from different plays by the same author. English part is the largest in terms of verification problems. The Greek corpus is a collection of opinion articles published in the online forum Protagon[1] where all documents are categorized into several thematic categories (e.g. Politics, Economy, Science, Health, Media, Sports, etc). The Spanish corpus consists of opinion articles taken from a variety of online newspapers and magazines, as well as personal web pages or blogs covering a variety of topics. It also includes literary essays. This is a mixed corpus meaning that in some verification problems there is a noticeable difference in topic and/or genre while in other problems the documents match for genre and they only differ in nuances of the topic.

3.4   Evaluation Results

In total, 18 teams submitted their software for this task. The submitted author verification approaches processed each part of the corpus separately. The majority of them were able to process all four parts of the evaluation corpus, one for each language. Table 2 provides the final score (AUC · c@1) for each part of corpus together with micro-averages and macro-averages (a more detailed view in the evaluation results can be found in [63]). Note that the English part is much

---

[1] http://www.protagon.gr

Table 2. Author identification results in terms of final score (AUC · c@1).

Team (alphabetically)	Dutch	English	Greek	Spanish	Micro-avg	Macro-avg
Bagnall	0.451	**0.614**	**0.750**	0.721	**0.608**	**0.628**
Bartoli et al.	0.518	0.323	0.458	**0.773**	0.417	0.506
Castro-Castro et al.	0.247	0.520	0.391	0.329	0.427	0.365
Gómez-Adorno et al.	0.390	0.281	0.348	0.281	0.308	0.323
Gutierrez et al.	0.329	0.513	0.581	0.509	0.479	0.478
Halvani	0.455	0.458	0.493	0.441	0.445	0.462
Hürlimann et al.	0.616	0.412	0.599	0.539	0.487	0.538
Kocher & Savoy	0.218	0.508	0.631	0.366	0.435	0.416
Maitra et al.	0.518	0.347	0.357	0.352	0.378	0.391
Mechti et al.	-	0.247	-	-	0.207	0.063
Moreau et al.	**0.635**	0.453	0.693	0.661	0.534	0.606
Nikolov et al.	0.089	0.258	0.454	0.095	0.217	0.201
Pacheco et al.	0.624	0.438	0.517	0.663	0.480	0.558
Pimas et al.	0.262	0.257	0.230	0.240	0.253	0.247
Posadas-Durán et al.	0.132	0.400	-	0.462	0.333	0.226
Sari & Stevenson	0.381	0.201	-	0.485	0.286	0.250
Solórzano et al.	0.153	0.259	0.330	0.218	0.242	0.235
Vartapetiance & Gillam	0.262	-	0.212	0.348	0.177	0.201
PAN15-ENSEMBLE	0.426	0.468	0.537	0.715	0.475	0.532
PAN14-BASELINE-1	0.255	0.249	0.198	0.443	0.269	0.280
PAN14-BASELINE-2	0.191	0.409	0.412	0.683	0.406	0.405
PAN13-BASELINE	0.242	0.404	0.384	0.367	0.358	0.347

larger with respect to the number of problems. Thus, macro-average provides a fair picture of the ability of submitted methods to handle all four sub-corpora. In average, the best results were produced for the cross-topic Greek part. Quite predictably, the cross-genre Dutch part proved to be the most challenging followed by the English part (this can be explained by the low number of known documents per problem). Note also that Greek and Spanish parts comprise longer texts (in average more than 500 words per document) while Dutch and English parts include shorter texts (less than 500 words per document).

The best performing approach, in terms of both micro-average and macro-average of final score, introduces a character-level Recurrent Neural Network model [3]. This method seems to be particularly effective for cross-topic verification cases while, based on the relatively low performance on the Dutch part, it seems to be affected by differences in genre. The second best overall performing approach by Moreau et al. is based on a heterogeneous ensemble combined with stacked generalization [34]. The success of this model verifies the conclusions of previous editions of PAN that different verification models when combined can achieve very good results [21,64].

In contrast to previous PAN editions, the majority of participants used eager supervised learning methods (e.g. SVMs, random forests) to model the verification process based on the training corpus. The best performing submitted methods belong to this category with the notable exception of the winner approach. The most successful methods also adopt the extrinsic verification paradigm where the one-class verification problem is transformed to a binary classification task by making use of texts from other authors [64]. The vast majority of submitted approaches attempt to combine a variety of text representation features. Most of them can be extracted from texts without any elaborate text analysis (e.g., word/sentence/paragraph length, character and word n-grams, etc.) The most common elaborate type of features depends on POS tagging. Only a couple of methods make use of full syntactic parsing. A more detailed review of the submitted approaches is given in [63].

The performance of the baseline models reflects the difficulty of the evaluation corpora. In the cross-genre Dutch part, all three baselines resemble a random-guessing classifier. PAN13-BASELINE and PAN14-BASELINE-2 provide relatively good results for the cross-topic English and Greek corpora while the performance of PAN14-BASELINE-1 is notably low. This may be explained by the fact that the latter method is based on eager supervised learning so it depends too much on the properties of the training corpus [12]. Both PAN14-BASELINE-1 and PAN14-BASELINE-2 are remarkably improved when applied to the mixed Spanish corpus where some verification problems match the properties of PAN-2014 corpora. In average, PAN13-BASELINE and PAN14-BASELINE-2 outperform almost half of the participant teams demonstrating their potential as generic approaches that can be used in any given corpus. On the other hand, the average performance of PAN14-BASELINE-2 resembles random-guessing.

Combining All Participants. Following the successful practice of previous PAN editions, we developed a simple meta-model combining all participant methods. This heterogeneous ensemble is based on the average of scores produced by all 18 participants for each verification problem. The evaluation results of this approach can also be seen in Table 2. In contrast to the corresponding results of PAN-2013 and PAN-2014 [21,64], the ensemble of all participants is not the best performing approach. When the micro-average and macro-average of final score is concerned, the ensemble is outperformed by 5 and 4 participants, respectively. This moderate performance of the meta-model can be partially explained by the low average performance of the submitted methods. This is demonstrated by the fact that all PAN-2014 participants acquired a micro-average final score greater than 0.3 while 6 out of 18 PAN-2015 participants get a micro-average final score lower than 0.3 (recall that the final score of a random-guessing model is 0.25).

4   Author Profiling

Author profiling distinguishes between classes of authors studying their sociolect aspect, that is, how language is shared by people. This helps in identifying profiling aspects such as gender, age, native language, or personality type. Author profiling is a problem of growing importance in applications in forensics, security, and marketing. E.g., from a forensic linguistics perspective one would like being able to know the linguistic profile of the author of a harassing text message (language used by a certain type of people) and identify certain characteristics (language as evidence). Similarly, from a marketing viewpoint, companies may be interested in knowing, on the basis of the analysis of blogs and online product reviews, the demographics of people that like or dislike their products.

4.1 Related Work

Pennebaker's [38] investigated how the style of writing is associated with personal attributes such as age, gender and personality traits, among others. In [2] the authors approached the task of gender identification from the British National Corpus and achieved approximately 80% accuracy. Similarly in [17] and [4] the authors investigated age and gender identification from formal texts. Recently most investigations focus on social media. For example, in [23] and [59] the authors investigated the style of writing in blogs. On the other hand, Zhang and Zhang [71] experimented with short segments of blog post and obtained 72.1% accuracy for gender prediction. Similarly, Nguyen et al. [35] studied the use of language and age among Dutch Twitter users. Since 2013 a shared task on author profiling has been organised at PAN [55,56]. It is worth mentioning the second order representation based on relationships between documents and profiles used by the best performing team at the PAN-AP 2013 and 2014 [27,28]. Recently, the EmoGraph [53] graph-based approach tried to capture how users convey verbal emotions in the morphosyntactic structure of the discourse, obtaining competitive results with the best performing systems at PAN 2013. Moreover with the PAN-AP-2013 dataset, the authors in [70] investigate a high variety of different features and show the contribution of IR-based features in age and gender identification and in [30] the authors approached the task with 3 million features in a MapReduce configuration, obtaining high accuracies with fractions of processing time.

With respect to automatically recognising personality from text, Argamon et al. [68] focused on two of the Big Five traits (Extraversion and Emotional Stability), measured by means of self-reports. They used Support Vector Machines (SVMs), trained on word categories and relative frequency of function words, to recognize these two traits. In a similar way, Oberlander and Nowson [36] worked on the classification of personality types of bloggers extracting patterns in a bottom-up fashion. Mairesse et al. [31], investigated systematically the usefulness of different sets of textual features exploiting psycholinguistic dictionaries such as LIWC and MRC. They extracted personality models from self-reports and observed data, and reported that the openness to experience trait yield the best performance. In more recent years, the interest in personality recognition has grown in two areas: the analysis of human behaviour and social network analysis. Several studies have started exploring the wealth of behavioral data made available by cameras, microphones [33], wearable sensors [22], and mobile phones [11] linking personality traits to dimensions such as face to face interaction, speech video and text transcriptions. From the other hand, researchers have also focused on personality prediction from corpora of social network data, like Twitter and Facebook, exploiting either linguistic features in status updates, social features such as friends count, and daily activity [9,51]. Kosinski et al. [26] made an extensive analysis of different features, including the size of friendship network, uploaded photos count and events attended, finding the correlations with the personality traits of 180000 Facebook users. They reported very good results in the automatic prediction of Extraversion. Bachrach et al. made an

Table 3. Distribution of Twitter users with respect to age classes per language.

	Training				Early birds				Test			
	EN	ES	IT	DU	EN	ES	IT	DU	EN	ES	IT	DU
18-24	58	22			16	6			56	18		
25-34	60	56			16	14			58	44		
35-49	22	22			6	6			20	18		
50+	12	10			4	4			8	8		
Σ	152	110	38	34	42	30	12	10	142	88	36	32

extensive analysis of the network traits (i.e. such as size of friendship network, uploaded photos, events attended, times user has been tagged in photos) that correlate with personality of 180000 Facebook users. They predicted personality scores using multivariate linear regression, and reported good results on extraversion. Schwartz *et al.* [60] analyzed 700 million words, phrases, and topic instances collected from the Facebook messages of 75000 volunteers, who also filled a standard Big Five personality test. In 2013 [8] and 2014 [7] evaluation campaigns on personality recognition have been organised in the framework of the workshop on computational personality recognition.

4.2 Experimental Settings

In the Author Profiling task at PAN 2015 participants approached the task of identifying age, gender and personality traits from Twitter in four different languages: English, Spanish, Dutch and Italian. The corpus was annotated with the help of an online questionnaire. In this test, users reported their age and gender and self-assessed their personality traits with the BFI-10 online test[2] [52]. For labelling age, the following classes were considered: 18-24; 25-34; 35-49; 50+. The dataset was split into training, early birds and test, as in previous editions. The number of authors per language and age class can be seen in Table 3. The corpus is balanced per gender but imbalanced per age.

We have used two different measures for evaluation: accuracy and Root Mean Square Error (RMSE). For the identification of age and gender, and also for the joint identification, the accuracy measure was used. The accuracy is calculated as the ratio between the number of authors correctly predicted and the total number of authors. RMSE was used to evaluate personality prediction. It measures how far is the predicted value to the actual value for each trait. RMSE is calculated as in Formula 1, where n is the number of authors, f_i the actual value for trait i and $\widehat{f_i}$ the predicted one.

$$RMSE = \sqrt{\frac{\sum_{i=1}^{n} (\widehat{f_i} - f_i)^2}{n}} \tag{1}$$

---

[2] In order to address ethical and privacy issues, authors were asked for their permission to use the tweets when answering the personality test. The dataset was anonymised, password protected, and released to task participants only.

Table 4. Global ranking as average of each language global accuracy.

Ranking	Team	Global	English	Spanish	Italian	Dutch
1	alvarezcarmona15	0.8404	0.7906	0.8215	0.8089	0.9406
2	gonzalesgallardo15	0.8346	0.7740	0.7745	0.8658	0.9242
3	grivas15	0.8078	0.7487	0.7471	0.8295	0.9058
4	kocher15	0.7875	0.7037	0.7735	0.8260	0.8469
5	sulea15	0.7755	0.7378	0.7496	0.7509	0.8637
6	miculicich15	0.7584	0.7115	0.7302	0.7442	0.8475
7	nowson15	0.7338	0.6039	0.6644	0.8270	0.8399
8	weren15	0.7223	0.6856	0.7449	0.7051	0.7536
9	poulston15	0.7130	0.6743	0.6918	0.8061	0.6796
10	maharjan15	0.7061	0.6623	0.6547	0.7411	0.7662
11	mccollister15	0.6960	0.6746	0.5727	0.7015	0.8353
12	arroju15	0.6875	0.6996	0.6535	0.7126	0.6843
13	gimenez15	0.6857	0.5917	0.6129	0.7590	0.7790
14	bartoli15	0.6809	0.6557	0.5867	0.6797	0.8016
15	ameer15	0.6685	0.6379	0.6044	0.7055	0.7260
16	cheema15	0.6495	0.6130	0.6353	0.6774	0.6723
17	teisseyre15	0.6401	0.7489	0.5049	0.6024	0.7042
18	mezaruiz15	0.6204	0.5217	0.6215	0.6682	0.6703
19	bayot15	0.6178	0.5253	0.5932	0.6644	0.6881
	ashraf15	-	0.5854	-	-	-
	kiprov15	-	0.7211	0.7889	-	-
	markov15	-	0.5890	0.5874	-	0.6798

We averaged the five RMSEs in order to obtain a global measure for personality prediction. The overall performance per language was obtained as the average between the joint identification accuracy and the (1-RMSE) for the personality recognition, as indicated in Formula 2.

$$rank = \frac{(1 - RMSE) + joint\_accuracy}{2} \tag{2}$$

Finally, the global ranking was obtained as the arithmetic average of the global measures per language.

4.3   Evaluation Results

This year 22 have been the teams who submitted software and notebook papers. In this section we show a summary of the obtained results. In Table 4 the overall performance per language and users' ranking are shown. The approach of [1] performs best overall and it is on the top 3 in every language. The authors combine the second order representation that allowed them to obtain the best results in PAN task in 2013 and 2014 together with Latent Semantic Analysis. We can observe that the highest accuracies were obtained in the Dutch dataset, with values over 90% in some cases, although it is the dataset with the lower number of authors. On the other hand, the worst results were obtained in the English dataset, although it has the highest number of authors. This may be due to the absence of age identification in Dutch that makes the task easier for

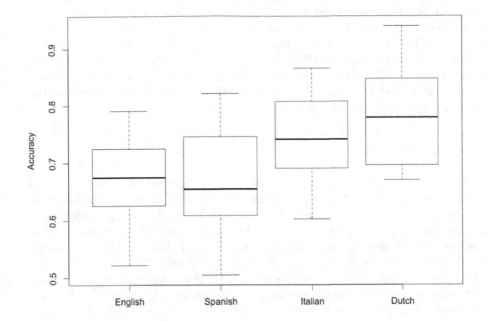

Fig. 1. Distribution accuracies per language.

that language. Something similar happens with more related languages such as Italian and Spanish, where accuracies in the first one are higher.

In Figure 1 the distribution of accuracies per language is shown. As can be seen, results in Spanish are the most sparse ones. Concretely, participants obtained accuracies from 0.5049 to 0.8215. Furthermore, results are more concentrated below the median (0.6547). Except in Dutch, there are slightly more extreme results in the lower bound. However in Dutch, the outliers occur in the upper bound, for instance with accuracies over 90% .

In Table 5 the best results per language and task are shown. In comparison to previous years of PAN, systems obtained much higher accuracy value in both age

Table 5. Best results per language and tasks

	Age and Gender			Personality Traits					
Language	*Joint*	Gender	Age	*RMSE*	E	S	A	C	O
English	0.7254	0.8592	0.8380	0.1442	0.1250	0.1951	0.1305	0.1101	0.1198
Spanish	0.7727	0.9659	0.7955	0.1235	0.1319	0.1631	0.1034	0.1017	0.1108
Italian	-	0.8611	-	0.1044	0.0726	0.1555	0.0527	0.1093	0.0972
Dutch	-	0.9688	-	0.0563	0.0750	0.0637	0.0000	0.0619	0.0354

and gender identification. This may suggest that, although the shorter length of individual tweets and their informality, the amount of tweets per author is good enough to profile age and gender with high accuracy. With respect to personality recognition, we can see that the best results were obtained for Italian and Dutch. This is contrary to what we may have expected due to the smaller number of authors for both languages both in training and test. With respect to each trait, it seems that the *Stable* one is the most difficult to predict as opposed to maybe *Conscientious* and *Openness*. A more in-depth analysis of the results and the different approaches can be found in [54].

5   Conclusions

PAN/CLEF 2015 evaluation lab attracted a high number of teams from all around the world. This demonstrates that the topics of the shared tasks are of particular interest for researchers. New corpora have been developed covering multiple languages for plagiarism detection, author identification and author profiling. These new resources together with the produced evaluation results largely define the state of the art in the respective areas.

In the last editions of PAN, the same basic tasks are repeated. However, each year variations of these tasks are taken into account and significant novelties are introduced. This practice enables us to establish a suitable evaluation framework composed by large scale corpora and appropriate evaluation measures without having to start from scratch every year. In addition, it permits participants from past years to improve their method and adopt it in order to handle the peculiarities of certain variations of tasks.

PAN requires software submissions to be evaluated within the TIRA experimentation platform. This procedure proved to be quite successful. It ensures credibility and reproducibility of the reported results while it enables to perform cross-year experiments where the submitted methods of one year are evaluated on a corpus of another year. That way, it is possible to establish challenging baselines (applying past methods to new corpora) and combine different models for the same task.

Acknowledgments. We thank the organizing committees of PAN's shared tasks Fabio Celli, Walter Daelemans, Ben Verhoeven, Patrick Juola, and Aurelio López-López. Our special thanks go to all of PAN's participants. This work was partially supported by the WIQ-EI IRSES project (Grant No. 269180) within the FP7 Marie Curie action.

References

1. Álvarez-Carmona, M.A., López-Monroy, A.P., Montes-Y-Gómez, M., Villaseñor-Pineda, L., Jair-Escalante, H.: INAOE's participation at PAN 2015: author profiling task–notebook for PAN at CLEF 2015. In: CLEF 2013 Working Notes. CEUR (2015)

2. Argamon, S., Koppel, M., Fine, J., Shimoni, A.R.: Gender, Genre, and Writing Style in Formal Written Texts. TEXT **23**, 321–346 (2003)
3. Bagnall, D.: Author identification using multi-headed recurrent neural networks. In: CLEF 2015 Working Notes. CEUR (2015)
4. Burger, J.D., Henderson, J., Kim, G., Zarrella, G.: Discriminating gender on twitter. In: Proceedings of EMNLP 2011. ACL (2011)
5. Burrows, S., Potthast, M., Stein, B.: Paraphrase Acquisition via Crowdsourcing and Machine Learning. ACM TIST **4**(3), 43:1–43:21 (2013)
6. Castillo, E., Cervantes, O., Vilariño, D., Pinto, D., León, S.: Unsupervised method for the authorship identification task. In: CLEF 2014 Labs and Workshops, Notebook Papers. CEUR (2014)
7. Celli, F., Lepri, B., Biel, J.I., Gatica-Perez, D., Riccardi, G., Pianesi, F.: The workshop on computational personality recognition 2014. In: Proceedings of ACM MM 2014 (2014)
8. Celli, F., Pianesi, F., Stillwell, D., Kosinski, M.: Workshop on computational personality recognition: shared task. In: Proceedings of WCPR at ICWSM 2013 (2013)
9. Celli, F., Polonio, L.: Relationships between personality and interactions in facebook. In: Social Networking: Recent Trends, Emerging Issues and Future Outlook. Nova Science Publishers, Inc. (2013)
10. Chaski, C.E.: Who's at the Keyboard: Authorship Attribution in Digital Evidence Invesigations. International Journal of Digital Evidence **4** (2005)
11. Chittaranjan, G., Blom, J., Gatica-Perez, D.: Mining Large-scale Smartphone Data for Personality Studies. Personal and Ubiquitous Computing **17**(3), 433–450 (2013)
12. Fréry, J., Largeron, C., Juganaru-Mathieu, M.: UJM at clef in author identification. In: CLEF 2014 Labs and Workshops, Notebook Papers. CEUR (2014)
13. Gollub, T., Potthast, M., Beyer, A., Busse, M., Rangel, F., Rosso, P., Stamatatos, E., Stein, B.: Recent trends in digital text forensics and its evaluation. In: Forner, P., Müller, H., Paredes, R., Rosso, P., Stein, B. (eds.) CLEF 2013. LNCS, vol. 8138, pp. 282–302. Springer, Heidelberg (2013)
14. Gollub, T., Stein, B., Burrows, S.: Ousting ivory tower research: towards a web framework for providing experiments as a service. In: Proceedings of SIGIR 2012. ACM (2012)
15. Hagen, M., Potthast, M., Stein, B.: Source retrieval for plagiarism detection from large web corpora: recent approaches. In: CLEF 2015 Working Notes. CEUR (2015)
16. van Halteren, H.: Linguistic profiling for author recognition and verification. In: Proceedings of ACL 2004. ACL (2004)
17. Holmes, J., Meyerhoff, M.: The Handbook of Language and Gender. Blackwell Handbooks in Linguistics. Wiley (2003)
18. Jankowska, M., Keselj, V., Milios, E.: CNG text classification for authorship profiling task–notebook for PAN at CLEF 2013. In: CLEF 2013 Working Notes. CEUR (2013)
19. Juola, P.: Authorship Attribution. Foundations and Trends in Information Retrieval **1**, 234–334 (2008)
20. Juola, P.: How a Computer Program Helped Reveal J.K. Rowling as Author of A Cuckoo's Calling. Scientific American (2013)
21. Juola, P., Stamatatos, E.: Overview of the author identification task at PAN-2013. In: CLEF 2013 Working Notes. CEUR (2013)
22. Kalimeri, K., Lepri, B., Pianesi, F.: Going beyond traits: multimodal classification of personality states in the wild. In: Proceedings of ICMI 2013. ACM (2013)
23. Koppel, M., Argamon, S., Shimoni, A.R.: Automatically Categorizing Written Texts by Author Gender. Literary and Linguistic Computing **17**(4) (2002)

24. Koppel, M., Schler, J., Bonchek-Dokow, E.: Measuring Differentiability: Unmasking Pseudonymous Authors. J. Mach. Learn. Res. **8**, 1261–1276 (2007)
25. Koppel, M., Winter, Y.: Determining if Two Documents are Written by the same Author. Journal of the American Society for Information Science and Technology **65**(1), 178–187 (2014)
26. Kosinski, M., Bachrach, Y., Kohli, P., Stillwell, D., Graepel, T.: Manifestations of User Personality in Website Choice and Behaviour on Online Social Networks. Machine Learning (2013)
27. López-Monroy, A.P., y Gómez, M.M., Jair-Escalante, H., Villaseñor-Pineda, L.: Using intra-profile information for author profiling–notebook for PAN at CLEF 2014. In: CLEF 2014 Working Notes. CEUR (2014)
28. Lopez-Monroy, A.P., Montes-Y-Gomez, M., Escalante, H.J., Villasenor-Pineda, L., Villatoro-Tello, E.: INAOE's participation at PAN 2013: author profiling task–notebook for PAN at CLEF 2013. In: CLEF 2013 Working Notes. CEUR (2013)
29. Luyckx, K., Daelemans, W.: Authorship attribution and verification with many authors and limited data. In: Proceedings of COLING 2008 (2008)
30. Maharjan, S., Shrestha, P., Solorio, T., Hasan, R.: A straightforward author profiling approach in mapreduce. In: Bazzan, A.L.C., Pichara, K. (eds.) IBERAMIA 2014. LNCS, vol. 8864, pp. 95–107. Springer, Heidelberg (2014)
31. Mairesse, F., Walker, M.A., Mehl, M.R., Moore, R.K.: Using Linguistic Cues for the Automatic Recognition of Personality in Conversation and Text. Journal of Artificial Intelligence Research **30**(1), 457–500 (2007)
32. Eissen, S.M., Stein, B.: Intrinsic plagiarism detection. In: Lalmas, M., MacFarlane, A., Rüger, S.M., Tombros, A., Tsikrika, T., Yavlinsky, A. (eds.) ECIR 2006. LNCS, vol. 3936, pp. 565–569. Springer, Heidelberg (2006)
33. Mohammadi, G., Vinciarelli, A.: Automatic personality perception: Prediction of Trait Attribution Based on Prosodic Features. IEEE Transactions on Affective Computing **3**(3), 273–284 (2012)
34. Moreau, E., Jayapal, A., Lynch, G., Vogel, C.: Author verification: basic stacked generalization applied to predictions from a set of heterogeneous learners. In: CLEF 2015 Working Notes. CEUR (2015)
35. Nguyen, D., Gravel, R., Trieschnigg, D., Meder, T.: "How old do you think I am?"; a study of language and age in twitter. In: Proceedings of ICWSM 2013. AAAI (2013)
36. Oberlander, J., Nowson, S.: Whose thumb is it anyway?: classifying author personality from weblog text. In: Proceedings of COLING 2006. ACL (2006)
37. Peñas, A., Rodrigo, A.: A simple measure to assess non-response. In: Proceedings of HLT 2011. ACL (2011)
38. Pennebaker, J.W., Mehl, M.R., Niederhoffer, K.G.: Psychological Aspects of Natural Language Use: Our Words. Our Selves. Annual Review of Psychology **54**(1), 547–577 (2003)
39. Potthast, M., Barrón-Cedeño, A., Eiselt, A., Stein, B., Rosso, P.: Overview of the 2nd international competition on plagiarism detection. In: CLEF 2010 Working Notes. CEUR (2010)
40. Potthast, M., Barrón-Cedeño, A., Stein, B., Rosso, P.: Cross-Language Plagiarism Detection. Language Resources and Evaluation (LRE) **45**, 45–62 (2011)
41. Potthast, M., Eiselt, A., Barrón-Cedeño, A., Stein, B., Rosso, P.: Overview of the 3rd international competition on plagiarism detection. In: CLEF 2011 Working Notes (2011)

42. Potthast, M., Gollub, T., Hagen, M., Graßegger, J., Kiesel, J., Michel, M., Oberländer, A., Tippmann, M., Barrón-Cedeño, A., Gupta, P., Rosso, P., Stein, B.: Overview of the 4th international competition on plagiarism detection. In: CLEF 2012 Working Notes. CEUR (2012)
43. Potthast, M., Gollub, T., Hagen, M., Tippmann, M., Kiesel, J., Rosso, P., Stamatatos, E., Stein, B.: Overview of the 5th international competition on plagiarism detection. In: CLEF 2013 Working Notes. CEUR (2013)
44. Potthast, M., Gollub, T., Rangel, F., Rosso, P., Stamatatos, E., Stein, B.: Improving the reproducibility of PAN's shared tasks: plagiarism detection, author identification, and author profiling. In: Kanoulas, E., Lupu, M., Clough, P., Sanderson, M., Hall, M., Hanbury, A., Toms, E. (eds.) CLEF 2014. LNCS, vol. 8685, pp. 268–299. Springer, Heidelberg (2014)
45. Potthast, M., Hagen, M., Beyer, A., Busse, M., Tippmann, M., Rosso, P., Stein, B.: Overview of the 6th international competition on plagiarism detection. In: CLEF 2014 Working Notes. CEUR (2014)
46. Potthast, M., Göring, S., Rosso, P., Stein, B.: Towards data submissions for shared tasks: first experiences for the task of text alignment. In: CLEF 2015 Working Notes. CEUR (2015)
47. Potthast, M., Hagen, M., Stein, B., Graßegger, J., Michel, M., Tippmann, M., Welsch, C.: ChatNoir: a search engine for the clueweb09 corpus. In: Proceedings of SIGIR 2012. ACM (2012)
48. Potthast, M., Hagen, M., Völske, M., Stein, B.: Crowdsourcing interaction logs to understand text reuse from the web. In: Proceedings of ACL 2013. ACL (2013)
49. Potthast, M., Stein, B., Barrón-Cedeño, A., Rosso, P.: An evaluation framework for plagiarism detection. In: Proceedings of COLING 2010. ACL (2010)
50. Potthast, M., Stein, B., Eiselt, A., Barrón-Cedeño, A., Rosso, P.: Overview of the 1st international competition on plagiarism detection. In: Proceedings of PAN at SEPLN 2009. CEUR (2009)
51. Quercia, D., Lambiotte, R., Stillwell, D., Kosinski, M., Crowcroft, J.: The personality of popular facebook users. In: Proceedings of CSCW 2012. ACM (2012)
52. Rammstedt, B., John, O.: Measuring Personality in One Minute or Less: A 10 Item Short Version of the Big Five Inventory in English and German. Journal of Research in Personality (2007)
53. Rangel, F., Rosso, P.: On the impact of emotions on author profiling. In: Information Processing & Management, Special Issue on Emotion and Sentiment in Social and Expressive Media (2014) (in press)
54. Rangel, F., Rosso, P., Celli, F., Potthast, M., Stein, B., Daelemans, W.: Overview of the 3rd author profiling task at PAN 2015. In: CLEF 2015 Working Notes. CEUR (2015)
55. Rangel, F., Rosso, P., Chugur, I., Potthast, M., Trenkmann, M., Stein, B., Verhoeven, B., Daelemans, W.: Overview of the 2nd author profiling task at PAN 2014. In: CLEF 2014 Working Notes. CEUR (2014)
56. Rangel, F., Rosso, P., Koppel, M., Stamatatos, E., Inches, G.: Overview of the author profiling task at PAN 2013–notebook for PAN at CLEF 2013. In: CLEF 2013 Working Notes. CEUR (2013)
57. Sapkota, U., Bethard, S., Montes-y-Gómez, M., Solorio, T.: Not all character N-grams are created equal: a study in authorship attribution. In: Proceedings of NAACL 2015. ACL (2015)
58. Sapkota, U., Solorio, T., Montes-y-Gómez, M., Bethard, S., Rosso, P.: Cross-topic authorship attribution: will out-of-topic data help? In: Proceedings of COLING 2014 (2014)

59. Schler, J., Koppel, M., Argamon, S., Pennebaker, J.W.: Effects of age and gender on blogging. In: AAAI Spring Symposium: Computational Approaches to Analyzing Weblogs. AAAI (2006)
60. Schwartz, H.A., Eichstaedt, J.C., Kern, M.L., Dziurzynski, L., Ramones, S.M., Agrawal, M., Shah, A., Kosinski, M., Stillwell, D., Seligman, M.E., et al.: Personality, Gender, and Age in the Language of Social Media: The Open-Vocabulary Approach. PloS one **8**(9), 773–791 (2013)
61. Stamatatos, E.: A Survey of Modern Authorship Attribution Methods. Journal of the American Society for Information Science and Technology **60**, 538–556 (2009)
62. Stamatatos, E.: On the Robustness of Authorship Attribution Based on Character N-gram Features. Journal of Law and Policy **21**, 421–439 (2013)
63. Stamatatos, E., Daelemans, W., Verhoeven, B., Juola, P., López-López, A., Potthast, M., Stein, B.: Overview of the author identification task at PAN 2015. In: Working Notes Papers of the CLEF 2015 Evaluation Labs. CEUR (2015)
64. Stamatatos, E., Daelemans, W., Verhoeven, B., Stein, B., Potthast, M., Juola, P., Sánchez-Pérez, M.A., Barrón-Cedeño, A.: Overview of the author identification task at PAN 2014. In: CLEF 2014 Working Notes. CEUR (2014)
65. Stamatatos, E., Fakotakis, N., Kokkinakis, G.: Automatic Text Categorization in Terms of Genre and Author. Comput. Linguist. **26**(4), 471–495 (2000)
66. Stein, B., Lipka, N., Prettenhofer, P.: Intrinsic Plagiarism Analysis. Language Resources and Evaluation (LRE) **45**, 63–82 (2011)
67. Stein, B., Meyer zu Eißen, S.: Near similarity search and plagiarism analysis. In: Proceedings of GFKL 2005. Springer (2006)
68. Sushant, S.A., Argamon, S., Dhawle, S., Pennebaker, J.W.: Lexical predictors of personality type. In: Proceedings of Joint Interface/CSNA 2005
69. Verhoeven, B., Daelemans, W.: Clips stylometry investigation (CSI) corpus: a dutch corpus for the detection of age, gender, personality, sentiment and deception in text. In: Proceedings of LREC 2014. ACL (2014)
70. Weren, E., Kauer, A., Mizusaki, L., Moreira, V., de Oliveira, P., Wives, L.: Examining Multiple Features for Author Profiling. Journal of Information and Data Management (2014)
71. Zhang, C., Zhang, P.: Predicting gender from blog posts. Tech. rep., Technical Report. University of Massachusetts Amherst, USA (2010)

Overview of the CLEF Question Answering Track 2015

Anselmo Peñas[1(✉)], Christina Unger[2], Georgios Paliouras[3], and Ioannis Kakadiaris[4]

[1] NLP&IR Group, UNED, Madrid, Spain
anselmo@lsi.uned.es
[2] CITEC, Bielefeld University, Bielefeld, Germany
cunger@techfak.uni-bielefeld.de
[3] IIT, NCSR Demokritos, Athens, Greece
paliourg@iit.demokritos.gr
[4] CBL, Deptartment of Computer Science, University of Houston, Houston, TX, USA
ioannisk@uh.edu

Abstract. This paper describes the CLEF QA Track 2015. Following the scenario stated last year for the CLEF QA Track, the starting point for accessing information is always a Natural Language question. However, answering some questions may need to query Linked Data (especially if aggregations or logical inferences are required), some questions may need textual inferences and querying free-text, and finally, answering some queries may require both sources of information. In this edition, the Track was divided into four tasks: (i) *QALD:* focused on translating natural language questions into SPARQL; (ii) *Entrance Exams:* focused on answering questions to assess machine reading capabilities; (iii) BioASQ1 focused on large-scale semantic indexing and (iv) BioASQ2 for Question Answering in the biomedical domain.

1 Introduction

Following last edition of the CLEF QA Track, the starting point is always a Natural Language question that has to be answered against Linked Data, Natural Language or both. Answering some questions may need to query Linked Data (especially if aggregations or logical inferences are required), some questions may need textual inferences and querying free-text, and finally, answering some queries may require both sources of information. The final goal is to help users understand the document by answering their questions.

Thus, given this general scenario, CLEF QA Track will work on two of its instances: one targeted to (bio)medical experts (BioASQ Tasks) and one targeted to Open Domains (QALD and Entrance Exams Tasks). In the former, medical knowledge bases, ontologies and articles must be considered. In the latter, textual documents and general resources such as Wikipedia articles and DBpedia are considered.

© Springer International Publishing Switzerland 2015
J. Mothe et al. (Eds.): CLEF 2015, LNCS 9283, pp. 539–544, 2015.
DOI: 10.1007/978-3-319-24027-5_50

2   Tasks

The CLEF QA Track 2015 was divided into the following tasks:

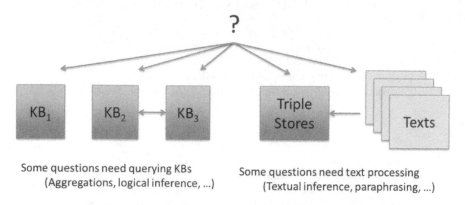

2.1   QALD: Question Answering Over Linked Data

QALD-5[1] [1] is the fifth in a series of evaluation campaigns on multilingual question answering over linked data, with a strong emphasis on multilingual question answering and hybrid approaches using information from both structured and unstructured data.

The challenge aims at all question answering systems that mediate between a user, expressing his or her information need in natural language, and semantic data. The general task is the following one: Given a natural language question or keywords, retrieve the correct answer(s) from a repository containing both RDF data and free text, in this case the English DBpedia 2014 dataset with free text abstracts.

The key challenge lies in translating the users' information needs into a form such that they can be evaluated using standard Semantic Web query processing and inference techniques.

QALD-5 provides a benchmark comprising two kinds of questions:

1. *Multilingual questions* are provided in seven different languages (English, German, Spanish, Italian, French, Dutch, and Romanian) and can be answered using the provided RDF data. They are annotated with corresponding SPARQL queries and answers retrieved from the provided SPARQL endpoint.

2. *Hybrid questions* are provided in English and can be answered only by integrating structured data (RDF) and unstructured data (free text available in the DBpedia abstracts). The questions thus all require information from both RDF and free text. They are annotated with pseudo-queries that show which part is contained in the RDF data and which part must be retrieved from the free text abstracts.

---

[1] http://www.sc.cit-ec.uni-bielefeld.de/qald

To get acquainted with the dataset and possible questions, a set of training questions was provided, comprising of 300 multilingual questions and 40 hybrid questions. Later, systems were evaluated on 60 different test questions, comprising of 50 multilingual ones and 10 hybrid ones. Overall, of the 350 training questions, 59 questions require aggregation (e.g., counting, filtering, ordering) and 102 questions require namespaces other than from the DBpedia ontology (21 of which use the YAGO namespace, 2 require FOAF, and all others rely on the DBpedia property namespace). Similarly, of the 60 test questions, 15 questions require aggregation and 12 cannot be answered with the DBpedia ontology only (3 of which use the YAGO namespace, all others rely on the DBpedia property namespace). As an additional challenge, 14 training and 1 test question are out of scope, i.e. they cannot be answered using the dataset.

The results submitted by participating systems were automatically compared to the gold standard results and evaluated using precision and recall metrics.

2.2   Entrance Exams Task

The challenge of Entrance Exams[2] [3] aims at evaluating systems reading capabilities under the same conditions humans are evaluated to enter the University.

Participant systems are asked to ingest a given document and answer a set of questions. Questions are provided in multiple-choice format, with several options from which a single answer must be selected. Systems must answer questions by referring to "common sense knowledge" that high school students who aim to enter the university are expected to have. The exercise does not intend to restrict question types, and the level of inference required to respond is very high.

Exams were created by the Japanese National Center for University Admissions Tests, and the "Entrance Exams" corpus is provided by NII's Todai Robot Project and NTCIR RITE.

For each examination, one text is given, and some (between 4 and 8) questions on the given text are asked. Each question has four choices. For this year's campaign, we reused as development data the 24 examinations from the last two years' campaigns. For testing, we provided 19 new documents where 89 questions and 356 candidate answers had to be validated.

Data sets for testing originally in English were manually translated into Russian, French, Spanish, German and Italian. They are parallel translations of texts, questions and candidate answers that offer a benchmark for evaluating systems in different languages.

In addition to the official data, we collected unofficial translations for each language. Although they preserve the original meaning, each translation has its particularities that produce different effects on systems performance: text simplification, lexical variation, different uses of anaphora, and overall quality. This data is useful to obtain insights about systems and their level of inference.

---

[2] http://nlp.uned.es/entrance-exams

Systems were evaluated from two different perspectives: question answering, where the relevant number is the overall number of questions being answered correctly; and reading comprehension, where results were grouped by test (document plus questionnaire) and we measure if machines were able to pass each test.

2.3 BioASQ: Biomedical Semantic Indexing and Question Answering

BioASQ [2] aims at assessing:

- large-scale classification of biomedical documents onto ontology concepts (semantic indexing),
- classification of biomedical questions onto relevant concepts,
- retrieval of relevant document snippets, concepts and knowledge base triples,
- delivery of the retrieved information in a concise and user-understandable form.

The challenge comprised two tasks: (i) a large-scale semantic indexing task and (ii) a question answering task.

2.3.1 Task BioASQ 1: Large-Scale Semantic Indexing

The goal was to classify documents from the MEDLINE digital library unto concepts of the MeSH2015 hierarchy. New MEDLINE articles not yet annotated are collected weekly. These articles are used as test sets for evaluating the participating systems. As soon as the annotations are available from the MEDLINE curators, the performance of each system is computed using standard information retrieval measures and hierarchical ones.

To provide an on-line and large-scale scenario, the task was divided into three independent batches. In each batch five test sets of biomedical articles were released consecutively. Each of these test sets were released in a weekly basis and the participants had 21 hours to provide their answers.

2.3.2 Task BioASQ 2: Biomedical Semantic QA

The goal of this task was to provide a large-scale question answering challenge where the systems should be able to cope with all the stages of a question-answering task, including the retrieval of relevant concepts and articles, and the provision of natural-language answers. This process involves a variety of technologies and methods, ranging from information retrieval from text and knowledge bases to information extraction and summarization.

It comprised two phases: In phase A, BioASQ released questions in English from benchmark datasets created by a group of biomedical experts. There were four types of questions: yes/no questions, factoid questions, list questions and summary questions. Participants had to respond with relevant concepts (from specific terminologies and ontologies), relevant articles (PubMed and PubMedCentral articles), relevant snippets extracted from the articles and relevant RDF triples (from specific ontologies).

In phase B, the released questions contained the correct answers for the required elements (concepts, articles, snippets and RDF triples) of the first phase. The participants had to answer with exact answers and with paragraph-sized summaries in natural language (dubbed ideal answers).

The task was split into five independent batches. The two phases for each batch were run during two consecutive days. For each phase, the participants had 24 hours to submit their answers. The evaluation in phase B was carried out manually by biomedical experts on the ideal answers provided by the systems. Each answer was evaluated along four dimensions: readability, recall, precision and repetition, using a scale from 1 to 5.

3   Participation

Table 1 shows the distribution of the participating teams among the exercises proposed by the CLEF QA Track 2015.

Table 1. Number of participants in CLEF QA Track 2015

Task	# Registered	Sub-task	# Participants
QALD	26	QALD	7 (English)
Entrance Exams	28	Entrance Exams	5 (English) 1 (French)
BioASQ	19	BioASQ 1	18 (English)
	23	BioASQ 2	12 (English)
Total	96	-	43

QALD-5, the fifth edition of the QALD challenge, has attracted seven participants. Two participants submitted results only for the multilingual questions, two participants submitted results only for the hybrid questions, and three participants submitted results for both kinds of questions. Although the overall number of participants is one less than in last year's challenge, the number of participating hybrid question answering systems increased from one to five, which is an important step towards advancement in the field. However, all systems still processed only the English questions, not yet addressing multilingualism.

Continuing the trend that appeared in the second edition of BioASQ, the number of participating teams increased further in the third BioASQ challenge. Particularly encouraging is the increase of participation in the hard QA task (BioASQ2), where by now a corpus of over 1,300 questions has been formed, including associated material (documents, snippets, concepts, triples) and correct answers produced by biomedical experts.

Concerning Entrance Exams, 18 systems were presented by the five participating teams. This represents a lower amount of runs than in the previous edition despite the fact that the number of participants was the same. Moreover, only one team has participated in the three editions of the task, while there has been two teams taking part also in the last two editions. Although the benchmarks were provided in Russian, Spanish, Italian, German and French, all systems run for English and only one for French.

4   Conclusions

Top systems performance appears to have improved in all tasks.

The average result in Entrance Exams was similar to the last edition, and only the best team from the last edition improved its score in English, obtaining similar results in French. From the reading perspective evaluation we had two systems (from the same team) able to pass at least half of the reading tests.

Concerning earlier challenges of QALD, question answering systems have made an important step towards hybrid question answering, querying not only RDF data but also including information in plain text sources. One of the biggest challenges remains the matching of natural language questions to correct vocabulary elements.

Something similar was also observed in Entrance Exams. In this task, there is a big lexical gap between the supporting text, the question and the candidate answer. The level of textual inferences that current systems perform is not adequate yet to solve the majority of questions.

In BioASQ the best systems increased their performance over last year and outperformed clearly all baselines, e.g. the difference between the best system in the semantic indexing task (by University of Fudan, China) and the MTI baseline was 5-6 percentage points throughout the challenge.

Acknowledgements. Anselmo Peñas was supported by CHIST-ERA READERS project (MINECO PCIN-2013-002-C02-01) and the Voxpopuli project (TIN2013-47090-C3-1-P). BioASQ started as an FP7 project, supported by the EC (contract number 318652). The third edition of BioASQ is supported by a conference grant from the NIH/NLM (number 1R13LM012214-01) and sponsored by Viseo.

References

1. Unger, C., Forascu, C., Lopez, L., Ngonga Ngomo, A., Cabrio, E., Cimiano, P., Walter, S.: Question answering over linked data (QALD-5). In: Cappellato, L., Ferro, N., Jones, G., San Juan, E. (eds) CLEF 2015 Labs and Workshops, Notebook Papers. CEUR Workshop Proceedings (CEUR-WS.org), ISSN 1613-0073 (2015)
2. Tsatsaronis, G., Balikas, G., Malakasiotis, P., Partalas, I., Zschunke, M., Alvers, M.R., Weissenborn, D., Krithara, A., Petridis, S., Polychronopoulos, D., Almirantis, Y., Pavlopoulos, J., Baskiotis, N., Gallinari, P., Artieres, T., Ngonga, A., Heino, N., Gaussier, E., Barrio-Alvers, L., Schroeder, M., Androutsopoulos, I., Paliouras, G.: An Overview of the BioASQ Large-Scale Biomedical Semantic Indexing and Question Answering Competition. BMC Bioinformatics **16**, 138 (2015)
3. Peñas, A., Miyao, Y., Rodrigo, Á., Hovy, E., Kando, N.: Overview of CLEF QA entrance exams task 2015. In: Cappellato, L., Ferro, N., Jones, G., San Juan, E. (eds) CLEF 2015 Labs and Workshops, Notebook Papers. CEUR Workshop Proceedings (CEUR-WS.org), ISSN 1613-0073 (2015)

Overview of the CLEF 2015 Social Book Search Lab

Marijn Koolen[1]([envelope]), Toine Bogers[2], Maria Gäde[3], Mark Hall[4],
Hugo Huurdeman[1], Jaap Kamps[1], Mette Skov[5], Elaine Toms[6],
and David Walsh[4]

[1] University of Amsterdam, Amsterdam, Netherlands
{marijn.koolen,h.c.huurdeman,kamps}@uva.nl
[2] Aalborg University Copehagen, Copenhagen, Denmark
toine@hum.aau.dk
[3] Humboldt University Berlin, Berlin, Germany
maria.gaede@ibi.hu-berlin.de
[4] Edge Hill University, Ormskirk, UK
{mark.hall,david.walsh}@edgehill.ac.uk
[5] Aalborg University, Aalborg, Denmark
skov@hum.aau.dk
[6] University of Sheffield, Sheffield, UK
e.toms@sheffield.ac.uk

Abstract. The Social Book Search (SBS) Lab investigates book search
in scenarios where users search with more than just a query, and look for
more than objective metadata. Real-world information needs are generally complex, yet almost all research focuses instead on either relatively
simple search based on queries or recommendation based on profiles.
The goal is to research and develop techniques to support users in complex book search tasks. The SBS Lab has two tracks. The aim of the
Suggestion Track is to develop test collections for evaluating ranking
effectiveness of book retrieval and recommender systems. The aim of
the Interactive Track is to develop user interfaces that support users
through each stage during complex search tasks and to investigate how
users exploit professional metadata and user-generated content.

1 Introduction

The goal of the Social Book Search (SBS) Lab[1] is to evaluate approaches for
supporting users in searching collections of books. The SBS Lab investigates the
complex nature of relevance in book search and the role of traditional and user-
generated book metadata in retrieval. The aims are 1) to develop test collections
for evaluating systems in terms of ranking search results and 2) to develop user
interfaces and conduct user studies to investigate book search in scenarios with
complex information need and book descriptions that combine heterogeneous
information from multiple sources.

---

[1] See: http://social-book-search.humanities.uva.nl/

© Springer International Publishing Switzerland 2015
J. Mothe et al. (Eds.): CLEF 2015, LNCS 9283, pp. 545–564, 2015.
DOI: 10.1007/978-3-319-24027-5_51

The SBS Lab runs two tracks:

- *Suggestion*: this is a system-centred track focused on the comparative evaluation of systems in terms of how well they rank search results for complex book search requests that consist of both extensive natural language expressions of information needs as well as example books that reflect important aspects of those information needs, using a large collection of book descriptions with both professional metadata and user-generated content.
- *Interactive*: this is a user-centred track investigating how searchers use different types of metadata at various stages in the search process and how a search interface can support each stage in that process.

In this paper, we report on the setup and results of the 2015 Suggestion and Interactive Tracks as part of the SBS Lab at CLEF 2015. The two tracks run in close collaboration as both focus on the complex nature of book search. The paper is structured as follows. First, in Section 2, we give a brief summary of the participating organisations. Then, in Section 3 we provide details on the Amazon/LibraryThing corpus of book descriptions that is used for both tracks. The setup and results of the Suggestion Track are described in Section 4, followed by the experiments and results of the Interactive Track in Sections 5. We close in Section 6 with a discussion of the overall findings and plans for 2016.

2   Participating Organisations

A total of 35 organisations registered for the SBS Lab, of which 27 registered for the Suggestion Track and 28 for the Interactive Track. In the Suggestion Track, 11 organisations submitted runs, compared to 8 in 2014. In the Interactive Track, 7 organisations recruited users, compared to 4 in 2014. The active organisations are listed in Table 1.

3   The Amazon/LibraryThing Corpus

We use and extend the Amazon/LibraryThing (A/LT) corpus crawled by the University of Duisburg-Essen for the INEX Interactive Track [1]. The corpus contains a large collection of book records with controlled subject headings and classification codes as well as social descriptions, such as tags and reviews.[2]

The collection consists of 2.8 million book records from Amazon, extended with social metadata from LT. This set represents the books available through Amazon. The records contain title information as well as a Dewey Decimal Classification (DDC) code (for 61% of the books) and category and subject information supplied by Amazon. Each book is identified by an ISBN. Note that since different editions of the same work have different ISBNs, there can be multiple records for a single intellectual work. Each book record is an XML file with fields

---

[2] See https://inex.mmci.uni-saarland.de/data/nd-agreements.jsp for information on how to gain access to the corpus.

Table 1. Active participants of the INEX 2014 Social Book Search Track and number of contributed runs

Institute	Acronym	Runs
Aalborg University Copenhagen	AAU	1
Aix-Marseille Université CNRS	LSIS	6
Chaoyang University of Technology	CSIE	4
Laboratoire d'Informatique de Grenoble	MRIM	6
Laboratoire Hubert Curien, Université de Saint-Etienne	LaHC	6
Oslo & Akershus University College of Applied Sciences	Oslo_SBS	4
Research Center on Scientific and Technical Information	CERIST	4
University of Amsterdam	UvA	3
Université de Neuchâtel, Institut de Recherche en Informatique de Toulouse	MIIB	6
University of Jordan	IR@JU	2
University of Science and Technology Beijing	USTB_PRIR	6
Total		48

Institute		# users
Aalborg University	AAU	36
University of Amsterdam	UvA	22
Edge Hill University	Edge_Hill	20
Humboldt University	Humboldt	67
Manchester Metropolitan University	MMU	23
Oslo & Akershus University College	Oslo_SBS	20
Stockholm University	Stockholm	1
Other		3
Total		192

like *isbn*, *title*, *author*, *publisher*, *dimensions*, *numberofpages* and *publicationdate*. Curated metadata comes in the form of a Dewey Decimal Classification in the *dewey* field, Amazon subject headings in the *subject* field, and Amazon category labels in the *browseNode* fields. The social metadata from Amazon and LT is stored in the *tag*, *rating*, and *review* fields.

To ensure that there is enough high-quality metadata from traditional library catalogues, we extended the A/LT data set with library catalogue records from the Library of Congress (LoC) and the British Library (BL). We only use library records of ISBNs that are already in the A/LT collection. There are 1,248,816 records from the LoC and 1,158,070 records in MARC format from the BL. Combined, there are 2,406,886 records covering 1,823,998 of the ISBNs in the A/LT collection (66%).

4   The SBS Suggestion Track

The goal of the Social Book Search 2015 Suggestion Track[3] is to investigate techniques to support users in searching for books in catalogues of professional metadata and complementary social media. Towards this goal the track is building appropriate evaluation benchmarks, complete with test collections for social, semantic and focused search tasks. The track provides opportunities to explore research questions around two key areas:

- Evaluation methodologies for book search tasks that combine aspects of retrieval and recommendation,
- Information retrieval techniques for dealing with professional and user-generated metadata,

The *Social Book Search* (SBS) 2015 Suggestion Track, framed within the scenario of a user searching a large online book catalogue for a given topic of interest, aims at exploring techniques to deal with complex information needs— that go beyond topical relevance and can include aspects such as genre, recency, engagement, interestingness, and quality of writing—and complex information sources that include user profiles, personal catalogues, and book descriptions containing both professional metadata and user-generated content.

The 2015 Suggestion Track is a continuation of of the INEX SBS Track that ran from 2011 up to 2014. For this fifth edition the focus is on search requests that combine a natural language description of the information need as well as example books, combining traditional ad hoc retrieval and query-by-document. The information needs are derived from the LibraryThing (LT) discussion forums. LibraryThing forum requests for book suggestions, combined with annotation of these requests resulted in a topic set of 208 topics with graded relevance judgments. A test collection is constructed around these information needs and the Amazon/LibraryThing collection [1] described in the previous section.

Through social media, book descriptions have extended far beyond what is traditionally stored in professional catalogues. Not only are books described in the users' own vocabulary, but they are also reviewed and discussed online, and added to online personal catalogues of individual readers. This additional information is subjective and personal, and opens up opportunities to aid users in searching for books in different ways that go beyond the traditional editorial metadata based search scenarios, such as known-item and subject search. For example, readers use many more aspects of books to help them decide which book to read next [9], such as how engaging, fun, educational or well-written a book is. In addition, readers leave a trail of rich information about themselves in the form of online profiles, which contain personal catalogues of the books they have read or want to read, personally assigned tags and ratings for those books and social network connections to other readers. This results in a search task that may require a different model than traditional ad hoc search [6] or recommendation.

---

[3] See http://social-book-search.humanities.uva.nl/#/suggestion

The SBS Suggestion Track aims to address the following research questions:

- Can we build reliable and reusable test collections for social book search based on book requests and suggestions from the LT discussion forums?
- Can user profiles provide a good source of information to capture personal, affective aspects of book search information needs?
- How can systems use both specific information needs and general user profiles to combine the retrieval and recommendation aspects of social book search?
- What is the relative value of social and controlled metadata for book search?

Task Description. The task is to reply to a user request posted on a LT forum (see Section 4.1) by returning a list of recommended books matching the user's information need. More specifically, the task assumes a user who issues a query to a retrieval system, which then returns a (ranked) list of relevant book records. The user is assumed to inspect the results list starting from the top, working down the list until the information need has been satisfied or until the user gives up. The retrieval system is expected to order the search results by relevance to the user's information need. Participants of the Suggestion track are provided with a set of book search requests and user profiles and are asked to submit the results returned by their systems as ranked lists. The track thus combines aspects from retrieval and recommendation.

4.1   Information Needs

LT users discuss their books on the discussion forums. Many of the topic threads are started with a request from a member for interesting, fun new books to read. Users typically describe what they are looking for, give examples of what they like and do not like, indicate which books they already know and ask other members for recommendations. Members often reply with links to works catalogued on LT, which, in turn, have direct links to the corresponding records on Amazon. These requests for recommendations are natural expressions of information needs for a large collection of online book records. We use a sample of these forum topics to evaluate systems participating in the Suggestion Track.

Each topic has a title and is associated with a group on the discussion forums. For instance, topic 99309 in Figure 1 has the title *Politics of Multiculturalism Recommendations?* and was posted in the group *Political Philosophy*. The books suggested by members in the thread are collected in a list on the side of the topic thread (see Figure 1). A feature called *touchstone* can be used by members to easily identify books they mention in the topic thread, giving other readers of the thread direct access to a book record in LT, with associated ISBNs and links to Amazon. We use these suggested books as initial relevance judgements for evaluation. In the rest of this paper, we use the term *suggestion* to refer to a book that has been identified in a touchstone list for a given forum topic. Since all suggestions are made by forum members, we assume they are valuable judgements on the relevance of books. We note that LT users may discuss their search requests and suggestions outside of the LT forums as well, e.g. share links

Fig. 1. A topic thread in LibraryThing, with suggested books listed on the right hand side.

of their forum request posts on Twitter. To what extent the suggestions made outside of LT differ or complement those on the forums requires investigation. Additional relevance information can be gleaned from the discussions on the threads. Consider, for example, topic 129939[4]. The topic starter first explains what sort of books he is looking for, and which relevant books he has already read or is reading. Other members post responses with book suggestions. The topic starter posts a reply describing which suggestions he likes and which books he has ordered and plans to read. Later on, the topic starter provides feedback on the suggested books that he has now read. Such feedback can be used to estimate the relevance of a suggestion to the user.

Topic Selection. The topic set of 2015 is a subset of the 2014 topic set, focusing on topics where the requester gives both a narrative description of the information need and one or more example books to guide the suggestions. The 2015 topic set has 208 topics, where the narrative and examples are combined with all the books of the topic creators' profiles up to the time of posting the request on the forum. This topic set was distributed to participating groups.

Each topic has at least one example book provided by the requester that helps other forum members understand in which direction the requester is thinking. The number of examples ranges from 1 to 21, with a median and mean of 2 and 2.48 respectively. Further, annotators indicated whether an example book was given as a positive example—i.e. they are looking for something along the lines

---

[4] URL: http://www.librarything.com/topic/129939

of the example—or as a negative example, where the example is broadly relevant but has aspects that the requester does not want in the suggested books.

After annotation, the topic in Figure 1 (topic 99309) is distributed to participants in the following format:

```
<topic id="99309">
  <query>Politics of Multiculturalism</query>
  <title>Politics of Multiculturalism Recommendations?</title>
  <group>Political Philosophy</group>
  <narrative> I'm new, and would appreciate any recommended reading on
    the politics of multiculturalism. <a href="/author/parekh">Parekh
    </a>'s <a href="/work/164382">Rethinking Multiculturalism: Cultural
    Diversity and Political Theory</a> (which I just finished) in the end
    left me unconvinced, though I did find much of value I thought he
    depended way too much on being able to talk out the details later. It
    may be that I found his writing style really irritating so adopted a
    defiant skepticism, but still... Anyway, I've read
    <a href="/author/sen">Sen</a>, <a href="/author/rawles">Rawls</a>,
    <a href="/author/habermas">Habermas</a>, and
    <a href="/author/nussbaum">Nussbaum</a>, still don't feel like I've
    wrapped my little brain around the issue very well and would
    appreciate any suggestions for further anyone might offer.
  </narrative>
  <examples>
    <example>
      <LT_id>164382</LT_id>
      <hasRead>yes</hasRead>
      <sentiment>neutral</sentiment>
    </example>
  </examples>
  <catalog>
    <book>
      <LT_id>9036</LT_id>
      <entry_date>2007-09</entry_date>
      <rating>0.0</rating>
      <tags></tags>
    </book>
    <book>
      ...
```

The hyperlink markup, represented by the <a> tags, is added by the *Touchstone* technology of LT. The rest of the markup is generated specifically for the Suggestion Track. Above, the example book with *LT_id* 164382 is annotated as one the requester is neutral about. It has positive and negative aspects. From the request, forum members can understand how to interpret this example.

We had 8 annotators label each example provided by the requester and each suggestion provided by LT members. They had to indicate whether the suggester *has read* the book. For the *has read* question, the possible answers were *Yes*, *No*, *Can't tell* and *It seems like this is not a book*. They also had to judge the attitude of the suggester towards the book. Possible answers were *Positively*, *Neutrally*,

Negatively, Not sure or *This book is not mentioned as a relevant suggestion!* The latter can be chosen when someone mentions a book for another reason than to suggest it as a relevant book for the topic of request.

In addition to the explicitly marked up books, e.g. the examples and suggestions, we noticed that there are other book titles that are not marked up but are intended as suggestions. In some cases this is because the suggester is not aware of the *Touchstone* syntax or because it fails to identify the correct book and they cannot manually correct it. To investigate the extent of this issue and to make the list of identified suggestions more complete, in 2015 we manually labeled all suggested book that were not marked up by *Touchstone* in each forum thread of the 208 topics. This resulted in 830 new suggestions (a mean of 4 per topic). From the touchstones we extracted 4240 suggestions (20.4 per topic), so the manually extracted suggestions bring the total to 5070 (24.4), an increase of 20%. Multiple users may suggest the same books, so the total number of suggested books is lower. The 4240 touchstone suggestion represent 3255 books (15.6 per topic). With the manually extracted suggestions, this increases to 3687 (17.7 per topic), an increase of 13%. The newly added suggestions therefore increase the recall base but also increase the number of recommendations for some of the touchstone suggestions.

Operationalisation of Forum Judgement Labels. The mapping from annotated suggestions to relevance judgements uses the same process as in 2014. Some of the books mentioned in the forums are not part of the 2.8 million books in our collection. We removed from the suggestions any books that are not in the A/LT collection. The numbers reported in the previous section were calculated after this filtering step.

Forum members can mention books for many different reasons. We want the relevance values to distinguish between books that were mentioned as positive recommendations, negative recommendations (books to avoid), neutral suggestions (mentioned as possibly relevant but not necessarily recommended) and books mentioned for some other reason (not relevant at all). We also want to differentiate between recommendations from members who have read the book they recommend and members who have not. We assume a recommendation based on having read the book to be of more value to the searcher. For the mapping to relevance values, we refer to the first mention of work as the *suggestion* and subsequent mentions of the same work as *replies*. We use *has read* when the forum members have read the book they mention and *not read* when they have not. Furthermore, we use a number of simplifying assumptions:

- When the annotator was *not sure* if the person mentioning a book has read it, we treat it as *not read*. We argue that for the topic starter there is no clear difference in the value of such recommendations.
- When the annotator was *not sure* if a suggestion was positive, negative or neutral, we treat it as *neutral*. Again, for the topic starter there is no clear signal that there is difference in value.

- *has read* recommendations overrule *not read* recommendations. Someone who has read the book is in a better position to judge a book than someone who has not.
- *positive* and *negative* recommendations neutralise each other. I.e. a *positive* and a *negative* recommendation together are the same as two *neutral* recommendations.
- If the topic starter *has read* a book she mentions, the relevance value is $rv = 0$. We assume such books have no value as suggestions.
- The attitude of the topic starter towards a book overrules those of others. The system should retrieve books for the topic starter, not for others.
- When forum members mention a single work multiple times, we use the last mention as judgement.

This leads to the following graded relevance values:

- $rv = 0$: not relevant
- $rv = 1$: relevant but more negative than positive mentions
- $rv = 2$: neutral mention
- $rv = 3$: positive mention (but not read by suggester(s))
- $rv = 4$: positive mention (but not read by suggester(s))
- $rv = 6$: positive mention (read by suggester(s))
- $rv = 8$: suggestion that is afterwards catalogued by requester

More details about this mapping are provided on the Track website.[5]

User Profiles and Personal Catalogues. From LT we can not only extract the information needs of social book search topics, but also the rich user profiles of the topic creators and other LT users, which contain information on which books they have in their personal catalogue on LT, which ratings and tags they assigned to them and a social network of friendship relations, interesting library relations and group memberships. In total, over 94,000 user profiles with 34 million cataloguing transactions were scraped from the LT site, anonymised and made available to participants. To anonymise all user profiles, we removed all friendship and group membership connections and replaced the user name with a randomly generated string. The cataloguing date of each book was reduced to the year and month. What is left is an anonymised user name, book ID, month of cataloguing, rating and tags.

4.2   Evaluation

This year, 11 teams submitted a total of 48 automatic runs (see Table 1) and one manual run. We omit the manual run, as it is a ranking of last year's Qrels. The official evaluation measure for this task is nDCG@10. It takes graded relevance values into account and is designed for evaluation based on the top retrieved results. In addition, P@10, MAP and MRR scores will also be reported, with the evaluation results shown in Table 2.

---

[5] See: http://social-book-search.humanities.uva.nl/#/results15

Table 2. Evaluation results for the official submissions. Shown are the topic scoring runs for each participating team.

Rank	Group	Run	nDCG@10	P@10	MRR	MAP	Profiles
1	MIIB	Run6	0.186	0.394	0.105	0.374	no
2	CERIST	CERIST_TOPICS_EXP_NO	0.137	0.285	0.093	0.562	yes
3	USTB_PRIR	run5-Rerank-RF-example	0.106	0.232	0.068	0.365	no
4	MRIM	LIG_3	0.098	0.189	0.069	0.514	yes
5	LaHC_Saint-Etienne	UJM_2	0.088	0.174	0.065	0.483	no
6	AAU	allfields-jm	0.087	0.191	0.061	0.420	yes
7	Oslo_SBS_iTrack_group	baseLine	0.082	0.182	0.052	0.341	no
8	CSIE	0.95AverageType2QTGN	0.082	0.194	0.050	0.319	no
9	LSIS-OpenEdition	INL2_SDM_Graph_LSIS	0.081	0.183	0.058	0.401	no
10	UAmsterdam	UAmsQTG_KNN_L.070	0.068	0.160	0.051	0.388	yes
11	IR@JU	KASIT_1	0.011	0.023	0.006	0.009	no

The best run of the top 5 groups are described below:

1. *MIIB - Run6* (rank 1): For this run, queries are generated from all topic fields and applied on a BM25 index with all textual document fields merged into a single field. A Learning-to-rank framework is applied using random forest on 6 result lists as well as the price, the book length and the ratings. Results are re-ranked based on tags and ratings.
2. *CERIST - CERIST_TOPICS_EXP_NO* (rank 2): The terms of topics have been combined with the top tags extracted from the example books mentioned in the book search request then the BM15 model has been used to rank books. The books which have been catalogued by the users topics have been removed.
3. *USTB_PRIR - run5-Rerank-RF-example* (rank 5): This run is a mixture of two runs (*run1-example* and *run4-Rerank-RF*). The former ranks the example books for each topic. The latter is a complex run based on re-ranking with 11 strategies and learning-to-rank with random forest.
4. *MRIM - LIG_3* (rank 6): This run is a weighted linear fusion of a BM25F run on all fields, an LGD run on all fields, and the topic profile (from top tf terms of books in catalog), and the two "best friends" profiles according to similarity of marks on books.
5. *LaHC_Saint-Etienne - UJM_2* (rank 17): This run is based on the Log Logistic LGD model, with an index based on all document fields. For retrieval, the query is constructed from the title, mediated query, group and narrative fields in the topic statement.

Most of the top performing systems, including the best (MIIB's *Run6*) make no use of user profile information. There are 11 systems that made use of the user profiles, with 4 in the top 10 (at ranks 2, 4, 6 and 9). So far, the additional value of user profiles has not been established. The best systems combine various topic fields, with parameters trained for optimal performance. Several of the best performing systems make use of learning-to-rank approaches, suggesting book search is a domain where systems need to learn from user behaviour what the right balance is for the multiple and diverse sources of information, both from the collection and the user side.

5   The SBS Interactive Track

The goal of the interactive Social Book Search (ISBS) track is to investigate how searchers make use of and appreciate professional metadata and user-generated content for book search on the Web and to develop interfaces that support searchers through the various stages of their search task. The user has a specific information need against a background of personal tastes, interests and previously seen books. Through social media, book descriptions are extended far beyond what is traditionally stored in professional catalogues. Not only are books described in the users' own vocabulary, but they are also reviewed and discussed online. As described in Section 4, this subjective user-generated content can help users during search tasks where their personal preferences, interests and background knowledge play a role. User reviews can contain information on how engaging, fun, educational or well-written a book is.

The ISBS track investigates book requests and suggestions from the Library-Thing (LT) discussion forums as a way to model book search in a social environment. The discussions in these forums show that readers frequently turn to others to get recommendations and tap into the collective knowledge of a group of readers interested in the same topic. The track builds on the INEX Amazon/LibraryThing (A/LT) collection, described in Section 3, using a subset of 1.5 million of the total 2.8 million book descriptions for which a thumbnail cover image is available.

5.1   User Tasks

This year in addition to the two main user tasks, a training task was developed to ensure that participants are familiar with all the functions offered by the two interfaces. The queries and topics used in the training task were chosen so as not to overlap with the *goal-oriented* task. However, a potential influence on the *non-goal* task cannot be ruled out.

Similar to last year, two tasks were created to investigate the impact of different task types on the participants interactions with the interfaces and the professional and user-generated book metadata. For both tasks, participants were asked to motivate each book selection in the book-bag.

The *Goal-Oriented* Task. contains five sub-tasks ensuring that participants spend enough time on finding relevant books. While the first sub-tasks defines a clear goal, the other sub-tasks are more open giving the user enough room to interact with and the available content and met-data options. The following instruction text was provided to participants:

> Imagine you participate in an experiment at a desert-island for one month. There will be no people, no TV, radio or other distraction. The only things you are allowed to take with you are 5 books. Please search for and add 5 books to your book-bag that you would want to read during your stay at the desert-island:

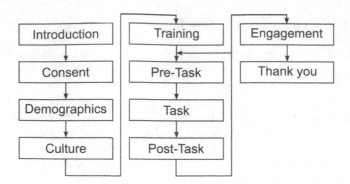

Fig. 2. The path participants took through the experiment. Each participant completed the *Pre-Task, Task, Post-Task* twice (once for each of the tasks). The SPIRE system automatically balanced the task order. No data was acquired in the *Introduction, Pre-Task,* and *Thank you* steps.

- Select one book about surviving on a desert island
- Select one book that will teach you something new
- Select one book about one of your personal hobbies or interests
- Select one book that is highly recommended by other users (based on user ratings and reviews)
- Select one book for fun

Please add a note (in the book-bag) explaining why you selected each of the five books.

The *Non-goal* Task. was developed based on the open-ended task used in the iCHiC task at CLEF 2013 [10] and the ISBS task at CLEF 2014 [4]. The aim of this task is to investigate how users interact with the system when they have no pre-defined goal in a more exploratory search context. It also allows the participants to bring their own goals or sub-tasks to the experiment in line with the "simulated work task" idea [2]. The following instruction text was provided to participants:

Imagine you are waiting to meet a friend in a coffee shop or pub or the airport or your office. While waiting, you come across this website and explore it looking for any book that you find interesting, or engaging or relevant. Explore anything you wish until you are completely and utterly bored. When you find something interesting, add it to the book-bag. Please add a note (in the book-bag) explaining why you selected each of the books.

5.2   Experiment Structure

The experiment was conducted using the SPIRE system[6] [5], using the flow shown in Figure 2. Each participant ran through the *Pre-Task*, *Task*, *Post-Task* steps once for each of the two tasks. When a new participant started the experiment, the SPIRE system automatically allocated them to one of the two tested interfaces and to a given task order. Interface allocation and task order were automatically balanced to minimise bias in the resulting data. Participants were not explicitly instructed to use only the interface and collection provided, so it is possible some users used other websites as well. However, given the lack of incentive to use external websites, we expect this issue to be negligible.

Participant responses were collected in the following five steps using a selection of questionnaires:

- *Consent* – participants had to confirm that they understood the tasks and the types of data collected in the experiment.
- *Demographics* – gender, age, achieved education level, current education level, and employment status;
- *Culture* – country of birth, country of residence, mother tongue, primary language spoken at home, languages used to search the web;
- *Post-Task* – after each task, participants judged the usefulness of interface components and meta-data parts, using 5-point Likert-like scales;
- *Engagement* – after completing both tasks, they were asked to complete O'Brien et al.'s [8] engagement scale.

5.3   System and Interfaces

The two tested interfaces (*baseline* and *multi-stage*) were both built using the PyIRE[7] workbench, which provides the required functionality for creating interactive IR interfaces and logging all interactions between the participants and the system. This includes any queries they enter, the books shown for the queries, pagination, facets selected, books viewed in detail, metadata facets viewed, books added to the book-bag, and books removed from the book-bag. All log-data is automatically timestamped and linked to the participant and task.

Both interfaces used a shared IR backend implemented using ElasticSearch[8], which provided free-text search, faceted search, and access to the individual books complete metadata. The 1.5 million book descriptions are indexed with all professional metadata and user-generated content. For indexing and retrieval the default parameters are used, which means stopwords are removed, but no stemming is performed. The Dewey Decimal Classification numbers are replaced by their natural language description. That is, the DDC number 573 is replaced

---

[6] Based on the Experiment Support System – https://bitbucket.org/mhall/experiment-support-system

[7] Python interactive Information Retrieval Evaluation workbench – https://bitbucket.org/mhall/pyire

[8] ElasticSearch – http://www.elasticsearch.org/

Fig. 3. *Baseline* interface – uses a standard faceted search interface, consisting of a search box, search facets based on the Amazon subject classifications and user tags, and the book-bag on the right.

by the descriptor *Physical anthropology*. User tags from LibraryThing are indexed both as text strings, such that complex terms are broken down into individual terms (e.g. *physical anthropology* is indexed as *physical* and *anthropology*) and as non-analyzed terms, which leaves complex terms intact and is used for faceted search.

The *Baseline* Interface. shown in figure 3 represents a standard faceted web-search interface, the only additions being the task information (top-left) and the list of past searches (top-right). The main interface consists of a search box at the top, two facets on the left, and the search results list (center). On the right-hand side is the book-bag, which shows the participants which books they have collected for their task and also provides the notes field, which the participants were instructed to use to explain why they had chosen that book.

The two facets provided on the left use the Amazon subject classification and the user tags to generate the two lists together with numeric indicators for how many books each facet contained. Selecting a facet restricted the search results to books with that facet. Participants could select multiple facets from both lists. In the search results list each book consisted of a thumbnail image, title, authors, aggregate user rating, a description, publication information (type, publisher, pages, year, ISBN ...), user reviews, and user tags (where available). The aggregate user rating was displayed using 1 to 5 stars in half-star steps, calculated by aggregating the 1-5 star ratings for each user review. If the book had no user reviews, then no stars were shown. Additionally each book had a "Add to Bookbag" button that participants used to add that book into their bookbag.

Fig. 4. *Multistage* interface – *Browse* view – subject browse hierarchy derived from the Amazon subject classifications on the left and the dense search results list on the right with thumbnail, title, and aggregate ratings for each book.

The *Multi-stage* Interface. aims to support users by taking the different stages of the search process into account. The idea behind the *multi-stage* interface design is supported by two theoretical components.

Firstly, several information search process models look at stages in the search process. A well-known example is [7], who discovered "common patterns in users' experience" during task performance. She developed a model consisting of six stages, which describe users' evolving thoughts, feelings and actions in the context of complex tasks. [11] later summarized Kuhlthau's stages into three categories (pre-focus, focus formulation, and post-focus), and points to the types of information searched for in the different stages. The multi-stage search interface constructed for iSBS was inspired by [11]. It includes three distinct panels, potentially supporting different stages: *browse*, in which users can explore categories of books, *search*, supporting in-depth searching, and *book-bag*, in which users can review and refine their book-bag selections.

Secondly, when designing a new search interface for social book search it has also been relevant to look more specifically at the process of choosing a book to read. A model of decision stages in book selection [9] identifies the following decision stages: browse category, selecting, judging, sampling, and sustained reading. This work supports the need for a user interface that takes the different search and decision stages into account. However, the different stages in [9] closely relate to a specific full text digital library, and therefore the model was not applicable to the present collection.

When the *multi-stage* interface first loads, participants are shown the *browse* stage (fig. 4), which is aimed at supporting the initial exploration of the dataset. The main feature to support the free exploration is the hierarchy browsing component on the left, which shows a hierarchical tree of Amazon subject classifications. This was generated using the algorithm described in [3], which uses the relative frequencies of the subjects to arrange them into the tree-structure

Fig. 5. *Multistage* interface – *Search* view – faceted search interface that matches the interface used in the *Baseline* interface. Differences are the inclusion of the Amazon subject selection box next to the search box and the removal of the book-bag.

Fig. 6. *Multistage* interface – *Book-bag* view – books added to the book-bag are listed on the left together with the note areas for each book. On the right the list of similar books using the dense result list from the *Browse* view.

with the most-frequent subjects at the top of the tree. The search result list is designed to be more compact to allow the user to browse books quickly and shows only the book's title, thumbnail image, and aggregate ratings (if available). Clicking on the book title showed a popup window with the book's full meta-data using the same layout and content as used in the *baseline* interface's search result list.

Participants switched to the *search* stage by clicking on the "Search" section in the gray bar at the top. The *search* stage (fig. 5 uses the same interface as the *baseline* with only two differences. The first is that as the book-bag is a separate stage, it is not shown on the *search* stage interface itself. The second is that if the participants select a topic in the *browse* stage, this topic is pre-selected as a filter for any queries in the blow box to the left of the search box. Participants can click on that box to see a drop-down menu of the selected topic and its parent topics. Participants can select a higher-level topic to widen their search.

The final stage is the *book-bag* shown in Figure 6, where participants review the books they have collected and can provide notes for each book. For each book, buttons were provided that allow the user to search for similar books by title, author, topic, and user tags. The similar books are shown on the right using the same compact layout as in the *browse* stage. As in the *browse* stage, clicking on a book in that list shows a popup window with the book's details.

5.4 Participants

A total of 192 participants were recruited (see Table 1), 120 female and 72 male. 72 were between 18 and 25, 80 between 26 and 35, 25 between 36 and 45, 8 between 46 and 55, 6 between 56 and 65 and 1 over 65. 60 were in employment, 3 unemployed, 128 were students and 1 selected *other*. Participants came from 36 different countries (country of birth) including Germany (63 participants), UK (33), Denmark (21), Norway (20), the Netherlands (11), resident in 13 different countries, again mainly in Germany, UK, Denmark, Norway and the Netherlands. Participants mother tongues included German, Dutch, English, Danish, Romanian, Farsi, Portuguese and 23 others. The majority of participants executed the tasks remotely (136) and only 56 users in a lab. 95 participants used the novel *multi-stage* interface, while 97 used the *baseline* interface.

5.5 Procedure

Participants were invited by the individual teams, either using e-mail or by recruiting students from a lecture or lab. Where participants were invited by e-mail, the e-mail contained a link to the online experiment, which would open in the participant's browser. Where participants were recruited in a lecture or lab, the experiment URL was distributed using e-learning platforms. The following browsers and operating systems had been tested: Windows, OS X, Linux using Internet Explorer, Chrome, Mozilla Firefox, and Safari. The only difference between browsers was that some of the graphical refinements such as shadows are not supported on Internet Explorer and fall back to a simpler line-based display.

After participants had completed the experiment as outlined above (5.2), they were provided with additional information on the tasks they had completed and with contact information, should they wish to learn more about the experiment. Where participants that completed the experiment in a lab, teams were able to conduct their own post-experiment process, which mostly focused on gathering additional feedback on the system from the participants.

5.6 Results

Based on the participant responses and log data we have aggregated summary statistics for a number of basic performance metrics.

Session Length. was measured automatically using JavaScript and stored with the participants' responses. Table 3 shows median and inter-quartile ranges for all interface and task combinations. Session lengths are significantly lower for the *baseline* interface (wilcoxon signed rank $p < 0.05$). Also all session lengths are significantly longer than in the iSBS 2014 experiment [4].

Table 3. Session lengths, number of queries executed, and number of books collected for the two interfaces and tasks. Times are in minutes:seconds, numbers reported are median and inter-quartile range.

Interface	Goal-oriented		Non-goal	
	Median	inter-quartile	Median	inter-quartile
Session length				
Baseline	10:30min	10:25min	5:33min	7:37min
Multi-Stage	12:52min	9:20min	7:18min	10:52min
Number of queries				
Baseline	8	5	2	3
Multi-Stage	6	6.5	1	3
Number of books				
Baseline	5	0	3	3
Multi-Stage	5	0	3	3

Number of Queries. was extracted from the log-data. In both interfaces it was possible to issue queries by typing keywords into the search box or by clicking on a meta-data field to search for other books with that meta-data field value. Both types of query have been aggregated and Table 3 shows the number of queries for each interface and task. The number of queries per session is significantly higher for the *baseline* interface over the *multi-stage* interface for both tasks (wilcox $p < 0.05$) and also for the *goal-oriented* over the *non-goal* task in both interfaces (wilcox $p < 0.01$).

Number of Books Collected. was extracted from the log-data. Participants collected those books that they felt were of use to them. The numbers reported in Table 3 are based on the number of books participants had in their book-bag when they completed the session, not the total number of books collected over the course of their session, as participants could always remove books from their book-bag in the course of the session.

Unlike the other metrics, there is no significant difference between the two interfaces. On the *goal-oriented* task this was expected as participants were asked to collect five books. On the *non-goal* task this indicates that the interface had no impact on what participants felt were enough books to complete the task.

6   Conclusions and Plans

This was the first year of the SBS Lab, which is a continuation from the SBS and iSBS Tracks at INEX 2014. The overall goal remains to investigate the relative value of professional metadata, user-generated content and user profiles. The number of active participants increased in both tracks, from 8 to 11 in the Suggestion Track and from 4 to 7 for the Interactive Track, indicating there is strong interest in the IR community for research in the domain of books and social media.

In the Suggestion Track, the setup was mostly the same as in 2014. Topic statements have both a natural language narrative of the information need and one or more books provided as positive or negative examples of what the user is looking for. In addition to the explicitly marked up book suggestions in the forum threads, We included manually extracted suggestions that were not marked up. With the examples participants can investigate the value of query-by-example techniques in combination with more traditional text-based queries. In terms of systems evaluation, the most effective systems include some form of learning-to-rank. It seems that the complex nature of the requests and the book descriptions, with multiple sources of evidence, requires a careful balancing of system parameters. Next year, we continue this focus on complex topics with example books and consider including an recommendation-type evaluation. We also consider extending the task by asking systems to select which part of the book description—e.g. a certain set of reviews or tags—is most useful to show to the user, given her information need.

The interactive track investigated how searchers make use of and appreciate professional metadata and user-generated content for book search on the Web. Two interfaces were tested to identify and analyse the different stages in the search process. This was the second year of the Interactive Track, in which we improved the two interfaces to identify and analyse the different stages in the search process in the domain of book search. One interface resembles traditional search interfaces familiar from Amazon and LibraryThing, the other is a *multistage* interface where the first part provides a broad overview of the collection, the second part allows the user to look at search results in a more detailed view and the final part allows the user to directly compare selected books in great detail. This year seven teams collaborated to get a shared data pool of 192 participants from many different backgrounds and countries. We found that users spent significantly more time searching the multistage interface than the baseline interface but issued fewer queries, probably because the multistage interface allows browsing as an extra mode of exploring the collection. For the next year, we plan to have multiple experiments focused on specific research questions, with fewer users per experiment. Another option is to let individual teams plan their own experiments.

One possibility for synergy between the two tracks that we intend to investigate next year is how to define experiment tasks that will enable the comparison of results and approaches between the two tracks. Sharing tasks would allow us to evaluate results from the *Suggestion* track based on the users' performances in the *Interactive* track. Another possibility could be to investigate whether some of the successful (re-)ranking techniques used in the Suggestion track could be implemented in the search engine used in the Interactive track.

References

1. Beckers, T., Fuhr, N., Pharo, N., Nordlie, R., Fachry, K.N.: Overview and results of the INEX 2009 interactive track. In: Lalmas, M., Jose, J., Rauber, A., Sebastiani, F., Frommholz, I. (eds.) ECDL 2010. LNCS, vol. 6273, pp. 409–412. Springer, Heidelberg (2010)
2. Borlund, P., Ingwersen, P.: The development of a method for the evaluation of interactive information retrieval systems. Journal of Documentation 53(3), 225–250 (1997)
3. Hall, M.M., Fernando, S., Clough, P.D., Soroa, A., Agirre, E., Stevenson, M.: Evaluating hierarchical organisation structures for exploring digital libraries. Information Retrieval 17(4), 351–379 (2014)
4. Hall, M.M., Huurdeman, H.C., Koolen, M., Skov, M., Walsh, D.: Overview of the INEX 2014 interactive social book search track. In: Cappellato, L., Ferro, N., Halvey, M., Kraaij, W. (eds.) Working Notes for CLEF 2014 Conference. CEUR Workshop Proceedings, Sheffield, UK, September 15–18, 2014, vol. 1180, pp. 480–493. CEUR-WS.org (2014)
5. Hall, M.M., Toms, E.: Building a common framework for IIR evaluation. In: Forner, P., Müller, H., Paredes, R., Rosso, P., Stein, B. (eds.) CLEF 2013. LNCS, vol. 8138, pp. 17–28. Springer, Heidelberg (2013)
6. Koolen, M., Kamps, J., Kazai, G.: Social book search: the impact of professional and user-generated content on book suggestions. In: Proceedings of the International Conference on Information and Knowledge Management (CIKM 2012). ACM (2012)
7. Kuhlthau, C.C.: Inside the search process: Information seeking from the user's perspective. Journal of the American Society for Information Science 42(5), 361–371 (1991)
8. O'Brien, H.L., Toms, E.G.: The development and evaluation of a survey to measure user engagement. Journal of the American Society for Information Science and Technology 61(1), 50–69 (2009)
9. Reuter, K.: Assessing aesthetic relevance: Children's book selection in a digital library. JASIST 58(12), 1745–1763 (2007)
10. Toms, E., Hall, M.M.: The chic interactive task (chici) at clef2013 (2013). http://www.clef-initiative.eu/documents/71612/1713e643-27c3-4d76-9a6f-926cdb1db0f4
11. Vakkari, P.: A theory of the task-based information retrieval process: a summary and generalisation of a longitudinal study. Journal of Documentation 57(1), 44–60 (2001)

Author Index

Printed in the United States
By Bookmasters